# DAVID BUSCH'S NIKON® D5200

## GUIDE TO DIGITAL SLR PHOTOGRAPHY

David D. Busch

**Cengage Learning PTR**

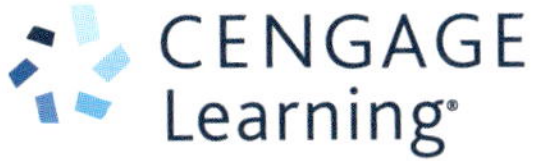

Professional • Technical • Reference

Australia, Brazil, Japan, Korea, Mexico, Singapore, Spain, United Kingdom, United States

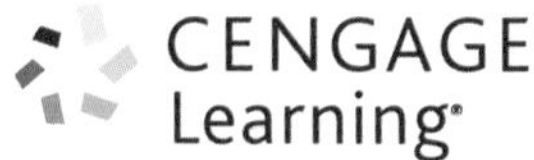

*For Cathy*

# Acknowledgments

Once again thanks to the folks at Cengage Learning PTR, who recognized that a camera as popular as the Nikon D5200 deserves in-depth, full-color coverage at a price anyone can afford. Special thanks to executive editor Kevin Harreld, who always gives me the freedom to let my imagination run free with a topic, as well as my veteran production team including project editor Jenny Davidson and series technical editor Mike Sullivan. Also thanks to Bill Hartman, layout; Katherine Stimson, indexing; Michael Beady, proofreading; Mike Tanamachi, cover design; and my agent, Carole Jelen, who has the amazing ability to keep both publishers and authors happy.

# About the Author

With more than a million books in print, **David D. Busch** is the world's #1 selling digital camera guide author, and the originator of popular digital photography series like *David Busch's Pro Secrets* and *David Busch's Quick Snap Guides*. He has written nearly two dozen hugely successful guidebooks and compact guides for Nikon digital SLR models, and several dozen additional user guides for other camera models, as well as many popular books devoted to dSLRs, including *Mastering Digital SLR Photography, Third Edition* and *Digital SLR Pro Secrets*. As a roving photojournalist for more than 20 years, he illustrated his books, magazine articles, and newspaper reports with award-winning images. He's operated his own commercial studio, suffocated in formal dress while shooting weddings-for-hire, and shot sports for a daily newspaper and upstate New York college. His photos have been published in magazines as diverse as *Scientific American* and *Petersen's PhotoGraphic*, and his articles have appeared in *Popular Photography, Rangefinder, Professional Photographer*, and hundreds of other publications. He's also reviewed dozens of digital cameras for CNet and other Ziff-Davis publications. His advice has been featured on National Public Radio's *All Tech Considered*.

When About.com named its top five books on Beginning Digital Photography, debuting at the #1 and #2 slots were Busch's *Digital Photography All-In-One Desk Reference for Dummies* and *Mastering Digital Photography*. During the past year, he's had as many as five of his books listed in the Top 20 of Amazon.com's Digital Photography Bestseller list—simultaneously! Busch's 100-plus other books published since 1983 include bestsellers like *David Busch's Quick Snap Guide to Digital SLR Lenses*.

Busch earned top category honors in the Computer Press Awards the first two years they were given (for *Sorry About The Explosion* and *Secrets of MacWrite, MacPaint and MacDraw*), and he later served as Master of Ceremonies for the awards.

Visit his website at http://www.dslrguides.com/blog.

# Contents



## PART I: GETTING STARTED WITH YOUR NIKON D5200

## Chapter 1
## Thinking Outside of the Box     3



## Chapter 2
## Nikon D5200 Quick Start     19

# Chapter 3
# Nikon D5200 Roadmap         39



# PART II: MASTERING YOUR TOOLS

# Chapter 4
# Nailing the Right Exposure       71

# Chapter 5
# Mastering Autofocus Options

**103**



# Chapter 6
# Live View and Movies

**117**

# Chapter 7
# Advanced Techniques
# 143



## PART III: ADVANCED TOOLS

# Chapter 8
# Playback and Shooting Menus
# 173

# Chapter 9
# The Custom Setting Menu     213

# Chapter 10
# The Setup Menu, Retouch Menu, and My Menu   229

# Chapter 11
# Working with Lenses                                      255

# Chapter 12
# Making Light Work for You     285

# Chapter 13
# Troubleshooting and Prevention    315



# Glossary    339

# Index    349

# Preface

Your new Nikon D5200 will give you great shots right out of the box—but why stop there? With a little guidance, you can easily take *outstanding* photos with your D5200, the most advanced entry-level camera that Nikon has ever introduced. It's aimed at enthusiasts like you, and boasts 24 megapixels of resolution, sophisticated full high-definition, movie-making capabilities, and blazing-fast automatic focus. But your gateway to pixel proficiency is dragged down by the slim booklet included in the box as a manual.

You're convinced that everything you need to know is in there, *somewhere*, but you don't know where to start. In addition, the official Nikon camera manual gives you basic information on the buttons, dials, and menus, but doesn't offer much information about digital photography that directly applies to your D5200.

What you *really* need is a guide that explains the purpose and function of each of the D5200's basic controls, how you should use them, and *why*. Ideally, there should be information about file formats, resolution, exposure, and special autofocus modes, but you'd prefer to read about those topics only after you've had the chance to go out and take a few hundred great pictures with your new camera. Why isn't there a book that summarizes the most important information, with lots of illustrations showing what your results will look like when you use this setting or that?

If you can't decide on what basic settings to use with your camera because you can't figure out how changing ISO or white balance or focus defaults will affect your pictures, you need this guide. I won't talk down to you, either; this book isn't padded with dozens of pages of checklists telling you how to take a travel picture, a sports photo, or how to take a snapshot of your kids in overly simplistic terms. There are no special sections devoted to "real world" recipes here. All of us do 100 percent of our shooting in the real world! So, I give you all the information you need to cook up great photos on your own!

# Introduction

What part of "entry level" doesn't Nikon understand? This new, affordable model is aimed at apprentice digital photographers who make up in enthusiasm what they may lack in experience. The D5200 is remarkably easy to use, whether you're capturing tack-sharp 24 megapixel still images or working with its full high-definition 1920 × 1080 movie-making capabilities to shoot video clips you'll be proud of. Nikon has stuffed an amazing array of photographer-friendly features into a compact body that, along with the D5200's slightly stripped-down sibling, the D3200 (also a 24MP model), elevates entry level to a new high.

But, despite its growing feature list, these "beginner" cameras retain the ease of use that smoothes the transition for those new to digital photography. For those just dipping their toes into the digital pond, the experience is warm and inviting. The Nikon D5200, especially, isn't a snapshot camera—it's a point-and-shoot (if you want to use it in that mode) for the thinking photographer.

Once you've confirmed that you made a wise purchase decision, the question comes up, *how do I use this thing?* All those cool features can be mind numbing to learn, if all you have as a guide is the manual furnished with the camera. Help is on the way. I sincerely believe that this book is your best bet for learning how to use your new camera, and for learning how to use it well.

If you're a Nikon D5200 owner who's looking to learn more about how to use this great camera, you've probably already explored your options. There are DVDs and online tutorials—but who can learn how to use a camera by sitting in front of a television or computer screen? Do you want to watch a movie or click on HTML links, or do you want to go out and take photos with your camera? Videos are fun, but not the best answer.

There's always the manual furnished with the D5200. It's compact and filled with information, but there's really very little about *why* you should use particular settings or features. Its organization may make it difficult to find what you need. Multiple cross-references may send you searching back and forth between two or three sections of the book to find what you want to know. The basic manual is also hobbled by black-and-white line drawings and tiny monochrome pictures that aren't very good examples of what you can do.

Also available are third-party guides to the D5200, like this one. I haven't been happy with some of these guidebooks, which is why I wrote this book. The existing books range from skimpy and illustrated by black-and-white photos to lushly illustrated in full color but too generic to do much good. Photography instruction is useful, but it needs to be related directly to the Nikon D5200 as much as possible.

I've tried to make *David Busch's Nikon D5200 Guide to Digital SLR Photography* different from your other D5200 learn-up options. The roadmap sections use larger, color pictures to show you where all the buttons and dials are, and the explanations of what they do are longer and more comprehensive. I've tried to avoid overly general advice, including the two-page checklists on how to take a "sports picture" or a "portrait picture" or a "travel picture." Instead, you'll find tips and techniques for using all the features of your Nikon D5200 to take *any kind of picture* you want. If you want to know where you should stand to take a picture of a quarterback dropping back to unleash a pass, there are plenty of books that will tell you that. This one concentrates on teaching you how to select the best autofocus mode, shutter speed, f/stop, or flash capability to take, say, a great sports picture under any conditions.

This book is not a lame rewriting of the manual that came with the camera. Some folks spend five minutes with a book like this one, spot some information that also appears in the original manual, and decide "Rehash!" without really understanding the differences. Yes, you'll find information here that is also in the owner's manual, such as the parameters you can enter when changing your D5200's operation in the various menus. Basic descriptions—before I dig in and start providing in-depth tips and information—may also be vaguely similar. There are only so many ways you can say, for example, "Hold the shutter release down halfway to lock in exposure." But not *everything* in the manual is included in this book. If you need advice on when and how to use the most important functions, you'll find the information here.

*David Busch's Nikon D5200 Guide to Digital SLR Photography* is aimed at both Nikon and dSLR veterans as well as newcomers to digital photography and digital SLRs. Both groups can be overwhelmed by the options the D5200 offers, while underwhelmed by the explanations they receive in their user's manual. The manuals are great if you already know what you don't know, and you can find an answer somewhere in a booklet arranged by menu listings and written by a camera vendor employee who last threw together instructions on how to operate a camcorder.

Once you've read this book and are ready to learn more, I hope you pick up one of my other guides to digital SLR photography. Five of them are offered by Cengage Learning PTR, each approaching the topic from a different perspective. They include:

### David Busch's Compact Field Guide for the Nikon D5200

Readers have told me they love my big guidebooks written specifically for their cameras, but asked me to condense the most essential information about settings, menus, and options into a pocket-sized format they can tuck in a camera bag. Well, you can throw away your cheat sheets and command cards. My *Compact Field Guide* for your D5200 is an on-the-go reference you can refer to as you shoot. It's a spiral-bound, lay-flat book with advice on using every setting and control your D5200 offers. While my "big books" contain everything you need to know, the compact versions make sure you'll have everything you need to know, when you need it.

### Quick Snap Guide to Digital SLR Photography

Consider this a prequel to the book you're holding in your hands. It might make a good gift for a spouse or friend who may be using your D5200, but who lacks even basic knowledge about digital photography, digital SLR photography, and Nikon photography. It serves as an introduction that summarizes the basic features of digital SLR cameras in general (not just the D5200), and what settings to use and when, such as continuous autofocus/single autofocus, aperture/shutter priority, EV settings, and so forth. The guide also includes recipes for shooting the most common kinds of pictures, with step-by-step instructions for capturing effective sports photos, portraits, landscapes, and other types of images.

### *David Busch's Quick Snap Guide to Using Digital SLR Lenses*

A bit overwhelmed by the features and controls of digital SLR lenses, and not quite sure when to use each type? This book explains lenses, their use, and lens technology in easy-to-access two- and four-page spreads, each devoted to a different topic, such as depth-of-field, lens aberrations, or using zoom lenses. If you have a friend or significant other who is less versed in photography, but who wants to borrow and use your Nikon D5200 from time to time, this book can save you a ton of explanation.

### *David Busch's Quick Snap Guide to Photo Gear*

Which three filters *must* you own—and which filters are obsolete in the era of digital photography? What's the best type of tripod or monopod for sports, landscape, or wildlife photography? Shoulder bags, sling bags, backpacks, and travel cases: which make the most sense to you? Of all the different gadgets for close-up photography, which are the best? Do I need a special memory card for my camera? What does a radio trigger do? You'll find the answers to all these questions in my guidebook for choosing and using the best photo gear and accessories.

### *David Busch's Mastering Digital SLR Photography, Third Edition*

This book, completely revamped with six brand new chapters for this latest edition, is an introduction to digital SLR photography, with nuts-and-bolts explanations of the technology, more in-depth coverage of settings, and whole chapters on the most common types of photography. While not specific to the D5200, this book can show you how to get more from its capabilities.

## Family Resemblance

If you've owned previous models in the Nikon digital camera line, and copies of my books for those cameras, you're bound to notice a certain family resemblance. Nikon has been very crafty in introducing upgraded cameras that share the best features of the models they replace, while adding new capabilities and options. You benefit in two ways. If you used a Nikon D5000 prior to switching to the latest D5200 model, you'll find that parts that haven't changed have a certain familiarity for you, making it easy to make the transition to the newest model. There are lots of features and menu choices of the D5200 that are exactly the same as those in the most recent models, or even "big siblings" like the D7000. This family resemblance will help level the learning curve for you.

Similarly, when writing books for each new model, I try to retain the easy-to-understand explanations that worked for previous books dedicated to earlier camera models, and concentrate on expanded descriptions of things readers have told me they want to know more about, a solid helping of fresh sample photos, and lots of details about the latest and greatest new features. So, even though a description of how to use a universal feature like, say, Shutter-priority is similar to my discussion last time around, rest assured, this book was written expressly for you, and tailored especially for the Nikon D5200.

# Who Are You?

When preparing a guidebook for a specific camera, it's always wise to consider exactly who will be reading the book. Indeed, thinking about the potential audience for *David Busch's Nikon D5200 Guide to Digital SLR Photography* is what led me to taking the approach and format I use for this book. I realized that the needs of readers like you had to be addressed both from a functional level (what you will use the D5200 for) as well as from a skill level (how much experience you may have with digital photography, dSLRs, or Nikon cameras specifically).

Addressing your needs from a skills level can be tricky, because the D5200 is such a great camera that a full spectrum of photographers will be buying it, from absolute beginners who have never owned a digital camera before up to the occasional professional with years of shooting experience who will be using the Nikon D5200 as a backup body. (I have to admit I tend to carry my D5200 with me everywhere, even if I intend to take most of my photos with another camera.)

Before tackling this book, it would be helpful for you to understand the following:

- **What a digital SLR is:** It's a camera that shows an optical (not LCD) view of the picture that's being taken through the (interchangeable) lens that actually takes the photo, thanks to a mirror that reflects an image to a viewfinder, but flips up out of the way to allow the sensor to be exposed. Today, such cameras also offer an optional live view feature if you want to preview your images on the LCD, especially when prepping to shoot movies.

- **How digital photography differs from film:** The image is stored not on film (which I call the *first* write-once optical media), but on a memory card as pixels that can be transferred to your computer, and then edited, corrected, and printed without the need for chemical processing.

- **What the basic tools of correct exposure are:** Don't worry if you don't understand these; I'll explain them later in this book. But if you already know something about shutter speed, aperture, and ISO sensitivity, you'll be ahead of the game. If not, you'll soon learn that shutter speed determines the amount of time the sensor is exposed to incoming light; the f/stop or aperture is like a valve that governs the quantity of light that can flow through the lens; and the sensor's sensitivity (ISO setting) controls how easily the sensor responds to light. All three factors can be varied individually and proportionately to produce a picture that is properly exposed (neither too light nor too dark).

It's tough to provide something for everybody, but I am going to try to address the needs of each of the following groups and skill levels:

- **Digital photography newbies:** If you've used only point-and-shoot digital cameras, or have worked only with non-SLR film cameras, you're to be congratulated for selecting one of the very best entry-level digital SLRs available as your first dSLR camera. This book can help you understand the controls and features of your D5200, and lead you down the path to better photography with your camera. I'll provide all the information you need, but if you want to do some additional reading for extra credit, you can also try one of the other books I mentioned earlier. They complement this book well.

- **Advanced point-and-shooters moving on up:** There are some quite sophisticated pocket-sized digital cameras available, including those with many user-definable options and settings, so it's possible you are already a knowledgeable photographer, even though you're new to the world of the digital SLR. You've recognized the limitations of the point-and-shoot camera: even the best of them have more noise at higher sensitivity (ISO) settings than a camera like the Nikon D5200; the speediest still have an unacceptable delay between the time you press the shutter and when the photo is actually taken; even a non-interchangeable super-zoom camera with 12X to 20X magnification often won't focus close enough, include an aperture suitable for low-light photography, or take in the really wide view you must have. Interchangeable lenses and other accessories available for the Nikon D5200 are another one of the reasons you moved up. Because you're an avid photographer already, you should pick up the finer points of using the D5200 from this book with no trouble.

- **Film SLR veterans new to the digital world:** You understand photography, you know about f/stops and shutter speeds, and thrive on interchangeable lenses. If you have used a newer film SLR, it probably has lots of electronic features already, including autofocus and sophisticated exposure metering. Perhaps you've even been using a Nikon film SLR and understand many of the available accessories that work with both film and digital cameras. All you need is information on using digital-specific features, working with the D5200 itself, and how to match—and exceed—the capabilities of your film camera with your new Nikon D5200.

- **Experienced dSLR users broadening their experience to include the D5200:** Perhaps you started out with the Nikon D70 back in 2004, or a D100 before that. It's very likely that some of you used a Nikon D40, D60, D3000, or even D5000 before the bug to advance to more megapixels bit you. You may have used a digital SLR from Nikon or another vendor and are making the switch. You understand basic photography, and want to learn more. And, most of all, you want to transfer the skills you already have to the Nikon D5200, as quickly and seamlessly as possible.

- **Pro photographers and other advanced shooters:** I expect my most discerning readers will be those who already have extensive experience with Nikon intermediate and pro-level cameras. I may not be able to teach you folks much about photography. But, even so, an amazing number of D5200 cameras have been purchased by those who feel it is a good complement to their favorite advanced dSLR. Others (like myself) own a camera like the Nikon D800 and find that the D5200 fills a specific niche incredibly well, and, is useful as a backup camera, because the D5200's 24-megapixel images are often just as good as those produced by more "advanced" models. You pros and semi-pros, despite your depth of knowledge, should find this book useful for learning about the features the D5200 has that your previous cameras lack or implement in a different way.

# Who Am I?

After spending years as the world's most successful unknown author, I've become slightly less obscure in the past few years, thanks to a horde of camera guidebooks and other photographically oriented tomes. You may have seen my photography articles in *Popular Photography* magazine. I've also written about 2,000 articles for magazines like *Petersen's PhotoGraphic* (which is now defunct through no fault of my own), plus *Rangefinder*, *Professional Photographer*, and dozens of other photographic publications. But, first, and foremost, I'm a photojournalist and made my living in the field until I began devoting most of my time to writing books. Although I love writing, I'm happiest when I'm out taking pictures, which is why I took off prior to writing this book to travel to Salamanca, Spain, and a visit to Old San Juan in Puerto Rico. Before that, my recent travels also took me to "exotic" locations that included Florida, San Diego, and Ireland. You'll find photos of some of these visual treasures within the pages of this book.

Like all my digital photography books, this one was written by a Nikon devotee with an incurable photography bug. My first Nikon SLR was a venerable Nikon F back in the 1960s, and I've owned most of the newer digital models since then.

Over the years, I've worked as a sports photographer for an Ohio newspaper and for an upstate New York college. I've operated my own commercial studio and photo lab, cranking out product shots on demand and then printing a few hundred glossy 8 × 10s on a tight deadline for a press kit. I've served as a photo-posing instructor for a modeling agency. People have actually paid me to shoot their weddings and immortalize them with portraits. I even prepared press kits and articles on photography as a PR consultant for a large Rochester, N.Y., company, which shall remain nameless. My trials and travails with imaging and computer technology have made their way into print in book form an alarming number of times, including a few dozen on scanners and photography.

Like you, I love photography for its own merits, and I view technology as just another tool to help me get the images I see in my mind's eye. But, also like you, I had to master this technology before I could apply it to my work. This book is the result of what I've learned, and I hope it will help you master your Nikon D5200 digital SLR, too.

As I write this, I'm currently in the throes of upgrading my website, which you can find at www.nikonguides.com, adding tutorials and information about my other books. There's a lot of information about several Nikon models right now, but I'll be adding tips and recommendations about the Nikon D5200 (including a list of equipment and accessories that I can't live without) in the next few months. I hope you'll stop by for a visit. I've also set up a wish list of Nikon cameras, lenses, and accessories on Amazon.com for those who want to begin shopping now. I hope you'll stop by for a visit to my blog at http://www.dslrguides.com/blog, where you'll find a list of any typos sharp-eyed readers have reported. You'll find my equipment recommendations at http://astore.amazon.com/nikonphoto-20.

# Part I

# Getting Started with Your Nikon D5200

This first part of the book, consisting of just three short chapters, is designed to familiarize you with the basics of your Nikon D5200 as quickly as possible, even though I have no doubt that you've already been out shooting a few hundred (or thousand) photographs with your pride and joy.

After all, inserting a memory card, mounting a lens, stuffing a charged battery into the base, and removing the lens cap to fire off a shot or two isn't rocket science. Even the rawest neophyte can rotate the mode dial (located at top right on the camera body) to the P (Programmed auto) indicator or green Auto icon, point the D5200 at something interesting, and press the shutter release. Presto! A pretty good picture will pop up on the color LCD monitor on the back of the camera. It's easy!

But in digital photography, there is such a thing as *too* easy. If you bought a D5200, you certainly had no intention of using the camera as a point-and-shoot snapshooter. After all, the D5200 is a tool suitable for the most advanced photographic pursuits, with an extensive array of customization possibilities. As such, you don't want the camera's operation to be brainless; you want *access* to the advanced features to be easy.

You get that easy access with the Nikon D5200. However, you'll still need to take the time to learn how to use these features, and I'm going to provide everything you need to know in these first three chapters to begin shooting:

- **Chapter 1:** This is a "Meet Your D5200" introduction, where you'll find information about what came in the box with your camera and, more importantly, what *didn't* come with the camera that you seriously should consider adding to your arsenal. I'll also cover some things you might not have known about charging the D5200's battery, choosing a memory card, setting the time and date, and a few other pre-flight tasks. This is basic stuff, and if you're a Nikon veteran, you can skim over it quickly. A lot of this first chapter is intended for newbies, and even if you personally don't find it essential, you'll probably agree that there was some point during your photographic development (so to speak) that you wished this information was spelled out for you. There's no extra charge!

- **Chapter 2:** Here, you'll find a Quick Start aimed at those who may not be old hands with Nikon cameras having this level of sophistication. The D5200 has some interesting new features, including a nifty built-in HDR (high dynamic range) capability. But even with all the goodies to play with and learning curve still to climb, you'll find that Chapter 2 will get you shooting quickly with a minimum of fuss.

- **Chapter 3:** This is a Streetsmart Roadmap to the Nikon D5200. Confused by the tiny little diagrams and multiple cross-references for each and every control that send you scurrying around looking for information you know is buried somewhere in the small and inadequate manual stuffed in the box? This chapter uses multiple large full-color pictures that show every dial, knob, and button, and explain the basics of using each in clear, easy-to-understand language. I'll give you the basics up front, and, even if I have to send you deeper into the book for a full discussion of a complex topic, you'll have what you need to use a control right away.

# 1

# Thinking Outside of the Box

Whether you subscribe to the "my camera is just a tool" theory, or belong to the "an exquisite camera adds new capabilities to my shooting arsenal" camp, picking up a new Nikon D5200 is a special experience. Those who simply wield tools will find this camera as comforting as an old friend, a solid piece of fine machinery ready and able to do their bidding as part of the creative process.

Other photographers see the low-light capabilities (up to ISO 25600), the rapid-fire 5 frames-per-second continuous shooting, commendable ruggedness, and ultra-high 20-megapixel resolution of the D5200, and gain a sense of empowerment. *Here* is a camera with fewer limitations and more capabilities for exercising renewed creative vision. In either case, using less mawkish terms, the D5200 is one of the coolest cameras Nikon has ever offered. Whether you're upgrading from another brand, from another Nikon model, or (O brave one!) your D5200 is your first digital camera and/or SLR, welcome to the club.

But, now that you've unwrapped and recharged the beast, mounted a lens, and fueled it with a memory card, what do you *do* with it? That's where this chapter—and the chapters that follow— should come in handy. Like many of you, I am a Nikon user of long standing. And, like other members of our club, I had to learn at least some aspects of my newest camera for the very first time at some point. Experienced pro, or Nikon newbie, you bought this book because you wanted to get the most from a very powerful tool, and I'm here to help.

Depending on your path to the camera, the Nikon D5200 is either the company's most ambitious entry-level (although it is several steps up from the very basic D3200) or most affordable intermediate camera, which are both distinctions that I find almost meaningless in the greater scheme of things. I know consummate professionals who produce amazing images with a D90; experienced wedding photographers who evoke the most romantic photos from an old Nikon D200. But whether your *images* are of professional quality, both technically and inspirationally, depends on what's between your ears, and how you apply it. The goal of this book is to provide you with the information you need to put your brain cells together with your Nikon's electro-mechanical components to work productively.

There's a lot to learn, but you don't have to master every detail all at once. Some of the other camera guides I've seen winnow this information down to about one-third as many pages. Indeed, I find it odd that those guidebooks use the same basic template for the advanced D5200 cameras as for a resolutely amateur-level model like the Nikon D3200. A camera like the D5200 has a lot more depth than that, and deserves the in-depth coverage you'll find here.

Whether you've already taken a dozen or twelve hundred photos with your new camera, now that you've got that initial creative burst out of your system, you'll want to take a more considered approach to operating the camera. This chapter and the next are designed to get your camera fired up and ready for shooting as quickly as possible. After all, the D5200 is not a point-and-shoot camera, even though it does boast easy-to-use Auto and Scene mode options.

Even if you're a long-time Nikon shooter, I hope you won't be tempted to skip this chapter or the next one. I realize that you probably didn't purchase this book the same day you bought your camera and that, even if you did, the urge to go out and take a few hundred—or thousand—photos with your new camera is enticing. As valuable as a book like this one is, nobody can suppress their excitement long enough to read the instructions before initiating play with a new toy.

No matter how extensive your experience level is, you don't need to fret about wading through a manual to find out what you must know to take those first few tentative snaps. I'm going to help you hit the ground running with this chapter, which will help you set up your camera and begin shooting in minutes. You won't find a lot of detail in this chapter. Indeed, I'm going to give you the basics, accompanied by some interesting tidbits that will help you become acclimated. I'll go into more depth and even repeat some of what I explain here in later chapters, so you don't have to memorize everything you see. Because I realize that some of you may already have experience with Nikon cameras similar to the D5200, each of the major sections in this chapter will begin with a brief description of what is covered in that section, so you can easily jump ahead to the next if you are in a hurry to get started.

## First Things First

This section helps get you oriented with all the things that come in the box with your Nikon D5200, including what they do. I'll also describe some optional equipment you might want to have. If you want to get started immediately, skim through this section and jump ahead to "Initial Setup" later in the chapter.

The Nikon D5200 comes in an impressive gold box filled with stuff, including connecting cords, booklets, a CD, and lots of paperwork. The most important components are the camera and lens (if you purchased your D5200 with a lens), battery, battery charger, and, if you're the nervous type, the neck strap. You'll also need a memory card as one is not included. If you purchased your D5200 from a camera shop, as I did, the store personnel probably attached the neck strap for you, ran through some basic operational advice that you've already forgotten, tried to sell you a memory card, and then, after they'd given you all the help you could absorb, sent you on your way with a handshake.

Perhaps you purchased your D5200 from one of those mass merchandisers that also sell washing machines and vacuum cleaners. In that case, you might have been sent on your way with only the handshake, or, maybe, not even that if you resisted the efforts to sell you an extended warranty. You save a few bucks at the big box stores, but you don't get the personal service a professional photo retailer provides. It's your choice. There's a third alternative, of course. You might have purchased your camera from a mail order or Internet source, and your D5200 arrived in a big brown (or purple/red) truck. Your only interaction when you took possession of your camera was to scrawl your signature on an electronic clipboard.

In all three cases, the first thing to do is to carefully unpack the camera and double-check the contents with the checklist on one end of the box, helpfully designated under a "This package includes" listing. While this level of setup detail may seem as superfluous as the instructions on a bottle of shampoo, checking the contents *first* is always a good idea. No matter who sells a camera, it's common to open boxes, use a particular camera for a demonstration, and then repack the box without replacing all the pieces and parts afterward. Someone might actually have helpfully checked out your camera on your behalf—and then mispacked the box. It's better to know *now* that something is missing so you can seek redress immediately, rather than discover two months from now that the video cable you thought you'd never use (but now *must* have) was never in the box. I once purchased a brand-new Nikon dSLR kit that was supposed to include a second focusing screen; it wasn't in the box, but because I discovered the deficiency right away, the dealer ordered a replacement for me posthaste.

At a minimum, the box should have the following:

- **Nikon D5200 digital camera.** It almost goes without saying that you should check out the camera immediately, making sure the back- and top-panel LCDs aren't scratched or cracked, the memory and battery doors open properly, and, when a charged battery is inserted and lens mounted, the camera powers up and reports for duty. Out-of-the-box defects like these are rare, but they can happen. It's probably more common that your dealer played with the camera or, perhaps, it was a customer return. That's why it's best to buy your D5200 from a retailer you trust to supply a factory-fresh camera.

- **Rechargeable Li-ion battery EN-EL14.** You'll need to charge this 7.0V, 1030mAh (milliampere hour) battery before you use it. You'll want a second EN-EL14 battery as a spare (trust me), so buy one as soon as possible.

- **Quick charger MH-24.** This charger plugs directly into a wall outlet.

- **EG-CP16 audio/video cable.** Use this supplied cable to connect your D5200 to a standard-definition (analog) television through the set's yellow RCA video jack when you want to view the camera's output on a larger screen. Although the D5200 can be connected to a high-definition television, you'll need to buy a high-definition multimedia interface (HDMI) cable to do that. No HDMI cable is included with the camera.

- **USB cable UC-E17.** You can use this cable to transfer photos from the camera to your computer (I don't recommend that because direct transfer uses a lot of battery power), to upload and download settings between the camera and your computer (highly recommended), and to operate your camera remotely using Nikon Camera Control Pro software (not included in the box). This cable is a standard one that works with the majority of digital cameras—Nikon and otherwise—so if you already own one, you now have a spare.

- **AN-DC3 neck strap.** Nikon provides you with a neck strap emblazoned with your camera model. It's not very adjustable, and, while useful for showing off to your friends exactly which nifty new camera you bought, the Nikon strap also can serve to alert observant unsavory types that you're sporting a higher-end model that's worthy of their attention. I never attach the Nikon strap to my cameras, and instead opt for a more serviceable strap from UPstrap (www.upstrap-pro.com). An UPstrap is shown in Figure 1.1, with its patented non-slip pad that keeps your D5200 on your shoulder, and not crashing to the ground. If you order one of these, tell inventor-photographer Al Stegmeyer that I sent you.

- **BF-1B body cap.** The body cap keeps dust from infiltrating your camera when a lens is not mounted. Always carry a body cap (and rear lens cap) in your camera bag for those times when you need to have the camera bare of optics for more than a minute or two. (That usually happens when repacking a bag efficiently for transport, or when you are carrying an extra body or two for backup.) The body cap/lens cap nest together for compact storage.

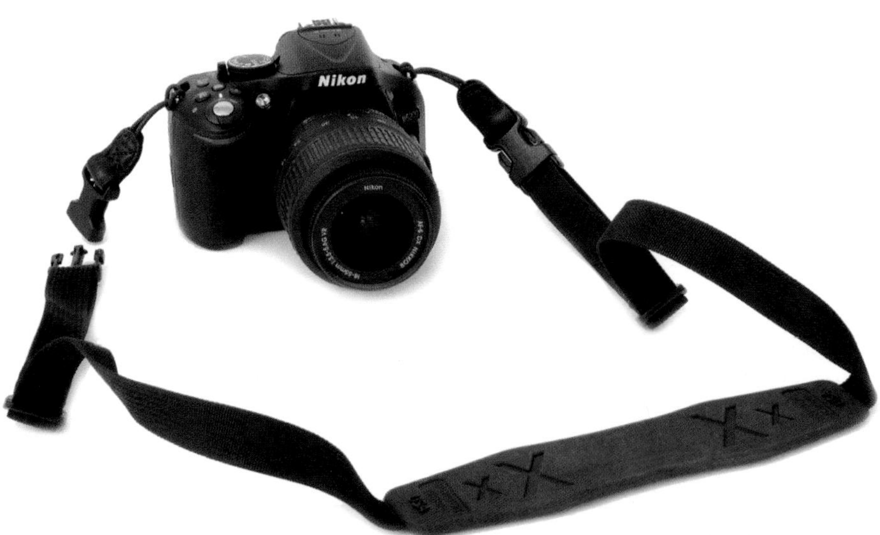

**Figure 1.1**
Third-party neck straps like this UPstrap model are often preferable to the Nikon-supplied strap.

- **DK-20 eyecup.** This is the square rubber eyecup that comes installed on the D5200. It slides on and off the viewfinder. If you prefer, you can also use round, screw-in eyepiece accessories, such as the DK-3 circular rubber eyecup or DG-2 eyepiece 2x magnifier by substituting the Nikon No. 2370 eyepiece adapter for the DK-23 eyecup.

- **DK-5 eyepiece cap.** This small piece can be clipped over the viewfinder window to prevent strong light sources from entering the viewing system when your eye is not pressed up against it, potentially affecting exposure measurement. That can be a special problem when the camera is mounted on a tripod, because additional illumination from the rear can make its way to the 1005-segment CCD that interprets light reaching the focusing screen. I pack this widget away to keep from losing it. As a practical matter, you'll never find it when you really need it, and covering the viewfinder with your hand (hover *near* the viewfinder window rather than touch it, to avoid shaking a tripod-mounted camera) works almost as well.

- **BS-1 accessory shoe cover.** This little piece of plastic protects the electrical contacts of the "hot" shoe on top of the D5200. You can remove it when mounting an electronic flash, Nikon GP-1 GPS device, or other accessory, and then safely leave it off for the rest of your life. I've never had an accessory shoe receive damage in normal use, even when not protected. The paranoid among you who use accessories frequently can keep removing/mounting the shoe cover as required. Find a safe place to keep it between uses, or purchase replacements for this easily mislaid item. (Visit www.bocaphoto.com for many Nikon-related items.)

- **User's manuals.** Even if you have this book, you'll probably want to check the user's guide that Nikon provides, if only to verify the actual nomenclature for some obscure accessory, or to double-check an error code. Google "Nikon D5200 manual PDF" to find a downloadable, non-printable version that you can store on your laptop, a CD-ROM, or other media in case you want to access this reference when the paper version isn't handy. If you have an old memory card that's too small to be usable on a modern dSLR (I still have some 128MB and 256MB cards), you can store the PDF on that. But an even better choice is to put the manual on a low-capacity USB "thumb" drive, which you can buy for less than $10. You'll then be able to access the reference anywhere you are, because you can always find someone with a computer that has a USB port and Adobe Acrobat Reader available. You might not be lucky enough to locate a computer with a memory reader.

- **Quick Start guide.** This little booklet tucked away in the camera's paperwork offers a summary of the Nikon D5200's basic commands and settings.

- **Software CD-ROM.** Here you'll find the Nikon ViewNX 2 software, a useful image management program.

- **Warranty and registration card.** Don't lose these! You can register your Nikon D5200 by mail or online (in the USA, the URL is www.nikonusa.com/register), and you may need the information in this paperwork (plus the purchase receipt/invoice from your retailer) should you require Nikon service support.

Don't bother rooting around in the box for anything beyond what I've listed previously. There are a few things Nikon classifies as optional accessories, even though you (and I) might consider some of them essential. Here's a list of what you *don't* get in the box, but might want to think about as an impending purchase. I'll list them roughly in the order of importance:

- **Secure Digital card.** First-time digital camera buyers are sometimes shocked that their new tool doesn't come with a memory card. Why should it? The manufacturer doesn't have the slightest idea of what capacity or speed card you prefer, so why should they pack one in the box and charge you for it? That's especially true for the Nikon D5200, which is likely to be purchased by photographers who have quite definite ideas about their ideal memory card. Perhaps you want to use tiny 4GB cards—and lots of them. I've met many paranoid wedding photographers who like to work with a horde of smaller cards (and then watch over them *very* protectively), on the theory that they are reducing their chances of losing a significant chunk of the event or reception at one time (of course, that's why you hire a second shooter as backup). Others, especially sports photographers, instead prefer a 16GB or 32GB card with room to spare. If you are shooting fast action at high frame rates, or transfer lots of photos to your computer with a speedy card reader, you might opt for the speediest possible memory card. Buy one (or two, or three) of your own and have your flash memory ready when you unpack your D5200.

- **Extra EN-EL14 battery.** I mentioned the need for an extra battery earlier, and I'll mention it here, again. Even though you might get 1,000 or more shots from a single battery, it's easy to exceed that figure in a few hours of shooting sports at 6 fps. Batteries can unexpectedly fail, too, or simply lose their charge from sitting around unused for a week or two. Buy an extra, keep it charged, and free your mind from worry. I own four, in total, because the same battery also fits my Nikon D3200, which I have converted to full-time infrared operation, as well as a Nikon D5100 I've turned over to other members of my family.

- **Nikon Capture NX 2 software.** You can download a free try-out copy of this software from Nikon's website, but if you want to use it after the free period expires, you'll need to buy it.

- **Camera Control Pro 2 software.** This is the utility you'll use to operate your camera remotely from your computer. Nikon charges extra for this software, but you'll find it invaluable if you're hiding near a tethered, tripod-mounted camera while shooting, say, close-ups of hummingbirds. There are lots of applications for remote shooting, and you'll need Camera Control Pro to operate your camera. Buy a suitably longer USB cable, too, unless you plan to use the Nikon WT4a wireless transmitter (described below).

- **Add-on Speedlight.** Your built-in flash can function as the main light, diffused and used for fill, or dialed down in power so it has virtually no effect on the finished photo at all. But, you'll have to own one or two (or more) external flash units to gain the most flexibility. If you do much flash photography at all, consider an add-on Speedlight as an important accessory.

- **Remote control cable MC-DC2.** You can plug this one-meter long accessory electronic release cable into the socket hidden behind a rubber cover on the side of the D5200, and then fire off the camera without the need to touch the camera itself. In a pinch, you can use the D5200's self-timer to minimize vibration when triggering the camera, or even take advantage of the delayed release features to reduce camera shake. (These are all described later in this book.) But when you want to take a photo at the exact moment you desire (and not when the self-timer happens to trip), or need to eliminate all possibility of human-induced camera shake, you need this release cord.

■ **ML-L3 infrared remote.** The D5200 has an infrared sensor on the front and rear that can receive signals from this optional remote control. It works best when used while facing the front or back of the camera (rather than from one side), but, unlike the MC-DC2 remote, you can be positioned farther away than one meter. (See Figure 1.2.)

■ **Nikon GP-1 global positioning system (GPS) device.** This accessory attaches to the accessory shoe on top of the Nikon D5200 and captures latitude, longitude, and altitude information, which is imprinted in a special data area of your image files. The "geotagging" data can be plotted on a map in Nikon ViewNX 2 or other software programs. I'll explain more about this feature in Chapter 7.

■ **AC adapter EH-5b/EP-5a power connector.** There are several typical situations where this AC adapter and connector for your D5200 can come in handy: when you're cleaning the sensor manually and want to totally eliminate the possibility that a lack of juice will cause the fragile shutter and mirror to spring to life during the process; when in the studio shooting product photos, portraits, class pictures, and so forth for hours on end; when using your D5200 for remote shooting as well as time-lapse photography; for extensive review of images on your standard-definition or high-definition television; or for file transfer to your computer. These all use prodigious amounts of power, which can be provided by this AC adapter. (Beware of power outages and blackouts when cleaning your sensor, however!)

**Figure 1.2** The ML-L3 infrared remote can trigger your camera from a dozen feet away, or more.

■ **DR-6 right-angle viewer.** Fastens in place of the standard square rubber eyecup and provides a 90-degree view for framing and composing your image at right angles to the original viewfinder, useful for low-level (or high-level) shooting. (Or, maybe, shooting around corners!)

■ **DK-21M magnifying eyepiece.** Provides a 1.17X magnification factor of the entire viewing area (unlike the 2X DG-2 eyepiece, which enlarges the center of the image), making it easier to check focus. You might have to move your eye around a little to see all the indicators outside the image frame, but this magnifier is still suitable for everyday use.

■ **SC-28 TTL flash cord.** Allows using Nikon Speedlights off-camera, while retaining all the automated features.

■ **SC-29 TTL flash cord.** Similar to the SC-28, this unit has its own AF-assist lamp, which can provide extra illumination for the D5200's autofocus system in dim light (which, not coincidentally, is when you'll probably be using an electronic flash).

# Initial Setup

This section helps you become familiar with the two important controls most used to make adjustments: the multi selector and the command dial. You'll also find information on charging the battery, setting the clock, mounting a lens, and making diopter vision adjustments. If you're comfortable with all these things, skim through and skip ahead to "Changing Default Settings" in the next section.

Once you've unpacked and inspected your camera, the initial setup of your Nikon D5200 is fast and easy. Basically, you just need to charge the battery, attach a lens, and insert a memory card. I'll address each of these steps separately, but if you already are confident you can manage these setup tasks without further instructions, feel free to skip this section entirely. While most buyers of a D5200 tend to be experienced photographers, I realize that some readers are ambitious, if inexperienced, and should, at the minimum, skim the contents of the next section, because I'm going to list a few options that you might not be aware of.

## Mastering the Multi Selector and Command Dials

I'll be saving descriptions of most of the controls used with the Nikon D5200 until Chapter 2, which provides a complete "roadmap" of the camera's buttons and dials and switches. However, you may need to perform a few tasks during this initial setup process, and most of them will require the MENU button and the multi selector pad. The MENU button is easy to find: it's located to the left of the viewfinder eyepiece. It requires almost no explanation; when you want to access a menu, press it. To exit most menus, press it again.

The multi selector pad may remind you of the similar control found on many point-and-shoot cameras, and other digital SLRs. It consists of a thumbpad-sized button with projections at the North, South, East, and West positions, plus a button in the center. It can also be pushed in diagonal directions to give you Northeast, Southeast, Southwest, and Northwest orientations. (See Figure 1.3.)

The multi selector on the D5200 functions slightly differently than its counterpart on some other cameras. For example, some point-and-shoot models assign a function, such as white balance or ISO setting, to one of the directional buttons (usually in conjunction with a function key of some sort). The use of the multi selector varies, even within the Nikon dSLR line up. For example, many earlier Nikon digital SLRs (such as the Nikon D50/D70/D80) have no center button in the multi selector at all. Other Nikon cameras (such as pro models like the Nikon D4) allow assigning a function of your choice to the multi selector center button.

With the D5200, the multi selector is used extensively for navigation—for example, to navigate among menus on the

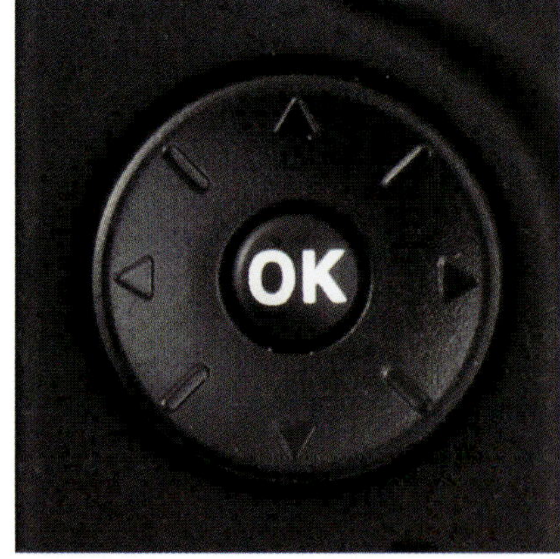

**Figure 1.3** The multi selector pad has four directional positions for navigating up/down/left/right, and a center button to confirm your selection.

LCD or to choose one of the 39 focus points, to advance or reverse display of a series of images during picture review, or to change the kind of photo information displayed on the screen. The center button is used to display the current image in the Retouch menu, as described in Chapter 10.

So, from time to time in this chapter (and throughout this book) I'll be referring to the multi selector and its left/right/up/down buttons, and center OK button.

The command dial is located on the rear of the D5200. The command dial is used to change settings such as shutter speed when rotated; spinning the same dial while pressing the aperture/exposure compensation button (located just southeast of the shutter release) adjusts an alternate or secondary setting. For example, in Manual exposure mode, you'd use the aperture button + command dial to adjust the aperture, while the command dial alone is used to change the shutter speed. (In both cases, the dial is "active" for these adjustments only when the D5200's exposure meter is On.) The meter will automatically go to sleep after an interval (you'll learn how to specify the length of time in Chapter 9), and you must waken the camera (just tap the shutter release button) to switch the meter back on and activate the command dial.

## Setting the Clock

It's likely that your Nikon D5200's internal clock hasn't been set to your local time, so you may need to do that first. You'll find complete instructions for setting the four options for the date/time (time zone, actual date and time, the date format, and whether you want the D5200 to conform to Daylight Savings Time) in Chapter 10. However, if you think you can handle this step without instruction, press the MENU button (at the far left corner of the back panel), use the multi selector (that thumb-friendly button I just described, located to the immediate right of the back-panel LCD) to scroll down to the Setup menu, press the multi selector button to the right, and scroll down to Time Zone and Date choice, and press right again. The options will appear on the screen that appears next. Keep in mind that you'll need to reset your camera's internal clock from time to time, as it is not 100-percent accurate.

## Battery Included

Your Nikon D5200 is a sophisticated hunk of machinery and electronics, but it needs a charged battery to function, so rejuvenating the EN-EL14 lithium-ion battery pack furnished with the camera should be your first step. A fully charged power source should be good for approximately 660 shots, based on standard tests defined by the Camera & Imaging Products Association (CIPA) document DC-002. Nikon's own standards are quite a bit more optimistic (it predicts as many as 2,200 shots from a single charge). In the real world, of course, the life of the battery will depend on how much image review you do, how many shots you take with the built-in flash, and many other factors. You'll want to keep track of how many pictures *you* are able to take in your own typical circumstances, and use that figure as a guideline, instead.

## A BATTERY AND A SPARE

I always recommend purchasing Nikon brand batteries (for about $50) over less-expensive third-party packs, even though the $30 substitute batteries may offer more capacity at a lower price (some may even top the 1,030 mAh offered by the Nikon battery). My reasoning is that it doesn't make sense to save $20 on a component for a sophisticated camera, especially since batteries have been known to fail in potentially harmful ways. You need only look as far as Nikon's own recall of its earlier EN-EL3 batteries, which forced the company to ship out thousands of free replacement cells. You're unlikely to get the same support from a third-party battery supplier that sells under a half-dozen or more different product labels and brands, and may not even have an easy way to get the word out that a recall has been issued.

If your pictures are important to you, always have at least one spare battery available, and make sure it is an authentic Nikon product.

All rechargeable batteries undergo some degree of self-discharge just sitting idle in the camera or in the original packaging. Lithium-ion power packs of this type typically lose a few percent of their charge every few days, even when the camera isn't turned on. The small amount of juice used to provide the "shots remaining" figure on the top-panel monochrome LCD when the D5200 is turned off isn't the culprit; Li-ion cells lose their power through a chemical reaction that continues when the camera is switched off. So, it's very likely that the battery purchased with your camera is at least partially pooped out, so you'll want to revive it before going out for some serious shooting.

### Charging the Battery

When the battery is inserted into the MH-24 charger properly (it's impossible to insert it incorrectly), a Charge light begins flashing, and remains flashing until the status lamp glows steadily, indicating that charging is finished (takes about 1.5 hours). (See Figure 1.4.) When the battery is charged, flip the lever on the bottom of the camera and slide the battery in, as shown in Figure 1.5. Check the Setup menu's Battery Info entry as I recommended earlier to make sure the battery is fully charged. If not, try putting it in the charger again. One of three things may be the culprit: a.) the actual charging cycle sometimes takes longer than you (or the charger) expected; b.) the battery is new and needs to be "seasoned" for a few charging cycles, after which it will accept a full charge and deliver more shots; c.) you've got a defective battery. The last is fairly rare, but before you start counting on getting a particular number of exposures from a battery, it's best to make sure it's fully charged, seasoned, and ready to deliver.

# Final Steps

Your Nikon D5200 is almost ready to fire up and shoot. You'll need to select and mount a lens, adjust the viewfinder for your vision, and insert a memory card. Each of these steps is easy, and if you've used any Nikon before, you already know exactly what to do. I'm going to provide a little extra detail for those of you who are new to the Nikon or SLR worlds.

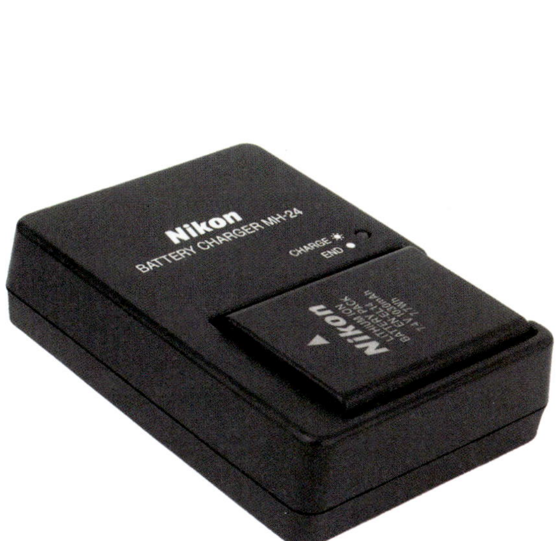

**Figure 1.4** Charge the battery before use.

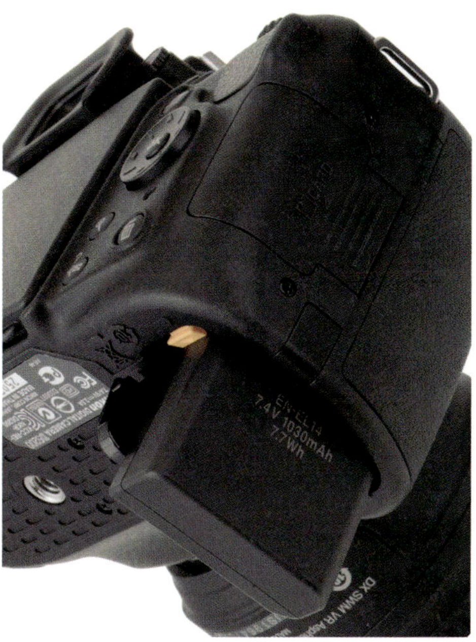

**Figure 1.5** Insert the battery in the camera; it only fits one way.

## Mounting the Lens

As you'll see, my recommended lens mounting procedure emphasizes protecting your equipment from accidental damage and minimizing the intrusion of dust. If your D5200 has no lens attached, select the lens you want to use and loosen (but do not remove) the rear lens cap. I generally place the lens I am planning to mount vertically in a slot in my camera bag, where it's protected from mishaps, but ready to pick up quickly. By loosening the rear lens cap, you'll be able to lift it off the back of the lens at the last instant, so the rear element of the lens is covered until then.

After that, remove the body cap by rotating the cap away from the release button. You should always mount the body cap when there is no lens on the camera, because it helps keep dust out of the interior of the camera, where it can settle on the mirror, focusing screen, interior mirror box, and potentially find its way past the shutter onto the sensor. (While the D5200's sensor cleaning mechanism works fine, the less dust it has to contend with, the better.) The body cap also protects the vulnerable mirror from damage caused by intruding objects (including your fingers, if you're not cautious).

Once the body cap has been removed, remove the rear lens cap from the lens, set it aside, and then mount the lens on the camera by matching the alignment indicator on the lens barrel with the raised white bump on the camera's lens mount. (See Figure 1.6.) Rotate the lens toward the shutter release until it seats securely. Some lenses are trickier to mount than others, particularly telephotos and telephoto zooms with swiveling collars that allow the lens to be fastened to a tripod. You might need to rotate the collar so the tripod foot doesn't bump into the front overhang of the D5200's prism.

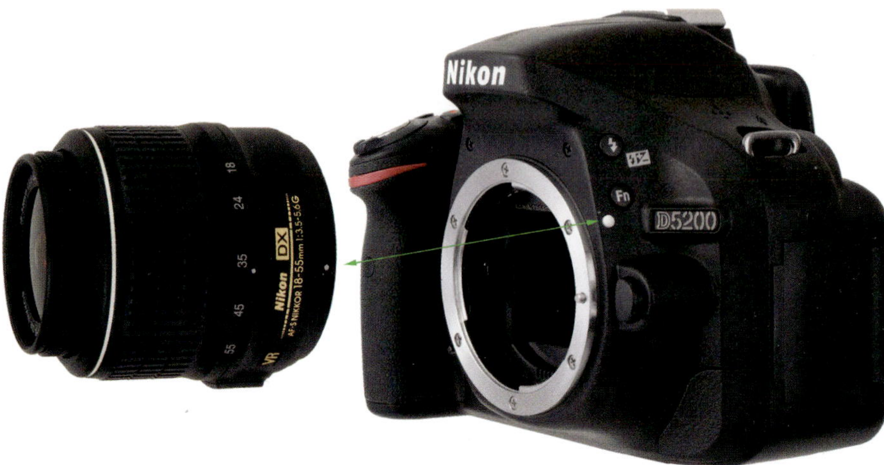

**Figure 1.6**
Match the indicator on the lens with the white dot on the camera mount to properly align the lens with the bayonet mount.

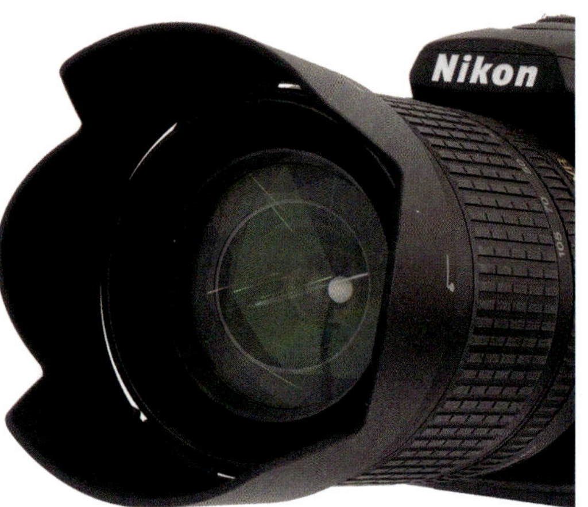

**Figure 1.7**
A lens hood protects the lens from extraneous light and accidental bumps.

Set the focus mode switch on the lens to AF or M-AF (autofocus). If the lens hood is bayoneted on the lens in the reversed position (which makes the lens/hood combination more compact for transport), twist it off and remount with the "petals" (found on virtually all Nikon lens hoods) facing outward. (See Figure 1.7.) A lens hood protects the front of the lens from accidental bumps, and reduces flare caused by extraneous light arriving at the front element of the lens from outside the picture area.

## Adjusting Diopter Correction

Those of us with less than perfect eyesight can often benefit from a little optical correction in the viewfinder. Your contact lenses or glasses may provide all the correction you need, but if you are a glasses wearer and want to use the D5200 without your glasses, you can take advantage of the camera's built-in diopter adjustment, which can be varied from −3 to +1 correction. Press the shutter release halfway to illuminate the indicators in the viewfinder, then rotate the diopter adjustment dial next to the viewfinder (see Figure 1.8) while looking through the viewfinder until the indicators appear sharp.

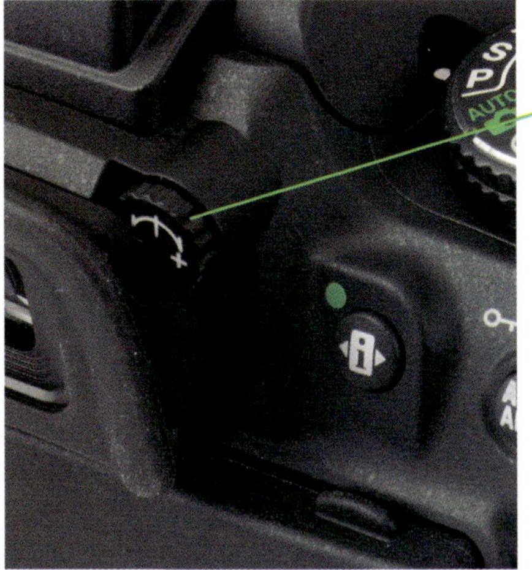


**Figure 1.8**
Viewfinder
diopter correction
from –3 to +1 can
be dialed in.

If more than one person uses your D5200, and each requires a different diopter setting on the camera itself, you can save a little time by noting the number of clicks and direction (clockwise to increase the diopter power; counterclockwise to decrease the diopter value) required to change from one user to the other. Should the available correction be insufficient, Nikon offers nine different Diopter-Adjustment Viewfinder Correction lenses for the viewfinder window, ranging from –5 to +3, at a cost of $15–$20 each.

## Inserting a Secure Digital Memory Card

You've probably set up your D5200 so you can't take photos without a memory card inserted. (There is a Slot Empty Release Lock entry, Custom Setting f4, that enables/disables shutter release functions when a memory card is absent—learn about that in Chapter 9.) So, your final step will be to insert a memory card. Slide the door on the back right edge of the body toward the back of the camera to release the cover, and then open it. (You should only remove a memory card when the camera is switched off, or, at the very least, the yellow-green memory access light that indicates the camera is writing to the card is not illuminated.)

### MORE ABOUT CUSTOM SETTING OPTIONS IN CHAPTER 9

The next section will suggest other "default" settings you might want to adjust before you get started. You'll find a complete list of Custom Setting menu options and parameters in Chapter 9.

Inside, you'll find one SD card slot. (See Figure 1.9.) Insert the memory card with the label facing the back of the camera oriented so the edge with the contacts (metallic "fingers") goes into the slot first. Close the door, and, if necessary, format the card. A Secure Digital card can be removed just by pressing it inward; it will pop out far enough that you can extract it.

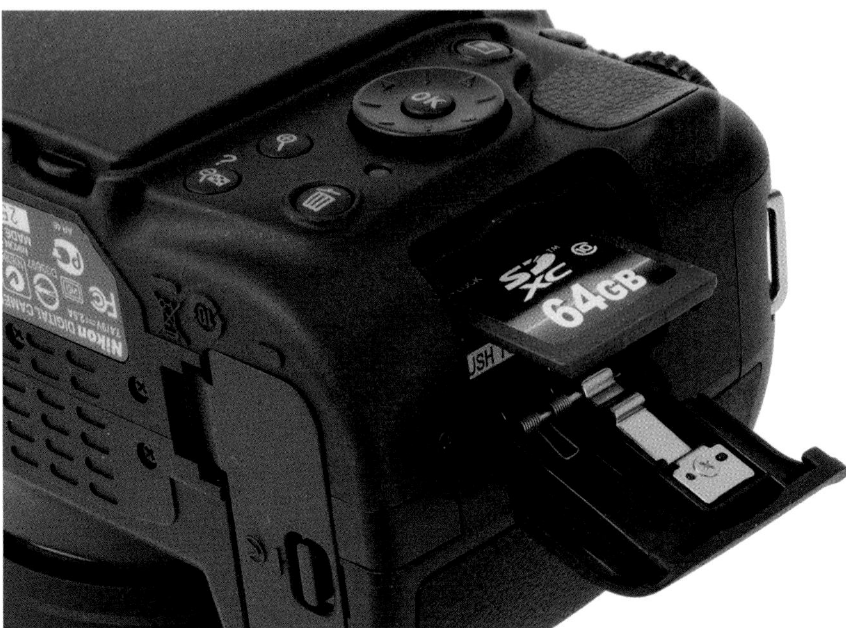

**Figure 1.9**
The memory card in either slot is always inserted with the label facing the back of the camera.

## Formatting a Memory Card

There are three ways to create a blank memory card for your D5200, and two of them are wrong. Here are your options, both correct and incorrect:

- **Transfer (move) files to your computer.** When you transfer (rather than copy) all the image files to your computer from the memory card (either using a direct cable transfer or with a card reader, as described later in this chapter), the old image files are erased from the card, leaving the card blank. Theoretically. Unfortunately, this method does *not* remove files that you've labeled as Protected by pressing the Protect button to the left of the command dial (it's marked with a key icon) while viewing the image on the LCD, nor does it identify and lock out parts of your memory card that have become corrupted or unusable since the last time you formatted the card. Therefore, I recommend always formatting the card, rather than simply moving the image files, each time you want to make a blank card. The only exception is when you *want* to leave the protected/unerased images on the card for awhile longer, say, to share with friends, family, and colleagues.

- **(Don't) Format in your computer.** With the memory card inserted in a card reader or card slot in your computer, you can use Windows or Mac OS to reformat the memory card. Don't! The operating system won't necessarily install the correct file system. The only way to ensure that the card has been properly formatted for your camera is to perform the format in the camera itself. The only exception to this rule is when you have a seriously munged memory card that your camera refuses to format. Sometimes it is possible to revive such a corrupted card by allowing the operating system to reformat it first, then trying again in the camera.

■ **Setup menu format.** To use one of the recommended methods to format a memory card, press the MENU button, use the up/down buttons of the multi selector (that thumb-pad-sized control to the right of the LCD) to choose the Setup menu (which is represented by a wrench icon), navigate to the Format Memory Card entry with the right button of the multi selector, and select Yes from the screen that appears. Press OK to begin the format process.

Table 1.1 shows the typical number of shots you can expect using 14-bit color depth and an 8GB memory card. If you'd like to change image quality settings now (without waiting for more complete instructions that come later in the book), press the MENU button, use the directional buttons to navigate to the Shooting menu (marked with a green camera icon), scroll down to Image Quality, and select JPEG Fine, JPEG Normal, JPEG Basic, RAW, or RAW+JPEG Fine, RAW+JPEG Normal, or RAW+JPEG Basic. I'll explain how to set image quality parameters in more detail in Chapter 8.

At this point, your camera is set up and ready to shoot. You can move on to Chapter 2, where I show you how to make basic settings.

### Table 1.1  File Capacity of 8GB Card

|  | Large | Medium | Small |
|---|---|---|---|
| JPEG Fine | 504 | 848 | 1,650 |
| JPEG Normal | 1,004 | 1,674 | 3,200 |
| JPEG Basic | 1,976 | 3,200 | 6,100 |
| RAW | 216 | N/A | N/A |
| RAW+JPEG Fine | 150 | 172 | 190 |
| RAW+JPEG Normal | 178 | 190 | 202 |
| RAW+JPEG Basic | 194 | 202 | 208 |

# Nikon D5200 Quick Start

Now it's time to fire up your Nikon D5200 and take some photos. The easy part is turning on the power—the Off-On switch is on the right side, concentric with the shutter release button. Turn on the camera, and, if you mounted a lens and inserted a fresh battery and memory card—as I prompted you in the last chapter—you're ready to begin. You'll need to select a release mode, exposure mode, metering mode, focus mode, and, if need be, elevate the D5200's built-in flash.

## Choosing a Release Mode

This section shows you how to choose from single frame, continuous mode, self-timer mode, delayed remote, quick response remote, and quiet shutter release mode.

The shooting mode determines when (and how often) the D5200 makes an exposure. If you're coming to the dSLR world from a point-and-shoot camera, you might have used a model that labels these options as drive modes, dating back to the film era when cameras could be set for single shot or "motor drive" (continuous) shooting modes. Your D5200 has seven release (shooting) modes: single frame, continuous low and high, self-timer, delayed remote, quick response remote, and quiet shutter release. The release modes are as follows:

- **Single frame.** In this mode, the D5200 takes one picture each time you press the shutter release button down all the way. If you press the shutter and nothing happens (which is very frustrating!), you may be using a focus mode that requires sharp focus to be achieved before a picture can be taken. This is called focus priority, and is discussed in more detail under "Choosing a Focus Mode," later in this chapter.

- **Continuous L/Continuous H.** These modes fire off shots at up to 3 or 5 frames per second, respectively. The frame rate can slow down as your D5200's memory buffer fills, which forces the camera to wait until some of the pictures you have already taken are written to the memory card, freeing up more space in the buffer. The frame rate may also decrease at shutter speeds slower than 1/200th second, or when operations like continuous-servo autofocus (described later in this chapter) force the D5200 to work at a slightly slower interval.

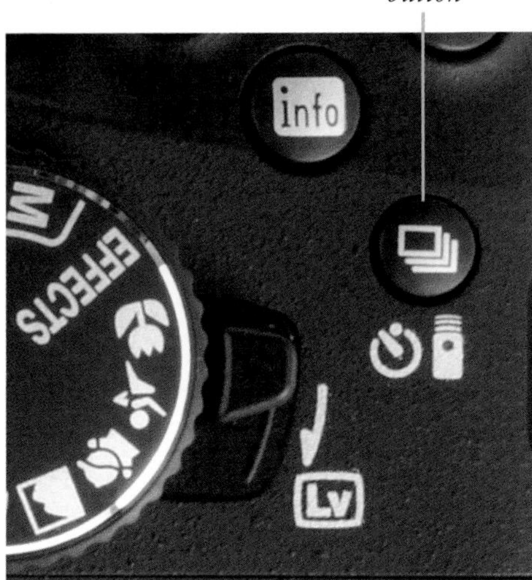



**Figure 2.1** Press the release mode button and use the multi selector navigation buttons to choose a mode. Press OK to confirm.

- **Self-timer.** You can use the self-timer as a replacement for a remote release, to reduce the effects of camera/user shake when the D5200 is mounted on a tripod or, say, set on a firm surface, or when you want to get in the picture yourself. Use Custom Setting c3 to specify delays of 2, 5, 10, or 20 seconds. You can also specify the number of shots taken at the end of the elapsed period, and the interval between those shots (see Chapter 9 for instructions). Any time you use the camera on a tripod (with the self-timer or otherwise) make sure there is no bright light shining on the viewfinder window; if so, cover it or locate that DK-5 eyepiece cap and block the window.

- **Delayed remote/Quick response remote.** No special setting of the release mode is necessary when you plug the wired MC-DC2 remote into the side of the camera. However, if you want to use the ML-L3 infrared remote, you'll need to change the release mode to either of these two settings: delayed remote (shutter releases two seconds after you press the button on the ML-L3 IR remote) or quick response remote (the shutter trips immediately when the button is pressed). Once you've selected either of these two release modes, the camera then "looks" for the remote signal for a period of time you specify using Custom Setting c4 (select from 1, 5, 10, or 15 minutes). As with the self-timer, make sure there is no bright light shining on the viewfinder window; if so, cover it or locate that DK-5 eyepiece cap and block the window.

- **Quiet shutter release.** This setting, marked with a Q symbol, activates the D5200's "quiet mode," which silences the camera's beep noise during autofocus, reduces the sound the mirror makes when it flips back down, and delays that "noise" until you release the shutter button.

## SHOOTING MOVIES

You'll learn more about shooting high-definition movie clips with your D5200 later in Chapter 6. But if you want to get started right away, it's easy. Just select live view mode by rotating the Live View (Lv) switch located next to the mode dial on the top right of the camera. When you want to start shooting, press the red button on top of the camera, located southwest of the shutter release button. Press the button again to stop shooting. That's it!

> **Note**
>
> If you plan to dash in front of the camera to join the scene when working with the self-timer, consider using manual focus so the D5200 won't refocus on your fleeing form and produce unintended results. (Nikon really needs to offer an option to autofocus at the *end* of the self-timer cycle.) An alternative is to use the ML-L3 IR remote, because the camera focuses when you press the button (after you've ensconced yourself safely in the frame).

To set a release mode, press the release mode button on top of the camera, immediately to the right of the mode dial. Then, use the multi selector navigation keys to highlight the mode you want. Press the OK button to confirm your choice.

## Adjusting ISO

Here you'll learn to use the information edit screen, which allows you to quickly change settings, including ISO sensitivity.

To start out, it's best to set the ISO (how sensitive the sensor is to light) to ISO 200 for daylight photos, and ISO 400 for pictures in dimmer light. (Don't be afraid of ISO 1600 or even higher; however, the D5200 does a *much* better job of producing low-noise photos at higher ISOs than earlier generations.) You can also set the D5200 to automatically select an appropriate ISO setting, using the menu system, as I'll describe in Chapter 4. Adjust ISO sensitivity now using the information edit screen.

1. **Access information edit screen.** If the information display screen (see Figure 2.2, left) is not visible on the LCD, press the information edit button (located to the right of the viewfinder window). When the information display is visible, press the information edit button again to access the information edit screen (see Figure 2.2, right).

2. **Navigate to ISO settings.** Use the left/right/up/down cursor keys to navigate to the ISO settings entry in the two bottom rows of the information edit screen. It's located in the right-hand corner.

3. **Select setting.** Press OK. A screen with the available ISO settings appears. Use the up/down buttons to choose the sensitivity you want, from ISO 100 to ISO 6400, plus four "extended" settings. Hi1 and Hi2 are the equivalent of ISO 12800 and 25600, respectively.

4. **Confirm or cancel.** Press the OK button to confirm, or the information edit button to cancel.

Other settings on the information edit screen, including image quality, white balance, and autofocus modes can also be selected using this basic procedure.

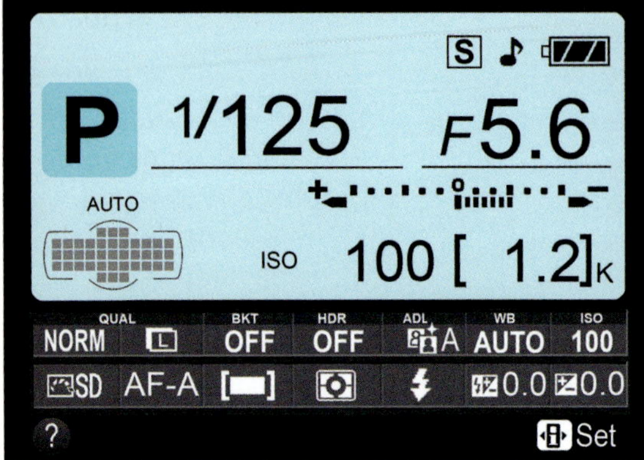
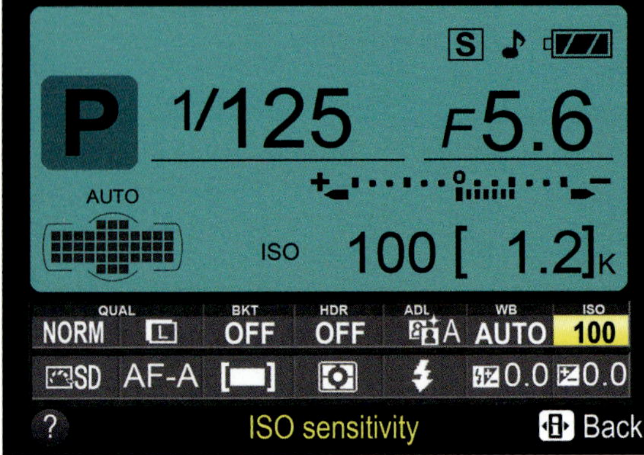

**Figure 2.2** Press the information edit button located to the right of the viewfinder to view this shooting information screen (right). Press a second time to access the information edit screen, where you can change settings.

# Selecting an Exposure Mode

This section shows you how to choose an exposure mode. If you'd rather have the D5200 make all of the decisions for you, just rotate the mode dial to Auto or Auto (Flash Off) and jump to the section titled "Reviewing the Pictures You've Taken." If you'd rather choose one of the scene modes, tailored to specific types of shooting situations, or try out the camera's semi-automatic modes, continue reading this section.

The Nikon D5200 has four types of shooting modes: advanced modes/exposure modes, Auto modes, which includes Auto and Auto (Flash Off), and a third set, which Nikon labels scene modes. Also available is a fourth option, Special Effects, which allows you to process your images with some retouching effects, such as Color Sketch or Miniature Effect, as the picture is actually taken. (See Figure 2.3.)

**Advanced modes.** The advanced manual and semi-automatic modes include Programmed-auto (or Program mode), Shutter-priority auto, Aperture-priority auto, and Manual exposure mode. These are the modes you'll use most often after you've learned all your D5200's features, because they allow you to specify how the camera chooses its settings when making an exposure, for greater creative control.

**Auto/Scene modes.** The two Auto and various scene modes take full control of the camera, make all the decisions for you, and don't allow you to override the D5200's settings. They are most useful while you're learning to use the camera, because you can select an appropriate mode. The Auto modes include Auto and Auto (Flash Off). Five scene modes reside on the mode dial itself: Portrait, Landscape, Child, Sports, and Close Up. Eleven additional scene modes are available when you rotate the mode dial to the SCENE position, and then rotate the command dial to select from Night Portrait, Night Landscape, Party/Indoor, Beach/Snow, Sunset, Dusk/Dawn, Pet Portrait, Candlelight, Blossom, Autumn Colors, and Food. Scene modes can give you decent photos using appropriate settings, but your opportunities to use a little creativity (say, to overexpose an image to create a silhouette, or to deliberately use a slow shutter speed to add a little blur to an action shot) are minimal.

**Special Effects modes.** The seven Special Effects modes add special looks to your images. They include Night Vision, Color Sketch, Miniature Effect, Selective Color, Silhouette, High Key, and Low Key. These are all applied as you take the picture, and can't be reversed. However, three of them, Color Sketch, Miniature Effect, and Selective Color, can be applied after the fact on a *copy* of your original image, using the Retouch menu, as described in Chapter 10.

## Choosing an Auto/Scene or Effects Mode

The 18 scene and Auto modes can be selected by rotating the mode dial on the top right of the Nikon D5200. The first seven have their own positions on the mode dial. The others can be selected by rotating the mode dial to the SCENE position, and then rotating the main command dial to select one of the additional modes. The options on the mode dial include:

- **Auto.** In this mode, the D5200 makes all the exposure decisions for you, and will pop up the internal flash if necessary under low-light conditions. The camera automatically focuses on the subject closest to the camera (unless you've set the lens to manual focus), and the autofocus-assist illuminator lamp on the front of the camera will light up to help the camera focus in low-light conditions.

- **Auto (Flash Off).** Identical to Auto mode, except that the flash will not pop up under any circumstances. You'd want to use this in a museum, during religious ceremonies, concerts, or any environment where flash is forbidden or distracting.

- **Portrait.** Use this mode when you're taking a portrait of a subject standing relatively close to the camera and want to de-emphasize the background, maximize sharpness, and produce flattering skin tones. The built-in flash will pop up if needed.

- **Landscape.** Select this mode when you want extra sharpness and rich colors of distant scenes. The built-in flash and AF-assist illuminator are disabled.

- **Child.** Use this mode to accentuate the vivid colors often found in children's clothing, and to render skin tones with a soft, natural-looking texture. The D5200 focuses on the closest subject to the camera. The built-in flash will pop up if needed.

- **Sports.** Use this mode to freeze fast-moving subjects. The D5200 selects a fast shutter speed to stop action, and focuses continuously on the center focus point while you have the shutter release button pressed halfway. However, you can select one of the other two focus points to the left or right of the center by pressing the multi selector left/right buttons. The built-in electronic flash and focus assist illuminator lamp are disabled.

- **Close Up.** This mode is helpful when you are shooting close-up pictures of a subject from about one foot away or less, such as flowers, bugs, and small items. The D5200 focuses on the closest subject in the center of the frame, but you can use the multi selector right and left buttons to focus on a different point. Use a tripod in this mode, as exposures may be long enough to cause blurring from camera movement. The built-in flash will pop up if needed.

When the camera is set to the SCENE position, you can select additional modes:

- **Night Portrait.** Choose this mode when you want to illuminate a subject in the foreground with flash (it will pop up automatically, if needed), but still allow the background to be exposed properly by the available light. The camera focuses on the closest main subject. Be prepared to use a tripod or a vibration-resistant lens like the 18-55 VR kit lens to reduce the effects of camera shake.

- **Night Landscape.** Mount your camera on a tripod and use this mode for longer exposure times to produce images with more natural colors and reduced visual noise in scenes with street lights or neon signs.

- **Party/Indoor.** For indoor scenes with typical background lighting.

- **Beach/Snow.** Useful for bright high-contrast scenes with sand or snow. The built-in flash and AF assist lamp are disabled.

- **Sunset.** Emphasizes the rich colors at sunset or sunrise, disables the flash, and may use a slow shutter speed, so consider working with a tripod.

- **Dusk/Dawn.** Similar to Sunset mode, but preserves the subtle colors in the sky just after sunset, or just prior to dawn.

- **Pet Portrait.** An "action" mode specifically for fast-moving, erratic subjects, such as pets.

- **Candlelight.** Disables your flash to allow photographs by candle; a tripod is recommended.

- **Blossom.** Uses a small f/stop to expand depth-of-field when shooting landscapes with broad expanses of blossoms. This scene mode may result in longer shutter speeds, so consider using a tripod.

- **Autumn Colors.** Makes reds and yellows in fall foliage richer.

- **Food.** Boosts saturation to make food look more appetizing in your snaps.

Special Effects mode provides additional special looks. Of the following, Color Sketch, Miniature Effect, and Selective Color are available in both still and live view/movie shooting modes. I'll describe these interesting modes in more detail in Chapter 10.

- **Night Vision.** Produces images of the darkest scenes using the D5200's high ISO sensitivity settings. Use a tripod, because blur is likely with the longer shutter speeds. Under this dim lighting, you'll need to focus manually if working with the optical viewfinder; autofocus is available only in live view.

- **Color Sketch.** Outlines your image's areas and fills them with color.

- **Miniature Effect.** This effect is widely becoming known as "Tilt/Shift" because it can be reproduced with special lenses that tilt and shift the plane of focus. By throwing backgrounds and foregrounds out of focus, the subjects in the middle of the frame appear to be miniatures photographed with shallow depth-of-field. A cool effect, but it's already starting to be over-used.

- **Selective Color.** You choose the colors that you want to dominate the main subject in your image, and everything else is rendered in black-and-white.

- **Silhouette.** Exposes for bright backgrounds, turning foreground objects into underexposed silhouettes.

- **High Key.** Exposes for bright scenes with lots of highlight areas.

- **Low Key.** Tailors exposure for darker scenes, retaining murky shadows while allowing highlights to remain.

## Choosing an Advanced Mode

If you're very new to digital photography, you might want to set the camera to P (Program mode) and start snapping away. That mode will make all the appropriate settings for you for many shooting situations. If you have more photographic experience, you might want to opt for one of the semi-automatic modes, shown on the mode dial in Figure 2.3. These, too, are described in more detail in Chapter 4. These modes all let you apply a little more creativity to your camera's settings.

- **P (Program).** This mode allows the D5200 to select the basic exposure settings, but you can still override the camera's choices to fine-tune your image, while maintaining metered exposure, as I'll explain in Chapter 4.

- **S (Shutter-priority).** This mode is useful when you want to use a particular shutter speed to stop action or produce creative blur effects. Choose your preferred shutter speed by rotating the main command dial when the meter is active, and the D5200 will select the appropriate f/stop for you.

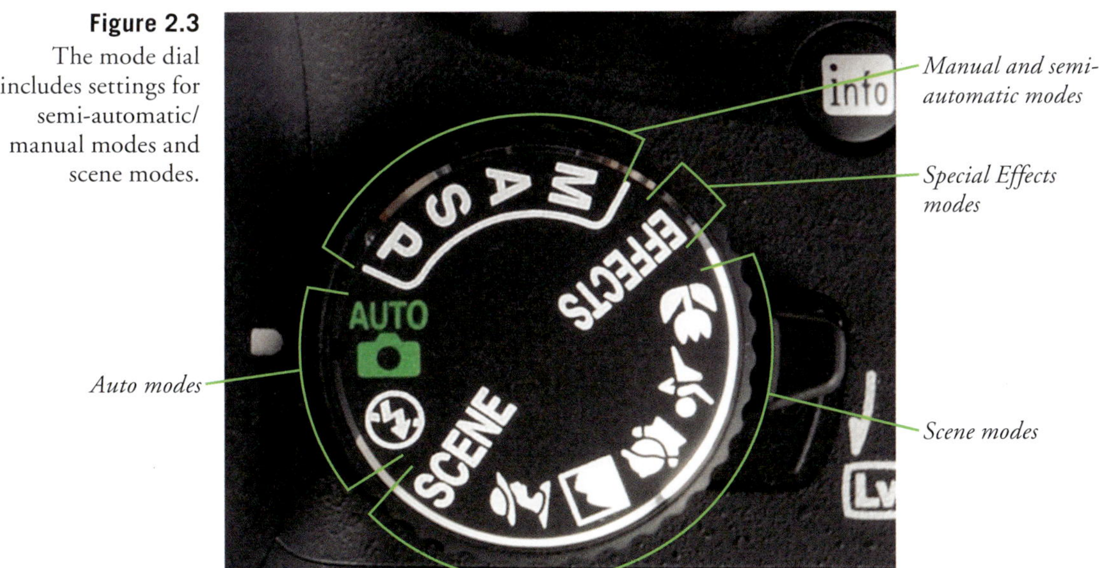


**Figure 2.3**
The mode dial includes settings for semi-automatic/ manual modes and scene modes.

*Manual and semi-automatic modes*

*Special Effects modes*

*Auto modes*

*Scene modes*

- **A (Aperture-priority).** Choose when you want to use a particular lens opening, especially to control sharpness or how much of your image is in focus. Specify the f/stop you want using the command dial when the meter is "awake" (tap the shutter release to activate the meter, if necessary), and the D5200 will select the appropriate shutter speed for you.

- **M (Manual).** Select when you want full control over the shutter speed and lens opening, either for creative effects or because you are using a studio flash or other flash unit not compatible with the D5200's automatic flash metering. Use the command dial (for shutter speed) and command dial+EV button when the exposure meter is active to specify the shutter speed and f/stop (respectively).

# Choosing a Metering Mode

This section shows you how to choose the area the D5200 will use to measure exposure, giving emphasis to the center of the frame; evaluating many different areas of the frame; or measuring light from a small spot in the center of the frame.

The metering mode you select determines how the D5200 calculates exposure. You might want to select a particular metering mode for your first shots, although the default Matrix metering is probably the best choice as you get to know your camera. I'll explain when and how to use each of the three metering modes later. To change metering modes, use the information edit screen as described earlier. When using any PSAM mode, press the information edit button, navigate the screen to Metering Mode (it's fourth from the left in the bottom row), press OK, and then use the left/right directional buttons to select one of the following, represented by the icons seen in Figure 2.4.

- **Matrix metering.** The standard metering mode; the D5200 attempts to intelligently classify your image and choose the best exposure based on readings from a 2016-segment color CCD sensor that interprets light reaching the viewfinder using a database of hundreds of thousands of patterns.

- **Center-weighted metering.** The D5200 meters the entire scene, but gives 75% of the emphasis to the central area of the frame, measuring about 8mm.

- **Spot metering.** Exposure is calculated from a smaller 3.5mm central spot, about 2.5 percent of the image area.

You'll find a detailed description of each of these modes in Chapter 4.

**Figure 2.4** Metering mode icons representing Matrix, Center-weighted, and Spot metering.

# Choosing a Focus Mode

This section shows how to select *when* the D5200 calculates focus, either all the time (continuously), only once when you press a control like the shutter release button (single autofocus), or manually when you rotate a focus ring on the lens. This section describes setting focus modes when using the optical viewfinder. Focus settings when working in live view are slightly different, and will be covered in Chapter 6, rather than this Quick Start.

You can easily switch between automatic and manual focus by moving the AF/MF, A/M, or M-AF/ MF switch on the lens mounted on your camera. You can select the autofocus mode (*when* the D5200 measures and locks in focus) and autofocus pattern (*which* of the 39 available autofocus points or zones are used to interpret correct focus). To specify when the D5200 locks in focus when using the optical viewfinder, follow these steps:

1. **Activate autofocus.** Make sure the camera is set for autofocus mode by sliding any M-AF/M or AF/M switch on the lens to the MA, A, or AF position.

2. **Enter setting mode.** Press the information edit button until you see the information edit screen shown earlier in Figure 2.2.

3. **Choose AF mode entry.** Navigate to the AF mode entry (it's second from the left in the bottom row), and press OK.

4. **Choose AF mode.** Select from AF-C, AF-S, or AF-A. The three focus modes are described in more detail next.

The three autofocus modes are as follows:

- **(AF-C) Continuous-servo autofocus.** This mode, sometimes called *continuous autofocus*, or AF-C, sets focus when you partially depress the shutter button (or other autofocus activation button), but continues to monitor the frame and refocuses if the camera or subject is moved. This is a useful mode for photographing sports and moving subjects. As you'll learn in Chapter 9, you can set your Nikon D5200 using Custom Setting a1 so that the camera will not take a photo unless sharp focus is achieved (*focus priority*), or so that it will go ahead and snap a photo while still adjusting focus (*release priority*).

- **(AF-S) Single-servo autofocus.** This mode, sometimes called *single autofocus*, or AF-S, locks in a focus point when the shutter button is pressed down halfway (there are other autofocus activation button options, described in Chapter 9), and the focus confirmation light glows at bottom left in the viewfinder. The focus will remain locked until you release the button or take the picture. This mode is best when your subject is relatively motionless.

- **(AF-A) Automatic autofocus.** In this mode, the D5200 will select from AF-S or AF-C, depending on whether your subject is stationary or moving.

# Choosing the Focus Area Mode

The Nikon D5200 uses up to 39 different focus points to calculate correct focus, using one or more points you can select yourself, or which the camera can choose. To choose a focus area mode used while working with the optical viewfinder, follow these steps:

1. **Activate autofocus.** Make sure the camera is set for autofocus mode by sliding any M-AF/M, A/M, or AF/M switch on the lens to the MA or AF position.

2. **Enter setting mode.** Press the information edit button until you see the information edit screen shown earlier in Figure 2.2.

3. **Choose AF-area mode.** Navigate to the AF-area mode entry (it's third from the left in the bottom row), and press OK.

4. **Choose AF-area mode selection method.** Select from up to six different modes, depending on whether you chose AF-S, AF-C, or AF-A focus modes. The six focus area modes are described in more detail next.

The six AF area modes are as follows. The first and last listed are the only ones available in AF-S focus mode.

- **Single-point.** The camera focuses on a point you select, using the multi selector directional buttons. The focus zones are shown in Figure 2.5, highlighted in red so you can see them more easily. (Available in AF-S, AF-C, AF-A modes.)

- **Dynamic-area AF (9 points).** You select the focus point, and the camera also uses information from surrounding AF points (nine points, total) to calculate focus. (Available in AF-C, AF-A modes only.)

- **Dynamic-area AF (21 points).** You select the focus point, and the camera also uses information from surrounding AF points (21 points, total) to calculate focus. (Available in AF-C, AF-A modes only.)

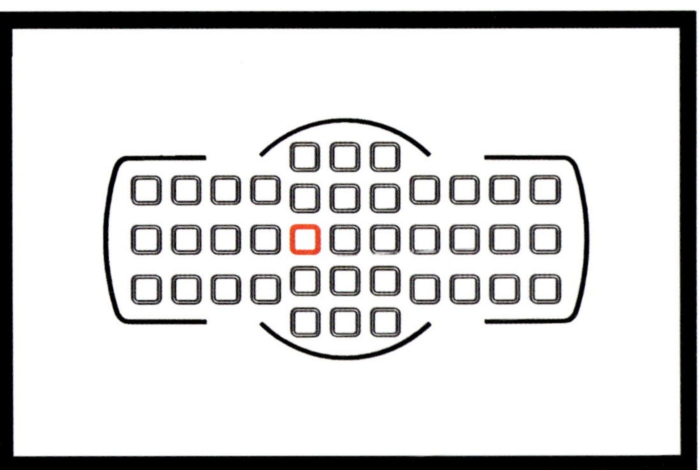

**Figure 2.5**
The D5200 has 39 focus zones.

- **Dynamic-area AF (39 points).** You select the focus point, and the camera also uses information from surrounding AF points (39 points, total) to calculate focus. (Available in AF-C, AF-A modes only.)

- **3D-tracking.** You select the focus point, and the camera will track your subject, using any of the other focus points, as needed, when using AF-A and AF-C modes. (In AF-S mode, focus tracking is not used, as focus is locked in when you press the shutter release halfway.) (Available in AF-C, AF-A modes only.)

- **Auto-area AF.** The D5200 chooses a focus point. (Available in AF-S, AF-C, AF-A modes.)

# Reviewing the Images You've Taken

Read this section when you're ready to take a closer look at the images you've taken, and want to know how to review pictures and zoom in.

The Nikon D5200 has a broad range of playback and image review options, and I'll cover them in more detail in Chapter 8. For now, you'll want to learn just the basics. Here is all you really need to know at this time, as shown in Figure 2.6:

- **View image.** Press the Playback button (marked with a white right-pointing triangle) at the upper-right corner of the back of the camera to display the most recent image on the LCD.

- **View additional images.** Press the multi selector left or right or rotate the command dial to review additional images. Press/rotate right to advance to the next image, or left to go back to a previous image.

- **Change information display.** Press the multi selector button up or down to change among overlays of basic image information or detailed shooting information. (I'll explain how to specify which information is shown in Chapter 8.)

- **Change magnification.** Press the Zoom In button repeatedly to zoom in on the image displayed; the Zoom Out button reduces the image. A thumbnail representation of the whole image appears in the lower-right corner with a yellow rectangle showing the relative level of zoom. At intermediate zoom positions, the yellow rectangle can be moved around within the frame using the multi selector.

- **Exit image review.** Press the Playback button again, or just tap the shutter release button to exit playback view.

You'll find information on viewing thumbnail indexes of images, automated playback, and other options in Chapter 8.

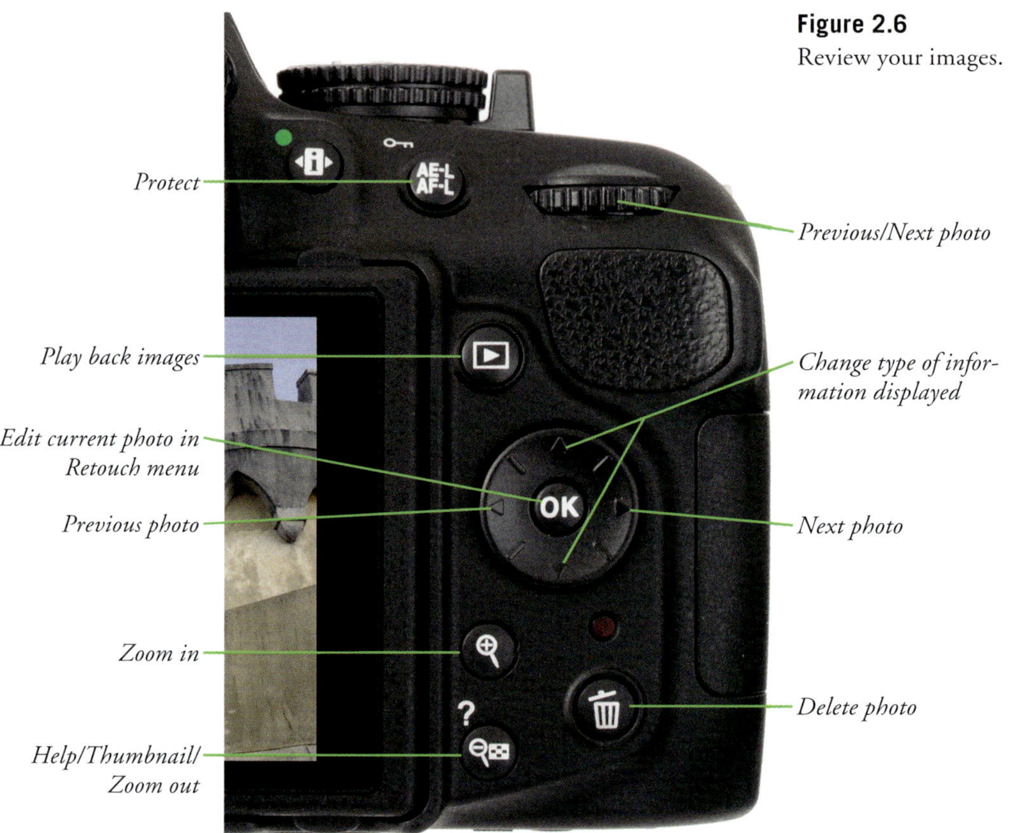


**Figure 2.6**
Review your images.

# Using the Built-in Flash

Working with the D5200's built-in flash (as well as external flash units like the Nikon SB-700) deserves detailed coverage, and I'm providing the information you need (see Chapter 12). But the built-in flash is easy enough to work with that you can begin using it right away, either to provide the main lighting of a scene or as supplementary illumination to fill in the shadows. For example, if you choose Matrix or Center-weighted metering (as described earlier), you can even use the flash in full daylight, as the D5200 will even automatically balance the amount of light emitted from the flash so that it illuminates the shadows nicely, without overwhelming the highlights and producing a glaring "flash" look. (Think *Baywatch* when they're using too many reflectors on the lifeguards!)

The D5200's flash has a power rating of 12/39 (meters/feet) at ISO 100, using the GN (guide number) system that dates back to the film era and before electronic flash units had any sort of automatic features. I'll explain guide numbers (which can be a little confusing) in more detail in Chapter 12, but in plain terms, the flash's rating means that the unit is powerful enough to allow proper illumination of a subject that's 10 feet away at f/4 at the ISO 100 (sensitivity) setting of your camera. Boost the ISO (or use a wider f/stop) and you can shoot subjects that are located at a great distance. For example, at ISO 800, the D5200's flash is good enough for a subject at 20 feet using f/5.6 or, alternatively, you can expose that scene at the original 10 feet distance at f/11. Ordinarily, the D5200 takes care of all these calculations for you. If you need a bigger blast of light, you can add an external flash, like the Nikon SB-700 or the top-of-the-line SB-910, which lets you reach out to 32–45 feet at ISO 200 and f/5.6 (or even farther at larger f/stops).

When using Auto, Portrait, Child, Close Up, Night Portrait, Party/Indoor, or Pet Portrait scene modes and Color Sketch Effects mode, the flash will pop up when needed. To use the built-in flash, for Program, Shutter-priority, Aperture-priority, Manual modes, or Food Scene mode, just press the flash pop-up button (shown in Figure 2.7). When you're finished using it, you need to push it back down. When the flash is fully charged, a lightning bolt symbol will flash at the right side of the viewfinder display. When using P (Program) or A (Aperture-priority) exposure modes, the D5200 will select a shutter speed for you automatically from the range 1/200th to 1/60th seconds (with a couple exceptions described in Chapter 12). In S (Shutter-priority) and M (Manual) modes, you select the shutter speed from 1/200th to 30 seconds (again, with a couple exceptions that I won't get into here). When using the built-in flash, if you select a shutter speed higher than 1/200th second (which prevents the camera from synchronizing with the shutter; see Chapter 12), the D5200 will set 1/200th second for you automatically.

You'll also learn in Chapter 12 how to change the flash syncing mode (and why you might want to do so), as well as how to increase/reduce the effects of the flash on your scene using *flash compensation* adjustments.

**Figure 2.7**
The pop-up electronic flash can be used as the main light source or for supplemental illumination.

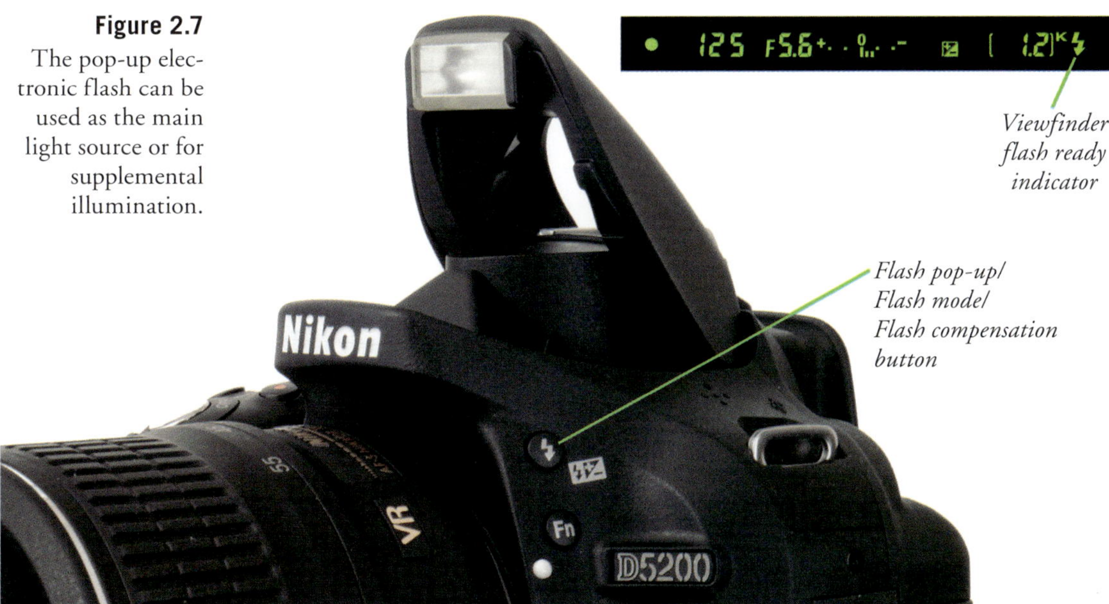


*Viewfinder flash ready indicator*

*Flash pop-up/ Flash mode/ Flash compensation button*

# Transferring Photos to Your Computer

The final step in your picture-taking session will be to transfer the photos you've taken to your computer for printing, further review, or image editing. Your D5200 allows you to print directly to PictBridge-compatible printers and to create print orders right in the camera, plus you can select which images to transfer to your computer. I'll outline those options in Chapter 8.

I always recommend using a card reader attached to your computer to transfer files, because that process is generally a lot faster and doesn't drain the D5200's battery. However, you can also use a cable for direct transfer, which may be your only option when you have the cable and a computer, but no card reader (perhaps you're using the computer of a friend or colleague, or at an Internet café).

To transfer images from the camera to a Mac or PC computer using the USB cable:

1. Turn off the camera.
2. Pry back the rubber cover that protects the D5200's USB port, and plug the USB cable furnished with the camera into the USB port. (See Figure 2.8.)
3. Connect the other end of the USB cable to a USB port on your computer.
4. Turn on the camera. The operating system itself, or installed software such as Nikon Transfer or Adobe Photoshop Elements Transfer, usually detects the camera and offers to copy or move the pictures. Or, the camera appears on your desktop as a mass storage device, enabling you to drag and drop the files to your computer.

To transfer images from a memory card to the computer using a card reader, as shown in Figure 2.9:

1. Turn off the camera.
2. Open the memory card door and extract the Secure Digital card.
3. Insert the memory card into your memory card reader. Your installed software detects the files on the card and offers to transfer them. The card can also appear as a mass storage device on your desktop, which you can open and then drag and drop the files to your computer.

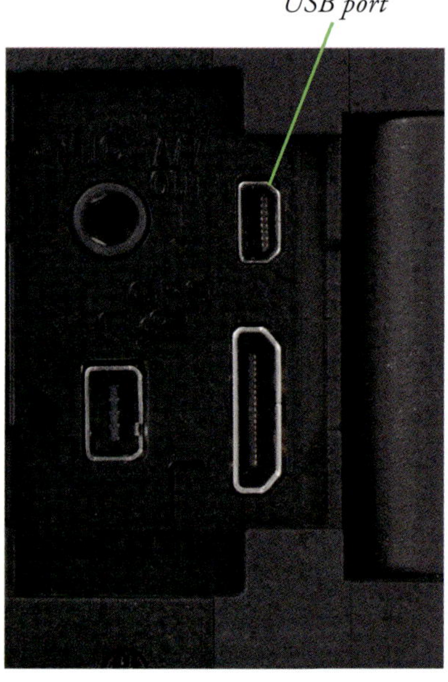


**Figure 2.8** Images can be transferred to your computer using a USB cable connected to this port.

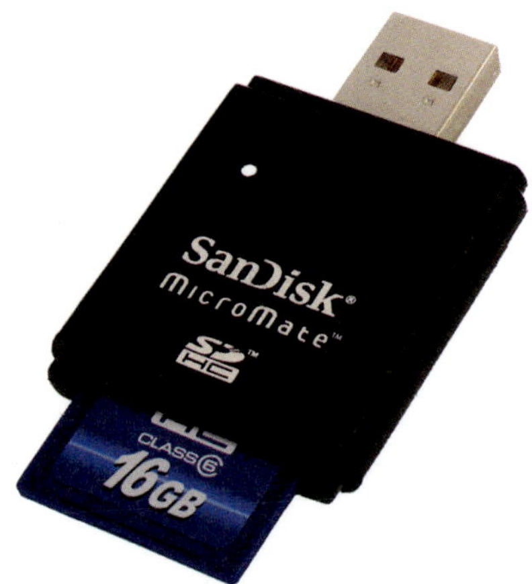


**Figure 2.9** A card reader is the fastest way to transfer photos.

# Changing Default Settings

> This section is purely optional, especially for true beginners, who should skip it entirely for now, and return when they've gained some experience with this full-featured camera. This section is for the benefit of those who want to know *now* some of the most common changes I recommend to the default settings of your D5200. Nikon has excellent reasons for using these settings as a default; I have better reasons for changing them.

Even if this is your first experience with a Nikon digital SLR, you can easily make a few changes to the default settings that I'm going to recommend, and then take your time learning *why* I suggest these changes when they're explained in the more detailed chapters of this book. I'm not going to provide step-by-step instructions for changing settings here; I'll give you an overview of how to make any setting adjustment, and leave you to navigate through the fairly intuitive D5200 menu system to make the changes yourself.

## Resetting the Nikon D5200

If you want to change from the factory default values, you might think that it would be a good idea to make sure that the Nikon D5200 is set to the factory defaults in the first place. After all, even a brand-new camera might have had its settings changed at the retailer, or during a demo. Unfortunately, Nikon doesn't make it easy to reset *all* settings in the camera to their factory defaults. In fact, there are no fewer than *four* different ways to "reset" the D5200, each of which does slightly different things. Those ways include:

- **Two-button reset.** This type of "rebooting" changes ten of the most basic settings in your camera, and is useful when you want to cancel the most common changes you make when adjusting your camera. It does not affect all Shooting menu settings, or any of the Custom Setting memory banks, described next. I'll show you how to perform the two-button reset shortly.

- **Shooting menu bank reset.** The Shooting menu has a separate Reset Shooting menu option that zeroes out the changes you've made to the default options.

- **Custom Setting menu bank reset.** The Custom Setting menu also has a separate Reset Custom Settings option that zeroes out most of the changes you've made to the default options. A two-button reset does not affect any of the settings in the Custom Setting menu banks.

- **Cold reset.** The only way to reset *all* of the D5200's internal settings is to remove the battery and allow the internal backup battery to run down until the settings are lost, which can take as long as several weeks. You can remove the battery and then turn on the camera briefly to reset *most* settings, but this won't zero out all settings to the factory defaults as long as some juice remains in the backup battery (which is tucked deep inside the camera and not user-accessible). You might want to try a cold reset if your camera is hopelessly locked up, and you'd like to make one last attempt at restoring it to factory operation before sending it in for service.

## Two-Button Reset

Just follow these steps to perform a two-button reset of the camera:

1. **Find reset buttons.** Locate the MENU button on the back left side of the camera, and the information edit button on the right side of the D5200, just to the right of the viewfinder window. Each is marked with a green dot. Figure 2.10 shows the two buttons highlighted in yellow.

2. **Start reset.** Press and hold the two buttons for more than two seconds. The LCD monitor switches off momentarily while the settings are reset.

3. **Release the two buttons.** Your camera's settings have been returned to the factory default, as described below.

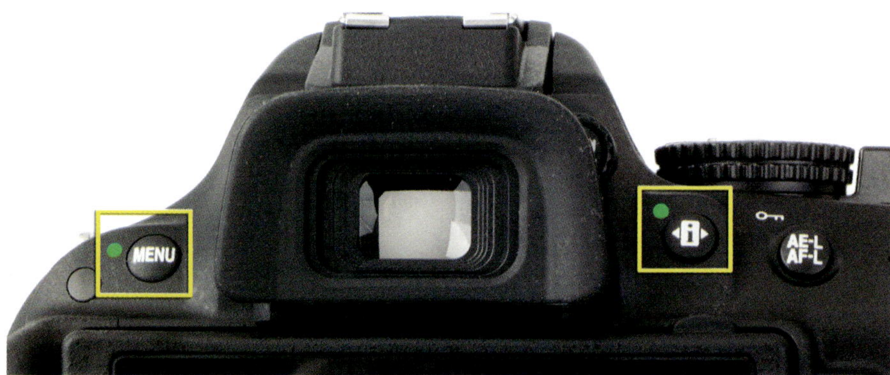

**Figure 2.10**
Perform a two-button reset by holding down the MENU and information edit buttons for more than two seconds.

Once a two-button reset has been performed, the following settings will be restored to their defaults (all these options, plus additional Special Effects options that are reset as well, are described in Chapters 8, 9, and 10):

- **Image quality:** Normal

- **Image size:** L (Large)

- **White balance:**
  *Auto*>Normal
  *White balance Fine Tuning*: 0

- **ISO sensitivity:**
  *Auto and Scene modes*: Auto
  *Program, Shutter-priority, Aperture-priority, Manual modes:* 100

- **Autofocus/Viewfinder:**
  *Autofocus mode:* AF-A
  *AF-area mode:* Close Up, Candlelight, Food, Beach/Snow, High Kcy, Low Key—Single-point AF
  *AF-area mode:* Sports, Pet Portrait—Dynamic-area AF
  *AF-area mode:* All others—Auto-area AF

- **Autofocus/Live View, Movie:**

    *Autofocus mode:* AF-S

    *AF-area mode:* Sports, Night Landscape, Pet Portrait, Beach/Snow, High Key, Low Key—Wide-area AF

    *AF-area mode:* Close Up, Food—Normal-area AF

    *AF-area mode:* All others—Face-priority AF

    *Focus point:* Center

- **Metering:** Matrix

- **AE/AF Lock hold:** Off

- **HDR mode:** P, S, A, M: Off

- **Active D-Lighting:** P, S, A, M: Off

- **Bracketing:** P, S, A, M: Off

- **Picture Control Settings:** P, S, A, M: Current Picture Control retained

- **Flash compensation:** Off

- **Exposure compensation:** Off

- **Flash mode:**

    *Auto/Portrait/Child/Close Up/Pet:* Auto front-curtain sync

    *Party:* Auto/Red-eye reduction

    *Night Portrait:* Auto slow sync

    *Food, Program, Shutter-priority, Aperture-priority, Manual:* Front-curtain sync

- **Multiple exposure:** Off

- **Flexible Program:** Off

## Shooting Menu/Custom Setting Menu Reset

If you'd like to reset all the options in the Shooting menu and Custom Setting menu individually, follow these steps:

1. **Access menus.** Press the MENU button located to the immediate left of viewfinder.

2. **Choose Shooting menu or Custom Setting menu.** Press the multi selector down button to scroll down to either the Shooting menu (represented by a camera icon; the second icon from the top in the left-column of the menus) or the Custom Setting menu (represented by a pencil icon; the third icon from the top). Press the right multi selector button to reveal the Shooting or Custom Setting menus.

3. **Reset menu.** Use the down button to scroll to the Reset Shooting Menu or Reset Custom Settings choices, then press the right button to reveal a screen with Yes and No choices. Press the up button to highlight Yes, and press OK (or the center button of the multi selector) to reset the active bank.

4. **Exit.** Press MENU or tap the shutter release to exit.

# Recommended Default Changes

Although I won't be explaining how to use the Nikon D5200's menu system in detail until Chapter 8, you can make some simple changes now. These general instructions will serve you to make any of the default setting changes I recommend next. To change any menu setting, follow these steps:

1. **Access menus.** Press the MENU button at left of the viewfinder window.

2. **Choose the main menu you need to access.** Press the multi selector down button to scroll down to the menu containing the entry you want to change. The available menus include (from top to bottom in the left column of the menu screen: Playback menu (right-pointing triangle icon); Shooting menu (camera icon); Custom Setting menu (pencil icon); Setup menu (wrench icon); Retouch menu (paintbrush icon); My Menu (text page/text page with checkmark icon).

3. **Select main menu.** Press the right multi selector button to choose the menu heading containing the submenu entry you want to change.

4. **Choose menu entry.** Press the down multi selector button to move within the main menu to the entry you want to change. A scroll bar at the right side shows your progress through the menu, as all the main menus except for the Custom Setting menu and My Menu (if it contains fewer than five custom entries) have more items than can fit on a single screen.

5. **Choose options.** Press the right multi selector button to choose the highlighted menu entry, and view a screen with options. Select the options you want, and press OK to confirm. Some menus allow you to confirm by pressing the right button again, or require you to move to a Done selection and choose that before exiting.

6. **Exit menus.** Usually you can exit the menu system by pressing the MENU button. If an option has variations, I'll explain them when I discuss each of the menu choices in Chapters 8, 9, and 10.

Here are some of the changes I recommend you make to the defaults that Nikon sets up for you. (I have no changes to recommend for the Playback, Setup, and My Menu settings, which are fine the way they are for most people, nor for the Retouch menu, which doesn't have parameters that can be stored.)

## Shooting Menu

Make these changes to the Shooting menu entries listed:

- **Image Quality.** Change from JPEG Normal to JPEG Fine, to produce better image quality.

- **High ISO NR.** Change from default Normal to Off, until you've had a chance to evaluate whether the D5200 performs to your liking at high sensitivity settings. Off produces the least amount of noise reduction, but also doesn't degrade the amount of detail as much as any of the On settings.

## Custom Setting Menu

Make these changes to the Custom Setting menu entries listed:

- **CSM a3: Built-in AF-assist illumination.** Change from the default On to Off. This feature doesn't work well, except at close distances and when the lamp isn't blocked by your fingers, and is annoying at other times.

- **CSM c2: Auto Off Timers.** If you shoot sports or other events where you don't want the camera going to sleep and delaying your ability to snap off a shot *now*, choose Custom and change the Auto Meter Off setting from the default 6 seconds to 30 seconds, 1 minute, 5 minutes, or 10 minutes. You'll use more power, but won't lose a shot from a split-second delay while the camera wakes up.

- **CSM d1: Beep.** Turn to OFF to quiet the camera during self-timer countdowns and single-servo autofocus confirmation. If you decide you need this reminder, you can always turn it back on, but most of the time it's annoying and calls attention to your shooting.

- **CSM f4: Slot empty release lock.** This controls what happens when you press the shutter release while no memory card is loaded in the camera. Double-check and make sure this is set to LOCK. Why would you want to be able to take pictures with no memory card in the camera, other than to demonstrate the camera or a few other reasons? Even though a DEMO label appears on the LCD when you "take" pictures with no memory card inserted, it's easy to overlook.

# 3

# Nikon D5200 Roadmap

Most of the Nikon D5200's key functions and settings that are changed frequently can be accessed using the array of dials, buttons, and knobs that populate the camera's surface. If you want to operate your D5200 efficiently, you'll need to learn the location, function, and application of all these controls. What you really need is a street-level roadmap that shows where everything is, and how it's used. But what Nikon gives you in the user's manual is akin to a world globe with an overall view and many cross-references to the pages that will tell you what you really need to know. Check out the Getting to Know the Camera pages in Nikon's manual, which offers four tiny black-and-white line drawings of the camera body that show front (see Figure 3.1), back, two sides, and the top and bottom of the D5200. There are about six dozen callouts pointing to various buttons and dials. If you can find the control you want in this cramped layout, you'll still need to flip back and

**Figure 3.1**

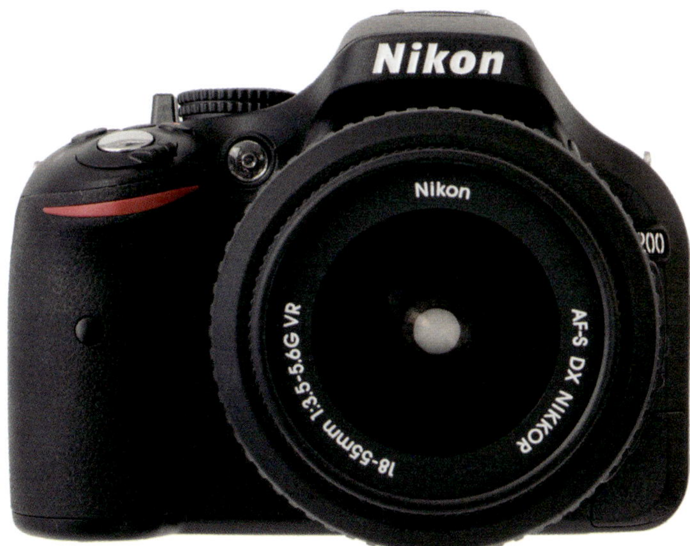

forth among multiple pages (individual buttons can have several different cross-references!) to locate the information.

Most other third-party books follow this format, featuring black-and-white photos or line drawings of front, back, and top views, and many labels. I originated the up-close-and-personal, full-color, street-level roadmap (rather than a satellite view) that I use in this book and my previous camera guidebooks. I provide you with many different views and lots of explanation accompanying each zone of the camera, so that by the time you finish this chapter, you'll have a basic understanding of every control and what it does. I'm not going to delve into menu functions here—you'll find a discussion of your Playback, Shooting, Custom Setting, and Setup options in Chapters 8, 9, and 10. Everything here is devoted to the button pusher and dial twirler in you.

You'll also find this "roadmap" chapter a good guide to the rest of the book, as well. I'll try to provide as much detail here about the use of the main controls as I can, but some topics (such as autofocus and exposure) are too complex to address in depth right away. So, I'll point you to the relevant chapters that discuss things like setup options, exposure, use of electronic flash, and working with lenses with the occasional cross-reference.

# Nikon D5200: Full Frontal

This is the side seen by your victims as you snap away. For the photographer, though, the front is the surface your fingers curl around as you hold the camera, and there are really only a few buttons to press, all within easy reach of the fingers of your left and right hands. There are additional controls on the lens itself. You'll need to look at several different views to see everything.

Figure 3.2 shows a view of the left side of the Nikon D5200, as seen from the front. The main components you need to know about are as follows:

- **Shutter release.** Angled on top of the hand grip is the shutter release button, which has multiple functions. Press this button down halfway to lock focus. Press it down all the way to actually take a photo or sequence of photos if you've changed to continuous shooting modes, or if you've redefined the behavior of the self-timer to take 1 to 9 exposures when its delay has expired. (I'll show you how to take multiple shots with the self-timer in Chapter 9.) Tapping the shutter button when the D5200's exposure meters have turned themselves off reactivates them, and a tap can be used to remove the display of a menu or image from the rear color LCD.

- **On/Off switch.** Rotating this switch to the detent turns the camera on.

- **AF-assist illuminator/Red-eye reduction/Self-timer lamp.** This LED provides a blip of light shortly before a flash exposure to cause the subjects' pupils to close down, reducing the effect of red-eye reflections off their retinas. When using the self-timer, this lamp also flashes to mark the countdown until the photo is taken. It can also illuminate to provide assistance for the D5200's autofocus mechanism at fairly close distances.

- **Infrared receiver.** This IR sensor receives a signal from the optional Nikon ML-L3 infrared remote control while standing in front of the camera (say, when you want to get in the picture yourself). Another IR receiver is located on the back of the camera.

**Figure 3.2**

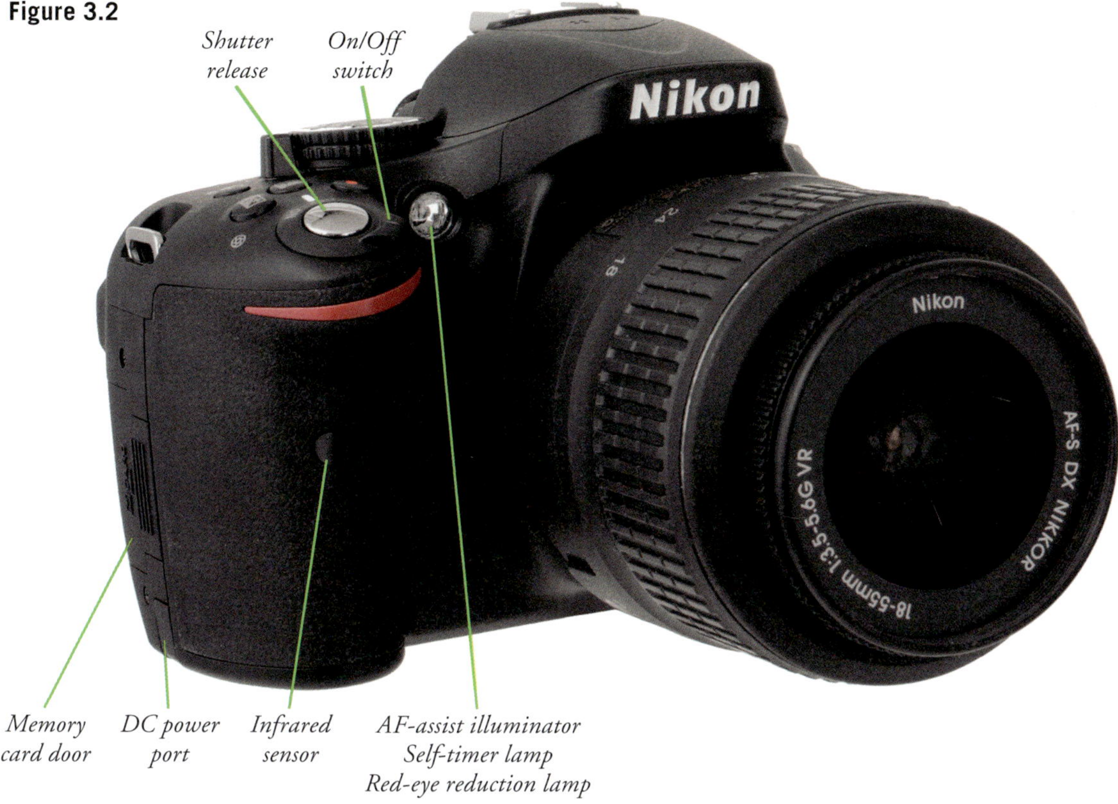


- **Hand grip.** This provides a comfortable hand hold, and also contains the D5200's battery.
- **Memory card door.** Your Secure Digital memory card can be inserted here when you slide the door toward the rear of the camera to open it.
- **DC power access.** Connect the optional AC adapter to the battery compartment through this opening.

You'll find more controls on the other side of the D5200, shown in Figure 3.3. In the illustration, you can see the mode dial on top, and the rubber covers on the side that protect the camera's USB, TV, HDMI, microphone ports, and GPS/accessory terminal. The main points of interest shown include:

- **Lens release button.** Press this button to unlock the lens, then rotate the lens away from the shutter release button to dismount your optics.
- **Lens mount index mark.** Line up the mark on the lens with this raised bump to align the lens when mounting it on the camera.
- **Lens autofocus/manual switch.** You can change from autofocus mode to manual using this switch.
- **Vibration reduction switch.** Turn your lens's image stabilization feature (if present) on or off using this switch.

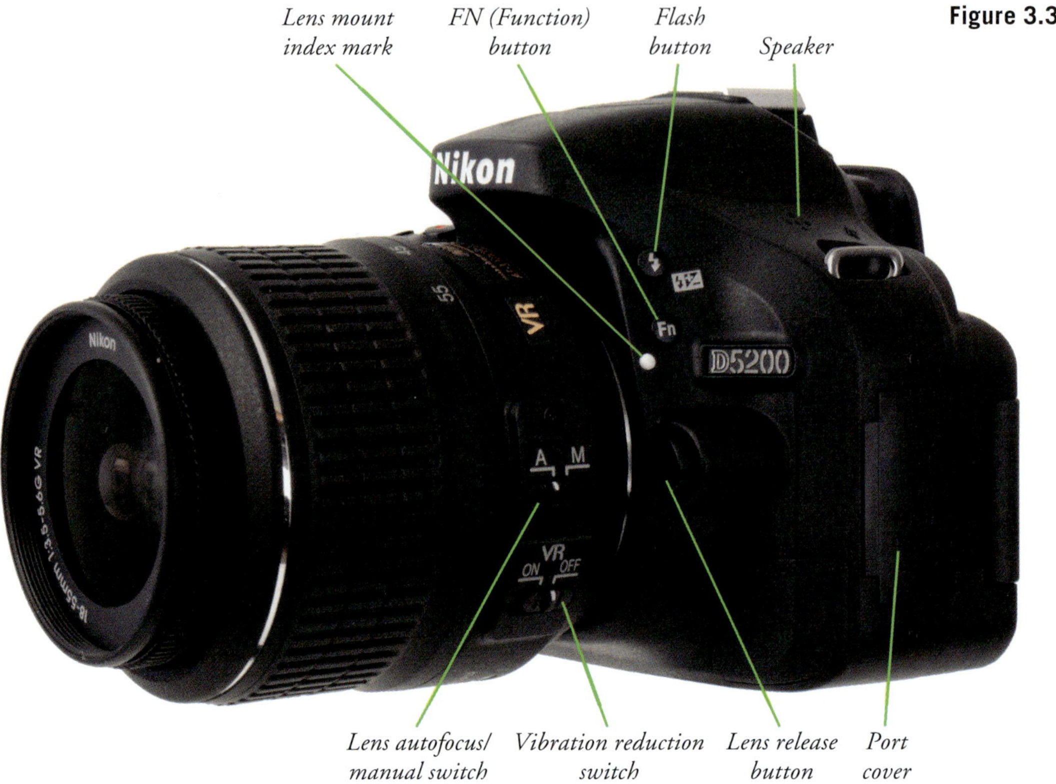


- **Speaker.** Sounds emitted by the camera, including audio during movie clip playback, are produced here.

- **Port cover.** The rubber cover protects the USB/AV, HDMI, microphone ports, and GPS/accessory terminals when not in use.

- **Fn (Function) button.** This conveniently located button activates the self-timer by default, but can be programmed to perform any one of several other different actions instead, including adjustment of image quality, bracketing, or white balance.

Controls for using the D5200's built-in electronic flash (also called a strobe or speedlight) are shown in Figure 3.4. These components include:

- **Pop-up flash.** The flash elevates from the top of the camera, theoretically reducing the chances of red-eye reflections, because the higher light source is less likely to reflect back from your subjects' eyes into the camera lens. In practice, the red-eye effect is still possible (and likely), and can be further minimized with the D5200's red-eye reduction lamp (which flashes before the exposure, causing the subjects' pupils to contract) and the after-shot red-eye elimination offered in the Retouch menu. (Your image editor may also have anti-red-eye tools.) Of course, the best strategy is to use an external Speedlight that mounts on the accessory shoe on top of the camera (and thus is even higher) or a flash that is off-camera entirely.

**Figure 3.4**

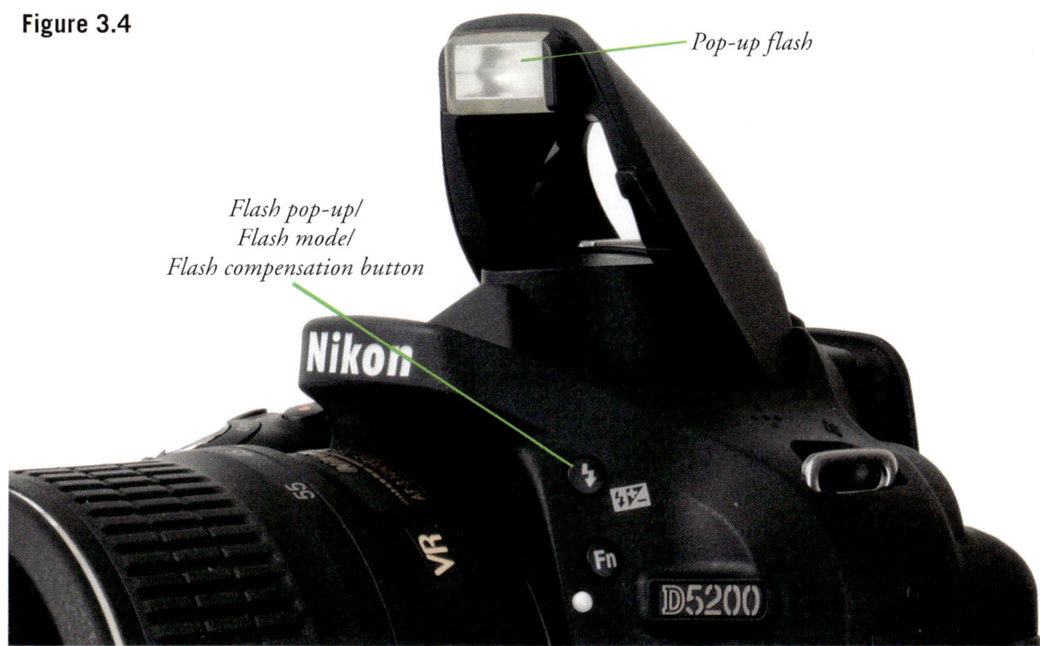


- **Flash pop-up/Flash mode/Flash compensation button.** If the flash does not pop up auto-matically when needed (when using Auto and some scene modes), this button can be used to release the built-in flash so it can elevate and start the charging process. If you decide you do not want to use the flash, you can turn it off by pressing the flash head back down. This button is held down while spinning the command dial (to choose flash compensation). I'll explain how to use the various flash modes (red-eye reduction, front/rear curtain sync, and slow sync, which are set using the information edit screen) in Chapter 12, along with some tips for adjusting flash exposure.

The main features on the side of the Nikon D5200 are a rubber cover that protects the four con-nector ports underneath from dust and moisture. The four connectors, shown in Figure 3.5, with the rubber covers removed, are as follows:

- **USB/AV port.** Plug in the USB cable furnished with your Nikon D5200 and connect the other end to a USB port in your computer to transfer photos, to upload Picture Control settings, or to upload/download other settings between your camera and computer. The included AV cable can be connected to link the camera to a standard-definition television or monitor to view your photos and movies on a large screen. Connect the red/white RCA plugs on the cable to the audio input jacks of your monitor/TV, and the yellow plug to the video jack.

- **HDMI port.** You need to buy an accessory cable to connect your D5200 to an HDTV, as one to fit this port is not provided with the camera. If you have a high-resolution television, it's worth the expenditure to be able to view your camera's output in all its glory.

- **GPS/Accessory terminal.** Connect the Nikon GP-1 Global Positioning Service device here, or plug in the MC-DC2 wired remote control here or WR-10 wireless remote, instead. If you want to use both, connect the GP-1 and then plug the remote into a pass-through connector on the GPS device. The optional WU-1a Wi-Fi accessory also plugs into this terminal. I'll describe key accessories in more detail in Chapter 7.

- **Microphone connector.** Although the D5200 has a built-in stereo microphone on the top panel, if you want better quality (and want to shield your video clip soundtracks from noises emanating from the camera and/or your handling of it), you can plug in an accessory mic here.

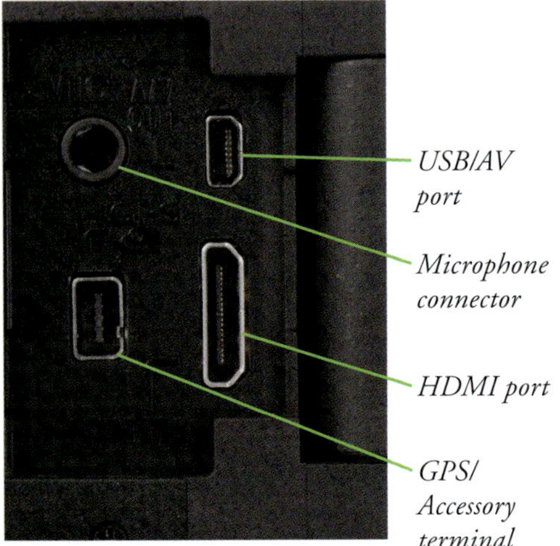


**Figure 3.5**

# The Nikon D5200's Business End

The back panel of the Nikon D5200 bristles with more than a dozen different controls, buttons, and knobs. That might seem like a lot of controls to learn, but you'll find it's a lot easier to press a button and spin a dial than to jump to a menu every time you want to change a setting. A key component is the swiveling LCD monitor, shown in some of its various configurations in Figure 3.6.

You can swivel the LCD around to face the back of the camera, as seen at upper left in Figure 3.6. In that position, the LCD is protected from hard knocks. You'll most often reverse it (Figure 3.6, upper right) to view settings, navigate menus, review images, or view the actual sensor in live view/ movie modes. The LCD monitor swings out (Figure 3.6, lower left) to allow waist level or over-head viewing, and can even be completely flipped around for self-portraits or to display images/previews to your subjects (Figure 3.6, lower right).

You can see the controls clustered along the top edge of the back panel in Figure 3.7, while those on the right side are shown in Figure 3.8. The key buttons and components and their functions are as follows:

- **MENU/Reset #1 button.** Summons/exits the menu displayed on the rear LCD of the D5200. When you're working with submenus, this button also serves to exit a submenu and return to the main menu. Holding down this button at the same time as the information edit/Reset #2 button returns the settings of your camera to their default values.

- **Information edit/Reset #2 button.** Press this button to activate the shooting information display. Press it again to change any of the parameters in the bottom rows of the display, using the multi selector to highlight the option. Then, press OK to summon a screen that lets you

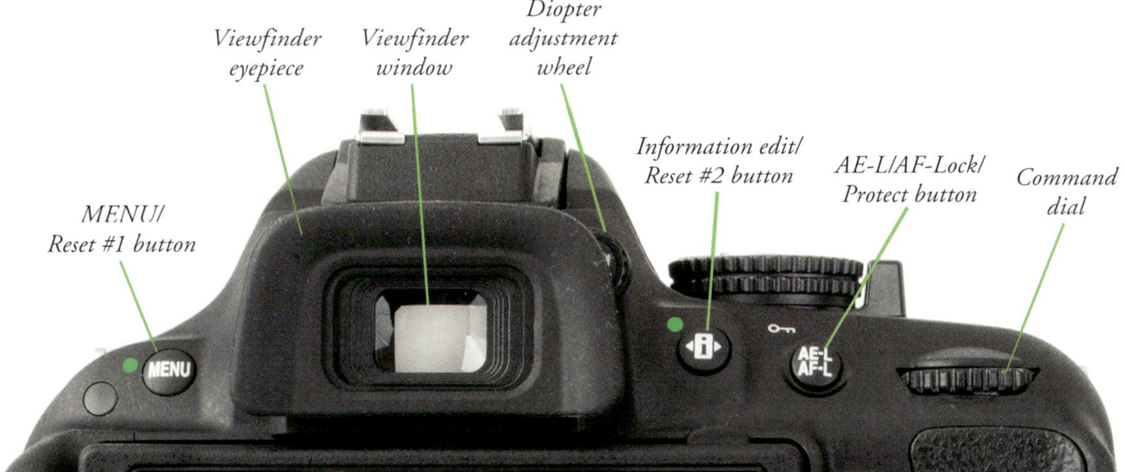

Figure 3.6



Figure 3.7

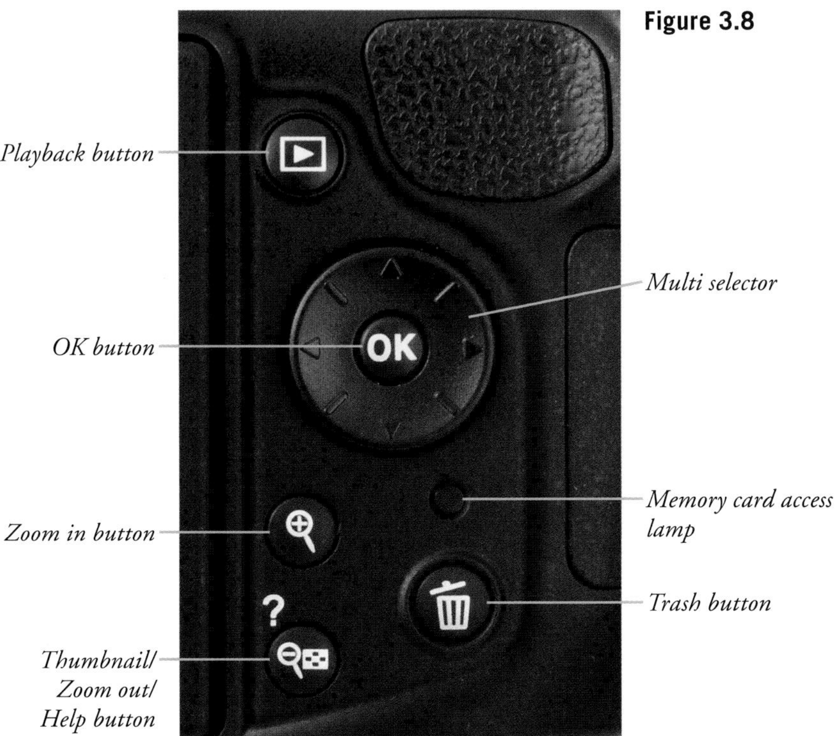


make the changes. Or, press it a third time to remove the information display (or simply tap the shutter release button). The display will also clear after the period you've set for LCD display (the default value is 20 seconds). I'll describe the use of the shooting information display in more detail later in this chapter. Don't confuse this button with the Info button on top of the camera, which simply turns the LCD display on or off. Note that Nikon doesn't assign "Reset #1" or "Reset #2" nomenclature to these buttons; I've done so to help differentiate between the two.

- **Viewfinder eyepiece.** You can frame your composition by peering into the viewfinder. It's surrounded by a soft rubber frame that seals out extraneous light when pressing your eye tightly up to the viewfinder, and it also protects your eyeglass lenses (if worn) from scratching. It can be removed and replaced by the DK-5 eyepiece cap when you use the camera on a tripod, to ensure that light coming from the back of the camera doesn't venture inside and possibly affect the exposure reading. Shielding the viewfinder with your hand may be more convenient (unless you're using the self-timer to get in the photo yourself).

- **Diopter adjustment wheel.** Rotate this to adjust the diopter correction for your eyesight, as described in Chapter 1.

- **AE-L/AF-L (autoexposure/autofocus) lock/Protect button.** This button can be programmed by you to provide a variety of autoexposure/autofocus locking functions, which I'll explain in Chapter 9. By default, it locks the exposure or focus that the camera sets when you partially depress the shutter button. The exposure lock indication (AE-L icon) appears in the viewfinder. If you want to recalculate exposure or autofocus with the shutter button still partially depressed, press the button again. The exposure/autofocus will be unlocked when you release the shutter button or take the picture. To retain the exposure/autofocus lock for subsequent photos, keep the button pressed while shooting. This double-duty button also can be used to protect an image from accidental erasure when reviewing a picture on the LCD. Press once to protect the image, a second time to unprotect it. A key symbol appears when the image is displayed to show that it is protected. (This feature safeguards an image from erasure when deleting or transferring pictures only; when you format a card, protected images are removed along with all the others.)

- **Command dial.** This is the main control dial of the D5200, used to set or adjust most functions, such as shutter speed, bracketing sequence, white balance, ISO, and so forth, either alone or when another button is depressed simultaneously. It is often used in conjunction with the EV/aperture button on top of the camera when pairs of settings can be made, such as exposure (command dial: shutter speed; EV/aperture button+command dial: aperture).

- **LCD monitor.** (Not shown) View your images and navigate through the menus on this screen. The screen reverses to protect the LCD, swivels to allow shooting from high or low vantage points, and even can be turned around to shoot a self-portrait or a group shot, as mentioned earlier.

You'll be using the buttons to the right of the LCD monitor quite frequently, so learn their functions now.

- **Multi selector.** This joypad-like button can be moved up, down, side to side, or pressed. It can be used for several functions, including AF-point selection, scrolling around a magnified image, trimming a photo, or setting white balance correction. Within menus, pressing the up/down arrows moves the on-screen cursor up or down; pressing toward the right selects the highlighted item and displays its options; pressing left cancels and returns to the previous menu. During image review, the up/down buttons change the type of information displayed about each image.

- **OK button.** Press to confirm your selections, and to display the current review image in the Retouch menu.

- **Memory card access lamp.** When lit or blinking, this lamp indicates that a memory card is being accessed.

- **Thumbnail/Zoom Out/Help.** During image review, use this button to change from full-screen view to six, nine, or 72 thumbnails, calendar view, or to zoom out. I'll explain zooming and other playback options in the next section. When viewing most menu items on the LCD, pressing this button produces a concise Help screen with tips on how to make the relevant setting.

- **Zoom In button.** Press to zoom in on an image, and to select image quality settings.

- **Trash.** Press to erase the image shown on the LCD. A display will pop up on the LCD asking you to press the Trash button once more to delete the photo, or press the Playback button to cancel.

# Playing Back Images

Reviewing images is a joy on the Nikon D5200's big three-inch LCD. The display is big and bright, and there is abundant detail on that 920,000-dot, VGA-resolution screen.

Here are the basics involved in reviewing images on the LCD screen (or on a television/HDTV screen you have connected with a cable). You'll find more details about some of these functions later in this chapter, or, for more complex capabilities, in the chapters that I point you to. This section just lists the must-know information.

- **Start review.** To begin review, press the Playback button at the right of the LCD. The most recently viewed image will appear on the LCD.

- **Playback folder.** Image review generally shows you the images in the currently selected folder on your Secure Digital card. A given card can contain several folders (a new one is created anytime you exceed 999 images in the current folder). You can use the Playback folder menu option in the Playback menu (as I'll explain in Chapter 8) to select a specific folder or direct the D5200 to display images from all the folders on the memory card.

- **View thumbnail images.** To change the view from a single image to four, nine, or 72 thumbnails, follow the instructions in the "Viewing Thumbnails" section that follows.

- **Zoom in and out.** To zoom in or out, press the Zoom In or Zoom Out/Thumbnail key, following the instructions in the "Zooming the Nikon D5200 Playback Display" section. (It also shows you how to move the zoomed area around using the multi selector keypad.)

- **Move back and forth.** To advance to the next image, press the right edge of the multi selector pad or rotate the command dial to the right; to go back to a previous shot, press the left edge or rotate the command dial left. When you reach the beginning/end of the photos in your folder, the display "wraps around" to the end/beginning of the available shots.

- **See different types of data.** To change the type of information about the displayed image that is shown, press the up and down portions of the multi selector pad. To learn what data is available, read the "Using Shooting Data" section later in this chapter.

- **Remove images.** To delete an image that's currently on the screen, press the Trash button once, then press it again to confirm the deletion. To select and delete a group of images, use the Delete option in the Playback menu to specify particular photos to remove, as described in more detail in Chapter 8.

- **Cancel playback.** To cancel image review, press the Playback button again, or simply tap the shutter release button.

## Zooming the Nikon D5200 Playback Display

The Nikon D5200 zooms in and out of preview images using the procedure that follows:

1. When an image is displayed (use the Playback button to start), press the Zoom In button to fill the screen with a slightly magnified version of the image.

2. A navigation window appears in the lower-right corner of the LCD showing the entire image. Keep pressing to continue zooming in to the maximum of 31X enlargement (with a full resolution large image).

3. A yellow box in the navigation window shows the zoomed area within the full image. The entire navigation window vanishes from the screen after a few seconds, leaving you with a full-screen view of the zoomed portion of the image. (See Figure 3.9.)

4. To detect faces, use the multi selector buttons while an image is zoomed to highlight the main face in the image. Up to 35 faces will be detected by the D5200, indicated by white borders in the navigation window.

5. Use the command dial to move to the same zoomed area of the next/previous image.

6. Use the Zoom Out/Thumbnail button to zoom back out of the image.

7. Use the multi selector buttons to move the zoomed area around within the image. The navigation window will reappear for reference when zooming or scrolling around within the display.

8. To exit the zoom in/zoom out display, keep pressing the Zoom Out button until the full screen/full image/information display appears again.

**Figure 3.9**
The Nikon D5200 incorporates a small thumbnail image with a yellow box showing the current zoom area.

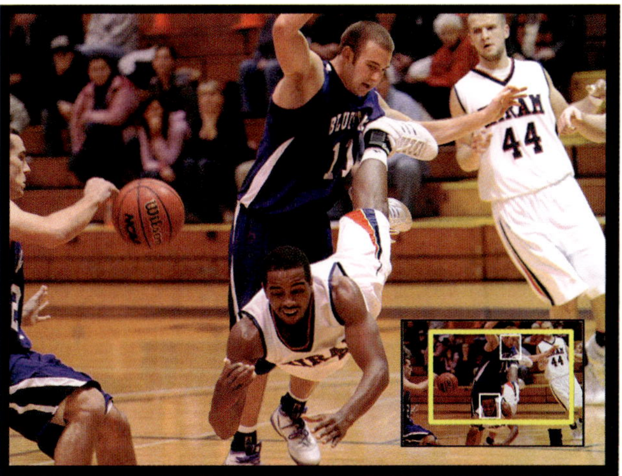

# Viewing Thumbnails

The Nikon D5200 provides other options for reviewing images in addition to zooming in and out. You can switch between single image view and either four, nine, or 72 reduced-size thumbnail images on a single LCD screen. There's also a calendar view that shows images grouped by the date they were shot.

Pages of thumbnail images offer a quick way to scroll through a large number of pictures quickly to find the one you want to examine in more detail. The D5200 lets you switch quickly from single- to four- to nine- to 72-image views, with a scroll bar displayed at the right side of the screen to show you the relative position of the displayed thumbnails within the full collection of images in the active folder on your memory card. Figure 3.10 offers a comparison between the three levels of thumbnail views. The Zoom In and Zoom Out/Thumbnail buttons are used.

- **Add thumbnails.** To increase the number of thumbnails on the screen, press the Zoom Out button. The D5200 will switch from single image to four thumbnails to nine thumbnails to 72 thumbnails, and then on to calendar view, described next. (The display doesn't cycle back to single image again.)

- **Reduce number of thumbnails.** To decrease the number of thumbnails on the screen, press the Zoom In button to change from calendar view to 72 to nine thumbnails to four thumbnails, or from four to single-image display. Continuing to press the Zoom In button once you've returned to single-image display starts the zoom process described in the previous section.

- **Switch between thumbnails and full image.** When viewing thumbnails, you can quickly switch between thumbnail view and full image display by pressing the OK button in the center of the multi selector. Pressing it again brings up the Retouch menu (described in Chapter 10). If you want to return to thumbnail views instead, press the Zoom In button.

- **Change highlighted thumbnail area.** Use the multi selector to move the yellow highlight box around among the thumbnails.

- **Protect and delete images.** When viewing thumbnails or a single page image, press the Protect button to preserve the image against accidental deletion (a key icon is overlaid over the full-page image; press Protect again to remove protection).

- **Exit image review.** Tap the shutter release button or press the Playback button to exit image review. You don't have to worry about missing a shot because you were reviewing images; a half-press of the shutter release automatically brings back the D5200's exposure meters, the autofocus system, and, unless you've redefined your controls or are using manual focus, cancels image review.

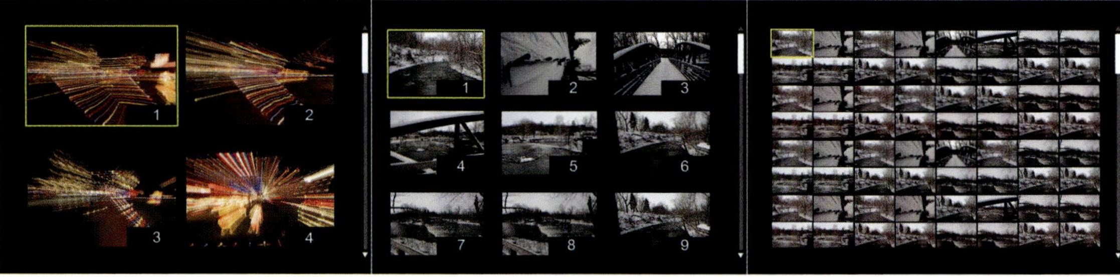

**Figure 3.10** Switch between four thumbnails (left), nine thumbnails (center), or 72 thumbnails (right), by pressing the Zoom Out and Zoom In buttons.

# Working with Calendar View

When you're in 72 thumbnail mode, pressing the Zoom Out button one more times takes you to calendar view, where you can sort through images arranged by the date they were taken. This feature is especially useful when you're traveling and want to see only the pictures you took in, say, a particular city on a certain day.

- **View dates and images taken on that date.** A yellow highlight box appears around a selected date in the date list calendar, as shown in Figure 3.11. When there are images available that were taken on that date, a scrolling thumbnail column appears at the right of the screen. The thumbnail column disappears if there are no photos taken on the highlighted date.

- **Change dates.** Use the multi selector keys to move through the date list.

- **View a date's images.** Press the Zoom In button to toggle between the date list to the scrolling thumbnail list of images taken on that date at the right of the screen. When viewing the thumbnail list, you can use the multi selector up/down keys to scroll through the available images. Press the Zoom In button again to return to the date list calendar when you want to select a different date.

- **Preview an image.** In the thumbnail list, when you've highlighted an image you want to look at, press the Zoom In button to see an enlarged view of that image without leaving the calendar view mode. The zoomed image replaces the date list.

- **Delete images.** Pressing the Trash button deletes a highlighted image in the thumbnail list. In the date view, pressing the Trash button removes all the images taken on that date (use with caution!).

- **Exit calendar view.** In thumbnail list view, if you highlight an image and press the OK button, you'll exit calendar view and the highlighted image will be shown on the LCD in the display mode you've chosen. (See "Working with Photo Information" to learn about the various display modes.) In date list view, pressing the Zoom In button exits calendar view and returns to 72 thumbnails view. You can also exit calendar view by tapping the shutter release (to turn off the LCD to ready the camera for shooting) or by pressing the MENU button.

**Figure 3.11**
Calendar view allows you to browse through all images on your memory card taken on a certain date.

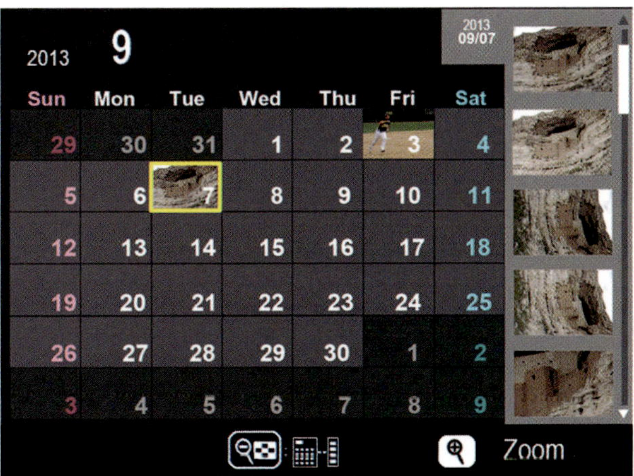

# Working with the Shooting Information/Photo Data Displays

Your Nikon D5200 can display two types of information on the color LCD as you are reviewing or taking pictures:

- **Shooting information display.** This is the screen of information that provides a readout of various settings for the D5200's shooting parameters. It appears when you press the information edit button on the back of the camera, just to the right of the viewfinder window.

- **Photo information.** These are a series of up to eight screens (including GPS data, which appears only if you used a GPS device to take the picture) that provide various types of shooting and other information *about a particular image* that you are reviewing. The data shown applies only to that image, and does not reflect your D5200's current shooting settings (unless you're viewing an image you've just taken). I'll show you each of these screens, too, and explain how you can use them.

## Using the Shooting Information Display

The shooting information display appears when you press the information edit button to the right of the viewfinder window. This display shows for about 10 seconds by default, but you can change this to a period of up to 10 minutes using Custom Setting c2, as described in Chapter 9. Hide this display by pressing the information edit button twice, by pressing the Info button on top of the camera, or by tapping the shutter release button. (The D5200 will always clear the LCD screen when you depress the shutter release button, and activate the exposure meter at the same time, so you'll be ready to take a shot if you want.)

The shooting information display provides a lot of basic shooting data. Figure 3.12 shows the various shooting information indicators. I've applied some labels highlighting the basic kinds of settings you'll find on this screen. This rendition just provides an overview of the kind of data you'll find on the color LCD; not every readout will appear on your screen, and certainly not all at once.

When the shooting information display is shown, press the information edit button a second time, and you'll be able to change the parameters in the bottom row and right-hand column, shown in Figure 3.13. Use the multi selector buttons to navigate to the parameter you want to adjust and press the OK button or the multi selector center button to produce a menu with your options. The specs you can change include the following. (I'll describe the options for each of them in Chapters 8–10.)

- **Image quality.** Choose JPEG Fine, Normal, Basic, RAW, or RAW+JPEG Fine, Normal, or Basic.

- **Image size.** Select from Large, Medium, or Small resolutions.

- **White balance.** Choose any of the white balance modes, including Auto and Preset, as described in Chapter 8.

- **ISO sensitivity.** Select ISO sensitivity from ISO 100 to H2 (ISO 25600 equivalent).

- **Release mode.** Choose one of the release modes described in Chapter 2, including single frame, continuous, self-timer, delayed remote, quick-response remote, and quiet shutter release.

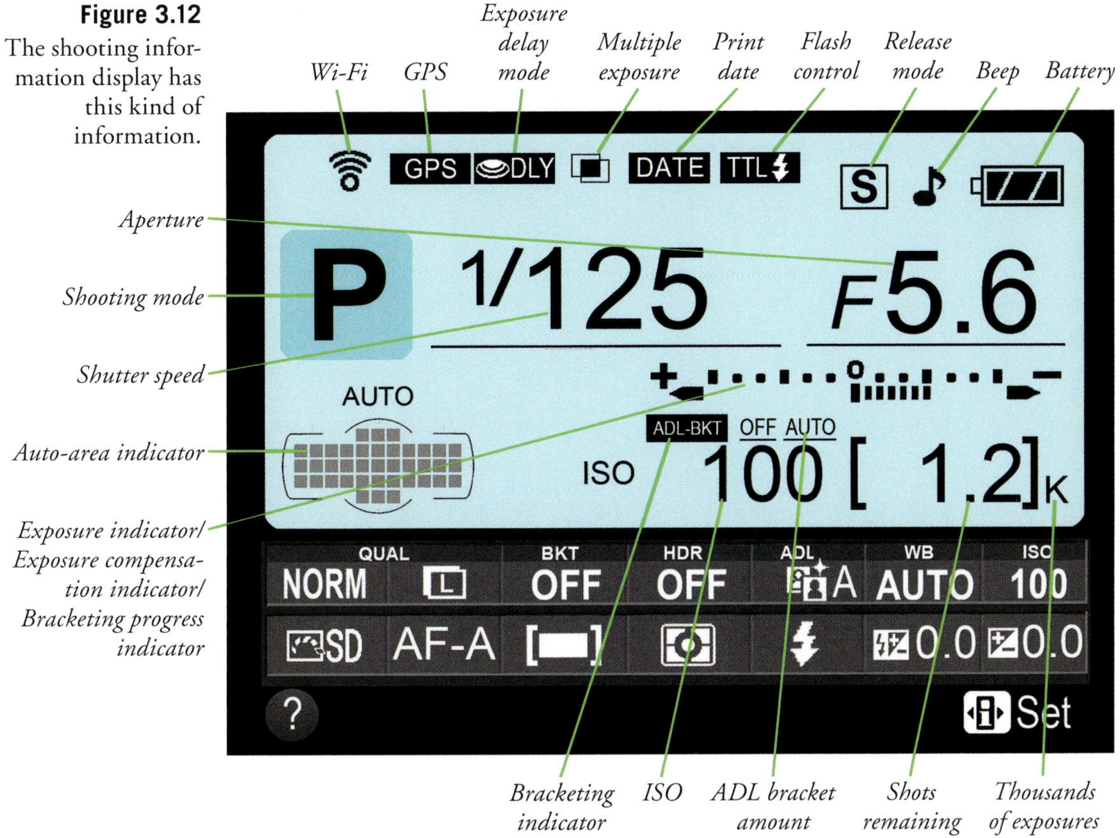


**Figure 3.12** The shooting information display has this kind of information.

- **Autofocus mode.** Select from AF-S, AF-C, and AF-A autofocus modes.
- **AF-area mode.** Choose single-point AF area mode, dynamic-area AF, 3D-tracking (11 points), and auto-area AF, as described in Chapter 2 and explained in more detail in Chapter 5.
- **Metering mode.** Select from Matrix, Center-weighted, and Spot metering.
- **Active D-Lighting.** Choose to extend the dynamic range of your image to one of four levels (Low, Normal, High, Extra High), plus Off. I'll explain the pitfalls/advantages of Active D-Lighting in Chapter 8.
- **Bracketing increment.** Select a bracketing increment for 0.3 (one-third stop) to 2 full stops, or off. Bracketing is explained in more detail in Chapter 4.
- **Flash mode.** You can choose a flash mode, including flash on, red-eye, slow sync with red-eye prevention, slow sync, and rear sync. When the flash is elevated, you can also choose one of these modes by pressing the flash button and rotating the command dial. The selected mode will be displayed on the shooting information screen.
- **Flash exposure compensation.** You can choose a flash exposure compensation amount from –3 to +1 EV. When the flash is elevated, you can also choose flash compensation by holding down the flash button and the aperture/compensation button and rotating the command dial. The selected mode will be displayed on the shooting information screen.

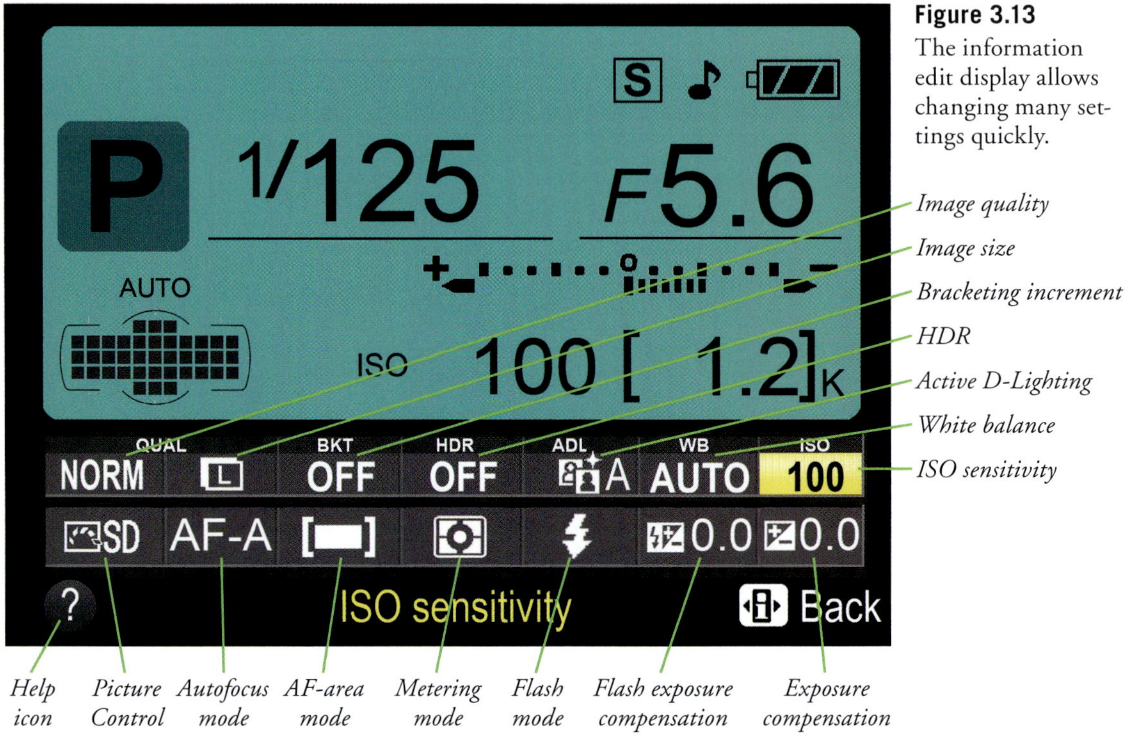



**Figure 3.13**
The information edit display allows changing many settings quickly.

*Image quality*
*Image size*
*Bracketing increment*
*HDR*
*Active D-Lighting*
*White balance*
*ISO sensitivity*

*Help icon*  *Picture Control*  *Autofocus mode*  *AF-area mode*  *Metering mode*  *Flash mode*  *Flash exposure compensation*  *Exposure compensation*

- **Exposure compensation.** You can choose an exposure compensation amount from −5 to +5 EV. You can also choose exposure compensation by holding down the aperture/compensation button and rotating the command dial. The selected mode will be displayed on the shooting information screen.
- **Picture Control.** Choose a Picture Control style.

## Using the Photo Data Displays

When reviewing an image on the screen, your D5200 can supplement the image itself with a variety of shooting data, ranging from basic information presented at the bottom of the LCD display, to three text overlays that detail virtually every shooting option you've selected. There is also a display for GPS data if you're using a GPS device, and two views of histograms. I'll explain how to do that and how to work with histograms in the discussion on achieving optimum exposure in Chapter 4. However, this is a good place to provide an overview of the kind of information you can view when playing back your photos.

You can change the *types* of information displayed using the Playback Display Options entry in the Playback menu. There you will find checkboxes you can mark for both basic photo information (overexposed highlights and the focus point used when the image was captured) and detailed photo information (which includes an RGB histogram and various data screens). You can also specify

None, which activates a screen that shows *only* the image, with no additional information. I'll show you how to activate these info options in Chapter 8, and provide more detailed reasons why you might want to see this data when you review your pictures. This section will simply show you the type of information available. Most of the data is self-explanatory, so the labels in the accompanying figures should tell you most of what you need to know. To change to any of these views while an image is on the screen in Playback mode, press the multi selector up/down buttons.

- **Image only.** If you specify None in the Playback menu's Playback Display Options entry, the D5200 will add a screen that shows only the image itself, with no extraneous information. (It does not nullify the other screens, in other words. You get an additional plain-vanilla screen.) I'm not providing a figure that illustrates this mode.

- **File information screen.** The basic full image review display is officially called the file information screen, and looks like Figure 3.14. Press the multi selector down button to advance to the next information screen.

- **Highlights.** When highlights display is active (after being chosen in the Display Mode entry of the Playback menu, as described in Chapter 8), any overexposed areas will be indicated by a flashing black border. As I am unable to make the printed page flash, you'll have to check out this effect for yourself. You can visualize what these "blinkies" look like in Figure 3.15.

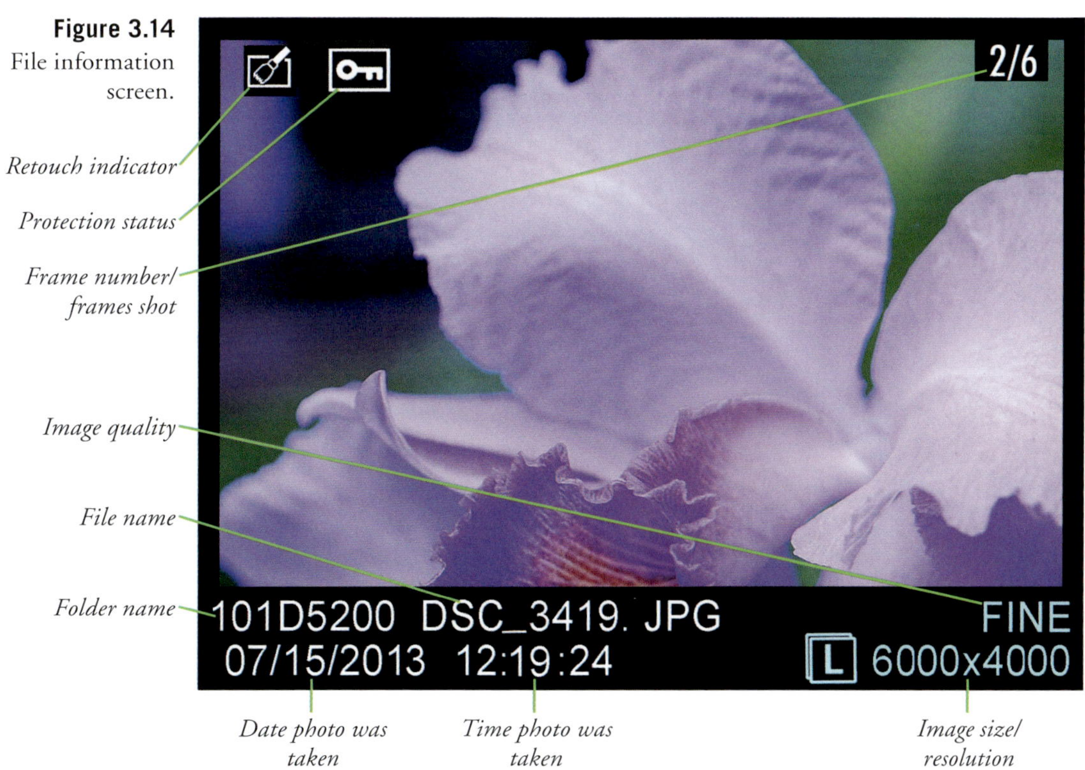


**Figure 3.14** File information screen.

Retouch indicator

Protection status

Frame number/ frames shot

Image quality

File name

Folder name

Date photo was taken

Time photo was taken

Image size/ resolution

- **RGB histogram.** Another optional screen is the RGB histogram, which you can see in Figure 3.16. I'm going to leave the discussion of histograms for Chapter 4.

- **Shooting Data 1.** This is the first in a series of three screens that collectively provide everything else you might want to know about a picture you've taken. I'm not providing any labels in Figure 3.17, because the information in the first seven lines in the screen should be obvious.

- **Shooting Data 2.** This screen shows white balance data and adjustments, the color space you've selected, and lists any Picture Control tweaks you've entered. (See Figure 3.18.)

- **Shooting Data 3.** The next screen shows any noise reduction you've specified, Active D-Lighting status, and any Retouch menu changes you may have made. Although none of them apply to the background image shown in Figure 3.19, I've added a few entries to show the kind of changes that can be made. You'll learn more about the Retouch menu in Chapter 10, which also will tell you how to create an image comment, like the one shown in the figure.

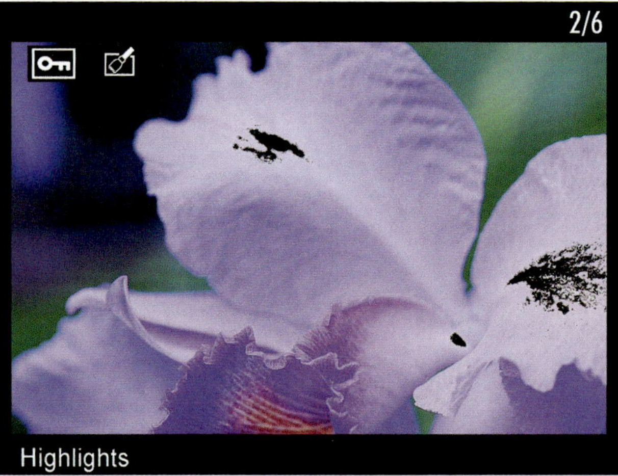


**Figure 3.15**
Highlights screen.

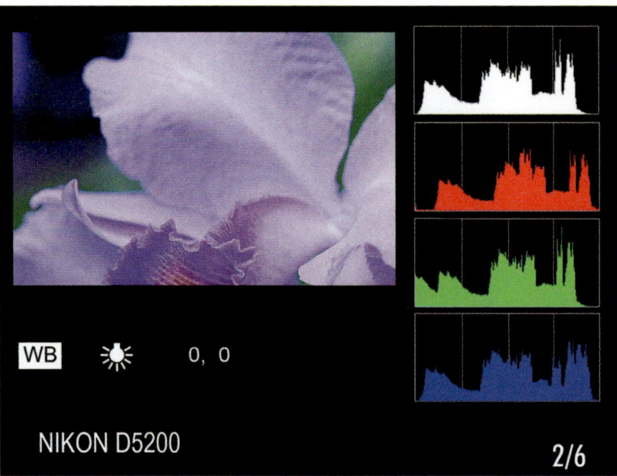


**Figure 3.16**
RGB histogram screen.

**Figure 3.17**
Shooting Data 1
screen.

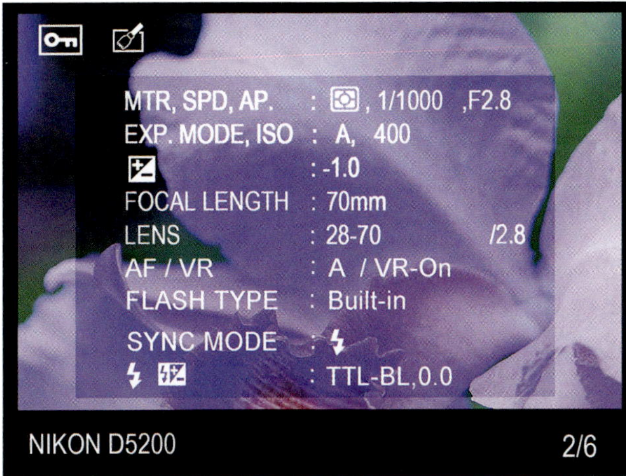


**Figure 3.18**
Shooting Data 2
screen.

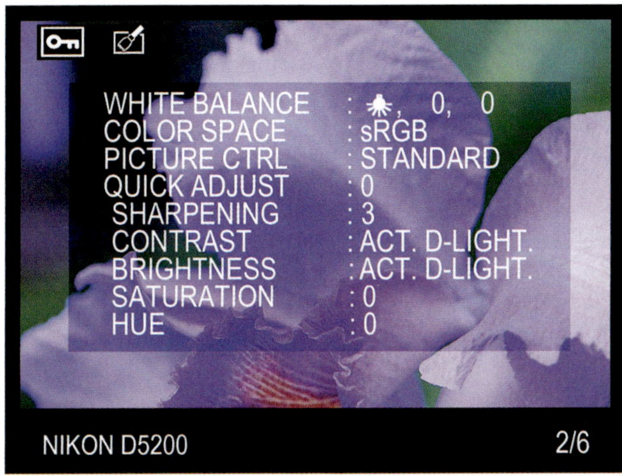


**Figure 3.19**
Shooting Data 3
screen.

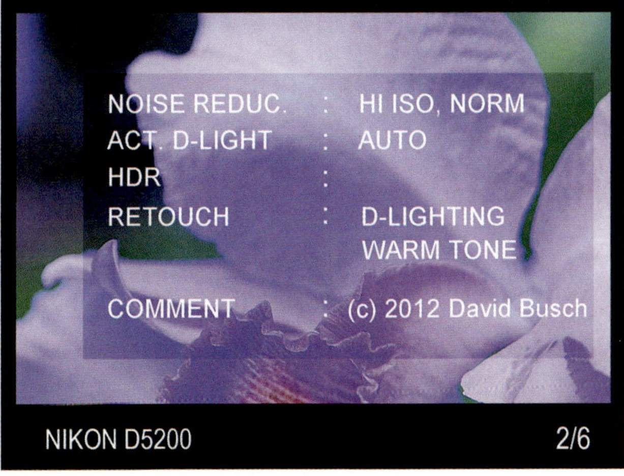

- **Overview data.** This screen, shown in Figure 3.20, provides a smaller image of your photo, but more information, including a luminance (brightness) histogram, metering mode used, lens focal length, exposure compensation, flash compensation, and lots of other data that's self-explanatory.

- **GPS data.** This screen appears *only* if the image was taken using the GPS device. It includes latitude, longitude, altitude, and time information, as shown in Figure 3.21.

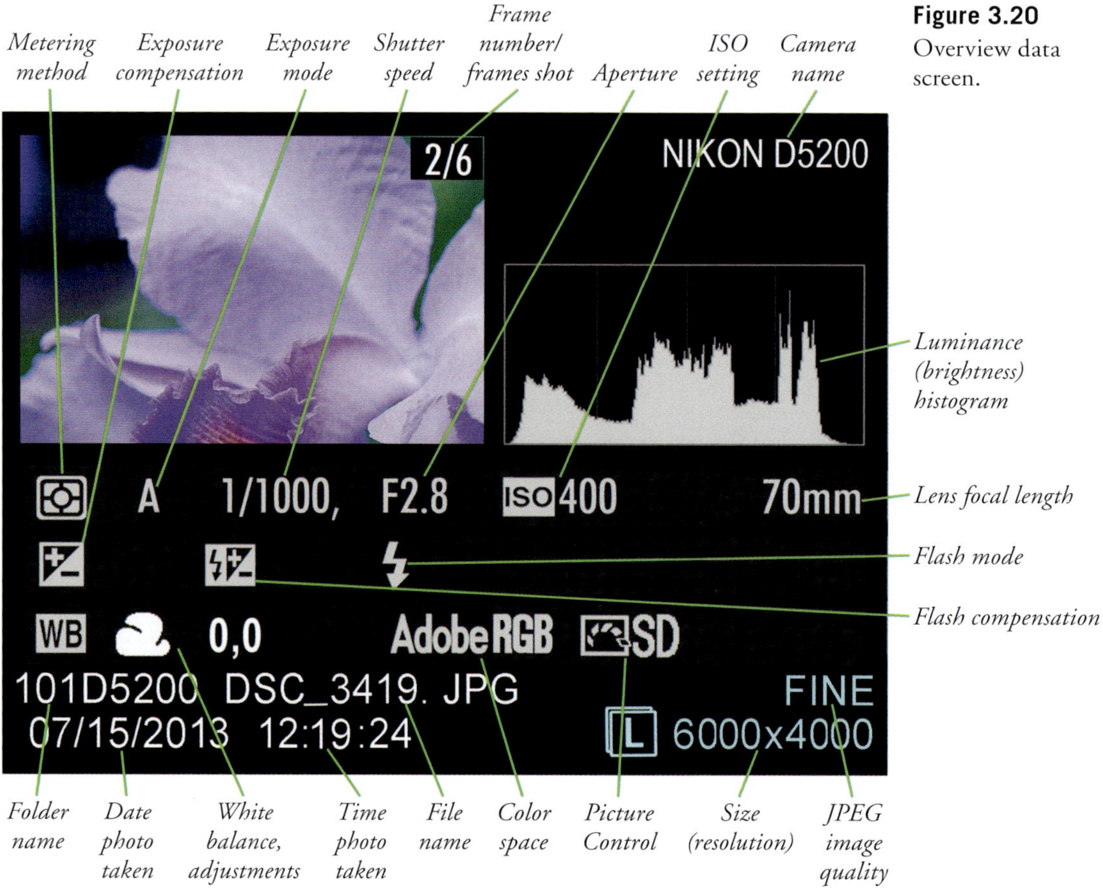


**Figure 3.20**
Overview data screen.

**Figure 3.21**
GPS data screen.

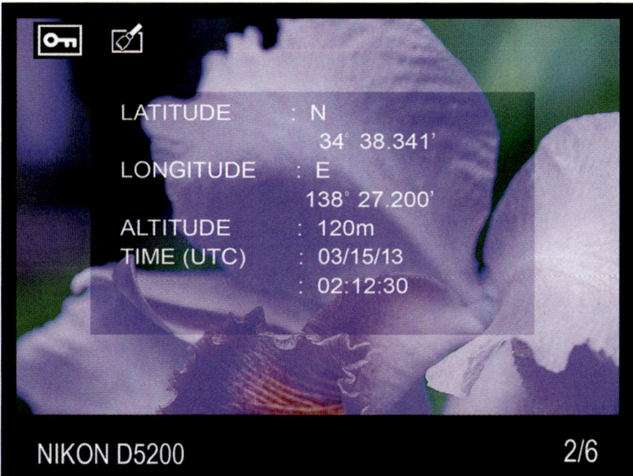


# Going Topside

The top surface of the Nikon D5200 (see Figures 3.22 and 3.23) has its own set of frequently accessed controls.

- **Sensor focal plane indicator.** This indicator shows the *plane* of the sensor, for use in applications where exact measurement of the distance from the focal plane to the subject is necessary. (These are mostly scientific/close-up applications.)

- **Accessory shoe.** Slide an electronic flash into this mount when you need a more powerful Speedlight. A dedicated flash unit, like the Nikon SB-900, can use the multiple contact points shown to communicate exposure, zoom setting, white balance information, and other data between the flash and the camera. There's more on using electronic flash in Chapter 12. You can also mount other accessories on this shoe, such as the Nikon GP-1 GPS adapter.

- **Microphones.** The D5200 has a pair of stereo microphones built into the electronic flash housing on top of the camera, seen as two quartets of holes.

- **Mode dial.** Rotate this dial to select from two fully automatic modes (Auto and Auto No Flash), four advanced exposure modes (Manual, Aperture-priority, Shutter-priority, and Program), five different scene modes (first described in Chapter 2, and next in Chapter 4) selected by rotating the command dial, plus additional modes available when the mode dial is set to the SCENE or EFFECTS positions.

- **Power switch.** Rotate this switch clockwise to turn on the Nikon D5200 (and virtually all other Nikon dSLRs).

- **Shutter release button.** Partially depress this button to activate the exposure meter, lock in exposure, and focus (unless you've redefined the focus activation button, as outlined in Chapter 9). Press all the way to take the picture. Tapping the shutter release when the camera has turned off the autoexposure and autofocus mechanisms reactivates both. When a review image is displayed on the back-panel color LCD, tapping this button removes the image from the display and reactivates the autoexposure and autofocus mechanisms.

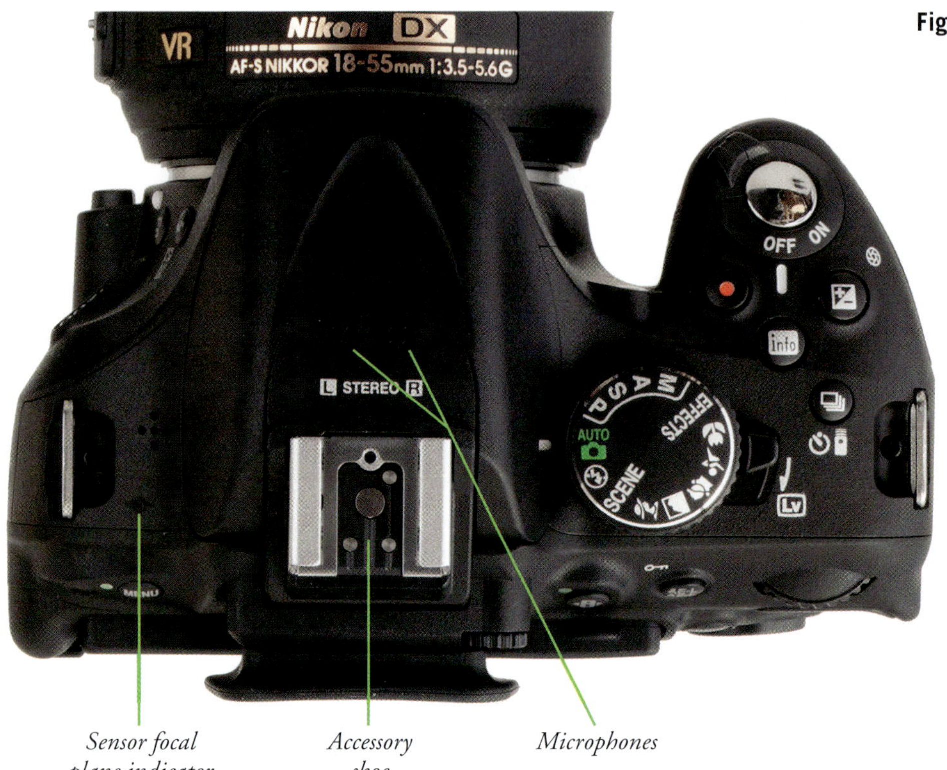

**Figure 3.22**

Sensor focal
plane indicator

Accessory
shoe

Microphones

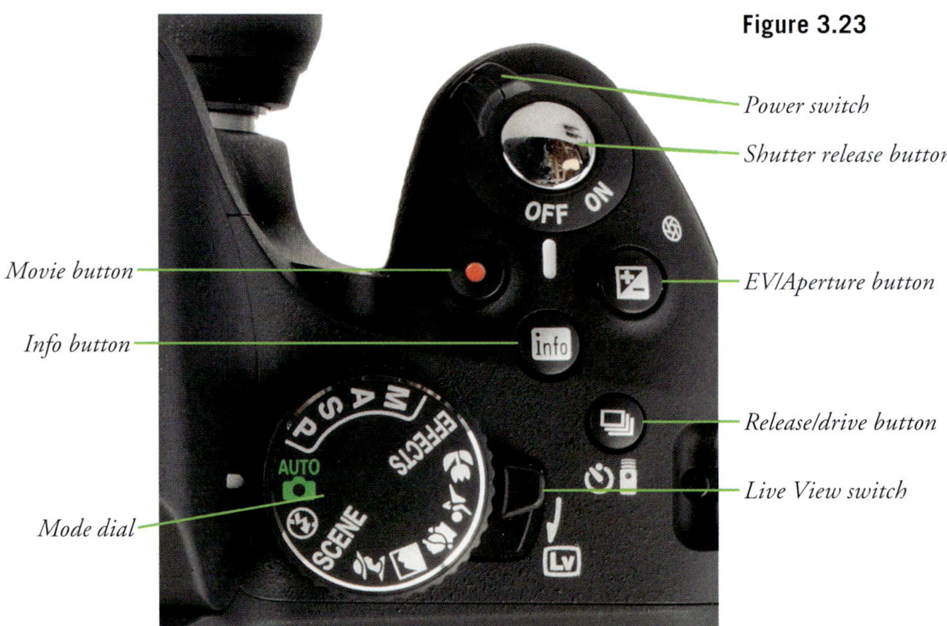

**Figure 3.23**

Power switch

Shutter release button

Movie button

EV/Aperture button

Info button

Release/drive button

Live View switch

Mode dial

- **Exposure compensation/Aperture button.** Hold down this button and spin the command dial to add or subtract exposure when using Program, Aperture-priority, or Shutter-priority modes. (In Manual mode, the exposure remains the same, but the "ideal" exposure shown in the electronic analog display [more on that in the next section] is modified to reflect the extra/ reduced exposure you're calling for.) The button is also used to make secondary settings, such as aperture when the camera is in Manual exposure mode. (The command dial changes shutter speed, and holding down the aperture button while rotating the command dial changes aperture.)

- **Info button.** Turns the LCD display on/off. Don't confuse with the information edit button on the back panel of the camera.

- **Live View switch.** Rotate this momentary-contact switch toward the back of the camera to turn on live view and enable movie shooting. Rotate it again to turn live view/moving shooting off.

- **Movie record button.** Press the red button to start movie shooting, and again to stop shooting.

## Lens Components

The lens shown at left in Figure 3.24 is a typical lens that might be mounted on a Nikon dSLR. Unfortunately, this particular lens doesn't include all the common features found on the various Nikon lenses available for your camera, so I am including a second lens (shown at right in the figure) that *does* have more features and components. It's not a typical lens that a D5200 user might work with, however. This 17-35mm zoom is a pricey "pro" lens that costs about half as much as the entire D5200 camera. Nevertheless, it makes a good example. Components found on this pair of lenses include:

- **Filter thread.** Most lenses have a thread on the front for attaching filters and other add-ons. Some, like the 18-55 VR kit lens shown, also use this thread for attaching a lens hood (you screw on the filter first, and then attach the hood to the screw thread on the front of the filter). Some lenses, such as the AF-S Nikkor 14-24mm f/2.8G ED lens, have no front filter thread, either because their front elements are too curved to allow mounting a filter and/or because the front element is so large that huge filters would be prohibitively expensive. Some of these front-filter-hostile lenses allow using smaller filters that drop into a slot at the back of the lens.

- **Lens hood bayonet.** Lenses like the 17-35mm zoom shown in the figure use this bayonet to mount the lens hood. Such lenses generally will have a dot on the edge showing how to align the lens hood with the bayonet mount.

- **Focus ring.** This is the ring you turn when you manually focus the lens, or fine-tune autofocus adjustment. It's a narrow ring at the very front of the lens (on the 18-55mm kit lens), or a wider ring located somewhere else.

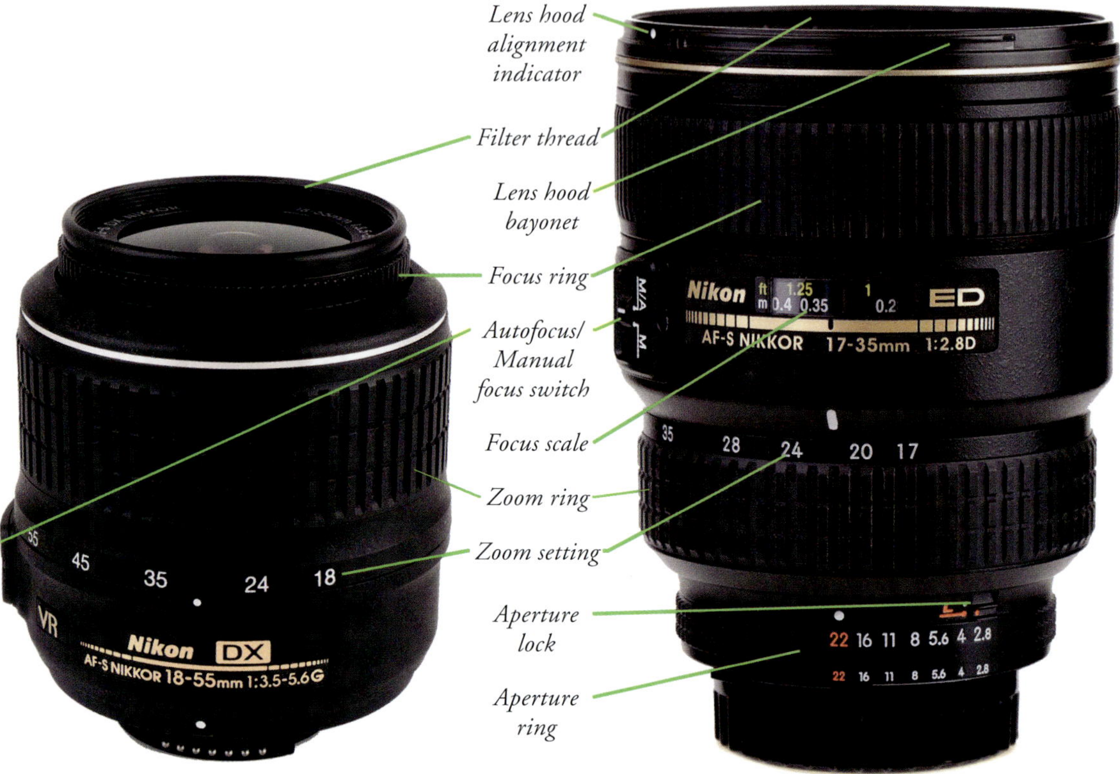


**Figure 3.24**

- **Focus scale.** This is a readout found on many lenses that rotates in unison with the lens's focus mechanism to show the distance at which the lens has been focused. It's a useful indicator for double-checking autofocus, roughly evaluating depth-of-field, and for setting manual focus guesstimates. Chapter 11 deals with the mysteries of lenses and their controls in more detail.

- **Zoom setting.** These markings on the lens show the current focal length selected.

- **Zoom ring.** Turn this ring to change the zoom setting.

- **Autofocus/Manual focus switch.** Allows you to change from automatic focus to manual focus.

- **Aperture ring.** Some lenses have a ring that allows you to set a specific f/stop manually, rather than use the camera's internal electronic aperture control. An aperture ring is useful when a lens is mounted on a non-automatic extension ring, bellows, or other accessory that doesn't couple electronically with the camera. Aperture rings also allow using a lens on an older camera that lacks electronic control. In recent years, Nikon has been replacing lenses that have aperture rings with versions that only allow setting the aperture with camera controls.

- **Aperture lock.** If you want your D5200 (or other Nikon dSLR) to control the aperture electronically, you must set the lens to its smallest aperture (usually f/22 or f/32) and lock it with this control.

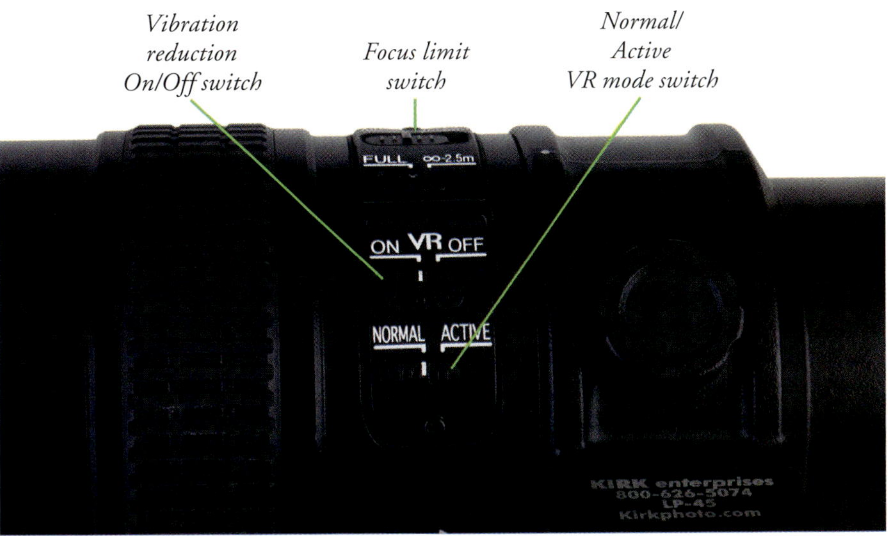


**Figure 3.25**
Some lenses have focus limit switches and controls for vibration reduction (VR) features.

- **Focus limit switch.** Some lenses have this switch (shown in Figure 3.25), which limits the focus range of the lens, thus potentially reducing focus seeking when shooting distant subjects. The limiter stops the lens from trying to focus at closer distances (in this case, closer than 2.5 meters).

- **Vibration reduction switch.** Lenses with Nikon's Vibration Reduction (VR) feature include a switch for turning the stabilization feature on and off, and, in some cases, for changing from normal vibration reduction to a more aggressive "active" VR mode useful for, say, shooting from moving vehicles. More on VR and other lens topics in Chapter 11.

The back end of a lens intended for use on a Nikon camera has other components that you seldom see (except when you swap lenses), shown in Figure 3.26, but still should know about:

- **Lens bayonet mount.** This is the mounting mechanism that attaches to a matching mount on the camera. Although the lens bayonet is usually metal, some lower-priced lenses use a rugged plastic for this key component.

- **Automatic diaphragm lever.** This lever is moved by a matching lever in the camera to adjust the f/stop from wide open (which makes for the brightest view) to the *taking aperture* or *working aperture*, which is the f/stop that will be used to take the picture. The actual taking aperture is determined by the camera's metering system (or by you when the D5200 is in Manual mode), and is communicated to the lens through the electronic contacts described next. (An exception is when the aperture ring on the lens itself is unlocked and used to specify the f/stop.) However, the spring-loaded physical levers are what actually push the aperture to the selected f/stop— even with advanced cameras like the D5200 or D3. The aperture lever is also activated when you press the DOF button.

- **Electronic contacts.** These metal contacts pass information to matching contacts located in the camera body allowing a firm electrical connection so that exposure, distance, and other information can be exchanged between the camera and lens.

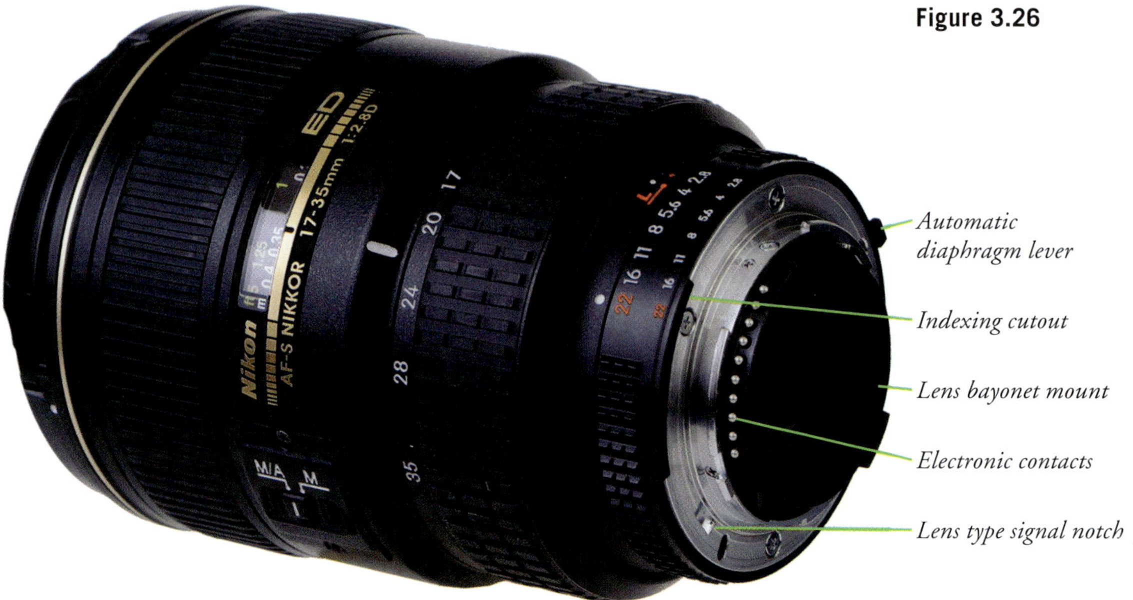



- **Lens type signal notch.** This is a machined groove in the lens mount, designed to tell older (non-dSLR) cameras that the aperture stops were linear. Today, this information would be conveyed electronically, except that all current lenses already have linear f/stops.

- **Indexing cutout.** The base of any Nikon lens made after 1977 that has an aperture ring includes a cutout notch that mates with a ring around the lens mount of Nikon's advanced cameras, but not entry-level models like the D5200. It tells the camera what the maximum aperture is and what f/stop has been set. For owners of those cameras, this means that older manual focus lenses (including pre-1977 lenses that have been converted to this system) can be used for automatic metering with the Aperture-priority exposure mode, and for manual metering in Manual exposure mode.

## Looking Inside the Viewfinder

Much of the important shooting status information is shown inside the viewfinder of the Nikon D5200. Not all of this information will be shown at any one time. Figure 3.27 shows what you can expect to see. These readouts include:

- **Focus points.** Can display the 39 areas used by the D5200 to focus. The camera can select the appropriate focus zone for you, or you can manually select one or all of the zones.

- **Active focus point.** The currently selected focus point can be highlighted with red illumination, depending on focus mode.

- **AF-area bracket.** Shows the area covered by the autofocus sensors.

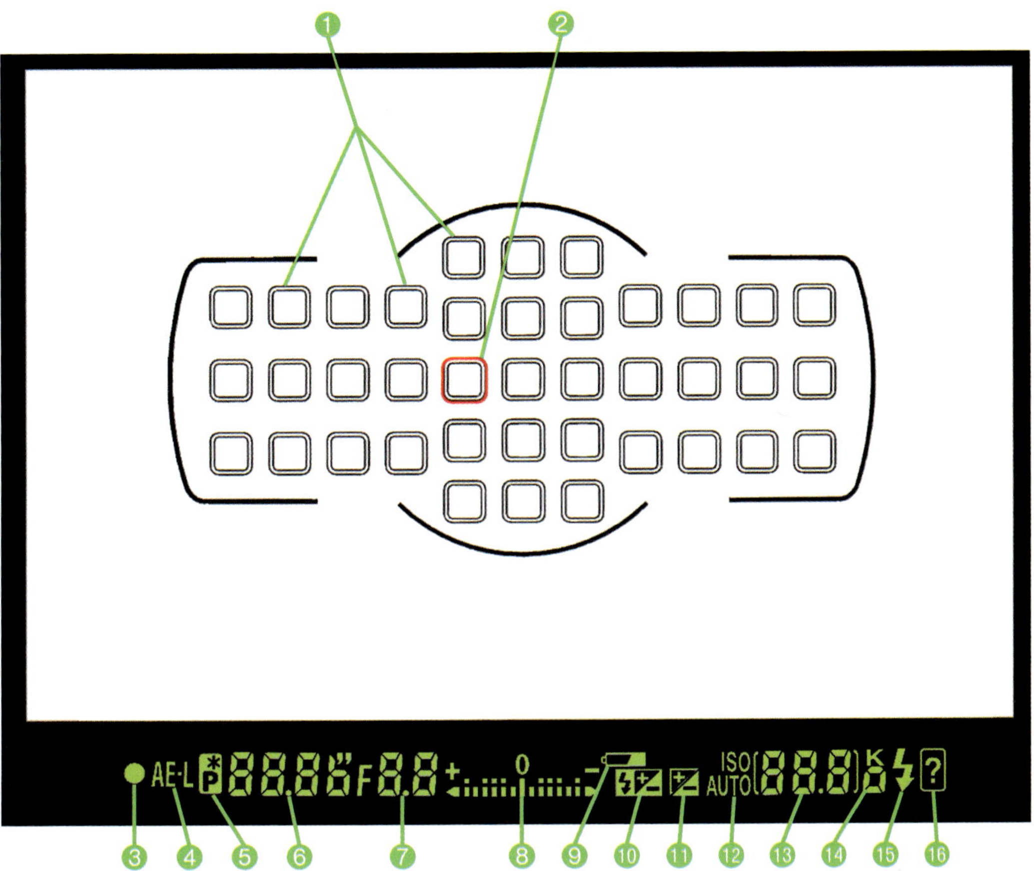


1 Focus points

2 Selected focus point

3 Focus indicator

4 Autoexposure lock indicator

5 Flexible program indicator

6 Shutter speed

7 Aperture

8 Exposure indicator/Exposure compensation display/Electronic rangefinder

9 Battery indicator

10 Flash exposure compensation

11 Exposure compensation

12 Auto ISO sensitivity indicator

13 Number of exposures remaining/Number of shots remaining before buffer fills/White balance recording indicator/Exposure compensation value/Flash compensation value/ISO sensitivity

14 Thousands of exposures

15 Flash ready indicator

16 Warning indicator

**Figure 3.27**

- **Focus indicator.** This green dot will glow steadily when the subject covered by the active autofocus zone is in sharp focus, whether focus was achieved by the AF system, or by you using manual focusing. Left and right arrows show whether focus is set ahead of or behind the subject.

- **Autoexposure (AE) lock/Flash value lock indicator.** Shows that exposure or flash exposure has been locked.

- **Shutter speed.** Displays the current shutter speed selected by the camera, or by you in Manual exposure mode.

- **Aperture.** Shows the current aperture chosen by the D5200's autoexposure system, or specified by you when using Manual exposure mode.

- **Automatic ISO indicator.** Is shown as a reminder that the D5200 has been set to adjust ISO sensitivity automatically.

- **Flash compensation indicator.** Appears when flash EV changes have been made.

- **Exposure compensation indicator.** This is shown when exposure compensation (EV) changes have been made. It's easy to forget you've dialed in a little more or less exposure, and then shoot a whole series of pictures of a different scene that doesn't require such compensation. Beware!

- **Electronic analog exposure display.** This scale shows the current exposure level, with the bottom indicator centered when the exposure is correct as metered. The indicator may also move to the left or right to indicate over- or underexposure (respectively). The scale is also used to show the amount of exposure compensation dialed in. Also shows exposure compensation and degree of horizontal tilt.

- **Exposures remaining/maximum burst available/other data.** Normally displays the number of exposures remaining on your memory card, but while shooting it changes to show a number that indicates the number of frames that can be taken in continuous shooting mode using the current settings. This indicator also shows other information, such as ISO sensitivity, exposure compensation value, and Active D-Lighting amount.

- **Thousands of exposures.** Displayed when more than 999 exposures remain; the readout to the left will then show number of shots remaining in thousands.

- **Flash ready indicator.** This icon appears when the flash is fully charged.

- **Battery status.** Shows amount of remaining power.

- **Bracketing indicator.** Shows when Active D-Lighting, exposure, flash, or white balance bracketing is underway.

- **ISO sensitivity.** This useful indicator shows the current ISO setting value. Those who have accidentally taken dozens of shots under bright sunlight at ISO 1600 because they forgot to change the setting back after some indoor shooting will treasure this addition.

# Underneath Your Nikon D5200

There's not a lot going on with the bottom panel of your Nikon D5200. You'll find the battery compartment access door, and a tripod socket, which secures the camera to a tripod. The socket accepts other accessories, such as quick-release plates that allow rapid attaching and detaching the D5200 from a matching platform affixed to your tripod. Figure 3.28 shows the underside view of the camera.

**Figure 3.28**

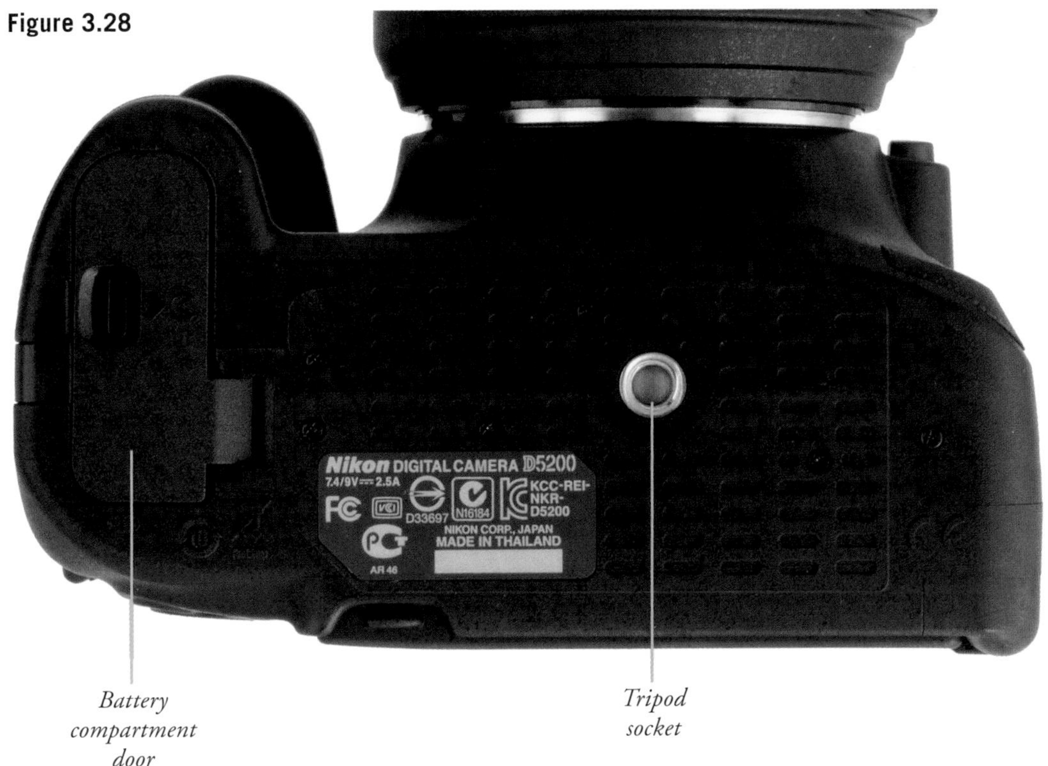


*Battery*
*compartment*
*door*

*Tripod*
*socket*

# Part II

## Mastering Your Tools

Even if you've learned the fundamentals and controls of the D5200 there is lots of room to learn more and master the features of the camera so you can use them to their fullest. Even if you're getting great exposures a high percentage of the time, you can fine-tune tonal values and use your shutter speed, aperture, and ISO controls creatively. Your camera's high performance autofocus system may zero in on your subject in most situations—but you still need to be able to tell the D5200 *what* to focus on, and *when*. Other tools at your disposal let you freeze an instant of time, create multiple exposures on a single frame, and improve your images in other imaginative ways. The chapters in this part will help you move your photography to the next level by understanding exposure, mastering the mysteries of autofocus, and using the Nikon D5200's advanced features.

> This part of the book contains the core chapters that will help you improve your images by nailing the best exposure, every time; using the (often confusing, sometimes conflicting) features of the camera's advanced autofocus system and exploring some advanced techniques like trap focus, stacked focus, and in-camera HDR.

- **Chapter 4:** This chapter explores all your options for fine-tuning exposure with the Nikon D5200. You'll learn when to use—and not use—each of the camera's metering modes, how to work with histograms, and the rationale for choosing the built-in HDR feature, or whether to capture high dynamic range images "manually." I'm also going to explode the myth of the 18-percent gray card.

- **Chapter 5:** As autofocus features are added, this useful capability often becomes more confusing, even for veteran photographers. I'm going to show you exactly how autofocus works so you can better understand the strengths and limitations of each mode. You'll discover how to select the mode that will give you tack-sharp focus time after time, and learn how to use fine-tuning (with the included focus chart) to correct lenses with front- and back-focus problems.

- **Chapter 6:** Learn how to use live view and shoot movies that will capture moments, as they happen, for presentations and video shows.

- **Chapter 7:** Here you'll find discussions of some more advanced techniques, including how to make people "invisible" with long exposures, getting the most from the D5200's continuous shooting capabilities, and some clever ways to create multiple exposures.

# 4

# Nailing the Right Exposure

When you bought your Nikon D5200, you probably thought your days of worrying about getting the correct exposure were over. To paraphrase an old Kodak tagline (remember Kodak?) dating back to the 19th Century—the goal is, "you press the button, and the camera does the rest." For the most part, that's a realistic objective. The D5200 is one of the smartest cameras available when it comes to calculating the right exposure for most situations. You can simply rotate the mode dial to switch to Program (P), Aperture-priority (A), or Shutter-priority (S) and shoot away. Even Manual (M) mode doesn't leave you up a creek without a paddle: the D5200's analog exposure display at the bottom of the viewfinder provides feedback about how much your selected settings vary from what the D5200 *would* have used if you'd opted for one of the semi-automated exposure modes.

For example, when you shoot with the main light source behind the subject, you end up with *backlighting*, which can result in an overexposed background and/or an underexposed subject. The Nikon D5200 recognizes backlit situations nicely, and can properly base exposure on the main subject, producing a decent photo. Features like Active D-Lighting (discussed in Chapter 8) can fine-tune exposure as you take photos, to preserve detail in the highlights and shadows.

But what if you *want* to underexpose the subject, to produce a silhouette effect? Or, perhaps, you might want to flip up the D5200's built-in flash unit to fill in the shadows on your subject. The more you know about how to use your D5200, the more you'll run into situations where you want to creatively tweak the exposure to provide a different look than you'd get with a straight shot.

This chapter shows you the fundamentals of exposure, so you'll be better equipped to override the Nikon D5200's default settings when you want to, or need to. After all, correct exposure is one of the foundations of good photography, along with accurate focus and sharpness, appropriate color balance, freedom from unwanted noise and excessive contrast, as well as pleasing composition.

The Nikon D5200 gives you a great deal of control over all of these, although composition is entirely up to you. You must still frame the photograph to create an interesting arrangement of subject matter, but all the other parameters are basic functions of the camera. You can let your D5200 set them for you automatically, you can fine-tune how the camera applies its automatic settings, or you can make them yourself, manually. The amount of control you have over exposure, sensitivity (ISO settings), color balance, focus, and image parameters like sharpness and contrast make the D5200 a versatile tool for creating images.

In the next few pages, I'm going to give you a grounding in one of those foundations, and explain the basics of exposure, either as an introduction or as a refresher course, depending on your current level of expertise. When you finish this chapter, you'll understand most of what you need to know to take well-exposed photographs creatively in a broad range of situations.

# Getting a Handle on Exposure

In the most basic sense, exposure is all about light. Exposure can make or break your photo. Correct exposure brings out the detail in the areas you want to picture, providing the range of tones and colors you need to create the desired image. Poor exposure can cloak important details in shadow, or wash them out in glare-filled featureless expanses of white. However, getting the perfect exposure requires some intelligence—either that built into the camera, or the smarts in your head—because digital sensors can't capture all the tones we are able to see. If the range of tones in an image is extensive, embracing both inky black shadows and bright highlights, we often must settle for an exposure that renders most of those tones—but not all—in a way that best suits the photo we want to produce. One solution is to use High Dynamic Range (HDR) photography—combining two (or more) exposures to create a single image will a full range of tones. The Nikon D5200 is especially adept at this technique, because it includes an HDR feature built right into the camera.

For example, look at two bracketed exposures presented in Figure 4.1. For the image on the left, the highlights (chiefly the clouds at upper left and the top-left edge of the skyscraper) are well exposed, but everything else in the shot is seriously underexposed. The version on the right, taken an instant later with the tripod-mounted camera, shows detail in the shadow areas of the buildings, but the highlights are completely washed out. The camera's sensor simply can't capture detail in both dark areas and bright areas in a single shot. The final image is shown in Figure 4.2. I'll explain more about HDR photography later in this chapter. For now, though, I'm going to concentrate on showing you how to get the best exposures possible without resorting to such tools, using only the features of your Nikon D5200.

To understand exposure, you need to understand the six aspects of light that combine to produce an image. Start with a light source—the sun, an interior lamp, or the glow from a campfire—and trace its path to your camera, through the lens, and finally to the sensor that captures the illumination.

Here's a brief review of the things within our control that affect exposure, listed in "chronological" order (that is, as the light moves from the subject to the sensor):

■ **Light at its source.** Our eyes and our cameras—film or digital—are most sensitive to that portion of the electromagnetic spectrum we call *visible light*. That light has several important aspects that are relevant to photography, such as color and harshness (which is determined primarily by the apparent size of the light source as it illuminates a subject). But, in terms of exposure, the important attribute of a light source is its *intensity*. We may have direct control over intensity, which might be the case with an interior light that can be brightened or dimmed. Or, we might have only indirect control over intensity, as with sunlight, which can be made to appear dimmer by introducing translucent light-absorbing or reflective materials in its path.

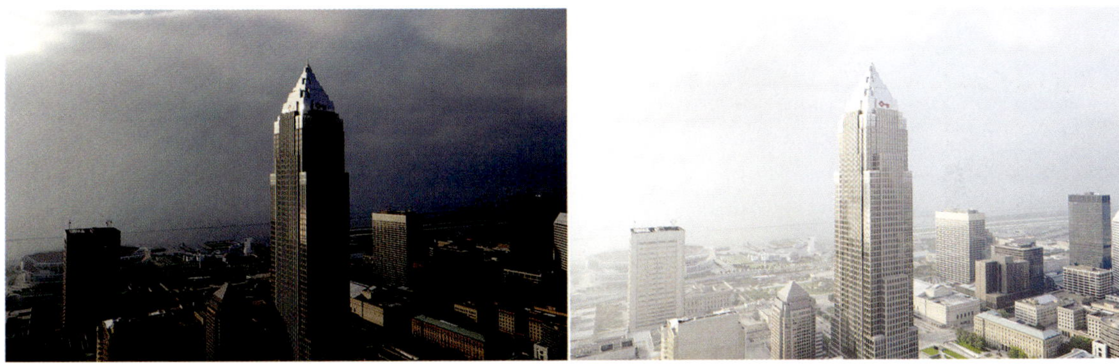

**Figure 4.1** At left, the image is exposed for the highlights, losing shadow detail. At right, the exposure captures detail in the shadows, but the highlights are washed out.

**Figure 4.2**
Combining the two exposures produces the best compromise image.

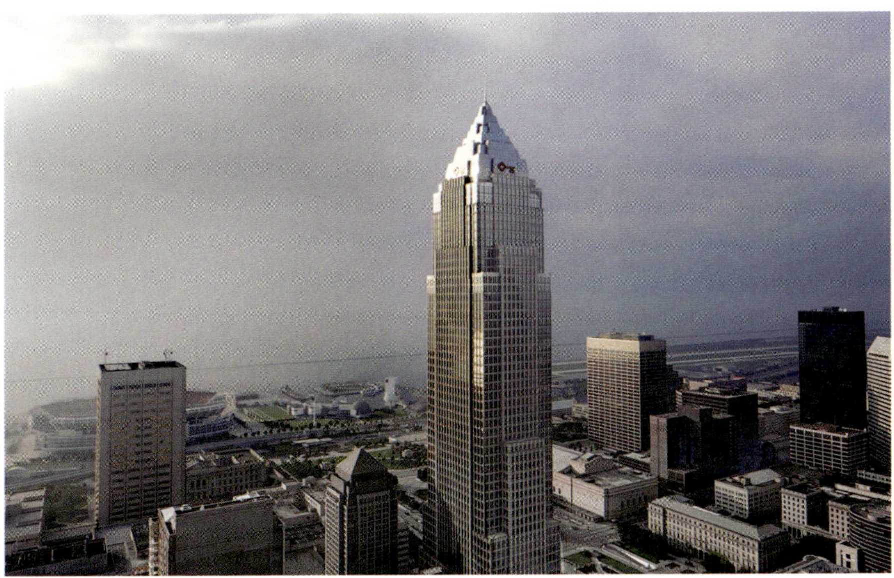

- **Light's duration.** We tend to think of most light sources as continuous. But, as you'll learn in Chapter 12, the duration of light can change quickly enough to modify the exposure, as when the main illumination in a photograph comes from an intermittent source, such as an electronic flash.

- **Light reflected, transmitted, or emitted.** Once light is produced by its source, either continuously or in a brief burst, we are able to see and photograph objects by the light that is reflected from our subjects toward the camera lens; transmitted (say, from translucent objects that are lit from behind); or emitted (by a candle or television screen). When more or less light reaches the lens from the subject, we need to adjust the exposure. This part of the equation is under our control to the extent we can increase the amount of light falling on or passing through the subject (by adding extra light sources or using reflectors), or by pumping up the light that's emitted (by increasing the brightness of the glowing object).

- **Light passed by the lens.** Not all the illumination that reaches the front of the lens makes it all the way through. Filters can remove some of the light before it enters the lens. Inside the lens barrel is a variable-sized diaphragm that produces an opening called an *aperture* that dilates and contracts to control the amount of light that enters the lens. You, or the D5200's autoexposure system, can control exposure by varying the size of the aperture. The relative size of the aperture is called the *f/stop*. (See Figure 4.3.)

- **Light passing through the shutter.** Once light passes through the lens, the amount of time the sensor receives it is determined by the D5200's shutter, which can remain open for as long as 30 seconds (or even longer if you use the Bulb setting) or as briefly as 1/4,000th second.

- **Light captured by the sensor.** Not all the light falling onto the sensor is captured. If the number of photons reaching a particular photosite doesn't pass a set threshold, no information is recorded. Similarly, if too much light illuminates a pixel in the sensor, then the excess isn't recorded or, worse, spills over to contaminate adjacent pixels. We can modify the minimum and maximum number of pixels that contribute to image detail by adjusting the ISO setting. At higher ISOs, the incoming light is amplified to boost the effective sensitivity of the sensor.

These four factors—quantity of light, light passed by the lens, the amount of time the shutter is open, and the sensitivity of the sensor—all work proportionately and reciprocally to produce an exposure. That is, if you double the amount of light, increase the aperture by one stop, make the shutter speed twice as long, or boost the ISO setting 2X, you'll get twice as much exposure. Similarly, you can increase any of these factors while decreasing one of the others by a similar amount to keep the same exposure.

Most commonly, exposure settings are made using the aperture and shutter speed, followed by adjusting the ISO sensitivity, if it's not possible to get the preferred exposure (that is, the one that uses the "best" f/stop or shutter speed for the depth-of-field or action stopping we want). Table 4.1 shows equivalent exposure settings using various shutter speeds and f/stops.

## Table 4.1 Equivalent Exposures

| Shutter speed | f/stop | Shutter speed | f/stop |
|---|---|---|---|
| 1/30th second | f/22 | 1/500th second | f/5.6 |
| 1/60th second | f/16 | 1/1,000th second | f/4 |
| 1/125th second | f/11 | 1/2,000th second | f/2.8 |
| 1/250th second | f/8 | 1/4,000th second | f/2 |

## F/STOPS AND SHUTTER SPEEDS

If you're *really* new to more advanced cameras (and I realize that some ambitious amateurs do purchase the D5200 as their first digital SLR), you might need to know that the lens aperture, or f/stop, is a ratio, much like a fraction, which is why f/2 is larger than f/4, just as 1/2 is larger than 1/4. However, f/2 is actually *four times* as large as f/4. (If you remember your high school geometry, you'll know that to double the area of a circle, you multiply its diameter by the square root of two: 1.4.)

Lenses are usually marked with intermediate f/stops that represent a size that's twice as much/half as much as the previous aperture. So, a lens might be marked: f/2, f/2.8, f/4, f/5.6, f/8, f/11, f/16, f/22, with each larger number representing an aperture that admits half as much light as the one before, as shown in Figure 4.3.

Shutter speeds are actual fractions (of a second), but the numerator is omitted, so that 60, 125, 250, 500, 1,000, and so forth represent 1/60th, 1/125th, 1/250th, 1/500th, and 1/1,000th second. To avoid confusion, Nikon uses quotation marks to signify longer exposures: 2", 2"5, 4", and so forth representing 2.0-, 2.5-, and 4.0-second exposures, respectively.

**Figure 4.3**
Top row (left to right): f/2, f/2.8, f/4, f/5.6; bottom row, f/8, f/11, f/16, f/22.

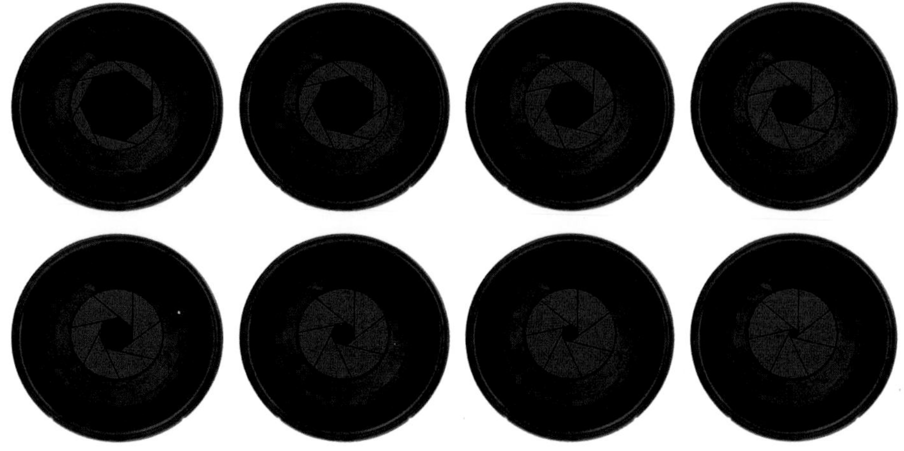

When the D5200 is set for P mode, the metering system selects the correct exposure for you automatically, but you can change quickly to an equivalent exposure by spinning the command dial until the desired equivalent exposure combination is displayed. You can use this Flexible Program feature more easily if you remember that you need to rotate the command dial toward the left when you want to increase the amount of depth-of-field or use a slower shutter speed; rotate to the right when you want to reduce the depth-of-field or use a faster shutter speed. The need for more/less DOF and slower/faster shutter speed are the primary reasons you'd want to use Flexible Program. This program shift mode does not work when you're using flash.

In Aperture-priority (A) and Shutter-priority (S) modes, you can change to an equivalent exposure, but only by either adjusting the aperture (the camera chooses the shutter speed) or shutter speed (the camera selects the aperture). I'll cover all these exposure modes later in the chapter.

## F/STOPS VERSUS STOPS

In photography parlance, *f/stop* always means the aperture or lens opening. However, for lack of a current commonly used word for one exposure increment, the term *stop* is often used. (In the past, EV served this purpose, but exposure value and its abbreviation have since been inextricably intertwined with its use in describing exposure compensation.) In this book, when I say "stop" by itself (no *f/*), I mean one whole unit of exposure, and am not necessarily referring to an actual f/stop or lens aperture. So, adjusting the exposure by "one stop" can mean both changing to the next shutter speed increment (say, from 1/125th second to 1/250th second) or the next aperture (such as f/4 to f/5.6). Similarly, 1/3 stop or 1/2 stop increments can mean either shutter speed or aperture changes, depending on the context. Be forewarned.

# How the D5200 Calculates Exposure

Your D5200 calculates exposure by measuring the light that passes through the lens and is bounced up by the mirror to sensors located near the focusing surface, using a pattern you can select (more on that later) and based on the assumption that each area being measured reflects about the same amount of light as a neutral gray card that reflects a "middle" gray of about 12- to 18-percent reflectance. (The photographic "gray cards" you buy at a camera store have an 18-percent gray tone; your camera is calibrated to interpret a somewhat darker 12-percent gray; I'll explain more about this later.) That "average" 12- to 18-percent gray assumption is necessary, because different subjects reflect different amounts of light. In a photo containing, say, a white cat and a dark gray cat, the white cat might reflect five times as much light as the gray cat. An exposure based on the white cat will cause the gray cat to appear to be black, while an exposure based only on the gray cat will make the white cat washed out.

This is more easily understood if you look at some photos of subjects that are dark (they reflect little light), those that have predominantly middle tones, and subjects that are highly reflective. The next few figures show some images of actual cats (actually, the *same* cat rendered in black, gray, and white varieties through the magic of Photoshop), with each of the three strips exposed using a different cat for reference.

## Correctly Exposed

The three pictures shown in Figure 4.4 represent how the black, gray, and white cats would appear if the exposure were calculated by measuring the light reflecting from the middle, gray cat, which, for the sake of illustration, we'll assume reflects approximately 12 to 18 percent of the light that strikes it. The exposure meter sees an object that it thinks is a middle gray, calculates an exposure based on that, and the feline in the center of the strip is rendered at its proper tonal value. Best of all, because the resulting exposure is correct, the black cat at left and white cat at right are rendered properly as well.

When you're shooting pictures with your D5200, and the meter happens to base its exposure on a subject that averages that "ideal" middle gray, then you'll end up with similar (accurate) results. The camera's exposure algorithms are concocted to ensure this kind of result as often as possible, barring any unusual subjects (that is, those that are backlit, or have uneven illumination). The D5200 has three different metering modes (described next), plus scene modes, each of which is equipped to handle certain types of unusual subjects, as I'll outline.

**Figure 4.4**
When exposure is calculated based on the middle-gray cat in the center, the black and white cats are rendered accurately, too.

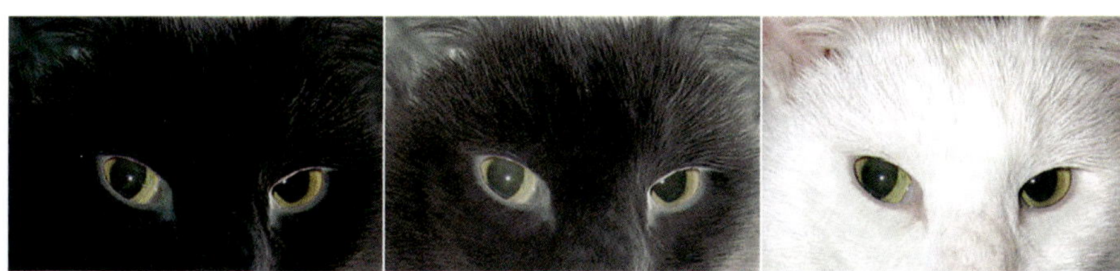

## Overexposed

The strip of three images in Figure 4.5 shows what would happen if the exposure were calculated based on metering the leftmost, black cat. The light meter sees less light reflecting from the black cat than it would see from a gray middle-tone subject, and so figures, "Aha! I need to add exposure to brighten this subject up to a middle gray!" That lightens the black cat, so it now appears to be gray.

But now the cat in the middle that was *originally* middle gray is overexposed and becomes light gray. And the white cat at right is now seriously overexposed, and loses detail in the highlights, which have become a featureless white.

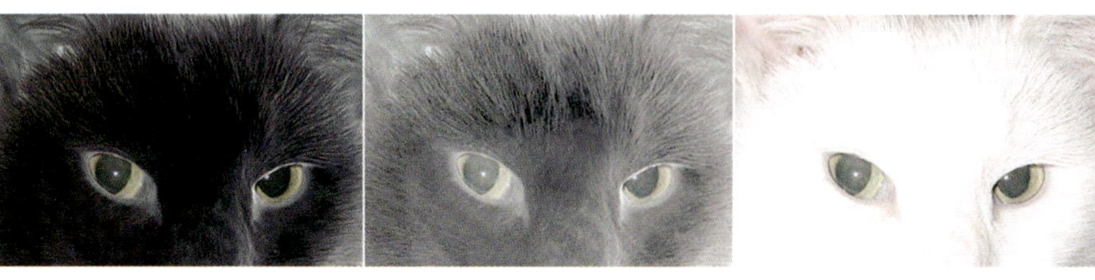

**Figure 4.5**
When exposure is calculated based on the black cat at the left, the black cat looks gray, the gray cat appears to be a light gray, and the white cat is seriously overexposed.

## Underexposed

The third possibility in this simplified scenario is that the light meter might measure the illumination bouncing off the white cat, and try to render that feline as a middle gray. A lot of light is reflected by the white kitty, so the exposure is *reduced*, bringing that cat closer to a middle gray tone. The cats that were originally gray and black are now rendered too dark. Clearly, measuring the gray cat—or a substitute that reflects about the same amount of light, is the only way to ensure that the exposure is precisely correct. (See Figure 4.6.)

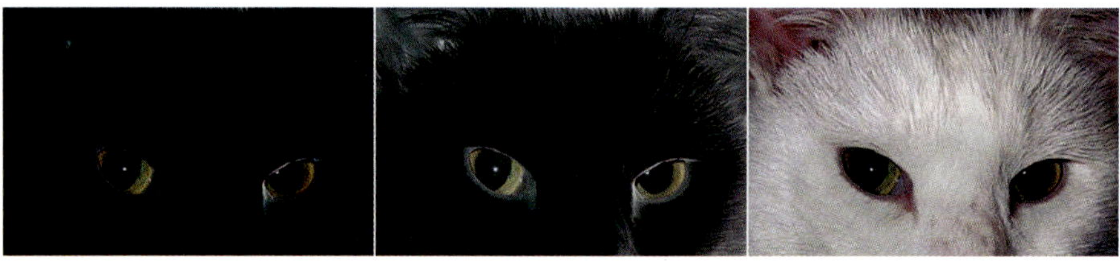

**Figure 4.6**
When exposure is calculated based on the white cat on the right, the other two cats are underexposed.

As you can see, the ideal way to measure exposure is to meter from a subject that reflects 12 to 18 percent of the light that reaches it. If you want the most precise exposure calculations, if you don't have a gray cat handy, the solution is to use a stand-in, such as the evenly illuminated gray card I mentioned earlier. But, because the standard Kodak gray card reflects 18 percent of the light that reaches it and, as I said, your camera is calibrated for a somewhat darker 12-percent tone, you would need to add about one-half stop *more* exposure than the value metered from the card.

Another substitute for a gray card is the palm of a human hand (the backside of the hand is too variable). But a human palm, regardless of ethnic group, is even brighter than a standard gray card, so instead of one-half stop more exposure, you need to add one additional stop. That is, if your meter reading is 1/500th of a second at f/11, use 1/500th second at f/8 or 1/250th second at f/11 instead. (Both exposures are equivalent.)

If you actually wanted to use a gray card, place it in your frame near your main subject, facing the camera, and with the exact same even illumination falling on it that is falling on your subject. Then, use the spot metering function (described in the next section) to calculate exposure. Of course, in most situations, it's not necessary to do this. Your camera's light meter will do a good job of calculating the right exposure, especially if you use the exposure tips in the next section. But, I felt that explaining exactly what is going on during exposure calculation would help you understand how your D5200's metering system works.

To meter properly you'll want to choose both the *metering method* (how light is evaluated) and *exposure method* (how the appropriate shutter speeds and apertures are chosen). I'll describe both in the following sections.

## WHY THE GRAY CARD CONFUSION?

Why are so many photographers under the impression that cameras and meters are calibrated to the 18-percent "standard," rather than the true value, which may be 12 to 14 percent, depending on the vendor? You'll find this misinformation in an alarming number of places. I've seen the 18-percent "myth" taught in camera classes; I've found it in books, and even been given this wrong information from the technical staff of camera vendors. (They should know better—the same vendors' engineers who design and calibrate the cameras have the right figure.)

The most common explanation is that during a revision of Kodak's instructions for its gray cards in the 1970s, the advice to open up an extra half stop was omitted, and a whole generation of shooters grew up thinking that a measurement off a gray card could be used as-is. The proviso returned to the instructions by 1987, it's said, but by then it was too late. Next to me is a (c)2006 version of the instructions for KODAK Gray Cards, Publication R-27Q, and the current directions read (with a bit of paraphrasing from me in italics):

■ For subjects of normal reflectance increase the indicated exposure by 1/2 stop.

■ For light subjects use the indicated exposure; for very light subjects, decrease the exposure by 1/2 stop. (*That is, you're measuring a cat that's lighter than middle gray.*)

■ If the subject is dark to very dark, increase the indicated exposure by 1 to 1-1/2 stops. (*You're shooting a black cat.*)

## MODES, MODES, AND MORE MODES

Call them modes or methods, the Nikon D5200 seems to have a lot of different sets of options that are described using similar terms. Here's how to sort them out:

■ **Metering method.** These modes determine the *parts of the image* within the 2016-segment RGB sensor array that are examined in order to calculate exposure. The D5200 may look at many different points within the image, segregating them by zone (Matrix metering); examine the same number of points, but give greater weight to those located in the middle of the frame (Center-weighted metering); or evaluate only a limited number of points in a limited area (Spot metering).

■ **Exposure method.** These modes determine *which* settings are used to expose the image. The D5200 may adjust the shutter speed, the aperture, or both, depending on the method you choose.

# Choosing a Metering Method

The D5200 has three different schemes for evaluating the light received by its exposure sensors: Matrix (with several variations, depending on what lens you have attached), Center-weighted, and Spot metering. Select the mode you want to use from the information edit screen. Here is what you need to know about each metering method:

## Matrix Metering

For its various Matrix metering modes, the D5200 slices up the frame into 2016 different zones in an RGB (red/green/blue) array that covers most of the sensor area, shown in Figure 4.7. When Matrix metering is active, an icon appears in the information display screen (enlarged in the upper-left corner of the figure). In all cases, the D5200 evaluates the differences between the zones, and compares them with a built-in database of several hundred thousand images to make an educated guess about what kind of picture you're taking. For example, if the top sections of a picture are much lighter than the bottom portions, the algorithm can assume that the scene is a landscape photo with lots of sky. An image that includes most of the lighter portions in the center area may be a portrait. A typical image suitable for Matrix metering is shown in Figure 4.8.

The Nikon D5200 also uses information other than brightness to make its evaluation:

- **3D Color Matrix metering II.** This metering mode is used by default when the D5200 is equipped with a lens that has a type G or type D designator in its name, such as the AF-S DX Nikkor 16-85mm f/3.5-5.6G ED VR lens. The G after the f/5.6 is the giveaway. (More on lens nomenclature in Chapter 11.) The camera calculates exposure based on brightness, colors of the subject matter (that is, blue pixels in the upper part of the image are probably sky; green pixels in the lower half probably foliage), focus point, and distance information. The D5200 is able to use that additional distance data to better calculate what kind of scene you have framed.

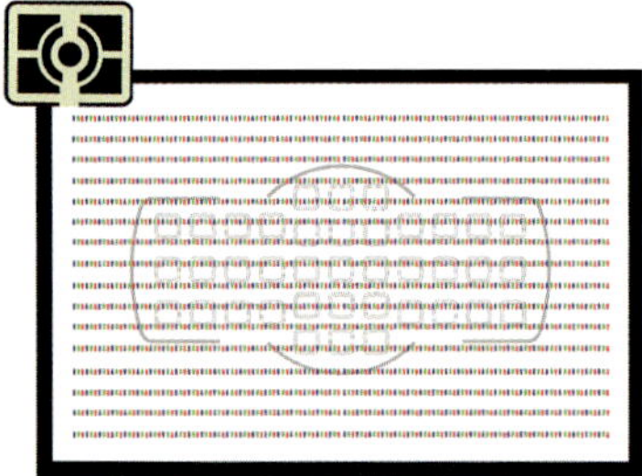

**Figure 4.7** Matrix metering calculates exposure based on 2016 points in the frame.

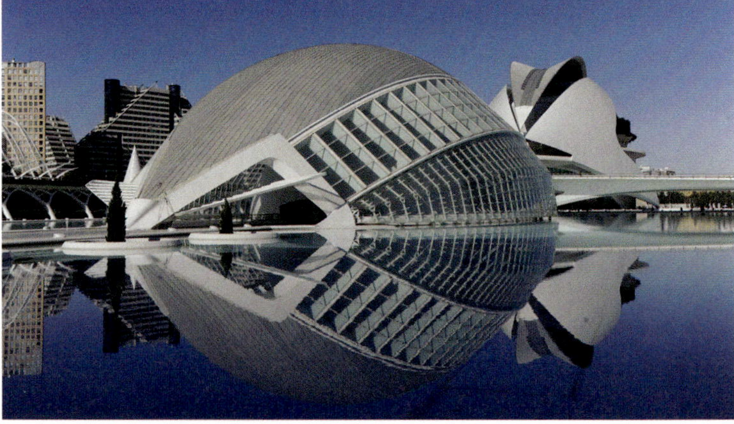

**Figure 4.8** Complex scenes lend themselves to the exposure interpretation provided by Matrix metering.

For example, if you're shooting a portrait with a longer focal-length lens focused to about 5 to 12 feet from the camera, and the upper half of the scene is very bright, the camera assumes you would prefer to meter for the rest of the image, and discount the bright area. However, if the camera has a wide-angle lens attached and is focused at infinity, the D5200 can assume you're taking a landscape photo and take the bright upper area into account to produce better looking sky and clouds.

■ **Color Matrix metering II.** If you have a non-G or non-D lens equipped with a CPU chip (these are generally older lenses, although chips can sometimes be added to optics that lack them), the distance range is not used. Instead, only focus, brightness, and color information is taken into account to calculate an appropriate exposure.

Matrix metering is best for most general subjects, because it is able to intelligently analyze a scene and make an excellent guess of what kind of subject you're shooting a great deal of the time. The camera can tell the difference between low-contrast and high-contrast subjects by looking at the range of differences in brightness across the scene. Because the D5200 has a fairly good idea about what kind of subject matter you are shooting, it can underexpose slightly when appropriate to preserve highlight detail when image contrast is high. (It's often possible to pull detail out of shadows that are too dark using an image editor, but once highlights are converted to white pixels, they are gone forever.)

> **CAUTION**
>
> If you're using a strong filter, including a polarizing filter, split-color filter, or neutral-density filter (particularly a graduated neutral-density filter), you should switch from Matrix metering to Center-weighted, because the filter can affect the relationships between the different areas of the frame used to calculate a Matrix exposure. For example, a polarizing filter produces a sky that is darker than usual, hindering the Matrix algorithm's recognition of a landscape photo. Extra dark or colored filters disturb the color relationships used for color Matrix metering, too.

## Center-Weighted Metering

In this mode, the exposure meter emphasizes a zone in the center of the frame to calculate exposure, as shown in Figure 4.9. About 75 percent of the exposure is based on that central area, and the remaining exposure is based on the rest of the frame. The theory, here, is that, for most pictures, the main subject will be located in the center. So, if the D5200 reads the center portion and determines that the exposure for that region should be f/8 at 1/250th second, while the outer area, which is a bit darker, calls for f/4 at 1/125th second, the camera will give the center portion the most weight and arrive at a final exposure of f/5.6 at 1/250th second.

Center-weighting works best for portraits, architectural photos, backlit subjects with extra-bright backgrounds (such as snow or sand), and other pictures in which the most important subject is located in the middle of the frame, as in Figure 4.10. As the name suggests, the light reading is

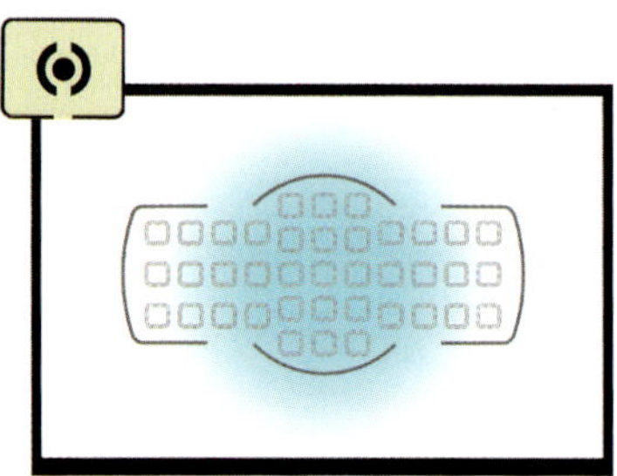

**Figure 4.9** Center-weighted metering calculates exposure based on the full frame, but gives 75 percent of the weight to the center area shown; the remaining 25 percent of the exposure is determined by the rest of the image area.

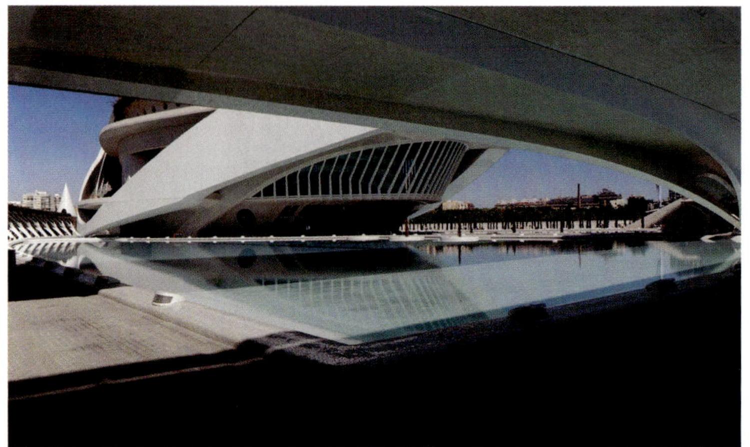

**Figure 4.10**  Scenes with the main subject in the center, surrounded by areas that are significantly darker or lighter, are perfect for Center-weighted metering.

*weighted* toward the central portion, but information is also used from the rest of the frame. If your main subject is surrounded by very bright or very dark areas, the exposure might not be exactly right. However, this scheme works well in many situations if you don't want to use one of the other modes. This mode can be useful for close-ups of subjects like flowers, or for portraits.

## Spot Metering

Spot metering is favored by those of us who used a hand-held light meter to measure exposure at various points (such as metering highlights and shadows separately). However, you can use Spot metering in any situation where you want to individually measure the light reflecting from light, midtone, or dark areas of your subject—or any combination of areas.

This mode confines the reading to a limited 3.5mm area in the viewfinder, making up only 2.5 percent of the image, as shown in Figure 4.11. The circle is centered on the *current focus point* (which can be *any* of the 39 focus points, *not* just the center one shown in Figure 4.11), *but is larger than the focus point*, so don't fall into the trap of believing that exposure is being measured only within the brackets that represent the active focus point. This is the only metering method you can use to tell the D5200 exactly where to measure exposure when using the optical viewfinder. However, if a non-CPU lens is mounted, or you have selected Auto-area AF, only the center focus point is used to spot meter.

You'll find Spot metering useful when you want to base exposure on a small area in the frame. If that area is in the center of the frame, so much the better. If not, you'll have to make your meter reading for an off-center subject using an appropriate focus point, and then lock exposure by pressing the shutter release halfway, or by pressing the AE-L/AF-L button. This mode is best for subjects where the background is significantly brighter or darker, as in Figure 4.12.

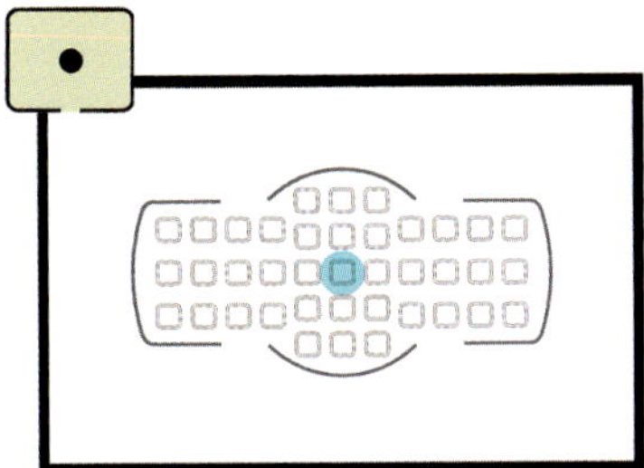

**Figure 4.11** Spot metering calculates exposure based on a center spot that's only two 2.5 percent of the image area, centered around the current focus point.

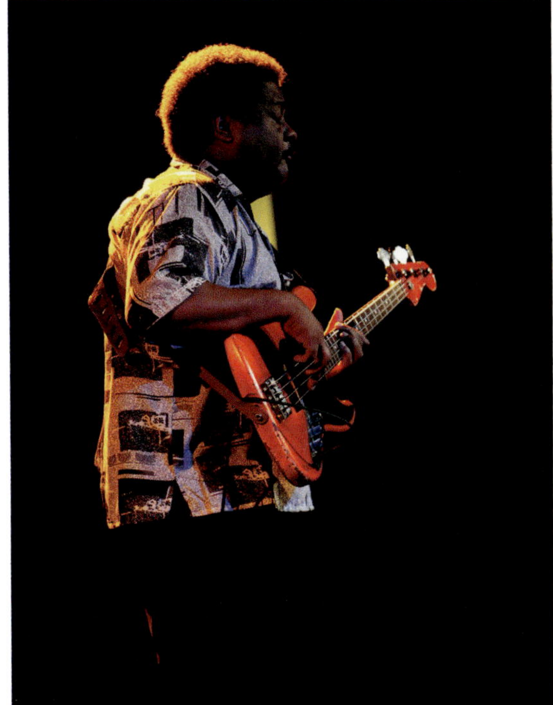

**Figure 4.12** Spot metering allowed measuring exposure from this performer's shirt.

# Choosing an Exposure Method

You'll find four methods for choosing the appropriate shutter speed and aperture, when using the semi-automatic/manual modes. (Scene modes, which use their own exposure biases, are described next.) You can choose among Program, Aperture-priority, Shutter-priority, or Manual options by rotating the mode dial on top of the camera. Your choice of which is best for a given shooting situation will depend on things like your need for lots of (or less) depth-of-field, a desire to freeze action or allow motion blur, or how much noise you find acceptable in an image. Each of the D5200's exposure methods emphasizes one aspect of image capture or another. This section introduces you to all four.

## Aperture-Priority

In A mode, you specify the lens opening used, and the D5200 selects the shutter speed. Aperture-priority is especially good when you want to use a particular lens opening to achieve a desired effect. Perhaps you'd like to use the smallest f/stop possible to maximize depth-of-field in a close-up picture. Or, you might want to use a large f/stop to throw everything except your main subject out of focus, as in Figure 4.13. Maybe you'd just like to "lock in" a particular f/stop because it's the sharpest available aperture with that lens. Or, you might prefer to use, say, f/2.8 on a lens with a maximum aperture of f/1.4, because you want the best compromise between speed and sharpness.

Aperture-priority can even be used to specify a *range* of shutter speeds you want to use under varying lighting conditions, which seems almost contradictory. But think about it. You're shooting a soccer game outdoors with a telephoto lens and want a relatively high shutter speed, but you don't care if the speed changes a little should the sun duck behind a cloud. Set your D5200 to A, and adjust the aperture until a shutter speed of, say, 1/1,000th second is selected at your current ISO setting. (In bright sunlight at ISO 400, that aperture is likely to be around f/11.) Then, go ahead and shoot, knowing that your D5200 will maintain that f/11 aperture (for sufficient DOF as the soccer players move about the field), but will drop down to 1/750th or 1/500th second if necessary should the lighting change a little.

A question mark indicator in the viewfinder and LCD blinks to indicate that the D5200 is unable to select an appropriate shutter speed at the selected aperture and that over- and underexposure will occur at the current ISO setting. In addition, a message will appear in the LCD stating

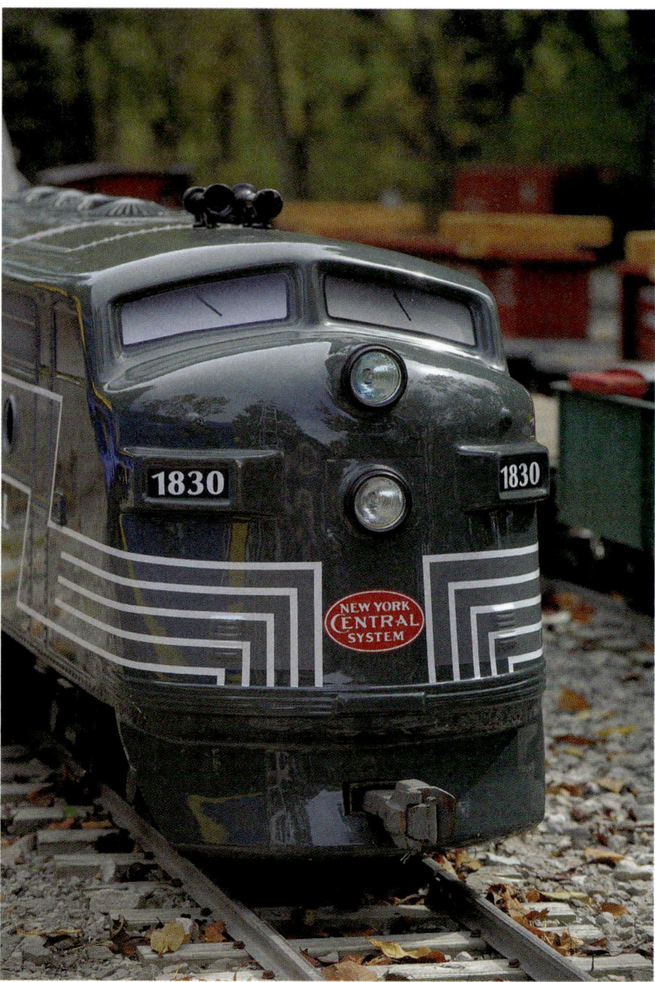

**Figure 4.13** Use Aperture-priority to "lock in" a large f/stop when you want to blur the background.

that the subject is too light or too dark. That's the major pitfall of using A: you might select an f/stop that is too small or too large to allow an optimal exposure with the available shutter speeds. For example, if you choose f/2.8 as your aperture and the illumination is quite bright (say, at the beach or in snow), even your camera's fastest shutter speed might not be able to cut down the amount of light reaching the sensor to provide the right exposure. Or, if you select f/8 in a dimly lit room, you might find yourself shooting with a very slow shutter speed that can cause blurring from subject movement or camera shake. Aperture-priority is best used by those with a bit of experience in choosing settings. Many seasoned photographers leave their D5200 set on A all the time. The exposure indicator scale in the LCD and viewfinder indicate the amount of under- or overexposure.

# Shutter-Priority

Shutter-priority (S) is the inverse of Aperture-priority: you choose the shutter speed you'd like to use, and the camera's metering system selects the appropriate f/stop. Perhaps you're shooting action photos and you want to use the absolute fastest shutter speed available with your camera; in other cases, you might want to use a slow shutter speed to add some blur to a sports photo that would be mundane if the action were completely frozen. (See the ends of the hockey sticks in Figure 4.14.) Shutter-priority mode gives you some control over how much action-freezing capability your digital camera brings to bear in a particular situation.

**Figure 4.14**
Lock the shutter at a specific speed to introduce blur into an action shot.

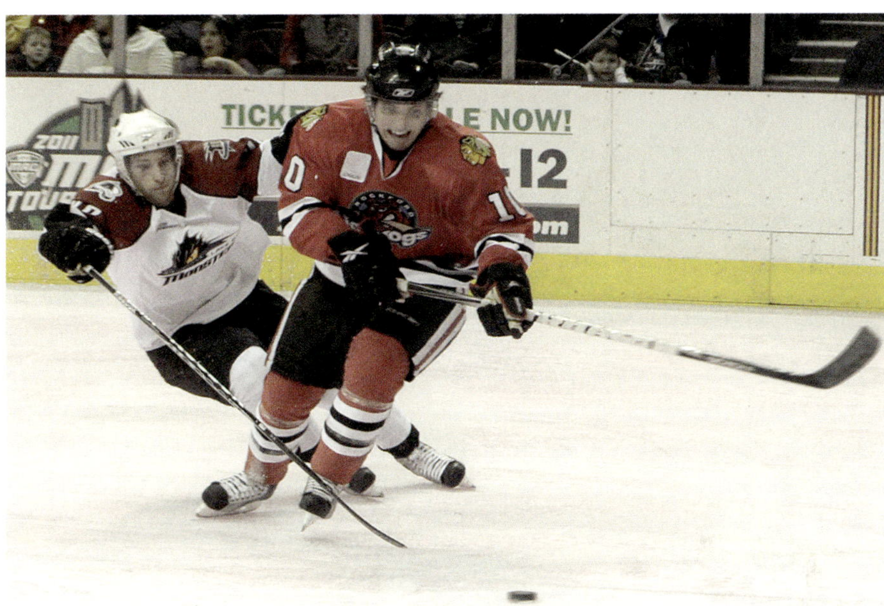

You'll also encounter the same problem as with Aperture-priority when you select a shutter speed that's too long or too short for correct exposure under some conditions. I've shot outdoor soccer games on sunny fall evenings and used Shutter-priority mode to lock in a 1/1,000th second shutter speed, and was unable to continue when the sun dipped behind some trees and there was no longer enough light to shoot at that speed, even with the lens wide open.

Like A mode, it's possible to choose an inappropriate shutter speed. If that's the case, the displays will flash.

# Program Mode

Program mode (P) uses the D5200's built-in smarts to select the correct f/stop and shutter speed using a database of picture information that tells it which combination of shutter speed and aperture will work best for a particular photo. If the correct exposure cannot be achieved at the current ISO setting, the question mark indicator in the viewfinder and shown on the LCD monitor will blink. You can then boost or reduce the ISO to increase or decrease sensitivity.

The D5200's recommended exposure can be overridden if you want. Use the EV (exposure value) setting feature (described later, because it also applies to S and A modes) to add or subtract exposure from the metered value. And, as I mentioned earlier in this chapter, in Program mode you can rotate the command dial to change from the recommended setting to an equivalent setting (as shown in Table 6.1) that produces the same exposure, but using a different combination of f/stop and shutter speed.

This is called "Flexible Program" by Nikon. Rotate the command dial left to reduce the size of the aperture (going from, say, f/4 to f/5.6), so that the D5200 will automatically use a slower shutter speed (going from, say, 1/250th second to 1/125th second). Rotate the command dial right to use a larger f/stop, while automatically producing a shorter shutter speed that provides the same equivalent exposure as metered in P mode. An asterisk appears next to the P in the LCD so you'll know you've overridden the D5200's default program setting. Your adjustment remains in force until you rotate the command dial until the asterisk disappears, or you switch to a different exposure mode, or turn the D5200 off.

## MAKING EV CHANGES

Sometimes you'll want more or less exposure than indicated by the D5200's metering system. Perhaps you want to underexpose to create a silhouette effect, or overexpose to produce a high key look. It's easy to use the D5200's exposure compensation system to override the exposure recommendations. Press the EV button on the top of the camera (just southeast of the shutter release). Then rotate the command dial right to add exposure, and left to subtract exposure. The EV change you've made remains for the exposures that follow, until you manually zero out the EV setting. The EV plus/minus icon appears in the viewfinder and LCD to warn you that an exposure compensation change has been entered. You can increase or decrease exposure over a range of plus or minus five stops.

# Manual Exposure

Part of being an experienced photographer comes from knowing when to rely on your D5200's automation (with P mode), when to go semiautomatic (with S or A), and when to set exposure manually (using M). Some photographers actually prefer to set their exposure manually, as the D5200 will be happy to provide an indication of when its metering system judges your manual settings provide the proper exposure, using the analog exposure scale at the bottom of the viewfinder.

Manual exposure can come in handy in some situations. You might be taking a silhouette photo and find that none of the exposure modes or EV correction features give you exactly the effect you want. Set the exposure manually to use the exact shutter speed and f/stop you need. Or, you might be working in a studio environment using multiple flash units. The additional flash are triggered by slave devices (gadgets that set off the flash when they sense the light from another flash unit, or, perhaps from a radio or infrared remote control). Your camera's exposure meter doesn't compensate for the extra illumination, so you need to set the aperture manually.

Because, depending on your proclivities, you might not need to set exposure manually very often, you should still make sure you understand how it works. Fortunately, the D5200 makes setting exposure manually very easy. Just rotate the mode dial to change to Manual mode, and then turn the command dial to set the shutter speed, and hold down the EV button while rotating the command dial to adjust the aperture. Press the shutter release halfway or press the AE lock button, and the exposure scale in the viewfinder shows you how far your chosen setting diverges from the metered exposure.

## Using Scene Modes

As described in Chapter 2, the D5200 retains the "quickie" exposure modes found in Nikon's entry-level cameras (like the D5200 and D3100), but absent from the company's "pro" and "semi-pro" models.

As an avid photographer, you probably won't use scene modes much, except when you're in a hurry to capture a grab shot and don't have time to make any decisions about what advanced exposure mode to use. You're on a beach, so you rotate the mode dial on the top left of the camera to SCENE, then use the command dial to select Beach/Snow, and you're all set. Nothing could be easier and—surprise, surprise—you will probably end up with some nice snapshots. You don't have all the creative control you might need for a more studied image, but a grab shot that's not perfect trumps any photo you don't take because you're fiddling with settings.

Scene modes are also useful when you loan your camera to someone and don't want to explain to them how to use the D5200. Scene modes not only make decisions about basic exposure, but they select some focusing options, whether or not to use flash, and what shutter speeds/apertures are best for a particular type of subject. Nearly anyone can make the right choice based on the 19 different scene modes (plus two Auto modes) available at the spin of the command dial. I'll recap the descriptions of these modes that I originally provided in Chapter 2:

- **Auto.** In this mode, the D5200 makes all the exposure decisions for you, and will pop up the internal flash if necessary under low-light conditions. The camera automatically focuses on the subject closest to the camera (unless you've set the lens to manual focus), and the autofocus assist illuminator lamp on the front of the camera will light up to help the camera focus in low-light conditions.

- **Auto (Flash Off).** Identical to Auto mode, except that the flash will not pop up under any circumstances. You'd want to use this in a museum, during religious ceremonies, concerts, or any environment where flash is forbidden or distracting.

- **Portrait.** Use this mode when you're taking a portrait of a subject standing relatively close to the camera and want to de-emphasize the background, maximize sharpness, and produce flattering skin tones. The built-in flash will pop up if needed.

- **Landscape.** Select this mode when you want extra sharpness and rich colors of distant scenes. The built-in flash and AF-assist illuminator are disabled.

- **Child.** Use this mode to accentuate the vivid colors often found in children's clothing, and to render skin tones with a soft, natural-looking texture. The D5200 focuses on the closest subject to the camera. The built-in flash will pop up if needed.

- **Sports.** Use this mode to freeze fast-moving subjects. The D5200 selects a fast shutter speed to stop action, and focuses continuously on the center focus point while you have the shutter release button pressed halfway. However, you can select one of the other two focus points to the left or right of the center by pressing the multi selector left/right buttons. The built-in electronic flash and focus assist illuminator lamp are disabled.

- **Close Up.** This mode is helpful when you are shooting close-up pictures of a subject from about one foot away or less, such as flowers, bugs, and small items. The D5200 focuses on the closest subject in the center of the frame, but you can use the multi selector right and left buttons to focus on a different point. Use a tripod in this mode, as exposures may be long enough to cause blurring from camera movement. The built-in flash will pop up if needed.

- **Night Portrait.** Choose this mode when you want to illuminate a subject in the foreground with flash (it will pop up automatically, if needed), but still allow the background to be exposed properly by the available light. The camera focuses on the closest main subject. Be prepared to use a tripod or a vibration-resistant lens like the 18-55 VR kit lens to reduce the effects of camera shake. (You'll find more about VR and camera shake in Chapter 11.)

- **Night Landscape.** Mount your camera on a tripod and use this mode for longer exposure times to produce images with more natural colors and reduced visual noise in scenes with street lights or neon signs.

- **Party/Indoor.** For indoor scenes with typical background lighting.

- **Beach/Snow.** Useful for bright high-contrast scenes with sand or snow.

- **Sunset.** Emphasizes the rich colors at sunset or sunrise, disables the flash, and may use a slow shutter speed, so consider working with a tripod.

- **Dusk/Dawn.** Similar to Sunset mode, but preserves the subtle colors in the sky just after sunset, or just prior to dawn.

- **Pet Portrait.** An "action" mode specifically for fast-moving, erratic subjects, such as pets.

- **Candlelight.** Disables your flash to allow photographs by candle; a tripod is recommended.

- **Blossom.** Uses a small f/stop to expand depth-of-field when shooting landscapes with broad expanses of blossoms. This scene mode may result in longer shutter speeds, so consider using a tripod.

- **Autumn Colors.** Makes reds and yellows in fall foliage richer.

- **Food.** Boosts saturation to make food look more appetizing in your snaps.

- **Silhouette.** Exposes for bright backgrounds, turning foreground objects into underexposed silhouettes.

- **High Key.** Exposes for bright scenes with lots of highlight areas.
- **Low Key.** Tailors exposure for darker scenes, retaining murky shadows while allowing highlights to remain.

# Adjusting Exposure with ISO Settings

Another way of adjusting exposures is by changing the ISO sensitivity setting. Sometimes photographers forget about this option, because the common practice is to set the ISO once for a particular shooting session (say, at ISO 200 for bright sunlight outdoors, or ISO 800 when shooting indoors) and then forget about ISO. ISOs higher than ISO 200 or 400 are seen as "bad" or "necessary evils." However, changing the ISO is a valid way of adjusting exposure settings, particularly with the Nikon D5200, which produces good results at ISO settings that create grainy, unusable pictures with some other camera models.

Indeed, I find myself using ISO adjustment as a convenient alternate way of adding or subtracting EV when shooting in Manual mode, and as a quick way of choosing equivalent exposures when in Program or Shutter-priority or Aperture-priority modes. For example, I've selected a Manual exposure with both f/stop and shutter speed suitable for my image using, say, ISO 200. I can change the exposure in 1/3 stop increments using the information edit screen. The difference in image quality/noise at ISO 200 is negligible if I dial in ISO 160 or ISO 125 to reduce exposure a little, or change to ISO 250 or 320 to increase exposure. I keep my preferred f/stop and shutter speed, but still adjust the exposure.

Or, perhaps, I am using S mode and the metered exposure at ISO 200 is 1/500th second at f/11. If I decide on the spur of the moment I'd rather use 1/500th second at f/8, I can use the information edit screen to switch to ISO 100. Of course, it's a good idea to monitor your ISO changes, so you don't end up at ISO 6400 accidentally. An ISO indicator appears in the LCD monitor and in the viewfinder to remind you what sensitivity setting has been dialed in.

ISO settings can, of course, also be used to boost or reduce sensitivity in particular shooting situations. The D5200 can use ISO settings from ISO 100 up to ISO 6400, plus Hi 0.3, 0.7, 1.0 and Hi 2.0 (Hi 1 and Hi 2 are ISO 12800 and 25600 equivalent). The camera can also adjust the ISO automatically as appropriate for various lighting conditions. When you choose the Auto ISO setting in the Shooting menu, as described in Chapter 8, the D5200 adjusts the sensitivity dynamically to suit the subject matter, based on minimum shutter speed and ISO limits you have prescribed. As I note in Chapter 8, you should use Auto ISO cautiously if you don't want the D5200 to use an ISO higher than you might otherwise have selected.

# Dealing with Noise

Visual image noise is that random grainy effect that some like to use as a special effect, but which, most of the time, is objectionable because it robs your image of detail even as it adds that "interesting" texture. Noise is caused by two different phenomena: high ISO settings and long exposures.

High ISO noise commonly appears when you raise your camera's sensitivity setting above ISO 400. With the Nikon D5200, noise may become visible at ISO 1600, and is often fairly noticeable at ISO 3200. At ISO 6400 and above, noise is usually quite bothersome. Nikon tips you off that ISO 12800 and 25600 may be tools used in special circumstances only by labeling them "Hi." You can expect noise and increase in contrast in any pictures taken at these lofty ratings. High ISO noise appears as a result of the amplification needed to increase the sensitivity of the sensor. While higher ISOs do pull details out of dark areas, they also amplify non-signal information randomly, creating noise. You'll find a High ISO NR choice in the Shooting menu, where you can specify High, Norm, or Low noise reduction, or turn the feature off entirely. Because noise reduction tends to soften the grainy look while robbing an image of detail, you may want to disable the feature if you're willing to accept a little noise in exchange for more details.

A similar noisy phenomenon occurs during long time exposures, which allow more photons to reach the sensor, increasing your ability to capture a picture under low light conditions. However, the longer exposures also increase the likelihood that some pixels will register random phantom photons, often because the longer an imager is "hot," the warmer it gets, and that heat can be mistaken for photons. There's also a special kind of noise that CMOS sensors like the one used in the D5200 are potentially susceptible to. With a CCD, the entire signal is conveyed off the chip and funneled through a single amplifier and analog-to-digital conversion circuit. Any noise introduced there is, at least, consistent. CMOS imagers, on the other hand, contain millions of individual amplifiers and A/D converters, all working in unison. Because these circuits don't necessarily all process in precisely the same way all the time, they can introduce something called fixed-pattern noise into the image data.

Fortunately, Nikon's electronics geniuses have done an exceptional job minimizing noise from all causes in the D5200. Even so, you might still want to apply the optional long exposure noise reduction that can be activated using Long Exp. NR in the Shooting menu, where the feature can be turned On or Off. This type of noise reduction involves the D5200 taking a second, blank exposure, and comparing the random pixels in that image with the photograph you just took. Pixels that coincide in the two represent noise and can safely be suppressed. This noise reduction system, called *dark frame subtraction,* effectively doubles the amount of time required to take a picture, and is used only for exposures longer than one second. Noise reduction can reduce the amount of detail in your picture, as some image information may be removed along with the noise. So, you might want to use this feature with moderation.

You can also apply noise reduction to a lesser extent using Photoshop, and when converting RAW files to some other format, using your favorite RAW converter, or an industrial-strength product like Noise Ninja (www.picturecode.com), to wipe out noise after you've already taken the picture.

# Fixing Exposures with Histograms

While you can often recover poorly exposed photos in your image editor, your best bet is to arrive at the correct exposure in the camera, minimizing the tweaks that you have to make in post-processing. However, you can't always judge exposure just by viewing the image on your D5200's

LCD monitor after the shot is made. Nor can you get a 100 percent accurately exposed picture by using the D5200's Live View feature. Ambient light may make the LCD difficult to see, and the brightness level you've set can affect the appearance of the playback image.

Instead, you can use a histogram, which is a chart displayed on the D5200's LCD monitor that shows the number of tones being captured at each brightness level. You can use the information to provide correction for the next shot you take. The D5200 offers four histogram variations in three screens: three histograms that show overall brightness levels for an image and an alternate version that separates the red, green, and blue channels of your image into separate histograms.

## DISPLAYING HISTOGRAMS

To view all the available histograms on your screen, you must have the D5200 set up properly. First, you'll need to mark Histograms using the Display Mode entry in the Playback menu, as described in Chapter 8. That will make the histograms screen visible when you cycle among the informational screens while pressing the multi selector up/down buttons while an image is displayed.

The most basic histogram is displayed during playback when you press the multi selector up/down buttons to produce the overview data screen, as described briefly in Chapter 3. This screen provides a small histogram at the right side that displays the distribution of luminance or brightness. The most useful histogram screen is the one shown in Figure 4.15, which displays both a luminance chart and separate red, green, and blue charts.

Both luminance and RGB histograms are charts that include a representation of up to 256 vertical lines on a horizontal axis that show the number of pixels in the image at each brightness level, from 0 (black) on the left side to 255 (white) on the right. (The three-inch LCD doesn't have enough pixels to show each and every one of the 256 lines, but, instead provides a representation of the shape of the curve formed.) The more pixels at a given level, the taller the bar at that position. If no

**Figure 4.15**
The D5200's most complete histogram screen shows both luminance and separate red, green, and blue histograms.

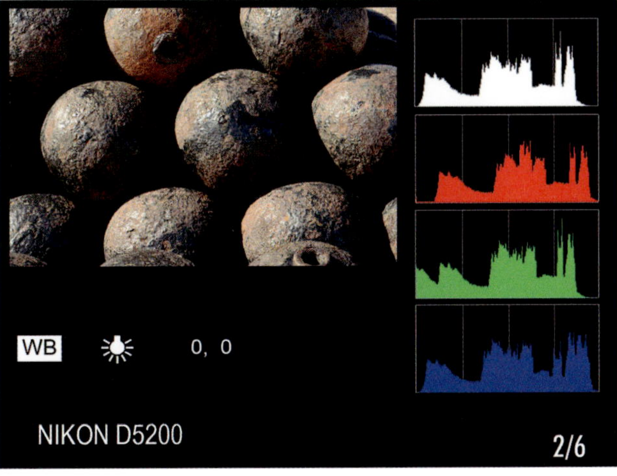

bar appears at a particular position on the scale from left to right, there are no pixels at that particular brightness level.

As you can see, a typical histogram produces a mountain-like shape, with most of the pixels bunched in the middle tones, with fewer pixels at the dark and light ends of the scale. Ideally, though, there will be at least some pixels at either extreme, so that your image has both a true black and a true white representing some details. Learn to spot histograms that represent over- and underexposure, and add or subtract exposure using an EV modification to compensate.

For example, Figure 4.16 shows the histogram (in the inset) for an image that is badly underexposed. You can guess from the shape of the histogram that many of the dark tones to the left of the graph have been clipped off. There's plenty of room on the right side for additional pixels to reside without having them become overexposed. Or, a histogram might look like the insert in Figure 4.17, which is overexposed. In either case, you can increase or decrease the exposure (either by changing the f/stop or shutter speed in Manual mode or by adding or subtracting an EV value in A or S modes) to produce the corrected histogram shown inset in Figure 4.18, in which the tones "hug" the right side of the histogram to produce as many highlight details as possible. See "Making EV Changes," above for information on dialing in exposure compensation.

The histogram can also be used to aid in fixing the contrast of an image, although gauging incorrect contrast is more difficult. For example, if the histogram shows all the tones bunched up in one place in the image, the photo will be low in contrast. If the tones are spread out more or less evenly, the image is probably high in contrast. In either case, your best bet may be to switch to RAW (if you're not already using that format) so you can adjust contrast in post-processing. However, you can also change to a user-defined Picture Control with contrast set lower (–1 to –3) or higher (+1 to +3) as required. You'll find instructions for creating Picture Controls in Chapter 8.

One useful, but often overlooked tool in evaluating histograms is the Highlights display, which shows blown out highlights with a black blinking border for the selected active channel. Highlights can give you a better picture of what information is being lost to overexposure. By default, the Highlights display shows "blinkies" for the luminance channel.

In working with histograms, your goal should be to have all the tones in an image spread out between the edges, with none clipped off at the left and right sides. Underexposing (to preserve highlights) should be done only as a last resort, because retrieving the underexposed shadows in your image editor will frequently increase the noise, even if you're working with RAW files. A better course of action is to expose for the highlights, but, when the subject matter makes it practical, fill in the shadows with additional light, using reflectors, fill flash, or other techniques rather than allowing them to be seriously underexposed.

The more you work with histograms, the more useful they become. One of the first things that histogram veterans notice is that it's possible to overexpose one channel even if the overall exposure appears to be correct. For example, flower photographers soon discover that it's really, really difficult to get a good picture of a rose, like the one shown in Figure 4.19. The exposure looks okay—but there's no detail in the rose's petals. Looking at the histogram (see Figure 4.20) shows why: the red

**Figure 4.16**
This histogram shows an underexposed image.

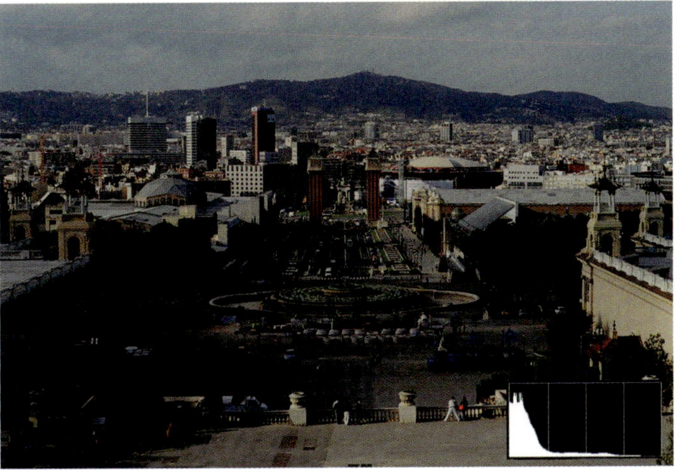

**Figure 4.17**
This histogram reveals that the image is overexposed.

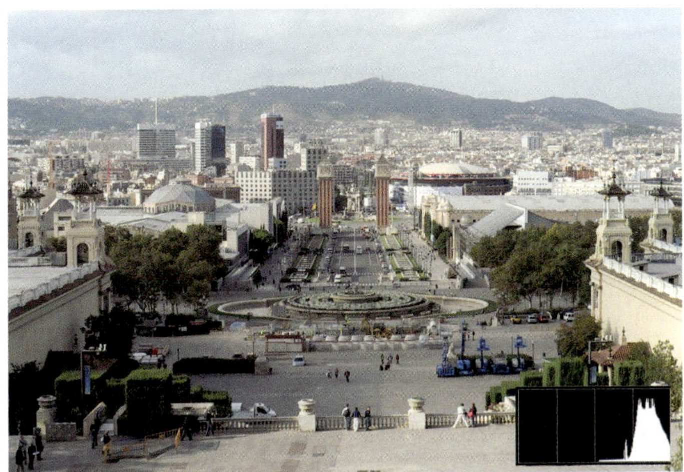

**Figure 4.18**
A histogram for a properly exposed image should look like this.

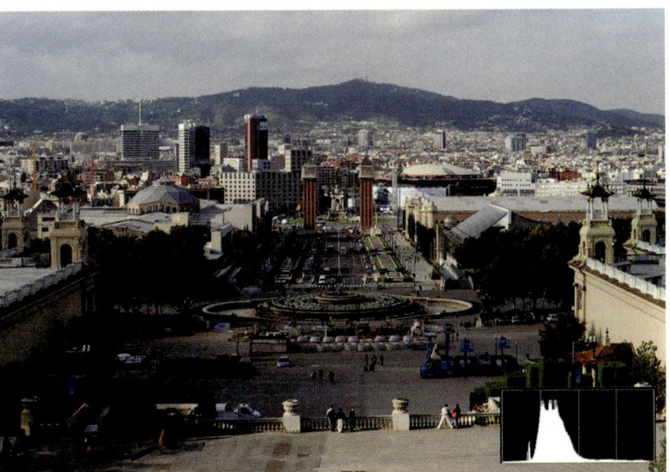

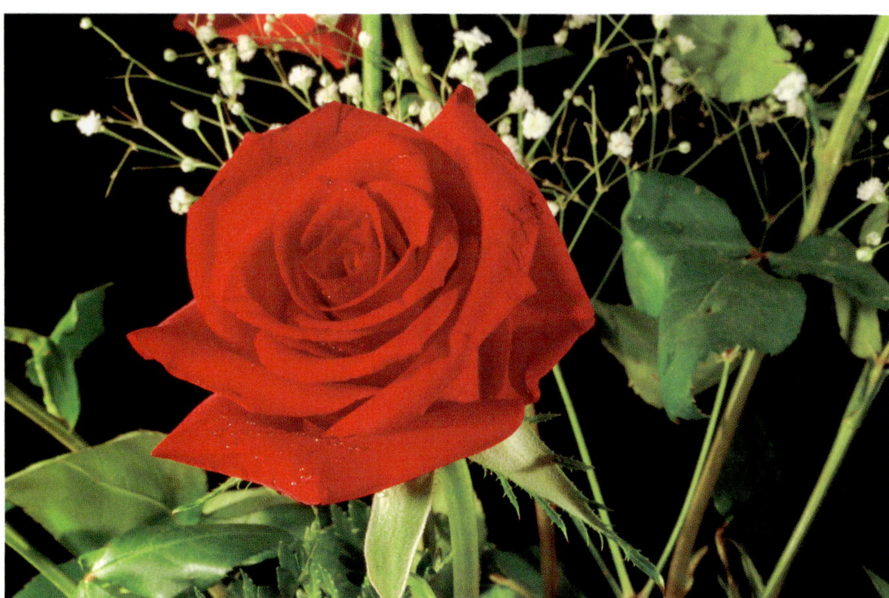

**Figure 4.19**
It's common to lose detail in bright red flowers because the red channel becomes overexposed even when the other channels are properly exposed.

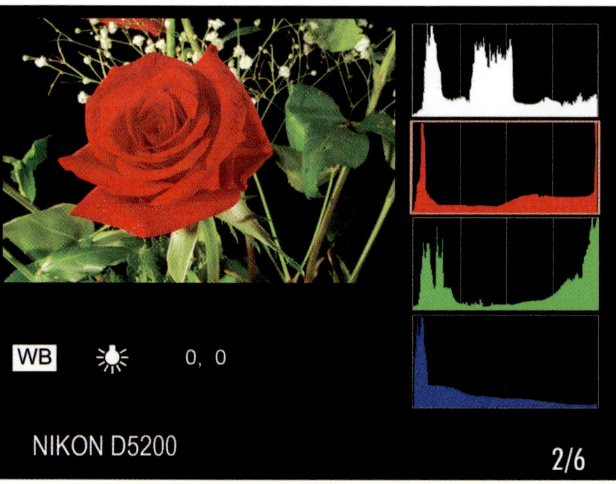


**Figure 4.20**
The RGB histograms show that both the red and green channels are overexposed.

channel is blown out. If you look at the red histogram, there's a peak at the right edge that indicates that highlight information has been lost. In fact, the green channel has been blown, too, and so the green parts of the flower also lack detail. Only the blue channel's histogram is entirely contained within the boundaries of the chart, and, on first glance, the white luminance histogram at top of the column of graphs seems fairly normal.

Any of the primary channels, red, green, or blue, can blow out all by themselves, although bright reds seem to be the most common problem area. More difficult to diagnose are overexposed tones in one of the "in-between" hues on the color wheel. Overexposed yellows (which are very common) will be shown by blowouts in *both* the red and green channels. Too-bright cyans will manifest as excessive blue and green highlights, while overexposure in the red and blue channels reduces detail in magenta colors. As you gain experience, you'll be able to see exactly how anomalies in the RGB channels translate into poor highlights and murky shadows.

The only way to correct for color channel blowouts is to reduce exposure. As I mentioned earlier, you might want to consider filling in the shadows with additional light to keep them from becoming too dark when you decrease exposure. In practice, you'll want to monitor the red channel most closely, followed by the blue channel, and slightly decrease exposure to see if that helps. Because of the way our eyes perceive color, we are more sensitive to variations in green, so green channel blowouts are less of a problem, unless your main subject is heavily colored in that hue. If you plan on photographing a frog hopping around on your front lawn, you'll want to be extra careful to preserve detail in the green channel, using bracketing or other exposure techniques outlined in this chapter.

# Bracketing

Bracketing is a method for shooting several consecutive exposures using different settings, as a way of improving the odds that one will be exactly right. Alternatively, bracketing can be used to create a series of photos with slightly different exposures (or white balances) in anticipation that one of the exposures will be "better" from a creative standpoint. For example, bracketing can supply you with a normal exposure of a backlit subject, one that's "underexposed," producing a silhouette effect, and a third that's "overexposed" to create still another look.

Before digital cameras took over the universe, it was common to bracket exposures, shooting, say, a series of three photos at 1/125th second, but varying the f/stop from f/8 to f/11 to f/16. In practice, smaller than whole-stop increments were used for greater precision, and lenses with apertures that were set manually commonly had half-stop detents on their aperture rings, or could easily be set to a mid-way position between whole f/stops. It was just as common to keep the same aperture and vary the shutter speed, although in the days before electronic shutters, film cameras often had only whole increment shutter speeds available.

Today, cameras like the D5200 can bracket exposures much more precisely, and bracket white balance and Active D-Lighting (ADL) as well. While WB bracketing is sometimes used when getting color absolutely correct in the camera is important, and ADL bracketing allows you to have the camera adjust the contrast of difficult images as they are exposed, autoexposure bracketing (AEB) is used much more often.

When AEB is activated, the D5200 takes three consecutive photos: one at the metered "correct" exposure, one with less exposure, and one with more exposure, using an increment of from 0.3 to 2EV stops. In S mode, the aperture will change, while in A mode, the shutter speed will change.

Using autoexposure bracketing is trickier than it needs to be, but you can follow these steps to get results like those shown in Figure 4.21:

1. **Choose the type of bracketing.** First, select the type of bracketing you want to do, using CSM e2, as explained in Chapter 9. You can select autoexposure, white balance, or ADL bracketing.

2. **Access the information edit display.** Press the Info button if it's not visible, and then press the Info button again to view the information edit display.

3. **Navigate to the bracketing settings.** Bracketing is located in the top row of settings, third from the left. Press OK.

4. **Choose bracket increment.** Select AE0.3, AE0.7, AE1.0, AE1.3, AE1.7, or AE2.0 to choose an exposure increment of 0.3, 0.7, 1.0, 1.3, 1.7, or 2.0EV. BKT will be displayed in the LCD monitor. Select OFF to disable bracketing.

5. **Frame and shoot.** As you take your photos, the camera will vary exposure, flash level, or white balance for each image, based on the bracketing "program" you selected. In Single frame mode, you'll need to press the shutter release button the number of times you specified for the exposures in your bracketed burst of three shots. I've found it easy to forget that I am shooting bracketed pictures, stop taking my sequence, and then wonder why the remaining pictures in my defined burst are "incorrectly" exposed. To avoid that, I often set the D5200 to its continuous shooting mode, so that all my bracketed pictures are taken at once. The D5200 does provide a BKT indicator as well as a bracketing progress indicator in the viewfinder, but they may be overlooked.

6. **Turn bracketing off.** When you're finished bracketing shots, remember to repeat steps 3–4, but choose OFF.

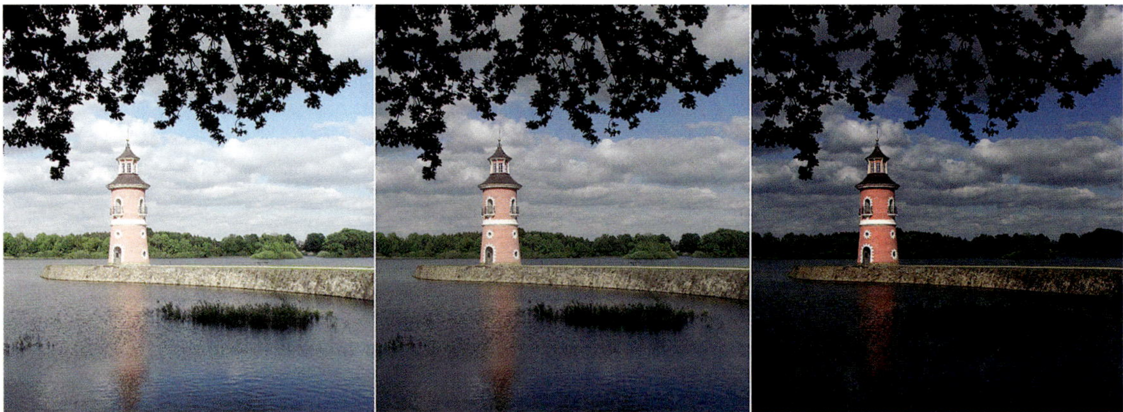

**Figure 4.21** Bracketing can give you three different exposures of the same subject.

## White Balance Bracketing/ADL Bracketing

When you choose white balance bracketing, the D5200 does not take three different exposures. There's no need, if you think about it. The camera always takes a RAW exposure first, no matter whether the camera is set to JPEG, RAW, or RAW+JPEG. If you've selected JPEG-only mode, the camera converts the initial RAW exposure to JPEG format using the settings you've opted for in the camera, and then discards the RAW data. In RAW mode, the camera stores the RAW data as a NEF file, and also creates a Basic JPEG version of the image that is embedded in the RAW file as a thumbnail. That thumbnail is what you're actually looking at on the back-panel LCD when you review your pictures; you never actually see the RAW file itself until you import it into your image editor. Your computer may also use the embedded JPEG file, when it displays a RAW image. Finally, if you save in RAW+JPEG, you end up with two files: the NEF RAW file (with its embedded JPEG image) and a separate JPEG file at the quality level you specify (Fine, Normal, or Basic).

Since the RAW file that the camera initially captures contains all the digital information captured during exposure, when you specify white balance bracketing, the D5200 needs to take only one picture—and then save a JPEG file at each of the required white balance settings. One snap, and you get either two or three JPEG files at the quality level you specified, bracketed as you directed. Very slick. As you might guess, WB bracketing is applied only to JPEG files; you can't specify WB bracketing if you've chosen RAW or RAW+JPEG. RAW files created are always unmodified, and will be converted according to the white balance settings you opted for in the camera when the photo is imported into your image editor (if you make no white balance changes during importation).

White balance bracketing produces JPEG files that vary, not by f/stops (which is the case with exposure bracketing), but by units called *mireds* (micro reciprocal degrees) that are used to specify color temperature. You don't really need to understand mireds at all, other than to know that WB bracketing varies the color temperature of your images by 5, 10, or 15 mireds when you select increments of 1, 2, or 3, respectively. Changes are made only in the amber-blue range; bracketing isn't applied to the green-magenta color bias.

Active D-Lighting bracketing produces two different shots, one with ADL turned off (your "control," so to speak), and a second shot with ADL applied at the setting you specified in the Shooting menu (Auto, Extra High, High, Normal, or Low). *However,* if you have turned ADL off in the Shooting menu, the D5200 will take the second shot using Auto, in effect overriding the Off setting you made. Confusing, but this provision allows you to keep ADL turned off, and then temporarily activate it in Auto mode just by selecting an ADL bracket burst. As with exposure and WB bracketing, remember to turn off ADL bracketing when you no longer want to use it.

## HDR Photography

High dynamic range (HDR) photography has fomented a bit of controversy in recent years, dividing many photographers into one of two camps: those that love it and use it, or wish they knew *how* to use it, and those who hate it. I'm not really in either camp; I see HDR as simply a tool that has definite uses, but which has become a bit of a fad that's often used (or over-used) to create some cartoonish, almost bizarre photographic clichés. HDR exists because sensors (or film, for that matter) can't capture the full range of tones that we see (or think we see) in real life.

If you're an architectural photographer shooting indoors and want to show both the interior and outdoor scenes as viewed through the windows, you really have only a limited number of choices. You can gel the windows with sheets of plastic that cut down the amount of light while balancing the exterior illumination for the interior light. You can use artificial lighting to balance the indoor/outdoor portions of your compositions (and, remember, the outdoor vistas may be night scenes, too). Or, you can use HDR photography to combine one or more images to get the balance you seek.

If you're a creative photographer, especially one doing landscapes, you're faced with your own challenges. How do you show the foreground and sky in the same image, when the difference may be eight or nine stops? Again, HDR may be an answer. Entire books have been written about the topic, and I've got only a portion of a chapter to address HDR. But, since Nikon has added an HDR feature to the Nikon D5200, the subject deserves a look. I only hope you'll use your new-found powers to benefit human-kind, and not succumb to the clichés that have graced the covers of every photography magazine every single month for the past year or two.

**My Five Simple Rules for Creating a High Dynamic Range Photo:**

1. Set up your tripod at dawn or dusk with a good view of a stunning panorama, preferably with dramatic clouds and a rising/setting sun.

2. Mount an ultrawide-angle lens on your camera (no longer than 10mm on a camera like the D5200).

3. Rotate the camera to achieve a vertical composition, with lots of foreground and sky.

4. Use Aperture-priority and a very small f/stop to maximize depth-of-field.

5. Take an HDR photograph, exactly like all the others you've seen recently.

That's not to say that there aren't very good vertically composed, ultrawide dawn/dusk landscape HDR photos. You'll just have to be extra creative to come up with one that's truly original.

This section will look at two ways of combining images using HDR: slow and versatile; and fast, easy, and slightly less flexible (using the D5200's built-in HDR feature). First, we'll look at the slow, versatile, traditional way of creating HDR photographs.

It's the same deal in the digital age. Suppose you wanted to photograph a dimly lit room that had a bright window showing an outdoors scene. Proper exposure for the room might be on the order of 1/60th second at f/2.8 at ISO 200, while the outdoors scene probably would require f/11 at 1/400th second. That's almost a 7EV step difference (approximately 7 f/stops) and well beyond the dynamic range of any digital camera, including the Nikon D5200.

Until camera sensors gain much higher dynamic ranges (which may not be as far into the distant future as we think), special tricks like Active D-Lighting and HDR photography will remain basic tools. With the Nikon D5200, you can create in-camera HDR exposures, or shoot HDR the old-fashioned way—with separate bracketed exposures that are later combined in a tool like Photomatix or Adobe's Merge to HDR image-editing feature. I'm going to show you how to use both.

# Auto HDR

The D5200's in-camera HDR feature is simple, not particularly flexible, but still surprisingly effective in creating high dynamic range images. It's also remarkably easy to use. It combines only two images to create a single HDR photograph.

Figure 4.23 illustrates how the two shots (see Figure 4.22) that the D5200's HDR feature merges might look. There is a three-stop differential between the underexposed image at left, and the overexposed image at right. The in-camera HDR processing is able to combine the two to derive an image that has a much fuller range of tones.

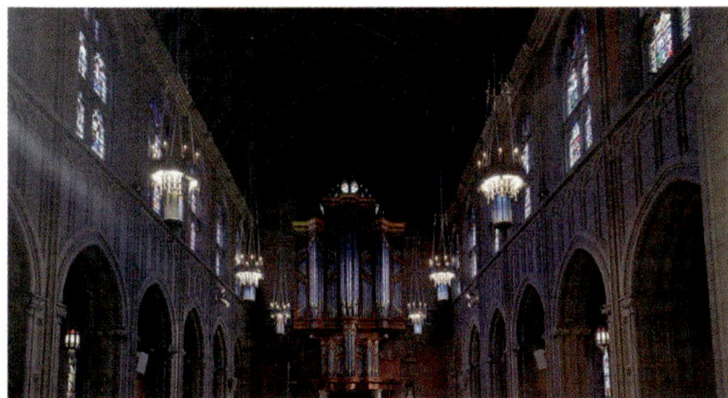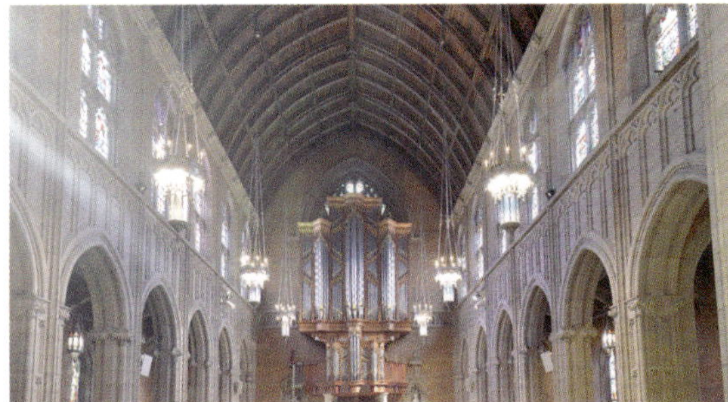

**Figure 4.22**  The underexposed image (left) can be combined with the overexposed version (right); ….

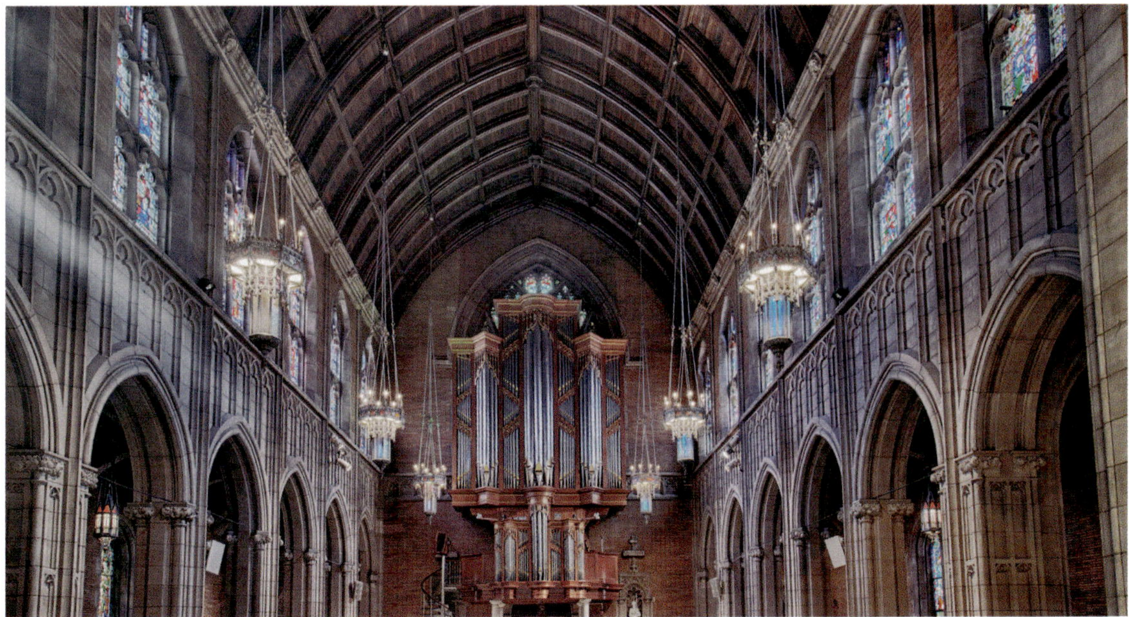

**Figure 4.23**  …to produce this merged high dynamic range (HDR) image.

There are two ways to activate the HDR feature. You can use the information edit screen (HDR is in the top row, fourth from the left) or work with the D5200's menu. The feature does not work if you have selected RAW or RAW+JPEG formats, or have one of the bracketing features turned on. Follow these steps to activate using the menu:

1. **Activate the menu.** Press the MENU button and navigate to the Shooting menu, represented by a camera icon. (If you need more help using the D5200's menu system, you'll find an introduction at the beginning of Chapter 8.)

2. **Scroll down to HDR (high dynamic range).** Press the right multi selector button.

3. **Turn on HDR.** Choose your HDR mode. Select from Auto, Extra High, High, Normal, Low, or Off. You'll need to experiment to discover exactly how much of the HDR effect is needed under various lighting/contrast conditions.

4. **Confirm your choice.** Press OK to confirm your selection.

5. **Take your shot.** Although you can shoot HDR hand-held, you'll get the best results with the D5200 mounted on a tripod, and with subjects that don't display a lot of motion. (That is, waterfalls are a poor choice.) While the D5200 is combining your two shots, the message Job Hdr will be shown at the bottom of the viewfinder.

## Bracketing and Merge to HDR

If your credo is "If you want something done right, do it yourself," you can also shoot HDR manually, without resorting to the D5200's HDR mode. Instead, you can shoot individual images either by manually bracketing or using the D5200's auto bracketing modes, described earlier in this chapter.

While my goal in this book is to show you how to take great photos *in the camera* rather than how to fix your errors in Photoshop, the Merge to HDR Pro feature in Adobe's flagship image editor is too cool to ignore. The ability to have a bracketed set of exposures that are identical except for exposure is key to getting good results with this Photoshop feature, which allows you to produce images with a full, rich dynamic range that includes a level of detail in the highlights and shadows that is almost impossible to achieve with digital cameras.

When you're using Merge to HDR Pro, you'd take several pictures, some exposed for the shadows, some for the middle tones, and some for the highlights. The exact number of images to combine is up to you. Four to seven is a good number. Then, you'd use the Merge to HDR Pro command to combine all of the images into one HDR image that integrates the well-exposed sections of each version. Here's how.

The images should be as identical as possible, except for exposure. So, it's a good idea to mount the D5200 on a tripod, use a remote release like ML-L3, and take all the exposures in one burst.

Just follow these steps:

1. **Set up the camera.** Mount the D5200 on a tripod.

2. **Set the camera to shoot a bracketed burst with an increment of 1EV to 3EV.** The description of how to do this will be found earlier in this chapter. Usually, 3EV is best, but experimentation may show you that for subjects that don't have dramatic tonal differences, an increment of 1EV or 2EV might provide more subtle effects.

3. **Choose an f/stop.** Set the camera for Aperture-priority and select an aperture that will provide a correct exposure at your initial settings for the series of bracketed shots. *And then leave this adjustment alone!* You don't want the aperture to change for your series, as that would change the depth-of-field. You want the D5200 to adjust exposure *only* using the shutter speed.

4. **Choose manual focus.** You don't want the focus to change between shots, so set the D5200 to manual focus, and carefully focus your shot.

5. **Choose RAW exposures.** Set the camera to take RAW files, which will give you the widest range of tones in your images.

6. **Take your bracketed set.** Press the button on the remote (or carefully press the shutter release or use the self-timer) and take the set of bracketed exposures. You can use "bracketing burst" or set the D5200 to continuous shooting mode.

7. **Continue with the Merge to HDR Pro steps listed next.** You can also use a different program, such as Photomatix, if you know how to use it.

## DETERMINING THE BEST EXPOSURE DIFFERENTIAL

How do you choose the number of EV/stops to separate your exposures? You can use histograms, described at the end of this chapter, to determine the correct bracketing range. Take a test shot and examine the histogram. Reduce the exposure until dark tones are clipped off at the left of the resulting histogram. Then, increase the exposure until the lighter tones are clipped off at the right of the histogram. The number of stops between the two is the range that should be covered using your bracketed exposures.

The next steps show you how to combine the separate exposures into one merged high dynamic range image. The sample images in Figure 4.24 show the results you can get from a bracketed sequence.

1. **Copy your images to your computer.** If you use an application to transfer the files to your computer, make sure it does not make any adjustments to brightness, contrast, or exposure. You want the real raw information for Merge to HDR Pro to work with.

2. **Activate Merge to HDR Pro.** Choose File > Automate > Merge to HDR Pro.

3. **Select the photos to be merged.** Use the Browse feature to locate and select your photos to be merged. You'll note a checkbox that can be used to automatically align the images if they were not taken with the camera mounted on a rock-steady support. This will adjust for any slight movement of the camera that might have occurred when you changed exposure settings.

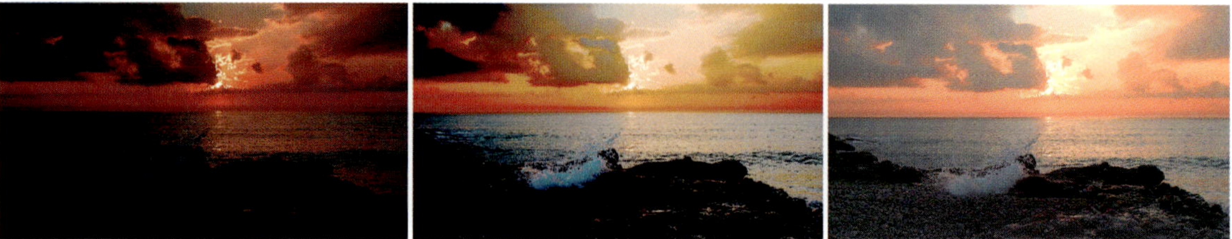

**Figure 4.24** Three bracketed photos should look like this.

4. **Choose parameters (optional).** The first time you use Merge to HDR Pro, you can let the program work with its default parameters. Once you've played with the feature a few times, you can read the Adobe help files and learn more about the options than I can present in this non-software-oriented camera guide.

5. **Click OK.** The merger begins.

6. **Save.** Once HDR merge has done its thing, save the file to your computer.

If you do everything correctly, you'll end up with a photo like the one shown in Figure 4.25.

What if you don't have the opportunity, inclination, or skills to create several images at different exposures, as described? If you shoot in RAW format, you can still use Merge to HDR, working with a *single* original image file. What you do is import the image into Photoshop several times, using Adobe Camera Raw to create multiple copies of the file at different exposure levels.

For example, you'd create one copy that's too dark, so the shadows lose detail, but the highlights are preserved. Create another copy with the shadows intact and allow the highlights to wash out. Then, you can use Merge to HDR to combine the two and end up with a finished image that has the extended dynamic range you're looking for.

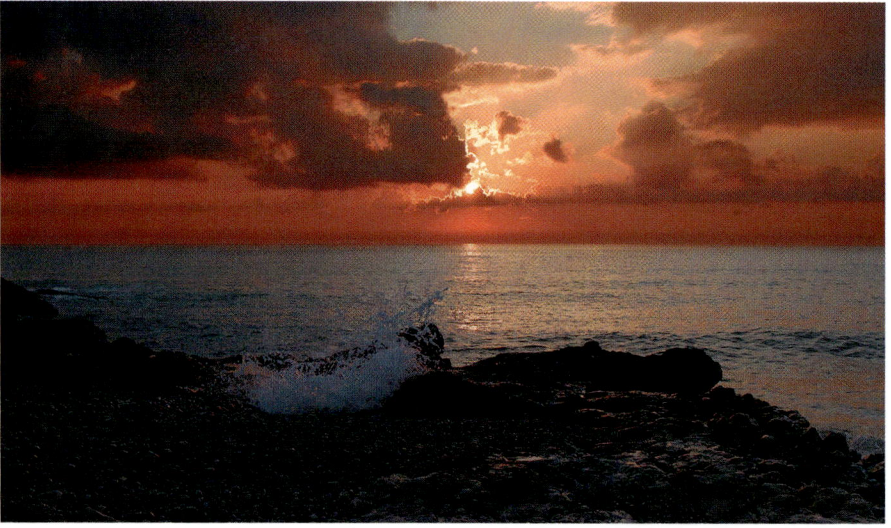

**Figure 4.25**
You'll end up with an extended dynamic range photo like this one.

# 5

# Mastering Autofocus Options

One of the most useful and powerful features of modern digital SLR cameras is their ability to lock in sharp focus faster than the blink of an eye. Sometimes. Although autofocus has been with us for more than 20 years, it continues to be problematic. While vendors like Nikon are giving us faster and more precise autofocus systems, with many more options, it's common for the sheer number of options to confuse even the most advanced photographers.

One key problem is that the camera doesn't really know, for certain, what subject you want to be in sharp focus. It may select an object and lock in focus with lightning speed—even though the subject is not the one that's the center of interest of your photograph. Or, the camera may lock focus too soon, or too late. This chapter will help you choose the options available with your Nikon D5200 that will help the camera understand what you want to focus on, when, and maybe even why.

## How Focus Works

Although Nikon added autofocus capabilities in the 1980s, back in the day of film cameras, prior to that focusing was always done manually. Honest. Even though viewfinders were bigger and brighter than they are today, special focusing screens, magnifiers, and other gadgets were often used to help the photographer achieve correct focus. Imagine what it must have been like to focus manually under demanding, fast-moving conditions such as sports photography.

Focusing was problematic because our eyes and brains have poor memory for correct focus, which is why your eye doctor must shift back and forth between sets of lenses and ask "Does that look sharper—or was it sharper before?" in determining your correct prescription. Similarly, manual focusing involves jogging the focus ring back and forth as you go from almost in focus, to sharp focus, to almost focused again. The little clockwise and counterclockwise arcs decrease in size until you've zeroed in on the point of correct focus. What you're looking for is the image with the most contrast between the edges of elements in the image.

The camera also looks for these contrast differences among pixels to determine relative sharpness. There are two ways that sharp focus is determined: Phase Detection (used when framing your image through the optical viewfinder) and Contrast Detection (used when shooting stills and movies with Live View).

## Phase Detection

The 39 autofocus sensors of Nikon's Multi-CAM 4800DX autofocus module are located in the "floor" of the mirror box, just under the flip-up mirror, which is partially silvered so that most of the light reaching it from the lens is bounced upward to the viewfinder, while some light is directed downward toward the focus sensors. If you lock up the mirror of your camera (using the Lock Mirror Up for Cleaning option in the Setup menu), you can see where these sensors are located. The focus zones cover an area on the center of the viewing frame, as shown in Figure 5.1. The horizontal lines and crosses in the center of the focus points in the diagram do not appear in your viewfinder; they represent the two different types of focus sensors: *linear* and *cross-type*. (More on the difference between them shortly.)

In phase detection mode, the autofocus sampling area for each autofocus sensor is divided into two halves by a prism-like optical component in front of the focus sensor. The two halves are compared, much like (actually, *exactly* like) a two-window rangefinder used in surveying, weaponry—and non-SLR cameras like the venerable Leica M film models. The relative positions between the two images change as focus is moved in or out, until sharp focus is achieved when the images are "in phase," or lined up.

You can visualize how phase detection autofocus works if you look at Figures 5.2 and 5.3. (However, the action of your camera's actual autofocus sensors don't look *anything* like this; I'm providing a greatly simplified view just for illustration.) In Figure 5.2, a typical horizontally oriented focus sensor is looking at a series of parallel vertical lines in a weathered piece of wood. The lines are broken into two halves by the sensor's rangefinder prism, and you can see that they don't line up exactly; the image is slightly out of focus.

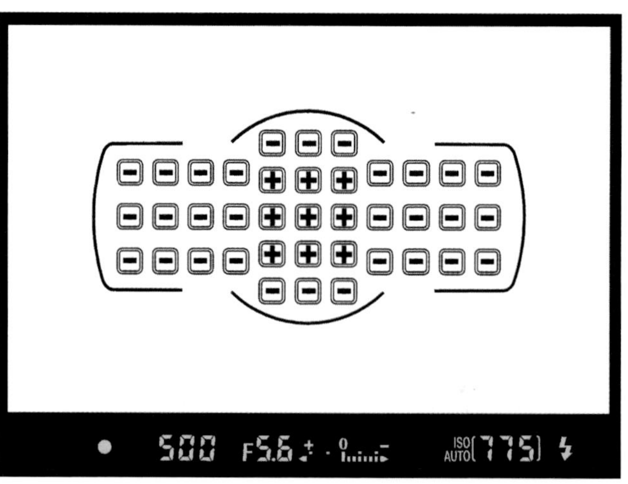

**Figure 5.1**
The D5200's focus sensors cover an area in the center of the frame.

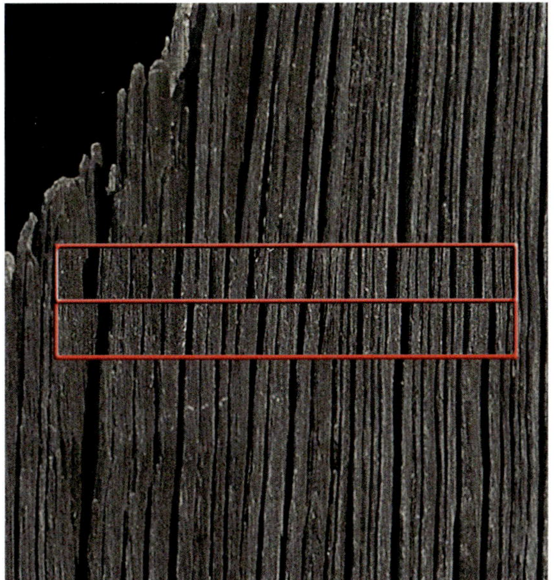

**Figure 5.2** When an image is out of focus, the split lines don't align precisely.

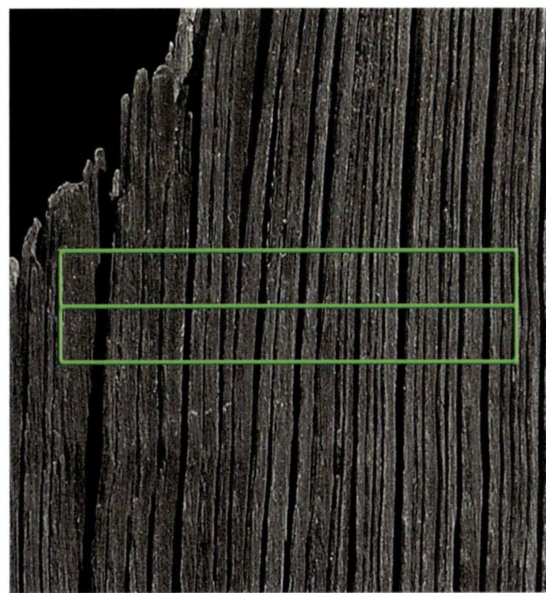

**Figure 5.3** Using phase detection, the D5200 is able to align the features of the image and achieve sharp focus quickly.

Fortunately, the rangefinder approach of phase detection tells the D5200 exactly how out of focus the image is, and in which direction (focus is too near, or too far) thanks to the amount and direction of the displacement of the split image. The camera can quickly and precisely snap the image into sharp focus and line up the vertical lines, as shown in Figure 5.3. Of course, this scenario— vertical lines being interpreted by a horizontally oriented sensor—is ideal. When the same sensor is asked to measure focus for, say, horizontal lines that don't split up quite so conveniently, or, in the worst case, subjects such as the sky (which may have neither vertical nor horizontal lines), focus can slow down drastically, or even become impossible.

Phase detection is the normal mode used by the D5200. As with any rangefinder-like function, accuracy is better when the "base length" between the two images is larger. (Think back to your high school trigonometry; you could calculate a distance more accurately when the separation between the two points where the angles were measured was greater.) For that reason, phase detection autofocus is more accurate with larger (wider) lens openings—especially those with maximum f/stops of f/2.8 or better—than with smaller lens openings, and may not work at all when the f/stop is smaller than f/5.6. As I noted, the D5200 is able to perform these comparisons very quickly.

## Improved Cross-Type Focus Point

One improvement that Nikon D5200 owners sometimes overlook is the upgrade to nine cross-type focus points clustered around the center position, represented in Figure 5.1 by plus signs. Why is this important? It helps to take a closer look at the phase detection system when presented with a non-ideal subject.

Figure 5.4 shows the same weathered wood pictured earlier, except in this case we've chosen to rotate the camera 90 degrees (say, because we want a vertically oriented composition). In the illustration, the image within the focus sensor's area is split in two and displaced slightly side-to-side, but the amount and direction of the misalignment is far from obvious. A horizontally oriented focus sensor will be forced to look for less obvious vertical lines to match up. Our best-case subject has been transformed into a *worst*-case subject for a horizontal focus sensor.

The value of the cross-type focus sensor, which can interpret contrast in both horizontal and vertical directions, can be seen in Figure 5.5. The horizontal lines are still giving the horizontal portion of the cross sensor fits, but the vertical bar can easily split and align the subject to achieve optimum focus. Cross-type sensors can handle horizontal and vertical lines with equal aplomb and, if you think about it, lines at any diagonal angle as well. In lower light levels, with subjects that were moving, or with subjects that have no pattern and less contrast to begin with, the cross-type sensor not only works faster but can focus subjects that a horizontal- or vertical-only sensor can't handle at all. So, you can see that having a center cross-type focus sensor that is extra-sensitive with faster lenses is a definite advantage for the D5200.

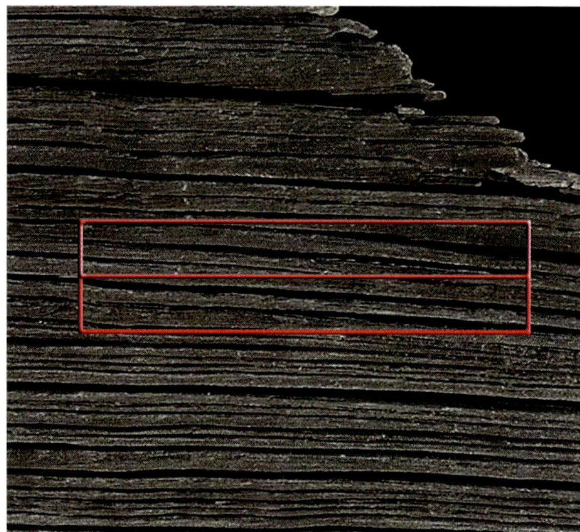

**Figure 5.4** A horizontal focus sensor doesn't handle horizontal lines very well.

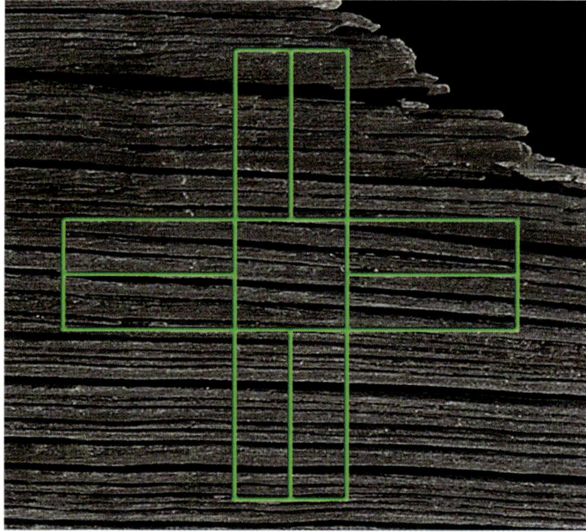

**Figure 5.5** Cross-type sensors can evaluate contrast in both horizontal and vertical directions, as well as diagonally.

## Contrast Detection

This is a slower mode, suitable for static subjects, and used by the D5200 in live view and movie modes. It's a bit easier to understand, and is illustrated by Figure 5.6. At top in the figure, the transitions between the edges found in the image are soft and blurred because of the low contrast between them. Although the illustration uses the same vertical lines used with the phase detection example, the orientation of the features doesn't matter. The focus system looks only for contrast between edges, and those edges can run in any direction.

**Figure 5.6**

Focus in contrast detection mode evaluates the increase in contrast in the edges of subjects, starting with a blurry image (top) and producing a sharp, contrasty image (bottom).

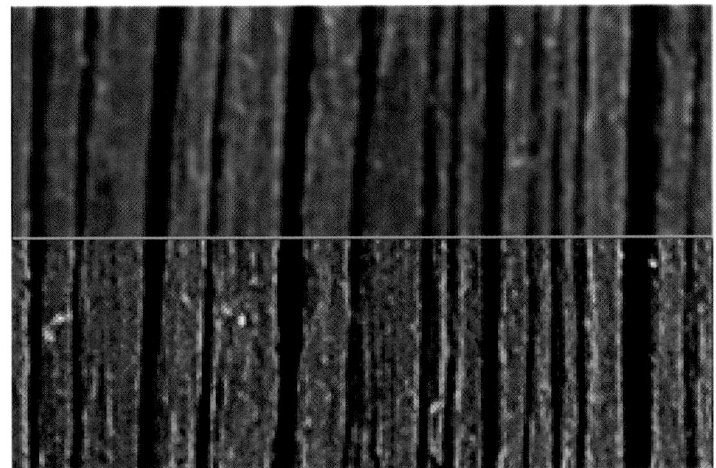

At the bottom of Figure 5.6, the image has been brought into sharp focus, and the edges have much more contrast; the transitions are sharp and clear. Although this example is a bit exaggerated so you can see the results on the printed page, it's easy to understand that when maximum contrast in a subject is achieved, it can be deemed to be in sharp focus. Although achieving focus with contrast detection is generally quite a bit slower, there are several advantages to this method:

- **Works with more image types.** Contrast detection doesn't require subject matter rotated 90 degrees from the sensor's orientation to operate optimally. Any subject that has edges will work.

- **Focus on any point.** While phase detection focus can be achieved *only* at the points that fall under one of the 39 autofocus sensors, with contrast detection, any portion of the image can be used. Focus is achieved with the actual sensor image, so focus point selection is simply a matter of choosing which part of the sensor image to use. As you'll learn in Chapter 6, you can move the focus frame around on the screen when working with live view.

- **Potentially more accurate.** Phase detection can fall prey to the vagaries of uncooperative subject matter: if suitable lines aren't available, the system may have to hunt for focus or achieve less than optimal focus. Contrast detection is more clear-cut. The camera can clearly see when the highest contrast has been achieved, as long as there is sufficient light to allow the camera to examine the image produced by the sensor. (The focus assist lamp can help when shooting subjects close enough to the camera for the focus assist illumination to provide extra contrast.)

The D5200's autofocus mechanism, like all such systems found in SLR cameras, evaluates the degree of focus, but, unlike the human eye, it is able to remember the progression perfectly, so that autofocus can lock in much more quickly and, with an image that has sufficient contrast, more precisely. Unfortunately, while the D5200's focus system finds it easy to measure degrees of apparent focus at each of the focus points in the viewfinder, it doesn't really know with any certainty *which* object should be in sharpest focus. Is it the closest object? The subject in the center? Something lurking *behind* the closest subject? A person standing over at the side of the picture? Many of the techniques for using autofocus effectively involve telling the Nikon D5200 exactly what it should be focusing on, by choosing a focus zone or by allowing the camera to choose a focus zone for you. I'll address that topic shortly.

As the camera collects focus information from the sensors, it then evaluates it to determine whether the desired sharp focus has been achieved. The calculations may include whether the subject is moving, and whether the camera needs to "predict" where the subject will be when the shutter release button is fully depressed and the picture is taken. The speed with which the camera is able to evaluate focus and then move the lens elements into the proper position to achieve the sharpest focus determines how fast the autofocus mechanism is. Although your D5200 will almost always focus more quickly than a human, there are types of shooting situations where that's not fast enough. For example, if you're having problems shooting sports because the D5200's autofocus system manically follows each moving subject, a better choice might be to switch Autofocus modes or shift into Manual and prefocus on a spot where you anticipate the action will be, such as a goal line or soccer net.

## Adding Circles of Confusion

But there are other factors in play, as well. You know that increased depth-of-field brings more of your subject into focus. But more depth-of-field also makes autofocusing (or manual focusing) more difficult because the contrast is lower between objects at different distances. So, autofocus with a 200mm lens (or zoom setting) may be easier than at a 28mm focal length (or zoom setting) because the longer lens has less apparent depth-of-field. By the same token, a lens with a maximum aperture of f/1.8 will be easier to autofocus (or manually focus) than one of the same focal length with an f/4 maximum aperture, because the f/4 lens has more depth-of-field *and* a dimmer view. That's why lenses with a maximum aperture smaller than f/5.6 can give your D5200's autofocus system fits.

To make things even more complicated, many subjects aren't polite enough to remain still. They move around in the frame, so that even if the D5200 is sharply focused on your main subject, it may change position and require refocusing. An intervening subject may pop into the frame and pass between you and the subject you meant to photograph. You (or the D5200) have to decide whether to lock focus on this new subject, or remain focused on the original subject. Finally, there are some kinds of subjects that are difficult to bring into sharp focus because they lack enough contrast to allow the D5200's AF system (or our eyes) to lock in. Blank walls, a clear blue sky, or other subject matter may make focusing difficult.

If you find all these focus factors confusing, you're on the right track. Focus is, in fact, measured using something called a *circle of confusion*. An ideal image consists of zillions of tiny little points, which, like all points, theoretically have no height or width. There is perfect contrast between the point and its surroundings. You can think of each point as a pinpoint of light in a darkened room. When a given point is out of focus, its edges decrease in contrast and it changes from a perfect point to a tiny disc with blurry edges (remember, blur is the lack of contrast between boundaries in an image). (See Figure 5.7.)

If this blurry disc—the circle of confusion—is small enough, our eye still perceives it as a point. It's only when the disc grows large enough that we can see it as a blur rather than a sharp point that a given point is viewed as out of focus. You can see, then, that enlarging an image, either by displaying it larger on your computer monitor or by making a large print, also enlarges the size of each circle of confusion. Moving closer to the image does the same thing. So, parts of an image that may look perfectly sharp in a 5 × 7–inch print viewed at arm's length, might appear blurry when blown up to 39 × 14 inches and examined at the same distance. Take a few steps back, however, and it may look sharp again.

To a lesser extent, the viewer also affects the apparent size of these circles of confusion. Some people see details better at a given distance and may perceive smaller circles of confusion than someone standing next to them. For the most part, however, such differences are small. Truly blurry images will look blurry to just about everyone under the same conditions.

Technically, there is just one plane within your picture area, parallel to the back of the camera (or sensor, in the case

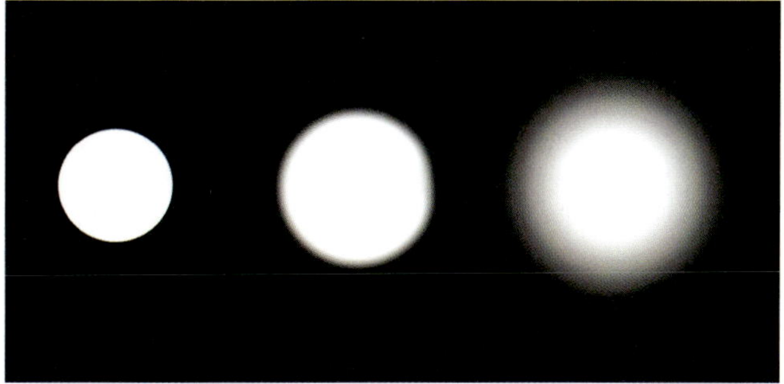

**Figure 5.7** When a pinpoint of light (left) goes out of focus, its blurry edges form a circle of confusion (center and right).

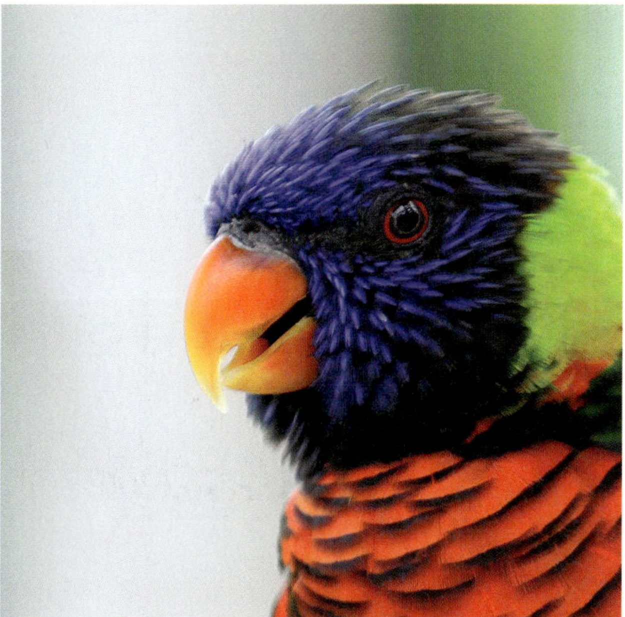

**Figure 5.8** Only the parts of the bird are in focus—the area behind it appears blurry because the depth-of-field is limited.

of a digital camera), that is in sharp focus. That's the plane in which the points of the image are rendered as precise points. At every other plane in front of or behind the focus plane, the points show up as discs that range from slightly blurry to extremely blurry (see Figure 5.8). In practice, the discs in many of these planes will still be so small that we see them as points, and that's where we get depth-of-field. Depth-of-field is just the range of planes that include discs that we perceive as points rather than blurred splotches. The size of this range increases as the aperture is reduced in size and is allocated roughly one-third in front of the plane of sharpest focus, and two-thirds behind it. The range of sharp focus is always greater behind your subject than in front of it.

# Using Autofocus with the Nikon D5200

Autofocus can sometimes be frustrating for the new digital SLR photographer, especially those coming from the point-and-shoot world. That's because correct focus plays a greater role among your creative options with a dSLR, even when photographing the same subjects. Most non-dSLR digital cameras have sensors that are much tinier than the sensor in the D5200. Those smaller sensors require shorter focal length lenses, which have, effectively, more depth-of-field.

The bottom line is that with the average point-and-shoot camera, *everything* is in focus from about one foot to infinity and at virtually every f/stop. Unless you're shooting close-up photos a few inches from the camera, the depth-of-field is prodigious, and autofocus is almost a non-factor. The D5200, on the other hand, uses longer focal length lenses to achieve the same field of view with its larger sensor, so there is less depth-of-field. That's a *good* thing, creatively, because you have the choice to use selective focus to isolate subjects. But it does make the correct use of autofocus more critical.

To maintain the most creative control, you have to choose three attributes:

- **How much is in focus.** Generally, by choosing the f/stop used, you'll determine the *range* of sharpness/amount of depth-of-field. The larger the DOF, the "easier" it is for the autofocus system's locked-in focus point to be appropriate (even though, strictly speaking, there is only one actual plane of sharp focus). With less depth-of-field, the accuracy of the focus point becomes more critical, because even a small error will result in an out-of-focus shot.

- **What subject is in focus.** The portion of your subject that is zeroed in for autofocus is determined by the autofocus zone that is active, and which is chosen either by you or by the Nikon D5200 (as described next). For example, when shooting portraits, it's actually okay for part of the subject—or even part of the subject's face—to be slightly out of focus as long as the eyes (or even just the *nearest* eye) appear sharp.

- **When focus is applied.** For static shots of objects that aren't moving, *when* focus is applied doesn't matter much. But when you're shooting sports, or birds in flight, or children, the subject may move within the viewfinder as you're framing the image. Whether that movement is across the frame or headed right toward you, timing the instant when autofocus is applied can be important.

## Autofocus Simplifies Our Lives...Doesn't It?

Manual focus is tricky, requires judgment, and fast reflexes. So, we're all better off now that autofocus has become almost universal, right? On the one hand, AF does save time and allows us to capture subjects (particularly fast-moving sports) that are difficult to image sharply using manual focusing (unless you have training and know certain techniques). On the other hand, learning to apply the Nikon D5200's autofocus system most effectively requires a bit of study and some practice. Then, once you're comfortable with autofocus, you'll know when it's appropriate to use the manual focus option, too.

The important thing to remember is that focus isn't absolute. For example, some things that look in sharp focus at a given viewing size and distance might not be in focus at a larger size and/or closer distance. In addition, the goal of optimum focus isn't always to make things look sharp. Not all of an image will be or should be sharp. Controlling exactly what is sharp and what is not is part of your creative palette. Use of depth-of-field characteristics to throw part of an image out of focus while other parts are sharply focused is one of the most valuable tools available to a photographer. But selective focus works only when the desired areas of an image are in focus properly. For the digital SLR photographer, correct focus can be one of the trickiest parts of the technical and creative process.

The D5200 now uses Nikon's 39-zone Multi-CAM 4800DX autofocus system. Like all camera autofocus sensors, those in your D5200 require a minimum amount of light as well as a minimum aperture size to operate, which is why autofocus capabilities are possible only with lenses having an f/5.6 or larger maximum aperture. While there's not a lot you can do to "fix" a lens that has a maximum aperture that's too small, if your subject's focus is difficult to evaluate because of waning light levels, the AF-assist beam built into the D5200 (usually of minimal aid because it is relatively weak) and the assist beams of Nikon's dedicated flash units provide additional light that helps assure enough illumination for autofocus under some circumstances.

## Bringing the Multi-CAM 4800DX AF System into Focus

I've explained individual bits and pieces of the Nikon D5200's autofocus system earlier in this book, particularly in the "roadmap" sections that showed you where all the controls were located, and the "setup" chapters that explained the key autofocus options. Now it's time to round out the coverage as we tie everything together. There are three aspects of autofocus that you need to understand to use this essential feature productively. They apply—in slightly different ways—to both autofocus when using the optical viewfinder, and in live view. In this chapter, I'm going to emphasize the optical viewfinder/phase detection system, and explore autofocus in live view in more detail in Chapter 6.

- **Autofocus point selection.** This aspect controls how the D5200 selects which areas of the frame are used to evaluate focus. Point selection allows the camera (or you) to specify a subject and lock focus in on that subject.

- **Autofocus mode and priority.** This governs *when* during the framing and shooting process autofocus is achieved. Should the camera focus once when activated, or continue to monitor your subject and refocus should the subject move? Is it okay to take a picture even if sharp focus isn't yet achieved, or should the camera lock out the shutter release until the image is sharp?

- **Autofocus activation.** When should the autofocus process begin, and when should it be locked? This aspect is related to the autofocus mode, but uses controls that you can specify to activate and/or lock the autofocus process.

# Autofocus Point Selection Overview

I'm discussing this aspect of autofocus first, because, in many ways, it is the most important. If your D5200 isn't focusing on the correct subject, autofocus speed and activation are pretty much wasted effort. As you've learned, the D5200 has up to 39 different points on the screen that can be individually selected by you or the camera as the active focus zone.

The number and type of autofocus sensors in use can affect how well the system operates. The focus sensors can consist of lines of pixels, cross-shapes, and/or a mixture of these types within a single camera, as with the D5200. The more AF points available, the more easily the camera can differentiate among areas of the frame, and the more precisely you can specify the area you want to be in focus if you're manually choosing a focus spot.

As the camera collects contrast information from the sensors, it then evaluates the data to determine whether the desired sharp focus has been achieved. The calculations may include whether the subject is moving, and whether the camera needs to "predict" where the subject will be when the shutter release button is fully depressed and the picture is taken. (Predictive focus tracking kicks in when the camera is set to AF-C continuous autofocus, or when you're using AF-A and the D5200 shifts from AF-S to AF-C. I'll explain these modes in more detail in the next section.)

The speed with which the camera is able to evaluate focus and then move the lens elements into the proper position to achieve the sharpest focus determines how fast the autofocus mechanism is. Although your D5200 will almost always focus more quickly than a human, there are types of shooting situations where that's not fast enough. As I mentioned, if you're having problems shooting sports because the D5200's autofocus system follows each moving subject, a better choice might be to switch autofocus modes or shift into manual and prefocus on a spot where you anticipate the action will be, such as a goal line or soccer net. At night football games, for example, when I am shooting with a telephoto lens almost wide open, I often focus manually on one of the referees who happens to be standing where I expect the action to be taking place (say, a halfback run or a pass reception).

# Choosing Autofocus Point Selection Mode

The D5200 has six different focus point selection modes. I'm going to describe each of the six modes, and explain how to use them. You can set any of the half-dozen point selection modes using the information edit screen, accessed by pressing the information edit button (twice, if necessary) and scrolling to the AF-point selection option in the bottom row of the screen.

### Single-Point AF

In this mode, you always select the focus point manually, using the multi selector button. The D5200 evaluates focus based solely on the point you select, making this a good choice for subjects that don't move much. You can temporarily lock the focus point by partially depressing the shutter release, or pressing the AE-L/AF-L button (unless you've redefined this behavior to some other controls in the Custom Setting menu).

## Dynamic-Area AF (9-, 21-,or 39-point Versions)

In any of these three separate modes, you still select the focus point yourself using the multi selector button. In that respect, the D5200 behaves exactly as it does in single-point AF mode. However, if you have chosen continuous-servo autofocus (AF-C) or are using automatic autofocus (AF-A) and the camera shifts from AF-S to AF-C, the D5200's "smarts" spring to life if your subject leaves the selected focus zone. When that happens, the camera re-evaluates focus based on the other focus points surrounding the one you chose. This choice is available only when using AF-C or AF-A modes. The number of points that are evaluated can be specified by you—9, 21, or all 39 focus zones.

- **9 points.** This mode is useful when photographing subjects with predictable paths of motion, such as runners at a track meet, or NASCAR racers. The D5200's focus seeking is limited to a fairly small area that you can control in the amount of time available as the subject moves across the frame.

- **21 points.** This mode comes in handy when the motion of your subjects is not so easy to predict, and you may not have enough time to select a precise focus point manually. You only need to "be close" when tracking, say, basketball players who are tossing the ball back and forth among their teammates and may suddenly dart for the hoop.

- **39 points.** Choose this mode for birds in flight and other wildly erratic subjects, such as children. All 39 focus points will be used if the subject moves outside of the focus point you've selected in the frame.

## 3D-Tracking

In this mode, all 39 points are used, and you can select the focus point as described for the other modes. Should the subject leave your selected focus zone, the D5200 uses distance information to calculate the path of the subject and select a new focus point. Nikon recommends using this setting to focus subjects that move erratically from side to side, because the camera can use the distance information to differentiate the original subject from objects that are closer or farther away. Tracking will abort if your subject leaves the viewfinder entirely; in that case, release the shutter button and reframe your image with your subject in the selected focus point. This choice is available only when using AF-C or AF-A modes.

## Automatic-Area AF

In this mode, autofocus point selection is out of your hands; the D5200 performs the task for you using its own intelligence. If you are using a type G or D lens, the camera can even work with the supplied distance information to distinguish humans from their background, so a person standing at the side of the frame will be detected and used to evaluate focus, while the camera ignores the background area in the frame.

The D5200 tends to keep the active focus point somewhat of a mystery (although it will be displayed during picture review if you've activated that option). In AF-S mode, the active focus point is highlighted in the viewfinder for about one second after focus is achieved. In AF-C mode, the active focus point is not shown.

# Autofocus Mode and Priority

Choosing the right autofocus mode (AF-S, AF-C, or Manual) is another key to focusing success. To save battery power, your D5200 doesn't start to focus the lens until you partially depress the shutter release or press the AE-L/AF-L button on the back of the camera. But, autofocus isn't some mindless beast out there snapping your pictures in and out of focus with no feedback from you after you press that button. There are several settings you can modify that return at least a modicum of control to you. Your first decision should be whether you set the D5200 to AF-S, AF-C, or Manual.

You can set any of the three modes using the information edit screen, as described previously. Navigate to the focus mode area of the screen, and select one of the three modes described next.

## Autofocus Mode

This choice determines *when* your D5200 starts to autofocus, and what it does when focus is achieved. Automatic focus is not something that happens all the time when your camera is turned on. To save battery power, your D5200 generally doesn't start to focus the lens until you partially depress the shutter release. (You can also use the AE/AL lock button to start autofocus, as described in Chapter 9.)

### Single-Servo Autofocus (AF-S)

In this mode, also called *AF-S*, focus is set once and remains at that setting until the button is fully depressed, taking the picture, or until you release the shutter button without taking a shot. For non-action photography, this setting is usually your best choice, as it minimizes out-of-focus pictures (at the expense of spontaneity). The drawback here is that you might not be able to take a picture at all while the camera is seeking focus; you're locked out until the autofocus mechanism is happy with the current setting.

When sharp focus is achieved, the selected focus point will flash red in the viewfinder, and the focus confirmation light at the lower left will show a steady green. If you're using Matrix metering, the exposure will be locked at the same time. By keeping the shutter button depressed halfway, you'll find you can reframe the image while retaining the focus (and exposure) that's been set. You can also use the AE-L/AF-L button (described in Chapter 9) if you've set that button to lock focus when pressed. Because of the small delay while the camera zeroes in on correct focus, you might experience slightly more shutter lag. This mode uses less battery power.

### Continuous-Servo Autofocus (AF-C)

This mode, also known as *AF-C*, is the mode to use for sports and other fast-moving subjects. In this mode, once the shutter release is partially depressed, the camera sets the focus but continues to monitor the subject, so that if it moves or you move, the lens will be refocused to suit. Focus and exposure aren't really locked until you press the shutter release down all the way to take the picture. You'll find that AF-C produces the least amount of shutter lag of any autofocus mode when set to release priority: press the button and the camera fires. It also uses the most battery power, because the autofocus system operates as long as the shutter release button is partially depressed.

Continuous-servo autofocus uses a technology called *predictive tracking AF*, which allows the D5200 to calculate the correct focus if the subject is moving toward or away from the camera at a constant rate. (Automatic autofocus, AF-A, described next, also uses predictive tracking when operating in AF-C mode.) It uses either the automatically selected AF point or the point you select manually to set focus. As described in Chapter 9, you can set AF-C mode to use release priority (the default), or focus priority using Custom Setting a1.

If you want to lock the focus point you've selected for a series of shots, rotate the focus selector lock lever up to the L position. You can also temporarily lock the focus point by partially depressing the shutter release, or pressing the AE-L/AF-L button (unless you've redefined this behavior to some other controls in the Custom Setting menu).

## Automatic Autofocus (AF-A)

This setting is actually a combination of the first two. When selected, the camera focuses using AF-S AF and locks in the focus setting. But, if the subject begins moving, it will switch automatically to AF-C and change the focus to keep the subject sharp. AF-A is a good choice when you're shooting a mixture of action pictures and less dynamic shots and want to use AF-S when possible. The camera will default to that mode, yet switch automatically to AF-C when it would be useful for subjects that might begin moving unexpectedly. However, as with AF-S, the shutter can be released only when the subject at the selected focus point is in focus.

## Manual Focus

With manual focus activated by sliding the switch on the lens to the M position (or choosing manual focus from the information edit screen), your D5200 lets you set the focus yourself. There are some advantages and disadvantages to this approach. While your batteries will last longer in manual focus mode, it will take you longer to focus the camera for each photo, a process that can be difficult. Modern digital cameras, even dSLRs, depend so much on autofocus that the viewfinders of models that have less than full-frame-sized sensors are no longer designed for optimum manual focus. Pick up any film camera and you'll see a bigger, brighter viewfinder with a focusing screen that's a joy to focus on manually.

In manual focus mode, you can use the rangefinder feature to help you achieve sharp focus when you're shooting in Program, Aperture-priority, or Shutter-priority mode. You'll find a complete description of how to activate the feature in Chapter 9, under the Custom Setting a4 setting. The rangefinder supplements the focus confirmation indicator at the left edge of the viewfinder by using the analog exposure indicator as a focusing "scale."

With a manual focus lens and the rangefinder operating, the analog exposure display at bottom center in the viewfinder will be replaced by a rangefinder focusing scale. Indicators on the scale like those in Figure 5.9 show when the image is in sharp focus, as well as when you have focused somewhat in front of or behind the subject. Follow these steps to use the rangefinder:

1. **Activate.** Use Custom Setting a4 to turn on the rangefinder, as described in Chapter 9.

2. **Select a focus point.** Use the multi selector to move the highlighting around in the frame.

3. **Rotate the lens focus ring.** Zoom lenses will have *two* rings; there's no fixed convention as to whether the wider or narrower ring is the focus ring. Choose the one farthest from the zoom scale.

4. **Watch the rangefinder.** If the indicator is pointing toward the left, focus farther away. If the scale points toward the right, focus more closely.

5. **Achieve sharp focus.** When the subject you've selected with the focus zone bracket is in sharp focus, only two bars will appear, centered under the 0, and the focus confirmation indicator will stop blinking. If no 0 appears, the camera cannot determine focus.

The readout in the viewfinder is not analog (that is, continuous). Only the six indicators shown in Figure 5.9 are displayed. Two centered rectangles indicate that correct focus has been achieved; when all 12 are shown, it means that correct focus cannot be indicated. Three and six rectangles show that slight or major focus corrections are needed, respectively.

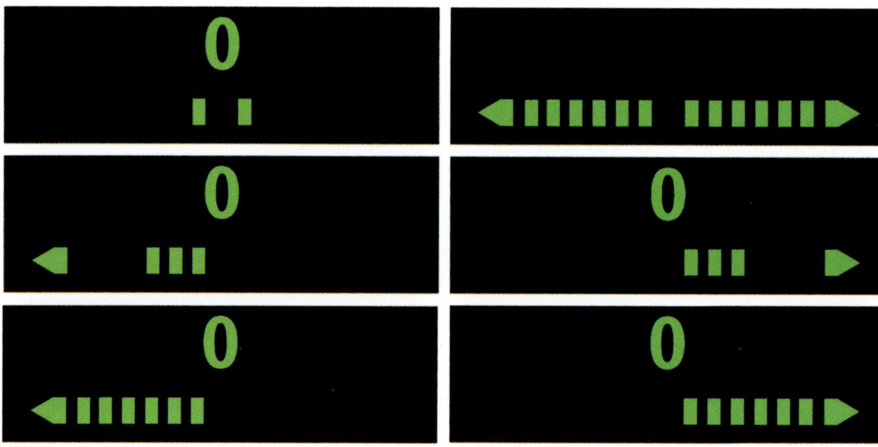

**Figure 5.9**
Upper left: Correct focus; upper right: focus is grossly incorrect; center left: focus slightly in front of the subject; center right: focus slightly behind the subject; bottom left: focus significantly in front of the sub-ject; bottom right: focus significantly behind the subject.

6

# Live View and Movies

The Nikon D5200's superior level of performance is not limited to still images. It can also shoot high-definition video with stereo sound at 1920 × 1080 resolution, or Standard HD video at 1280 × 720 resolution. VGA movies can also be captured at an e-mail-friendly 640 × 480 resolution. Whether you're looking to record informal clips of the family on vacation, the latest viral video for YouTube, or a clip that will be painstakingly crafted into a cinematic masterpiece using editing software and displayed on a giant HDTV screen, you'll find the basics quite easy.

While the D5200 is not intended to compete with a sophisticated dedicated video camcorder, its compact size means you'll have it with you often, and it can certainly shoot very nice 1080p video clips with stereo sound provided by the pair of built-in mics or an optional external microphone. So, if you're out and about and develop a sudden need to make a video record of an event, from a school sports contest to a breaking news story, you can save footage of very fine quality to your SD card.

Movie making evolved from the camera's live view still mode, so I'm going to cover both aspects in this chapter. We'll start off with some information on using live view preview to shoot still photographs.

## The New Perspective of Live View and Movies

Both live view and movie making are features that experienced SLR users originally thought they didn't need—until they tried them. Live view, in particular, is also one of those features (like truly "silent" shooting, without any shutter click) that point-and-shoot refugees are surprised that digital SLRs (until relatively recently) have lacked. As I noted earlier, SLRs have actual, mechanical shutters that can't be completely silenced (even with the D5200's "quiet shutter" mode), as can be done with point-and-shoot cameras. I've fielded almost as many queries from those who want to know how to preview their images on the LCD monitor—just as they did with their point-and-shoot cameras. Indeed, many P & S models don't even *have* optical viewfinders, engendering a whole generation of amateur photographers who think the only way to frame and compose an image is to hold the camera out at arm's length so the back-panel LCD monitor can be viewed more easily.

While dSLR veterans didn't really miss live view, it was at least, in part, because they didn't have it and couldn't miss what they never had. After all, why would you eschew a big, bright, magnified through-the-lens optical view that showed depth-of-field fairly well, and which was easily visible under virtually all ambient light conditions? LCD monitor displays, after all, were small, tended to wash out in bright light, and didn't really provide you with an accurate view of what your picture was going to look like.

Fortunately, the Nikon D5200 has a gorgeous three-inch LCD monitor that can be viewed under a variety of lighting conditions and from wide-ranging angles, so you don't have to be exactly behind the display to see it clearly. It offers a 100-percent view of the sensor's capture area, even better than the D5200's optical viewfinder (at 95%). Indeed, while the D5200 crops the sensor image slightly when recording movies at HD resolution, the actual image area is enlarged to fill the LCD monitor during shooting.

# Beginning Live View

Activate live view prior to shooting stills or movies by rotating the Lv switch on top of the camera (just to the right of the mode dial) clockwise until the mirror flips up and the live view preview is shown on the display. Rotate the switch again to turn live view off. The first thing to do when entering live view is to double-check three important settings that affect how your image or movie is taken. These settings include:

## Metering Mode

While using live view, you can press the information edit button (just to the right of the viewfinder window) once, navigate to the metering icon in the second row, and select Matrix, Center-weighted, or Spot metering.

## Focus Mode

Focus mode is chosen using the same information edit screen controls, using icons that are also located in the second row. The available modes differ slightly from those possible when not shooting in live view: AF-S, AF-F, and MF. To use manual focus, you can also set the focus mode selector switch on the lens to M.

- **AF-S.** This single autofocus mode, which Nikon calls single-servo AF, locks focus when the shutter release is pressed halfway. This mode uses *focus priority;* the focus frame turns red and blinks if the D5200 is unable to achieve sharp focus.

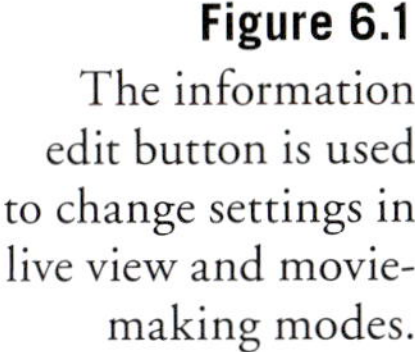

**Figure 6.1**
The information edit button is used to change settings in live view and movie-making modes.

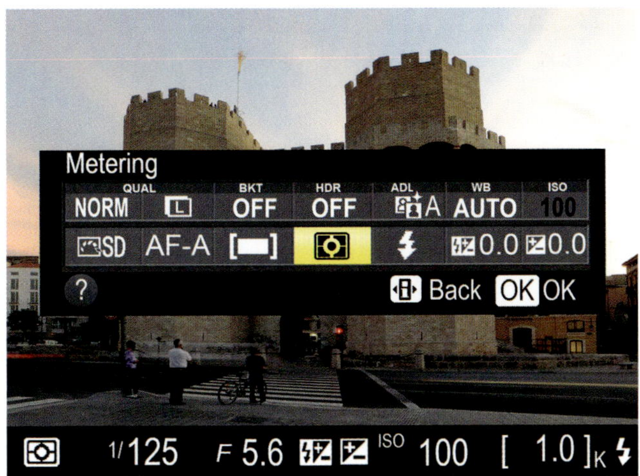


- **AF-F.** This mode is roughly the equivalent of AF-C. Nikon calls it full-time servo AF. The D5200 focuses and refocuses continually as you shoot stills in live view modes or record movies. Unlike AF-C, this mode also uses focus priority. You can't release the shutter unless the camera has achieved sharp focus.

- **MF.** Manual focus. You focus the image by rotating the focus ring on the camera.

## Focus Area

Using the information edit screen, you can choose the focus area modes available from the second row of icons. They are different from those used when working with the optical viewfinder. Your choices are as follows:

- **Face-priority AF.** The camera automatically detects faces, and focuses on subjects facing the camera, as when you're shooting a portrait. You can't select the focus zone yourself. Instead, a double yellow border will be displayed on the LCD monitor when the camera detects a face. You don't need to press the shutter release to activate this behavior. (Up to 35 faces may be detected; the D5200 focuses on the face that is closest to the camera.) When you press down the shutter release halfway, the camera attempts to focus the face. As sharp focus is achieved, the border turns green. (See Figure 6.2.) If the camera is unable to focus, the border blinks red. Focus may also be lost if the subject turns away from the camera and is no longer detectable by Face-priority.

- **Wide-area AF.** This is the mode to use for non-portrait subjects, such as landscapes, as you can select the focus zone to be used manually. It's good for shooting hand-held, because the subjects may change as you reframe the image with a hand-held camera, and the wide-area zones are forgiving of these changes. The focus zone will be outlined in red. You can move the focus zone around the screen with the multi selector buttons. When sharp focus is achieved, the focus zone box will turn green. (See Figure 6.3.)

- **Normal-area AF.** This mode uses smaller focus zones, and so is best suited for tripod-mounted images where the camera is held fairly steady. As with Wide-area AF, the focus zone will be outlined in red. You can move the focus zone around the screen with the multi selector buttons. When sharp focus is achieved, the focus zone box will turn green. (See Figure 6.4.)

- **Subject-tracking AF.** This mode allows the camera to "grab" a subject, focus, and then follow the subject as it moves within the frame. You can use this mode for subjects that don't remain stationary, such as small children. When using Subject-tracking AF, a white border appears in the center of the frame, and turns yellow when focus is locked in (as described in the section that follows). To activate focus or refocus, press the multi selector up button. I'll explain Subject-tracking in more detail next. (See Figure 6.5.)

- **Manual focus.** In this non-automatic focus mode, you can move the focus area around the frame with the multi selector buttons, press the shutter release halfway, and then adjust focus manually by rotating the focus ring on the lens. When sharp focus is achieved, the red focus zone box will turn green, and the camera's beeper, if enabled, will sound.

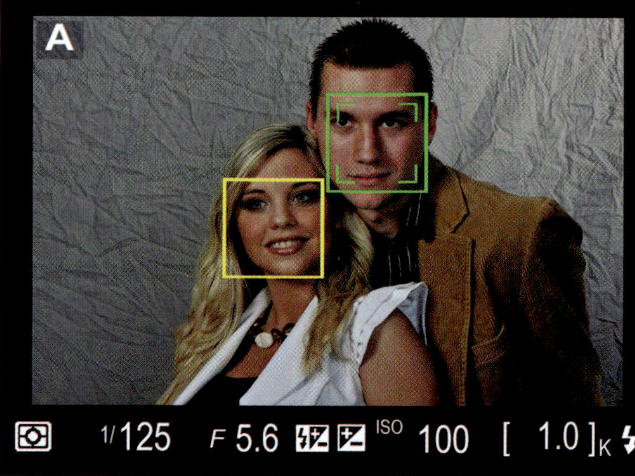

**Figure 6.2**
Face-priority AF attempts to focus on the face that's closest to the camera.

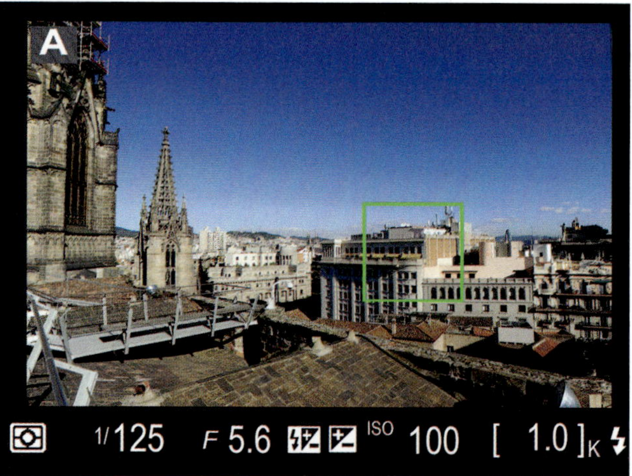

**Figure 6.3**
Wide-area AF is best for landscapes and other subjects with large elements.

**Figure 6.4**
Normal-area AF allows you to zero in on a specific point of focus.

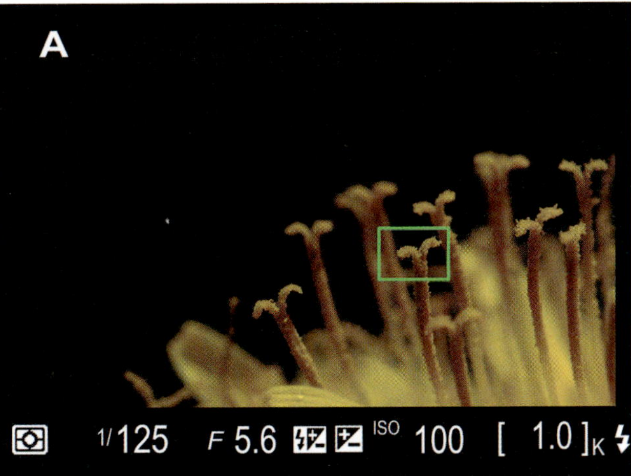

**Figure 6.5**
Subject-tracking can keep focus as it follows your subject around in the frame.

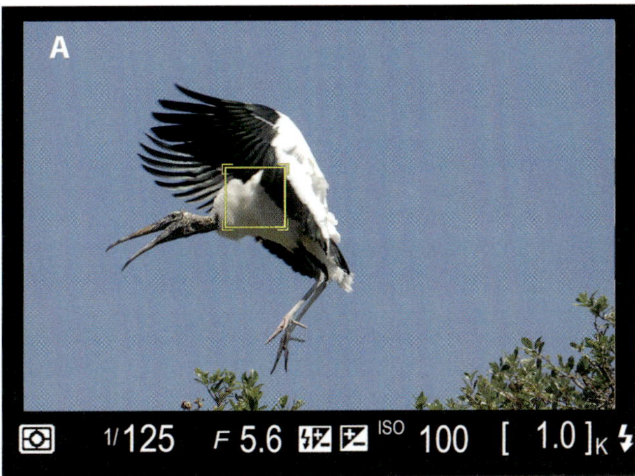

# Introducing Subject-Tracking

The useful Subject-tracking autofocus feature is one of those features that can be confusing at first, but once you get the hang of it, it's remarkably easy to use. Face-priority, in comparison, is almost intuitive to learn. Here's the quick introduction you need to Subject-tracking.

- **Ready, aim…** When you've activated Subject-tracking, a white border appears in the center of the frame. Use that border to "aim" the camera until the subject you want to focus on and track is located within the border.

- **…Focus.** When you've pinpointed your subject, press the OK button to activate the D5200's contrast detection autofocus feature. The focus frame will turn yellow and the camera will emit a beep (unless you've disabled the beep within the Setup menu) when locked in.

- **Reframe as desired.** Once the focus frame has turned yellow, it seemingly takes on a life of its own, and will "follow" your subject around on the LCD monitor as you reframe your image.

(See Figure 6.5.) (In other words, the subject being tracked doesn't have to be in the center of the frame for the actual photo.) Best of all, if your subject moves, the D5200 will follow it and keep focus as required.

- **Tracking continues.** The only glitches that may pop up might occur if your subject is small and difficult to track, or is too close in tonal value to its background, or if the subject approaches the camera or recedes sufficiently to change its relative size on the LCD monitor significantly.

- **Grab a new subject.** If you want to refocus or grab a new subject, press the OK button again.

## Viewing Live View Information

Once you've activated live view, a display like the one shown in Figure 6.6 appears. Not all of the information appears all the time (in fact, it's *impossible* for all these indicators to be active at the same time). For example, the Time Remaining indicator shows only when there are 30 seconds or less remaining for live view shooting. The indicators overlaid on the image can be displayed or suppressed by pressing the Info button (that's the one that's *on top* of the camera, and which is *not* the information edit button). As you press the button, the LCD monitor cycles among these screen variations:

- **Live view screen overlaid with shooting information.** Nikon calls this mode Show Photo Indicators. (See Figure 6.7.)

- **Live view screen overlaid with information relevant to movie shooting.** Nikon calls this mode Show Movie Indicators. The area used to capture HD movies is shown, with other parts of the frame darkened, before you begin video capture. When you press the movie button, the highlighted area expands to fill the entire LCD monitor, as shown in Figure 6.8.

- **Live view screen overlaid with only minimal information**, including markers for the 16:9 aspect ratio of the HD movie format. Nikon calls this Hide Indicators. (See Figure 6.9.)

- **Live view screen overlaid with basic information**, plus a 16-segment alignment grid. Nikon calls this Framing Grid view. (See Figure 6.10.)

The overlaid indicators include:

- **Shooting mode.** This indicator shows the mode dial position you've selected, including any of the PASM (Program, Aperture-priority, Shutter-priority, and Manual) modes, as well as one of the scene modes. You can change modes while live view is active. This indicator appears on the LCD monitor even when shooting information is turned off.

- **Sound Level.** Shows when a microphone is being used.

- **No Movies Possible.** This shows that it is not possible to shoot movies, because there is not enough space remaining on your memory card.

- **Live view time remaining.** This is displayed when the amount of shooting time in live view mode is 30 seconds or less. Although live view is possible for 60 minutes, if the D5200 overheats, this countdown display appears and the camera exits live view before damage is done.

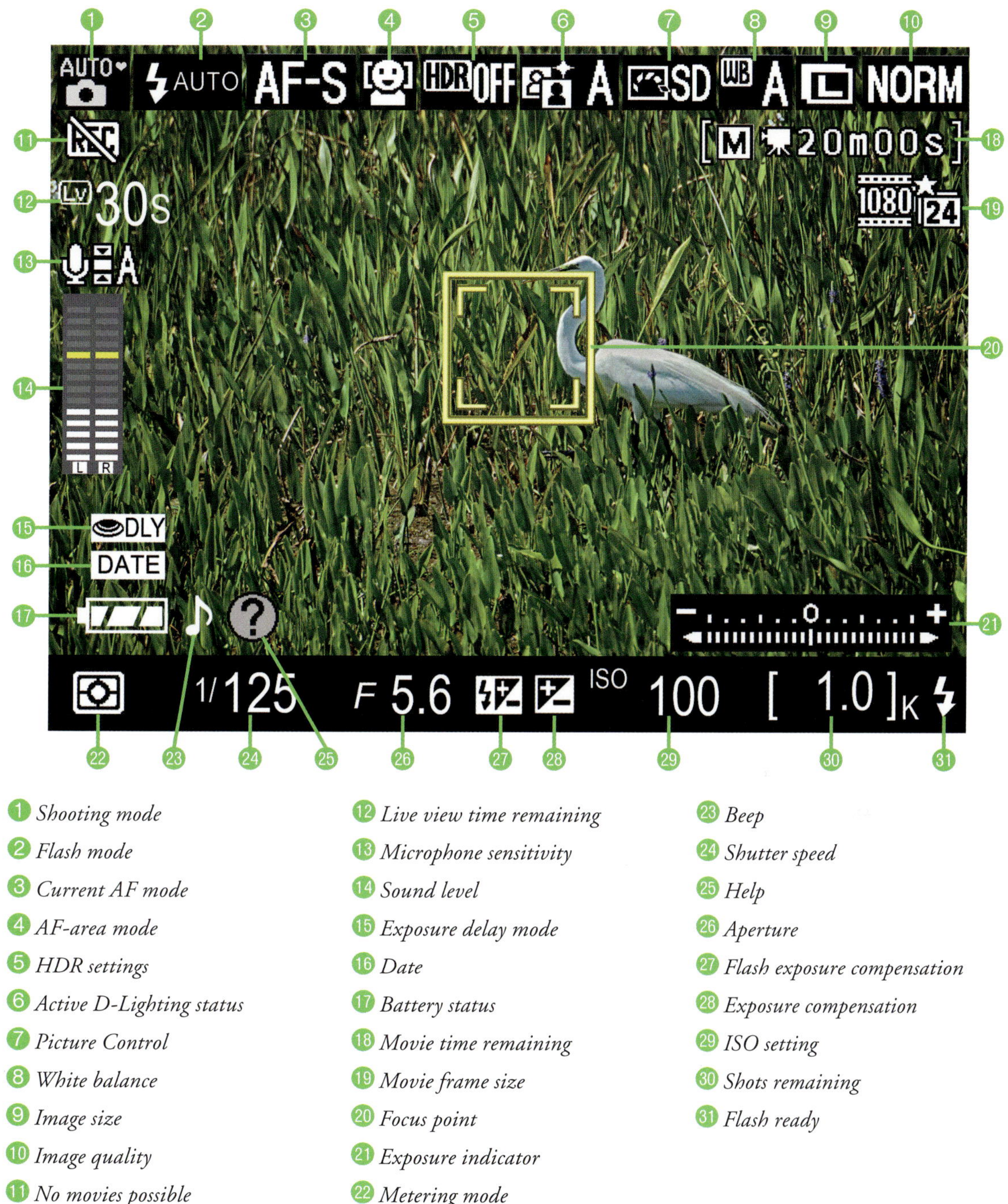




1. Shooting mode
2. Flash mode
3. Current AF mode
4. AF-area mode
5. HDR settings
6. Active D-Lighting status
7. Picture Control
8. White balance
9. Image size
10. Image quality
11. No movies possible
12. Live view time remaining
13. Microphone sensitivity
14. Sound level
15. Exposure delay mode
16. Date
17. Battery status
18. Movie time remaining
19. Movie frame size
20. Focus point
21. Exposure indicator
22. Metering mode
23. Beep
24. Shutter speed
25. Help
26. Aperture
27. Flash exposure compensation
28. Exposure compensation
29. ISO setting
30. Shots remaining
31. Flash ready

**Figure 6.6** The live view display includes a lot of information, some of which can be hidden.

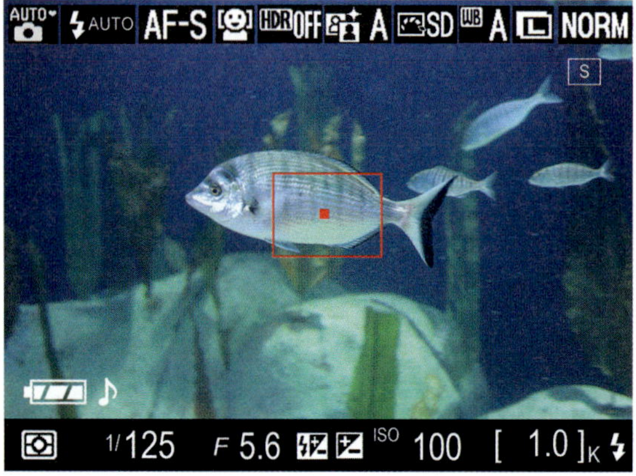

**Figure 6.7**  The live view display with information.

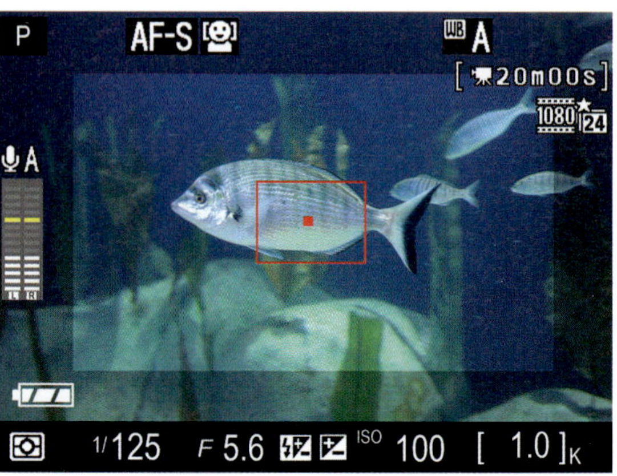

**Figure 6.8**  The live view display with 16:9 HDTV frame shown.

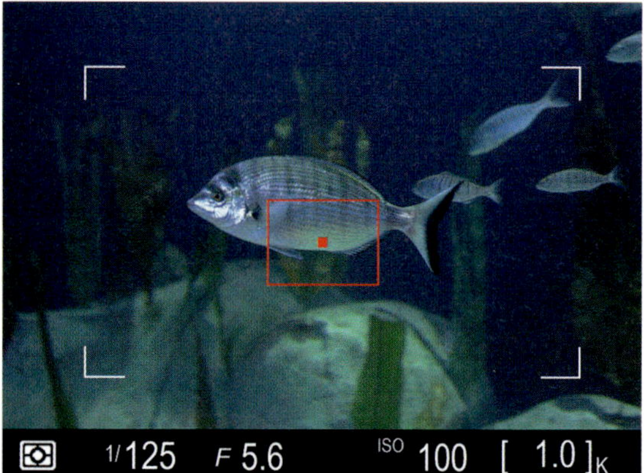

**Figure 6.9**  The live view display with 16:9 "corner" markers.

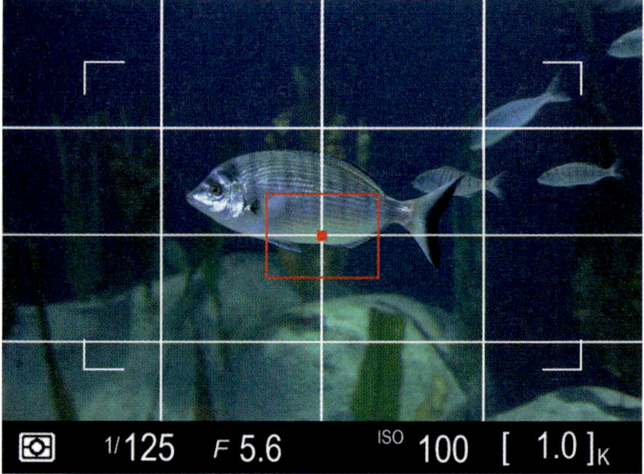

**Figure 6.10**  The live view display with alignment grid.

- **Flash mode.** Displays the flash mode.
- **Release mode.** Shows the current release mode.
- **Picture Control.** Currently selected Picture Control.
- **Current AF mode.** Shows AF-S, AF-F, or M focus.
- **Current AF-area.** Shows whether Face-priority, Wide-area, Normal-area, or Subject-tracking autofocus will be used. This indicator still appears when the alignment grid is displayed, even when other shooting information is turned off.
- **Active D-Lighting status.** Shows the D-Lighting that will be applied.
- **Focus point.** Shows the appropriate focus indicator for the AF-area mode in use.
- **Image size.** Displays the current resolution, L (Large), M (Medium), or S (Small).

- **Image quality.** Shows JPEG image quality: Fine, Norm, or Basic.

- **White balance.** Displays the current white balance preset or WB Auto.

- **Movie time remaining.** Indicates the number of minutes and seconds remaining for movie shooting.

- **Movie frame size.** Displays the resolution of the movie frame and frames per second rate, from 1920 × 1080 pixels to 1280 × 720, down to 640 × 424, at either 24 or 30 fps (depending on what you've selected in the Movie Settings entry in the Shooting menu). (See Chapter 8.)

- **Alignment grid.** (Shown in Figure 6.9.) This set of guides can be used to help line up horizontal or vertical lines.

- **Self-timer.** (Not shown in figure.) A self-timer icon appears at right when the self-timer is active.

- **Battery status.** Current power level of the battery.

- **Beep status.** Shows whether the beeper is turned on or off.

- **Wi-Fi.** (Not shown in figure.) Displayed when a Wi-Fi memory card is installed.

- **DATE.** Shown when Date Imprint is activated.

Additional information is arrayed along the bottom of the LCD monitor image, more or less duplicating much of the data in the LED display that is seen through the viewfinder when not using live view. These indicators include:

- **Metering method.** Shows whether Matrix, Center-weighted, or Spot metering is selected. Choose before entering live view.

- **Shutter speed.** The currently selected shutter speed.

- **F/stop.** The current f/stop

- **ISO value.** Shows the ISO sensitivity setting, or ISO Auto

- **Shots remaining.** Indicates the number of images remaining on your memory card at the current Image Size and Image Quality settings.

- **Flash ready.** (Not shown.) Shows the electronic flash is fully charged and ready to shoot.

## Shooting in Live View

Shooting stills and movies in live view is easy. Just follow these steps:

1. **Rotate Lv switch.** Activate live view by rotating the switch on top of the camera. The D5200 can be hand-held or mounted on a tripod. (Using a tripod mode makes it easier to obtain and keep sharp focus.) You can exit live view at any time by rotating the Lv button again. It's a momentary contact switch that springs back to its original position when you release it.

2. **Automatic scene selection.** You can choose P, S, A, M, or one of the scene modes manually, but if you choose Auto or Auto (Flash Off), the D5200 will analyze the scene and choose a mode for you automatically, choosing from Portrait, Landscape, Close Up, Night Portrait, or, if none of those apply, it will use the default Auto or Auto (Flash Off) settings.

3. **Zoom in/out.** Check your view by pressing the Zoom In and Zoom Out buttons (located to the right of the color LCD monitor). Five levels of magnification are available, up to 6.7X zoom. A navigation box appears in the lower right of the LCD monitor with a yellow box representing the portion of the image zoomed, just as when you're reviewing photos you've already taken using Playback mode. Use the multi selector keys to change the zoomed area within the full frame. Press the Zoom Out button to zoom out again.

4. **Make exposure adjustments.** While using an automatic exposure mode, you can add or subtract exposure using the EV settings, as described in Chapter 4. Hold down the EV button (just southeast of the shutter release) and rotate the main command dial to add or subtract exposure when using P, S, and A modes. The back-panel color LCD monitor will brighten or darken to represent the exposure change you make.

5. **Shoot.** Press the shutter release all the way down to take a still picture, or press the red movie button to start motion picture filming. Stop filming by pressing the movie button again. Movies up to 4GB in size can be taken (assuming there is sufficient room on your memory card), which limits you to 20 minutes for an HDTV clip.

# Shooting Movies with the D5200

As you've probably gathered, movie making is an extension of the live view concept. Once you've directed the output of the sensor to the LCD monitor, capturing it as a video file—with audio—is relatively easy. All the focus modes and AF-area modes described for plain old live view mode can be applied to movie making, too. Here are some considerations to think about:

- **Stills, too.** You can take a still photograph even while you're shooting a movie clip by pressing the shutter release all the way down. You won't miss a still shot because you're shooting video. However, movie shooting will cease after you take the still, and must be re-activated by pressing the red movie button again.

- **Exposure compensation.** When shooting movies, exposure compensation is available in plus/minus 3EV steps in 1/3EV increments.

- **Size matters.** Individual movie files can be up to 4GB in size (this will vary according to the resolution you select), and no more than 20 or 29 minutes in length (at High and Normal quality, respectively). The speed and capacity of your memory card may provide additional restrictions on size/length.

In the Movie Settings entry of the Shooting menu, you can make the following choices:

- **Movie Quality.** Choose your resolution. Use the Movie Settings entry in the Shooting menu. Or, when live view is activated, and before you start shooting your video clip, you can select the resolution/frame rate of your movie. All use *progressive scan,* in which all the lines are captured one after another in order, except for the single *interlaced scan* choice (60i), which interweaves odd/even lines of two fields per frame.

## WHAT FRAME RATE: 24 fps, 30 fps, or 60 fps?

Even intermediate movie shooters can be confused by the choice between 24 fps and 30 or 60 fps, especially since those are only nominal figures (with the D5200, the 24 fps setting actually yields 23.976 frames per second; 30 fps gives you 29.97 actual "frames" per second; 60 fps is 59.24 fps).

The difference lies in the two "worlds" of motion images, film and video. The standard frame rate for motion picture film is 24 fps, while the video rate, at least in the United States, Japan, and other places using the NTSC standard is 30 fps (actually 60 interlaced *fields* per second) and also manifested as 60 fps. In countries using the PAL system, 25 and 50 fps options are available.

Computer editing software can handle any of these types, and convert between them. The choice between 24 fps and 30/60 fps is determined by what you plan to do with your video.

The short explanation is that, for technical reasons I won't go into here, shooting at 24 fps gives your movie a "film" look, excellent for showing fine detail. However, if your clip has moving subjects, or you pan the camera, 24 fps can produce a jerky effect called "judder." A 30/60 fps rate produces a home-video look that some feel is less desirable, but which is smoother and less jittery when displayed on an electronic monitor. I suggest you try both and use the frame rate that best suits your tastes and video editing software.

Your choices are as follows:

- 1920 × 1080 at 60 fps, interlaced scan (60i)
- 1920 × 1080 at 30 fps, progressive scan (30p)
- 1920 × 1080 at 24 fps, progressive scan (24p)
- 1280 × 720 at 24 fps, progressive scan (24p)
- 640 × 424 at 30 fps, progressive scan (30p) (Useful for video clips displayed on web pages.)

- **Movie Quality.** Choose High quality (to capture up to 20 minutes of action) or Normal quality (for up to 29 minutes, 59 seconds of video per clip). The High setting has a maximum bit rate requirement of 24 Mbps; if your memory card won't handle that, the Normal setting reduces the demand to 12 Mbps, at the cost of some additional compression that reduces the size of the file and cuts resolution/image quality slightly.

- **Microphone.** Here you can set audio sensitivity for the built-in stereo microphones or an optional external mic like the Nikon ME-1. Choose from Auto, High Sensitivity, Medium Sensitivity, Low Sensitivity, or Off. With the Manual Sensitivity setting, a set of volume unit (VU) meter bars appears on the menu screen showing the current sound levels. Press the right directional button to access a screen where you can select a manual sensitivity level from 1 to 20.

- **Manual Movie Settings.** Select On or Off.

## NOT MUCH OF A LIMITATION

Unless you are shooting an entire performance from a fixed position, such as a stage play, the 20/29-minute limitation on HDTV movie duration won't put much of a crimp in your style. Good motion picture practice calls for each production to consist of a series of relatively *short* clips, with 10 to 20 seconds a good average. You can assemble and edit your D5200 movies into one long, finished production using one of the many movie-editing software packages available. Andy Warhol might have been successful with his 1963 five-hour epic *Sleep*, but the rest of us will do better with short sequences of the type produced by the Nikon D5200.

To shoot your movies, follow these steps, which are similar to those for using live view:

1. **Plug in microphone.** If you want to use an external monaural or stereo microphone with a 3.5mm stereo mini plug, attach it to the microphone jack on the left side of the camera.

2. **Start live view.** Activate live view by rotating the live view switch.

3. **Choose a focus mode.** Select from AF-S, AF-F, or M, as described earlier.

4. **Choose an AF-area mode.** Choices include Face-priority AF, Wide-area AF, Normal-area AF, Subject-tracking AF, or Manual focus, as described earlier.

5. **Activate and lock in focus.** This was also described under the live view instructions.

6. **Preview framing.** If you want to preview the image area that will be captured when shooting video, you can press the Info button (the one *on top* of the camera) to show movie indicators. During actual capture, the movie frame area will be enlarged to fill the LCD monitor, so what you see is what you get.

7. **Start/Stop recording.** Press the red movie recording button. Press again to stop recording.

## Viewing Your Movies

Once you've finished recording your movies, they are available for review. Film clips show up during picture review the same as still photos, but they are differentiated by a sprocket holes overlay. Press the OK button to start playback.

During playback, you can perform the following functions:

- **Pause.** Press the multi selector down button to pause the clip during playback. Press the multi selector center button to resume playback.

- **Rewind/Advance.** Press the left/right multi selector buttons to rewind or advance (respectively). Press once for 2X speed, twice for 8X speed, or three times for 16X speed. Hold down the left/right buttons to move to the end or beginning of the clip.

- **Single Frame Rewind/Advance.** Press the multi selector down key to pause the clip, then use the left/right buttons to rewind or advance one frame at a time.

- **Change volume.** Press the Zoom In and Zoom Out buttons to increase/decrease volume.

- **Trim movie.** Press the AE-L/AF-L button while the movie is paused. If you press the button before pausing, it simply adds the Protect attribute to the clip. You must first pause the movie to access the editing features.

- **Exit Playback.** Press the multi selector up button or press the shutter release halfway to exit playback.

- **View menus.** Press the MENU button to interrupt playback to access menus.

## Editing Your Movies

In-camera editing is limited to trimming the beginning or end from a clip, and the clip must be at least two seconds long. For more advanced editing, you'll need an application capable of editing AVI movie clips. Google "AVI Editor" to locate any of the hundreds of free video editors available, or use a commercial product like Corel Video Studio, Adobe Premiere Elements, or Pinnacle Studio. These will let you combine several clips into one movie, add titles, special effects, and transitions between scenes.

To do in-camera editing/trimming, follow these steps:

1. **Start movie clip.** Use the Playback button to start image review, and press OK when the LCD monitor shows a clip you want to edit. It will begin playing.

2. **Activate edit.** To remove video from the beginning of a clip, view the movie until you reach the first frame you want to keep, and then press the down button to pause. To trim video from the end of a clip, watch the movie until you reach the last frame you want to keep and then press the down button to pause.

3. **Access edit screen.** Press the AE-L/AF-L button to display the Edit Movie prompt. (See Figure 6.11.)

4. **Select start/end point.** To remove video from the beginning of the clip, press the up/down multi selector button and highlight either Choose Start Point or Choose End Point, and press OK. The screen shown in Figure 6.12 appears.

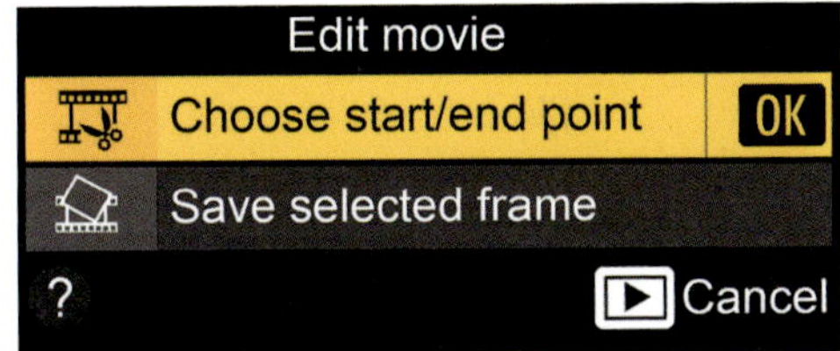


**Figure 6.11** Choose editing options from this menu.

5. **Resume playback.** Press the center button of the multi selector to start or resume playback. You can use the Pause, Rewind, Advance, and Single frame controls described previously to move around within your clip. Rotate the command dial to skip ahead or back 10 seconds in the clip. You can switch back and forth between selecting the start and end points by pressing the AE-L/AF-L button.

6. **Mark trim point.** When you reach the point where you want to trim, press the Pause button (if the movie is not already paused), and then press the multi selector up button. All frames prior to the pause will be deleted if you're in Choose Start Point mode; all frames *after* the pause will be deleted if you're in Choose End Point mode. Your trimmed movie must be at least two seconds long.

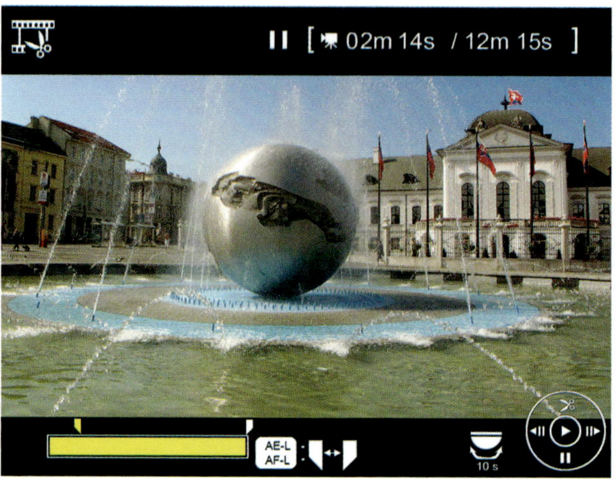

**Figure 6.12**
Edit from this screen.

7. **Confirm trim.** You can choose between saving the trimmed clip as a new file, overwriting the existing file, canceling to return to the trimming screen, or Preview to see the clip that will be saved.

8. **Save movie.** You'll see a Saving Movie message and a green progress bar as the D5200 stores the trimmed clip to your memory card. Storage takes some time, and you don't want to interrupt it to avoid losing your saved clip. So, make sure your camera has a fully charged battery before you start to edit a clip.

## Saving a Frame

You can store any frame from one of your movies as a JPEG still, using the resolution of the video format. Just follow these steps:

1. Pause your movie at the frame you want to save. Press the AE-L/AF-L button to access the Edit Movie screen.

2. Choose Save Selected Frame and press OK.

3. Press the up button to choose Proceed and confirm.

4. Your frame will be stored on the memory card, and will be marked with a scissors icon.

# Tips for Shooting Better Movies

Producing high-quality movies can be a real challenge for amateur photographers. After all, by comparison we're used to watching the best productions that television, video, and motion pictures can offer. Whether it's fair or not, our efforts are compared to what we're used to seeing produced by experts. While this chapter can't make you into a pro videographer, it can help you improve your efforts.

There are a number of different things to consider when planning a video shoot, and when possible, a shooting script and storyboard can help you produce a higher quality video.

## Make a Shooting Script

A shooting script is nothing more than a coordinated plan that covers both audio and video and provides order and structure for your video. A detailed script will cover what types of shots you're going after, what dialogue you're going to use, audio effects, transitions, and graphics. When you first begin shooting movies, your shooting scripts will be very simple. As you gain experience, you'll learn how to tell stories with video, and will map out your script in more detail before you even begin to capture the first sequence.

A shooting script will also help you if you need to shoot out of sequence. For example, you may have several scenes that take place on different days at the same location. It probably will make sense to shoot all those scenes at one time, rather than in the movie's chronological order. You can check the shooting script to see what types of video and audio you need for the separate scenes, as well as what dialogue your "actors" need to deliver (even, if, as is the case for most informal videos, the "lines" are ad-libbed as you shoot).

## Use Storyboards

A storyboard is a series of panels providing visuals of what each scene should look like. While the ones produced by Hollywood are generally of very high quality, there's nothing that says drawing skills are important for this step. Stick figures work just fine if that's the best you can do. The storyboard just helps you visualize locations, placement of actors/actresses, props and furniture, and also helps everyone involved get an idea of what you're trying to show. It also helps show how you want to frame or compose a shot. You can even shoot a series of still photos and transform them into a "storyboard" if you want, as I did in Figure 6.13. In this case, I took pictures of a parade, and then used them to assemble a storyboard to follow when I shot video at a similar parade on a later date.

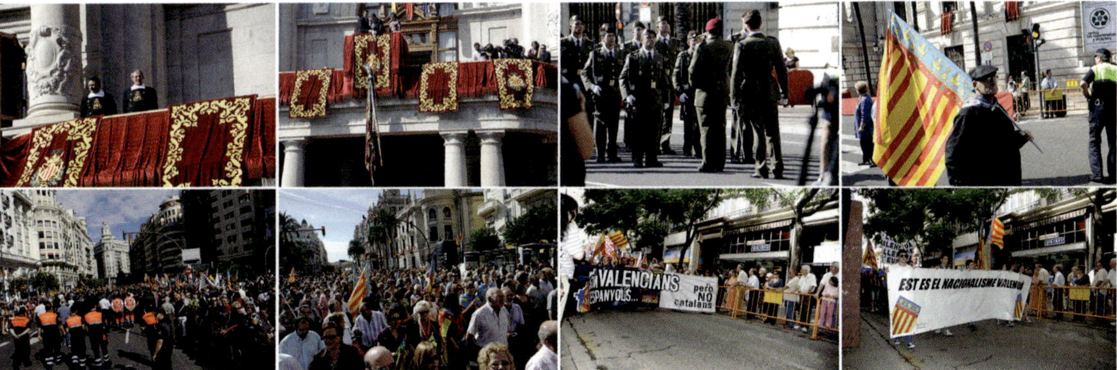

**Figure 6.13** A storyboard is a series of simple sketches or photos to help visualize a segment of video.

# Storytelling in Video

Today's audience is accustomed to fast-paced, short scene storytelling. In order to produce interesting video for such viewers, it's important to view video storytelling as a kind of shorthand code for the more leisurely efforts print media offers. Audio and video should always be advancing the story. While it's okay to let the camera linger from time to time, it should only be for a compelling reason and only briefly.

Composition is one of the most important tools available to you for telling a story in video. However, while you can crop a still frame any old way you like, in movie shooting, several factors restrict your composition, and impose requirements you just don't always have in still photography (although other rules of good composition do apply). Here are some of the key differences to keep in mind when composing movie frames:

- **Horizontal compositions only.** Some subjects, such as basketball players and tall buildings, just lend themselves to vertical compositions. But movies are shown in horizontal format only. So if you're interviewing a local basketball star, you can end up with a worst-case situation like the one shown in Figure 6.14. Using the D5200's FH (1920 × 1080) format, or 1280 × 720 formats, you are limited to relatively wide frames. If you want to show how tall your subject is, it's often impractical to move back far enough to show him full-length. You really can't capture a vertical composition. Tricks like getting down on the floor and shooting up at your subject can exaggerate the perspective, but aren't a perfect solution.

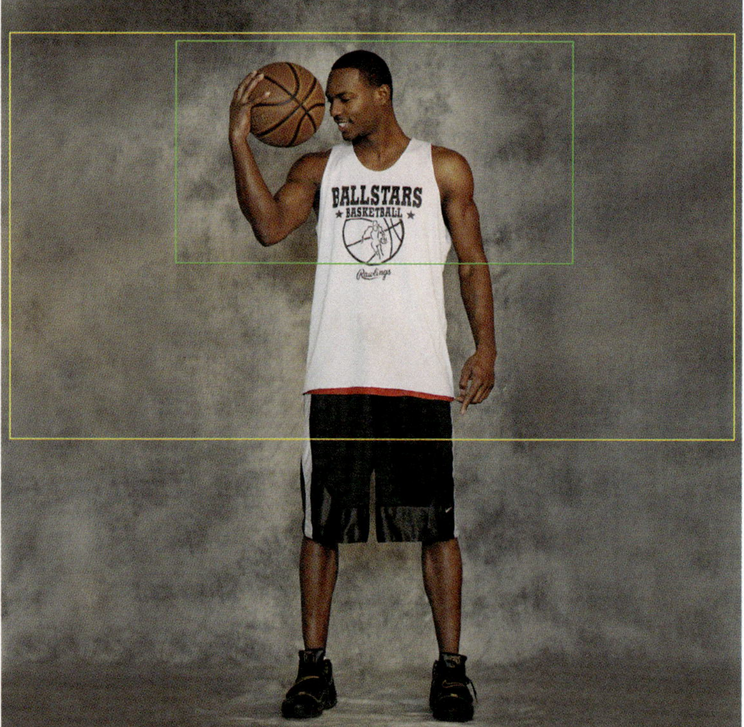


**Figure 6.14**

Movie shooting requires you to fit all your subjects into a horizontally oriented frame.

- **Wasted space at the sides.** Moving in to frame the basketball player as outlined by the yellow box in Figure 6.14, means that you're still forced to leave a lot of empty space on either side. (Of course, you can fill that space with other people and/or interesting stuff, but that defeats your intent of concentrating on your main subject.) So when faced with some types of subjects in a horizontal frame, you can be creative, or move in *really* tight. For example, if I was willing to give up the "height" aspect of my composition, I could have framed the shot as shown by the green box in the figure, and wasted less of the image area at either side of the model. The least attractive option is to switch to a movie-recording format that has less "wide-screen" perspective, specifically 640 × 424 pixels, in which case you lose the resolution advantage of the HD aspect ratio.

- **Seamless (or seamed) transitions.** Unless you're telling a picture story with a photo essay, still pictures often stand alone. But with movies, each of your compositions must relate to the shot that preceded it, and the one that follows. It can be jarring to jump from a long shot to a tight close-up unless the director—you—is very creative. Another common error is the "jump cut" in which successive shots vary only slightly in camera angle, making it appear that the main subject has "jumped" from one place to another. (Although everyone from French New Wave director Jean-Luc Goddard to Guy Ritchie—Madonna's ex—has used jump cuts effectively in their films.) The rule of thumb is to vary the camera angle by at least 30 degrees between shots to make it appear to be seamless. Unless you prefer that your images flaunt convention and appear to be "seamy."

- **The time dimension.** Unlike still photography, with motion pictures there's a lot more emphasis on using a series of images to build on each other to tell a story. Static shots where the camera is mounted on a tripod and everything is shot from the same distance are a recipe for dull videos. Watch a television program sometime and notice how often camera shots change distances and directions. Viewers are used to this variety and have come to expect it. Professional video productions are often done with multiple cameras shooting from different angles and positions. But many professional productions are shot with just one camera and careful planning, and you can do just fine with your camera.

Within those compositional restraints, you still have a great deal of flexibility. It only takes a second or two for an establishing shot to impart the necessary information. For example, many of the scenes for a video documenting a model being photographed in a Rock and Roll music setting might be close-ups and talking heads, but an establishing shot showing the studio where the video was captured helps set the scene.

Provide variety too. Change camera angles and perspectives often and never leave a static scene on the screen for a long period of time. (You can record a static scene for a reasonably long period and then edit in other shots that cut away and back to the longer scene with close-ups that show each person talking.)

When editing, keep transitions basic! I can't stress this one enough. Watch a television program or movie. The action "jumps" from one scene or person to the next. Fancy transitions that involve exotic "wipes," dissolves, or cross fades take too long for the average viewer and make your video ponderous.

Here's a look at the different types of commonly used compositional tools:

- **Establishing shot.** Much like it sounds, this type of composition, as shown at left in Figure 6.15, establishes the scene and tells the viewer where the action is taking place. Let's say you're shooting a video of your offspring's move to college; the establishing shot could be a wide shot of the campus with a sign welcoming you to the school in the foreground. Another example would be for a child's birthday party; the establishing shot could be the front of the house decorated with birthday signs and streamers or a shot of the dining room table decked out with party favors and a candle-covered birthday cake. Or, in Figure 6.15, I wanted to show the studio where the video was shot.

- **Medium shot.** This shot is composed from about waist to head room (some space above the subject's head). It's useful for providing variety from a series of close-ups and also makes for a useful first look at a speaker. (See at right in Figure 6.15.)

- **Close-up.** The close-up, usually described as "from shirt pocket to head room," provides a good composition for someone talking directly to the camera. Although it's common to have your talking head centered in the shot, that's not a requirement. At left in Figure 6.16 the subject was offset to the right. This would allow other images, especially graphics or titles, to be superimposed in the frame in a "real" (professional) production. But the compositional technique can be used with your videos, too, even if special effects are not going to be added.

- **Extreme close-up.** When I went through broadcast training back in the '70s, this shot was described as the "big talking face" shot and we were actively discouraged from employing it. Styles and tastes change over the years and now the big talking face is much more commonly used (maybe people are better looking these days?) and so this view may be appropriate. Just remember, your camera is capable of shooting in high-definition video and you may be playing the video on a high-def TV; be careful that you use this composition on a face that can stand up to high definition. (See right in Figure 6.16.)

- **"Two" shot.** A two shot shows a pair of subjects in one frame. (See Figure 6.17, left.) They can be side by side or one in the foreground and one in the background. This does not have to be a head to ground composition. Subjects can be standing or seated. A "three shot" is the same principle except that three people are in the frame.

- **Over-the-shoulder shot.** Long a composition of interview programs, the "over-the-shoulder shot" uses the rear of one person's head and shoulder to serve as a frame for the other person. This puts the viewer's perspective as that of the person facing away from the camera. (See Figure 6.17, right.)

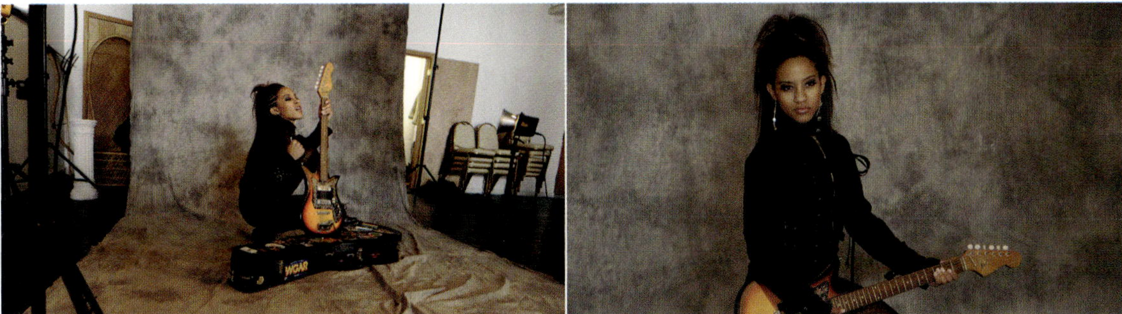

**Figure 6.15** (Left) An establishing shot from a distance sets the stage for closer views. (Right) A medium shot is used to bring the viewer into a scene without shocking them. It can be used to introduce a character and provide context via their surroundings.

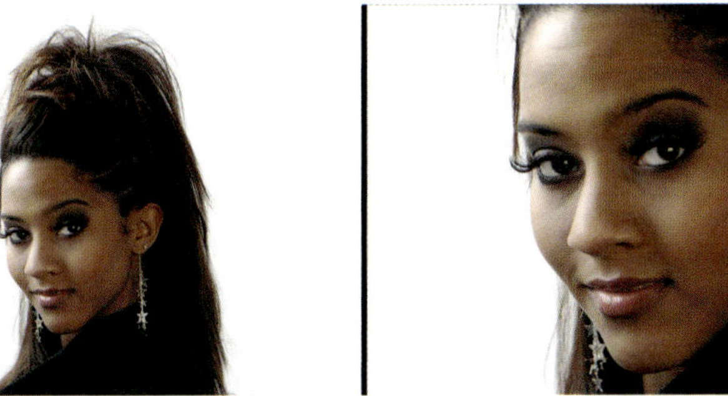

**Figure 6.16** (Left) A close-up generally shows the full face with a little head room at the top and down to the shoulders at the bottom of the frame. (Right) An extreme close-up is a very tight shot that cuts off everything above the top of the head and below the chin (or even closer!). Be careful using this shot since many of us look better from a distance!

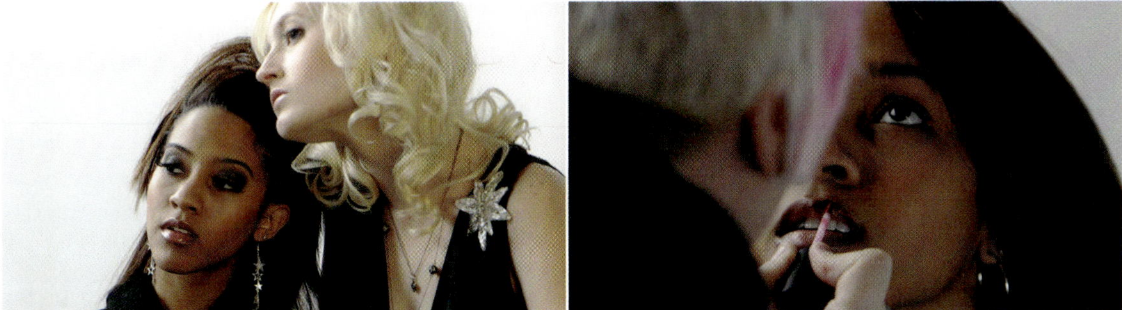

**Figure 6.17** At left, a "two-shot" features two people in the frame. This version can be framed at various distances such as medium or close up. At right, an "over-the-shoulder" shot is a popular shot for interview programs. It helps make the viewers feel like they're asking the questions.

# Lighting for Video

Much like in still photography, how you handle light pretty much can make or break your videography. Lighting for video can be more complicated than lighting for still photography, since both subject and camera movement is often part of the process.

Lighting for video presents several concerns. First off, you want enough illumination to create a useable video. Beyond that, you want to use light to help tell your story or increase drama. Let's take a better look at both.

## Illumination

You can significantly improve the quality of your video by increasing the light falling in the scene. This is true indoors or out, by the way. While it may seem like sunlight is more than enough, it depends on how much contrast you're dealing with. If your subject is in shadow (which can help them from squinting) or wearing a ball cap, a video light can help make them look a lot better.

Lighting choices for amateur videographers are a lot better these days than they were a decade or two ago. An inexpensive incandescent video light, which will easily fit in a camera bag, can be found for $15 or $20. You can even get a good-quality LED video light for less than $100. (See Figure 6.18.) Work lights sold at many home improvement stores can also serve as video lights since you can set the camera's white balance to correct for any color casts. You'll need to mount these lights on a tripod or other support, or, perhaps, to a bracket that fastens to the tripod socket on the bottom of the camera.

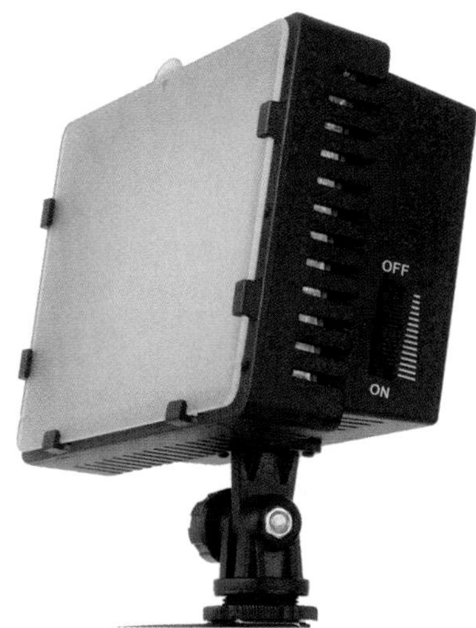


**Figure 6.18** Inexpensive LED lights work well for video.

Much of the challenge depends upon whether you're just trying to add some fill light on your subject versus trying to boost the light on an entire scene. A small video light will do just fine for the former. It won't handle the latter.

## Creative Lighting

While ramping up the light intensity will produce better technical quality in your video, it won't necessarily improve the artistic quality of it. Whether we're outdoors or indoors, we're used to seeing light come from above. Videographers need to consider how they position their lights to provide even illumination while up high enough to angle shadows down low and out of sight of the camera.

When considering lighting for video, there are several factors. One is the quality of the light. It can either be hard (direct) or soft (diffused). Hard light is good for showing detail, but can also be very harsh and unforgiving. "Softening" the light, but diffusing it somehow, can reduce the intensity of the light but make for a kinder, gentler light as well.

While mixing light sources isn't always a good idea, one approach is to combine window light with supplemental lighting. Position your subject with the window to one side and bring in either a supplemental light or a reflector to the other side for reasonably even lighting.

## Lighting Styles

Some lighting styles are more heavily used than others. Some forms are used for special effects, while others are designed to be invisible. At its most basic, lighting just illuminates the scene, but when used properly it can also create drama. Let's look at some types of lighting styles:

- **Three-point lighting.** This is a basic lighting setup for one person. A main light illuminates the strong side of a person's face, while a fill light lights up the other side. A third light is then positioned above and behind the subject to light the back of the head and shoulders. (See Figure 6.19.)

- **Flat lighting.** Use this type of lighting to provide illumination and nothing more. It calls for a variety of lights and diffusers set to raise the light level in a space enough for good video reproduction, but not to create a particular mood or emphasize a particular scene or individual. With flat lighting, you're trying to create even lighting levels throughout the video space and minimize any shadows. Generally, the lights are placed up high and angled downward (or possibly pointed straight up to bounce off of a white ceiling). (See Figure 6.20.)

- **"Ghoul lighting."** This is the style of lighting used for old horror movies. The idea is to position the light down low, pointed upward. It's such an unnatural style of lighting that it makes its targets seem weird and "ghoulish."

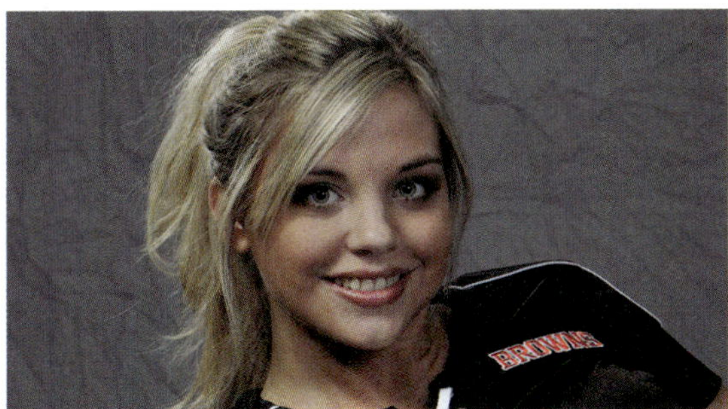

**Figure 6.19** With three-point lighting, two lights are placed in front and to the side of the subject (45-degree angles are ideal) and positioned about a foot higher than the subject's head. Another light is directed on the background in order to separate the subject and the background.

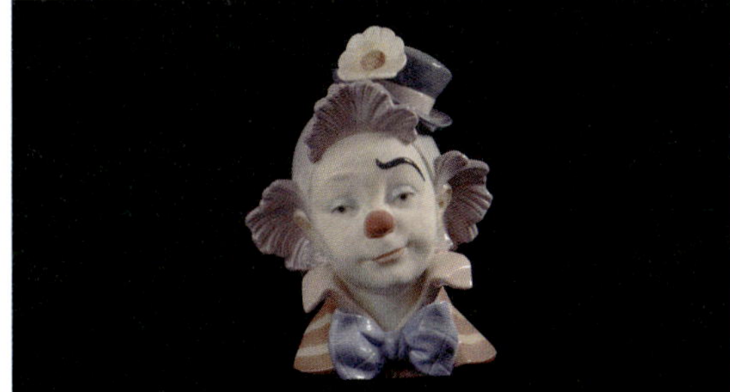

**Figure 6.20** Flat lighting is another approach for creating even illumination. Here the lights can be bounced off of a white ceiling and walls to fill in shadows as much as possible. It is a flexible lighting approach since the subject can change positions without needing a change in light direction.

- **Outdoor lighting.** While shooting outdoors may seem easier because the sun provides more light, it also presents its own problems. As a general rule of thumb, keep the sun behind you when you're shooting video outdoors, except when shooting faces (anything from a medium shot and closer) since the viewer won't want to see a squinting subject. When shooting another human this way, put the sun behind her and use a video light to balance light levels between the foreground and background. If the sun is simply too bright, position the subject in the shade and use the video light for your main illumination. Using reflectors (white board panels or aluminum foil covered cardboard panels are cheap options) can also help balance light effectively.

# Audio

When it comes to making a successful video, audio quality is one of those things that separates the professionals from the amateurs. We're used to watching top-quality productions on television and in the movies, yet the average person has no idea how much effort goes in to producing what seems to be "natural" sound. Much of the sound you hear in such productions is actually recorded on carefully controlled sound stages and "sweetened" with a variety of sound effects and other recordings of "natural" sound.

## Tips for Better Audio

Since recording high-quality audio is such a challenge, it's a good idea to do everything possible to maximize recording quality. Here are some ideas for improving the quality of the audio your camera records:

- **Get the camera and its microphone close to the speaker.** The farther the microphone is from the audio source, the less effective it will be in picking up that sound. While having to position the camera and its built-in microphone closer to the subject affects your lens choices and lens perspective options, it will make the most of your audio source. Of course, if you're using a very wide-angle lens, getting too close to your subject can have unflattering results, so don't take this advice too far. It's important to think carefully about what sounds you want to capture. If you're shooting video of an acoustic combo that's not using a PA system, you'll want the microphone close to them, but not so close that, say, only the lead singer or instrumentalist is picked up, while the players at either side fade off into the background.

- **Use an external microphone.** You'll recall the description of the camera's external microphone port in Chapter 2. As noted, this port accepts a stereo mini-plug from a standard external microphone, allowing you to achieve considerably higher audio quality for your movies than is possible with the camera's built-in microphones (which are disabled when an external mic is plugged in). An external microphone reduces the amount of camera-induced noise that is picked up and recorded on your audio track. (The action of the lens as it focuses can be audible when the built-in microphones are active.)

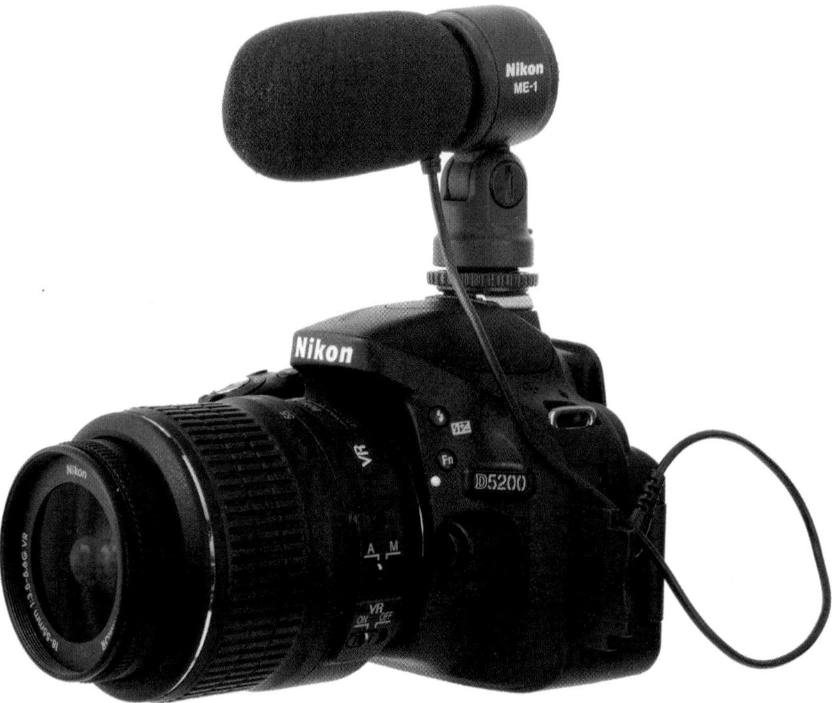

**Figure 6.21**
The Nikon ME-1 microphone provides much better sound than the D5200's built-in mics.

The external microphone port can provide plug-in power for microphones that can take their power from this sort of outlet rather than from a battery in the microphone. You may find suitable microphones from companies such as Shure and Audio-Technica. If you are on a quest for really superior audio quality, you can even obtain a portable mixer that can plug into this jack, such as the affordable Rolls MX124 (around $150) (www.rolls.com), letting you use multiple high-quality microphones (up to four) to record your soundtrack. Nikon offers the ME-1 microphone (see Figure 6.21) that provides good quality sound.

■ **Hide the microphone.** Combine the first few tips by using an external mic, and getting it as close to your subject as possible. If you're capturing a single person, you can always use a lapel microphone (described in the next section). But if you want a single mic to capture sound from multiple sources, your best bet may be to hide it somewhere in the shot. Put it behind a vase, using duct tape to fasten the microphone and fix the mic cable out of sight (if you're not using a wireless microphone).

■ **Turn off any sound makers you can.** Little things like fans and air handling units aren't obvious to the human ear, but will be picked up by the microphone. Turn off any machinery or devices that you can plus make sure cell phones are set to silent mode. Also, do what you can to minimize sounds such as wind, radio, television, or people talking in the background.

■ **Make sure to record some "natural" sound.** If you're shooting video at an event of some kind, make sure you get some background sound that you can add to your audio as desired in post-production.

- **Consider recording audio separately.** Lip-syncing is probably beyond most of the people you're going to be shooting, but there's nothing that says you can't record narration separately and add it later. It's relatively easy if you learn how to use simple software video-editing programs like iMovie (for the Macintosh) or Windows Movie Maker (for Windows PCs). Any time the speaker is off-camera, you can work with separately recorded narration rather than recording the speaker on-camera. This can produce much cleaner sound.

## External Microphones

The single most important thing you can do to improve your audio quality is to use an external microphone. The D5200's internal stereo microphones mounted on the front of the camera will do a decent job, but they have some significant drawbacks, partially spelled out in the previous section.

- **Camera noise.** There are plenty of noise sources emanating from the camera, including your own breathing and rustling around as the camera shifts in your hand. Manual zooming is bound to affect your sound, and your fingers will fall directly in front of the built-in mics as you change focal lengths. An external microphone isolates the sound recording from camera noise.

- **Distance.** Anytime your D5200 is located more than 6–8 feet from your subjects or sound source, the audio will suffer. An external unit allows you to place the mic right next to your subject.

- **Improved quality.** Obviously, Canon wasn't able to install a super-expensive, super high-quality microphone. Not all owners of the D5200 would be willing to pay the premium, especially if they didn't plan to shoot much video themselves. An external microphone will almost always be of better quality.

- **Directionality.** The D5200's internal microphones generally record only sounds directly in front of them. An external microphone can be either of the directional type or omnidirectional, depending on whether you want to "shotgun" your sound or record more ambient sound.

You can choose from several different types of microphones, each of which has its own advantages and disadvantages. If you're serious about movie making with your D5200, you might want to own more than one. Common configurations include:

- **Shotgun microphones.** These can be mounted directly on your D5200. I prefer to use a bracket, which further isolates the microphone from any camera noise. One thing to keep in mind is that while the shotgun mic will generally ignore any sound coming from *behind* it, it will pick up any sound it is pointed at, even *behind* your subject. You may be capturing video and audio of someone you're interviewing in a restaurant, and not realize you're picking up the lunchtime conversation of the diners seated in the table behind your subject. Outdoors, you may record your speaker, as well as the traffic on a busy street or freeway in the background.

- **Lapel microphones.** Also called *lavalieres*, these microphones attach to the subject's clothing and pick up their voice with the best quality. You'll need a long enough cord or a wireless mic (described later). These are especially good for video interviews, so whether you're producing a documentary or grilling relatives for a family history, you'll want one of these.

- **Hand-held microphones.** If you're capturing a singer crooning a tune, or want your subject to mimic famed faux newscaster Wally Ballou, a hand-held mic may be your best choice. They serve much the same purpose as a lapel microphone, and they're more intrusive—but that may be the point. A hand-held microphone can make a great prop for your fake newscast! The speaker can talk right into the microphone, point it at another person, or use it to record ambient sound. If your narrator is not going to appear on-camera, one of these can be an inexpensive way to improve sound.

- **Wired and wireless external microphones.** This option is the most expensive, but you get a receiver and a transmitter (both battery-powered, so you'll need to make sure you have enough batteries). The transmitter is connected to the microphone, and the receiver is connected to your D5200. In addition to being less klutzy and enabling you to avoid having wires on view in your scene, wireless mics let you record sounds that are physically located some distance from your camera. Of course, you need to keep in mind the range of your device, and be aware of possible signal interference from other electronic components in the vicinity.

## WIND NOISE REDUCTION

Always use the windscreen provided with an external microphone to reduce the effect of noise produced by even light breezes blowing over the microphone. Many mics include a low-cut filter to further reduce wind noise. However, these can also affect other sounds. External mics often have their own low-cut filter switch.

7

# Advanced Techniques

I've saved some advanced techniques for this chapter, which devotes a little extra space to some special features of the Nikon D5200. This chapter covers GPS techniques, Wi-Fi, and special exposure options, including time-lapse photography and very long and very short exposures.

## Continuous Shooting

The Nikon D5200's continuous shooting mode reminds me how far digital photography has brought us. The first accessory I purchased when I worked as a sports photographer some years ago was a motor drive for my film SLR. It enabled me to snap off a series of shots in rapid succession, which came in very handy when a fullback broke through the line and headed for the end zone. Even a seasoned action photographer can miss the decisive instant when a crucial block is made, or a baseball superstar's bat shatters and pieces of cork fly out. Continuous shooting simplifies taking a series of pictures, either to ensure that one has more or less the exact moment you want to capture or to capture a sequence that is interesting as a collection of successive images. Even simple plays, like a layup, seemed more exciting when captured in a sequence of shots, as in Figure 7.1.

To use the D5200's continuous shooting mode, press the drive mode button on top of the camera (to the immediate right of the mode dial) and choose Continuous L (up to 3 fps) or Continuous H (up to 5 fps). Thereafter, when you partially depress the shutter button, the viewfinder will display at the right side a number representing the maximum number of shots you can take at the current quality settings. The large buffer in the D5200 will generally allow you to take as many as 35 JPEG Fine shots in a single burst, or 8 RAW photos.

To increase this number, reduce the image-quality setting by switching to a lower JPEG quality setting, such as JPEG Normal, or by reducing the D5200's resolution from L to M or S. The reason the size of your bursts is limited is that continuous images are first shuttled into the D5200's internal memory buffer, then doled out to the Secure Digital card as quickly as they can be written to

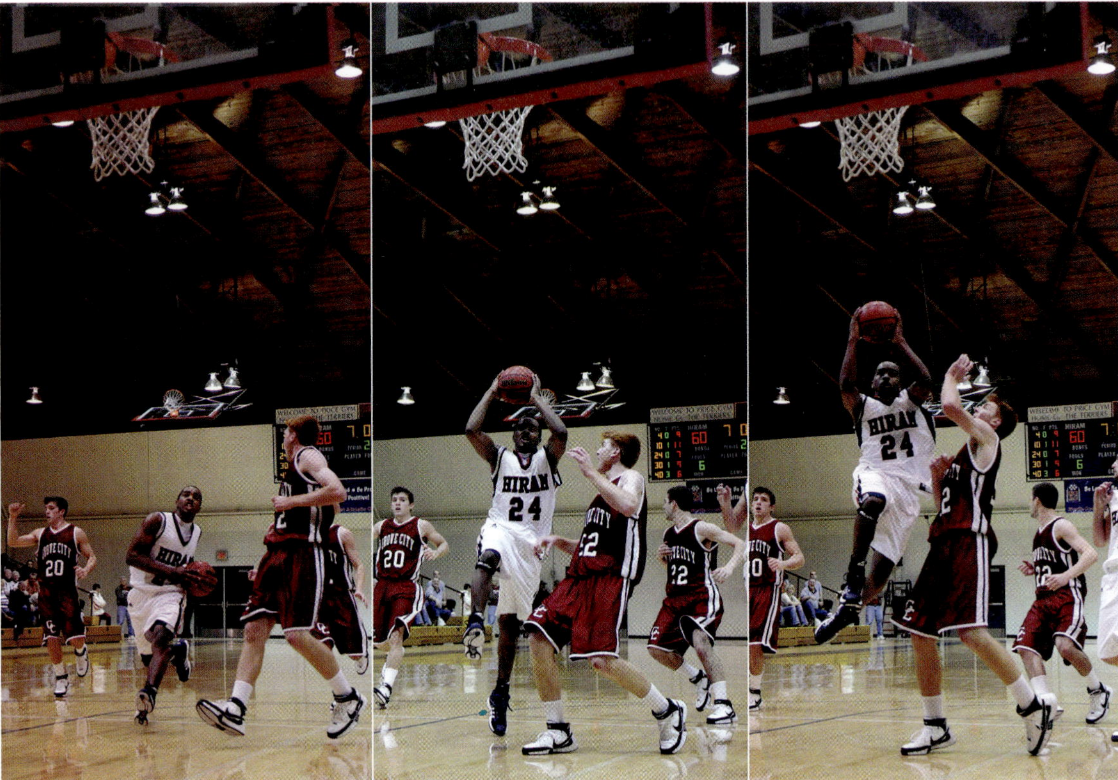

**Figure 7.1** Continuous shooting allows you to capture an entire sequence of exciting moments as they unfold.

the card. Technically, the D5200 takes the RAW data received from the digital image processor and converts it to the output format you've selected—either JPG or NEF (RAW)—and deposits it in the buffer ready to store on the card.

This internal "smart" buffer can suck up photos much more quickly than the SD card and, indeed, some memory cards are significantly faster or slower than others. When the buffer fills, you can't take any more continuous shots until the D5200 has written some of them to the card, making more room in the buffer. You should keep in mind that faster SD cards write images more quickly, freeing up buffer space faster. Today, SD cards are speed-rated using a "Class" figure, with Class 4 (4 megabits per second transfer speed) being the slowest units commonly available. Most SD cards on the market are at least Class 6 (6 megabits per second), with the most common "speedy" cards rated as Class 10 (at least 10 megabits per second). We're starting to see SDXC (Secure Digital Extra Capacity) memory cards given a Class 10 designation, but with read/write speeds that actually top out at 20 megabits per second. (Theoretically, SDXC cards could eventually have speeds that are 10 to 20 times faster.)

The choice between Continuous L or Continuous H will depend on the kind of shooting you want to do. Here are some guidelines:

- **5 fps.** The max rate of 5 fps is available when using Continuous H mode. Use this for sports and other subjects where you want to optimize your chances of capturing the decisive moment. Perhaps you're shooting some active kids and want to grab their most appealing expressions. This fast frame rate can improve the odds. However, there is no guarantee that even at 5 fps the crucial instant won't occur *between* frames. (A ball pitched at 90 miles per hour travels 18 feet between each frame when you're shooting at 5 fps.) For example, when shooting major league baseball games, if I want to shoot a batter, I keep both eyes open, and keep one of them on the pitcher. Then, I start taking my sequence just as the pitcher releases the ball. My goal is to capture the batter making contact with the ball. But even at 5 fps, I find that a hitter connects between frames. I usually must take pictures of a couple dozen at-bats to get a shot of bat and ball connecting.

- **3.0 fps.** When using Continuous L, the slower rate can be useful for activities that aren't quite so fast moving. But, there's another benefit. Using the fastest frame rate means that your camera may fill up its buffer and won't be ready for the next sequence. If you don't want to miss any sequences, using a slightly slower frame rate can help prevent buffer overload. Use this rate when you just want to be able to take pictures quickly, and aren't interested in filling up your memory card with mostly duplicated images. Slow frame rates are good for bracketing, too. Set the D5200 to take a three-frame bracket burst, and you can take all three with one press of the shutter release. The camera will stop shooting after three images, even if you continue to hold down the shutter release. You'll find that slower frame rates also come in handy for subjects that are moving around in interesting ways (photographic models come to mind) but don't change their looks or poses quickly enough to merit a 5 fps burst.

## A Tiny Slice of Time

Exposures that seem impossibly brief can reveal a world we didn't know existed. In the 1930s, Dr. Harold Edgerton, a professor of electrical engineering at MIT, pioneered high-speed photography using a repeating electronic flash unit he patented called the *stroboscope*. As the inventor of the electronic flash, he popularized its use to freeze objects in motion, and you've probably seen his photographs of bullets piercing balloons and drops of milk forming a coronet-shaped splash.

Electronic flash freezes action by virtue of its extremely short duration—as brief as 1/50,000th second or less. Although the D5200's built-in flash unit can give you these ultra-quick glimpses of moving subjects, an external flash, such as one of the Nikon Speedlights, offers even more versatility. You can read more about using electronic flash to stop action in Chapter 12.

Of course, the D5200 is fully capable of immobilizing all but the fastest movement using only its shutter speeds, which range all the way up to 1/4,000th second. Indeed, you'll rarely have need for such a brief shutter speed in ordinary shooting. (For the record, I don't believe I've *ever* used a shutter speed of 1/4,000th second.) But if you wanted to use an aperture of f/1.8 at ISO 200 outdoors in bright sunlight, for some reason, a shutter speed of 1/4,000th second would more than do the job. You'd need a faster shutter speed only if you moved the ISO setting to a higher sensitivity (but why would you do that?). Under less than full sunlight, 1/4,000th second is more than fast enough for any conditions you're likely to encounter.

Most sports action can be frozen at 1/2,000th second or slower, and for many sports a slower shutter speed is actually preferable—for example, to allow the wheels of a racing automobile or motorcycle, or the rotors on a helicopter to blur realistically, as shown in Figure 7.2. At top, a 1/1,000th second shutter speed effectively stopped the rotors of the helicopter, making it look like a crash was impending. At bottom, I used a slower 1/250th second shutter speed to allow enough blur to make this a true action picture.

But if you want to do some exotic action-freezing photography without resorting to electronic flash, the D5200's top shutter speed is at your disposal. Here are some things to think about when exploring this type of high-speed photography:

- **You'll need a lot of light.** High shutter speeds cut very fine slices of time and sharply reduce the amount of illumination that reaches your sensor. To use 1/4,000th second at an aperture of f/6.3, you'd need an ISO setting of 1600—even in full daylight. To use an f/stop smaller than f/6.3 or an ISO setting lower than 1600, you'd need *more* light than full daylight provides. (That's why electronic flash units work so well for high-speed photography when used as the sole illumination; they provide both the effect of a brief shutter speed and the high levels of illumination needed.)

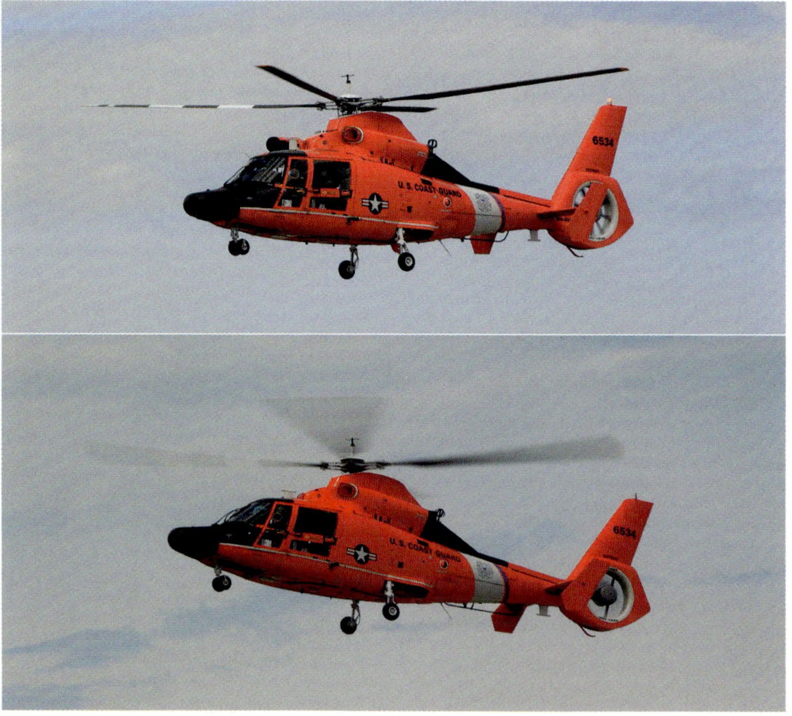

**Figure 7.2**
A little blur can be a good thing, as these shots of a helicopter at 1/1000th second (top) and 1/250th second (bottom) show.

- **Forget about reciprocity failure.** If you're an old-time film shooter, you might recall that very brief shutter speeds (as well as very high light levels and very *long* exposures) produced an effect called *reciprocity failure,* in which given exposures ended up providing less than the calculated value because of the way film responded to very short, very intense, or very long exposures of light. Solid-state sensors don't suffer from this defect, so you don't need to make an adjustment when using high shutter speeds (or brief flash bursts).

- **High shutter speeds with electronic flash.** You might be tempted to use an electronic flash with a high shutter speed. Perhaps you want to stop some action in daylight with a brief shutter speed and use electronic flash only as supplemental illumination to fill in the shadows. Unfortunately, under most conditions you can't use flash in subdued illumination with your D5200 at any shutter speed faster than 1/200th second. That's the fastest speed at which the camera's focal plane shutter is fully open: at shorter speeds, the "slit" described above comes into play, so that the flash will expose only the small portion of the sensor exposed by the slit throughout its duration. (Check out "High Speed Sync" in Chapter 12 if you want to see how you *can* use shutter speeds shorter than 1/250th second, albeit at much-reduced effective power levels.)

## Working with Short Exposures

You can have a lot of fun exploring the kinds of pictures you can take using very brief exposure times, whether you decide to take advantage of the action-stopping capabilities of your built-in or external electronic flash or work with the Nikon D5200's faster shutter speeds. Here are a few ideas to get you started:

- **Take revealing images.** Fast shutter speeds can help you reveal the real subject behind the façade, by freezing constant motion to capture an enlightening moment in time. Legendary fashion/portrait photographer Philippe Halsman used leaping photos of famous people, such as the Duke and Duchess of Windsor, Richard Nixon, and Salvador Dali to illuminate their real selves. Halsman said, "*When you ask a person to jump, his attention is mostly directed toward the act of jumping and the mask falls so that the real person appears.*" Try some high-speed portraits of people you know in motion to see how they appear when concentrating on something other than the portrait. (See Figure 7.3.)

- **Create unreal images.** High-speed photography can also produce photographs that show your subjects in ways that are quite unreal. A motocross cyclist leaping over a ramp, but with all motion stopped so that the rider and machine look as if they were frozen in mid-air, make for an unusual picture. When we're accustomed to seeing subjects in motion, seeing them stopped in time can verge on the surreal.

- **Capture unseen perspectives.** Some things are *never* seen in real life, except when viewed in a stop-action photograph. Edgerton's balloon bursts were only a starting point. Freeze a hummingbird in flight for a view of wings that never seem to stop. Or, capture the splashes as liquid falls into a bowl, as shown in Figure 7.4. No electronic flash was required for this image (and wouldn't have illuminated the water in the bowl as evenly). Instead, two high-intensity lamps and an ISO setting of 1600 allowed the camera to capture this image at 1/2,000th second.

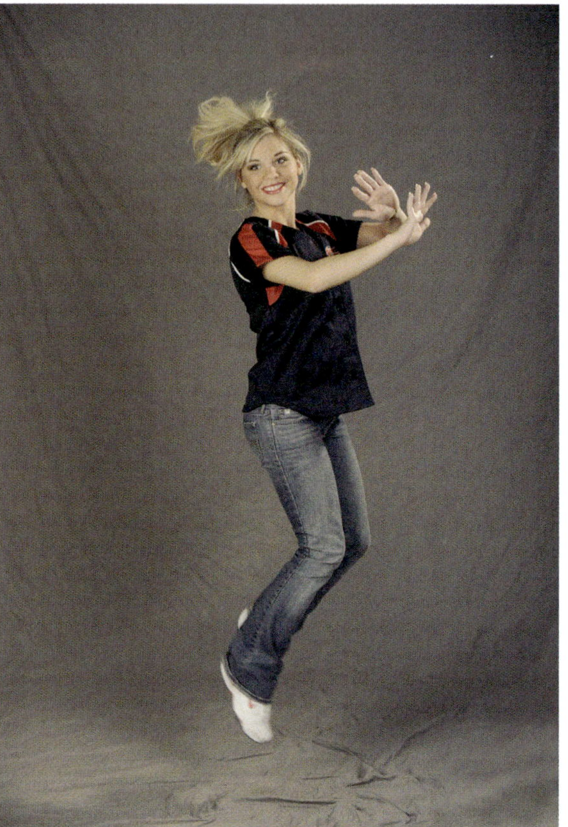

**Figure 7.3**
Freeze your subjects in mid-jump to reveal a whole new side of their personality.

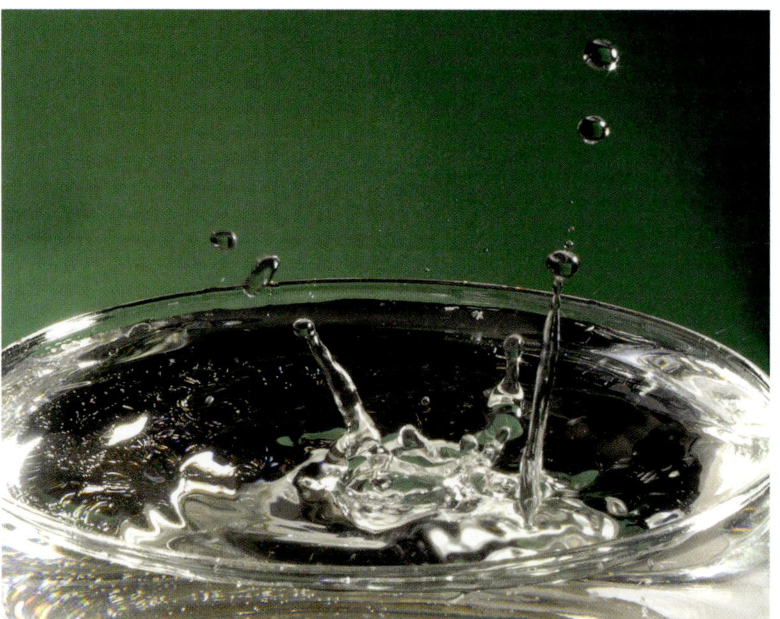

**Figure 7.4**
A large amount of artificial illumina-tion and an ISO 1600 sensitivity set-ting allowed captur-ing this shot at 1/2,000th second without use of an electronic flash.

■ **Vanquish camera shake and gain new angles.** Here's an idea that's so obvious it isn't always explored to its fullest extent. A high enough shutter speed can free you from the tyranny of a tripod, making it easier to capture new angles, or to shoot quickly while moving around, especially with longer lenses. I tend to use a monopod or tripod for almost everything when I'm not using an image-stabilized lens, and I end up missing some shots because of a reluctance to adjust my camera support to get a higher, lower, or different angle. If you have enough light and can use an f/stop wide enough to permit a high shutter speed, you'll find a new freedom to choose your shots (see Figure 7.5). I have a favored 170mm-500mm lens that I use for sports and wildlife photography, almost invariably with a tripod, as I don't find the "reciprocal of the focal length" rule particularly helpful in most cases. I would *not* hand-hold this hefty lens at its 500mm setting with a 1/500th second shutter speed under most circumstances. Nor, if you want to account for the crop factor, would I use 1/750th second. However, at 1/2,000th second or faster, it's entirely possible for a steady hand to use this lens without a tripod or monopod's extra support, and I've found that my whole approach to shooting animals and other elusive subjects changes in high-speed mode. Selective focus allows dramatically isolating my prey wide open at f/6.3, too. Of course, at such a high shutter speed, you may need to boost your ISO setting—even when shooting outdoors.

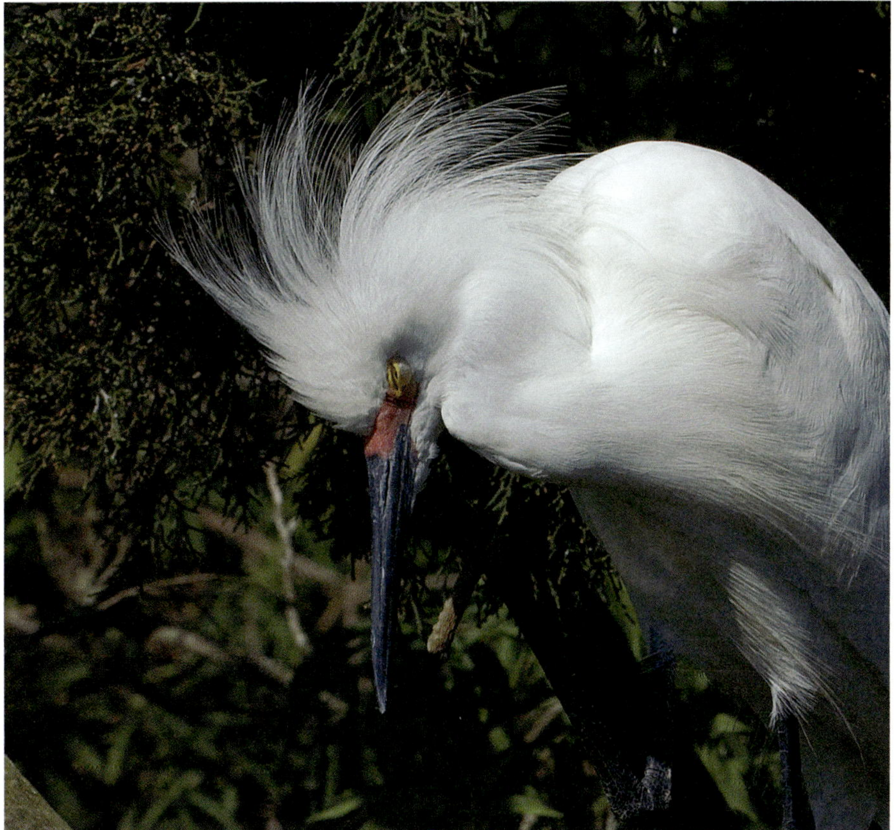

**Figure 7.5**
Outdoors, you may need a shutter speed of 1/2,000th second to hand-hold a 500mm lens to capture distant wildlife.

# Long Exposures

Longer exposures are a doorway into another world, showing us how even familiar scenes can look much different when photographed over periods measured in seconds. At night, long exposures produce streaks of light from moving, illuminated subjects like automobiles or amusement park rides. Extra-long exposures of seemingly pitch-dark subjects can reveal interesting views using light levels barely bright enough to see by. At any time of day, including daytime (in which case you'll often need the help of neutral-density filters to make the long exposure practical), long exposures can cause moving objects to vanish entirely, because they don't remain stationary long enough to register in a photograph.

## Three Ways to Take Long Exposures

There are actually three common types of lengthy exposures: *timed exposures*, *bulb exposures*, and *time exposures*. The D5200 offers only the first two, but once you understand all three, you'll see why Nikon made the choices it did. Because of the length of the exposure, all of the following techniques should be used with a tripod to hold the camera steady.

- **Timed exposures.** These are long exposures from 1 second to 30 seconds, measured by the camera itself. To take a picture in this range, simply use Manual or S modes and use the command dial to set the shutter speed to the length of time you want, choosing from preset speeds of 1.0, 1.5, 2.0, 3.0, 4.0, 6.0, 8.0, 10.0, 15.0, 20.0, or 30.0 seconds (if you've specified 1/2 stop increments for exposure adjustments), or 1.0, 1.3, 1.6, 2.0, 2.5, 3.2, 4.0, 5.0, 6.0, 8.0, 10.0, 13.0, 15.0, 20.0, 25.0, and 30.0 seconds (if you're using 1/3 stop increments). The advantage of timed exposures is that the camera does all the calculating for you. There's no need for a stop-watch. If you review your image on the LCD and decide to try again with the exposure doubled or halved, you can dial in the correct exposure with precision. The disadvantage of timed exposures is that you can't take a photo for longer than 30 seconds.

- **Bulb exposures.** This type of exposure is so-called because in the olden days the photographer squeezed and held an air bulb attached to a tube that provided the force necessary to keep the shutter open. Traditionally, a bulb exposure is one that lasts as long as the shutter release button is pressed; when you release the button, the exposure ends. To make a bulb exposure with the D5200, set the camera on Manual mode and use the command dial to select the shutter speed immediately after 30 seconds—buLb. Then, press the shutter to start the exposure, and press it again to close the shutter.

  Of course, holding down the shutter release on the camera can create camera motion blur. So you might want to use the WR-R10 (transceiver)/WR-T10 (transmitter) wireless remote control system, described in the section that follows. You can also use the corded MC-DC2 remote controller, which plugs into the accessory terminal on the camera, or the equivalent terminal on the GP-1 GPS unit (when using both). It has a locking button that can be used to keep the D5200's shutter open for long periods.

**Figure 7.6** A locking cable release can give you long time exposures, such as this 60 second shot in San Juan, Puerto Rico.

■ **Time exposures.** This is a setting found on some cameras to produce longer exposures. With cameras that implement this option, the shutter opens when you press the shutter release button, and remains open until you press the button again. With the Nikon D5200, you can produce this effect with a locking cable release, as I did for the shot in San Juan, Puerto Rico shown in Figure 7.6. You can press the shutter release button, go off for a few minutes, and come back to close the shutter (assuming your camera is still there). The disadvantages of this mode are exposures must be timed manually, and with shorter exposures it's possible for the vibration of manually opening and closing the shutter to register in the photo. For longer exposures, the period of vibration is relatively brief and not usually a problem.

## Using the WR-R10/WR-T10 TRANSCEIVER/TRANSMITTERS

Nikon has introduced a remarkably versatile radio control system with three components that can be used with many recent Nikon dSLRs, including the D5200. More than simply a shutter release device, the WR-*x*10 system allows controlling autofocus, video capture, continuous shooting, silent shooting, and bulb exposures at a range of up to 164 feet (50 meters).

The individual components include:

- **WR-R10 Wireless Remote Control Transceiver.** This $99 component plugs into your camera, either into the accessory port when used with cameras like the D5200 that have a remote/GPS/Wi-Fi accessory port on the side or into the 10-pin port of cameras like the D800 or D4, using the WR-A10 adapter described below. It's called a transceiver (rather than simply a receiver) because the WR-R10 receives signals from the WR-T10 transmitter, but also relays information over its radio channels. The transceiver has three RF channels (labeled 5, 10, and 15) so that several photographers can be working a scene simultaneously without interference. (Or, *you* can control several different cameras, each with its own WR-R10 transceiver set to a different channel.)

- **WR-T10 Wireless Remote Control Transmitter.** Like the WR-R10, this transmitter is available separately (for $79) or in kits with one or both of the other components. It sends signals to the transceivers using the same three channels. It can be used to autofocus (press the main button down part way) and trigger capture using any still photo mode (including continuous shooting, and quiet shutter release modes) plus movie making. An Fn button can be assigned to a specific function.

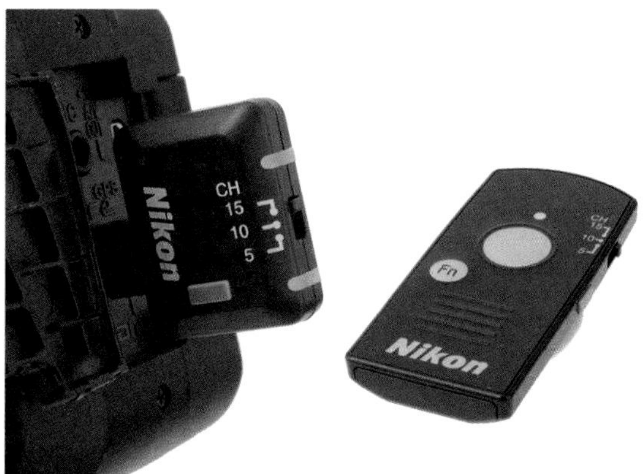

**Figure 7.7**  Nikon's WR-x10 remote control system.

- **WR-A10 Wireless Remote Adapter.** This is a $59 adapter with a terminal that accepts the WR-R10 transceiver, and a plug that can be inserted in the 10-pin connector of cameras like the Nikon D4 and D800/D800E. You won't need this unless you also own a camera requiring it, or later on upgrade/add one of those cameras to your arsenal.

You can specify whether the wireless remote takes still photos or records movies when the button is pressed, using the Remote Shutter Release option in the Accessory Terminal entry of the Setup menu. There, you can choose Take Photos or Record Movies. It's not possible to switch from one of these modes to the other using the WR-T10 transmitter; you'll need to visit the camera and access the menu to toggle from one to the other.

Nikon also has announced another option, the WR-1 transceiver, which can control multiple cameras in up to four separate groups for stills, videos, and time-lapse sequences, using its own controller as well as WR-10 units. The hot-shoe-mounted device has a range of 394 feet, or twice that distance using two additional WR-1 devices as relay controllers, and allows remotely adjusting the ISO, shooting mode, shutter speed, and aperture of the remote cameras. The WR-1 is likely to be beyond the means of someone who owns only a D5200; while the USA price hasn't been announced as I write this, it is likely to be well over $600.

# Working with Long Exposures

Because the D5200 produces such good images at longer exposures, and there are so many creative things you can do with long exposure techniques, you'll want to do some experimenting. Get yourself a tripod or another firm support and take some test shots with long exposure noise reduction both enabled and disabled (to see whether you prefer low noise or high detail) and get started. Here are some things to try:

- **Make people invisible.** One very cool thing about long exposures is that objects that move rapidly enough won't register at all in a photograph, while the subjects that remain stationary are portrayed in the normal way. That makes it easy to produce people-free landscape photos and architectural photos at night or, even, in full daylight if you use a neutral-density filter (or two) (or three) to allow an exposure of at least a few seconds. At ISO 100, f/22, and a pair of 8X (three-stop) neutral-density filters, you can use exposures of nearly two seconds; overcast days and/or even more neutral-density filtration would work even better if daylight people-vanishing is your goal. They'll have to be walking *very* briskly and across the field of view (rather than directly toward the camera) for this to work. At night, it's much easier to achieve this effect with the 20- to 30-second exposures that are possible, as you can see in Figure 7.8.

- **Create streaks.** If you aren't shooting for total invisibility, long exposures with the camera on a tripod can produce some interesting streaky effects. Even a single 8X ND filter will let you shoot at f/22 and 1/6th second in daylight.

**Figure 7.8**
This European alleyway is thronged with people, but with the camera on a tripod, a 30-second exposure rendered the passersby almost invisible.

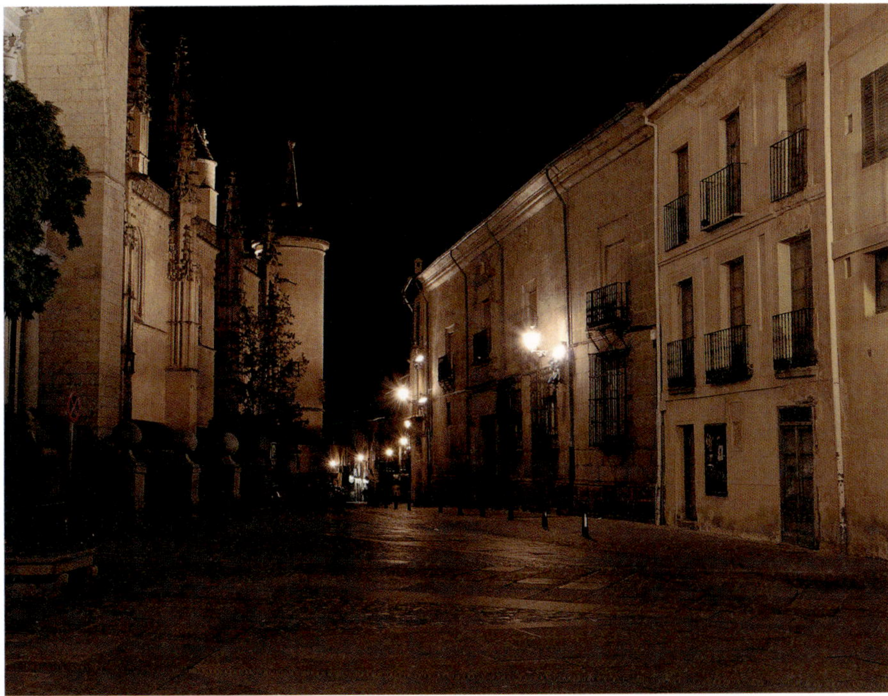

- **Produce light trails.** At night, car headlights and taillights and other moving sources of illumination can generate interesting light trails, as shown in Figure 7.9. Your camera doesn't even need to be mounted on a tripod; hand-holding the D5200 for longer exposures adds movement and patterns to your streaky trails. If you're shooting fireworks with the camera mounted on a tripod, a longer exposure may allow you to combine several bursts into one picture.

- **Blur waterfalls, etc.** You'll find that waterfalls and other sources of moving liquid produce a special type of long-exposure blur, because the water merges into a fantasy-like veil that looks different at different exposure times, and with different waterfalls. Cascades with turbulent flow produce a rougher look at a given longer exposure than falls that flow smoothly. Although blurred waterfalls have become almost a cliché, there are still plenty of variations for a creative photographer to explore. (See Figure 7.10.)

- **Show total darkness in new ways.** Even on the darkest, moonless nights, there is enough starlight or glow from distant illumination sources to see by, and, if you use a long exposure, there is enough light to take a picture, too.

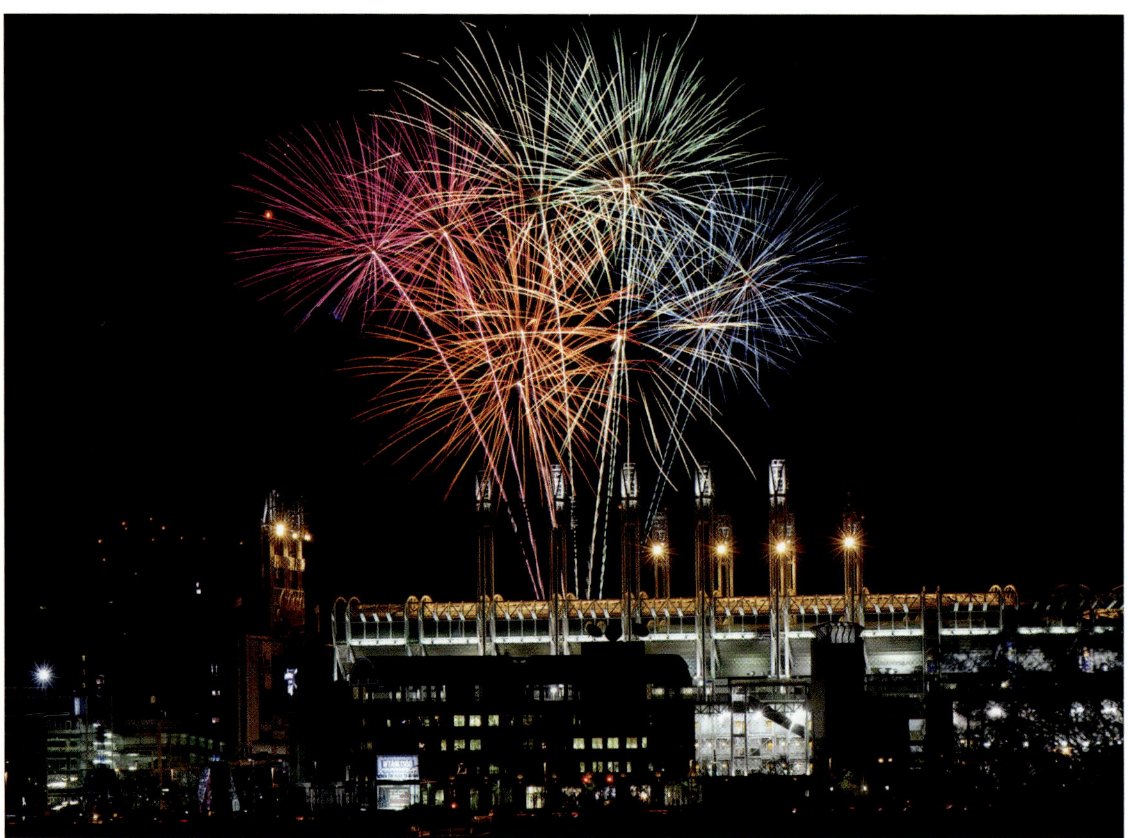

**Figure 7.9** Long exposures can capture several bursts of fireworks in one frame.

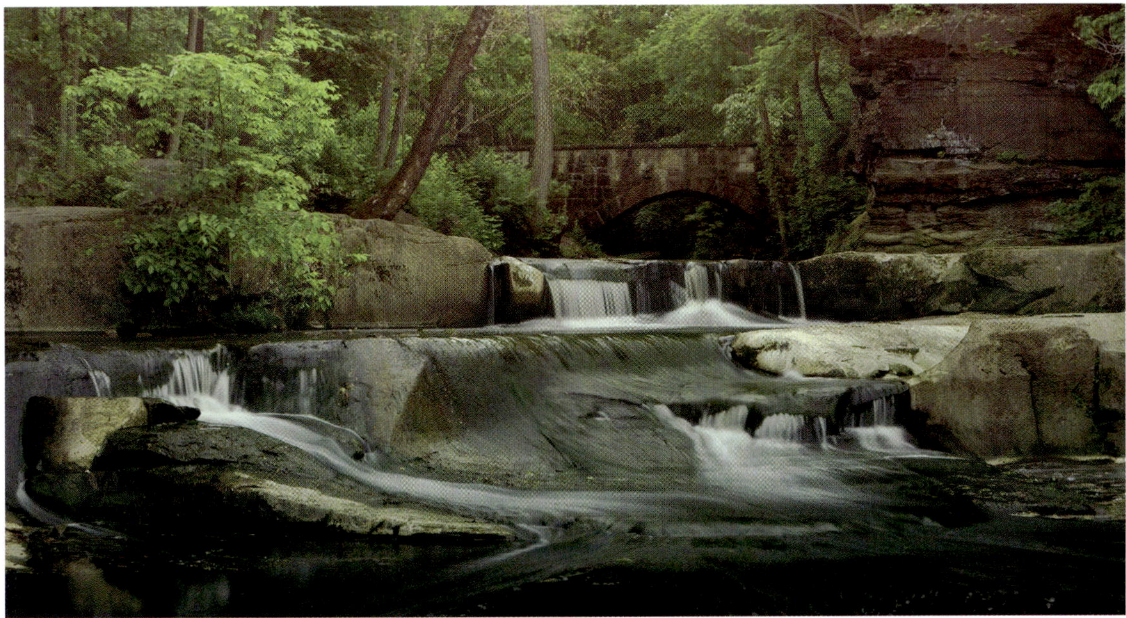

**Figure 7.10** A three-second exposure blurred this cascade of flowing water.

# Delayed Exposures

Sometimes it's desirable to have a delay of some sort before a picture is actually taken. Perhaps you'd like to get in the picture yourself, and would appreciate it if the camera waited 10 seconds after you press the shutter release to actually take the picture. Maybe you want to give a tripod-mounted camera time to settle down and damp any residual vibration after the release is pressed to improve sharpness for an exposure with a relatively slow shutter speed. It's possible you want to explore the world of time-lapse photography. The next sections present your delayed exposure options.

## Self-Timer

The D5200 has a built-in self-timer with a user-selectable delay. Activate the timer by pressing the drive button and selecting from the same screen used to activate continuous shooting mode. Press the shutter release button halfway to lock in focus on your subjects (if you're taking a self-portrait, focus on an object at a similar distance and use focus lock). When you're ready to take the photo, continue pressing the shutter release the rest of the way. The lamp on the front of the camera will blink slowly for eight seconds (when using the 10-second timer) and the beeper will chirp (if you haven't disabled it in the Custom Setting menu, as described in Chapter 9). During the final two seconds, the beeper sounds more rapidly and the lamp remains on until the picture is taken.

The self-timer is useful if you're shooting close-ups, landscapes, or other types of pictures and want to trip the shutter in the most vibration-free way possible. Forget to bring along your tripod, but still want to take a close-up picture with a precise focus setting? That happened to me when I encountered this colorful plant (see Figure 7.11) in a greenhouse when picking up some potted plants. I wheeled a planting cart over to the blossom, rested the D5200 on a soft bag of potting soil (a beanbag would have been better!), carefully focused, and let the self-timer trip the shutter at the appropriate moment. In such situations, the camera might teeter back and forth for a second or two, but it will settle back to its original position before the self-timer activates the shutter. The self-timer remains the active mode until you turn it off—even if you power down the D5200—so remember to change the release mode back to single frame mode when you're finished.

You can customize the settings of the self-timer. Your adjustments are "sticky" and remain in effect until you change them. Your options include:

- **Self-timer delay.** Choose 2, 5, 10, or 20 seconds. If I have the camera mounted on a tripod or other support and am too lazy to dig around for my wired remote, I can set a two-second delay that is sufficient to let the camera stop vibrating after I've pressed the shutter release.

- **Number of shots.** After the timer finishes counting down, the D5200 can take from 1 to 9 different shots. This is a godsend when shooting photos of groups, especially if you want to appear in the photo itself. You'll always want to shoot several pictures to ensure that everyone's eyes are open and there are smiling expressions on each face. Instead of racing back and forth between the camera to trigger the self-timer multiple times, you can select the number of shots taken after a single countdown. For small groups, I always take at least as many shots as there are people in the group—plus one. That gives everybody a chance to close their eyes.

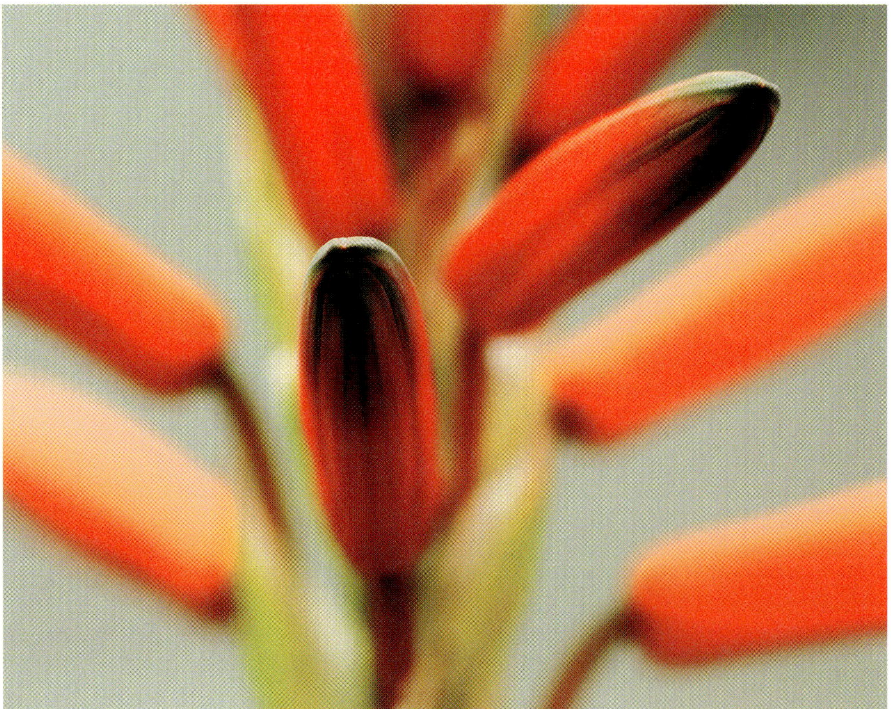

**Figure 7.11**
With the camera resting on a bag of potting soil on a cart, the self-timer triggered this vibration-free image of a bud about to open.

# Time-Lapse/Interval Photography

Who hasn't marveled at a time-lapse photograph of a flower opening, a series of shots of the moon marching across the sky, or one of those extreme time-lapse picture sets showing something that takes a very, very long time, such as a building under construction.

You probably won't be shooting such construction shots, unless you have a spare D5200 you don't need for a few months (or are willing to go through the rigmarole of figuring out how to set up your camera in precisely the same position using the same lens settings to shoot a series of pictures at intervals). However, other kinds of time-lapse photography are entirely within reach.

The D5200 can take time-lapse/interval photographs all by itself, using the Interval Timer Shooting entry found in the Shooting menu. You'll find step-by-step instructions for using this feature in Chapter 8. If you're willing to tether the camera to a computer (a laptop will do) using the USB cable, you can take time-lapse photos using the optional extra-cost Nikon Camera Control Pro.

Here is a recap of essential tips for effective time-lapse photography:

- **Use AC power.** If you're shooting a long sequence, consider connecting your camera to an AC adapter, as leaving the D5200 on for long periods of time will rapidly deplete the battery.

- **Make sure you have enough storage space.** Unless your memory card has enough capacity to hold all the images you'll be taking, you might want to change to a higher compression rate or reduced resolution to maximize the image count.

- **Make a movie.** While time-lapse stills are interesting, you can increase your fun factor by compiling all your shots into a motion picture using your favorite desktop movie-making software.

- **Protect your camera.** If your camera will be set up, make sure it's protected from weather, earthquakes, animals, young children, innocent bystanders, and theft.

- **Vary intervals.** Experiment with different time intervals. You don't want to take pictures too often or less often than necessary to capture the changes you hope to image.

# Geotagging with the Nikon GP-1A

A swarm of satellites in geosynchronous orbits above the Earth became a big part of my life even before I purchased the Nikon D5200. I use the GPS features of my iPhone and iPad and the GPS device in my car to track and plan my movements. When family members travel without me—most recently to Europe—I can use the Find my iPhone feature to see where they are roaming and vicariously accompany them with Google Maps' Street View features. And, since the introduction of the Nikon GP-1A accessory, GPS has become an integral part of my shooting regimen, too.

The GP-1A unit makes it easy to tag your images with the same kind of longitude, latitude, altitude, and time stamp information that is supplied by the GPS unit you use in your car. (Don't have a GPS? Photographers who get lost in the boonies as easily as I do *must* have one of these!) The geotagging information is stored in the metadata space within your image files, and can be accessed by Nikon ViewNX 2, or by online photo services such as mypicturetown.com and Flickr.

Geotagging can also be done by attaching geographic information to the photo after it's already been taken. This is often done with online sharing services, such as Flickr, which allow you to associate your uploaded photographs with a map, city, street address, or postal code. When properly geotagged and uploaded to sites like Flickr, users can browse through your photos using a map, finding pictures you've taken in a given area, or even searching through photos taken at the same location by other users. Of course, in this day and age it's probably wise not to include GPS information in photos of your home, especially if your photos can be viewed by an unrestricted audience.

Having this information available makes it easier to track where your pictures are taken. That can be essential, as I learned from a trip out West, where I found the red rocks, canyons, and arroyos of Nevada, Utah, Arizona, and Colorado all pretty much look alike to my untrained eye. I find the capability especially useful when I want to return to a spot I've photographed in the past and am not sure how to get there. I can enter the coordinates shown into my hand-held or auto GPS (or an app in my iPad or iPhone) and receive instructions on how to get there. That's handy if you're returning to a spot later in the same day, or months later.

Like all GPS units, the Nikon GP-1A obtains its data by triangulating signals from satellites orbiting the Earth. It works with the Nikon D5200, as well as many other Nikon cameras. At almost $200, it's not cheap, but those who need geotagging—especially for professional mapping or location applications—will find it to be a bargain.

The GP-1A (see Figure 7.12) slips onto the accessory shoe on top of the Nikon D5200. It connects to the GPS port on the camera using the Nikon GP1-CA90 cable, which plugs into the connector marked CAMERA on the GP-1A.

A third connector connects the GP-1A to your computer using a USB cable. Nikon has released a utility for Windows and Mac operating systems that allows you to read GPS data from the GP-1A directly in your computer—no camera required. I tried the driver, and discovered that the GP-1A couldn't "see" any satellites from inside my office (big surprise). I plan on trying it with my netbook outdoors, in a car, or in some other more satellite-

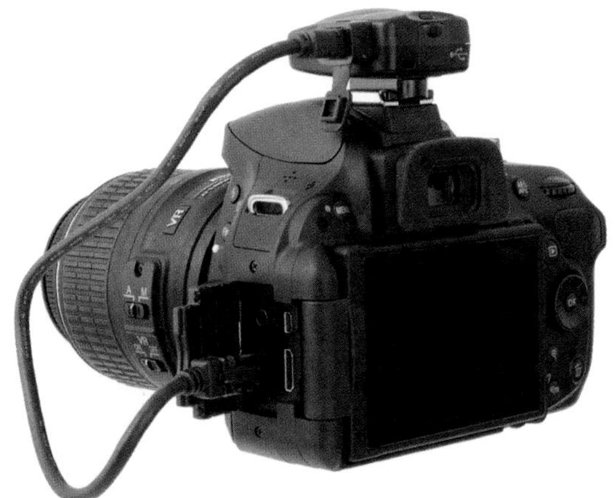

**Figure 7.12** Nikon GP-1A geotagging unit.

accessible location. Once attached, the device is very easy to use. You need to activate the Nikon D5200's GPS capabilities in the GPS choice within the Accessory Terminal entry of the Setup menu (it appears when the GPS device is attached), as described in Chapter 10.

The first step is to allow the GP-1A to acquire signals from at least three satellites. If you've used a GPS in your car, you'll know that satellite acquisition works best outdoors under a clear sky and out of the "shadow" of tall buildings, and the Nikon unit is no exception. It takes about 40-60 seconds for the GP-1A to "connect." A red blinking LED means that GPS data is not being recorded; a green blinking LED signifies that the unit has acquired three satellites and is recording data. When the LED is solid green, the unit has connected to four or more satellites, and is recording data with optimum accuracy.

Next, set up the camera by selecting the GPS option found under the Setup menu entry Accessory Terminal on the Nikon D5200. There are three choices:

- **Auto meter-off.** You can choose Enable or Disable. Enabling reduces battery drain by allowing the D5200 to turn off exposure meters while using the GP-1A after the time specified in Custom Setting c2 (Standby timer delay, discussed in Chapter 12) has elapsed. When the meters turn off, the GP-1A becomes inactive and must reacquire at least three satellite signals before it can begin recording GPS data once more. When you choose Disable, the exposure meters remain on while using the GP-1A, so that GPS data can be recorded at any time, despite increased battery drain.

- **Position.** This is an information display, rather than a selectable option. It appears when the GP-1A is connected and receiving satellite positioning data. It shows the latitude, longitude, altitude, and Coordinated Universal Time (UTC) values for your current location. I've found this feature to be more valuable than I expected. If I don't have my eTrex 20 with me and someone wants to know exactly where I am, say, to meet up, I can check this readout, make a quick phone call, and tell them to set their own GPS (car, hand-held, whatever) for those coordinates, and then make a bee-line for me.

- **Use GPS to set camera clock.** Select Yes or No. When enabled, your D5200's internal camera clock will be set using UTC values whenever the GP-1A is attached to the camera. If you use the device frequently, this will ensure that your camera's clock is always set accurately, and won't require a manual update periodically.

Once the unit is up and running, you can view GPS information using photo information screens available on the color monitor (and described in Chapter 2). The GPS screen appears only when a photo has been taken using the GPS unit.

# Wi-Fi

These days, GPS and Wi-Fi capabilities work together with your D5200 in interesting new ways. Wireless capabilities allow you to upload photos directly from your D5200 to your computer at home or in your studio, or, through a hotspot at your hotel or coffee shop back to your home computer or to a photo sharing service like Facebook or Flickr. A special Wi-Fi-enabled memory card that you slip in the SD slot of your camera performs the magic. GPS capabilities—built right into some of those Wi-Fi cards—allow you to mark your photographs with location information, so you don't have to guess where a picture was taken. Alternatively, you can also upload your images to a device, such as a smart phone, as you shoot them using the Nikon WU-1a gadget that plugs into the D5200's versatile accessory terminal.

Both capabilities are very cool. Wi-Fi uploads can provide instant backup of important shots and sharing. And, as noted in the previous section, geotagging is most important as a way to associate the geographical location where the photographer was when a picture was taken, with the actual photograph itself. It can be done with the location-mapping capabilities of the Wi-Fi card, or through add-on devices that third parties make available for your D5200. I'll cover a range of different hardware options in this section.

## Eye-Fi Cards and Alternatives

A relatively affordable solution has long been offered by Eye-Fi (www.eye.fi). The Eye-Fi card (see Figure 7.13) is an SDHC memory card with a wireless transmitter built in. You insert it in your camera just as with any ordinary card, and then specify which networks to use. You can add as many as 32 different networks. The next time your camera is on within range of a specified network, your photos and videos can be uploaded to your computer and/ or to your favorite sharing site. During setup, you can customize where you want your images uploaded. The Eye-Fi card will only send them to the computer and to the sharing site you choose. Upload to any of 25 popular sharing websites, including Flickr, Facebook, Picasa, Costco, Adorama, Smugmug, YouTube, Shutterfly, or Walmart. Online Sharing is included as a lifetime, unlimited service with all X2 cards.

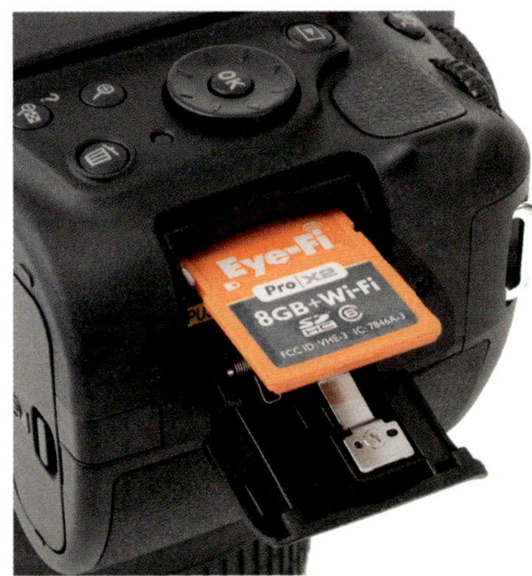

**Figure 7.13** Eye-Fi wireless memory card.

When uploading to online sites, you can specify not just where your images are sent, but how they are organized, by specifying preset album names, tags, descriptions, and even privacy preferences on certain sharing sites. Some Eye-Fi cards also include geotagging service, which helps you view uploaded photos on a map, and sort them by location. Eye-Fi's geotagging uses Wi-Fi Positioning System (WPS) technology. Using built-in Wi-Fi, the Eye-Fi card senses surrounding Wi-Fi networks as you take pictures. When photos are uploaded, the Eye-Fi service then adds the geotags to your photos. You don't need to have the password or a subscription for the Wi-Fi networks the card accesses; it can grab the location information directly without the need to "log in." You don't need to set up or control the Eye-Fi card from your camera. Software on your computer manages all the parameters.

Your D5200 has an Eye-Fi Upload entry in the Setup menu that allows you to enable or disable this capability. You'll want to turn off Eye-Fi when traveling on an airplane (just as you disable your cell phone, tablet, or laptop's wireless capabilities when required to do so). In addition, use of Wi-Fi cards may be restricted or banned outside the United States, because the telecommunications laws differ in other countries. Wi-Fi cards like the Eye-Fi offerings also use more battery power than plain old, "dumb" memory cards, so you might want to turn yours off when you don't really need its features.

While Eye-Fi has had the playing field all to itself for a long time, other vendors have been releasing similar products. Transcend is one of the latest, with fast Class 10 cards, currently in 16GB and 32GB sizes for around $70–$100. Like Eye-Fi, the Transcend cards are available with a free app for iOS and Android tablets and phones that allows direct sharing from your camera to the mobile device, where they can be e-mailed immediately, or uploaded to the Internet, including sites like Facebook. Other alternatives include the Toshiba FlashAir (which hasn't reached the USA yet), and EZ Share, a Wi-Fi SD card from a Chinese company called Lzeal. The EZ Share has its own on/off switch so you can activate it without a trip to Menuland.

## Nikon's WU-1a

Another option is the $59 WU-1a Wi-Fi adapter (shown in Figure 7.14), which slips into the USB port on the side of the camera, and transmits your photos directly to your iOS or Android smartphone or tablet, using a custom Nikon app. This gadget is a great idea, and has only one defect that bothers me. It sticks out of the camera and precludes closing the port door, making it a bit clumsy to use.

It's a tiny device and comes in a tiny case (about the size of a pair of dice) that clips onto your neck strap. It's easy to lose such a small component, so I recommend finding a zippered compartment in your camera bag to keep it in when not in use. To work with it, just follow these steps, which assume you've already installed the free Nikon Wireless Mobile Device app on your smartphone or tablet:

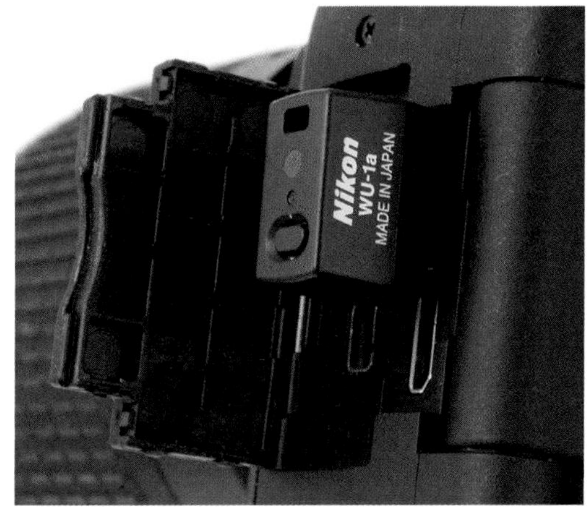
**Figure 7.14** Wireless mobile adapter.

1. **Insert.** Slide the gadget into the USB port of your D5200. The LED on the adapter will flash green, showing it is ready to connect.

2. **Enable.** If you haven't done this already, visit the Wireless Mobile Adapter entry in the Setup menu and choose Enable.

3. **Activate your phone/tablet.** Go to your device's Settings screen and choose the adapter's Wi-Fi network SSID as the device's current Wi-Fi connection. The name will be something on the order of Nikon_WU_*nnnnnnnn*. (This step will be different for each particular device. On my iPhone, there's a "Wi-Fi" entry between the Airplane Mode and Bluetooth entries in the main Settings screen.) The LED on the adapter plugged into your camera will turn green when the connection is made. If there is a connection error, the LED will flash red.

4. **Open the Wireless Mobile Adapter app.** You should be connected, and the Take Photos and View Photos menu will be visible. If you want to check your connection, battery level, and adapter firmware version, you can tap the gear icon in the upper-right corner of the app.

5. **Shift your phone/tablet to live view.** Tap the Take Photos entry and you'll hear the mirror of your D5200 flip up as the camera switches to live view and transmits the sensor image to your phone.

6. **Evaluate preview image.** The live view preview will show up on your device's screen (unless you choose to turn it off), with shooting data such as current f/stop, shutter speed, and remaining exposures displayed.

7. **Set focus.** A red focus frame is shown in the fame. You can tap anywhere in the frame to move the focus frame to another part of the image. The red frame turns green when the subject is in focus.

8. **Take photo.** Tap the camera icon in the lower part of the screen to take a picture.

9. **Download file.** The image you just took will automatically download to your device (unless you disable this feature) and become available for review in a strip at the bottom of the phone/tablet's live view screen. Note that as data is transmitted between the D5200 and your device, the adapter's LED will flash green rapidly. If the gadget flashes every five seconds, instead, it is in sleep mode and will wake when you resume using the app.

The app has a number of options, such as the ability to turn device live view on or off (you'll no longer see a real-time view of what the camera sees). You can also activate the self-timer (so you can get in the picture yourself without needing to have the phone/tablet in your hand) and activate/deactivate automatic downloading of the camera's shots to your device. Pictures that you take that are downloaded to your phone/tablet are also stored on the D5200's memory card, so you can use the app to *take* pictures (like a remote control) even if you don't want to download/store them on your phone or tablet.

If you've made several changes and want to restore the WU-1a adapter to its factory default settings, hold down the WPS button (located under the LED) for ten seconds. When the LED turns orange, press the button again to perform a reset. The LED stops flashing when the reset is complete.

# Tablets, Smart Phones, and the Nikon D5200

Although tablets and smart phones are still in their infancies, in the future, your iPhone, iPad/tablet computer, iPod Touch/MP3 player, smart phone, or Google Android portable device will be one of the most important accessories you can have for your D5200 (or other) digital camera. Even though these devices have been around for a few years, we're only now seeing the beginnings of the trend. The relevant platforms are these:

- **Old-style smart phones.** I include in this category all smart phones that are *not* iPhones or phones based on Google's Android operating system. You can buy lots of interesting apps for these phones, although not many applications specifically for photography. This type of phone is already on its way out, too, with iPhone and Android smart phones dominating, simply because it's easier to write applications for the iPhone's iOS and Android than to create them for multiple "old" smart phone platforms.

■ **Android smart phones.** There are already more Android-based smart phones on the market than for all other types, including iOS. Although Apple had a head start, the number of Android applications rapidly caught up, and continues to rise as Android-compatible tablets (described later) gain in popularity.

■ **iPhones.** To date, iOS has a commanding lead in number of applications, especially for photography apps. When my first apps were developed as guides for certain Nikon cameras, they appeared for the iOS platform first.

■ **iPod Touch.** Basically, the latest iPod Touch is an iPhone that can't make phone calls. (Although there are some hacks around that limitation.) Virtually all of the apps that run on the iPhone under iOS also run on the iPod Touch. You need a Wi-Fi connection to access features that use network capabilities, but, these days, Wi-Fi hot spots aren't that difficult to find. Tethering and Mi-Fi (which allows another device to serve as a hot spot for non-connected gadgets like the Touch), and *automobiles* that include built-in Wi-Fi (!) make connectivity almost universal. In my travels through Europe in the last year, I found free Wi-Fi connections in the smallest towns. (Indeed, the only time I was asked to pay for it was when staying in an upscale hotel.) So, for many who are tied to a non-iPhone cell phone, the iPod Touch is a viable alternative for iOS apps.

■ **Tablet computers: iOS edition.** I've been welded to my iPad (shown alongside my iPhone in Figure 7.15) since I bought it on the first day they became available. I use them to access e-mail and useful apps, and as a portable portfolio. Your iPad options became broader in October 2012, when Apple introduced its first iPad Mini, and replaced its six-months-old third-generation "New iPad" with a fourth-generation model it dubbed "iPad with Retina Display" (although its predecessor also had the 2048 × 1536–pixel screen).

The iPad Mini (7.9-inch screen) and its bigger sibling (9.7-inch screen) are available with 16, 32, or 64GB of internal storage (a new 128GB option for the full-size iPad became available early in 2013). You can't supplement that with any plug-in memory modules, but there are external hard drives that can sync with the iPads over Wi-Fi, effectively expanding your storage. Each model can be purchased both in Wi-Fi only and Cellular data versions.

■ **Tablet computers: Android edition.** Today, there are alternative tablet computers running Android. I recently picked up an Amazon Kindle Fire, which also does e-mail and a limited number of apps, and which has a Gallery feature (see Figure 7.16) that transforms it onto a compact portfolio almost as useful for that purpose as an iPad. The original Kindle Fire made only 6 of its 8GB of storage available to the user, so you had to limit the size of your portfolio. Newer versions, at this writing, can hold up to 32GB of data.

Like Apple, Amazon has expanded its Kindle Fire lineup to include models like the one I own, with a 7-inch screen, and "high-definition" alternatives with a 1920 × 1200 pixel, 8.9-inch screen that's larger than the iPad Mini's and more compact than that of a full-size iPad. Models are available for Wi-Fi only as well as Wi-Fi/Cellular. Of the other Android-based tablets, Google's Nexus seems to be the most popular right now. It's a 7-inch 1280 × 800-pixel model with 8 or 16GB of storage and Wi-Fi/Bluetooth connectivity.

■ **Tablet computers: Microsoft edition.** Neither of the two announced Microsoft Surface models have gained much traction as I write this, so it's too early to predict whether either or both will be able to overtake the lead carved out by the iOS and Android tablets. We'll have to see whether the Surface computers are Xboxes or Zunes in terms of popularity.

On the plus side, those who are switching from Windows 7 (or an earlier Microsoft OS) to Windows 8 will find the Windows RT and Windows 8 Pro operating systems to be highly compatible and familiar. Their 10.6-inch, 1366 × 768-pixel/1920 × 1080 screens (respectively), and storage that ranges from 32, or 64, to 128GB—on the Windows 8 Pro model—(expandable through a microSD card slot) are in the right ballpark. Only Wi-Fi (and USB) connectivity are possible, but the Windows 8 Pro model has a mini DisplayPort port that allows linking to a larger monitor, which is definitely a plus for photographers.

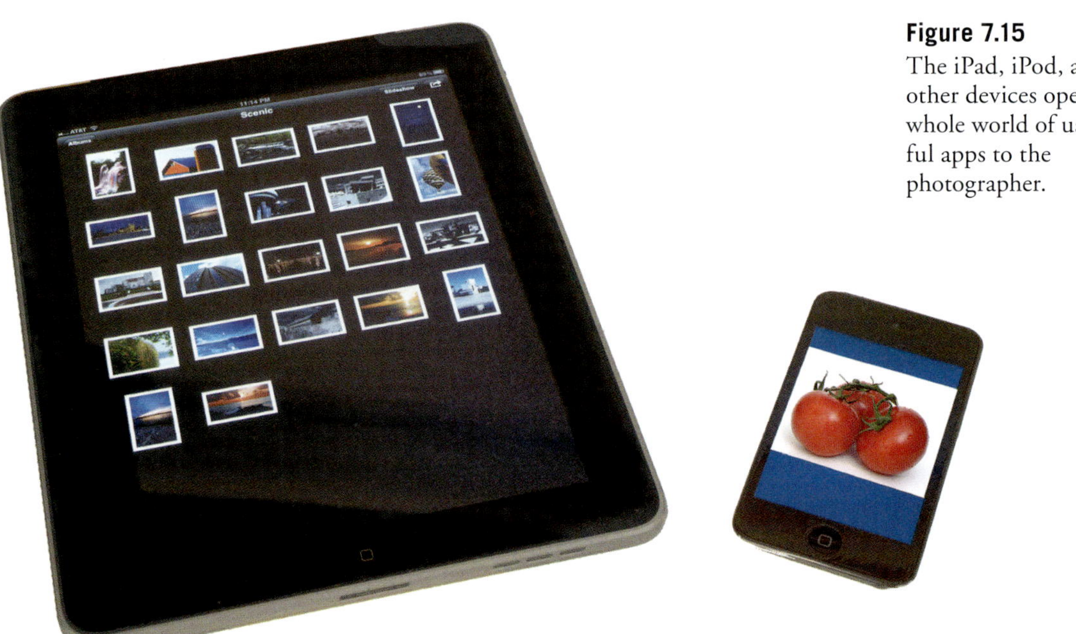

**Figure 7.15**
The iPad, iPod, and other devices open a whole world of useful apps to the photographer.

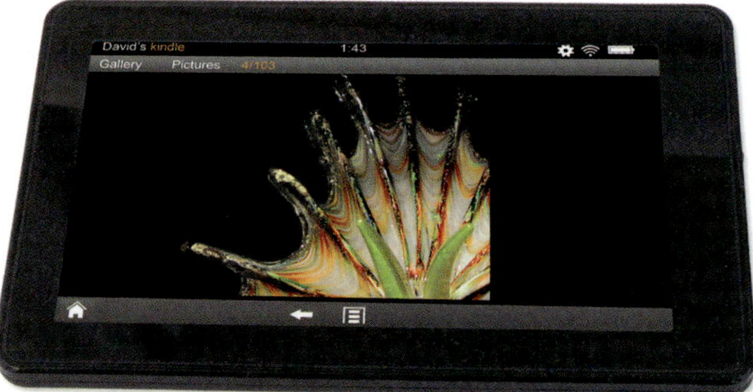

**Figure 7.16**
The Kindle Fire is a smaller, more affordable alternative to the iPad.

# Wi-Fi or Cellular

Choosing a Wi-Fi-only model, versus one with cellular connectivity can have a significant impact on your pocketbook. The Wi-Fi tablets generally cost $100 to $150 less, particularly when compared to models with 4G coverage, and, while limited to locations with a Wi-Fi hot spot, won't cost you $25 (and up) for data transfer from a cellular carrier. Here's what I've discovered:

- **Are you often within range of free Wi-Fi?** About 80 percent of my tablet usage is at home, in my office/studio, or in other locations where Wi-Fi is available. I find I can use my Wi-Fi-only Kindle easily in just about any circumstances where I need my smaller tablet.

- **Are your access needs all over the map?** A great deal of my applications for my larger tablet involve roaming around, either in my car or trekking through outdoor shooting locations. While the relevant apps are often available on my smart phone, too, the larger screen is often preferable. And it's nice to be able to whip out your tablet and show off your portfolio to a friend, colleague, or client without thinking about whether there is a Wi-Fi hotspot nearby.

- **Can you carry a "free" hotspot in your pocket?** Many smartphones can be converted into a hotspot that any nearby computer or tablet can access. My own cellular carrier gives free hotspot service to every compatible phone on our plan; you can choose how much data (up to 6GB per month) you want to bundle in. Since my smartphone is always with me, I can connect a Wi-Fi-only tablet (like my Kindle) or my MacBook Air to the Internet from just about anywhere. Many carriers also offer a $50 gadget, like my Verizon JetPack, that can serve as a hotspot, in case you don't want to/can't use your phone. The advantage of the personal hotspot is that it has a much larger battery, which is a standard battery that is user replaceable if it goes bad. The JetPack keeps my phone from running out of juice when I want a hotspot for a lengthy period.

- **Do you need to separate your tablet/phone data usage?** My iPhone uses Verizon's network, and my iPad, introduced before Verizon joined the party, uses AT&T's network. Ne'er the twain shall meet, because they use different communication standards (CDMA and GSM, respectively). I decided to stop paying for separate cellular coverage with AT&T, and now use my iPad in Wi-Fi mode through my iPhone's personal hotspot, or use my JetPack.

# What Else Can You Do with Them?

Many of these devices can serve as a backup for your D5200's memory cards. I've got Apple's camera connection kit, and can offload my pictures to my iPad's 64GB of memory, then upload them to Flickr or Facebook, or send to anyone through e-mail. My iPad also makes a perfect portable portfolio, too. I have hundreds of photos stored on mine, arranged into albums ready for instant display, either individually or in slide shows. I have the same photo library on my iPhone and iPod Touch, and more than a few pictures available for showing on my Kindle Fire.

But the real potential for using these devices comes from specialized apps written specifically to serve photographic needs. Here are some of the kinds of apps you can expect in the future. (I'm working on more than a few of them myself.)

- **Camera guides.** Even the inadequate manual that came with your camera is too large to carry around in your camera bag all day. I'm converting many of my own camera-specific guides to app form, while adding interactive elements, including hyperlinks and videos. You can already put a PDF version of your camera manual on your portable device and read it, if you like. In the future, you should be able to read any of the more useful third-party guides anywhere, anytime.

- **Lens selector.** Wonder what's the best lens to use in a specific situation? Enter information about your scene, and your app will advise you.

- **Exposure estimator.** Choose a situation and the estimated exposure will be provided. Useful as a reality check and in difficult situations, such as fireworks, where the camera's meters may falter.

- **Shutter speed advisor.** The correct shutter speed for a scene varies depending on whether you want to freeze action, or add a little blur to express motion. Other variables include whether the subject is crossing the frame, moving diagonally, or headed toward you. The photographer also needs to consider the focal length of the lens, and presence/absence of image stabilization features, tripod, monopod, etc. This app will allow you to tap in all the factors and receive advice about what shutter speed to use.

- **Hyperfocal length calculator.** In any given situation, set the focus point at the distance specified for your lens's current focal length setting, and everything from half that distance to infinity will be in focus. But the right setting differs at various focal lengths. This app tells you, and is a great tool for grab shots.

- **Accessory selector.** Confused about what flash, remote control, battery grip, lens hood, filter, or other accessory to use with your camera or lens? This selector lists the key gadgets, which ones fit which cameras, and explains how to use them.

- **Before and after.** Images showing before/after versions of dozens of situations with and without corrective/in-camera special effects applied.

- **Fill light.** Pesky shadows on faces from overhead lighting indoors? This turns your iPod/iPhone or (best of all) iPad into a bright, diffuse fill light panel. Choose from white fill light, or *colors* for special effects. Makes good illumination for viewing your camera's buttons and dials in dark locations, too. Some of these apps use the iPhone's flash for an especially bright light.

- **Gray card.** Turn your i-device into an 18-percent gray card for metering and color balance.

- **Super links.** If you don't find your answer in the Toolkit, you can link to websites, including mine, with more information.

- **How It's Made.** A collection of inspiring photos, with details on how they were taken in camera—or manipulated in Photoshop (if that's your thing).
- **Quickie guides.** Small apps that lead you, step-by-step, through everything you need to photograph lots of different types of scenes. Typical subjects would be sports, landscape photography, macro work, portraits, concerts/performances, flowers, wildlife, and nature.

As you can see, the potential for apps is virtually unlimited. You can expect your smart phone, tablet computer, or other device to be a mainstay in your camera bag within a very short time.

## Focus Stacking

If you are doing macro (close-up) photography of flowers, or other small objects at short distances, the depth-of-field often will be extremely narrow. In some cases, it will be so narrow that it will be impossible to keep the entire subject in focus in one photograph. Although having part of the image out of focus can be a pleasing effect for a portrait of a person, it is likely to be a hindrance when you are trying to make an accurate photographic record of a flower, or small piece of precision equipment. One solution to this problem is focus stacking, a procedure that can be considered like HDR translated for the world of focus—taking multiple shots with different settings, and, using software as explained below, combining the best parts from each image in order to make a whole that is better than the sum of the parts. Focus stacking requires a non-moving object, so some subjects, such as flowers, are best photographed in a breezeless environment, such as indoors.

For example, see Figures 7.17 through 7.19, in which I took photographs of three colorful crayons. As you can see from these images, the depth-of-field was extremely narrow, and only a small part of the subject was in focus for each shot.

Now look at Figure 7.20, in which the entire subject is in reasonably sharp focus. This image is a composite, made up of the three shots above, as well as 10 others, each one focused on the same scene, but at very gradually increasing distances from the camera's lens. All 13 images were then combined in Adobe Photoshop using the focus stacking procedure. Here are the steps you can take to combine shots for the purpose of achieving sharp focus in this sort of situation:

1. **Set the camera firmly on a solid tripod.** A tripod or other equally firm support is absolutely essential for this procedure.
2. **Attach a remote release, such as the MC-DC2.** You want to be able to trigger the camera without moving it.
3. **Set the camera to manual focus mode.** Use the procedure described in the previous section to activate manual focus.
4. **Set the exposure, ISO, and white balance manually.** Use test shots if necessary to determine the best values. This step in the Shooting menu will help prevent visible variations from arising among the multiple shots that you'll be taking. You don't want the D5200 to change the ISO setting or white balance between shots.

5. **Set the quality of the images to NEF (RAW) + JPEG FINE.** Use the Shooting menu to make this adjustment. Having both formats will give you flexibility when combining the images.

6. **Turn off vibration reduction.** Turn off VR using the switch on your lens. You don't need it when the camera is securely mounted on a tripod, and disabling VR will keep the D5200 from making any sort of image adjustment between exposures.

7. **Focus manually on the very closest point of the subject to the lens.** Rotate the multi selector dial to change the focus.

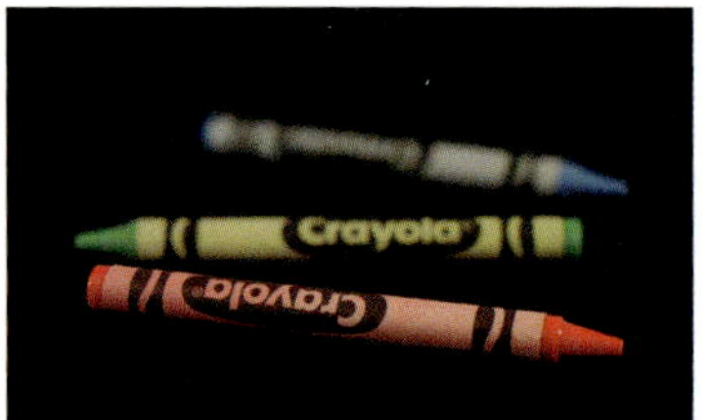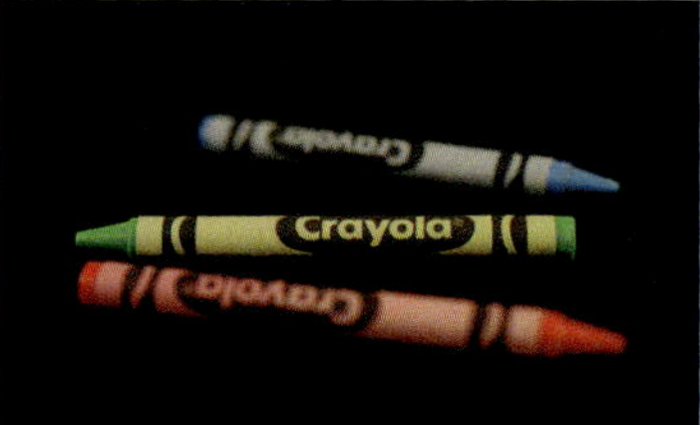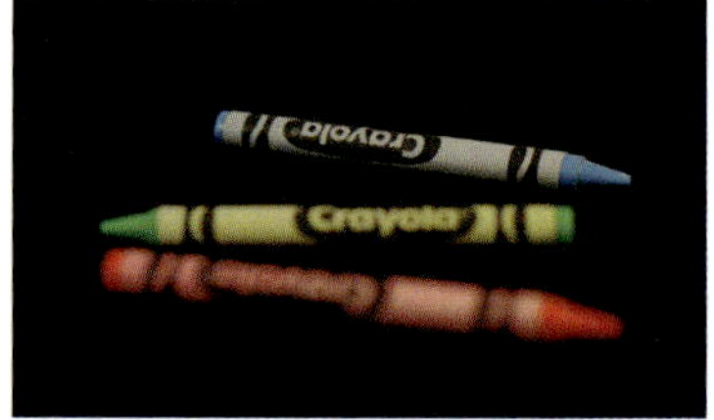

**Figures 7.17, 7.18, 7.19** These three shots were all focused on different distances within the same scene. No single shot could bring the entire subject into sharp focus.

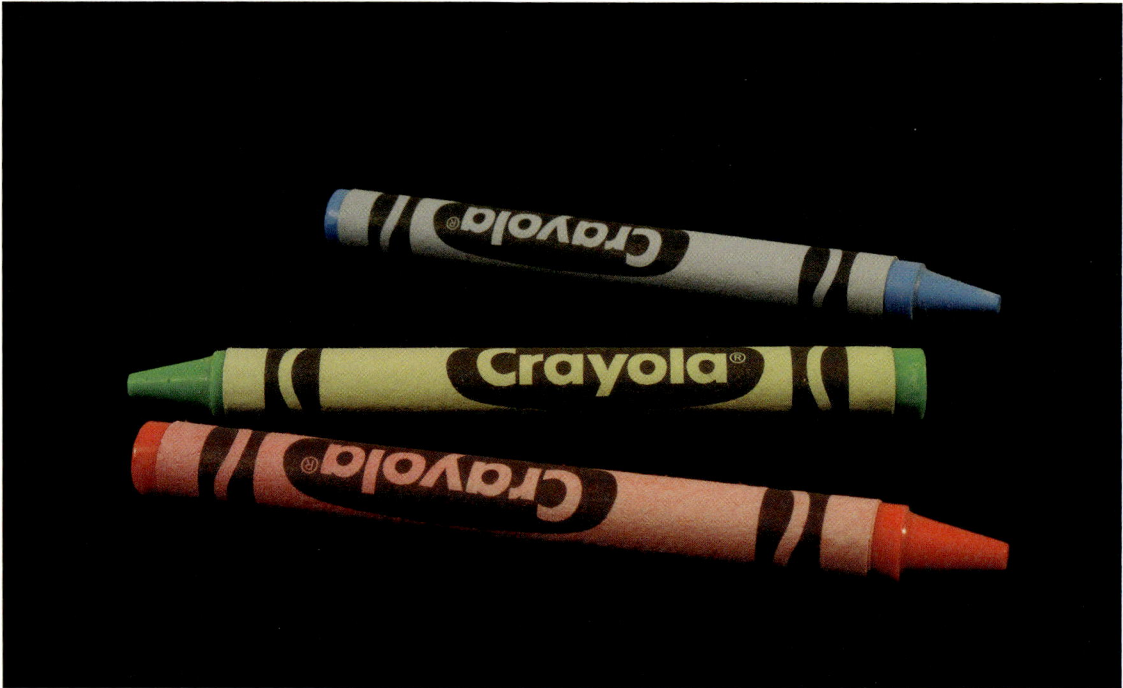

**Figure 7.20** Three partially out-of-focus shots have been merged, along with ten others, through a focus stacking procedure in Adobe Photoshop, to produce a single image with the entire subject in focus.

8. **Trip the shutter.** Use the remote.

9. **Carefully refocus.** Gently rotate the focus ring on the lens to focus on a point slightly farther away from the lens and trip the shutter again.

10. **Continue taking photographs** in this way until you have covered the entire subject with in-focus shots.

The next step is to process the images you've taken in Photoshop. Transfer the images to your computer, and then follow these steps:

1. In Photoshop, select File > Scripts > Load Files into Stack. In the dialog box that then appears, navigate on your computer to find the files for the photographs you have taken, and highlight them all.

2. At the bottom of the next dialog box that appears, check the box that says, "Attempt to Automatically Align Source Images," then click OK. The images will load; it may take several minutes for the program to load the images and attempt to arrange them into layers that are aligned based on their content.

3. Once the program has finished processing the images, go to the Layers panel and select all of the layers. You can do this by clicking on the top layer and then Shift-clicking on the bottom one.

4. While the layers are all selected, in Photoshop go to Edit > Auto-Blend Layers. In the dialog box that appears, select the two options, Stack Images and Seamless Tones and Colors, then click OK. The program will process the images, possibly for a considerable length of time.

5. If the procedure worked well, the result will be a single image made up of numerous layers that have been processed to produce a sharply focused rendering of your subject. If it did not work well, you may have to take additional images the next time, focusing very carefully on small slices of the subject as you move progressively farther away from the lens.

Although this procedure can work very well in Photoshop, you also may want to try it with programs that were developed more specifically for focus stacking and related procedures, such as Helicon Focus (www.heliconsoft.com), PhotoAcute (www.photoacute.com), or CombineZM (www.hadleyweb.pwp.blueyonder.co.uk).

# Part III

# Advanced Tools

The next six chapters are devoted to helping you dig deeper into the capabilities of your Nikon D5200, so you can exploit all those cool features that your previous camera lacked. Three cover all the configuration options available in the D5200's Playback, Shooting, Custom, Setup, Retouch, and My Menu entries, while the three final chapters in the book help you choose lenses, work with natural and flash illumination, and troubleshoot your camera.

- **Chapter 8:** In this chapter, you'll discover an easy way to specify exactly which information screens are displayed during playback, and how to create your own slide shows. Then, we'll move on to the Shooting menu, with its important tools including HDR, vignetting and distortion control, multiple exposures, and the magic of Picture Controls.

- **Chapter 9:** In this chapter, you'll find a mind-boggling number of entries in the Custom Setting menu, in six different categories (and many of those have three or more sub-options) that let you fine-tune everything from autofocus and metering to the functions assigned to various buttons and dials. If your D5200 doesn't behave exactly as you'd like, you can probably tweak it with one of the recommendations I provide in this chapter.

- **Chapter 10:** In this chapter, I'll cover the Setup and Retouch menus as well as My Menu. You'll be able to fine-tune your D5200's autofocus, work with an optional GPS attachment, manage monitor brightness, and manipulate your images *after* they are stored on your memory card. If you don't like the Nikon D5200's menu layout, you can create your own menu system, too.

- **Chapter 11:** In this chapter, I'll show you how to select the best lenses for the kinds of photography you want to do, with my recommendations for starter lenses as well as more advanced optics for specialized applications.

- **Chapter 12:** This chapter is devoted to the magic of light—your fundamental tool in creating any photograph. There are entire books devoted to working with electronic flash, but I hope to get you started with plenty of coverage of the Nikon D5200's capabilities. I'll show you how to master your camera's built-in flash—and avoid that "built-in flash" look, and offer an introduction to the use of external flash units, including the Nikon SB-910.

- **Chapter 13:** Learn how to upgrade your firmware, clean your sensor, and protect your images.

**8**

# Playback and Shooting Menus

The Nikon D5200 is undoubtedly one of the most customizable, tweakable, fine-tunable cameras Nikon has ever offered, and it provides an amazing degree of adjustments for a camera in its price range. This versatility has made the D5200 popular among professional photographers (if only as a versatile backup) as well as advanced amateurs.

You can enjoy this flexibility, too. If your camera doesn't behave in exactly the way you'd like, chances are you can make a small change in the Playback, Shooting, Custom Setting, and Setup menus that will tailor the D5200 to your needs. In fact, if you don't like the *menus*, you can create your own using the clever My Menu system.

This chapter will help you sort out the settings for the Playback and Shooting menus, which determine how the D5200 displays images on review, and how it uses many of its shooting features to take a photo. The following chapters will focus on the Custom Setting menu (Chapter 9), and Setup, Retouch, and My Menu options (Chapter 10).

As I've mentioned before, this book isn't intended to replace the manual you received with your D5200, nor have I any interest in rehashing its contents. You'll still find the original manual useful as a standby reference that lists every possible option in exhaustive (if mind-numbing) detail—without really telling you how to use those options to take better pictures. There is, however, some unavoidable duplication between the Nikon manual and the next three chapters, because I'm going to explain all the key menu choices and the options you may have in using them. You should find, though, that I will give you the information you need in a much more helpful format, with plenty of detail on why you should make some settings that are particularly cryptic.

I'm not going to waste a lot of space on some of the more obvious menu choices in these chapters. For example, you can probably figure out that the Beep option in Custom Setting d1 deals with the solid-state beeper in your camera that sounds off during various activities (such as the self-timer countdown). You can certainly decipher the import of the three options available for the Beep entry

(High, Low, and Off). In this chapter, I'll devote no more than a sentence or two to the blatantly obvious settings and concentrate on the more confusing aspects of the D5200 setup, such as automatic exposure bracketing. I'll start with an overview of using the D5200's menus themselves.

# Anatomy of the Nikon D5200's Menus

If you used any Nikon digital SLR before you purchased your Nikon D5200, you're probably already familiar with the basic menu system. The menus consist of a series of screens with entries, as shown in Figure 8.1. Navigating among the various menus is easy and follows a consistent set of rules:

- Press the MENU button to display the main menu screens.

- Use the multi selector's left/right/up/down buttons to navigate among the menu entries to highlight your choice. Moving the highlighting to the left column lets you scroll up and down among the six top-level menus. From the top in Figure 8.1, they are Playback, Shooting, Custom Setting, Setup, Retouch, and My Menu, with Help access represented by a question mark at the bottom of the column.

- A highlighted top-level menu's icon will change from black-and-white to yellow highlighting. Use the multi selector's right button to move into the column containing that menu's choices, and the top-level icon will change once again, to the color associated with that menu (Playback: Blue; Shooting: Green; Custom Setting: Red; Setup: Orange; Retouch: Purple; My Menu: Gray). Use the up/down buttons to scroll among the entries. If more than one screen full of choices is available, a scroll bar appears at the far right of the screen, with a position slider showing the relative position of the currently highlighted entry.

- To work with a highlighted menu entry, press the OK button in the center of the multi selector, or just press the right button on the multi selector. Any additional screens of choices will appear. You can move among them using the same multi selector movements.

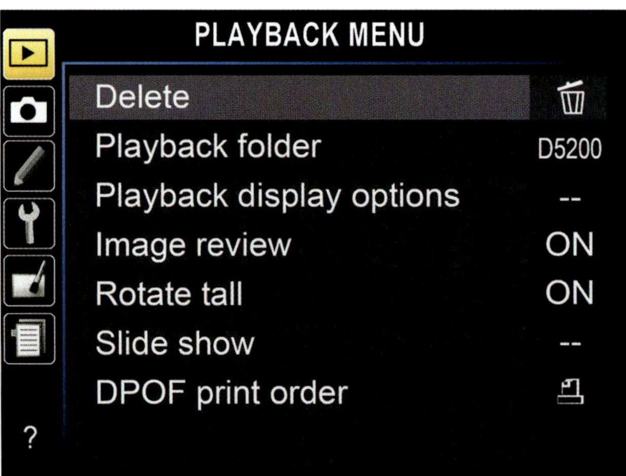


**Figure 8.1**
The multi selector's navigational buttons are used to move among the various menu entries.

■ You can confirm a selection by pressing the OK button or, frequently, by pressing the right button on the multi selector once again. Some functions require scrolling to a Done menu choice, or include an instruction to set a choice using some other button.

■ Pressing the multi selector left button usually backs you out of the current screen, and pressing the MENU button again usually does the same thing. You can exit the menu system at any time by tapping the shutter release button.

■ The Nikon D5200 "remembers" the top-level menu and specific menu entry you were using (but not any submenus) the last time the menu system was accessed, so pressing the MENU button brings you back to where you left off. So, if you were working with an entry in the Custom Setting menu's Autofocus section, then decided to take a photo, the next time you press the MENU button the Custom Setting menu and the Autofocus entry will be highlighted, but not the specific submenu (a1 to a3) that you might have selected.

As I mentioned, the top-level menus are color-coded, and a partial "frame" in that color is displayed underneath the menu title when one of those menus is highlighted. The colors are: Playback menu (blue); Shooting menu (green); Custom Setting menu (red); Setup menu (orange); Retouch menu (purple); and My Menu (gray). The Custom Setting menu has six submenus that are themselves color-coded to help you keep track of where you are located in the menu system. You'll learn about the Custom Setting, Setup, Retouch, and My Menu options in Chapters 9 and 10.

## Playback Menu Options

The blue-coded Playback menu has seven entries where you select options related to the display, review, transfer, and printing of the photos you've taken. The choices you'll find include the following entries pictured in Figure 8.1:

■ Delete
■ Playback Folder
■ Playback Display Options
■ Image Review

■ Rotate Tall
■ Slide Show
■ DPOF Print Order

## Delete

Choose this menu entry and you'll be given three choices: Selected, Select Date, and All. If you choose All, then all the pictures in the folder currently selected for playback (as described next) will be removed. To delete only some pictures from a folder, choose Selected; you'll see an image selection screen like the one shown in Figure 8.2. Then, follow these instructions:

1. Use the multi selector cursor keys to scroll among the available images.

2. When you highlight an image you think you might like to delete, press the Playback button to temporarily enlarge that image so you can evaluate it further. When you release the button, the selection screen returns.

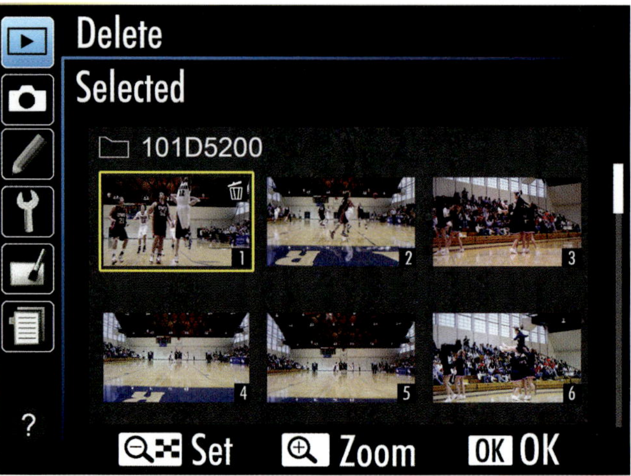



**Figure 8.2**
Select images to delete.

3. To mark an image for deletion, press the Zoom Out/Thumbnail button (*not* the Trash button). A trash can icon will appear overlaid on that image's thumbnail. To unmark an image, press the Zoom Out/Thumbnail button again.

4. When you've finished marking images to delete, press OK. A final screen will appear asking you to confirm the removal of the image(s). Choose Yes to delete the image(s) or No to cancel deletion, and then press OK. If you selected Yes, then you'll return to the Playback menu; if you chose No, you'll be taken back to the selection screen to mark/unmark images.

5. To back out of the selection screen, press the MENU button.

In the main Delete screen you can also choose Select Date. Highlight any of the available dates that have pictures, and press the multi selector right button to add a check mark to that date. Press the Zoom Out/Index button to view/confirm that the images for the date you've marked are those you want to delete, and press the button again to return to the Select Date screen. When you're finished choosing dates, press OK to delete the images from the confirmation screen.

Your final choice from the main Delete screen is All, which removes all the images from your memory card, except for those marked as Protected. Keep in mind that deleting images though the Delete process is slower than just wiping out the whole card with the Format command, so using Format is generally much faster than choosing Delete: All, and also is a safer way of returning your memory card to a fresh, blank state.

## Playback Folder

Your Nikon D5200 will create folders on your memory card to store the images that it creates. It assigns the first folder a number, like 100D5200, and when that folder fills with 999 images, the camera automatically creates a new folder numbered one higher, such as 101D5200. If you use the same memory card in another camera, that camera will also create its own folder. Thus, you can end up with several folders on the same memory card, until you eventually reformat the card and folder creation starts anew.

This menu item allows you to choose which folders are accessed when displaying images using the D5200's Playback facility. Your choices are as follows:

- **Current.** The D5200 will display only images in the current folder. For example, if you have been shooting heavily at an event and have already accumulated more than 999 shots in one folder and the D5200 has created a new folder for the overflow, you'd use this setting to view only the most recent photos, which reside in the current folder. You can change the current folder to any other folder on your memory card using the Active Folder option in the Shooting menu, described later in this chapter.

- **All.** All folders containing images that the D5200 can read will be accessed, regardless of which camera created them. You might want to use this setting if you swap memory cards among several cameras and want to be able to review all the photos (especially when considering reformatting the memory card). You will be able to view images even if they were created by a non-Nikon camera if those images conform to the Design Rule for Camera File system (DCF) specifications.

## Playback Display Options

You'll recall from Chapter 3 that a great deal of information, available on multiple screens, can be displayed when reviewing images. This menu item helps you reduce/increase the clutter by specifying which information and screens will be available. To activate or deactivate an info option, scroll to that option and press the OK button or right multi selector button to add a check mark to the box next to that item. Press the OK button or right button to unmark an item that has previously been checked. Important: when you're finished, you must scroll up to Done and press OK or the right multi selector button to confirm your choices. Exiting the Display mode menu any other way will cause any changes you may have made to be ignored. Your info options include:

- **None.** This choice does *not* mean that all information will be hidden. (To do that, you'd need to uncheck all the boxes on this screen.) When you select this option, an additional playback screen with *no shooting information* will be shown in the cycle displayed when you press the up/down multi selector buttons.

- **Highlights.** When enabled, overexposed highlight areas in your image will blink with a black border during picture review. That's your cue to consider using exposure compensation to reduce exposure, unless a minus-EV setting will cause loss of shadow detail that you want to preserve. You can read more about correcting exposure in Chapter 4.

- **RGB histogram.** Displays both luminance (brightness) and RGB histograms on a screen that can be displayed using the up/down multi selector buttons, as shown in Chapter 2.

- **Shooting data.** Activates the three pages of shooting data shown in Chapter 3. (Flip back if you need a refresher.)

- **Overview.** Marking this enables the Overview screen shown in Chapter 3.

# Image Review

There are certain shooting situations in which it's useful to have the picture you've just shot pop up on the LCD automatically for review. Perhaps you're fine-tuning exposure or autofocus and want to be able to see whether your most recent image is acceptable. Or, maybe you're the nervous type and just want confirmation that you actually took a picture. Instant review has saved my bacon a few times; for example, when I was shooting with studio flash in Manual mode and didn't notice that the shutter speed had been set to a (non-syncing) 1/500th second by mistake.

A lot of the time, however, it's a better idea to *not* automatically review your shots in order to conserve battery power (the LCD is one of the major juice drains in the camera) or to speed up or simplify operations. For example, if you've just fired off a burst of eight shots at 5 fps during a football game, do you *really* need to have each and every frame display as the D5200 clears its buffer and stores the photos on your memory card? This menu operation allows you to choose which mode to use:

- **On.** Image review is automatic after every shot is taken.
- **Off.** Images are displayed only when you press the Playback button. Nikon, in its wisdom, has made this the default setting.

# Rotate Tall

When you rotate the D5200 to photograph vertical subjects in portrait (tall), rather than landscape (wide) orientation, you probably don't want to view them tilted onto their sides later on, either on the camera LCD or within your image viewing/editing application on your computer. The D5200 is way ahead of you. It has a directional sensor built in that can detect whether the camera was rotated when the photo was taken and hide this information in the image file itself.

The orientation data is applied in two different ways. It can be used by the D5200 to automatically rotate images when they are displayed on the camera's LCD monitor, or you can ignore the data and let the images display in non-rotated fashion (so you have to rotate the camera to view them in their proper orientation). Your image-editing application, such as Adobe Photoshop Elements, can also use the embedded file data to automatically rotate images on your computer screen.

Rotation works only if you've set Auto Image Rotation to On in the Setup menu (I'll show you how to do that in Chapter 10). Once you've done that, the D5200 will embed information about orientation in the image file, and your image editor (such as Adobe Photoshop or Photoshop Elements) will rotate the images for you as the files are loaded.

This menu choice deals only with whether the image should be rotated when displayed on the *camera LCD monitor.* (If you de-activate this option, your image-editing software can still read the embedded rotation data and properly display your images.) When Rotate Tall is turned off, the Nikon D5200 does not rotate pictures taken in vertical orientation, displaying them as shown at left in Figure 8.3. The image is large on your LCD screen, but you must rotate the camera to view it upright.

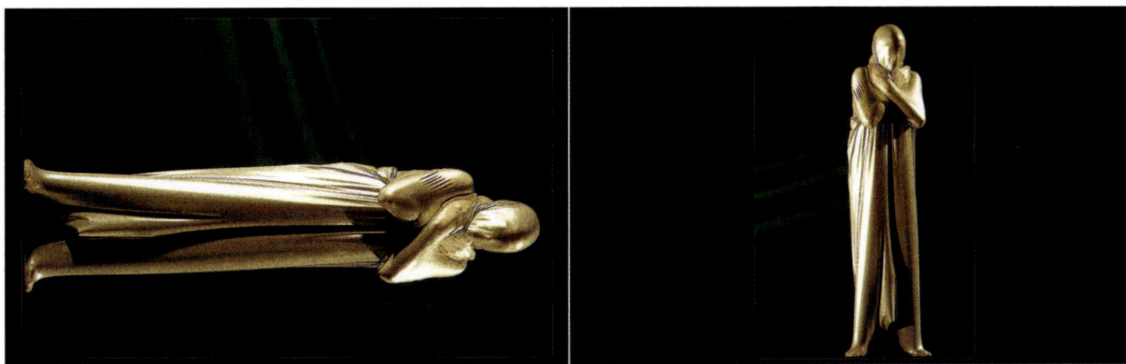

**Figure 8.3** With Rotate Tall turned off, vertical images appear large on the LCD, but you must turn the camera to view them upright. With Rotate Tall turned on, vertical images are shown in a smaller size, but oriented for viewing without turning the camera.

When Rotate Tall is turned on, the D5200 rotates pictures taken in vertical orientation on the LCD screen so you don't have to turn the camera to view them comfortably. However, this orientation also means that the longest dimension of the image is shown using the shortest dimension of the LCD, so the picture is reduced in size, as you can see at right in Figure 8.3.

So, turn this feature On (as well as Auto Image Rotation in the Setup menu), if you'd rather not turn your camera to view vertical shots in their natural orientation, and don't mind the smaller image. Turn the feature Off if, as I do, you'd rather see a larger image and are willing to rotate the camera to do so.

## Slide Show

The D5200's Slide Show feature is a convenient way to review images in the current playback folder one after another, without the need to manually switch between them.

To activate a slide show, just choose Start from this entry in the Playback menu. If you like, you can choose Frame Interval before commencing the show in order to select an interval of either 2, 3, 5, or 10 seconds between "slides." During playback, you can press the OK button to pause the "slide show." When the show is paused, a menu pops up, as shown in Figure 8.4, with choices to restart the show (by pressing the OK button again); change the interval between frames; or to exit the show entirely.

As the images are displayed, press the up/down multi selector buttons to change the amount of information presented on the screen with each image. For example, you might want to review a set of images and the settings used to shoot them. At any time during the show, press the up/down buttons until the informational screen you want is overlaid on the images.

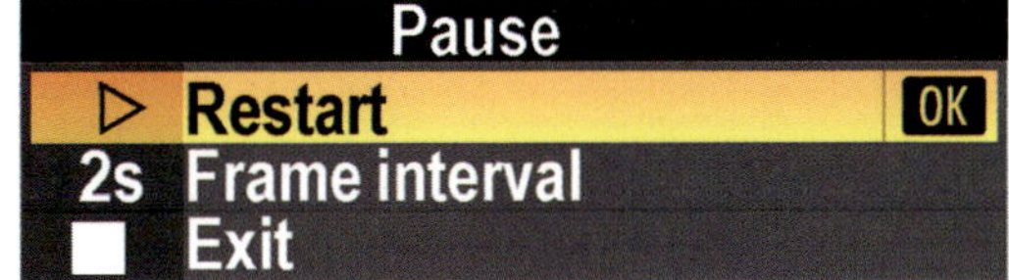


**Figure 8.4** Press the OK button to pause the slide show, change the interval between slides, or to exit the presentation.

As the slide show progresses, you can press the left/right multi selector buttons to move back to a previous frame or jump ahead to the next one. The slide show will then proceed as before. Press the MENU button to exit the slide show and return to the menu, or press the Playback button to exit the menu system totally. As always, while reviewing images you can tap the MENU button to exit the show and return to the menus, or tap the shutter release button if you want to remove everything from the screen and return to shooting mode.

At the end of the slide show, as when you've paused it, you'll be offered the choice of restarting the sequence, changing the frame interval, or exiting the Slide Show feature completely.

## DPOF Print Order

The Nikon D5200 supports the DPOF (Digital Print Order Format) that is now almost universally used by digital cameras to specify which images on your memory card should be printed, and the number of prints desired of each image. This information is recorded on the memory card and can be interpreted by a compatible printer when the camera is linked to the printer using the USB cable, or when the memory card is inserted into a card reader slot on the printer itself. Photo labs are also equipped to read this data and make prints when you supply your memory card to them.

When you choose this menu item, you're presented with a set of screens that look very much like the Delete Photos screens described earlier, only you're selecting pictures for printing rather than deleting them. The button sequences are slightly different, however:

1. Use the multi selector cursor keys to scroll among the available images.

2. When you highlight an image you might want to print, press the Playback Zoom In button to temporarily enlarge that image so you can evaluate it further. When you release the button, the selection screen returns.

3. To mark an image for printing, press the multi selector up buttons to choose the number of prints you want, up to 99 per image. To deselect an image, press the multi selector down button. A printer icon and the number specified will appear overlaid on that image's thumbnail. (See Figure 8.5.)

4. To unmark an image for printing press the down button until the number of prints reaches zero. The printer icon will vanish.

5. When you've finished marking images to print, press OK.

6. A final screen will appear in which you can request a data imprint (shutter speed and aperture) or imprint date (the date the photos were taken). Use the up/down buttons to select one or both of these options, if desired, and press the left/right buttons to mark or unmark the check boxes. When a box is marked, the imprint information for that option will be included on *all* prints in the print order.

7. Press OK when finished, and a Print Order Complete message appears on the LCD monitor.

**Figure 8.5**
Select images for
printing.

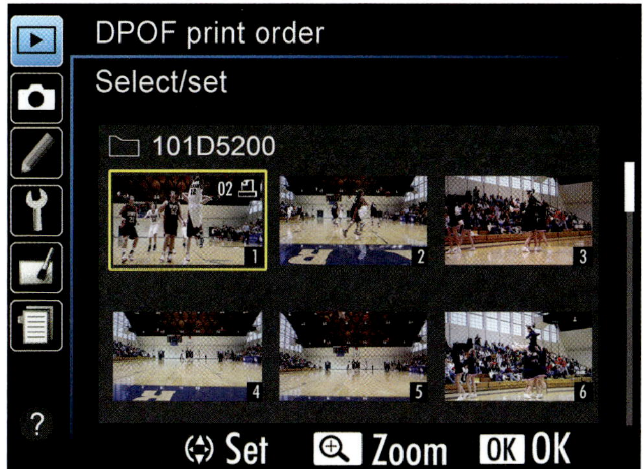


## Shooting Menu Options

This section explains the options of the Shooting menu (see Figure 8.6) and how to use them. The options you'll find in these green-coded menus include:

- Reset Shooting Menu
- Storage Folder
- Image Quality
- Image Size
- White Balance
- Set Picture Control
- Manage Picture Control
- Auto Distortion Control
- Color Space
- Active D-Lighting
- HDR (high dynamic range)
- Long Exp. NR
- High ISO NR
- ISO Sensitivity Settings
- Release Mode
- Multiple Exposure
- Interval Timer Shooting
- Movie Settings

## Reset Shooting Menu

Don't feel bad over being confused about what this menu item does. The Nikon D5200 has, in effect, *three* different kinds of resets. This is one of them.

- **Shooting menu reset.** Use this option to reset the values of the currently selected Shooting menu bank *except for image quality, image size, white balance, and ISO sensitivity* to their default values. When you select this menu item, your choices are Yes or No.

- **Custom Setting menu reset.** This option, which I'll describe in Chapter 9, is used to reset the four Custom Setting values. It has no effect on camera settings or shooting menu banks.

- **Two-button reset.** The Nikon D5200's two-button reset (holding down the MENU and information edit buttons [located on either side of the viewfinder and marked with a green dot] simultaneously for more than two seconds) will *not* reset your Shooting menu banks or Custom Setting menu banks. This particular reset is for basic settings, such as focus point, exposure mode, flexible program, exposure/flash compensation, bracketing, flash mode, flash value lock, and multiple exposure settings.

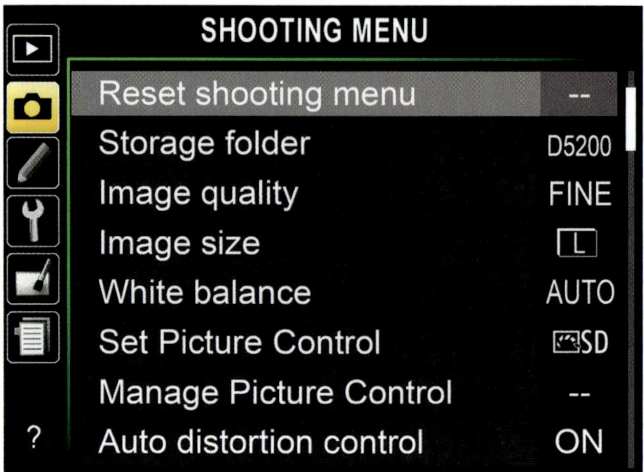



**Figure 8.6**
Common shooting settings can be changed in this menu.

Table 8.1 shows the default values that are set using Reset Shooting menu option. If you don't know what some of these settings are, I'll explain them later in this section.

## Storage Folder

If you want to store images in a folder other than the one created and selected by the Nikon D5200, you can switch among available folders on your Secure Digital card, or create your own folder. Remember that any folders you create will be deleted when you reformat your memory card.

To change the currently active folder:

1. Choose Storage Folder in the Shooting menu.
2. Scroll down to Select Folder and press the multi selector right button.
3. From among the available folders shown, scroll to the one that you want to become active for image storage and playback. (Handy when displaying slide shows.)
4. Press the OK button to confirm your choice, or press the multi selector right button to return to the Shooting menu.

Why create your own folders? Perhaps you're traveling and have a high-capacity memory card and want to store the images for each day (or for each city that you visit) in a separate folder. When I'm shooting images on the same card on consecutive days, I change the folder number so I can copy only that day's new pictures to my backup media back in my hotel room. The photos I shoot on January 25 go in a folder numbered 125; those shot on January 26 go in 126; and so forth. (Use some other system in October, November, and December, as folders can have only three-digit prefixes.)

### Table 8.1  Default Shooting Menu Values

| Function | Default Value | Function | Default Value |
|---|---|---|---|
| Reset Shooting Menu | None | Release mode | |
| Storage Folder | None | Sports, Pets | Continuous H |
| Image Quality | JPEG Normal | Other exposure modes | Singe-frame |
| Image Size | Large | Multiple Exposure | |
| White Balance | Auto | Multiple exposure mode | Off |
| Fluorescent | Cool-white | Number of shots | 2 |
| Set Picture Control | Standard | Auto gain | On |
| Manage Picture Control | None | Interval Timer Shooting | Off |
| Auto Distortion Control | Off | Movie Settings | |
| Color Space | sRGB | Frame size/frame rate | 1920 × 1080/60i |
| Active D-Lighting | Auto | Movie quality | High quality |
| HDR (high dynamic range) | Off | Microphone | Auto sensitivity |
| Long Exposure Noise Reduction | Off | Manual movie settings | Off |
| High ISO Noise Reduction | Normal | | |
| ISO Sensitivity Settings | | | |
| P, S, A, M modes | 100 | | |
| Other exposure modes | Auto | | |
| Auto ISO sensitivity control | Off | | |

Or, maybe you'd like to separate those wedding photos you snapped at the ceremony from those taken at the reception. As I mentioned earlier, the Nikon D5200 automatically creates a folder on a newly formatted memory card with a name like 100D5200, and when it fills with 999 images, it will automatically create a new folder with a number incremented by one (such as 101D5200). To create your own folder:

1. Choose Storage Folder in the Shooting menu.

2. Scroll down to New and press the multi selector right button.

3. A screen like the one shown in Figure 8.7 appears. You can enter a name for the folder, up to five characters long, as described next.

4. Press OK when finished to create and activate the new folder.

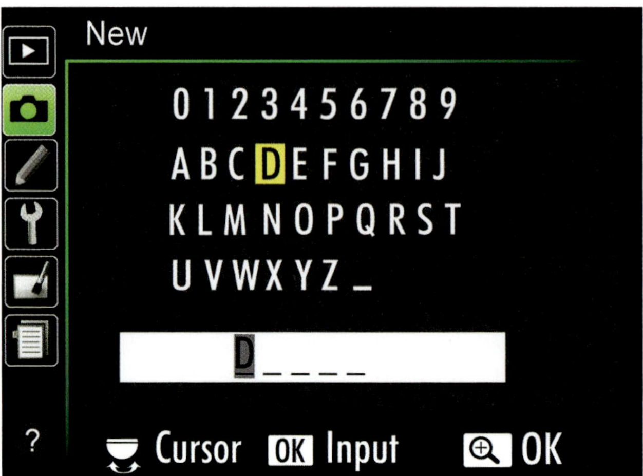



**Figure 8.7**
Use this D5200
screen to enter text.

## Entering Text on the Nikon D5200

Now is a good time to master text entry, because you can use it to enter comments, rename folders, and perform other functions. The Nikon D5200 uses a fairly standardized text entry screen to name files, Picture Controls, create new folder names, enter image comments, and other text. You'll be using text entry with other functions that I'll describe later in this book. The screen looks like the one shown in Figure 8.7, with some variations (for example, some functions have a less diverse character set, or offer more or fewer spaces for your entries). To name a Picture Control, first select File Naming, then use the right multi selector button to reveal the text entry screen. After that, you can use the multi selector navigational buttons to scroll around within the array of alphanumerics, and enter your text:

- **Highlight a character.** Use the multi selector keys to scroll around within the array of characters.

- **Insert highlighted character.** Press the multi selector center button, OK, to insert the highlighted character. The cursor will move one place to the right to accept the next character.

- **Non-destructively backspace.** Use the command dial to move the cursor within the naming field. This allows you to backspace and replace a character without disturbing the others you've entered.

- **Erase a highlighted character.** To remove a character you've already input, move the cursor to highlight that character, and then type in a replacement character or press the Trash button. If you want to remove the character or insert a blank, choose the blank character (located after the Z in the array).

- **Confirm your entry.** When you're finished entering text, press the Zoom In button to confirm your entry, then tap the shutter release to exit the menu system.

# Image Quality

As I noted in Chapter 1, you can choose the image quality settings used by the D5200 to store its files. The quickest way to do that is using the information edit screen. You can also use this menu option to make the quality settings using the bigger, brighter three-inch color LCD. You have two choices to make:

- **JPEG compression.** To reduce the size of your image files and allow more photos to be stored on a given memory card, the D5200 uses JPEG compression to squeeze the images down to a smaller size. This compacting reduces the image quality a little, so you're offered your choice of Fine (a 1:4 reduction), Normal (1:8 reduction), and Basic (1:16) compression. You can see an exaggerated version of the effects of JPEG compression in Figure 8.8. There is a further tweak you can make, specifying whether JPEG compression should be optimized for the smallest possible image size at a given compression level, or whether you'd prefer to sacrifice some compression for optimal quality. You won't find those options in this menu entry; instead, use the JPEG Compression menu item, described later in this section.

- **JPEG, RAW, or both.** You can elect to store only JPEG versions of the images you shoot, or you can save your photos as RAW files, which consume more than twice as much space on your memory card. Or, you can store both at once as you shoot. Many photographers elect to save *both* JPEG and a RAW, so they'll have a JPEG version that might be usable as-is, as well as the original "digital negative" RAW file in case they want to do some processing of the image later. You'll end up with two different versions of the same file: one with a JPG extension, and one with the NEF extension that signifies a Nikon RAW file.

**Figure 8.8**
At low levels of JPEG compression the image looks sharp even when you enlarge it enough to see the actual pixels (top); when using extreme JPEG compression (bottom), an image obviously loses quality.

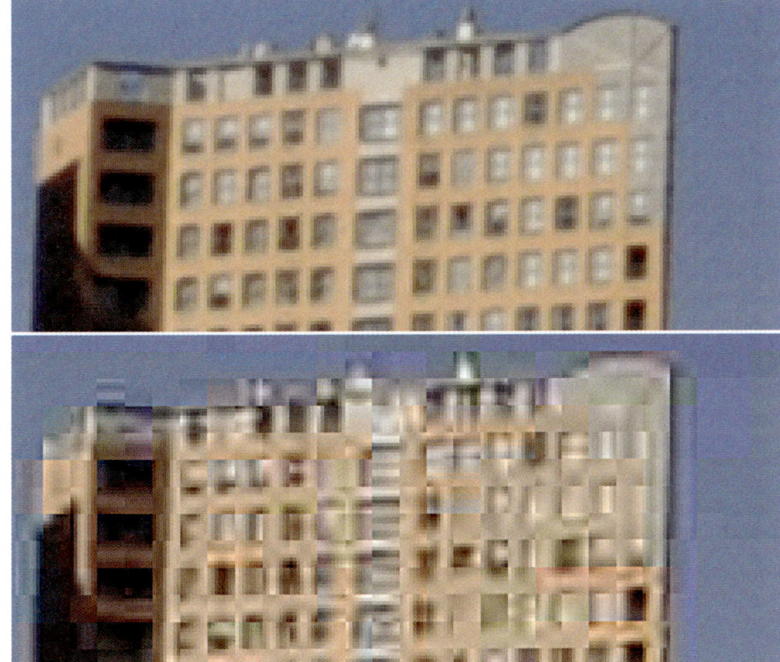

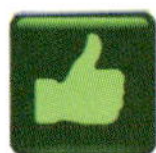

> **Tip**
>
> In any RAW+JPEG mode, the D5200 always saves a full-resolution 6000 × 4000 pixel RAW image, even if you choose a smaller image size (resolution) for the JPEG version (such as Medium (M) or Small (S)).

To choose the combination you want, access the Shooting menu, scroll to Image Quality, and select it. A screen similar to the one shown in Figure 8.9 will appear. Scroll to highlight the setting you want, and either press OK or push the multi selector right button to confirm your selection.

In practice, you'll probably use the JPEG Fine, RAW+JPEG Fine selections most often. Why so many choices, then? There are some limited advantages to using the JPEG Normal and JPEG Basic settings, either at full resolution (Large) or when using the Medium and Small resolution settings. Settings that are less than max allow stretching the capacity of your memory card so you can shoehorn quite a few more pictures onto a single memory card. That can come in useful when on vacation and you're running out of storage, or when you're shooting non-critical work that doesn't require 24 megapixels of resolution (such as photos taken for real estate listings, web page display, photo ID cards, or similar applications). Some photographers like to record RAW+JPEG Normal so they'll have a moderate-quality JPEG file for review only and no intention of using it for editing purposes, while retaining access to the original RAW file for serious editing.

For most work, using lower resolution and extra compression is false economy. You never know when you might actually need that extra bit of picture detail. Your best bet is to have enough memory cards to handle all the shooting you want to do until you have the chance to transfer your photos to your computer or a personal storage device.

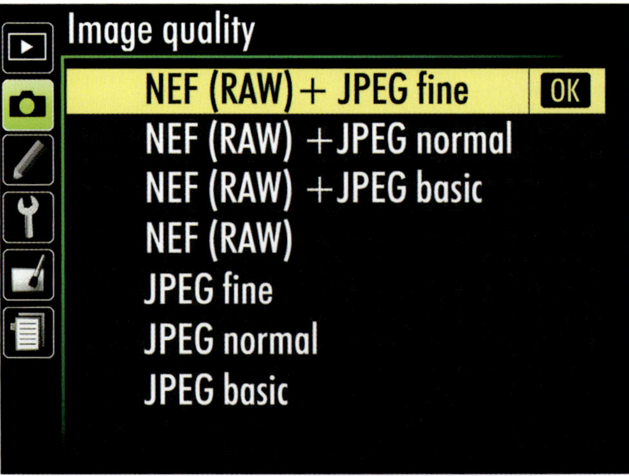


**Figure 8.9**
You can choose RAW, JPEG, or RAW+JPEG formats here.

However, reduced image quality can sometimes be beneficial if you're shooting sequences of photos rapidly, as the D5200 is able to hold more of them in its internal memory buffer before transferring to the memory card. Still, for most sports and other applications, you'd probably rather have better, sharper pictures than longer periods of continuous shooting. Do you really need 20 or 30 shots of a pass reception in a football game, or a dozen or two slightly different versions of your local basketball star driving in for a lay-up?

## JPEG vs. RAW

You'll sometimes be told that RAW files are the "unprocessed" image information your camera produces, before it's been modified. That's nonsense. RAW files are no more unprocessed than your camera film is after it's been through the chemicals to produce a negative or transparency. A lot can happen in the developer that can affect the quality of a film image—positively and negatively—and, similarly, your digital image undergoes a significant amount of processing before it is saved as a RAW file. Nikon even applies a name (EXPEED) to the digital image processing (DIP) chip used to perform this magic.

A RAW file is more similar to a film camera's processed negative. It contains all the information, captured in 14-bit channels per color (and stored in a 16-bit space), with no sharpening and no application of any special filters or other settings you might have specified when you took the picture. Those settings are *stored* with the RAW file so they can be applied when the image is converted to a form compatible with your favorite image editor. However, using RAW conversion software such as Adobe Camera Raw or Nikon Capture NX, you can override those settings and apply settings of your own. You can select essentially the same changes there that you might have specified in your camera's picture-taking options.

RAW exists because sometimes we want to have access to all the information captured by the camera, before the camera's internal logic has processed it and converted the image to a standard file format. Even compressed RAW doesn't save as much space as JPEG. What it does do is preserve all the information captured by your camera after it's been converted from analog to digital form.

So, why don't we always use RAW? Some photographers avoid using Nikon's RAW NEF files on the misguided conviction that they don't want to spend time in post-processing, forgetting that, if the camera settings you would have used for JPEG are correct, each RAW image's default attributes will use those settings and the RAW image will not need much manipulation. Post-processing in such cases is *optional*, and overwhelmingly helpful when an image needs to be fine-tuned.

Although some photographers do save *only* in RAW format, it's more common (and frequently more convenient) to use RAW plus one of the JPEG options, or, if you're confident about your settings, just shoot JPEG and eschew RAW altogether. In some situations, working with a RAW file can slow you down a little. RAW images take longer to store on the memory card, and must be converted from RAW to a format your image editor can handle, whether you elect to go with the default settings in force when the picture was taken, or make minor adjustments to the settings you specified in the camera.

As a result, those who depend on speedy access to images or who shoot large numbers of photos at once may prefer JPEG over RAW. Wedding photographers, for example, might expose several thousand photos during a bridal affair and offer hundreds to clients as electronic proofs for inclusion in an album. Wedding shooters take the time to make sure that their in-camera settings are correct, minimizing the need to post-process photos after the event. Given that their JPEGs are so good, there is little need to get bogged down shooting RAW.

Sports photographers also avoid RAW files. I visited a local Division III college one sunny September afternoon. I covered the first half of a football game, trotted down a hill to shoot a women's soccer match later that afternoon, and ended up in the adjacent field house shooting a volleyball invitational tournament an hour later. I managed to shoot 1,920 photos, most of them at a 5 fps clip, in about four hours. I certainly didn't have any plans to do post-processing on very many of those shots, and firing the camera at its maximum frame rate didn't allow RAW shooting, so carefully exposed and precisely focused JPEG images were my file format of choice that day.

JPEG was invented as a more compact file format that can store most of the information in a digital image, but in a much smaller size. JPEG predates most digital SLRs and was initially used to squeeze down files for transmission over slow dial-up connections. Even if you were using an early dSLR with 1.3 megapixel files for news photography, you didn't want to send them back to the office over a modem at 1,200 bps.

But, as I noted, JPEG provides smaller files by compressing the information in a way that loses some image data. JPEG remains a viable alternative because it offers several different quality levels. At the highest quality Fine level, you might not be able to tell the difference between the original RAW file and the JPEG version, even though a RAW file occupies, by Nikon's estimate, 24.6MB on your memory card, while the Fine JPEG takes up only 12.2MB of space. You've squeezed the image by roughly 50 percent without losing much visual information at all. If you don't mind losing some quality, you can use more aggressive Normal compression with JPEG to cut the size in half again, to 6.2MB.

In my case, I shoot virtually everything at RAW+JPEG Fine. Most of the time, I'm not concerned about filling up my memory cards, as I usually have a minimum of two 64GB cards and six 32GB memory cards with me. I often copy shots to my Apple iPad because, thanks to its 3G connectivity, I can e-mail them immediately or post them on Facebook or Flickr, no matter where I happen to be.

I also use an netbook with an external 320GB hard drive, and, most recently, a tiny MacBook Air with an 11.6 inch screen (it's not much bigger than my iPad). As I mentioned earlier, when shooting sports I'll shift to JPEG FINE (with no RAW file) to squeeze a little extra speed out of my camera's continuous shooting mode, and to reduce the need to wade through eight-photo bursts taken in RAW format.

### HIDDEN JPEGS

You may not be aware that your RAW file contains an embedded JPEG file, hidden inside in the JPEG Basic format. It's used to provide thumbnail previews of JPEG files, and to display images you've shot during picture review on the D5200's built-in screen. That's right, even if you're shooting RAW (only), the D5200 still creates a JPEG version, and that—not your RAW image—is displayed on the color LCD monitor.

This is also why you may notice an interesting phenomenon when loading a RAW image into a program like Nikon Capture NX 2 or Adobe Lightroom. When the software first starts interpreting the RAW image, it may immediately display this hidden JPEG view which has, as you might expect, all the settings applied that you dialed into the camera. Then, as it finishes loading the RAW file, the application (Lightroom in particular) uses its own intelligence to fine-tune the image and display what it thinks is a decent version of the image, replacing the embedded JPEG. That's why you may see complaints that Lightroom or another program is behaving oddly: the initial embedded JPEG may look better than the final version, so it looks as if the application is degrading the image quality as the file loads. Of course, in all cases, once the RAW file is available, you can make your own changes to optimize it to your taste.

There is a second use for these hidden JPEG files. If you shoot RAW without creating JPEG files and later decide you want a JPEG version, there are dozens of utility programs that will extract the embedded JPEG and save it as a separate file. (Google "JPEG extractor" to locate a freeware program that will perform this step for your Mac, PC, or other computer.)

# Image Size

The next menu command in the Shooting menu lets you select the resolution, or number of pixels captured as you shoot with your Nikon D5200. Your choices range from Large (L—6000 × 4000 pixels, 24 megapixels), Medium (M—4496 × 3000, 13 megapixels), and Small (S—2992 × 2000 pixels, 6.0 megapixels). Personally, I think it's pretty cool that after using a Nikon D70 (with 6MP) and a Nikon D200 (with 10MP) for several years, my D5200 has a *medium* resolution that exceeds both of them.

You can select image sizes using the information edit screen. Or, you can use this menu to perform the task. There are no additional options available from the Image Size menu screen.

# White Balance

This menu entry allows you to choose one of the white balance values from among Auto, incandescent, seven varieties of fluorescent illumination, direct sunlight, flash, cloudy, shade, or a preset value taken from an existing photograph, or a measurement you make. Some of the settings you make here can be duplicated using the information edit screen, but the menus offer even more choices, as you'll see. Your white balance settings can have a significant impact on the color rendition of your images, as you can see in Figure 8.10.

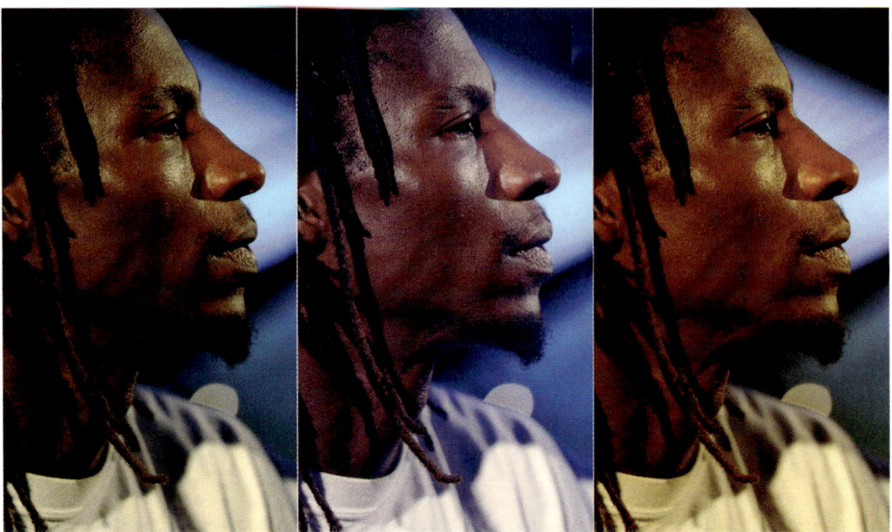

**Figure 8.10**
Adjusting color temperature can provide different results of the same subject at settings of 3,400K (left), 5,000K (middle), and 2,800K (right).

In this section, I'm going to describe only the menu commands at your disposal for setting white balance. To learn more about the theory behind why and when you should make white balance adjustments, check out the more complete description of white balance bracketing in Chapter 4.

When you select the White Balance entry on the Shooting menu, you'll see an array of choices like those shown in Figure 8.11. (One additional choice, PRE Preset Manual, is not visible until you scroll down to it.) If you choose Fluorescent, you'll be taken to another screen that presents seven different types of lamps, from sodium-vapor through warm-white fluorescent down to high-temperature mercury-vapor. If you know the exact type of non-incandescent lighting being used, you can select it, or settle on a likely compromise.

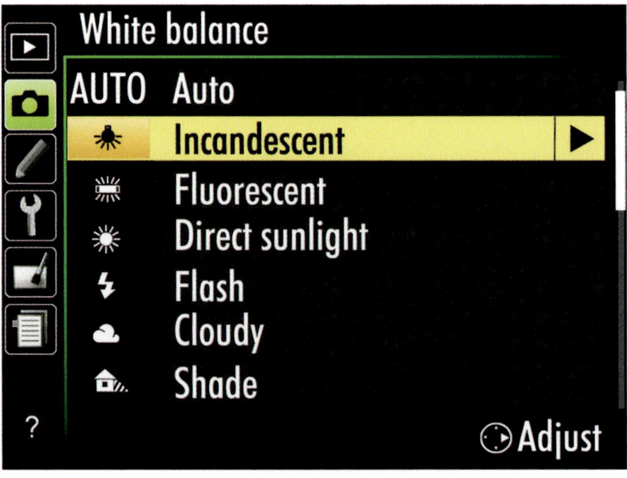


**Figure 8.11**
The White Balance menu has predefined values, plus the option of setting color temperature and presets you measure yourself.

For all other settings (Auto, Incandescent, Direct Sunlight, Flash, Cloudy, or Shade), highlight the white balance option you want, then press the multi selector right button (or press OK) to view the fine-tuning screen shown in Figure 8.12 (and which uses the Incandescent setting as an example). The screen shows a grid with two axes, a blue/amber axis extending left/right, and a green/magenta axis extending up and down the grid. By default, the grid's cursor is positioned in the middle, and a readout to the right of the grid shows the cursor's coordinates on the A-B axis (yes, I know the display has the end points reversed) and G-M axis at 0,0.

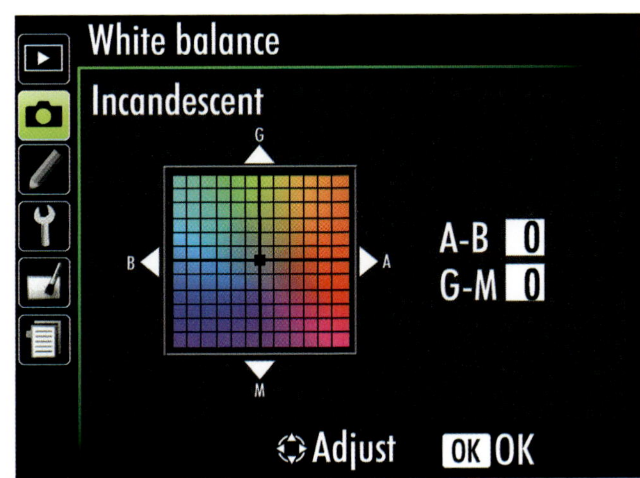


**Figure 8.12**
Specific white balance settings can be fine-tuned by changing their bias in the amber/blue, magenta/green directions—or along both axes simultaneously.

You can use the multi selector's up/down and right/left buttons to move the cursor to any coordinate in the grid, thereby biasing the white balance in the direction(s) you choose. The amber-blue axis makes the image warmer or colder (but not actually yellow or blue). Similarly, the green-magenta axis preserves all the colors in the original image, but gives them a tinge biased toward green or magenta. Each increment equals about five mired units, but you should know that mired values aren't linear; five mireds at 2,500K produces a much stronger effect than five mireds at 6,000K. If you really want to fine-tune your color balance, you're better off experimenting and evaluating the results of a particular change.

When you've fine-tuned white balance, either using the Shooting menu options or the WB button, left/right triangles appear in the white balance section of the LCD at lower right to remind you that this tweaking has taken place.

## Using Preset Manual White Balance

If automatic white balance or one of the predefined settings available aren't suitable, you can set a custom white balance using the Preset Manual menu option. You can apply the white balance from a scene, either by shooting a new picture on the spot and using the resulting white balance (Measure), or using an image you have already shot (Use Photo).

To perform direct measurement from your current scene using a reference object (preferably a neutral gray or white object), follow these steps:

1. **Position reference subject.** Place the neutral reference under the lighting you want to measure.

2. **Change to Preset Manual white balance.** Access the White Balance menu entry, scroll down to Preset Manual, and press the right multi selector button. There, you'll see a screen with a choice of Measure or Use Photo.

3. **Highlight Measure.** Press OK to confirm.

4. **Overwrite existing data.** A screen appears asking whether you want to overwrite the existing Preset Manual value. Highlight Yes and press OK to proceed.

5. **Take photo.** Take a picture of your neutral reference subject.

6. **Confirm successful capture of white balance.** If the camera successfully measured white balance, Gd will appear in the bottom line of the viewfinder, and Data Acquired will appear on the shooting information screen on the LCD. Otherwise, you'll see no Gd on viewfinder. White balance measurement can fail when the reference object is too brightly or poorly illuminated. In that case, repeat steps 2–5 until the measurement is successful.

7. **Use captured white balance.** You can immediately begin taking pictures using the captured white balance, until you use the information edit screen or the Shooting menu entry to switch to one of the other white balance settings, such as Tungsten, or Fluorescent. The next time you switch to Pre, the white balance you just captured will be used again.

If you want to use an existing photo, choose Use Photo, and a screen will appear offering to use the most recently taken image, or you can Select Image from a folder of your choice, accessing the standard D5200 selection screen.

## Set Picture Control

Nikon's Picture Control styles allow you to choose your own sharpness, contrast, color saturation, and hue settings and apply them to your images as they are taken. There are six predefined styles offered, which Nikon calls Original Picture Controls: Standard, Neutral, Vivid, Monochrome, Portrait, and Landscape. However, you can *edit* the settings of any of those styles so they better suit your taste. But that's only the beginning; the D5200 also offers *nine* (count 'em) user-definable Picture Control styles, which you can edit to your heart's content, assign descriptive names, and deploy at the press of a few buttons. Even better, you can *copy* these styles to a memory card, edit them on your computer, and reload them into your camera at any time. So, effectively, you can have a lot more than nine custom Picture Control styles available: the nine in your camera, as well as a virtually unlimited library of user-defined styles that you have stored on memory cards.

Moreover, Nikon insists that these styles have been standardized to the extent that if you re-use a style created for one camera (say, your D5200) and load it into a different compatible camera (such as a Nikon D800), you'll get substantially the same rendition. In a way, Picture Control styles are a bit like using a particular film. Do you want the look of Kodak Ektachrome or Fujifilm Velvia? Load the appropriate style created by you—or anyone else.

Using and managing Picture Control styles is accomplished using two different menu entries, Set Picture Control, which allows you to choose an existing style and to edit the predefined styles that Nikon provides, and Manage Picture Control, discussed in the next section, which gives you the capability of creating and editing user-defined styles.

## Choosing a Picture Control Style

To choose from one of the predefined styles (Standard, Neutral, Vivid, or Monochrome) or select a user-defined style (numbered C-1 to C-9), follow these steps:

1. **Choose Set Picture Control.** This option is located in the Shooting menu. The screen shown in Figure 8.13 appears. Note that Picture Controls that have been modified from their standard settings have an asterisk next to their name.

2. **Select style.** Scroll down to the Picture Control you'd like to use.

3. **Activate Picture Control.** Press OK to activate the highlighted style. (Although you can usually select a menu item by pressing the multi selector right button; in this case, that button activates editing instead.)

4. **Exit menu.** Press the MENU button or tap the shutter release to exit the menu system.

## Editing a Picture Control Style

You can change the parameters of any of Nikon's predefined Picture Controls in P, S, A, and M modes, or any of the nine user-defined styles you create. In other modes, the camera selects one of the pre-defined Picture Controls automatically. You are given the choice of using the quick adjust/fine-tune facility to modify a Picture Control with a few sliders, or to view the relationship of your Picture Controls on a grid.

**Figure 8.13**
You can choose from the six predefined Picture Controls, or select a user-defined style, such as *C-1 Concerts* shown at the bottom of the screen.

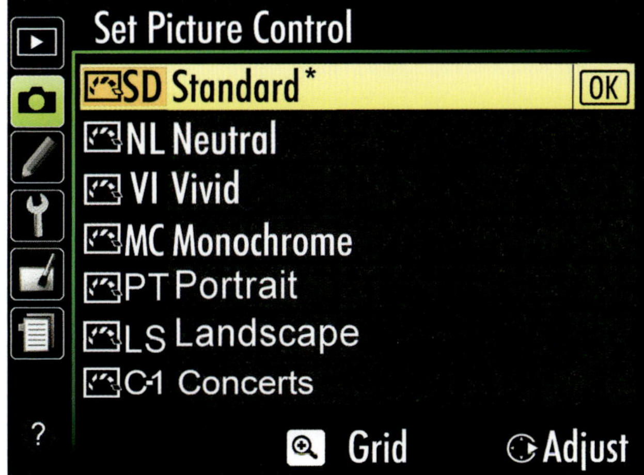

To make quick adjustments to any Picture Control except the Monochrome style, follow these steps:

1. **Access menu.** Choose Set Picture Control from the Shooting menu.

2. **Select style.** Scroll down to the Picture Control you'd like to edit.

3. **Access adjustment screen.** Press the multi selector right button to produce the adjustment screen shown in Figure 8.14.

4. **Make fast changes.** Use the Quick Adjust slider to exaggerate the attributes of the Standard or Vivid styles (Quick Adjustments are not available with other styles).

5. **Change other attributes.** Scroll down to the Sharpening, Contrast, Brightness, Saturation, and Hue sliders with the multi selector up/down buttons, then use the left/right buttons to decrease or increase the effects. A line will appear under the original setting in the slider whenever you've made a change from the defaults. **Note:** You can't adjust contrast and brightness when Active D-Lighting (discussed later in this chapter) is active. Turn it off to make those Picture Control adjustments. An icon at the upper right of the screen shows whether Active D-Lighting is on or off.

6. **Or use auto adjustments.** Instead of making changes with the slider's scale, you can move the cursor to the far left and choose A (for auto) instead when working with the Sharpening, Contrast, and Saturation sliders. The D5200 will adjust these parameters automatically, depending on the type of scene it detects.

7. **To reset values.** Press the Trash button to reset the values to their defaults.

8. **View adjustment grid.** Press the Zoom In button to view an adjustment grid (discussed next).

9. **Confirm changes.** Press OK when you're finished making adjustments.

The changes Picture Controls make to your images are more subtle than you realize, because the values that are applied among the various Picture Controls aren't absolute. Adjustments you make to, say, the Standard or Vivid styles are relative to the base values of those styles themselves. For example, the Standard style is inherently less saturated than the Vivid style, so if you move the Saturation slider two notches to the right, you'll end up with a modified Standard style that is *still*

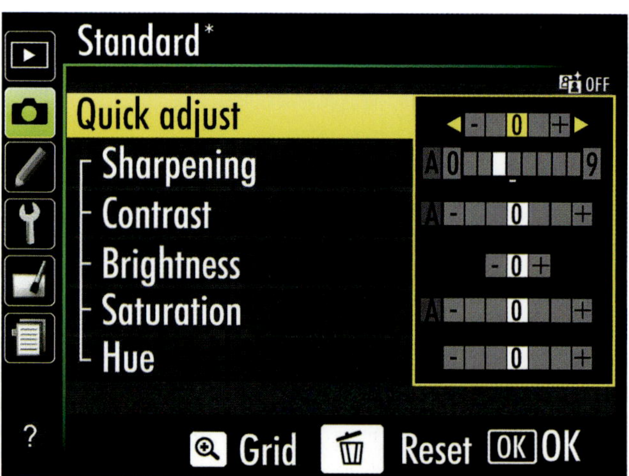


**Figure 8.14**
Sliders can be used to make quick adjustments to your Picture Control styles.

less saturated than the Vivid style's default. You'll want to learn exactly what happens to your images when you adjust each individual Picture Control, and, moreover, use the right Picture Control as your base or "parent" style when creating Picture Controls of your own. If you wanted a very, very saturated Picture Control, you'd start with the Vivid style, then adjust that and save it as Super Vivid (or something along those lines). Figure 8.15 shows pairs of images that compare four of the most frequently adjusted attributes.

Editing the Monochrome style is similar to modifying the other styles, except that the parameters differ slightly. Sharpening, Contrast, and Brightness are available, but, instead of Saturation and Hue, you can choose a filter effect (Yellow, Orange, Red, Green, or none) and a toning effect (black-and-white, plus seven levels of Sepia, Cyanotype, Red, Yellow, Green, Blue Green, Blue, Purple Blue, and Red Purple). (Keep in mind that once you've taken a JPEG photo using a Monochrome style, you can't convert the image back to full color.)

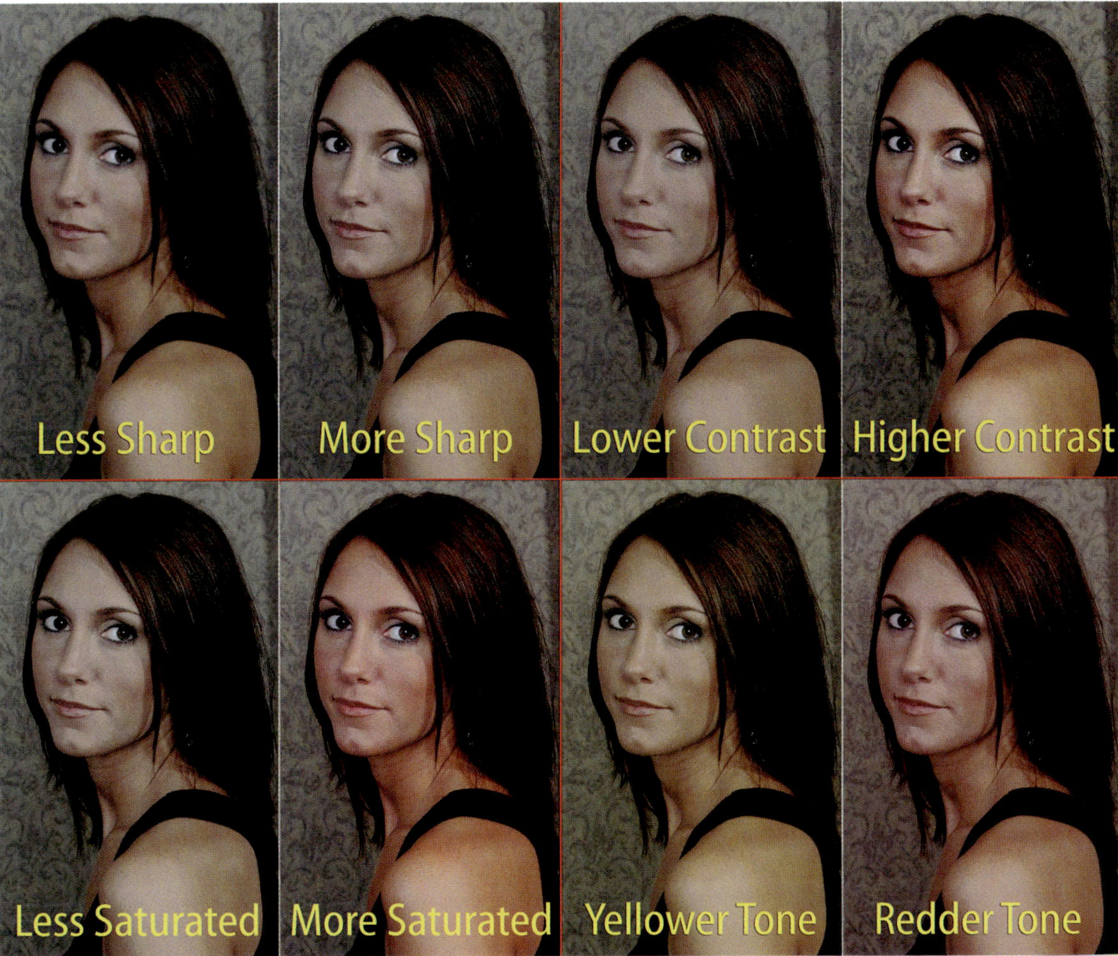


**Figure 8.15** Picture Controls allow you to adjust attributes like sharpness (upper-left pair); contrast (upper-right pair); saturation (lower-left pair); and hue (lower-right pair).

## FILTERS VS. TONING

Although some of the color choices seem to overlap, you'll get very different looks when choosing between Filter Effects and Toning. Filter Effects add no color to the monochrome image. Instead, they reproduce the look of black-and-white film that has been shot through a color filter. That is, Yellow will make the sky darker and the clouds will stand out more, while Orange makes the sky even darker and sunsets more full of detail. The Red filter produces the darkest sky of all and darkens green objects, such as leaves. Human skin may appear lighter than normal. The Green filter has the opposite effect on leaves, making them appear lighter in tone. Figure 8.16 shows a landscape scene shot with no filter, then Yellow, Green, and Red filters.

The Sepia, Blue, Green, and other toning effects, on the other hand, all add a color cast to your monochrome image. Use these when you want an old-time look or a special effect, without bothering to recolor your shots in an image editor. Several toning effects are shown in Figure 8.17.

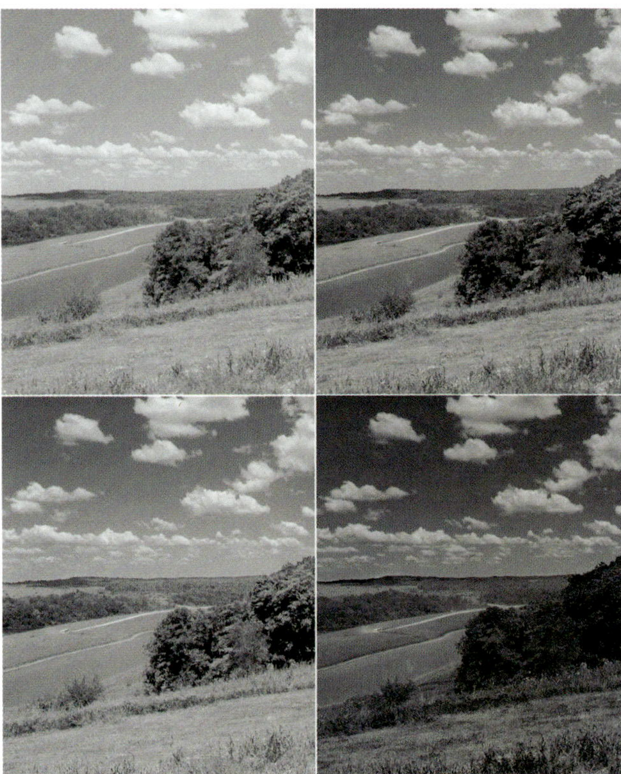

**Figure 8.16** No filter (upper left); Yellow filter (upper right); Green filter (lower left); and Red filter (lower right).

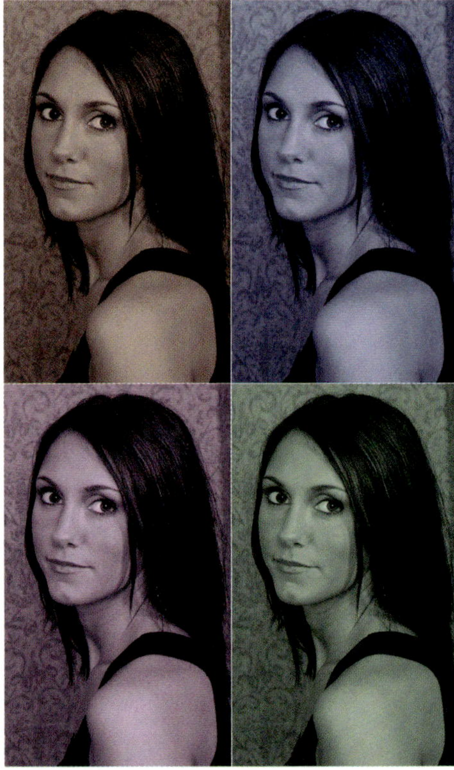

**Figure 8.17** Toning effects: Sepia (upper left); Purple Blue (upper right); Red Purple (lower left); and Green (lower right).

When you press the Zoom In button, a grid display, like the one shown in Figure 8.18, appears, showing the relative contrast and saturation of each of the predefined Picture Controls. If you've created your own custom Picture Controls, they will appear on this grid, too, represented by the numbers 1–9. Because the values for autocontrast and autosaturation may vary, the icons for any Picture Control that uses the Auto feature will be shown on the grid in green, with lines extending up and down from the icon to tip you off that the position within the coordinates may vary from the one shown.

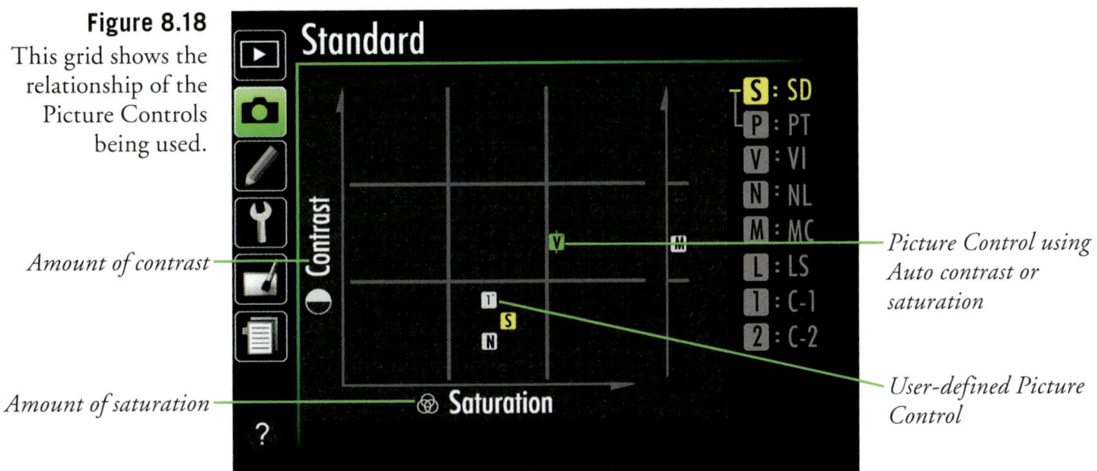


**Figure 8.18**
This grid shows the relationship of the Picture Controls being used.

*Amount of contrast*

*Amount of saturation*

*Picture Control using Auto contrast or saturation*

*User-defined Picture Control*

# Manage Picture Control

The Manage Picture Control menu entry can be used to create new styles, edit existing styles, rename or delete them, and store/retrieve them from the memory card. Here are the basic functions of this menu item, which can be found on the Shooting menu directly below the Set Picture Control entry:

- **Make a copy.** Choose Save/Edit, select from the list of available Picture Controls, and press OK to store that style in one of the user-defined slots C-1 to C-9 (with slots C1 to C7 shown in Figure 8.19).

- **Save an edited copy.** Choose Save/Edit, select from the list of available Picture Controls, and then press the multi selector right button to edit the style, as described in the previous section. Press OK when you've finished editing, and then save the modified style in one of the user-defined slots C-1 to C-9.

- **Rename a style.** Choose Rename, select from the list of user-defined Picture Controls (you cannot rename the default styles), and then enter the text used as the new label for the style, using the standard D5200 text entry screen like the one shown earlier in this chapter. You may use up to 19 characters for the name.

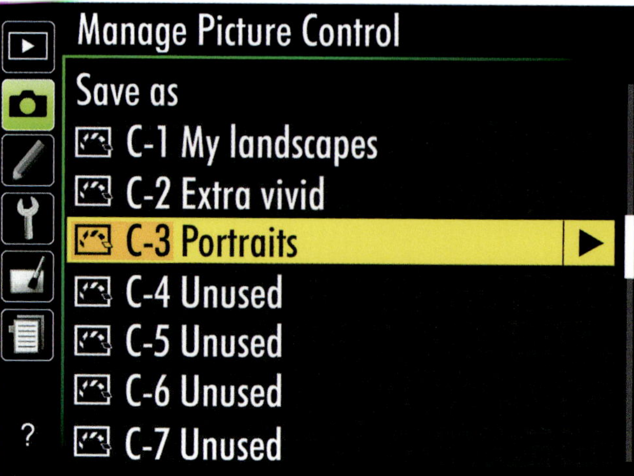


**Figure 8.19**
Save a custom
Picture Control.

- **Remove a style.** Select Delete, choose from the list of user-defined Picture Controls (you can't remove one of the default styles), press the multi selector right button, then highlight Yes in the screen that follows, and press OK to remove that Picture Control.

- **Store/retrieve style on card.** Choose Load/Save, then select Copy to Camera to locate a Picture Control on your Secure Digital card and copy it to the D5200; Delete from Card to select a Picture Control on your memory card and remove it; or Copy to Card to duplicate a style currently in your camera onto the Secure Digital card. This last option allows you to create and save Picture Controls in excess of the nine that can be loaded into the camera at one time. Once you've copied a style to your memory card, you can modify the version in the camera, give it a new name, and, in effect, create a whole new Picture Control.

## Auto Distortion Control

This option can correct barrel distortion (outward bowing of lines that should be straight) that sometimes occurs with telephoto lenses, and pincushion distortion (lines that curve inward, toward the center of the frame) that can appear when using wide-angle lenses. When turned on, the D5200 uses information about your Nikon-brand lens that is stored in the third (L) firmware module (and which can be updated with new firmware releases as lenses are introduced). Because this correction can result in cropping out part of your image, you may want to turn it off and use it only if you find the distortion produced by your lens is particularly bad.

Nikon recommends using this feature only with type G and D lenses (that is, lenses that have those designations as part of their names). Auto Distortion Control operates as you take the picture; you can also apply distortion control after a picture is taken using the Retouch menu (discussed in Chapter 10). Barrel and pincushion distortion can also be fully or partially corrected using an image editor like Photoshop. The in-camera feature is faster when you have lots of photos to process, because it performs its magic as the photo is saved to your memory card. You'll find more information about the L firmware module in Chapter 13.

# Color Space

The Nikon D5200's Color Space option, the first entry in the second page of the Shooting menu (see Figure 8.20), gives you two different color spaces (also called *color gamuts*), named Adobe RGB (because it was developed by Adobe Systems in 1998), and sRGB (supposedly because it is the *standard* RGB color space). These two color gamuts define a specific set of colors that can be applied to the images your D5200 captures.

You're probably surprised that the Nikon D5200 doesn't automatically capture *all* the colors we see. Unfortunately, that's impossible because of the limitations of the sensor and the filters used to capture the fundamental red, green, and blue colors, as well as that of the phosphors used to display those colors on your camera and computer monitors. Nor is it possible to *print* every color our eyes detect, because the inks or pigments used don't absorb and reflect colors perfectly.

On the other hand, the D5200 does capture quite a few more colors than we need. Even if you use 12-bit capture instead of the default 14-bit capture, an original 12-bit RAW image contains a possible 68 *billion* different hues, which are condensed down to a mere 16.8 million possible colors when converted to a 24-bit (eight bits per channel) image. While 16.8 million colors may seem like a lot, it's a small subset of 68 billion captured, and an even smaller subset of all the possible colors we can see.

The set of colors, or gamut, that can be reproduced or captured by a given device (scanner, digital camera, monitor, printer, or some other piece of equipment) is represented as a color space that exists within the larger full range of colors. That full range is represented by the odd-shaped splotch of color shown in Figure 8.21, as defined by scientists at an international organization back in 1931. The colors possible with Adobe RGB are represented by the larger, black triangle in the figure, while the sRGB gamut is represented by the smaller white triangle. Regardless of which triangle—or color space—is used by the D5200, you end up with some combination of 16.8 million different colors that can be used in your photograph. But, as you can see from the figure, the colors available will be *different*.

**Figure 8.20**

Color Space is the first entry on the second page of the Shooting menu.

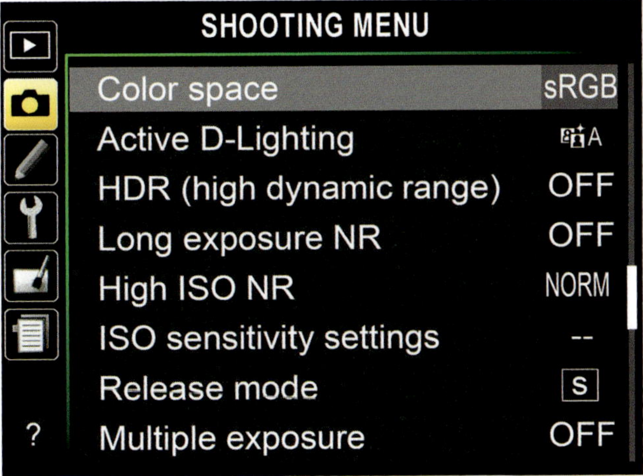

Adobe RGB is an expanded color space useful for commercial and professional printing, and it can reproduce a wider range of colors. It can also come in useful if an image is going to be extensively retouched, especially within an advanced image editor, like Adobe Photoshop, which has sophisticated color management capabilities that can be tailored to specific color spaces. As an advanced user, you don't need to automatically "upgrade" your D5200 to Adobe RGB, because images tend to look less saturated on your monitor and, it is likely, significantly different from what you will get if you output the photo to your personal inkjet. (You can *profile* your monitor for the Adobe RGB color space to improve your on-screen rendition, as I'll describe shortly.)

While both Adobe RGB and sRGB can reproduce the exact same 16.8 million absolute colors, Adobe RGB spreads those colors over a larger portion of the visible

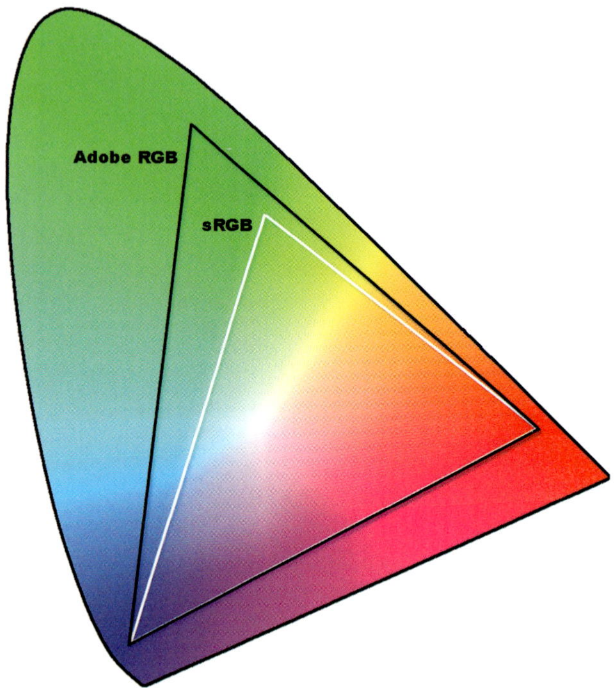


**Figure 8.21** The outer figure shows all the colors we can see; the two inner outlines show the boundaries of Adobe RGB (black triangle) and sRGB (white triangle).

spectrum. Think of a box of crayons (the jumbo 16.8 million crayon variety). Some of the basic crayons from the original sRGB set have been removed and replaced with new hues not contained in the original box. Your "new" box contains colors that can't be reproduced by your computer monitor, but which work just fine with a commercial printing press. For example, Adobe RGB has more "crayons" available in the cyan-green portion of the box, compared to sRGB, which is unlikely to be an advantage unless your image's final destination is the cyan, magenta, yellow, and black inks of a printing press.

The other color space, sRGB, is recommended for images that will be output locally on the user's own printer, as this color space matches that of the typical inkjet printer fairly closely. You might prefer sRGB, which is the default for the Nikon D5200 and most other cameras, as it is well suited for the range of colors that can be displayed on a computer screen and viewed over the Internet. If you plan to take your image file to a retailer's kiosk for printing, sRGB is your best choice, because those automated output devices are calibrated for the sRGB color space that consumers use.

Of course, choosing the right color space doesn't solve the problems that result from having each device in the image chain manipulating or producing a slightly different set of colors. To that end, you'll need to investigate the wonderful world of *color management*, which uses hardware and software tools to match or *calibrate* all your devices as closely as possible, so that what you see more closely resembles what you capture, what you see on your computer display, and what ends up on a printed hardcopy. Entire books have been devoted to color management, and most of what you need to know doesn't directly involve your Nikon D5200, so I won't detail the nuts and bolts here.

To manage your color, you'll need, at the bare minimum, some sort of calibration system for your computer display, so that your monitor can be adjusted to show a standardized set of colors that is repeatable over time. (What you see on the screen can vary as the monitor ages, or even when the room light changes.) I use the Spyder Pro4 monitor color correction system for my computer's main 26-inch wide-screen LCD display, as well as for my matching 26-inch wide-screen secondary display that flanks it. The device checks room light levels every five minutes, and reminds me to recalibrate every week or two; using at small sensor device that is suspended temporarily to the front of screen, it interprets test patches that the software displays during calibration. The rest of the time, the sensor sits in its stand, measuring the room illumination and adjusting my monitors for higher or lower ambient light levels.

## Active D-Lighting

Active D-Lighting is a feature that improves the rendition of detail in highlights and shadows when you're photographing high contrast scenes. It's been available as an internal retouching option in Nikon's lower-end cameras (by that I mean the Coolpix point-and-shoot line) for some time, and has gradually worked its way up through the company's dSLR products, eventually reaching the more advanced cameras, including the D5200. You'll find the "non-active" D-Lighting feature in the Retouch menu, which I'll describe in Chapter 10.

A new wrinkle, however, is the Active D-Lighting capability introduced with Nikon's new higher-end models, which, unlike the Retouch menu post-processing feature, applies its tonal improvements *while you are actually taking the photo.* That's good news and bad news. It means that, if you're taking photos in a contrasty environment, Active D-Lighting can automatically improve the apparent dynamic range of your image as you shoot, without additional effort on your part. However, you'll need to disable the feature once you leave the high contrast lighting behind, and the process does take some time. You wouldn't want to use Active D-Lighting for continuous shooting of sports subjects, for example. There are many situations in which the selective application of D-Lighting using the Retouch menu is a better choice.

You have six choices: Auto, Extra High, High, Normal, Low, and Off. You may need to experiment with the feature a little to discover how much D-Lighting you can apply to a high contrast image before the shadows start to darken objectionably. Note that when this feature is activated, brightness and contrast Picture Control settings cannot be changed. Figure 8.22 shows some examples of Active D-Light applied. By the time the sample images shown have been half-toned and rendered to the printed page, the differences may be fairly subtle. For that reason, I'm not illustrating the effects of the Auto setting (which varies, of course, depending on the scene) and Extra High, which is difficult to distinguish from High under normal circumstances. Look at the amount of detail in the overhanging rock in the upper-right area of each version.

For best results, use your D5200's Matrix metering mode, so the Active D-Lighting feature can work with a full range of exposure information from multiple points in the image. Active D-Lighting

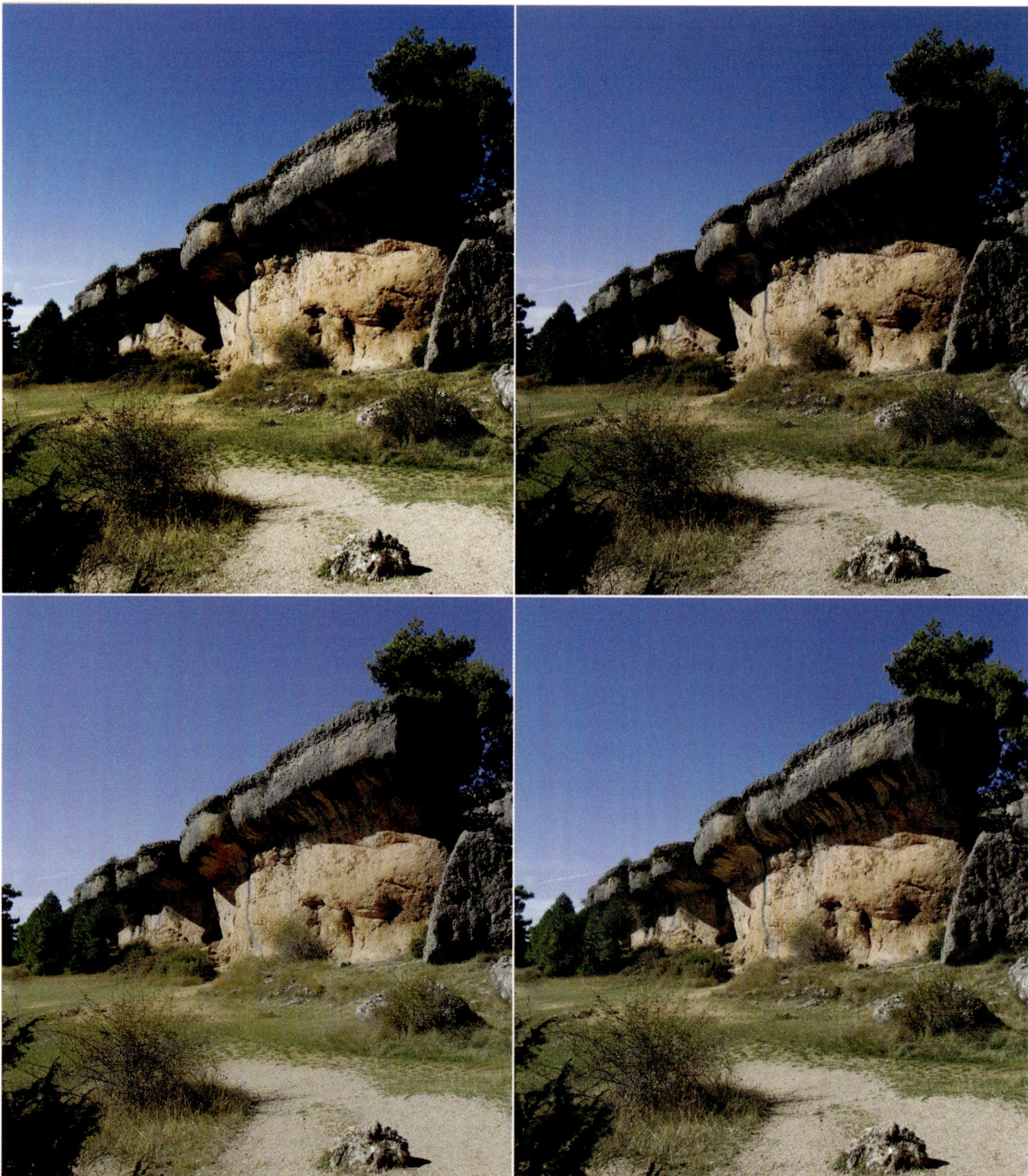

**Figure 8.22** No D-Lighting (upper left); low (upper right); normal (lower left); and high (lower right).

works its magic by subtly *underexposing* your image so that details in the highlights (which would normally be overexposed and become featureless white pixels) are not lost. At the same time, it adjusts the values of pixels located in midtone and shadow areas so they don't become too dark because of the underexposure. Highlight tones will be preserved, while shadows will eventually be allowed to go dark more readily. Bright beach or snow scenes, especially those with few shadows (think high noon, when the shadows are smaller) can benefit from using Active D-Lighting.

It's important to *always* keep in mind that Active D-Lighting not only adjusts the contrast automatically of your image (that's why you can't adjust the brightness/contrast of a Picture Control when Active D-Lighting is turned on), it modifies exposure for both existing light and flash as well, as I've noted. Exposure for both is reduced from about 1/3 stop (at the Low setting) to as much as 1 full stop less at the Extra High setting.

> **Tip**
>
> In Manual exposure mode, Active D-Lighting does not adjust the exposure of your image; it simply shifts the center (zero) point of the analog exposure indicator in the viewfinder/LCD.

Nikon gives you a lot of flexibility in using Active D-Lighting. You can choose the setting yourself, or let the camera *vary* the amount of tweaking by using Active D-Lighting Bracketing, which I explained in the general bracketing discussion in Chapter 4. You'll find this is a useful feature, if used with caution.

## HDR (High Dynamic Range)

The D5200's in-camera HDR feature was explained in Chapter 4, where you'll find a longer explanation of how to use it. I won't repeat that discussion here. When activated, the camera will take two exposures, which can be separated by no more than three stops' worth of exposure. The HDR entry has one set of options: you can choose Auto to allow the camera to decide how much HDR correction to apply; Off, to disable the feature; or select a level, using Low, Normal, High, or Extra High.

## Long Exp. NR

Visual noise is that awful graininess caused by long exposures and high ISO settings, and which shows up as multicolored specks in images. This setting helps you manage the kind of noise caused by lengthy exposure times. In some ways, noise is like the excessive grain found in some high-speed photographic films. However, while photographic grain is sometimes used as a special effect, it's rarely desirable in a digital photograph. There are easier ways to add texture to your photos.

Some noise is created when you're using shutter speeds longer than eight seconds to create a longer exposure. Extended exposure times allow more photons to reach the sensor, but increase the likelihood that some photosites will react randomly even though not struck by a particle of light.

Moreover, as the sensor remains switched on for the longer exposure, it heats, and this heat can be mistakenly recorded as if it were a barrage of photons. This menu setting can be used to activate the D5200's long exposure noise-canceling operation performed by the EXPEED digital signal processor.

- **Off.** This default setting disables long exposure noise reduction. Use it when you want the maximum amount of detail present in your photograph, even though higher noise levels will result. This setting also eliminates the extra time needed to take a picture caused by the noise reduction process. If you plan to use only lower ISO settings (thereby reducing the noise caused by ISO amplification), the noise levels produced by longer exposures may be acceptable. For example, you might be shooting a waterfall at ISO 100 with the camera mounted on a tripod, using a neutral-density filter and a long exposure to cause the water to blur. (Try exposures of 2 to 16 seconds, depending on the intensity of the light and how much blur you want.) (See Figure 8.23.) To maximize detail in the non-moving portions of your photos for the exposures that are eight seconds or longer, you can switch off long exposure noise reduction.

- **On.** When exposures are eight seconds or longer, the Nikon D5200 takes a second, blank exposure to compare that to the first image. (While the second image is taken, the warning Job nr appears on the monochrome LCD panel and in the viewfinder.) Noise (pixels that are bright in a frame that *should* be completely black) in the "dark frame" image is subtracted from your original picture, and only the noise-corrected image is saved to your memory card. Because the noise-reduction process effectively doubles the time required to take a picture, you won't want to use this setting when you're rushed. Some noise can be removed later on, using tools like the noise reduction features built into many image editors, or Nikon Capture NX 2.

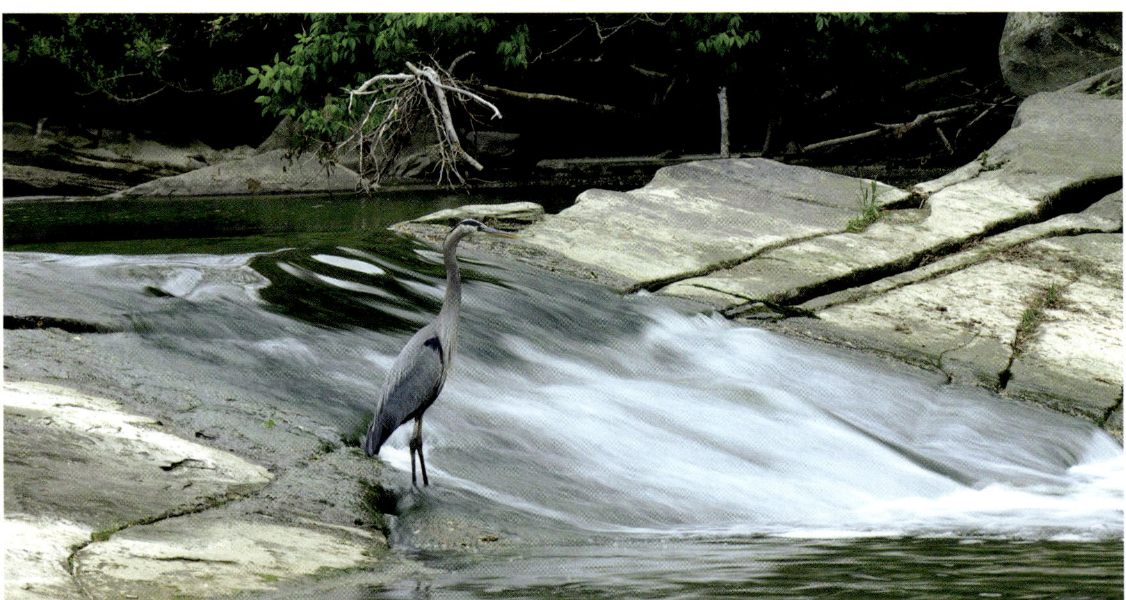

**Figure 8.23** A long exposure with the camera mounted on a tripod produces this traditional moving water photo.

# High ISO NR

Noise can also be caused by higher ISO sensitivity settings, and the Nikon D5200, which offers settings up to ISO 6400 (and thence up to the equivalent of ISO 12800 and 25600 with the Hi 1.0 and Hi 2.0 settings) has a loftier ISO ceiling than many cameras. Even so, high ISO noise reduction, which can be set with this menu option, may be a good option in many cases. You can choose Off when you want to preserve detail at the cost of some noise graininess, and the D5200 will apply high ISO NR only at the "boosted" settings of Hi 0.3 and above. Or, you can select On, which is applied when ISO sensitivity has been set to ISO 800 or higher.

The effects of high ISO noise are something like listening to a CD in your car, and then rolling down all the windows. You're adding sonic noise to the audio signal, and while increasing the CD player's volume may help a bit, you're still contending with an unfavorable signal to noise ratio that probably mutes tones (especially higher treble notes) that you really want to hear.

The same thing happens when the analog image signal is amplified: You're increasing the image information in the signal, but boosting the background fuzziness at the same time. Tune in a very faint or distant AM radio station on your car stereo. Then turn up the volume. After a certain point, turning up the volume further no longer helps you hear better. There's a similar point of diminishing returns for digital sensor ISO increases and signal amplification as well.

As the captured information is amplified to produce higher ISO sensitivities, some random noise in the signal is amplified along with the photon information. Increasing the ISO setting of your camera raises the threshold of sensitivity so that fewer and fewer photons are needed to register as an exposed pixel. Yet, that also increases the chances of one of those phantom photons being counted among the real-life light particles, too.

Fortunately, the Nikon D5200's CMOS sensor and its EXPEED digital processing chip are optimized to produce the low noise levels, so ratings as high as ISO 1600 to ISO 3200 can be used routinely (although there will be some noise, of course), and even ISO 6400 and higher can generate acceptable results. Some kinds of subjects may not require this kind of noise cancellation, such as those that have a texture of their own that tends to hide or mask the noise.

# ISO Sensitivity Settings

This menu entry has four parts: ISO Sensitivity, Auto ISO Sensitivity Control, Maximum Sensitivity, and Minimum Shutter Speed. You can select a specific ISO setting, or control how the D5200 chooses an ISO setting automatically. The Auto ISO Sensitivity Control menu entry lets you specify how and when the D5200 will adjust the ISO value for you automatically under certain conditions. This capability can be potentially useful, although experienced photographers tend to shy away from any feature that allows the camera to change basic settings like ISO that have been carefully selected. Fortunately, you can set some boundaries so the D5200 will use this adjustment in a fairly intelligent way.

When Auto ISO is activated, the camera can bump up the ISO sensitivity, if necessary, whenever an optimal exposure cannot be achieved at the current ISO setting. Of course, it can be disconcerting to think you're shooting at ISO 400 and then see a grainier ISO 1600 shot during LCD review. While the D5200 provides a flashing ISO-Auto alert in the viewfinder, the warning is easy to miss. Here are the important considerations to keep in mind when using the options available for this feature:

- **ISO Sensitivity.** This option allows you to choose specific ISO settings in one-third stop increments, from ISO 100 though ISO 6400, and then to the "extended" settings including Hi 0.3, Hi 0.7, Hi 1 (ISO 12800 equivalent), and Hi 2 (ISO 25600 equivalent).

- **Auto ISO Sensitivity.** Set ISO Sensitivity Auto Control to Off, and the ISO setting will not budge from whatever value you have specified. Use this setting when you don't want any ISO surprises, or when ISO increases are not needed to counter slow shutter speeds. For example, if the D5200 is mounted on a tripod, you can safely use slower shutter speeds at a relatively low ISO setting, so there is no need for a speed bump. On the other hand, if you're hand-holding the camera and the D5200 set for Program (P) or Aperture-priority (A) mode wants to use a shutter speed slower than, say, 1/30th second, it's probably a good idea to increase the ISO to avoid the effects of camera shake. If you're using a longer lens, a shutter speed of 1/125th second or higher might be the point where an ISO bump would be a good idea. In that case, you can turn the ISO Sensitivity Auto Control on, or remember to boost the ISO setting yourself.

- **Maximum Sensitivity.** Use this parameter, available only when Auto ISO Sensitivity is on, to indicate the highest ISO setting you're comfortable having the D5200 set on its own. You can choose from ISO 400, 800, 1600, 3200, 6400, and Hi 1 and Hi 2 as the max ISO setting the camera will use. Use a low number if you'd rather not take any photos at a high ISO without manually setting that value yourself. Dial in a higher ISO number if getting the photo at any sensitivity setting is more important than worrying about noise.

- **Minimum Shutter Speed.** This setting, accessible when Auto ISO Sensitivity is on, allows you to tell the D5200 how slow the shutter speed must be before the ISO boost kicks in, within the range 1 second to 1/2,000th second, plus Auto. The default value is 1/30th second, because for most shooters in most situations, any shutter speed longer than 1/30 is to be avoided, unless you're using a tripod, monopod, or looking for a special effect. If you have steady hands, or the camera is partially braced against movement (say, you're using that monopod), a slower shutter speed, down to 1 full second, can be specified. Similarly, if you're working with a telephoto lens and find even a relatively brief shutter speed "dangerous," you can set a minimum shutter speed threshold of, say, 1/250th second. When the shutter speed is faster than the minimum you enter, Auto ISO will not take effect.

# Release Mode

This entry duplicates the release mode settings available when the release mode/drive button is pressed. You can choose:

- **Single frame.** In single shot mode, the D5200 takes one picture each time you press the shutter release button down all the way.

- **Continuous L/Continuous H.** These modes fire off shots at up to 3 and 5 frames per second, respectively. The frame rate can slow down as your D5200's memory buffer fills, which forces the camera to wait until some of the pictures you have already taken are written to the memory card, freeing up more space in the buffer. The frame rate may also decrease at shutter speeds slower than 1/200th second, or when operations like continuous-servo autofocus (described later in this chapter) force the D5200 to work at a slightly slower interval.

- **10 second self-timer.** You can use the self-timer as a replacement for a remote release, to reduce the effects of camera/user shake when the D5200 is mounted on a tripod or, say, set on a firm surface, or when you want to get in the picture yourself. Use Custom Setting c3 to specify delays of 2, 5, 10, or 20 seconds. You can also specify the number of shots taken at the end of the elapsed period, and the interval between those shots. Any time you use the camera on a tripod (with the self-timer or otherwise) make sure there is no bright light shining on the viewfinder window; if so, cover it or locate that DK-5 eyepiece cap and block the window.

- **2s delayed remote/Quick response remote (ML-L3).** If you use the ML-L3 infrared remote, you'll need to change the release mode to either of these two settings: Delayed remote (shutter releases two seconds after you press the button on the ML-L3 IR remote) or quick response remote (the shutter trips immediately when the button is pressed). Once you've selected either of these two release modes, the camera then "looks" for the remote signal for a period of time you specify using Custom Setting c4 (select from 1, 5, 10, or 15 minutes). As with the self-timer, make sure there is no bright light shining on the viewfinder window; if so, cover it or locate that DK-5 eyepiece cap and block the window.

- **Quiet shutter release.** This setting, marked with a Q symbol, activates the D5200's "quiet mode," which silences the camera's beep noise during autofocus, reduces the sound the mirror makes when it flips back down, and delays that "noise" until you release the shutter button.

# Multiple Exposure

This option lets you combine two exposures into one image without the need for an image editor like Photoshop and can be an entertaining way to return to those thrilling days of yesteryear, when complex photos were created in the camera itself. In truth, prior to the digital age, multiple exposures were a cool, groovy, far-out, hep/hip, phat, sick, fabulous way of producing composite images. Today, it's more common to take the lazy way out, snap two or more pictures, and then assemble them in an image editor like Photoshop.

However, if you're willing to spend the time planning a multiple exposure (or are open to some happy accidents), there is a lot to recommend the multiple exposure capability that Nikon has bestowed on the D5200. For one thing, the camera is able to combine two or more images using the RAW data from the sensor, producing photos that are blended together more smoothly than is likely for anyone who's not a Photoshop guru. To take your own multiple exposures, just follow these steps (although it's probably a good idea to do a little planning and maybe even some sketching on paper first):

1. **Access Multiple Exposure setting.** Navigate to the option in the Shooting menu.
2. **Activate Multiple Exposure mode.** Highlight the Multiple Exposure Mode option, press the right directional button, and choose On. Press OK.
3. **Select Number of Shots.** Choose a value from 2 to 3 with the multi selector up/down buttons, and press OK.
4. **Choose Auto Gain.** Specify either On (the default) or Off. When On is selected, the D5200 will divide the total exposure of the image by the number of shots specified; for example, applying 1/3 of the exposure time to each shot in a three-image series. Choose Off, and the full exposure is applied to each picture. You'd want to use Off when using a dark background that would allow successive exposures to add details, as in Figure 8.24, and On to avoid the risk of overlapping images washing each other out. Press OK to set the gain.
5. **Finish.** Press the MENU button to exit. The multiple exposure icon appears at the top of the information screen on the LCD monitor.
6. **Take the multiple exposures.** Press the shutter release button multiple times until all the exposures in the series have been taken. (In continuous shooting mode, the entire series will be shot in a single burst.) The blinking multiple exposure icon vanishes when the series is finished. **Note:** you'll need to deactivate the Multiple Exposure feature once you've finished taking your exposures.

Keep in mind if you wait longer than 30 seconds between any two photos in the series, the sequence will terminate and combine the images taken so far. If you want a longer elapsed time between exposures, go to the Playback menu and make sure On has been specified for Image Review, and then extend the monitor display time using Custom Setting c2 to an appropriate Standby Timer maximum interval. The Multiple Exposure feature will then use the monitor-off delay as its maximum interval between shots. Figure 8.24 shows double exposure created at a ballet performance.

## Interval Timer Shooting

Nikon D5200's built-in time-lapse photography feature allows you to take pictures for up to 999 intervals in bursts of as many as nine shots, with a delay of up to 23 hours and 59 minutes between shots/bursts, and an initial start-up time of as long as 23 hours and 59 minutes from the time you activate the feature. That means that if you want to photograph a rosebud opening and would like to photograph the flower once every two minutes over the next 16 hours, you can do that easily. If you like, you can delay the first photo taken by a couple hours so you don't have to stand there by the D5200 waiting for the right moment.

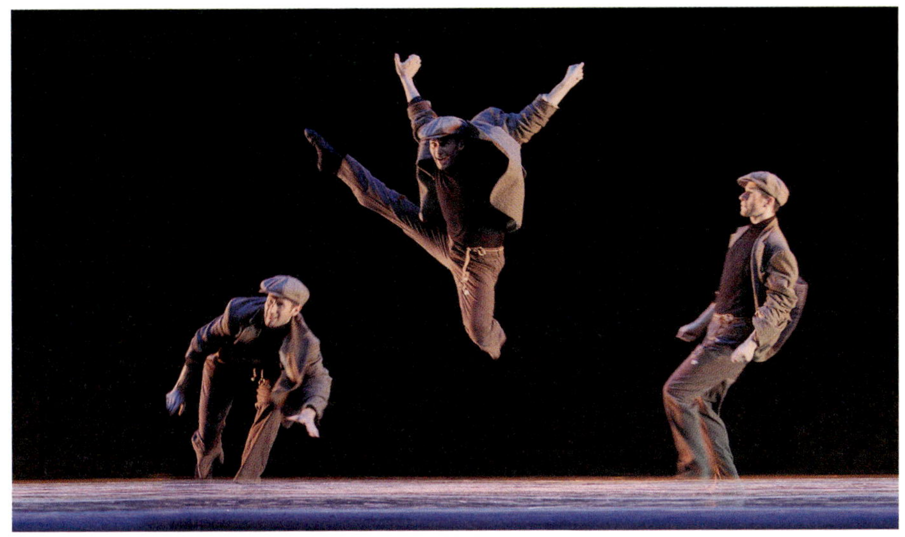

**Figure 8.24**
The D5200's Multiple Exposure capability allows combining images without an image editor.

Or, you might want to photograph a particular scene every hour for 24 hours to capture, say, a landscape from sunrise to sunset to the following day's sunrise again. The D5200 can do that, too. I will offer two practical tips right now, in case you want to run out and try interval timer shooting immediately: *use a tripod, and for best results over longer time periods, plan on connecting your D5200 to an external power source!*

The Interval Timer Shooting screen (see Figure 8.25) is confusingly designed, in my opinion. It's needlessly complex; the display changes in a quirky way depending on what information you're entering, and some portions of the screen aren't accessible until you've performed a prerequisite function. I would have set up this menu with nothing more than five entries, each with their own screen of options: On/Off, start time, interval delay, total number of shots to expose, and the number of shots in the burst per interval (if more than one image per interval is desired).

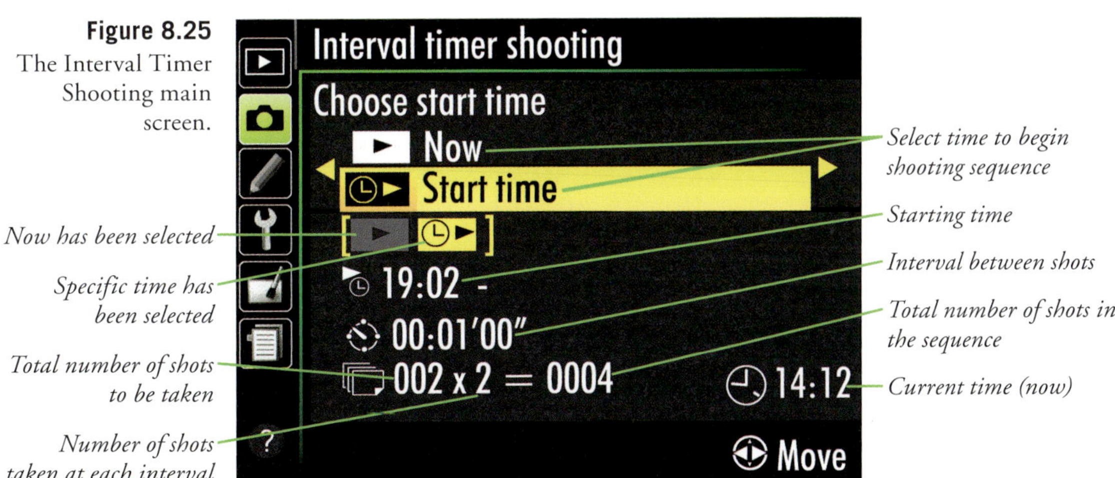


**Figure 8.25**
The Interval Timer Shooting main screen.

Now has been selected —

Specific time has been selected —

Total number of shots to be taken —

Number of shots taken at each interval —

— Select time to begin shooting sequence

— Starting time

— Interval between shots

— Total number of shots in the sequence

— Current time (now)

To set up interval timer shooting, just follow these steps.

Before you start:

1. **Set your clock.** The D5200 uses its internal World Time clock to activate, so make sure the time has been set accurately in the Setup menu before you begin.

2. **Select release mode.** If you want to shoot bursts of images each time an interval elapses, set the release mode to continuous shooting. If you prefer to take one picture per interval, set the release mode dial to S. However, you can still specify multiple shots per interval when using S.

3. **Bracket, if desired.** If you'd like to bracket exposures during interval shooting, set up bracketing prior to beginning. (You learned how to bracket in Chapter 4.)

4. **Fully charge the battery.** Although the camera more or less goes to sleep between intervals, some power is drawn, and long sequences with bursts of shots can drain power even when you're not using the interval timer feature.

5. **Protect your camera.** Make sure the camera is shielded from the elements, accidents, and theft, and that the viewfinder is covered (using the DK-5 eyepiece cap if necessary) if you need to keep strong ambient light from entering the viewfinder and affecting exposure.

When you're ready to go, set up the D5200 for interval shooting:

1. **Select timer.** Choose Interval Timer Shooting from the Shooting menu.

2. **Specify a starting time.** You must do this before the D5200 will let you set other parameters. Highlight either Now or Start Time and press the multi selector right button. If you choose Now, the interval shooting will begin approximately three seconds after you've finished setting the parameters beginning with Step 5. If you select Start Time, you'll be able to enter a specific time, as described in Steps 3 and 4.

3. **Choose start time.** When the Start Time sub-screen appears, use the multi selector left/right buttons to highlight the hours or minutes, and the up/down buttons to increase or decrease the hours/minutes entry. The 24-hour clock is used, so you can specify a time from 00:00 (midnight) to 23:59 (one minute to midnight). When both hours and minutes have been set, press the multi selector right button to move the highlighting to the Interval section of the sub-screen.

4. **Set the interval between exposures.** You can use the left/right buttons to move among hours, minutes, and seconds, and use the up/down buttons to choose an interval from one second to 24 hours. Press the right button when finished to move down to the number of intervals/shots per interval sub-screen.

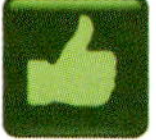

**Tip**

The interval cannot be shorter than the shutter speed; for example, you can not set one second as the interval if the images will be taken at two seconds or longer.

5. **Set number of intervals and shots per interval.** Use the left/right buttons to highlight the number of intervals, the number of shots taken after each interval has elapsed, and the total number of shots to be exposed overall. You can highlight each number column separately, so that to enter, say, 250 intervals you can set the 100s, 10s, and 1s columns individually (rather than press the up button 250 times!). You can select up to 999 intervals, and 9 shots per interval for a maximum of 8991 exposures with one interval shooting cycle.

6. **Start.** When all the parameters have been entered, press the multi selector right button once more, and the Start sub-screen appears, with the choices On or Off. Choose either one and press OK. If you activate interval shooting, a message is displayed on the monitor one minute before each series of shots begins.

## Movie Settings

This menu entry allows you to choose four movie-making parameters. To begin shooting, rotate the Lv switch, and then push the red Movie button. To recap the options explained in Chapter 6:

- **Frame size/rate.** Choose your resolution. Use the Movie Settings entry in the Shooting menu. Or, when live view is activated, and before you start shooting your video clip, you can select the resolution/frame rate of your movie. All use *progressive scan,* in which all the lines are captured one after another in order, except for the single *interlaced scan* choice (60i), which interweaves odd/even lines of two fields per frame. Your choices are as follows:
    - 1920 × 1080 at 60 fps, interlaced scan (60i)
    - 1920 × 1080 at 30 fps, progressive scan (30p)
    - 1920 × 1080 at 24 fps, progressive scan (24p)
    - 1280 × 720 at 24 fps, progressive scan (24p)
    - 640 × 424 at 30 fps, progressive scan (30p)
- **Movie Quality.** Choose High quality (to capture up to 20 minutes of action) or Normal quality (for up to 29 minutes, 59 seconds of video per clip). The High setting has a maximum bit rate requirement of 24 Mbps; if your memory card won't handle that, the Normal setting reduces the demand to 12 Mbps, at the cost of some additional compression that reduces the size of the file and cuts resolution/image quality slightly.
- **Microphone.** Here you can set audio sensitivity for the built-in stereo microphones or an optional external mic like the Nikon ME-1. Choose from Auto, High Sensitivity, Medium Sensitivity, Low Sensitivity, or Off. With the Manual Sensitivity setting, a set of volume unit (VU) meter bars appears on the screen showing the current sound levels. Press the right directional button to access a screen where you can select a manual sensitivity level from 1 to 20.
- **Manual Movie Settings.** Select On or Off

# 9

# The Custom Setting Menu

Unlike the Shooting menu options, which you are likely to modify frequently as your picture-taking environment changes, Custom Settings, found in the Custom Setting menu, are slightly more stable sets of preferences that let you tailor the behavior of your camera in a variety of different ways for longer-term use.

Some options are minor tweaks, useful for specific shooting situations. You can turn off the auto-focus assist lamp, the back-panel LCD's shooting information display, and the D5200's built-in beeper when you are shooting an acoustic music concert, when you'd rather not disrupt the environment. Others make the camera more convenient to use. Perhaps you'd like to assign a frequently used feature to the Fn button. This chapter concentrates on explaining all the options of the Custom Setting menu and, most importantly, when and why you might want to use each setting.

## Custom Setting Menu Layout

There are 22 different Custom Settings, arranged in six different categories, as shown in Figure 9.1: Autofocus, Exposure, Timers/AE Lock, Shooting/Display, Bracketing/Flash, and Controls. Some of those may seem to be an odd match. What does bracketing have to do with flash? Oh, wait! You can *bracket* flash (as well as non-flash) exposures. The category system does have an advantage. Once you've learned what settings are available within each category, you can select the Custom Setting menu, scroll down to the specific category you want, and enter the CSM system at that point, skipping the other entries.

However, once you get past the main CSM screen, the entries are one long scrolling list, so if you've guessed wrong about where you want to start, you can enter the list at any point and then scroll up or down until you find the entry you want. The CSM menu items are all color- and letter-coded: **a** (red) for autofocus functions; **b** (orange) for exposure; **c** (green) for timers and AE/Lock features;

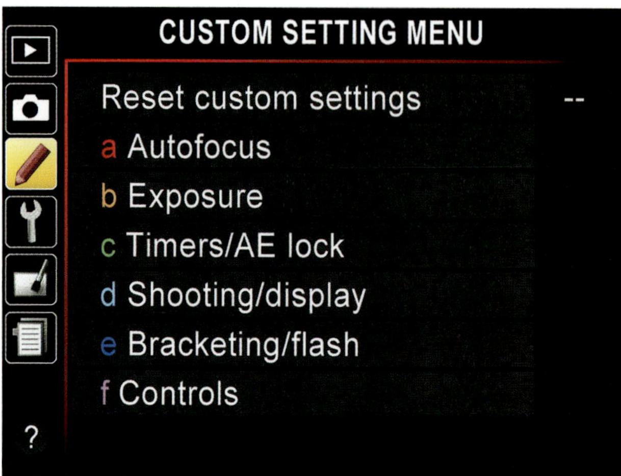


**Figure 9.1**

These six categories include 22 different entries in the Custom Settings menu.

**d** (light blue) for shooting/display functions; **e** (dark blue) for bracketing/flash; and **f** (purple) for adjustments to the D5200's controls.

For simplicity, in this book I have been consistently referring to the Custom Setting menu entries by their letter/names, so that you always know that when I mention Custom Setting a4, I am describing the fourth entry in the Autofocus menu, Rangefinder. That terminology makes it easy to jump quickly to the specific entry.

You can select a CSM function as you do any menu entry, by pressing the multi selector right button, and navigating through the screen that appears with the up/down (and sometimes left/right) buttons. Confirming an option is usually done by pressing the OK button, pushing the multi selector right button, or sometimes by choosing Done when a series of related options have been chosen.

At the top level, you'll see these entries:

- Reset Custom Settings
- a. Autofocus
- b. Exposure
- c. Timers/AE Lock

- d. Shooting/Display
- e. Bracketing/Flash
- f. Controls

## Reset Custom Settings

Although located in the Custom Setting menu, this entry is called Restore Custom Settings (plural). You can restore the settings of the Custom Setting banks to their default values by choosing this menu entry and selecting Yes or No. Tables 9.1 to 9.6 show the default values as the Nikon D5200 comes from the factory, and after a reset. If you don't know what some of these settings are, I'll explain them later in this chapter. Be careful when changing any of your carefully tailored customized settings back to the defaults.

## Table 9.1　Default Custom Setting Values: Autofocus

| Function | Option | Default |
|---|---|---|
| a1 | AF-C priority selection | Focus |
| a2 | Number of focus points | AF39 |
| a3 | Built-in AF-assist illuminator | On |
| a4 | Rangefinder | Off |

## Table 9.2　Default Custom Setting Bank Values: Metering/Exposure

| Function | Option | Default |
|---|---|---|
| b1 | ISO sensitivity step value | 1/3 step |

## Table 9.3　Default Custom Setting Bank Values: Timers/AE Lock

| Function | Option | Default |
|---|---|---|
| c1 | Shutter release button AE-L | Off |
| c2 | Auto off timers | Normal |
| c3 | Self-timer | |
| | Self-timer delay | 10 seconds |
| | Number of Shots | 1 |
| c4 | Remote on duration (ML-L3) | 1 minute |

## Table 9.4　Default Custom Setting Bank Values: Shooting/Display

| Function | Option | Default |
|---|---|---|
| d1 | Beep | Low |
| d2 | Viewfinder grid display | Off |
| d3 | ISO display | Off |
| d4 | File number sequence | Off |
| d5 | Exposure delay mode | Off |
| d6 | Print date | Off |

**Table 9.5  Default Custom Setting Bank Values: Bracketing/Flash**

| Function | Option | Default |
|---|---|---|
| e1 | Flash control for built-in flash | TTL |
| e2 | Auto bracketing set | AE bracketing |

**Table 9.6  Default Custom Setting Bank Values: Controls**

| Function | Option | Default |
|---|---|---|
| f1 | Fn button | ISO sensitivity |
| f2 | Assign AE-L/AF-L button | AE/AF lock |
| f3 | Reverse dial rotation | Exposure Compensation: No<br>Shutter speed/Aperture: No |
| f4 | Slot empty release lock | Release locked |
| f5 | Reverse indicators | - 0 + |

# a. Autofocus

The red-coded Autofocus options (see Figure 9.2) deal with some of the potentially most vexing settings available with the Nikon D5200. After all, incorrect focus is one of the most damaging picture-killers of all the attributes in an image. You may be able to compensate for bad exposure, partially fix errant color balance, and perhaps even incorporate motion blur into an image as a creative element. But if focus is wrong, the photograph doesn't look right, and no amount of "I meant to do that!" pleas are likely to work. The D5200's autofocus options enable you to choose how and when focus is applied (using the AF-S or AF-C focus mode you selected on the camera body), the controls used to activate the feature, and the way focus points are selected from the available 39 zones.

## a1 AF-C Priority Selection

As you learned in Chapter 5, the Nikon D5200 has three primary autofocus modes when using the optical viewfinder: Continuous-servo autofocus (AF-C) and single-servo autofocus (AF-S)—plus AF-A, which, in effect, flips between the two main modes as appropriate. (Live view has two similar modes, AF-S and AF-F.) This menu entry allows you to specify what takes precedence in optical viewfinder modes when you press the shutter release all the way down to take a picture.

You can give precedence to focus (called *focus priority*) or to the release button (called *release priority*).

**Figure 9.2**
The first eight entries in the Custom Setting menu.

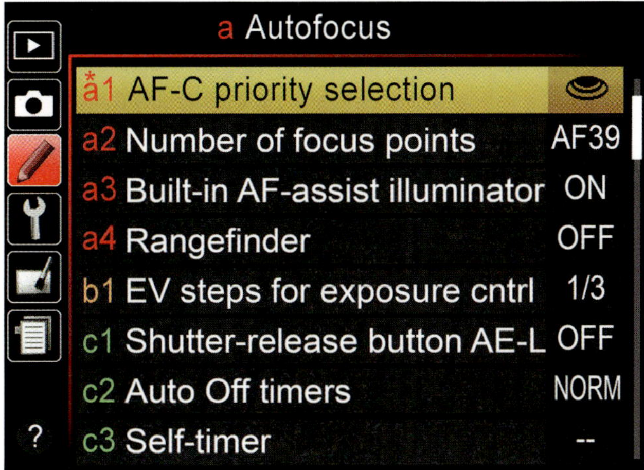


You can choose from:

- **Release.** When this option is selected, the shutter is activated when the release button is pushed down all the way, even if sharp focus has not yet been achieved. Because AF-C focuses and refocuses constantly when autofocus is active, you may find that an image is not quite in sharpest focus. Use this option when taking a picture is more important than absolute best focus, such as fast action or photojournalism applications. (You don't want to miss that record-setting home run, or the protestor's pie smashing into the Governor's face.) Using this setting doesn't mean that your image won't be sharply focused; it just means that you'll get a picture even if autofocusing isn't quite complete. If you've been poised with the shutter release pressed halfway, the D5200 probably has been tracking the focus of your image.

- **Focus.** With this default option, the shutter is not activated until sharp focus is achieved. This is best for subjects that are not moving rapidly. AF-C will continue to track your subjects' movement, but the D5200 won't take a picture until focus is locked in. You might miss a few shots, but you will have fewer out-of-focus images.

## a2 Number of Focus Points

You can choose the number of focus points available when you *manually* select a zone using the multi selector up/down and left/right buttons. (Note that this option is different from the 9, 21, or 39 points that may be selected *automatically* [dynamically] when using dynamic-area AF, as described in Chapter 5.) Your choices are as follows:

- **39 points.** This is the default. All 39 focus points can be selected.

- **11 points.** A more widely spaced array of points is available. This can be the best choice for faster focus point selection when taking pictures of relatively large, evenly illuminated subject matter such that choosing precise focus zones is not particularly beneficial. I often use the 11-point option when photographing basketball games.

# a3 Built-in AF-Assist Illuminator

Use this setting to control whether to use the AF-assist lamp built into the Nikon D5200, or rely on the more powerful AF-assist lamp built into Nikon electronic flash units (like the Nikon SB-910) and the Nikon SC-29 coiled remote flash cord (for firing the flash when not mounted on the camera).

- **On.** This default value will cause the AF-assist illuminator lamp to fire when lighting is poor, but only if single-servo autofocus (AF-S) is active, or you have selected the center focus point manually and either single-point or dynamic-area autofocus (rather than auto-area autofocus) has been chosen.

- **Off.** Use this to disable the AF-assist illuminator. You'd find that useful when the lamp might be distracting or discourteous (say, at a religious ceremony or acoustic music concert), or your subject is located closer than one foot, eight inches or farther than about 10 feet.

# a4 Rangefinder

Use this entry to set the manual focus rangefinder aid (described in detail in Chapter 5) on or off. The rangefinder scale helps you focus manually through the viewfinder by providing an indication of which direction the focus ring needs to be moved to achieve correct focus.

# b. Exposure

The orange-coded Exposure Custom Setting has just one entry.

# b1 EV Steps for Exposure Cntrl.

This setting tells the Nikon D5200 the size of the "jumps" it should use when making exposure adjustments—either one-third or one-half stop. The increment you specify here applies to f/stops, shutter speeds, EV changes, and autoexposure bracketing. As with ISO sensitivity step value, you can select from 1/3 step (the default); or 1/2 step.

Choose the 1/3 stop setting when you want the finest increments between shutter speeds and/or f/stops. For example, the D5200 will use shutter speeds such as 1/60th, 1/80th, 1/100th, 1/125th, and 1/160th second, and f/stops such as f/5.6, f/6.3, f/7.1, and f/8, giving you (and the autoexposure system) maximum flexibility.

With 1/2-stop increments, you will have larger and more noticeable changes between settings. The D5200 will apply shutter speeds such as 1/60th, 1/125th, 1/250th, and 1/500th second, and f/stops including f/5.6, f/6.7, f/8, f/9.5, and f/11. These coarser adjustments are useful when you want more dramatic changes between different exposures, or want to create a series of more widely spaced shots for high dynamic range (HDR) photography.

# c. Timers/AE Lock

This category is a mixed bag of settings, covering both entries that adjust delay times (c2 through c4) and how the shutter release and AE-L buttons interact (c1). I think the latter setting should have been placed in the purple f-coded Controls section. Go figure.

## c1 Shutter Release Button AE-L

This is another of Nikon's easily confusing options for controlling how and when autofocus and exposure are activated and locked. The intent is to allow you to separate autofocus and autoexposure activation and locking. All you need to know is:

- **Off.** Exposure is locked *only* when the AE-L/AF-L button is pressed. This is the default.
- **On.** Exposure locks when either the shutter release button is depressed halfway or the AE-L/AF-L button is held down.

## c2 Auto Off Timers

Use this setting to determine how long the D5200's displays and exposure meters continue to remain active after the last operation, such as autofocusing, focus point selection, and so forth, was performed. You can choose Short, Norm, or Long timings, or select Custom to specify timers for specific functions. Your options include:

- **Short.** Playback/menus: 12 seconds; Image review: 4 seconds; Live View: 3 minutes; Auto meter off: 4 seconds.
- **Normal.** Playback/menus: 20 seconds; Image review: 4 seconds; Live View: 3 minutes; Auto meter off: 8 seconds.
- **Long.** Playback/menus: 60 seconds; Image review: 20 seconds; Live View: 10 minutes; Auto meter off: 60 seconds.
- **Custom.** Select any combination, then choose Done to confirm: Playback/menus: 8, 12, 20, 60 seconds; Image review: 4, 8, 20, 60 seconds; Live View: 3, 5, 10, 15 minutes; Auto meter off: 4, 8, 20, 60 seconds, 10 minutes.

To save power, you should select an intermediate value, such as 8, 16, or 30 seconds if the default values are not long enough. When the Nikon EH5a/EP5b AC adapter is connected to the D5200, the exposure meter will remain on indefinitely, just as if you'd specified no limit. Absent an external power source, any setting longer than 8 seconds will definitely eat up power.

Even so, sports shooters and some others prefer longer delays, because they are able to keep their camera always "at the ready" with no delay to interfere with taking an action shot that unexpectedly presents itself. Extra battery consumption is just part of the price paid. For example, when I am shooting football, a meter-off delay of 16 seconds is plenty, because the players lining up for the snap is my signal to get ready to shoot. But for basketball or soccer, I typically set the meter-off delay to the longest interval, because action is virtually continuous. Of course, if the meters have shut off, and the power switch remains in the On position, you can bring the camera back to life by tapping the shutter button.

## c3 Self-Timer

This setting lets you choose the length of the self-timer shutter release delay, the number of shots taken, and the interval between those shots. Your options include:

- **Self-timer delay.** The default value is 10 seconds. You can choose 2, 5, 10, or 20 seconds. If I have the camera mounted on a tripod or other support and am too lazy to dig around for my wired or IR remote, I can set a two-second delay that is sufficient to let the camera stop vibrating after I've pressed the shutter release. I use a longer delay time if I am racing to get into the picture myself and am not sure I can make it in 10 seconds.

- **Number of shots.** After the timer finishes counting down, the D5200 can take from 1 to 9 different shots. This is a godsend when shooting photos of groups, especially if you want to appear in the photo itself. You'll always want to shoot several pictures to ensure that everyone's eyes are open and there are smiling expressions on each face. Instead of racing back and forth between the camera to trigger the self-timer multiple times, you can select the number of shots taken after a single countdown. For small groups of eight or fewer, I always take at least as many shots as there are people in the group—plus one. That gives everybody a chance to close their eyes. Of course, the ML-L3 IR remote is often your best choice, but this facility works well if you don't have one handy.

## c4 Remote on Duration (ML-L3)

You can adjust the amount of time the D5200 "looks" for an IR signal from its front and rear infrared sensors. You can select 1, 5, 10, or 15 minutes. Use a shorter active interval to save power.

# d. Shooting/Display

This menu section (see Figure 9.3) offers a variety of mostly unrelated shooting and display options not found elsewhere, but which are not frequently changed, making them suitable for a Custom Setting entry.

## d1 Beep

The Nikon D5200's internal beeper provides a (usually) superfluous chirp to signify various functions, such as the countdown of your camera's self-timer or autofocus confirmation in AF-S mode. You can (and probably should) switch it off if you want to avoid the beep because it's annoying, impolite, distracting (at a concert or museum), or undesired for any other reason. It's one of the few ways to make the D5200 a bit quieter. (I've actually had new dSLR owners ask me how to turn off the "shutter sound" the camera makes; such an option was available in the point-and-shoot camera they'd used previously.) Select d1: Beep from the menu, and select one of the following:

- **Volume.** High or Low. A quarter-note icon appears in the shooting information display.
- **Off.** Disables the beeper.

**Figure 9.3**

A mixed bag of entries is found in the Shooting/ Display submenu.

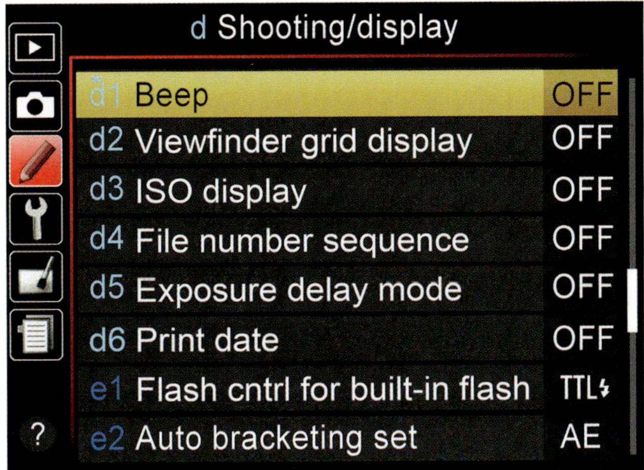


## d2 Viewfinder Grid Display

Activates the optional grid guidelines in the viewfinder (shown in Figure 9.4), which are useful for aligning the horizon, vertical lines, and, especially for framing architectural subjects.

## d3 ISO Display

This entry controls whether ISO or frame count are displayed in the viewfinder. You have two options.

- **On.** Choose this option, and the viewfinder will display the current ISO sensitivity in the position where the frame count is normally shown. Use it if knowing the ISO setting is more important than having ready access to the number of frames remaining. (For example, you're using a very large card with thousands of exposures available.)
- **Off.** In this default mode, the number of exposures remaining is shown in the viewfinder. You can always use the information display to view the ISO setting if this mode is set.

## d4 File Number Sequence

The Nikon D5200 will automatically apply a file number to each picture you take, using consecutive numbering for all your photos over a long period of time, spanning many different memory cards, starting over from scratch when you insert a new card, or when you manually reset the numbers. Numbers are applied from 0001 to 9999, at which time the D5200 "rolls over" to 0001 again.

The camera keeps track of the last number used in its internal memory and, if File Number Sequence is turned On, will apply a number that's one higher, or a number that's one higher than the largest number in the current folder on the memory card inserted in the camera. You can also start over each time a new folder has been created on the memory card, or reset the current counter back to 0001 at any time.

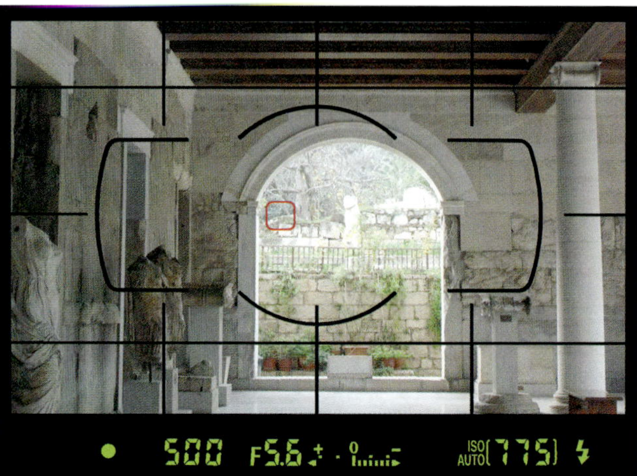

**Figure 9.4**
The optional grid display is useful for architectural subjects.

Here's how it works:

- **On.** At this default setting, the D5200 will use the number stored in its internal memory any time a new folder is created, a new memory card inserted, or an existing memory card formatted. If the card is not blank and contains images, then the next number will be one greater than the highest number on the card *or* in internal memory (whichever is higher). Here are some examples.

    - You've taken 1,235 shots with the camera, and you insert a blank/reformatted memory card. The next number assigned will be 1,236, based on the value stored in internal memory.

    - You've taken 1,235 shots with the camera, and you insert an old memory card you previously used with the D5200, but which has a picture numbered 0728. The next picture will be numbered 1,236.

    - You've taken more than 9,999 shots with the camera and the counter has rolled over to 0001 again, and your new total is 1,235 shots. You insert an old memory card with a picture from before the rollover that's numbered 8,281. The next picture will be numbered 8,282, and that value will be stored in the camera's menu as the "high" shot number (and will be applied when you next insert a blank card). This misnumbering makes it a good idea to always reformat your memory cards before taking a photo, if at all possible.

- **Off.** If you're using a blank/reformatted memory card, or a new folder is created, the next photo taken will be numbered 0001. File number sequences will be reset every time you use or format a card, or a new folder is created (which happens when an existing folder on the card contains 999 shots).

- **Reset.** The D5200 assigns a file number that's one larger than the largest file number in the current folder, unless the folder is empty, in which case numbering is reset to 0001. At this setting, new or reformatted memory cards will always have 0001 as the first file number.

**HOW MANY SHOTS, REALLY?**

The file numbers produced by the D5200 don't provide information about the actual number of times the camera's shutter has been tripped—called actuations. For that data, you'll need a third-party software solution, such as the free Opanda iExif (www.opanda.com) for Windows or the non-free ($34.95) GraphicConverter for Macintosh (www.lemkesoft.com). These utilities can be used to extract the true number of actuations from the Exif information embedded in a JPEG file.

## d5 Exposure Delay Mode

This is a marginally useful feature you can use to force the Nikon D5200 to snap a picture about one second after you've pressed the shutter release button all the way. It's useful when you are using shutter speeds of about 1/8th to 1/60th second hand-held and want to minimize the effects of the vibration that results when you depress the shutter button. It can also be used when the camera is mounted on a tripod, although the self-timer function, set to a two-second delay, is more useful in that scenario. When switched On, the camera will pause while you steady your steely grip on the camera, taking the picture about one second later. When turned Off, the picture is taken when the shutter release is pressed, as normal. One interesting side-effect of this mode is that it separates the normally invisible pre-flash produced by the D5200's internal flash (or any external flash that's connected) with the delay, so, if you're shooting living subjects (human or animal) they may be startled by the initial flash and close their eyes just before the main flash fires 1000 milliseconds later.

## d6 Print Date

You can superimpose the date, time, or both on your photographs, or imprint a date counter that shows the number of days (or years and days, or months, years, and days) between when the picture was taken and a date (in the past or future) that you select. The good news is that this feature can be useful for certain types of photographs used for documentation. While the D5200's time/date stamp may not be admissible in a court of law, it makes a convincing (or convenient) in-picture indication of when the shot was made. This feature works only with JPEG images; you cannot use Date Imprint with pictures taken using the RAW or RAW+Fine settings.

The bad news, especially if you use the feature accidentally, is that the imprint is a permanent part of the photograph. You'll have to polish up your Photoshop skills if you want to remove it, or, at the very least, crop it out of the picture area. Date and time are set using the format you specify in the Time and Date setting of the Setup menu. Your options are as follows:

- **Off.** Deactivates the date/time imprint feature.
- **Date.** The date is overlaid on your image in the bottom-right corner of the frame, and appears in the shooting information display. If you've turned on Auto Image Rotation the date is over-laid at the bottom-right corner of vertically oriented frames.

- **Date/Time.** Both date and time are imprinted, in the same positions.

- **Date Counter.** This option imprints the current date on the image, but also adds the number of days that have elapsed since a particular date in the past that you specify, *or* the days remaining until an upcoming date in the future.

Here are some applications for the Date Counter:

- **Tracking a newborn.** Enter the child's birthday as one of your three dates. Select Number of Days as your display option for a newborn. Then, as often as you like, activate the Date Counter and take a picture or two. The number of days since the baby's birth will be displayed right on the picture. (Remember to turn the feature off when shooting other pictures of the child, or of other subjects!)

- **Document construction.** Enter the start date of the project, activate the Date Counter, and take pictures of the construction progress. Each photo will show exactly how many days have elapsed since ground was broken (or the cornerstone laid, or that non-bearing wall demolished to begin remodeling).

- **Long-term documentation.** Perhaps you'd like to record the appearance of your favorite nature spot at different times of the year. Choose the first day of spring as your start date, then shoot pictures at intervals for an entire year, activating the Date Counter as needed. The results will be interesting—and maybe a revelation. With the Years, Months, and Days selected as a display option, you can continue your documentation for years!

- **Countdown.** Something big scheduled for a particular day? Choose that date in the future as your counter, and any photo you take with imprinting activated will show the days remaining until the big day.

# e. Bracketing/Flash

There are just two settings in this submenu that deal with bracketing and electronic flash (hence the cleverly concocted name). I'll provide a thorough description of using bracketing in Chapter 4, and a complete rundown of flash options in Chapter 12. Here, I'll offer an introduction to the settings at your disposal.

## e1 Flash Cntrl for Built-in Flash

The Nikon D5200's built-in flash has two modes, which I'll describe in a lot more detail in Chapter 12. When a Nikon SB-400 flash is attached and powered up, this menu choice changes to Optional Flash, and you can make these settings for the external unit instead. Your options are as follows:

- **TTL.** When the built-in flash is triggered, the D5200 first fires a pre-flash and measures the light reflected back and through the lens to calculate the proper exposure when the full flash is emitted a fraction of a second later.

- **Manual.** You can set the level of the built-in flash from full power to 1/32 power.

# e2 Auto Bracketing Set

The Nikon D5200 can automatically take several pictures using slightly different settings within a range that you specify, and apply the changes to automatic exposure, electronic flash, or white balance. This setting allows you to specify whether bracketing is used for automatic exposure only (AE), white balance color bracketing alone (WB bracketing), or Active D-Lighting bracketing. No autoexposure or flash bracketing will be performed when white balance bracketing is activated. Because you can specify white balance manually when importing a RAW file, WB bracketing is not available when Quality has been set to NEF (RAW) or NEF (RAW)+JPEG. The results you get with flash bracketing can vary quite a bit, depending on the amount of ambient illumination and flash mode you've chosen, but exposure bracketing is fairly consistent. I tend to leave this option set to AE most of the time. White balance bracketing is useful when you're not quite sure of the color balance of your illumination.

Bracketing is explained in detail in Chapter 4.

# f. Controls

You can modify the way various control buttons and dials perform by using the options in this submenu, shown in Figure 9.5.

# f1 Assign Fn. Button

You can define the function of the Fn button. Your choices are as follows:

- **Quality.** When this behavior is selected, pressing the Fn button produces the information edit screen, with Quality/Size options highlighted. You can rotate the command dial to cycle among all the combinations of image quality and size (resolution). Release the Fn button to lock the combination you've dialed in.

**Figure 9.5**

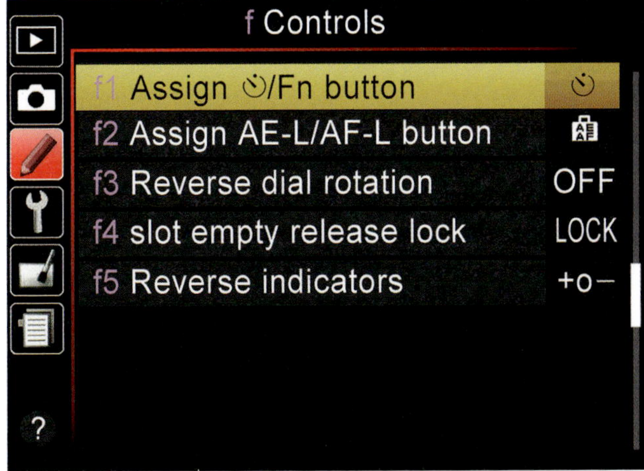

- **ISO.** Choose this option, the default, and pressing the Fn button produces the information edit screen, with ISO sensitivity settings highlighted. You can rotate the command dial to change values. Release the Fn button to lock the setting.

- **White balance.** When this behavior is selected, pressing the Fn button produces the information edit screen, with white balance highlighted. You can rotate the command dial to change the WB setting. Release the Fn button to lock the WB setting you've dialed in.

- **Active D-Lighting.** Press the Fn button and rotate the command dial to choose Active D-Lighting settings.

- **HDR.** Allows using the Fn button to turn HDR functions on or off when using P, S, A, or M modes. HDR is deactivated after you've taken a picture, or when you press the Fn button a second time.

- **+NEF (RAW).** If your D5200 is currently set to shoot JPEG only, use this setting so that when you press the Fn button, the next shot will be recorded as a RAW+JPEG set. I use this option when shooting sports or other fast-moving events, then decide to shoot an image, say, along the sidelines, that could benefit from RAW manipulation later.

- **BKT.** Press the Fn button when using P, S, A, M modes and rotate the control dial to choose bracketing increment for exposure or white balance bracketing, or to turn ADL bracketing on or off.

- **AF-area mode.** Press the Fn button when using P, S, A, M modes and rotate the control dial to choose any of the AF-area modes described in Chapter 5, including single-point, dynamic-area (9 points), dynamic-area (21 points), dynamic-area (39 points), or 3D tracking.

- **Live view.** Press the Fn button to switch into live view mode. You might find this handy when you want to keep your right finger glued to the shutter release to catch some impending action, and then decide you need to switch into live view mode. Rather than move your trigger finger, you can activate live view with your left hand by pressing the Fn button.

- **AE/AF Lock.** Lock both focus and exposure while the AE-L/AF-L button is pressed.

- **AE Lock only.** Lock only the exposure while the AE-L/AF-L button is pressed.

- **AF Lock only.** Focus is locked in while the AE-L/AF-L button is held down.

- **AE Lock (Hold).** Exposure is locked when the AE-L/AF-L button is pressed, and remains locked until the button is pressed again, or the exposure meter-off delay expires.

- **AF-ON.** The AE-L/AF-L button is used to initiate autofocus.

# f2 Assign AE-L/AF-L Button

As if the Nikon D5200 didn't have enough buttons that are user-definable, you can change the behavior of the AE-L/AF-L button, too! The default value for the AE-L/AF-L button is AE/AF Lock.

To recap your options:

- **AE/AF Lock.** Lock both focus and exposure while the AE-L/AF-L button is pressed.
- **AE Lock only.** Lock only the exposure while the AE-L/AF-L button is pressed.
- **AF Lock only.** Focus is locked in while the AE-L/AF-L button is held down.
- **AE Lock (Hold).** Exposure is locked when the AE-L/AF-L button is pressed, and remains locked until the button is pressed again, or the exposure meter-off delay expires.
- **AF-ON.** The AE-L/AF-L button is used to initiate autofocus.

## f3 Reverse Dial Rotation

You can use the options in this menu entry to change the behavior of the command dials. Use the available tweaks to change the behavior of the dials to better suit your preferences, or if you're coming to the Nikon world from another vendor's product that uses a different operational scheme. Keep in mind that redefining basic controls in this way can prove confusing if someone other than yourself uses your camera, or if you find yourself working with other Nikon cameras that have retained the normal command dial behavior. The reason that the dials are set for their default directions is to match the direction of rotation of the aperture ring/command dial (when changing the aperture). Turning any of the three to the left decreases exposure, while rotating to the right increases exposure.

You can reverse the rotation direction of the command dial separately for exposure compensation and shutter speed/aperture setting using the checkboxes that appear when this menu entry is selected.

## f4 Slot Empty Release Lock

This entry gives you the ability to snap off "pictures" without a memory card installed—or to lock the camera shutter release if that is the case. It is sometimes called Play mode, because you can experiment with your camera's features or even hand your D5200 to a friend to let him fool around, without any danger of pictures actually being taken.

Back in our film days, we'd sometimes finish a roll, rewind the film back into its cassette surreptitiously, and then hand the camera to a child to take a few pictures—without actually wasting any film. It's hard to waste digital film, but "shoot without card" mode is still appreciated by some, especially camera vendors who want to be able to demo a camera at a store or trade show, but don't want to have to equip each and every demonstrator model with a memory card. Choose Enable Release to activate "play" mode or Release Locked to disable it.

The pictures you actually "take" are displayed on the LCD with the legend "Demo" superimposed on the screen, and they are, of course, not saved. Note that if you are using the optional Camera Control Pro 2 software to record photos from a USB-tethered D5200 directly to a computer, no memory card is required to unlock the shutter even if Release Locked has been selected.

# f5 Reverse Indicators

Refugees from other dSLR product lines are sometimes put off that Nikon cameras place the plus exposure values on the left side of the analog exposure display in the control panel, viewfinder, and shooting information display, with the negative values on the right, to match the rotation of the aperture ring (if used). This setting (-0+) can be swapped for the opposite orientation (+0-) to change the display to the other orientation. My take is that if you've fled to Nikonland, you might as well get used to it. I suppose this adjustment is useful for a dedicated shooter who sometimes uses a Nikon dSLR, and who never needs to change exposure using an aperture ring.

# 10

# The Setup Menu, Retouch Menu, and My Menu

We're not done covering the Nikon D5200's Setup options yet. There are three more menus to deal with. These include the Setup menu (which deals with adjustments that are outside the actual shooting experience, such as formatting a memory card, adjusting the time, or checking your battery); the Retouch menu (which enables you to fine-tune the appearance of images by trimming, adding filter effects, or removing red-eye); and the My Menu system, which can help you set up a customized menu that contains only the entries you want.

## Setup Menu Options

There is a long list of entries in the orange-coded Setup menu (see Figure 10.1), in which you can make additional adjustments on how your camera *behaves* before or during your shooting session, as differentiated from the Shooting menu, which adjusts how the pictures are actually taken. Your choices include:

- Format Memory Card
- Monitor Brightness
- Info Display Format
- Auto Info Display
- Clean Image Sensor
- Lock Mirror Up for Cleaning

- Image Dust Off Ref Photo
- Video Mode
- HDMI
- Flicker Reduction
- Time Zone and Date
- Language
- Image Comment

- Auto Image Rotation
- Accessory Terminal/ Remote Shutter Release/ GPS
- Wireless Mobile Adapter
- Eye-Fi Upload
- Firmware Version

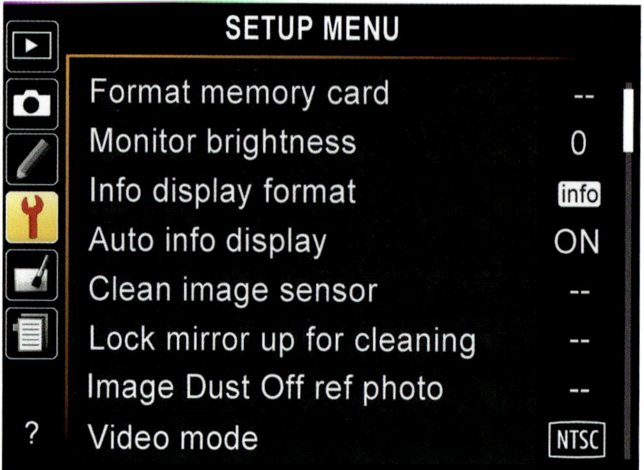


**Figure 10.1**
The Setup menu allows you to adjust how the D5200 behaves.

# Format Memory Card

I recommend using this menu entry to reformat your memory card after each shoot. While you can move files from the memory card to your computer, leaving behind a blank card, or delete files using the Playback menu's Delete feature, both of those options can leave behind stray files (such as those that have been marked as Protected). Format removes those files completely and beyond retrieval (unless you use a special utility program as described in Chapter 13) and establishes a fresh file system on the card, including a spanking-new DCIM (Digital Camera Images) folder, which will contain subfolders for each model camera that the card happens to be used in. (That's why you can remove a card from your D5200, use it in another model camera, and find that the images from each type of camera reside in folders of their own within the main DCIM folder.) Reformatting resets all the file allocation table (FAT) pointers (which tell the camera and your computer's operating system where all the images reside) efficiently pointing where they are supposed to on a blank card.

Or, select this menu entry and choose Yes from the screen that appears. Press OK to begin the format process.

# Monitor Brightness

Choose this menu option and a grayscale strip appears on the LCD, as shown in Figure 10.2. Use the multi selector up/down keys to adjust the brightness to a comfortable viewing level. Under the lighting conditions that exist when you make this adjustment, you should be able to see all 10 swatches from black to white. If the two end swatches blend together, the brightness has been set too low. If the two whitest swatches on the right end of the strip blend together, the brightness is too high. Brighter settings use more battery power, but can allow you to view an image on the LCD outdoors in bright sunlight. When you have the brightness you want, press OK to lock it in and return to the menu.

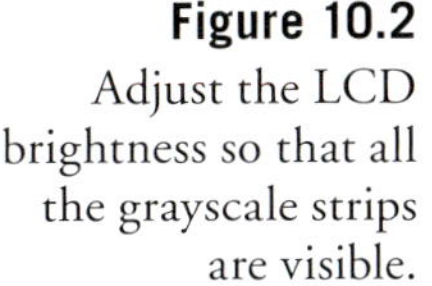

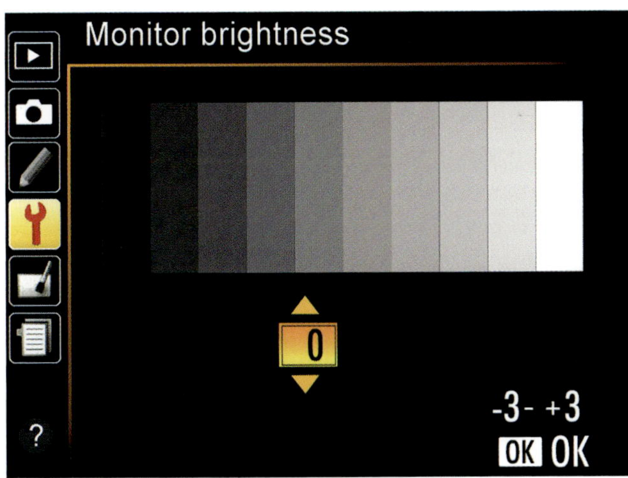


**Figure 10.2**
Adjust the LCD brightness so that all the grayscale strips are visible.

# Info Display Format

This entry allows you to choose the shooting information screen format and color scheme. You can select the Classic format, which I find easier to read and use, with background colors of blue, black, or orange, or the Graphic format with background colors of green, black, or brown. This is strictly a matter of personal preference.

# Auto Info Display

Choose On, and the shooting information display will appear automatically after the shutter release is pressed halfway, and after the picture is taken if image review has been turned off in the Playback menu. Choose Off, and the information display can be viewed by pressing the information edit button. Some find that Off is less distracting, because the information display is only shown when invoked by the user.

# Clean Image Sensor

This entry gives you some control over the Nikon D5200's automatic sensor cleaning feature, which removes dust through a vibration cycle that shakes the sensor until dust, presumably, falls off and is captured by a sticky surface at the bottom of the sensor area. If you happen to take a picture and notice an artifact in an area that contains little detail (such as the sky or a blank wall), you can access this menu choice, place the camera with its base downward, and choose Clean Now. A message Cleaning Sensor now appears, and the dust you noticed has probably been shaken off.

You can also tell the D5200 when you'd like it to perform automatic cleaning without specific instructions from you. Select from:

- **ON.** Clean at startup. This allows you to start off a particular shooting session with a clean sensor.

- **OFF.** Clean at shutdown. This removes any dust that may have accumulated since the camera has been turned on, say, from dust infiltration while changing lenses. Note that this choice does not turn off automatic cleaning; it simply moves the operation to the camera power-down sequence.

- **ON/OFF.** Clean at both startup and shutdown. Use this setting if you're paranoid about dust and don't mind the extra battery power consumed each time the camera is turned on or off. If you only turn off the D5200 when you're finished shooting, the power penalty is not large, but if you're the sort who turns off the camera every time you pause in shooting, the extra power consumed by the dust removal may exceed any savings you get from leaving the camera off.

- **Cleaning Off.** No automatic dust removal will be performed. Use this to preserve battery power, or if you prefer to use automatic dust removal only when you explicitly want to apply it.

## Lock Mirror Up for Cleaning

You can also clean the sensor manually. Use this menu entry to raise the mirror and open the shutter so you'll have access to the sensor for cleaning with a blower, brush, or swab, as described in Chapter 13. You don't want power to fail while you're poking around inside the camera, so this option is available only when sufficient battery power (at least 60 percent) is available. Using a fully charged battery or connecting the D5200 to an EH-5/EH5a AC adapter is an even better idea.

## Image Dust Off Ref Photo

This menu choice lets you "take a picture" of any dust or other particles that may be adhering to your sensor. The D5200 will then append information about the location of this dust to your photos, so that the Image Dust Off option in Capture NX 2 can be used to mask the dust in the NEF image.

To use this feature, select Image Dust Off Ref Photo, choose either Start or Clean Sensor and then Start, and then press OK. If directed to do so, the camera will first perform a self-cleaning operation by applying ultrasonic vibration to the low-pass filter that resides on top of the sensor. Then, a screen will appear asking you to take a photo of a bright featureless white object 10 cm from the lens. Nikon recommends using a lens with a focal length of at least 50mm. Point the D5200 at a solid white card and press the shutter release. An image with the extension NDF will be created, and can be used by Nikon Capture NX 2 as a reference photo if the "dust off" picture is placed in the same folder as an image to be processed for dust removal.

# Video Mode

This setting controls the output of the Nikon D5200 to a conventional video system through the video cable when you're displaying images on a monitor or connected to a VCR through the external device's yellow video input jack. You can select NTSC, used in the United States, Canada, Mexico, many Central, South American, and Caribbean countries, much of Asia, and other countries, or PAL, which is used in the UK, much of Europe, Africa, India, China, and parts of the Middle East.

# HDMI

The Nikon D5200 has a High-Definition Multimedia Interface (HDMI) video connection, so you can play back your camera's images on HDTV or HD monitors using a type C cable, which Nikon does not provide to you, but which is readily available from third parties. Before you link up you'll want to choose the HDMI resolution to be used, from 480p (640 × 480 progressive scan); 576p (720 × 576 progressive scan); 720p (1280 × 720 progressive scan); or 1080i (1920 × 1080 interlaced scan). Or, select the Auto option and the camera will choose the appropriate format for you. This entry is the first on the second page of the Setup menu (see Figure 10.3).

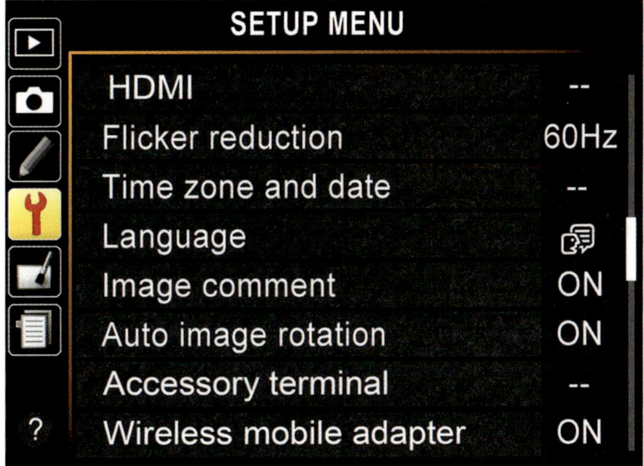


**Figure 10.3**
HDMI is the first entry on the second page of the Setup menu.

You can also choose to turn Device Control on or off. When On is chosen and the camera is connected to a television that supports the HDMI-CEC protocol (when both the TV and camera are turned on) you'll see PLAY and SLIDE SHOW messages on the television. You can then use the television's compatible remote control instead of the multi selector and OK buttons to review images and play slide shows. Choose Off, and this capability is disabled.

# Flicker Reduction

This menu entry reduces flicker and banding, which can occur when shooting in live view mode and movie mode under fluorescent and mercury vapor illumination, because the cycling of these light sources interacts with the frame rate of the camera's video system. In the United States, you'd choose the 60Hz frequency; in locations where 50Hz current is the norm, select that option instead. You can also select Auto and let the camera decide.

# Time Zone and Date

Use this menu entry to adjust the D5200's internal clock. Your options include:

- **Time zone.** A small map will pop up on the setting screen and you can choose your local time zone. I sometimes forget to change the time zone when I travel (especially when going to Europe), so my pictures are all time-stamped incorrectly. I like to use the time stamp to recall exactly when a photo was taken, so keeping this setting correct is important.

- **Date and time.** Use this setting to enter the exact year, month, day, hour, minute, and second, using a 24-hour clock.

- **Date format.** Choose from Y/M/D (year/month/day), M/D/Y (month/day/year), or D/M/Y (day/month/year) formats.

- **Daylight saving time.** Use this to turn daylight saving time On or Off. Because the date on which DST goes into effect each year has been changed from time to time, if you turn this feature on you may need to monitor your camera to make sure DST has been implemented correctly.

# Language

Choose your language for menu display, including Arabic, Chinese (Simplified and Traditional), Czech, Danish, Dutch, English, Finnish, French, German, Greek, Hindi, Hungarian, Indonesian, Italian, Japanese, Korean, Norwegian, Polish, Portuguese (Portugal and Brazil), Romanian, Russian, Spanish, Swedish, Thai, Turkish, and Ukrainian.

# Image Comment

The image comment is your opportunity to add a copyright notice, personal information about yourself (including contact info), or even a description of where the image was taken (e.g., Browns Super Bowl 2013), although text entry with the Nikon D5200 is a bit too clumsy for doing a lot of individual annotation of your photos. (But you still might want to change the comment each time, say, you change cities during your travels.) The embedded comments can be read by many software programs, including Nikon ViewNX 2 or Capture NX 2.

The standard text entry screen described in Chapter 8 can be used to enter your comment, with up to 36 characters available. For the copyright symbol, embed a lowercase "c" within opening and closing parentheses: (c). You can input the comment, turn attachment of the comment On or Off using the Attach Comment entry, and select Done when you're finished working with comments. If you find typing with a cursor too tedious, you can enter your comment in Nikon Capture NX 2 and upload it to the camera through a USB cable.

## Auto Image Rotation

Turning this setting On tells the Nikon D5200 to include camera orientation information in the image file. The orientation can be read by many software applications, including Adobe Photoshop, Nikon ViewNX 2, and Capture NX 2, as well as the Rotate Tall setting in the Playback menu. Turn this feature Off, and none of the software applications or Playback's Rotate Tall will be able to determine the correct orientation for the image. Nikon notes that only the first image's orientation is used when shooting continuous bursts; subsequent photos will be assigned the same orientation, even if you rotate the camera during the sequence (which is something I have been known to do myself when shooting sports like basketball).

## Accessory Terminal

This menu entry has options that allow you to control how devices plugged into the D5200's accessory terminal are used. It has two options, Remote Shutter Release and GPS. For remote shutter release you can specify whether pressing the button on the release (such as the MC-DC2) takes still photos or records movies. The additional Record Movies choice makes it possible for you to start movie capture without needing to first switch into live view mode and pressing the movie button on the camera.

The GPS option provides access to features of the Nikon GP-1 Global Positioning System (GPS) device. It has three choices, none of which turn GPS features on or off, despite the misleading "Enable" and "Disable" nomenclature (what you're enabling and disabling is the automatic exposure meter turn-off):

■ **Standby timer.** You can choose Enable or Disable. Enabling reduces battery drain by allowing the D5200 to turn off exposure meters while using the GP-1 after the time specified in CSM c2 (Auto Meter-off Delay, discussed in Chapter 9) has elapsed. When the meters turn off, the GP-1 becomes inactive and must reacquire at least three satellite signals before it can begin recording GPS data once more. When you choose Disable, the exposure meters to remain on while using the GP-1, so that GPS data can be recorded at any time, despite increased battery drain.

■ **Position.** This is an information display, rather than a selectable option. It appears when the GP-1 is connected and receiving satellite positioning data. It shows the latitude, longitude, altitude, and Coordinated Universal Time (UTC) values.

■ **Use GPS to set camera clock.** Select Yes or No. When enabled, your D5200's internal camera clock will be set using UTC values whenever the GP-1 is attached to the camera. If you use the device frequently, this will ensure that your camera's clock is always set accurately, and won't require a manual update periodically.

# Eye-Fi Upload

This option (not shown in Figure 10.3) is displayed in the menu *only* when a compatible Eye-Fi memory card is being used in the D5200. The Eye-Fi card looks like an ordinary SDHC memory card, but has built-in Wi-Fi capabilities, so it can be used to transmit your photos as they are taken directly to a computer over a Wi-Fi network. When an Eye-Fi card is inserted, and you've enabled the card by choosing Enable in this menu entry, one of four informational icons will appear in the shooting information screen, shown, left to right in Figure 10.4.

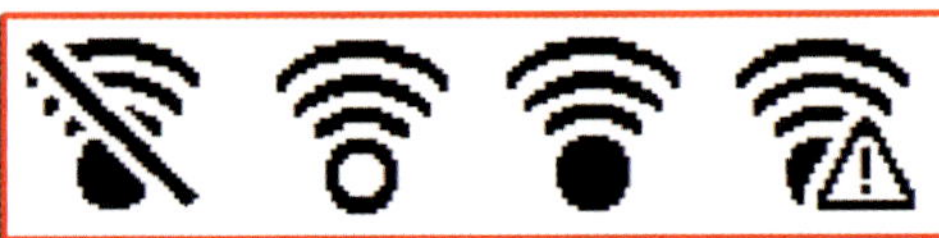

**Figure 10.4** The icons show the Eye-Fi card's status. Left to right: Eye-Fi upload disabled; Eye-Fi upload enabled, but no images available for upload; Waiting to begin upload (if static)/ Uploading (if animated); Error.

# Wireless Mobile Adapter

Allows you to Enable or Disable the WU-1a Wireless Mobile Adapter. I explained how to use this device in Chapter 7.

# Firmware Version

You can see the current firmware release in use in the menu listing. You can learn how to update firmware in Chapter 13.

# Retouch Menu Options

The Retouch Menu choices allow you to trim, resize, and combine images, or modify them with special effects. Movie-editing features can also be found here, along with the ability to compare a pair of images side by side.

- D-Lighting
- Red-Eye Correction
- Trim
- Monochrome
- Filter Effects
- Color Balance
- Image Overlay

- NEF (Raw) Processing
- Resize
- Quick Retouch
- Straighten
- Distortion Control
- Fisheye
- Color Outline

- Color Sketch
- Perspective Control
- Miniature Effect
- Selective Color
- Edit Movie
- Side-by-Side Comparison

The Retouch menu (see Figure 10.5) is most useful when you want to create a modified copy of an image on the spot, for immediate printing or e-mailing without first importing into your computer for more extensive editing. You can also use it to create a JPEG version of an image in the camera when you are shooting RAW-only photos. While you can retouch images that have already been processed by the Retouch menu, each retouch option can be applied only once, except for the Image

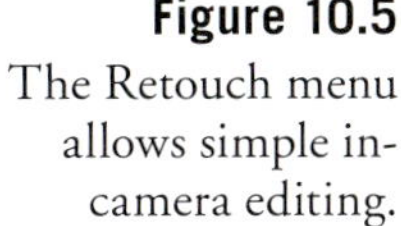

**Figure 10.5**
The Retouch menu allows simple in-camera editing.

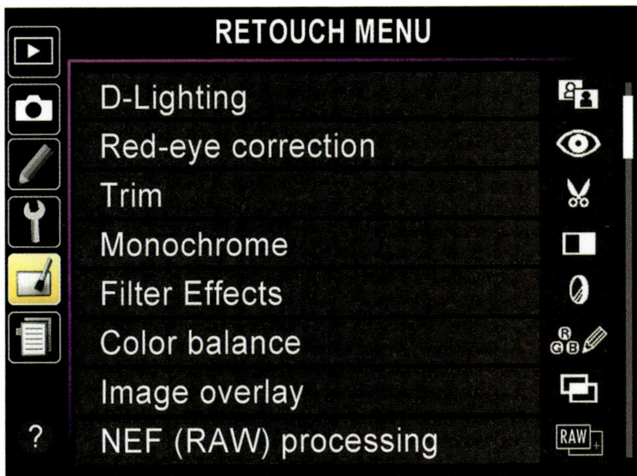


Overlay and Edit Movie tools. You may notice some quality loss when applying more than one retouch option. To create a retouched copy of an image:

1. While browsing among images in Playback mode, press OK when an image you want to retouch is displayed on the screen. The Retouch menu will pop up, and you can select a retouching option.

2. From the Retouch menu, select the option you want and press the multi selector right button. The Nikon D5200's standard image selection screen appears. Scroll among the images as usual with the left/right multi selector buttons, press the Zoom In button to examine a highlighted image more closely, and press OK to choose that image.

3. Work with the options available from that particular Retouch menu feature and press OK to create the modified copy, or Playback to cancel your changes.

4. A retouched JPEG image will be the same size and quality as the original, except for copies created from NEF images (which are always saved as JPEG Fine images).

## D-Lighting

This option brightens the shadows of pictures that have already been taken. Once you've selected your photo for modification, you'll be shown side-by-side images with the unaltered version on the left, and your adjusted version on the right. Press the multi selector's up/down buttons to choose from High, Normal, or Low corrections. Press the Zoom In button to magnify the image. When you're happy with the corrected image on the right, compared to the original on the left, press OK to save the copy to your memory card.

## Red-Eye Correction

This Retouch menu tool can be used to remove the residual red-eye look that remains after applying the Nikon D5200's other remedies, such as the red-eye reduction lamp. (You can use the red-eye tools found in most image editors, as well.)

Your Nikon D5200 has a fairly effective red-eye reduction flash mode. Unfortunately, your camera is unable, on its own, to totally *eliminate* the red-eye effects that occur when an electronic flash (or, rarely, illumination from other sources) bounces off the retinas of the eye and into the camera lens. Animals seem to suffer from yellow or green glowing pupils, instead; the effect is equally undesirable. The effect is worst under low-light conditions (exactly when you might be using a flash) as the pupils expand to allow more light to reach the retinas. The best you can hope for is to *reduce* or minimize the red-eye effect.

The best way to truly eliminate red-eye is to raise the flash up off the camera so its illumination approaches the eye from an angle that won't reflect directly back to the retina and into the lens. The extra height of the built-in flash may not be sufficient, however. That alone is a good reason for using an external flash. If you're working with your D5200's built-in flash, your only recourse may be to switch on the red-eye reduction flash mode. That causes a lamp on the front of the camera to illuminate with a half-press of the shutter release button, which may result in your subjects' pupils contracting, decreasing the amount of the red-eye effect. (You may have to ask your subject to look at the lamp to gain maximum effect.)

If your image still displays red-eye effects, you can use the Retouch menu to make a copy with red-eye reduced further. First, select a picture that was taken with flash (non-flash pictures won't be available for selection). After you've selected the picture to process, press OK. The image will be displayed on the LCD. You can magnify the image with the Zoom In button, scroll around the zoomed image with the multi selector buttons, and zoom out with the Zoom Out button. While zoomed, you can cancel the zoom by pressing the OK button.

When you are finished examining the image, press OK again. The D5200 will look for red-eye, and, if detected, create a copy that has been processed to reduce the effect. If no red-eye is found, a copy is not created. Figure 10.6 shows an original image (left) and its processed copy (right).

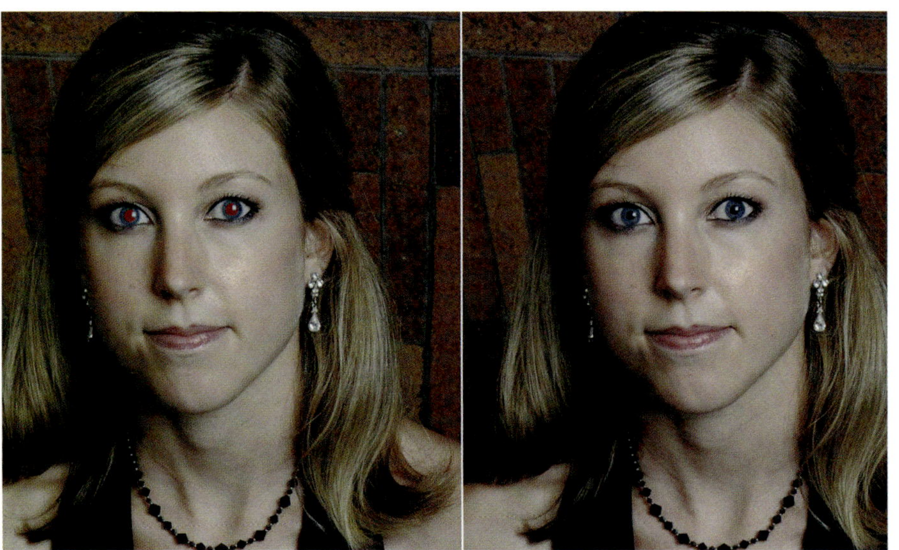

**Figure 10.6**
Wider pupils (left) can lead to red-eye effects; the Nikon D5200's red-eye reduction retouching feature can fix the image (right).

# Trim

This option creates copies in specific sizes based on the final size you select, chosen from among 3:2, 4:3, and 5:4 aspect ratios (proportions) (see Figure 10.7). You can use this feature to create smaller versions of a picture for e-mailing without the need to first transfer the image to your own computer. If you're traveling, create your smaller copy here, insert the memory card in a card reader at an Internet café, your library's public computers, or some other computer, and e-mail the reduced-size version. Just follow these steps:

1. **Select your photo.** Choose Trim from the Retouch menu. You'll be shown the standard Nikon D5200 image selection screen. Scroll among the photos using the multi selector left/right buttons, and press OK when the image you want to trim is highlighted. While selecting, you can temporarily enlarge the highlighted image by pressing the Zoom In button.

2. **Choose your aspect ratio.** Rotate the command dial to change from 3:2, 4:3, 5:4, 1:1, and 16:9 aspect ratios. These proportions happen to correspond to the proportions of common print sizes, including the two most popular sizes: 4 × 6 inches (3:2) and 8 × 10 inches (5:4).

3. **Crop in on your photo.** Press the Zoom In button to crop in on your picture. The pixel dimensions of the cropped image at the selected proportions will be displayed in the upper-left corner (see Figure 10.7 as you zoom). The current framed size is outlined in yellow.

4. **Move cropped area within the image.** Use the multi selector left/right and up/down buttons to relocate the yellow cropping border within the frame.

5. **Save the cropped image.** Press OK to save a copy of the image using the current crop and size, or press the Playback button to exit without creating a copy. Copies created from JPEG Fine, Normal, or Standard have the same Image Quality setting as the original; copies made from RAW files or any RAW+JPEG setting will use JPEG Fine compression.

**Figure 10.7**
The Trim feature of the Retouch menu allows in-camera cropping.

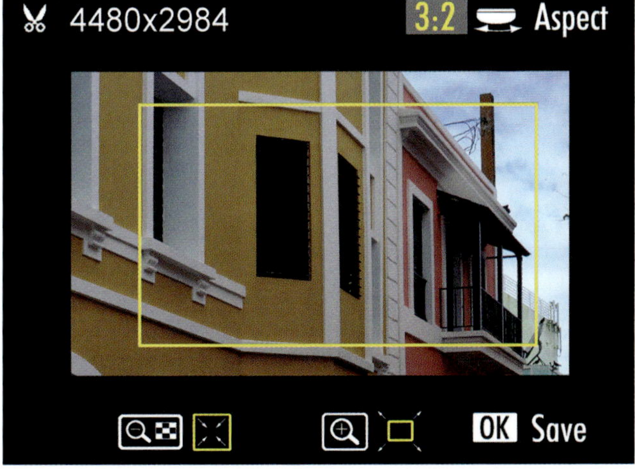

## Table 10.1 Trim Sizes

| Aspect Ratio | Sizes Available |
| --- | --- |
| 3:2 | 5760 × 3850, 5120 × 3416, 4480 × 2984, 3840 × 2560; 3200 × 2128; 2560 × 1704; 1920 × 1280; 1280 × 856; 960 × 640; 640 × 424 |
| 4:3 | 5328 × 4000, 5120 × 3840, 4480 × 3360, 3840 × 2880; 3200 × 2400; 2560 × 1920; 1920 × 1440; 1280 × 960; 960 × 720; 640 × 480 |
| 5:4 | 5008 × 4000, 4800 × 3840, 4208 × 3360, 3600 × 2880; 2992 × 2400; 2400 × 1920; 1808 × 1440; 1200 × 960; 896 × 720; 608 × 480 |
| 1:1 | 3840 × 3840, 3360 × 3360, 2880 × 2880; 2400 × 2400; 1920 × 1920; 1440 × 1440; 960 × 960; 720 × 720; 480 × 480 |
| 16:9 | 6016 × 3384, 5760 × 3240, 5120 × 2880, 4480 × 2520, 3840 × 2160; 3200 × 1800; 2560 × 1440; 1920 × 1080; 1280 × 720; 960 × 536; 640 × 360 |

# Monochrome

This Retouch choice allows you to produce a copy of the selected photo as a black-and-white image, sepia-toned image, or cyanotype (blue-and-white). You can fine-tune the color saturation of the previewed Sepia or Cyanotype version by pressing the multi selector up button to increase color richness, and the down button to decrease saturation. When satisfied, press OK to create the monochrome duplicate. Cancel by pressing the Playback button.

# Filter Effects

Add tones to your images using this Retouch option. You have seven choices: Skylight, Warm, Red/Green/Blue intensifiers, Cross Screen, and Soft. Preview the effects in the color LCD before pressing OK to create the modified copy using the selected effect.

# Color Balance

This Retouch effect allows you to create a copy with modified color balance. When you press the OK button while viewing a selected image, a screen like the one shown in Figure 10.8 appears with the photo shown in thumbnail size at the upper-left corner, and red/green/blue histograms at the right. You can bias the image along the magenta/green axis or blue/yellow (amber) axis based on your perception of the thumbnail or, as you gain experience, from your estimation of the distribution of tones as shown by the histograms.

Press the multi selector up button to increase the amount of green, the down button to increase the amount of magenta, the right button to increase the bias toward yellow/amber, and the left button to increase the amount of blue. As you make these modifications, the changes will be reflected in the histograms.

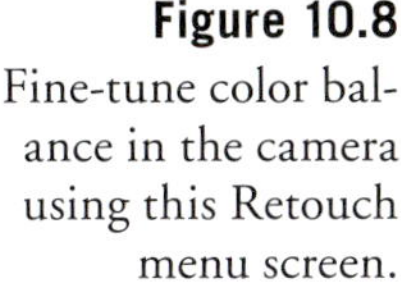

**Figure 10.8**
Fine-tune color balance in the camera using this Retouch menu screen.

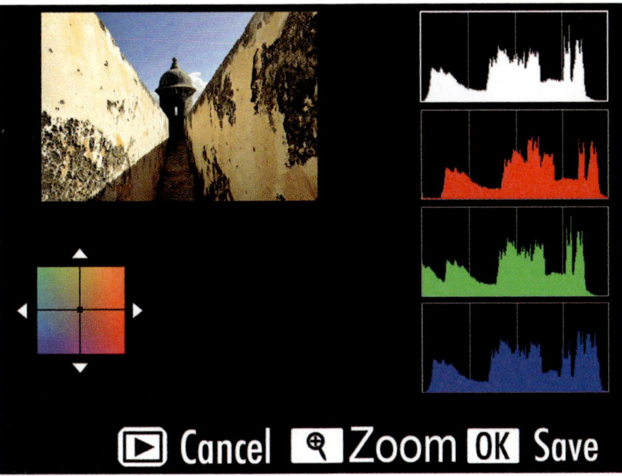

# Image Overlay

This feature allows you to combine two RAW photos (only NEF files can be used) in a composite image that Nikon claims is better than a "double exposure" created in an image-editing application, because the overlays are made using RAW data. To produce this composite image, follow these steps:

1. **Choose Image Overlay in the Retouch menu.** The screen shown in Figure 10.9 will be displayed, with the Image 1 box highlighted.
2. **Select first image.** Press OK and the Nikon D5200's image selection screen appears. Highlight the first image for the overlay with the multi selector and press OK to choose the photo and return to the preview display.
3. **Select second image.** Press the multi selector right button to highlight the Image 2 box, and press OK to produce the image selection screen. Choose the second image for the overlay.

**Figure 10.9**
Overlay two RAW images to produce a "double exposure."

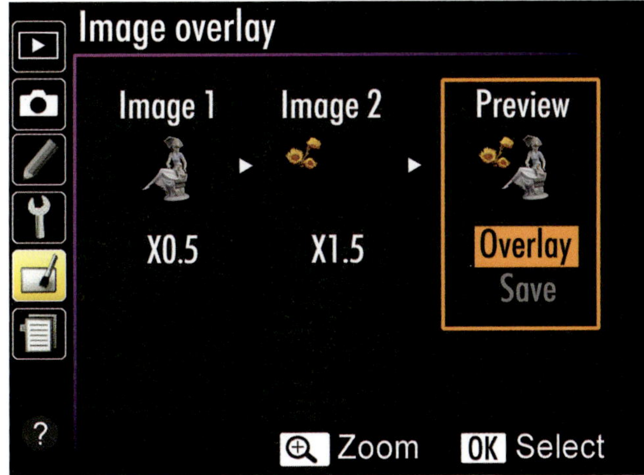

4. **Adjust gain.** By highlighting either the Image 1 or Image 2 boxes and pressing the multi selector up/down buttons, you can adjust the "gain," or how much of the final image will be "exposed" from the selected picture. You can choose from X0.5 (half-exposure) to X2.0 (twice the exposure) for each image. The default value is 1.0 for each, so that each image will contribute equally to the final exposure.

5. **Examine combined image.** Use the multi selector right button to highlight the Preview box and view the combined picture. Press the Zoom In button to enlarge the view.

6. **Save new image.** When you're ready to store your composite copy, press the multi selector down button when the Preview box is highlighted to select Save, and press OK. The combined image is stored on the memory card.

# NEF (RAW) Processing

Use this tool to create a JPEG version of any image saved in either straight RAW (with no JPEG version) or RAW+Basic (with a Basic JPEG version). You can select from among several parameters to "process" your new JPEG copy right in the camera.

1. Choose a RAW image. Select NEF (RAW) processing from the Retouch menu. You'll be shown the standard Nikon D5200 image selection screen. Use the left/right buttons to navigate among the RAW images displayed. Press OK to select the highlighted image.

2. In the NEF (RAW) processing screen, shown in Figure 10.10, you can use the multi selector up/down keys to select from seven different attributes of the RAW image information to apply to your JPEG copy. Choose Image Quality (Fine, Normal, or Basic), Image Size (Large, Medium, or Small), White Balance, Exposure Compensation, Picture Control, High ISO Noise Reduction, and D-Lighting parameters.

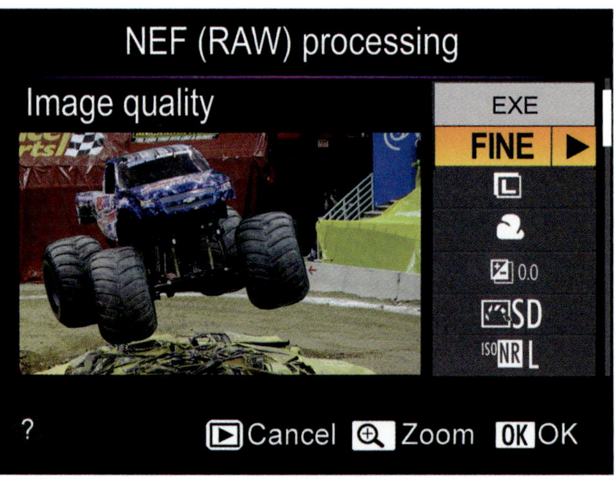


**Figure 10.10**
Adjust parameters and then save your JPEG copy from a RAW original file.

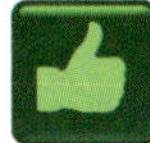

**Tip**

The White Balance parameter cannot be selected for images created with the Image Overlay tool, and the Preset manual white balance setting can be fine-tuned only with images that were originally shot using the Preset white balance setting. Exposure compensation cannot be adjusted for images taken using Active D-Lighting, and both white balance and optimize image settings cannot be applied to pictures taken using any of the scene modes.

3. Press the Zoom In button to magnify the image temporarily while the button is held down.

4. Press the Playback button if you change your mind, to exit from the processing screen.

5. When all parameters are set, highlight EXE (for Execute) and press OK. The D5200 will create a JPEG file with the settings you've specified, and show an Image Saved message on the LCD when finished.

# Resize

This option, the first on the second page of the Retouch menu (see Figure 10.11), creates smaller copies of the selected images. It can be applied while viewing a single image in full-frame mode (just press the OK button while viewing a photo), or accessed from the Retouch menu (especially useful if you'd like to select and resize multiple images).

1. **Select images.** If accessing from the Retouch menu, you can choose to select multiple images, or jump directly to the following two steps.

2. **Choose Size.** Next, select the size for the finished copy, from 2.5M (1920 × 1280 pixels), 1.1M (1280 × 856 pixels), 0.6M (960 × 640 pixels), 0.3M (640 × 424 pixels), or 0.1M (320 × 216 pixels).

3. **Confirm.** Press OK to create your copy.

**Figure 10.11**
Resize is the first entry on the second page of the Retouch menu.

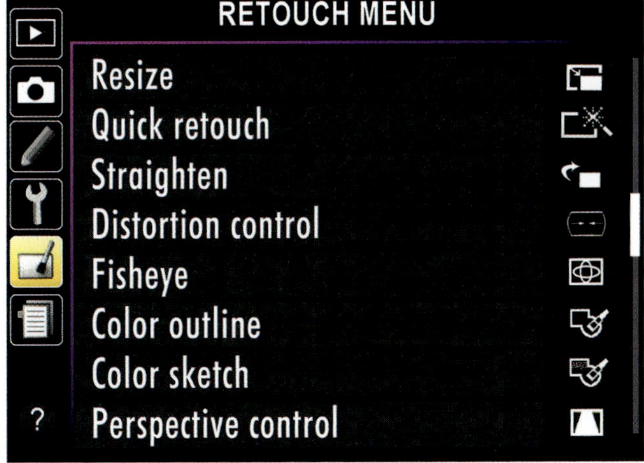

# Quick Retouch

This option brightens the shadows of pictures that have already been taken. Once you've selected your photo for processing, use the multi selector up/down keys in the screen that pops up (see Figure 10.12). The amount of correction that you select (High, Normal, or Low) will be applied to the version of the image shown at right. The left-hand version of the image shows the uncorrected version. While working on your image, you can press the Zoom In image to temporarily magnify the original photo.

Quick Retouch brightens shadows, enhances contrast, and adds color richness (saturation) to the image. Press OK to create a copy on your memory card with the retouching applied.

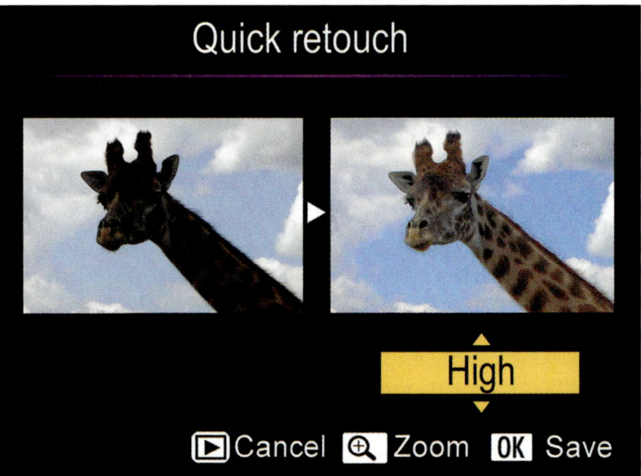


**Figure 10.12**
Quick Retouch applies D-Lighting, enhanced contrast, and added saturation to an image.

# Straighten

Use this to create a corrected copy of a crooked image, rotated by up to five degrees, in increments of one-quarter of a degree. Use the right directional button to rotate clockwise, and the left directional button to rotate counterclockwise. Press OK to make a corrected copy, or the Playback button to exit without saving a copy.

# Distortion Control

This option produces a copy with reduced barrel distortion (a bowing out effect) or pincushion distortion (an inward-bending effect), both most noticeable at the edges of a photo. You can select Auto to let the D5200 make this correction, or use Manual to make the fix yourself visually. Use the right directional button to reduce barrel distortion and the left directional button to reduce pincushion distortion. In both cases, some of the edges of the photo will be cropped out of your image. Press OK to make a corrected copy, or the Playback button to exit without saving a copy. Note that Auto cannot be used with images exposed using the Auto Distortion Control feature described earlier in this chapter. Auto works only with type G and type D lenses (see Chapter 11 for a description of what these lenses are), and does not work well with certain lenses, such as fisheye lenses and perspective control lenses.

# Fisheye

This feature emulates the extreme curving effect of a fisheye lens. Use the right directional button to increase the effect, and the left directional button to decrease it. Press OK to make a corrected copy, or the Playback button to exit without saving a copy. Figure 10.13 shows an example image.

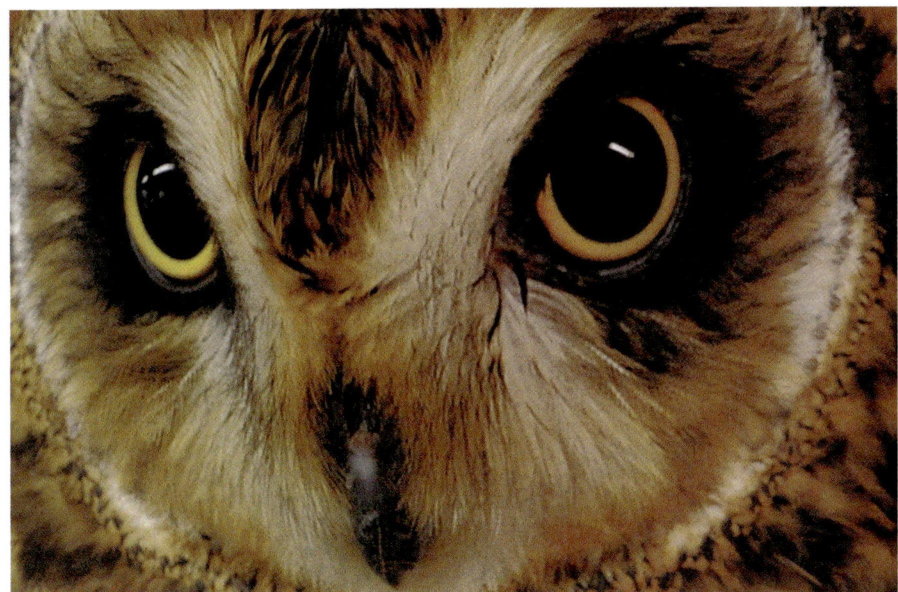

**Figure 10.13**
You can apply a fisheye effect to an image.

# Color Sketch

This option creates a copy of your image in outline form, too, but retains some of the colors of the original image.

# Color Outline

This option creates a copy of your image in outline form (see Figure 10.14), which Nikon says you can use for "painting." You might like the effect on its own. It's a little like the Find Edges command in Photoshop and Photoshop Elements, but you can perform this magic in your camera!

# Perspective Control

This option (shown in Figure 10.15) lets you adjust the perspective of an image, reducing the falling back effect produced when the camera is tilted to take in the top of a tall subject, such as a building. Use the multi selector buttons to "tilt" the image in various directions and visually correct the distortion.

**Figure 10.14**  The Color Outline retouching feature creates an outline image (right), but it's not in color (like the original, left).

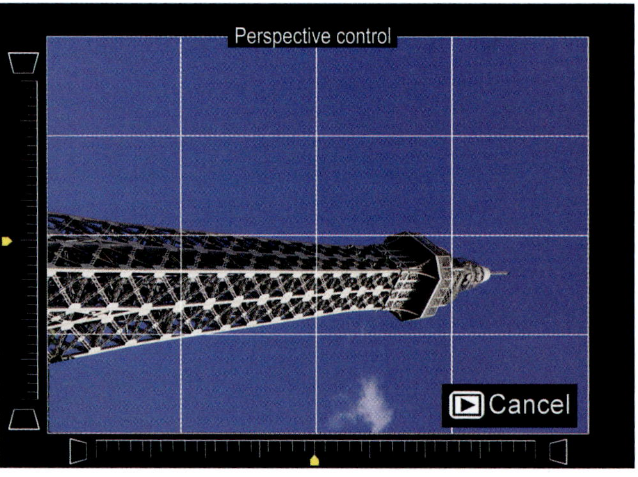


**Figure 10.15**
Perspective Control lets you fix "falling back" distortion when photographing tall subjects.

# Miniature Effect

This is a clever effect, and it's hampered by a misleading name and the fact that its properties are hard to visualize (which is not a great attribute for a visual effect). This tool doesn't create a "miniature" picture, as you might expect. What it does is mimic tilt/shift lens effects that angle the lens off the axis of the sensor plane to drastically change the plane of focus, producing the sort of look you get when viewing some photographs of a diorama, or miniature scene. Confused yet?

Perhaps the best way to understand this capability is to actually modify a picture using it. Just follow these steps:

1. **Take your best shot.** Capture an image of a distant landscape or other scene, preferably from a slightly elevated viewpoint.

2. **Access Miniature Effect.** When viewing the image during playback, press the multi selector center button to access the Retouch menu, and select Miniature Effect. A screen like the one shown in Figure 10.16 appears.

3. **Adjust selected area.** A wide yellow box (or a tall yellow box if the image is rotated to vertical perspective on playback) highlights a small section of the image. (No, we're not going to create a panorama from that slice; this Nikon super-tricky feature has fooled you yet again.) Use the up/down buttons (or left/right buttons if the image is displayed vertically) to move the yellow box, which represents the area of your image that will be rendered in (fairly) sharp focus. The rest of the image will be blurred.

4. **Preview area to be in sharp focus.** Press the Zoom In button to preview the area that will be rendered in sharp focus. Nikon labels this control Confirm, but that's just to mislead you. It's actually just a preview that lets you "confirm" that this is the area you want to emphasize.

5. **Apply the effect.** Press the OK button to apply the effect (or the Playback button to cancel). Your finished image will be rendered in a weird altered-focus way, as shown in Figure 10.17.

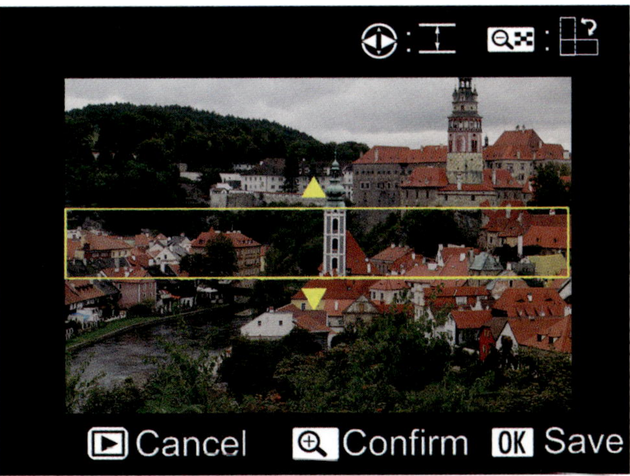


**Figure 10.16**

Choose the area for sharp focus by moving the yellow box within the frame.

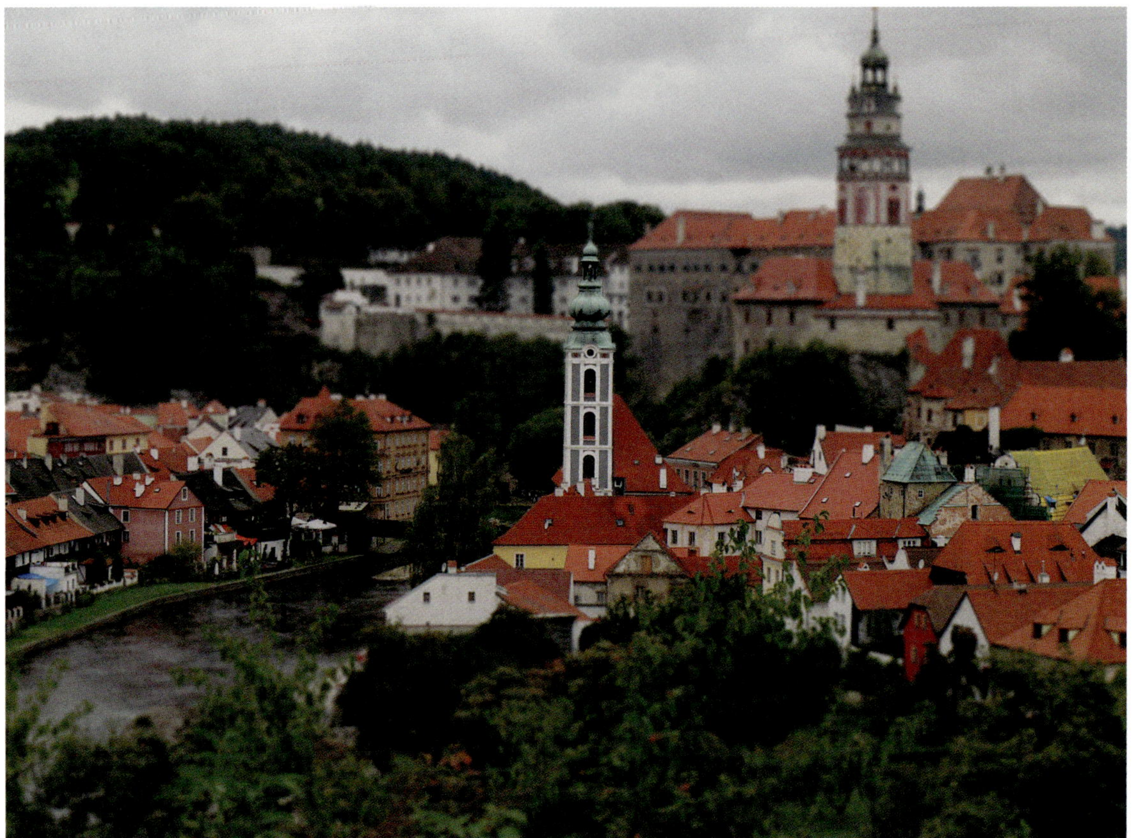

**Figure 10.17** The same photo with the diorama/miniature effect applied.

# Selective Color

This is a retouching effect that allows you to choose which colors appear in a finished image, with the other colors rendered in black-and-white, resembling the effects seen in movies like *Sin City*, and every single wedding picture of a monochrome bride holding a vivid red rose. Your D5200 gives you access to this effect, to use creatively, or to reproduce some of the most popular clichés. To use it:

1. **Access Selective Color feature.** Choose Selective Color from the Retouch menu.

2. **Choose image.** When the Select Photo screen appears, highlight the one you want to process. You can preview the image in full frame by pressing the Zoom In button. When you've decided on the image, press the OK button. A screen like the one shown in Figure 10.18 appears.

3. **Specify a color.** Next, use the multi selector buttons to move the on-screen cursor over an area of the object with the color you want to specify and press the Protect/AE-L/AF-L button. The effect works best if you choose a rich, highly saturated color. You can enlarge a portion of the image by pressing the Zoom In button.

4. **Add the selected color to a color range.** Rotate the command dial to choose one of the three color range boxes.

5. **Increase/decrease "tolerance."** Press the up/down multi selector buttons to increase or decrease the range of similar colors that will be included, with values from 1 to 7. A very broad range may extend the color selection into adjoining colors, say, embracing dark blues as well as lighter blues or even cyans.

6. **Choose a different color range box to add more colors.** Rotate the command dial again to highlight one of the other three color range boxes and repeat Steps 3 to 5 to add more colors.

7. **Save image.** Press OK to create a modified copy of your original photograph. (See Figure 10.19.)

**Figure 10.18**
Select your colors and color ranges here.

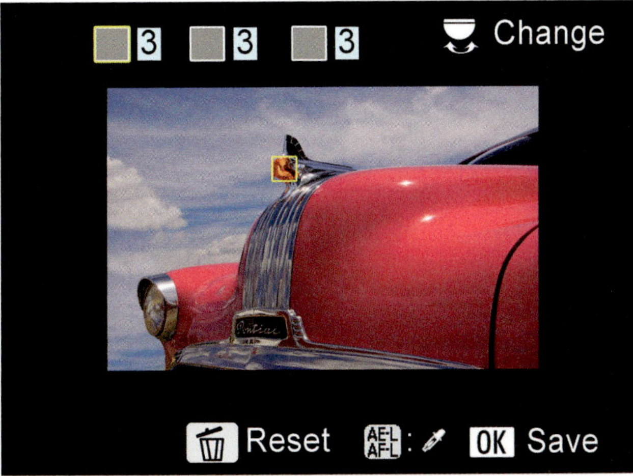


**Figure 10.19**
The finished effect looks like this.

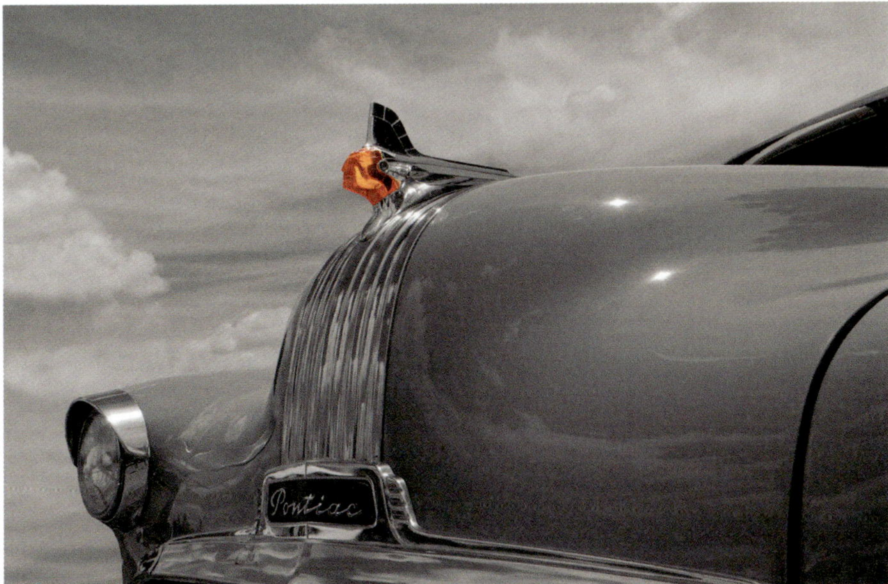

# Edit Movie

You can edit movies as you view them, pausing (using the down directional button) and clipping off portions from the beginning and/or end of the movie to create an edited version. Movie editing can be done from this menu entry, or accessed by pausing and pressing the AE-L/AF-L button to display a retouching menu.

I described editing movies using this capability in detail in Chapter 6.

# Side-by-Side Comparison

Use this option to compare a previously retouched or copied photo side-by-side with the original from which it was derived. Don't look for Side-by-Side Comparison in the Retouch menu. It doesn't appear there. Instead, this option is shown at the bottom of the pop-up menu that appears when you are viewing an image (or copy) full screen and press the OK button.

To use Side-by-Side Comparison:

1. Press the Playback button and review images in full-frame mode until you encounter a source image or retouched copy you want to compare. The retouched copy will have the retouching icon displayed in the upper-left corner. Press OK.

2. The original and retouched image will appear next to each other, with the retouching options you've used shown as a label above the images, as you can see in Figure 10.20.

3. Highlight the original or the copy with the multi selector left/right buttons, and press the Zoom In button to magnify the image to examine it more closely.

4. If you have created more than one copy of an original image, select the retouched version shown, and press the multi selector up/down buttons to view the other retouched copies. The up/down buttons will also let you view the other image used to create an Image Overlay copy.

5. When done comparing, press the Playback button to exit.

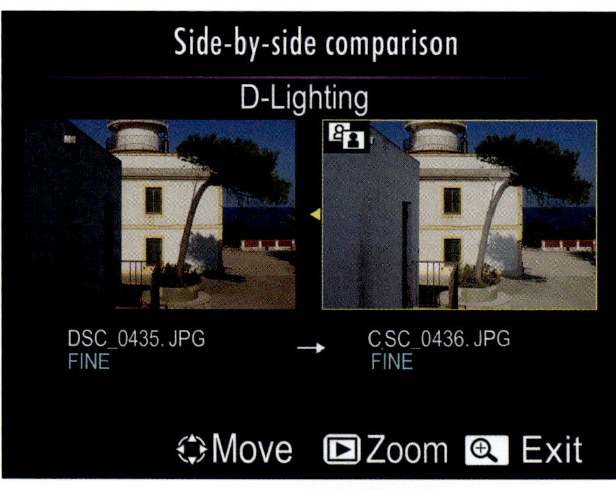


**Figure 10.20**
You can easily compare an original image and the retouched version side-by-side.

# Using Special Effects Modes

Although the D5200's seven Special Effects modes are a type of scene mode selection, I've elected to describe them here, because they are actually more closely related to the retouching effects we've explored in this chapter. Indeed, three of them are essentially identical, but are simply applied during shooting rather than after the image has already been captured.

To use Special Effects, set the mode dial to the EFFECTS position, and then rotate the command dial to cycle through the seven effects and select the one you want to use. Then, you can take pictures as always. However, when using Night Vision, Color Sketch, Miniature Effect, or Select Color special effects when RAW+JPEG has been selected for Image Quality, or if RAW (only) has been selected, only JPEG Fine images will be saved. No RAW image is created. The flash and AF-assist beam are disabled when using all these effects.

Your choices include:

- **Night Vision.** This effect gives you a monochrome image recorded at high ISO under very low light conditions. Because the light is so dim, autofocus is available only in live view mode. You can use manual focus. The D5200's flash and AF-assist beam are disabled. You'll probably want to use a tripod, because this mode can use longer shutter speeds that accentuate camera movement. (See upper left, Figure 10.21.)

- **Color Sketch.** This setting produces the same look as the Color Sketch retouching option described previously. This is a cool effect to apply to your movies, giving them a cartoon-like quality.

- **Miniature Effect.** This setting produces the same look as the Miniature Effect retouching option described earlier in this chapter. I've seen some great video clips shot with this effect, making, in one example, Disneyland appear to be a miniature amusement park. No sound is recorded, but you can add your own audio later. The built-in flash and AF-assist beam are disabled.

- **Selective Color.** This setting creates an image with the selective color effects described previously. As with the other special effects, the built-in flash is disabled.

- **Silhouette.** Produces silhouettes against bright backgrounds, and flash is disabled. (See Figure 10.23, upper right.)

- **High Key.** Creates bright scenes. This effects tool, like the Low Key effect described next, can't work miracles. It won't produce a high-key image from a low-key subject. But if you have a scene that is filled with bright light, this effect will accentuate that, as seen at lower left in Figure 10.21.

- **Low Key.** Gives you dark, foreboding images. You'll need contrasty lighting to achieve this effect, but given the right subject, you can end up with an image like the one at lower right in Figure 10.21.

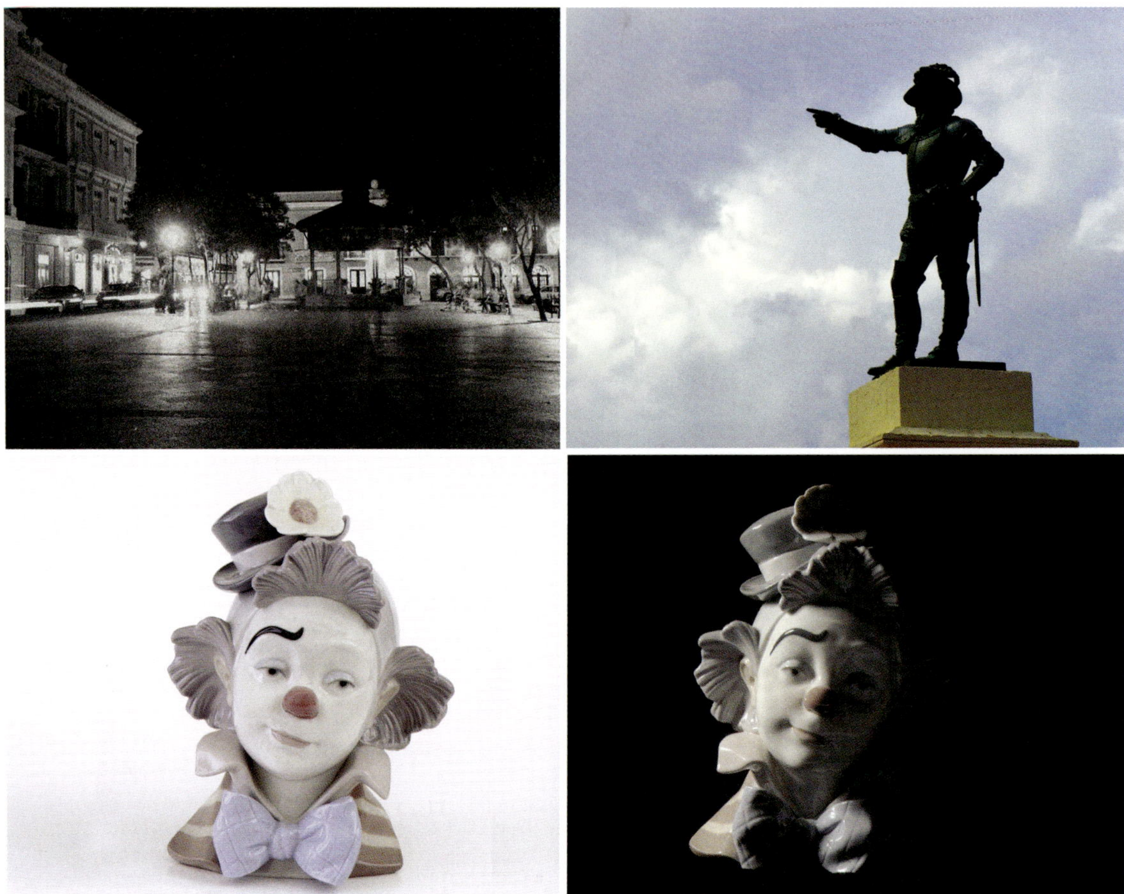

**Figure 10.21** Special effects include Night Vision (upper left); Silhouette (upper right); High Key (lower left); and Low Key (lower right).

# Using My Menu

The last menu in the D5200's main menu screen has two versions: Recent Settings and My Menu. The default mode is Recent Settings, which simply shows an ever-changing roster of the 20 menu items you used most recently. You'll probably find it more useful to activate the My Menu option instead, which contains only those menu items that you deposit there extracted from the Playback, Shooting, Custom Setting, Setup, and Retouch menus, based on your own decisions on which you use most. Remember that the D5200 always returns to the last menu and menu entry accessed when you press the MENU button. So you can set up My Menu (see Figure 10.22) to include just the items accessed most frequently, and (as long as you haven't used another menu), jump to those items instantly by pressing the MENU button.

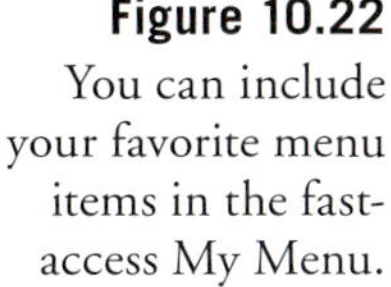

**Figure 10.22**
You can include your favorite menu items in the fast-access My Menu.

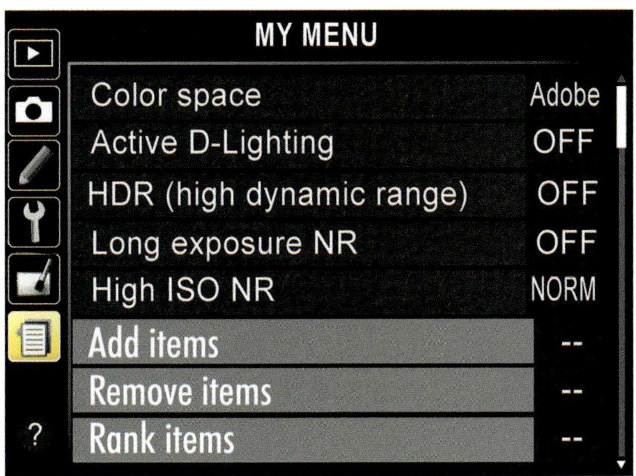


Switching back and forth is easy. The My Menu and Recent Settings menus each has a menu choice called Choose Tab. Highlight that entry and press the right multi selector button to view a screen that allows you to activate either the My Menu or Recent Settings menu. Press OK to confirm. If you find your needs change so often that My Menu is of little use, you might find the Recent Settings tab a better choice, because it displays the actual menu items you've been using recently.

I tend to include frequently used functions that aren't available using direct access buttons in My Menu. For example, I include High ISO NR and Long Exp. NR there, because I may want to turn noise reduction on or off during shooting.

You can add or subtract entries on My Menu at any time, and re-order (or rank) the entries so the ones you access most often are shown at the top of the list. Here's all you need to know to work with My Menu. To add entries to My Menu:

1. Select My Menu and choose Add Items.
2. A list of the available menus will appear (Playback, Shooting, Custom Setting, Setup, and Retouch menus). Highlight one and press the multi selector's right button.
3. Within the selected menu, choose the menu item you want to add and press OK.
4. The label Choose Position appears at the top of the My Menu screen. Use the up/down buttons to select a rank among the entries, and press OK to confirm and add the new item.
5. Repeat steps 1–4 if you want to add more entries to My Menu.

To reorder the menu listings:

1. Within the My Menu screen, choose Rank Items.
2. Use the up/down buttons to select the item to be moved, and press OK.
3. Use the up/down buttons to relocate the selected item, and press OK.
4. Repeat steps 2–3 to move additional entries.

To remove entries from the list, you can simply press the Trash button while an item is highlighted in the My Menu screen. To remove multiple items, follow these steps:

1. Within the My Menu screen, choose Remove Items.

2. A list with checkboxes next to the menu items appears. Scroll down to an item you want to remove and press the multi selector right button to mark its box. If you change your mind, highlight the item and press the right button again to unmark the box.

3. When finished, highlight Done and press the OK button.

4. Press OK to confirm the deletion.

# 11

# Working with Lenses

There's no disputing the fact that there is a key reason why many digital SLR buyers choose Nikon cameras: Nikon lenses. Some favor Nikon cameras because of the broad selection of quality lenses. Others already possess a large collection of Nikon optics (perhaps dating from the owner's photography during the film era), and the ability to use those lenses on the latest digital cameras is a big plus. A few may be attracted to the Nikon brand because there are many inexpensive lenses (including a few in the $100–$200 price range) that make it possible to assemble a basic kit for cameras like the D5200 without spending a lot of cash.

It's true that there is a mind-bending assortment of high-quality lenses available to enhance the capabilities of Nikon cameras. You can use thousands of current and older lenses introduced by Nikon and third-party vendors since 1959, although lenses made before 1977 may need an inexpensive modification for use with cameras *other* than your D5200 and those in the Nikon D5xxx-series, D3xxx-series, the D60, D40, and D40x. (More on this later.) These lenses can give you a wider view, bring distant subjects closer, let you focus closer, shoot under lower light conditions, or provide a more detailed, sharper image for critical work. Other than the sensor itself, the lens you choose for your dSLR is the most important component in determining image quality and perspective of your images.

This chapter explains how to select the best lenses for the kinds of photography you want to do.

## Sensor Sensibilities

From time to time, you've heard the term *crop factor*, and you've probably also heard the term *lens multiplier factor*. Both are misleading and inaccurate terms used to describe the same phenomenon: the fact that cameras like the D5200 (and most other affordable digital SLRs) provide a field of view that's smaller and narrower than that produced by certain other (usually much more expensive) cameras, when fitted with exactly the same lens.

Figure 11.1 quite clearly shows the phenomenon at work. The outer rectangle, marked 1X, shows the field of view you might expect with a 28mm lens mounted on one of Nikon's "full-frame" (non-cropped) cameras, like the Nikon D700, D3, or D3x. The area marked 1.5X shows the field of view you'd get with that 28mm lens installed on a D5200. It's easy to see from the illustration that the 1X rendition provides a wider, more expansive view, while the inner field of view is, in comparison, *cropped.*

The cropping effect is produced because the sensors of DX cameras like the Nikon D5200 are smaller than the sensors of the Nikon D4, D800/D800E, D600, and earlier full-frame cameras. The "full-frame" camera has a sensor that's the size of the standard 35mm film frame, 24mm × 36mm. Your D5200's sensor does *not* measure 24mm × 36mm; instead, it specs out at 23.5 mm × 15.6 mm, or about 66.7 percent of the area of a full-frame sensor, as shown by the boxes in the figure. You can calculate the relative field of view by dividing the focal length of the lens by .667. Thus, a 100mm lens mounted on a D5200 has the same field of view as a 150mm lens on the Nikon D800. We humans tend to perform multiplication operations in our heads more easily than division, so such field of view comparisons are usually calculated using the reciprocal of .667—1.5—so we can multiply instead. (100 / .667=150; 100 × 1.5=150.)

This translation is generally useful only if you're accustomed to using full-frame cameras (usually of the film variety) and want to know how a familiar lens will perform on a digital camera. I strongly prefer *crop factor* over *lens multiplier*, because nothing is being multiplied; a 100mm lens doesn't "become" a 150mm lens—the depth-of-field and lens aperture remain the same. (I'll explain more about these later in this chapter.) Only the field of view is cropped. But *crop factor* isn't much better, as it implies that the 24 mm × 36mm frame is "full" and anything else is "less." I get e-mails

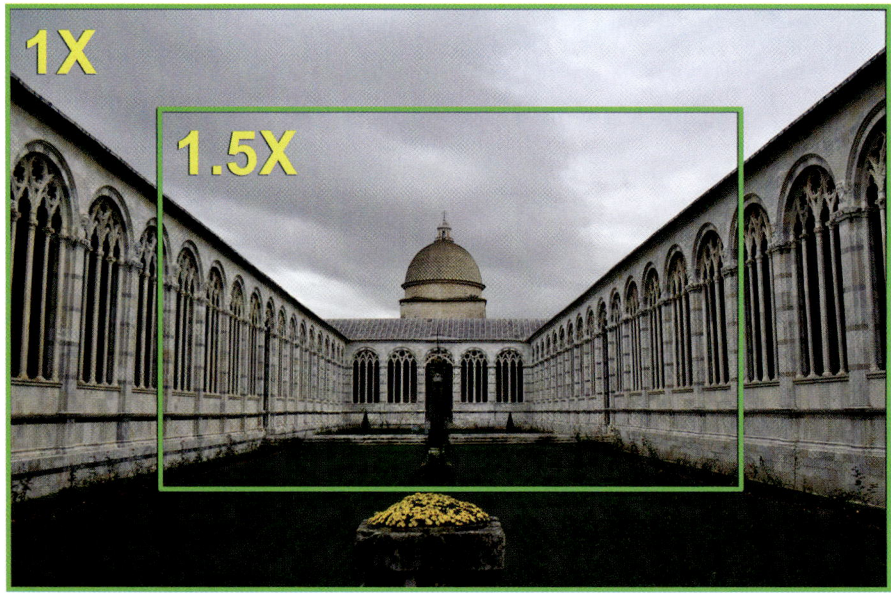


**Figure 11.1**
Nikon offers digital SLRs with full-frame (1X) crops, as well as 1.5X crops.

all the time from photographers who point out that they own full-frame cameras with 36mm × 48mm sensors (like the Mamiya 645ZD or Hasselblad H3D-39 medium-format digitals). By their reckoning, the "half-size" sensors found in cameras like the Nikon D800 and D4 are "cropped."

If you're accustomed to using full-frame film cameras, you might find it helpful to use the crop factor "multiplier" to translate a lens's real focal length into the full-frame equivalent, even though, as I said, nothing is actually being multiplied. Throughout most of this book, I've been using actual focal lengths and not equivalents, except when referring to specific wide-angle or telephoto focal length ranges and their fields of view.

## Crop or Not?

There's a lot of debate over the "advantages" and "disadvantages" of using a camera with a "cropped" sensor, versus one with a "full-frame" sensor. The arguments go like this:

- **"Free" 1.5X teleconverter.** The Nikon D5200 (and other cameras with the 1.5X crop factor), magically transform any telephoto lens you have into a longer lens, which can be useful for sports, wildlife photography, and other endeavors that benefit from more reach. Yet, your f/stop remains the same (that is, a 300mm f/4 becomes a very fast 450mm f/4 lens). Some discount this advantage, pointing out that the exact same field of view can be had by taking a full-frame image, and trimming it to the 1.5X equivalent. While that is strictly true, it doesn't take into account a factor called *pixel density*.

- **Dense pixels=more noise.** The other side of the pixel density coin is that the denser packing of pixels to achieve 24 megapixels in the D5200 sensor means that each pixel must be smaller, and will have less light-gathering capabilities. Larger pixels capture light more efficiently, reducing the need to amplify the signal when boosting ISO sensitivity, and, therefore, producing less noise. In an absolute sense, this is true, and cameras like the D4 *do* have sensational high ISO performance. However, the D5200's sensor is improved over earlier cameras (for one thing, it is a high-sensitivity CMOS sensor, rather than a noisier CCD sensor like that found in some earlier Nikon entry-level cameras), so you'll find it performs very well at higher ISOs.

- **Lack of wide-angle perspective.** Of course, the 1.5X "crop" factor applies to wide-angle lenses, too, so your 20mm ultrawide lens becomes a hum-drum 30mm near-wide-angle, and a 35mm focal length is transformed into what photographers call a "normal" lens. Zoom lenses, like the 18-105mm lens that is often purchased with the Nikon cameras in a kit, have less wide-angle perspective at their minimum focal length. The 18-105mm optic, for example, is the equivalent of a 27mm moderate wide angle when zoomed to its widest setting. Nikon has "fixed" this problem by providing several different extra-wide zooms specifically for the DX format, including the (relatively) affordable 12-24mm and 10-24mm DX Nikkors. You'll never really lack for wide-angle lenses, but some of us will need to buy wider optics to regain the expansive view we're looking for.

- **Mixed body mix-up.** The relatively small number of Nikon D5200 owners who also have a Nikon full-frame camera like the D700 or D800 can't ignore the focal-length mix-up factor. If you own both FX and DX-format cameras (some D5200 owners use them as a backup to a D600, for example), it's vexing to have to adjust to the different fields of view that the cameras provide. If you remove a given lens from one camera and put it on the other, the effective focal length/field of view changes. That 16-35mm zoom works as an ultrawide to wide angle on a D700, but functions more as a moderate wide-angle to normal lens on a D5200. To get the "look" on both cameras, you'd need to use a 12-24mm zoom on the D5200, and the 17-35mm zoom on the D700. It's possible to become accustomed to this field of view shake-up and, indeed, some photographers put it to work by mounting their longest telephoto lens on the D5200 and their wide-angle lenses on their full-frame camera. Even if you've never owned both an FX and DX camera, you should be aware of the possible confusion.

# Your First Lens

Some Nikon dSLRs are almost always purchased with a lens. The entry- and mid-level Nikon dSLRs, including the Nikon D5200, are often bought by those new to digital photography, frequently by first-time SLR or dSLR owners who find the AF-S DX Nikkor 18-105mm f/3.5-5.6G ED VR or AF-S DX Zoom-Nikkor 18-55mm f/3.5-5.6G ED II (shown in Figure 11.2), both with vibration reduction, irresistible bargains. Other Nikon models, including the Nikon D4 and D800, are generally purchased without a lens by veteran Nikon photographers who already have a complement of optics to use with their cameras.

I bought my D5200 with the 18-55mm VR lens, even though I already had a (large) collection of lenses, because the VR was an attractive feature, and the lens is perfect to mount on the camera when I loan it to family members who have little photographic experience. Depending on which category of photographer you fall into, you'll need to make a decision about what kit lens to buy, or decide what other kind of lenses you need to fill out your complement of Nikon optics. This section will cover "first lens" concerns, while later in the chapter we'll look at "add-on lens" considerations.

When deciding on a first lens, there are several factors you'll want to consider:

- **Cost.** You might have stretched your budget a bit to purchase your Nikon D5200, so the 18-55mm VR kit lens helps you keep the cost of your first lens fairly low. In addition, there are excellent moderately priced lenses available that will add from $100 to $300 to the price of your camera if purchased at the same time.

- **Zoom range.** If you have only one lens, you'll want a fairly long zoom range to provide as much flexibility as possible. Fortunately, several popular basic lenses for the D5200 have 3X to 5.8X zoom ranges (I'll list some of them next), extending from moderate wide-angle/normal out to medium telephoto. Either is fine for everyday shooting, portraits, and some types of sports.

- **Adequate maximum aperture.** You'll want an f/stop of at least f/3.5 to f/4 for shooting under fairly low light conditions. The thing to watch for is the maximum aperture when the lens is zoomed to its telephoto end. You may end up with no better than an f/5.6 maximum aperture. That's not great, but you can often live with it, particularly with a lens having vibration reduction (VR) capabilities, because you can often shoot at lower shutter speeds to compensate for the limited maximum aperture.

- **Image quality.** Your starter lens should have good image quality, because that's one of the primary factors that will be used to judge your photos. Even at a low price, several of the different lenses that can be used with the D5200 kit include extra-low dispersion glass and aspherical elements that minimize distortion and chromatic aberration; they are sharp enough for most applications. If you read the user evaluations in the online photography forums, you know that owners of the kit lenses have been very pleased with its image quality.

- **Size matters.** A good walking-around lens is compact in size and light in weight.

- **Fast/close focusing.** Your first lens should have a speedy autofocus system (which is where the Silent Wave motor found in all but the bargain basement lenses [older, non-AF-S models] is an advantage). Close focusing (to 12 inches or closer) will let you use your basic lens for some types of macro photography.

You can find comparisons of the lenses discussed in the next section, as well as evaluations of lenses I don't describe, third-party optics from Sigma, Tokina, Tamron, and other vendors, in online groups and websites.

## Buy Now, Expand Later

When the Nikon D5200 was introduced, it was available only in kit form with the 18-55mm VR lens. By the time this book is published, I expect to see it offered packaged with other lenses, including the terrific 18-105mm VR lens. These are all good, basic lenses that can serve you well as a "walk-around" lens (one you keep on the camera most of the time, especially when you're out and about without your camera bag). The number of options available to you is actually quite amazing, even if your budget is limited to about $100–$350 for your first lens. One other vendor, for example, offers only 18-70mm and 18-55mm kit lenses in that price range, plus a 24-85mm zoom. Here's a list of Nikon's best-bet "first" lenses. Don't worry about sorting out the alphabet soup right now; I provide a complete list of Nikon lens "codes" later in the chapter.

- **AF-S DX Nikkor 18-105mm f/3.5-5.6G ED VR.** This lens is one of my choices as a "walking-around" lens for this camera. I much prefer it over the 18-200mm VR (described later), even though it has a more limited zoom range. Its focal length range is quite sufficient for most general photography, and at around $400 with the camera, it's a real bargain (see Figure 11.2, left).

- **AF-S DX Nikkor 18-55mm f/3.5-5.6G VR.** This new VR version of the 18-55mm (see Figure 11.2, right) is a better choice than the basic 18-55mm optic, which remains available from many stores. That's because the vibration reduction ("anti-shake") feature of this lens partially offsets the relatively slow maximum aperture of the lens at the telephoto position. It can be mated with

Nikon's AF-S DX VR Zoom-Nikkor 55-200mm f/4-5.6G IF-ED to give you a two-lens VR pair that will handle everything from 18mm to 200mm, at a relatively low price of around $120.

■ **AF-S DX Nikkor 16-85mm f/3.5-5.6G ED VR.** The 16-85mm VR lens is the zoom that would make a lot of sense as a kit lens for the D5200 if price were no object. It costs a significant fraction of the price of the D5200 itself! If you really want to use just a single lens with your camera, this one provides an excellent combination of focal lengths, image quality, and features. Its zoom range extends from a true wide angle (equivalent to a 24mm lens on a full-frame camera) to useful medium telephoto (about 128mm equivalent), and so can be used for everything from architecture to portraiture to sports. If you think vibration reduction is useful only with longer telephoto lenses, you may be surprised at how much it helps you hand-hold your D5200 even at the widest focal lengths. The only disadvantage to this lens is its relatively slow speed (f/5.6) when you crank it out to the telephoto end.

■ **AF-S DX Zoom-Nikkor 18-70mm f/3.5-4.5G IF-ED.** If you don't plan on getting a longer zoom-range basic lens and can't afford the 16-85 zoom, I highly recommend this aging, but impressive lens, if you can find one in stock as a used item. Originally introduced as the kit lens for the venerable Nikon D70, the 18-70mm zoom quickly gained a reputation as a very sharp lens at a bargain price. It doesn't provide a view that's as long or as wide as the 16-85, but it's a half-stop faster at its maximum zoom position. You may have to hunt around to find one of these, but they are available for $250–$300 and well worth it. I own one to this day, and use it regularly, although it spends most of its time installed on my D3200, which has been converted to infrared-only photography.

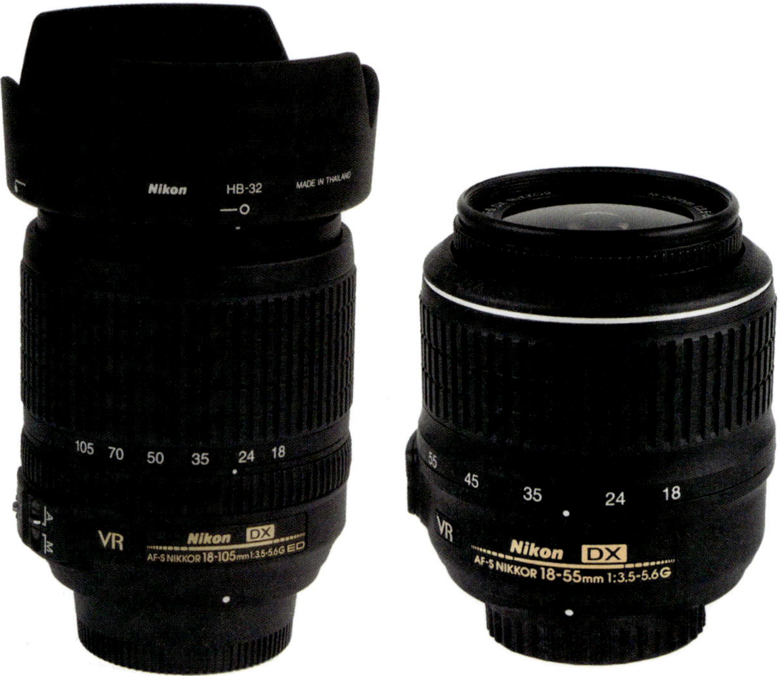

**Figure 11.2**
AF-S DX Nikkor 18-105mm f/3.5-5.6G ED VR and AF-S DX Nikkor 18-55mm f/3.5-5.6G VR can be purchased as the basic kit lens for the D5200.

- **AF-S DX Zoom-Nikkor 18-135mm f/3.5-5.6G IF-ED.** This lens has been sold as a kit lens for cameras aimed at intermediate amateur-level shooters, and some retailers with stock on hand are packaging it with the D5200 body as well. While decent, it's really best suited for the crowd who buy one do-everything lens and then never purchase another. Available for less than $300, you won't tie up a lot of money in this lens. There's no VR, so, for most, the 18-105mm VR lens is a better choice.

- **AF-S DX VR Zoom-Nikkor 18-200mm f/3.5-5.6G IF-ED.** I owned this lens for about three months, and decided it really didn't meet my needs. It was introduced as an ideal "kit" lens for the Nikon D200 a few years back, and, at the time had almost everything you might want. It's a holdover, more upscale kit lens for the D5200. Its stunning 11X zoom range covers everything from the equivalent of 27mm to 300mm when the 1.5X crop factor is figured in, and its VR capabilities plus light weight let you use it without a tripod most of the time. However, I found the image quality to be good, but not outstanding, and the slow maximum aperture at 200mm to be limiting when a fast shutter speed is required to stop action. The "zoom creep" (a tendency for the lens to zoom when the camera is tilted up or down) found in many examples will drive you nuts after a while (see Figure 11.3). Fortunately, a new version with improved VR and with the creep fixed is available.

- **AF-S VR II Zoom-Nikkor 24-120mm f/4G ED VR.** This one is a relatively new full-frame lens, but it works fine on a cropped sensor model like the D5200. It has a useful zoom range, and, as a bonus, if you ever decide to upgrade to a full-frame camera, you can take this lens along with you.

- **AF-S VR Zoom-Nikkor 24-85mm f/3.5-4.5G.** Priced at about $600, this lens is reasonably priced, and has the advantage (like the 24-120mm lens) of being a full-frame optic, so if you upgrade in the future to a Nikon FX camera, you can take this one along with you. (See Figure 11.4.)

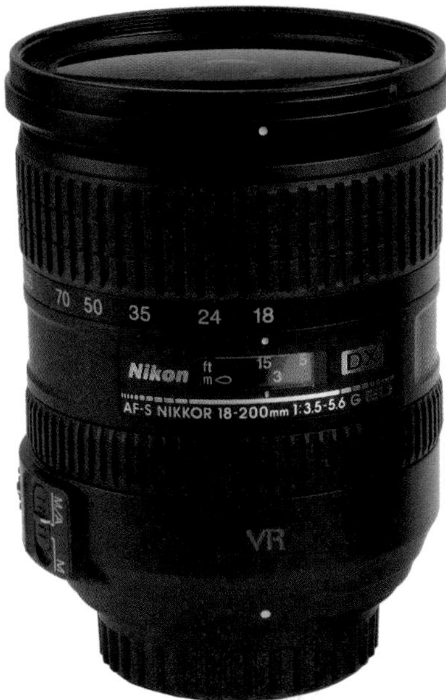

**Figure 11.3** The AF-S DX VR Zoom-Nikkor 18-200mm f/3.5-5.6G IF-ED is a lightweight "walking-around" lens.

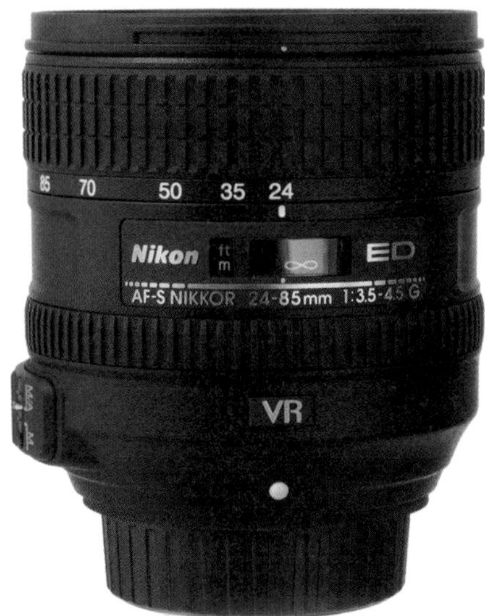

**Figure 11.4** This AF-S VR Zoom-Nikkor 24-85mm f/3.5-4.5G lens is affordable, and is compatible with full-frame cameras, too.

# Your Best Do-Everything Option?

In June 2012 Nikon introduced a DX lens at $999 that might actually be the best do-everything option for D5200 shooters. The new AF-S DX Nikkor 18-300mm f/3.5-5.6G ED VR zoom has an incredible 16.7X zoom range, yet is relatively light and compact, focuses close, and has image stabilization built in. (See Figure 11.5.) It's become a standard walk-around lens on my DX format cameras, because its 27-450mm equivalent focal length range is spectacular for sports and wildlife. It's not my sharpest lens at its maximum focal length, but it more than makes up for a little softness at the far end with versatility.

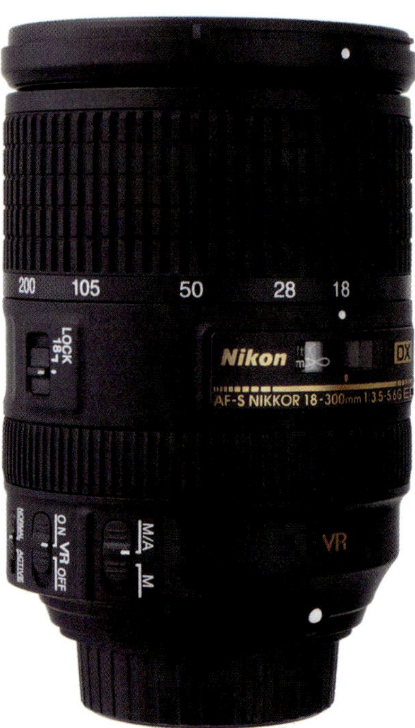


**Figure 11.5** Nikon's remarkable 18-300mm f/3.5-5.6 zoom lens.

- **Ultra-long zoom range.** Used on your D5200, this lens provides the equivalent field of view as a full-frame 27-400mm lens. That's sort of wide to super-telephoto, without the need to swap lenses. That versatility is important when shooting stills, of course, especially with sports and other rapidly changing scenes. But if you're shooting movies, the 18-300mm focal lengths come in especially handy. You can capture a wide establishing shot to set the scene, switch to a medium shot to draw viewer attention to your main subjects, then capture an extreme close-up. Even if you're collecting short clips, the action may be continuing between "takes," so if you had to switch lenses you might miss something. Not so with this lens. You can change field of view between each shot as quickly as you can rotate the zoom ring. The lens's long range has some possibilities for those mind-boggling quick zooms in or out *during* video capture, too. (Use with restraint!) The only drawback this lens has is that it is not especially sharp at its maximum telephoto setting. If most of your work requires 18-200mm focal lengths and you have an occasional need for the 200-300mm range (and don't want to shoot wide open), this lens can be very useful.

- **Vibration reduction.** It's so common to have VR in telephoto lenses these days, especially those with equivalent or actual focal lengths of 400mm or more that you might not stop to think how rare image stabilization is at the other end. Nikon's 24-120mm f/4, 16-35mm f/4 full-frame, and new 24-85mm VR lenses (discussed later in this chapter) along with DX lenses (the 18-55mm kit lenses, 16-85mm f/3.5-5.6G, and 18-200mm f/3.5-5.6) are *it* in the Nikon product line. While it's arguable that VR is less essential in a wide-angle lens because camera shake blur is less of a problem, having a lens that starts wide and goes all the way to supertele-photo with optical image stabilization built in is a definite plus.

- **Compact size.** Although it replaces a half-dozen or more lenses, the 18-300mm zoom measures just 3.3 × 4.7 inches and weighs 1 pound, 13 ounces, which is svelte for a 300mm lens (even if a bit large for an 18mm wide angle). However, it almost doubles in length when cranked out to its full 300mm setting, becoming lanky instead of svelte. Even so, in weight and size, your do-everything walk around lens compares favorably to its 18-200mm predecessor (3 × 3.8, 1 pound, four ounces), takes pro-standard 77mm filters (vs 72mm for the older model), and has a lock to totally prevent dreaded zoom creep, to boot. Mine doesn't exhibit creep even with the lock off, however.

- **Close focusing.** The 18-300mm has the ability to focus down to 1.48 feet at 300mm, giving you a 1:3.2X maximum reproduction ratio (about one-third life-size in DX format). The 18-300mm is not a true macro lens, but when you're venturing out with a single lens on your D5200, the ability to focus that closely at 300mm is the next best thing.

- **Good (not great) image quality.** Nikon says that three extra-low dispersion (ED) elements and three aspheric elements deliver the promised minimized chromatic aberration (which can be especially troublesome at wide-angle focal lengths), and the typical aberrations that appear when a lens is used at larger apertures (that's something that will probably happen given the relatively slow f/5.6 maximum aperture at 300mm). Nikon touts this lens's 9-bladed aperture for its pleasing bokeh, too. (I'll show you the effects of bokeh later in this chapter.) As I said earlier, this lens delivers useful image quality even if it's not the sharpest 300mm lens you own.

# What Lenses Can You Use?

The previous section helped you sort out what basic lens you need to buy with your Nikon D5200. Now, you're probably wondering what lenses can be added to your growing collection (trust me, it will grow). You need to know which lenses are suitable and, most importantly, which lenses are fully compatible with your Nikon D5200.

With the Nikon D5200, the compatibility issue is a simple one: It can use any modern-era Nikon lens with the AF-S designation, with full availability of all autofocus, auto aperture, autoexposure, and image stabilization features (if present). Older lenses with the AF designation won't autofocus on the D5200, but can still be used for automatic exposure. You can also use any Nikon AI, AI-S, or AI-P lens, which are manual focus lenses that were produced starting in 1977 and continue in production effectively through the present day, because Nikon continues to offer a limited number of manual focus lenses for those who need them. Just remember: AF-S—all features available; non-AF-S (including AF)–no autofocusing possible.

The Nikon D5200, as well as previous entry-level models D5100, D5000, D3100, D3200, D3000, D60, D40, and D40x, doesn't have an autofocusing motor built into the camera body itself. The motor, present in all other Nikon digital SLRs, allows the camera to adjust the lens focus mechanically. Without that motor in the body, cameras like the D5200 must communicate focus information to the lens, so that the lens's own built-in AF motor can take care of the autofocus process. Because virtually all newer Nikon-brand lenses are of the AF-S type, this means your D5200 will have problems only with older Nikon optics.

That's not true with third-party (non-Nikon) lenses. While your D5200 will accept virtually all modern lenses produced by Tokina, Tamron, Sigma, and other vendors, they will autofocus only with those lenses that contain an internal focusing motor, similar to Nikon's AF-S offerings. Vendors have different designators to indicate these lenses, such as HSM (for hypersonic motor). You'll have to check with the manufacturer of non-Nikon lenses to see if they are compatible with the D5200, particularly since some vendors have been gradually introducing revamped versions of their existing lenses with the addition of an internal motor.

There's some good news for those using one of Nikon's focus-motorless entry-level models. These cameras, *unlike* Nikon models that have the camera body focus motor, can safely use lenses offered prior to 1977 (although I expect that, while numerous, most of these aren't used much by those who have modern digital cameras). That's because cameras other than Nikon's entry-level quartet have a pin on the lens mount that can be damaged by an older, unmodified lens. John White at www.aiconversions.com will do the work for about $35 to allow these older lenses to be safely used on any Nikon digital camera. If you own or may someday purchase one of those other cameras, you'll want to consider having the lens conversion done, even though your D5200 doesn't require it to use the lens safely.

Today, in addition to its traditional full-frame lenses, Nikon offers lenses with the DX designation, which is intended for use only on DX-format cameras, like your D5200. While the lens mounting system is the same, DX lenses have a coverage area that fills only the smaller frame, allowing the design of more compact, less-expensive lenses especially for non-full-frame cameras. The AF-S DX Nikkor 35mm f/1.8G, a fixed focal length (non-zoom) lens with a fast f/1.8 maximum aperture, is an example of such a lens.

# Ingredients of Nikon's Alphanumeric Soup

Nikon has always been fond of appending cryptic letters and descriptors onto the names of its lenses. Here's an alphabetical list of lens terms you're likely to encounter, either as part of the lens name or in reference to the lens's capabilities. Not all of these are used as parts of a lens's name, but you may come across some of these terms in discussions of particular Nikon optics:

- **AF, AF-D, AF-I, AF-S.** In all cases, AF stands for *autofocus* when appended to the name of a Nikon lens. An extra letter is added to provide additional information. A plain old AF lens is an autofocus lens that uses a slot-drive motor in the camera body to provide autofocus functions (and so cannot be used in AF mode on the entry-level models noted earlier). The D means that it's a D-type lens (described later in this listing); the I indicates that focus is through a motor inside the lens; and the S means that a super-special (Silent Wave) motor in the lens provides focusing. (Don't confuse a Nikon AF-S lens with the AF-S [Single-Servo Autofocus mode].) Nikon is currently upgrading its older AF lenses with AF-S versions, but it's not safe to assume that all newer Nikkors are AF-S, or even offer autofocus. For example, the PC-E Nikkor 24mm f/3.5D ED perspective control lens must be focused manually, and Nikon offers a surprising collection of other manual focus lenses to meet specialized needs.

- **AI, AI-S.** All Nikkor lenses produced after 1977 have either automatic aperture indexing (AI) or automatic indexing-shutter (AI-S) features that eliminate the previous requirement to manually align the aperture ring on the camera when mounting a lens. Within a few years, all Nikkors had this automatic aperture indexing feature (except for G-type lenses, which have no aperture ring at all), including Nikon's budget-priced Series E lenses, so the designation was dropped at the time the first autofocus (AF) lenses were introduced.

- **E.** The E designation was used for Nikon's budget-priced E Series optics, five prime and three zoom manual focus lenses built using aluminum or plastic parts rather than the preferred brass parts of that era, so they were considered less rugged. All are effectively AI-S lenses. They do have good image quality, which makes them a bargain for those who treat their lenses gently and don't need the latest autofocus features. They were available in 28mm f/2.8, 35mm f/2.5, 50mm f/1.8, 100mm f/2.8, and 135mm f/2.8 focal lengths, plus 36-72mm f/3.5, 75-150mm f/3.5, and 70-210mm f/4 zooms. (All these would be considered fairly "fast" today.)

- **D.** Appended to the maximum f/stop of the lens (as in f/2.8D), a D-Series lens is able to send focus distance data to the camera, which uses the information for flash exposure calculation and 3D Color Matrix II metering.

- **DC.** The DC stands for defocus control, which allows managing the out-of-focus parts of an image to produce better-looking portraits and close-ups.

- **DX.** The DX lenses are designed for use with digital cameras using the APS-C–sized sensor having the 1.5X crop factor. The image circle they produce isn't large enough to fill up a full 35mm frame at all focal lengths, but they can be used on Nikon's full-frame models using the automatic/manual DX crop mode.

- **ED (or LD/UD).** The ED (extra-low dispersion) designation indicates that some lens elements are made of a special hard and scratch-resistant glass that minimizes the divergence of the different colors of light as they pass through, thus reducing chromatic aberration (color "fringing") and other image defects. A gold band around the front of the lens indicates an optic with ED elements. You sometimes find LD (low dispersion) or UD (ultra-low dispersion) designations.

- **FX.** When Nikon introduced the Nikon D3 as its first full-frame camera, it coined the term "FX," representing the 23.9mm × 36mm sensor format as a counterpart to "DX," which was used for its 15.8mm × 23.6mm APS-C-sized sensors. Although FX hasn't been officially applied to any Nikon lenses so far, expect to see the designation used more often to differentiate between lenses that are compatible with any Nikon digital SLR (FX) and those that operate only on DX-format cameras, or in DX mode when used on an FX camera like the D700, D800, D3, D3s, D3x, and D4.

- **G.** G-type lenses have no aperture ring, and you can use them at other than the maximum aperture only with electronic cameras like the D5200 that set the aperture automatically. Fortunately, this includes all Nikon digital dSLRs.

- **IF.** Nikon's *internal focusing* lenses change focus by shifting only small internal lens groups with no change required in the lens's physical length, unlike conventional double helicoid focusing systems that move all lens groups toward the front or rear during focusing. IF lenses are more compact and lighter in weight, provide better balance, focus more closely, and can be focused more quickly.

- **IX.** These lenses were produced for Nikon's long-discontinued Pronea 6i and S APS film cameras. While the Pronea could use many standard Nikon lenses, IX lenses cannot be mounted on any Nikon digital SLR.

- **Micro.** Nikon uses the term *micro* to designate its close-up lenses. Most other vendors use *macro* instead.

- **PC (Perspective Control).** A PC lens is capable of shifting the lens from side to side (and up/down) to provide a more realistic perspective when photographing architecture and other subjects that otherwise require tilting the camera so that the sensor plane is not parallel to the subject. Older Nikkor PC lenses offered shifting only, but more modern models, such as the PC-E Nikkor 24mm f/3.5D ED lens introduced early in 2008 allow both shifting and tilting.

- **UV.** This term is applied to special (and expensive) lenses designed to pass ultraviolet light.

- **UW.** Lenses with this designation are designed for underwater photography with Nikonos camera bodies, and cannot be used with Nikon digital SLRs.

- **VR.** Nikon has an expanding line of vibration reduction (VR) lenses, including several very affordable models and the AF-S DX Nikkor 16-85mm f/3.5-5.6G ED VR lens, which shifts lens elements internally to counteract camera shake. The VR feature allows using a shutter speed up to four stops slower than would be possible without vibration reduction.

# What Lenses Can Do for You

No one can afford to buy even a percentage of the lenses available. The sanest approach to expanding your lens collection is to consider what each of your options can do for you and then choose the type of lens and specific model that will really boost your creative opportunities. So, in the sections that follow, I'm going to provide a general guide to the sort of capabilities you can gain for your D5200 by adding a lens to your repertoire.

- **Wider perspective.** Your 18-105mm f/3.5-5.6, 18-55mm f/3.5-5.6, or 16-85mm f/4-5.6 lens has served you well for moderate wide-angle shots. Now you find your back is up against a wall and you *can't* take a step backward to take in more subject matter. Perhaps you're standing on the rim of the Grand Canyon, and you want to take in as much of the breathtaking view as you can. You might find yourself just behind the baseline at a high school basketball game and want an interesting shot with a little perspective distortion tossed in the mix.

- **Bring objects closer.** A long lens brings distant subjects closer to you, offers better control over depth-of-field, and avoids the perspective distortion that wide-angle lenses provide. They compress the apparent distance between objects in your frame. Don't forget that the Nikon D5200's crop factor narrows the field of view of all these lenses, so your 70-300mm lens looks more like a 105mm-450mm zoom through the viewfinder. The image shown in Figure 11.6 was taken using a wide 24mm lens, while Figures 11.7 and 11.8 were taken from the same position as Figure 11.6, but with focal lengths of 75mm and 200mm, respectively.

- **Bring your camera closer.** Macro lenses allow you to focus to within an inch or two of your subject. Nikon's best close-up lenses are all fixed focal length optics in the 60mm to 200mm range, but you'll find good macro zooms available from Sigma and others. They don't tend to focus quite as close, but they provide a bit of flexibility when you want to vary your subject distance (say, to avoid spooking a skittish creature).

- **Look sharp.** Many lenses are prized for their sharpness and overall image quality. While your run-of-the-mill lens is likely to be plenty sharp for most applications, the very best optics are even better over their entire field of view (which means no fuzzy corners), are sharper at a wider range of focal lengths (in the case of zooms), and have better correction for various types of distortion. Of course, these lenses cost a great deal more (sometimes $1,000 or more each).

- **More speed.** Your Nikon 70-300mm f/4.5-5.6 telephoto zoom lens might have the perfect focal length and sharpness for sports photography, but the maximum aperture won't cut it for night baseball or football games, or, even, any sports shooting in daylight if the weather is cloudy or you need to use some ungodly fast shutter speed, such as 1/4,000th second. You might be happier to gain a full f/stop with a (non-zooming) AF-S Nikkor 300mm f/4D IF-ED for a little more than $1,500. Or, maybe you just need the speed and can benefit from an f/1.8 or f/1.4 prime lens. They're all available in Nikon mounts (there's even an 85mm f/1.4 and 50mm f/1.4 for the real speed demons). With any of these lenses you can continue photographing under the dimmest of lighting conditions without the need for a tripod or flash.

- **Special features.** Accessory lenses give you special features, such as tilt/shift capabilities to correct for perspective distortion in architectural shots. You'll also find macro lenses, including the AF-S Micro-Nikkor 60mm f/2.8G ED. Fisheye lenses like the AF DX Fisheye-Nikkor 10.5mm f/2.8G ED, and all other VR (vibration reduction) lenses also count as special-feature optics.

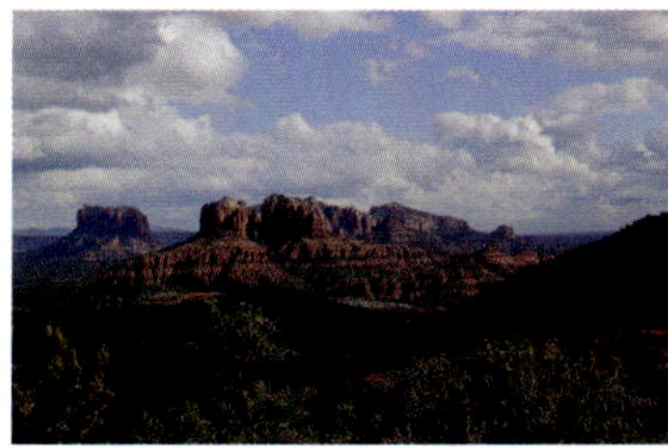

**Figure 11.6** A wide-angle lens provided this view of Castle Rock in Sedona, Arizona.

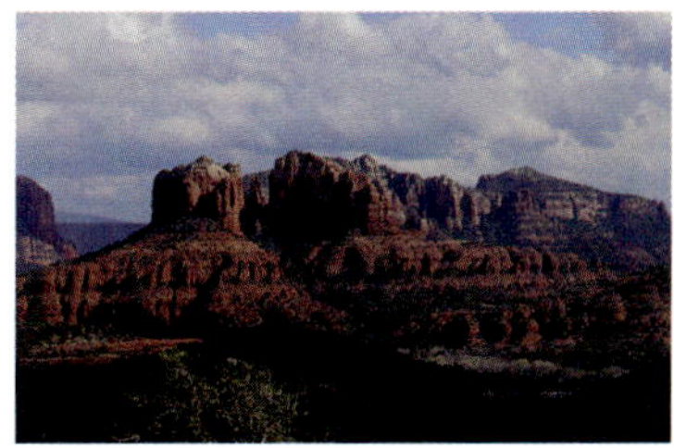

**Figure 11.7** This photo, taken from the same distance shows the view using a short telephoto lens.

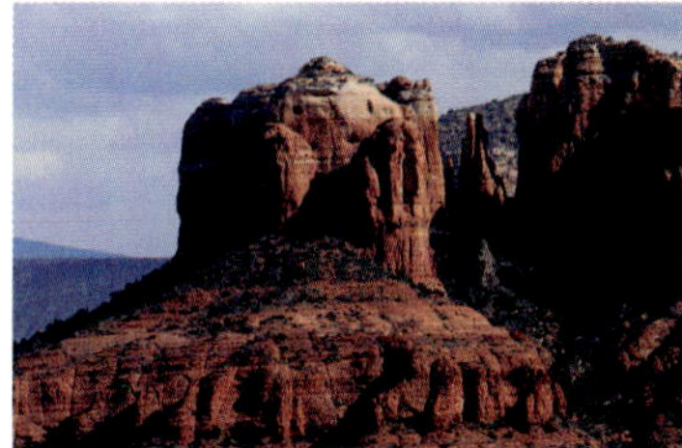

**Figure 11.8** A long telephoto lens captured this close-up view of the formation, from the same shooting position.

# Zoom or Prime?

Zoom lenses have changed the way serious photographers take pictures. One of the reasons that I still own 12 (almost worthless) SLR film bodies dating back to the pre-zoom days is that in ancient times it was common to mount a different fixed focal length prime lens on various cameras and take pictures with two or three cameras around your neck (or tucked in a camera case) so you'd be ready to take a long shot or an intimate close-up or wide-angle view on a moment's notice, without the need to switch lenses. It made sense (at the time) to have a half-dozen or so bodies (two to use, one in the shop, one in transit, and a couple backups). Zoom lenses of the time had a limited zoom range, were heavy, and not very sharp (especially when you tried to wield one of those monsters hand-held). That's all changed today. Smaller, longer, sharper zoom lenses, many with VR features, are available.

When selecting between zoom and prime lenses, there are several considerations to ponder. Here's a checklist of the most important factors. I already mentioned image quality and maximum aperture earlier, but those aspects take on additional meaning when comparing zooms and primes.

- **Logistics.** As prime lenses offer just a single focal length, you'll need more of them to encompass the full range offered by a single zoom. More lenses mean additional slots in your camera bag, and extra weight to carry. Just within Nikon's line alone you can choose from a good selection of general-purpose (if you can count AF lenses that won't autofocus with the D5200 as "general-purpose") prime lenses in 28mm, 35mm, 50mm, 85mm, 100mm, 135mm, and 200mm focal lengths, all of which are overlapped by the 18-200mm zoom I mentioned earlier. Even so, you might be willing to carry an extra prime lens or two in order to gain the speed or image quality that lens offers.

- **Image quality.** Prime lenses usually produce better image quality at their focal length than even the most sophisticated zoom lenses at the same magnification. Zoom lenses, with their shifting elements and f/stops that can vary from zoom position to zoom position, are in general more complex to design than fixed focal length lenses. That's not to say that the very best prime lenses can't be complicated as well. However, the exotic designs, aspheric elements, and low-dispersion glass can be applied to improving the quality of the lens, rather than wasting a lot of it on compensating for problems caused by the zoom process itself.

- **Maximum aperture.** Because of the same design constraints, zoom lenses usually have smaller maximum apertures than prime lenses, and the most affordable zooms have a lens opening that grows effectively smaller as you zoom in. The difference in lens speed verges on the ridiculous at some focal lengths. For example, the 18-55mm basic zoom gives you a 55mm f/5.6 lens when zoomed all the way out, while prime lenses in that focal length commonly have f/1.8 or faster maximum apertures. Indeed, the fastest f/2, f/1.8, f/1.4, and f/1.2 lenses are all manual focus primes (at least on the D5200, because they are AF models), and if you require speed, a fixed focal length lens is what you should rely on. Figure 11.9 shows an image taken with a Nikon 85mm f/1.4 lens.

**Figure 11.9**
An 85mm f/1.4 lens was perfect for this hand-held photo at a concert featuring British Invasion singer Peter Asher.

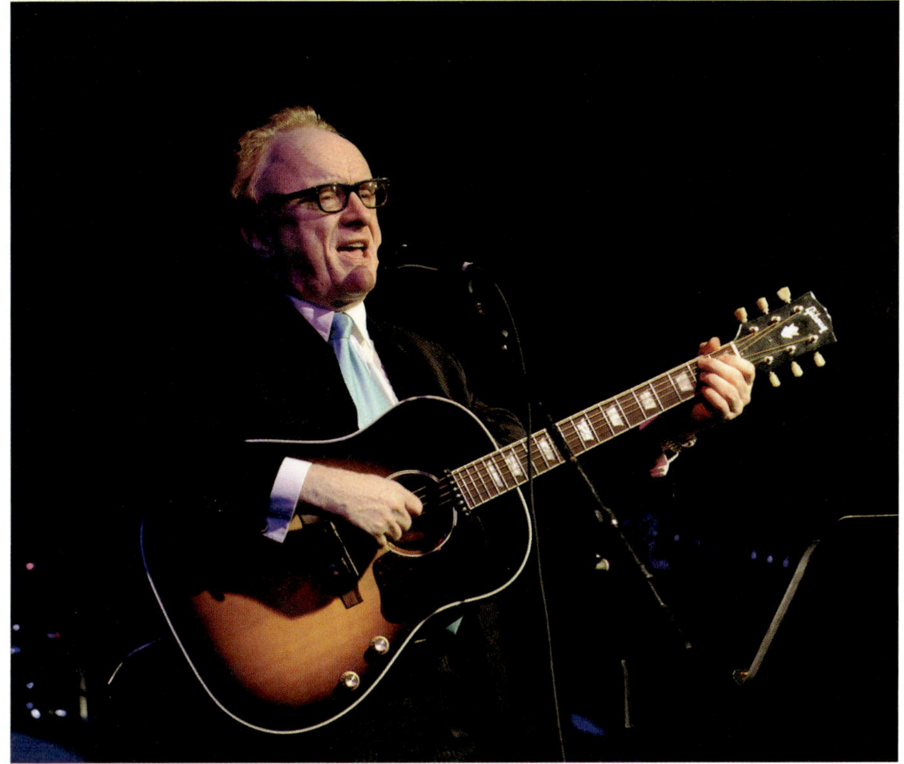

- **Speed.** Using prime lenses takes time and slows you down. It takes a few seconds to remove your current lens and mount a new one, and the more often you need to do that, the more time is wasted. If you choose not to swap lenses, when using a fixed focal length lens you'll still have to move closer or farther away from your subject to get the field of view you want. A zoom lens allows you to change magnifications and focal lengths with the twist of a ring and generally saves a great deal of time.

## Categories of Lenses

Lenses can be categorized by their intended purpose—general photography, macro photography, and so forth—or by their focal length. The range of available focal lengths is usually divided into three main groups: wide angle, normal, and telephoto. Prime lenses fall neatly into one of these classifications. Zooms can overlap designations, with a significant number falling into the catch-all, wide-to-telephoto zoom range. This section provides more information about focal length ranges, and how they are used.

When the 1.5X crop factor (mentioned at the beginning of this chapter) is figured in, any lens with an equivalent focal length of 10mm to 16mm is said to be an *ultrawide-angle lens*; from about 16mm to 30mm is said to be a *wide-angle lens*. *Normal lenses* have a focal length roughly equivalent to the diagonal of the film or sensor, in millimeters, and so fall into the range of about 30mm to

40mm on a D5200. *Short telephoto lenses* start at about 40mm to 70mm, with anything from 70mm to 250mm qualifying as a conventional *telephoto.* For the Nikon D5200, anything from about 300mm to 400mm or longer can be considered a *super-telephoto.*

# Using Wide-Angle and Wide-Zoom Lenses

To use wide-angle prime lenses and wide zooms, you need to understand how they affect your photography. Here's a quick summary of the things you need to know.

- **More depth-of-field.** Practically speaking, wide-angle lenses offer more depth-of-field at a particular subject distance and aperture. (But, see the sidebar below for an important note.) You'll find that helpful when you want to maximize sharpness of a large zone, but not very useful when you'd rather isolate your subject using selective focus (telephoto lenses are better for that).

- **Stepping back.** Wide-angle lenses have the effect of making it seem that you are standing farther from your subject than you really are. They're helpful when you don't want to back up, or can't because there are impediments in your way.

- **Wider field of view.** While making your subject seem farther away, as implied above, a wide-angle lens also provides a larger field of view, including more of the subject in your photos.

- **More foreground.** As background objects retreat, more of the foreground is brought into view by a wide-angle lens. That gives you extra emphasis on the area that's closest to the camera. Photograph your home with a normal lens/normal zoom setting, and the front yard probably looks fairly conventional in your photo (that's why they're called "normal" lenses). Switch to a wider lens and you'll discover that your lawn now makes up much more of the photo. So, wide-angle lenses are great when you want to emphasize that lake in the foreground, but problematic when your intended subject is located farther in the distance.

- **Super-sized subjects.** The tendency of a wide-angle lens to emphasize objects in the foreground, while de-emphasizing objects in the background can lead to a kind of size distortion that may be more objectionable for some types of subjects than others. Shoot a bed of flowers up close with a wide angle, and you might like the distorted effect of the larger blossoms nearer the lens. Take a photo of a family member with the same lens from the same distance, and you're likely to get some complaints about that gigantic nose in the foreground.

## DOF IN DEPTH

The DOF advantage of wide-angle lenses is diminished when you enlarge your picture; believe it or not, a wide-angle image enlarged and cropped to provide the same subject size as a telephoto shot would have the *same* depth-of-field. Try it: take a wide-angle photo of a friend from a fair distance, and then zoom in to duplicate the picture in a telephoto image. Then, enlarge the wide shot so your friend is the same size in both. The wide photo will have the same depth-of-field (and will have much less detail, too).

- **Perspective distortion.** When you tilt the camera so the plane of the sensor is no longer perpendicular to the vertical plane of your subject, some parts of the subject are now closer to the sensor than they were before, while other parts are farther away. So, buildings, flagpoles, or NBA players appear to be falling backward, as you can see in Figure 11.10. While this kind of apparent distortion (it's not caused by a defect in the lens) can happen with any lens, it's most apparent when a wide angle is used.

- **Steady cam.** You'll find that you can hand-hold a wide-angle lens at slower shutter speeds, without need for vibration reduction, than you can with a telephoto lens. The reduced magnification of the wide-lens or wide-zoom setting doesn't emphasize camera shake like a telephoto lens does.

- **Interesting angles.** Many of the factors already listed combine to produce more interesting angles when shooting with wide-angle lenses. Raising or lowering a telephoto lens a few feet probably will have little effect on the appearance of the distant subjects you're shooting. The same change in elevation can produce a dramatic effect for the much-closer subjects typically captured with a wide-angle lens or wide-zoom setting.

**Figure 11.10**
Tilting the camera back produces this "falling back" look in architectural photos.

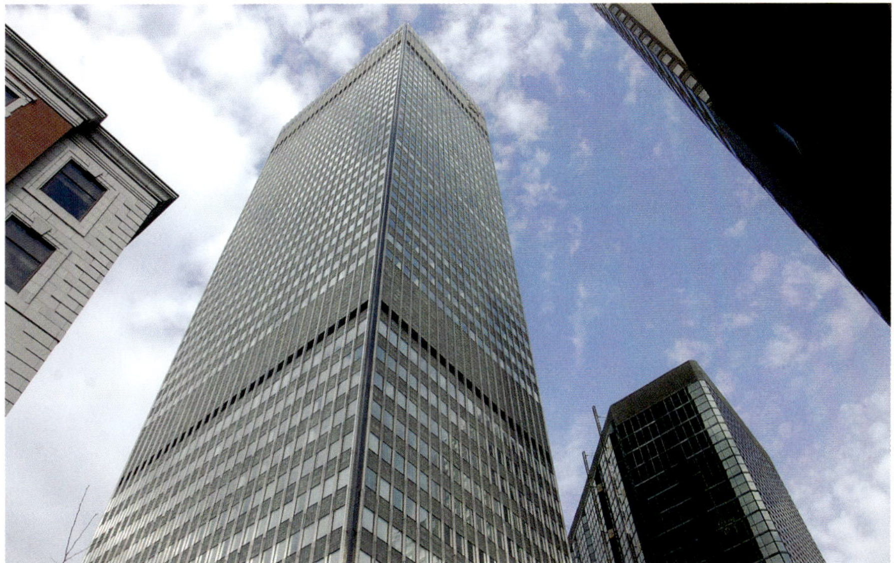

# Avoiding Potential Wide-Angle Problems

Wide-angle lenses have a few quirks that you'll want to keep in mind when shooting so you can avoid falling into some common traps. Here's a checklist of tips for avoiding common problems:

- **Symptom: converging lines.** Unless you want to use wildly diverging lines as a creative effect, it's a good idea to keep horizontal and vertical lines in landscapes, architecture, and other subjects carefully aligned with the sides, top, and bottom of the frame. That will help you avoid undesired perspective distortion. Sometimes it helps to shoot from a slightly elevated position so you don't have to tilt the camera up or down.

- **Symptom: color fringes around objects.** Lenses are often plagued with fringes of color around backlit objects, produced by *chromatic aberration*, which is produced when all the colors of light don't focus in the same plane or same lateral position (that is, the colors are offset to one side). This phenomenon is more common in wide-angle lenses and in photos of subjects with contrasty edges. Some kinds of chromatic aberration can be reduced by stopping down the lens, while all sorts can be reduced by using lenses with low diffraction index glass (or ED elements, in Nikon nomenclature) and by incorporating elements that cancel the chromatic aberration of other glass in the lens.

- **Symptom: lines that bow outward.** Some wide-angle lenses cause straight lines to bow outward, with the strongest effect at the edges. In fisheye (or *curvilinear*) lenses, this defect is a feature, as you can see in Figure 11.11. When distortion is not desired, you'll need to use a lens that has corrected barrel distortion. Manufacturers like Nikon do their best to minimize or eliminate it (producing a *rectilinear* lens), often using *aspherical* lens elements (which are not cross-sections of a sphere). You can also minimize barrel distortion simply by framing your photo with some extra space all around, so the edges where the defect is most obvious can be cropped out of the picture. Some image editors, including Photoshop and Photoshop Elements and Nikon Capture NX, have a lens distortion correction feature.

- **Symptom: dark corners and shadows in flash photos.** The Nikon D5200's built-in electronic flash is designed to provide even coverage for lenses as wide as 17mm. If you use a wider lens, you can expect darkening, or *vignetting*, in the corners of the frame. At wider focal lengths, the lens hood of some lenses (my 18-70mm lens is a prime offender) can cast a semi-circular shadow in the lower portion of the frame when using the built-in flash. Sometimes removing the lens hood or zooming in a bit can eliminate the shadow. Mounting an external flash unit, such as the mighty Nikon SB-910 can solve both problems, as this high-end flash unit (it costs almost half as much as the D5200 camera) has zoomable coverage up to as wide as the field of view of a 14mm lens when used with the included adapter. Its higher vantage point eliminates the problem of lens hood shadow and helps with red-eye, too.

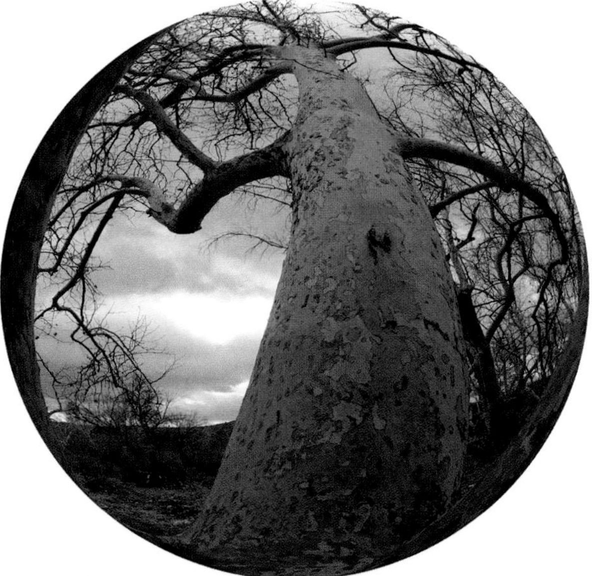

**Figure 11.11** Many wide-angle lenses cause lines to bow outward toward the edges of the image; with a fisheye lens, this tendency is considered an interesting feature.

# Using Telephoto and Tele-Zoom Lenses

Telephoto lenses also can have a dramatic effect on your photography, and Nikon is especially strong in the long-lens arena, with lots of choices in many focal lengths and zoom ranges. You should be able to find an affordable telephoto or tele-zoom to enhance your photography in several different ways. Here are the most important things you need to know. In the next section, I'll concentrate on telephoto considerations that can be problematic—and how to avoid those problems.

- **Selective focus.** Long lenses have reduced depth-of-field within the frame, allowing you to use selective focus to isolate your subject. You can open the lens up wide to create shallow depth-of-field, or close it down a bit to allow more to be in focus. The flip side of the coin is that when you *want* to make a range of objects sharp, you'll need to use a smaller f/stop to get the depth-of-field you need. Like fire, the depth-of-field of a telephoto lens can be friend or foe. Figure 11.12 shows a photo of a statue shot with a 200mm lens and a wider f/2.8 f/stop to de-emphasize the distracting background.

- **Getting closer.** Telephoto lenses bring you closer to wildlife, sports action, and candid subjects. No one wants to get a reputation as a surreptitious or "sneaky" photographer (except for paparazzi), but when applied to candids in an open and honest way, a long lens can help you capture memorable moments while retaining enough distance to stay out of the way of events as they transpire.

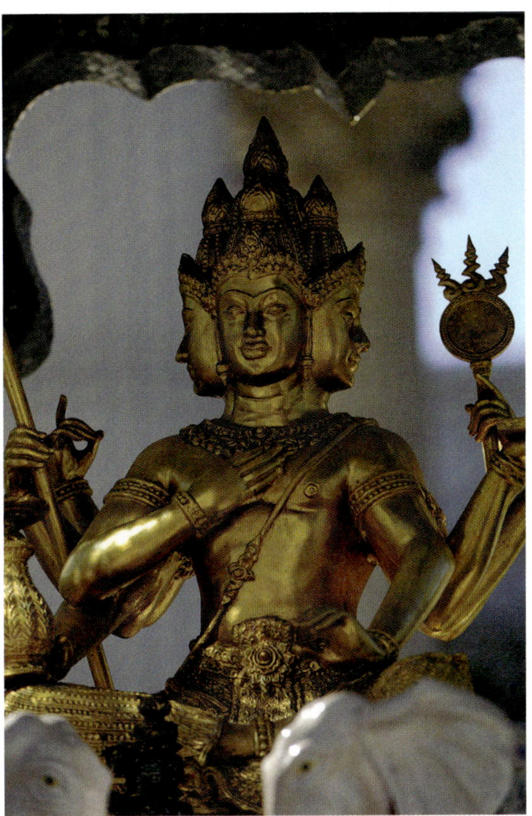

**Figure 11.12** A wide f/stop helped isolate the statue while allowing the background to go out of focus.

- **Reduced foreground/increased compression.** Telephoto lenses have the opposite effect of wide angles: they reduce the importance of things in the foreground by squeezing everything together. This compression even makes distant objects appear to be closer to subjects in the foreground and middle ranges. You can use this effect as a creative tool to squeeze subjects together.

- **Accentuates camera shakiness.** Telephoto focal lengths hit you with a double whammy in terms of camera/photographer shake. The lenses themselves are bulkier, more difficult to hold steady, and may even produce a barely perceptible see-saw rocking effect when you support them with one hand halfway down the lens barrel. Telephotos also magnify any camera shake. It's no wonder that vibration reduction is popular in longer lenses.

- **Interesting angles require creativity.** Telephoto lenses require more imagination in selecting interesting angles, because the "angle" you do get on your subjects is so narrow. Moving from side to side or a bit higher or lower can make a dramatic difference in a wide-angle shot, but raising or lowering a telephoto lens a few feet probably will have little effect on the appearance of the distant subjects you're shooting.

## Avoiding Telephoto Lens Problems

Many of the "problems" that telephoto lenses pose are really just challenges and are not that difficult to overcome. Here is a list of the seven most common picture maladies and suggested solutions.

- **Symptom: flat faces in portraits.** Head-and-shoulders portraits of humans tend to be more flattering when a focal length of 50mm to 85mm is used. Longer focal lengths compress the distance between features like noses and ears, making the face look wider and flat. A wide angle might make noses look huge and ears tiny when you fill the frame with a face. So stick with 50mm to 85mm focal lengths, going longer only when you're forced to shoot from a greater distance, and wider only when shooting three-quarters/full-length portraits, or group shots.

- **Symptom: blur due to camera shake.** Use a higher shutter speed (boosting ISO if necessary), consider an image-stabilized lens, or mount your camera on a tripod, monopod, or brace it with some other support. Of those three solutions, only the first will reduce blur caused by *subject* motion; a VR lens or tripod won't help you freeze a race car in mid-lap.

- **Symptom: color fringes.** Chromatic aberration is the most pernicious optical problem found in telephoto lenses. There are others, including spherical aberration, astigmatism, coma, curvature of field, and similarly scary-sounding phenomena. The best solution for any of these is to use a better lens that offers the proper degree of correction, or stop down the lens to minimize the problem. But that's not always possible. Your second-best choice may be to correct the fringing in your favorite RAW conversion tool or image editor. Photoshop's Lens Correction filter (found in the Filter menu's Distort submenu) offers sliders that minimize both red/cyan and blue/yellow fringing.

- **Symptom: lines that curve inward.** Pincushion distortion is found in many telephoto lenses. You might find after a bit of testing that it is worse at certain focal lengths with your particular zoom lens. Like chromatic aberration, it can be partially corrected using tools like the correction tools built into Photoshop and Photoshop Elements. You can see an exaggerated example in Figure 11.13, especially at the right edge where the walls of the tower bend noticeably; pincushion distortion isn't always this obvious.

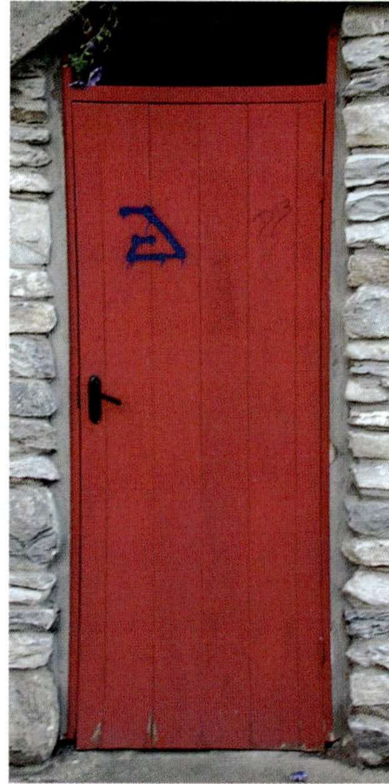

**Figure 11.13** Pincushion distortion in telephoto lenses causes lines to bow inward from the edges.

- **Symptom: low contrast from haze or fog.** When you're photographing distant objects, a long lens shoots through a lot more atmosphere, which generally is muddied up with extra haze and fog. That dirt or moisture in the atmosphere can reduce contrast and mute colors. Some feel that a skylight or UV filter can help, but this practice is mostly a holdover from the film days. Digital sensors are not sensitive enough to UV light for a UV filter to have much effect. So you should be prepared to boost contrast and color saturation in your Picture Controls menu or image editor if necessary.

- **Symptom: low contrast from flare.** Lenses are furnished with lens hoods for a good reason: to reduce flare from bright light sources at the periphery of the picture area, or completely outside it. Because telephoto lenses often create images that are lower in contrast in the first place, you'll want to be especially careful to use a lens hood to prevent further effects on your image (or shade the front of the lens with your hand).

- **Symptom: dark flash photos.** Edge-to-edge flash coverage isn't a problem with telephoto lenses as it is with wide angles. The shooting distance is. A long lens might make a subject that's 50 feet away look as if it's right next to you, but your camera's flash isn't fooled. You'll need extra power for distant flash shots, and probably more power than your D5200's built-in flash provides. The Nikon SB-900 Speedlight, for example, can automatically zoom its coverage to illuminate the area captured by a 200mm telephoto lens, with three light distribution patterns (Standard, Center-weighted, and Even). (Try *that* with the built-in flash!)

## Telephotos and Bokeh

*Bokeh* describes the aesthetic qualities of the out-of-focus parts of an image and whether out-of-focus points of light—circles of confusion—are rendered as distracting fuzzy discs or smoothly fade into the background. *Boke* is a Japanese word for "blur," and the h was added to keep English speakers from rendering it monosyllabically to rhyme with *broke.* Although bokeh is visible in blurry portions of any image, it's of particular concern with telephoto lenses, which, thanks to the magic of reduced depth-of-field, produce more obviously out-of-focus areas.

Bokeh can vary from lens to lens, or even within a given lens depending on the f/stop in use. Bokeh becomes objectionable when the circles of confusion are evenly illuminated, making them stand out as distinct discs, or, worse, when these circles are darker in the center, producing an ugly "doughnut" effect. A lens defect called spherical aberration may produce out-of-focus discs that are brighter on the edges and darker in the center, because the lens doesn't focus light passing through the edges of the lens exactly as it does light going through the center. (Mirror or *catadioptric* lenses also produce this effect.)

Other kinds of spherical aberration generate circles of confusion that are brightest in the center and fade out at the edges, producing a smooth blending effect, as you can see at bottom in Figure 11.14. Ironically, when no spherical aberration is present at all, the discs are a uniform shade, which, while better than the doughnut effect, is not as pleasing as the bright center/dark edge rendition. The shape of the disc also comes into play, with round smooth circles considered the best, and nonagonal or some other polygon (determined by the shape of the lens diaphragm) considered less desirable.

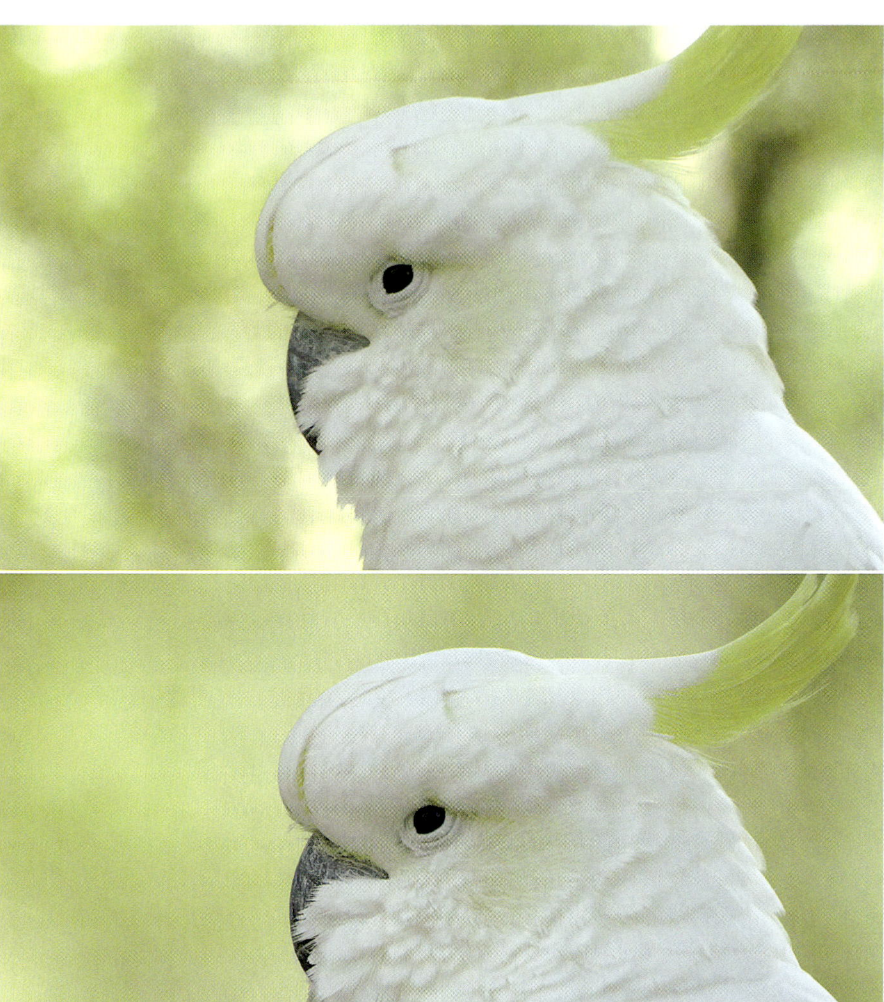

**Figure 11.14**
Bokeh is less pleasing when the discs are prominent (top), and less obtrusive when they blend into the background (bottom).

If you plan to use selective focus a lot, you should investigate the bokeh characteristics of a particular lens before you buy. Nikon user groups and forums will usually be full of comments and questions about bokeh, so the research is fairly easy.

# Add-ons and Special Features

Once you've purchased your telephoto lens, you'll want to think about some appropriate accessories for it. There are some handy add-ons available that can be valuable. Here are a couple of them to think about.

# Lens Hoods

Lens hoods are an important accessory for all lenses, but they're especially valuable with telephotos. As I mentioned earlier, lens hoods do a good job of preserving image contrast by keeping bright light sources outside the field of view from striking the lens and, potentially, bouncing around inside that long tube to generate flare that, when coupled with atmospheric haze, can rob your image of detail and snap. In addition, lens hoods serve as valuable protection for that large, vulnerable, front lens element. It's easy to forget that you've got that long tube sticking out in front of your camera and accidentally whack the front of your lens into something. It's cheaper to replace a lens hood than it is to have a lens repaired, so you might find that a good hood is valuable protection for your prized optics.

When choosing a lens hood, it's important to have the right hood for the lens, usually the one offered for that lens by Nikon or the third-party manufacturer. You want a hood that blocks precisely the right amount of light: neither too much light nor too little. A hood with a front diameter that is too small can show up in your pictures as vignetting. A hood that has a front diameter that's too large isn't stopping all the light it should. Generic lens hoods may not do the job.

When your telephoto is a zoom lens, it's even more important to get the right hood, because you need one that does what it is supposed to at both the wide-angle and telephoto ends of the zoom range. Lens hoods may be cylindrical, rectangular (shaped like the image frame), or petal shaped (that is, cylindrical, but with cut-out areas at the corners that correspond to the actual image area). Lens hoods should be mounted in the correct orientation (a bayonet mount for the hood usually takes care of this).

# Telephoto Converters

Teleconverters (often called telephoto extenders outside the Nikon world) multiply the actual focal length of your lens, giving you a longer telephoto for much less than the price of a lens with that actual focal length. These converters fit between the lens and your camera and contain optical elements that magnify the image produced by the lens. Available in 1.4X, 1.7X, and 2.0X configurations from Nikon, a teleconverter transforms, say, a 200mm lens into a 280mm, 340mm, or 400mm optic, respectively. Given the D5200's crop factor, your 200mm lens now has the same field of view as a 420mm, 510mm, or 600mm lens on a full-frame camera. At around $500 each, converters are quite a bargain, aren't they? You can also find less expensive telephoto extenders, like the one shown in Figure 11.15, from third-party suppliers.

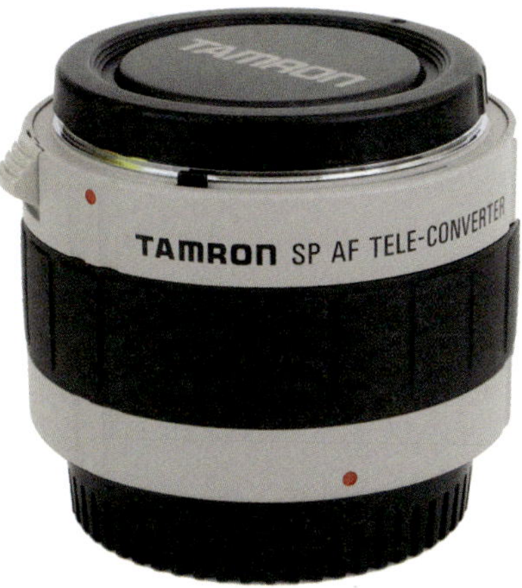


**Figure 11.15** Teleconverters multiply the true focal length of your lenses—but at a cost of some sharpness and aperture speed.

The only drawback is that Nikon's own TC II and TC III teleconverters can be used only with a limited number of Nikkor AF-S lenses. The compatible models include the 200mm f/2G ED-IF AF-S VR Nikkor, 300mm f/2.8G ED-IF AF-S VR Nikkor, 400mm f/2.8D ED-IF AF-S II Nikkor, 80-200mm f/2.8D ED-IF AF-S, 70-200mm f/2.8G ED-IF AF-S VR Zoom-Nikkor, 200-400mm f/4G ED-IF AF-S VR Zoom-Nikkor, 300mm f/4D ED-IF AF-S Nikkor, 500mm f/4D ED-IF AF-S II Nikkor, and 600mm f/4D ED-IF AF-S II Nikkor. These tend to be pricey (or ultra-pricey lenses). Teleconverters from Sigma, Kenko, Tamron, and others cost less, and may be compatible with a broader range of lenses. (They work especially well with lenses from the same vendor that produces the teleconverter.)

There are other downsides. While extenders retain the closest focusing distance of your original lens, autofocus is maintained only if the lens's original maximum aperture is f/4 or larger (for the 1.4X extender) or f/2.8 or larger (for the 2X extender). The components reduce the effective aperture of any lens they are used with, by one f/stop with the 1.4X converter, 1.5 f/stops with the 1.7X converter, and two f/stops with the 2X extender. So, your 200mm f/2.8 lens becomes a 280mm f/4 or 400mm f/5.6 lens. Although Nikon converters are precision optical devices, they do cost you a little sharpness, but that improves when you reduce the aperture by a stop or two. Each of the converters is compatible only with a particular set of lenses greater, so you'll want to check Nikon's compatibility chart to see if the component can be used with the lens you want to attach to it.

If your lenses are compatible and you're shooting under bright lighting conditions, the Nikon extenders make handy accessories. I recommend the 1.4X version because it robs you of very little sharpness and only one f/stop. The 1.7X version also works well, too, but I've found the 2X teleconverter to exact too much of a sharpness and speed penalty to be of much use.

## Macro Focusing

Some telephotos and telephoto zooms available for the Nikon D5200 have particularly close focusing capabilities, making them *macro* lenses. Of course, the object is not necessarily to get close (get too close and you'll find it difficult to light your subject). What you're really looking for in a macro lens is to magnify the apparent size of the subject in the final image. Camera-to-subject distance is most important when you want to back up farther from your subject (say, to avoid spooking skittish insects or small animals). In that case, you'll want a macro lens with a longer focal length to allow that distance while retaining the desired magnification.

Nikon makes five lenses that are officially designated as macro lenses. They include:

- **AF-S Micro-Nikkor 60mm f/2.8G ED.** This type-G lens supposedly replaces the type-D lens listed next, adding an internal Silent Wave autofocus motor that should operate faster, and which is also compatible with cameras lacking a body motor, such as the Nikon D40/D40x and D5200. It also has ED lens elements for improved image quality. However, because it lacks an aperture ring, you can control the f/stop only when the lens is mounted directly on the camera or used with automatic extension tubes. Should you want to reverse a macro lens using a special adapter (the Nikon BR2-A ring) to improve image quality or mount it on a bellows, you're better off with a lens having an aperture ring.

- **AF Micro-Nikkor 60mm f/2.8D.** This non-AF-S lens won't autofocus on the Nikon D5200, but, then, you might be manually focusing most of the time when shooting close-ups, and may appreciate the lower cost of an "obsolete" lens.

- **AF-S Micro-Nikkor 40mm f/2.8 DX.** The latest macro lens in the lineup, this one is an inexpensive (roughly $280) non-full-frame lens produced especially for DX-format cameras like the D5200. It's sharp and affordable.

- **AF-S VR Micro-Nikkor 105mm f/2.8G IF-ED.** This G-series lens did replace a similar D-type, non-AF-S version that also lacked VR. I own the older lens, too, and am keeping it because I find VR a rather specialized tool for macro work. Some 99 percent of the time, I shoot close-ups with my D5200 mounted on a tripod or, at the very least, on a monopod, so camera vibration is not much of a concern. Indeed, *subject* movement is a more serious problem, especially when shooting plant life outdoors on days plagued with even slight breezes. Because my outdoor subjects are likely to move while I am composing my photo, I find both VR and auto-focus not very useful. I end up focusing manually most of the time, too. This lens provides a little extra camera-to-subject distance, so you'll find it very useful, but consider the older non-G, non-VR version, too, if you're in the market and don't mind losing autofocus features.

- **AF Micro-Nikkor 200mm f/4D IF-ED.** With a price tag of about $1,800, you'd probably want this lens only if you planned a great deal of close-up shooting at greater distances. It focuses down to 1.6 feet, and is manual focus only with the D5200, but provides enough magnification to allow interesting close-ups of subjects that are farther away. A specialized tool for specialized shooting.

- **AF-S DX Micro 85mm f/3.5 ED VR.** This lens was designed especially for cropped sensor (DX) models like the D5200. It autofocuses on the D5200, it has vibration reduction, and it's relatively fast at f/3.5, making it an excellent choice for hand-held close-up photography.

- **PC Micro-Nikkor 85mm f/2.8D.** Priced about the same as the 200mm Micro-Nikkor, this is a manual focus lens (on *any* camera; it doesn't offer autofocus features) that has both tilt and shift capabilities, so you can adjust the perspective of the subject as you shoot. The tilt feature lets you "tilt" the plane of focus, providing the illusion of greater depth-of-field, while the shift capabilities make it possible to shoot down on a subject from an angle and still maintain its correct proportions. If you need one of these for perspective control, you already know it; if you're still wondering how you'd use one, you probably have no need for these specialized capabilities. However, I have recently watched some very creative fashion and wedding photographers use this lens for portraits, applying the tilting features to throw parts of the image wildly out of focus to concentrate interest on faces, and so forth. None of these are likely pursuits of the average Nikon D5200 photographer, but I couldn't resist mentioning this interesting lens.

You'll also find macro lenses, macro zooms, and other close-focusing lenses available from Sigma, Tamron, and Tokina. If you want to focus closer with a macro lens, or any other lens, you can add an accessory called an *extension tube*, like the one shown in Figure 11.16, or a *bellows extension*. These add-ons move the lens farther from the focal plane, allowing it to focus more closely. Nikon also sells add-on close-up lenses, which look like filters, and allow lenses to focus more closely.

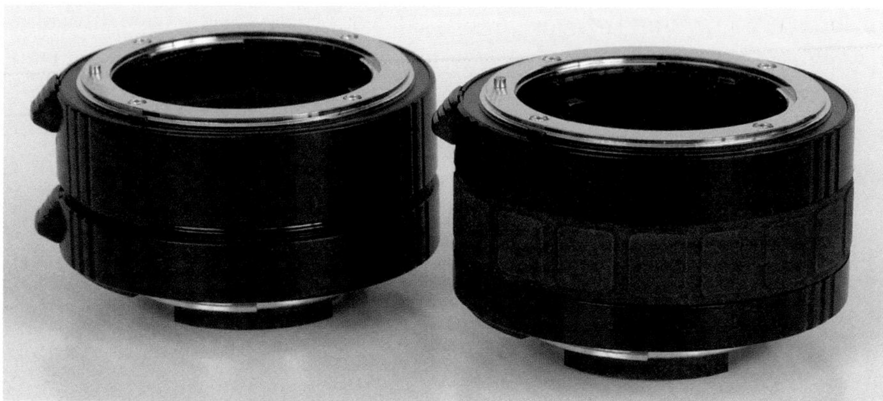

**Figure 11.16**
Extension tubes
enable any lens to
focus more closely to
the subject.

# Vibration Reduction

Nikon has a burgeoning line of more than 16 lenses with built-in vibration reduction (VR) capabilities. I probably shouldn't have mentioned a specific number, because I expect another half dozen or so new VR lenses to be introduced rather early in the life of this book.

The VR feature uses lens elements that are shifted internally in response to vertical or horizontal motion of the lens, which compensates for any camera shake in those directions. Vibration reduction is particularly effective when used with telephoto lenses, which magnify the effects of camera and photographer motion. However, VR can be useful for lenses of shorter focal lengths, such as Nikon's 16-85mm, 18-105mm, and 18-55mm VR lenses. Other Nikon VR lenses provide stabilization with zooms that are as wide as 24mm.

Vibration reduction offers two to three shutter speed increments' worth of shake reduction. (Nikon claims a four-stop gain, which I feel may be optimistic.) This extra margin can be invaluable when you're shooting under dim lighting conditions or hand-holding a lens for, say, wildlife photography. Perhaps that shot of a foraging deer would require a shutter speed of 1/2,000th second at f/5.6 with your AF-S VR Zoom-Nikkor 200-400mm f/4G IF-ED lens. Relax. You can shoot at 1/250th second at f/11 and get a photo that is just as sharp, as long as the deer doesn't decide to bound off. Or, perhaps you're shooting indoors and would prefer to shoot at 1/15th second at f/4. Your 16-85mm VR lens can grab the shot for you at its wide-angle position. However, consider these facts:

- **VR doesn't freeze subject motion.** Vibration reduction won't freeze moving subjects in their tracks, because it is effective only at compensating for *camera* motion. It's best used in reduced illumination, to steady the up-down swaying of telephoto lenses, and to improve close-up photography. If your subject is in motion, you'll still need a shutter speed that's fast enough to stop the action.

- **VR adds to shutter lag.** The process of adjusting the lens elements, like autofocus, takes time, so vibration reduction may contribute to a slight increase in shutter lag. If you're shooting sports, that delay may be annoying, but I still use my VR lenses for sports all the time!

- **Use when appropriate.** You may find that your results are worse when using VR while panning, although newer Nikon VR lenses work fine when the camera is deliberately moved from side to side during exposure. Older lenses can confuse the panning motion with camera wobble and provide too much compensation. You might want to switch off VR when panning or when your camera is mounted on a tripod.

- **Do you need VR at all?** Remember that an inexpensive monopod might be able to provide the same additional steadiness as a VR lens, at a much lower cost. If you're out in the field shooting wild animals or flowers and think a tripod isn't practical, try a monopod first.

The AF-S VR Zoom-Nikkor 70-200mm f/2.8G IF-ED, though atypical for the average D5200 owner, is typical of the VR lenses Nikon offers, so I'll use it as an example. It has the basic controls shown in Figure 11.17, to adjust focus range (full, or limited to infinity down to 2.5 meters); VR On/Off; and Normal VR/Active VR (the latter an aggressive mode used in extreme situations, such as a moving car). Not visible (it's over the horizon, so to speak) is the M/A-M focus mode switch, which allows changing from autofocus (with manual override) to manual focus.

**Figure 11.17**

On the Nikon 70-200mm VR zoom you'll find (top to bottom): the focus limit switch, VR on/off switch, and Normal/Active VR adjustment.

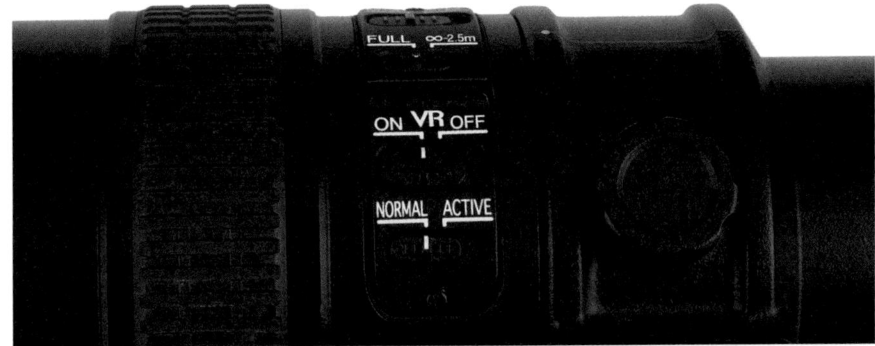


## VIBRATION REDUCTION: IN THE CAMERA OR IN THE LENS?

The adoption of image stabilization/anti-shake technology into the camera bodies of models from Sony, Olympus, Pentax, and Samsung has revived an old debate about whether VR belongs in the camera or in the lens. Perhaps it's my Nikon bias showing, but I am quite happy not to have vibration reduction available in the body itself. Here are some reasons:

- Should in-camera VR fail, you have to send the whole camera in for repair, and camera repairs are generally more expensive than lens repairs. I like being able to simply switch to another lens if I have a VR problem.

- VR in the camera doesn't steady your view in the viewfinder, whereas a VR lens shows you a steadied image as you shoot.

- You're stuck with the VR system built in to your camera. If an improved system is incorporated into a lens and the improvements are important to you, just trade in your old lens for the new one.

- When building VR in the camera, a compromise system that works with all lenses must be designed. VR in the lens, however, can be custom-tailored to each specific lens's needs.

# Using the Lensbaby

I'm going to depart from my Nikon-only regimen to include the wonderful Lensbaby line of optics, because Nikon doesn't offer anything similar, nor as delightfully affordable. The Lensbaby comes in several varieties, including Edge 80, a new shift-tilt model for about $300; the Composer Pro shown in Figure 11.18, uses distortion-heavy glass elements mounted on a system that allows you to bend, twist, and distort the lens's alignment to produce transmogrified images unlike anything else you've ever seen. Like the legendary cheap-o Diana and Holga cameras, the pictures are prized expressly because of their plastic image quality. Jack and Meg White (formerly of the White Stripes) have, in fact, sold per-sonalized Diana and Holga cameras on their website for wacky *lomography* (named after the Lomo, another low-quality/high-concept camera). The various Lensbaby models are for more serious photographers, if you can say that about anyone who yearns to take pictures that look like they were shot through a glob of corn syrup.

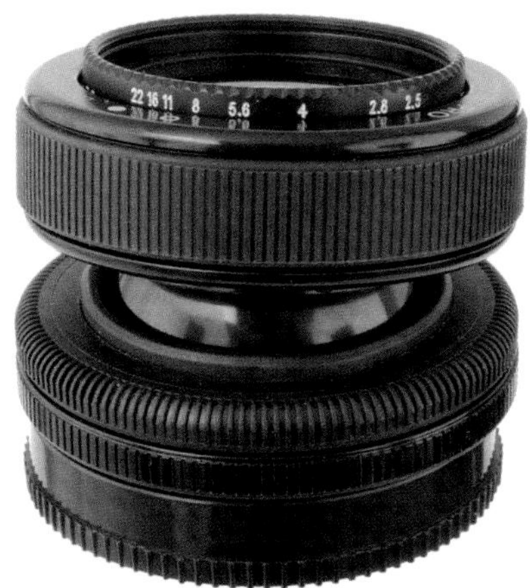

**Figure 11.18** The Lensbaby Composer Pro.

Lensbabies are capable of creating all sorts of special effects. You use a Lensbaby by shifting the front mount to move the lens's sweet spot to a particular point in the scene. This is basically a selective focus lens that gets very soft outside the sweet spot. There are several different types of Lensbabies, which can be interchanged using the system's Optic Swap technology.

- **Macro.** A Lensbaby accessory makes it possible to use this tool for macro photography.

- **Wide-angle/telephoto conversion.** Add-on lenses convert the basic Lensbaby into a wide-angle or telephoto version.

- **Edge 80.** This is an 80mm f/2.8 lens with a flat field of focus, and ideal for portraits. It has a 12-blade adjustable aperture, focuses as close as 17 inches, and functions as a tilt-shift lens. When canted, the Edge 80 delivers a slice of tack sharp focus through the image, bordered by a soft blur. When pointed straight ahead, Edge 80 can be used like a conventional lens. You can also use it in any of the traditional selective focus applications you'd use one of Nikon's PC-E lenses for—but *not* for perspective correction. (It tilts, but does not shift from side to side.)

- **Creative aperture kit.** Various shaped cutouts can be used in place of the regular aperture inserts that control depth-of-field. These shapes can include things like hearts, stars, and other shapes.

- **Optic swap kit.** This three-lens accessory kit provides different adapters that include a pinhole lens, plastic lens, and single glass lens.

Among the interchangeable components are the Sweet 35, Fisheye, Soft Focus, Double Glass, Single Glass, and Pinhole lenses. Models include the Composer Pro, Composer, Muse, Control Freak, and

Scout, each with varying amounts of adjustments. (The Scout does not bend at all, making it ideal for use with the fisheye component.)

The other Lensbaby models, like the Composer Pro, have the same tilting lens configuration as previous editions, but are designed for easier and more precise distorting movements. Hold the camera with your finger gripping the knobs as you bend the camera to move the central "sweet spot" (sharp area) to any portion of your image. With two (count 'em) multicoated optical glass lens elements, you'll get a blurry image, but the amount of distortion is under your control. F/stops from f/2 to f/22 are available to increase/decrease depth-of-field and allow you to adjust exposure. The 50mm lens focuses down to 12 inches and is strictly manual focus/manual exposure in operation. At $300 or so, these lenses are not cheap accessories, but there is really no other easy way to achieve the kind of looks you can get with a Lensbaby.

Figures 11.19 and 11.20 are examples of the type of effect you can get, in photographs crafted by Cleveland photographer Nancy Balluck. She also produced the back cover photography of yours truly, and one of her specialties is Lensbaby effects. Nancy regularly gives demonstrations and classes on the use of these optics, and you can follow her work at www.nancyballuckphotography.com.

**Figure 11.19**
Lensbabies are specialized lens replacements with some special soft-focus features.

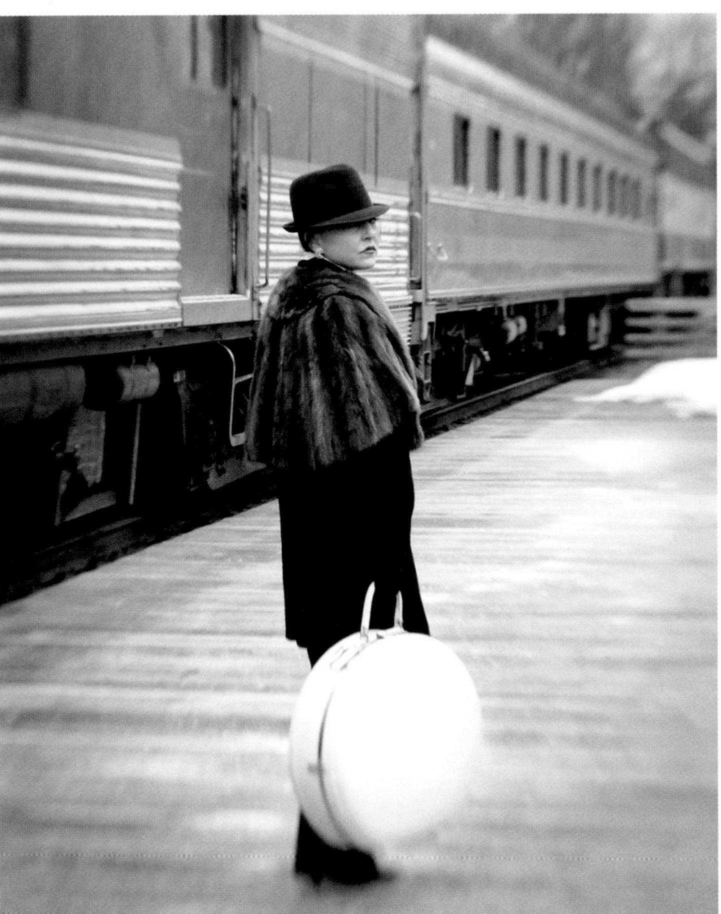

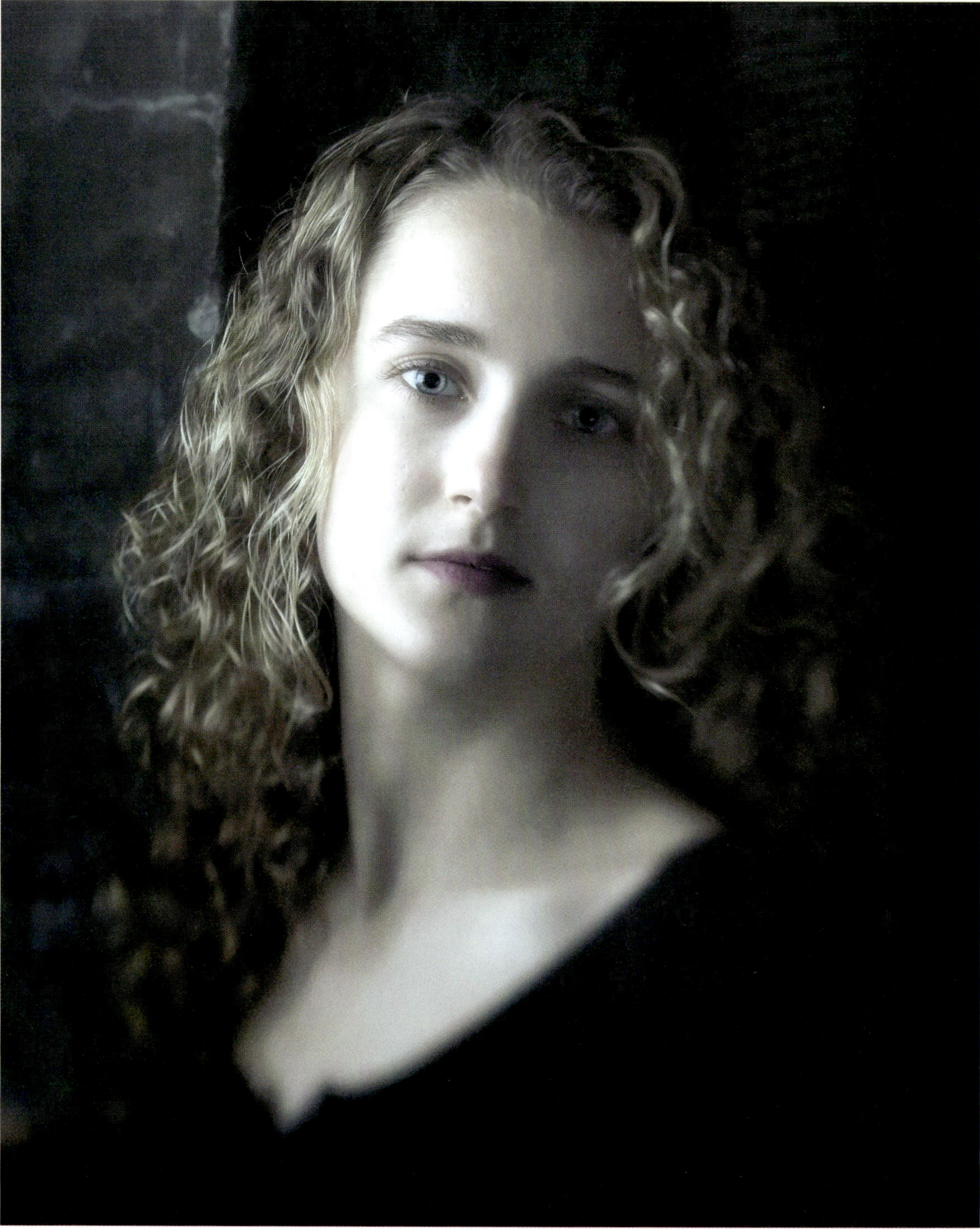

**Figure 11.20** Everything is uniquely blurry outside the Lensbaby's "sweet spot," but you can move that spot around within your frame at will. They can be used for selective focus effects, and can simulate the dreamy look of some old-style cameras.

# 12

# Making Light Work for You

Successful photographers and artists have an intimate understanding of the importance of light in shaping an image. Rembrandt was a master of using light to create moods and reveal the character of his subjects. Late artist Thomas Kinkade's official tagline was "Painter of Light." Dean Collins, co-founder of Finelight Studios, revolutionized how a whole generation of photographers learned and used lighting. It's impossible to underestimate how the use of light adds to—and how misuse can detract from—your photographs.

All forms of visual art use light to shape the finished product. Sculptors don't have control over the light used to illuminate their finished work, so they must create shapes using planes and curved surfaces so that the form envisioned by the artist comes to life from a variety of viewing and lighting angles. Painters, in contrast, have absolute control over both shape and light in their work, as well as the viewing angle, so they can use both the contours of their two-dimensional subjects and the qualities of the "light" they use to illuminate those subjects to evoke the image they want to produce.

Photography is a third form of art. The photographer may have little or no control over the subject (other than posing human subjects) but can often adjust both viewing angle *and* the nature of the light source to create a particular compelling image. The direction and intensity of the light sources create the shapes and textures that we see. The distribution and proportions determine the contrast and tonal values: whether the image is stark or high key, or muted and low in contrast. The colors of the light (because even "white" light has a color balance that the sensor can detect), and how much of those colors the subject reflects or absorbs, paint the hues visible in the image.

As a Nikon D5200 photographer, you must learn to be a painter and sculptor of light if you want to move from *taking* a picture to *making* a photograph. This chapter provides an introduction to using the two main types of illumination: *continuous* lighting (such as daylight, incandescent, or fluorescent sources) and the brief, but brilliant snippets of light we call *electronic flash.*

# Continuous Illumination versus Electronic Flash

Continuous lighting is exactly what you might think: uninterrupted illumination that is available all the time during a shooting session. Daylight, moonlight, and the artificial lighting encountered both indoors and outdoors count as continuous light sources (although all of them can be "interrupted" by passing clouds, solar eclipses, a blown fuse, or simply by switching off a lamp). Indoor continuous illumination includes both the lights that are there already (such as incandescent lamps or overhead fluorescent lights indoors) and fixtures you supply yourself, including photoflood lamps or reflectors used to bounce existing light onto your subject.

The surge of light we call electronic flash is produced by a burst of photons generated by an electrical charge that is accumulated in a component called a *capacitor* and then directed through a glass tube containing xenon gas, which absorbs the energy and emits the brief flash. Electronic flash is notable because it can be much more intense than continuous lighting, lasts only a brief moment, and can be much more portable than supplementary incandescent sources. It's a light source you can carry with you and use anywhere.

Indeed, your D5200 has a flip-up electronic flash unit built in, as shown in Figure 12.1. But you can also use an external flash, either mounted on the D5200's accessory shoe or used off-camera and linked with a cable or triggered by a slave light (which sets off a flash when it senses the firing of another unit). Studio flash units are electronic flash, too, and aren't limited to "professional" shooters, as there are economical "monolight" (one-piece flash/power supply) units available in the $200 price range. Serious photographers with some spare cash can buy a couple to store in a closet and use to set up a home studio, or use as supplementary lighting when traveling away from home. You'll need a remote trigger mounted on the D5200's accessory/hot shoe, or an accessory/hot shoe–to–PC connector adapter to use studio flash with your camera.

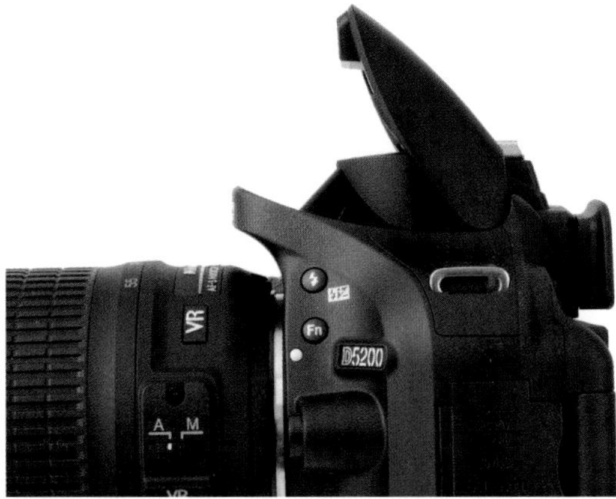

**Figure 12.1** One form of light that's always available is the flip-up flash on your D5200.

There are advantages and disadvantages to each type of illumination. Here's a quick checklist of pros and cons:

- **Lighting preview—Pro: continuous lighting.** With continuous lighting, you always know exactly what kind of lighting effect you're going to get and, if multiple lights are used, how they will interact with each other, as shown in Figure 12.2. With electronic flash, the general effect you're going to see may be a mystery until you've built some experience, and you may need to review a shot on the LCD, make some adjustments, and then reshoot to get the look you want. (In this sense, a digital camera's review capabilities replace the Polaroid test shots pro photographers relied on in decades past.)

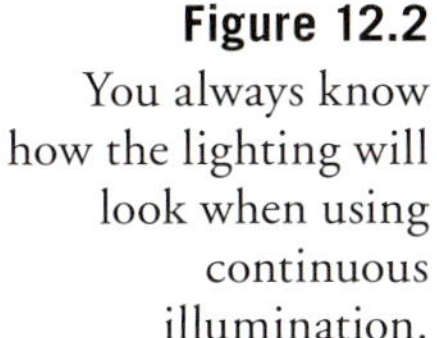

**Figure 12.2**
You always know how the lighting will look when using continuous illumination.

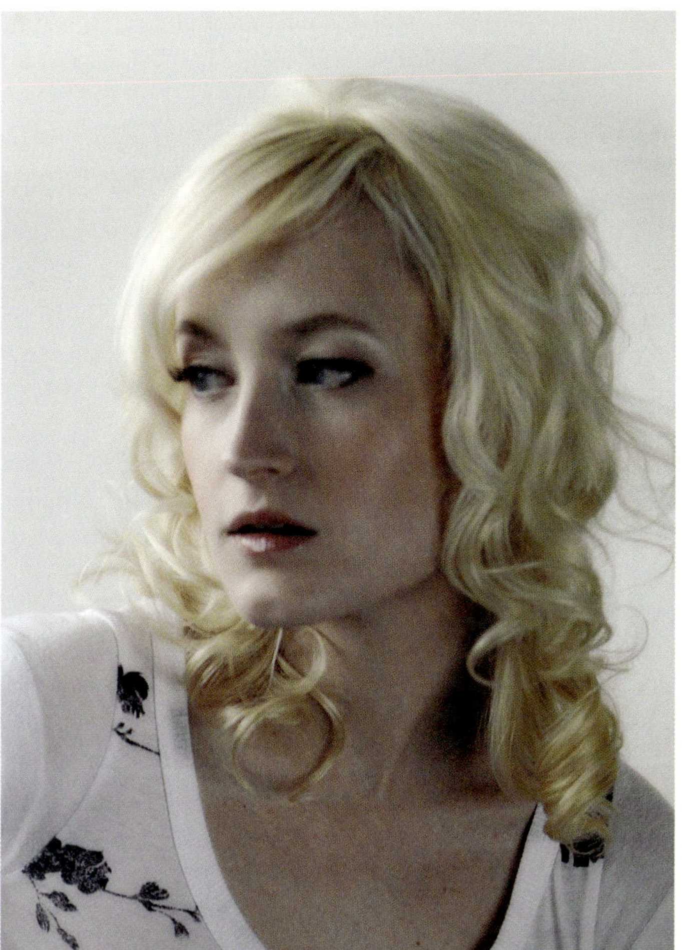

- **Lighting preview—Con: electronic flash.** With flash, the general effect you're going to see may be a mystery until you've built some experience, and you may need to review a shot on the LCD, make some adjustments, and then reshoot to get the look you want. (In this sense, a digital camera's review capabilities replace the Polaroid test shots pro photographers relied on in decades past.)

- **Exposure calculation—Pro: continuous lighting.** Your D5200 has no problem calculating exposure for continuous lighting, because it remains constant and can be measured through a sensor that interprets the light reaching the viewfinder. The amount of light available just before the exposure will, in almost all cases, be the same amount of light present when the shutter is released. The D5200's Spot metering mode can be used to measure and compare the proportions of light in the highlights and shadows, so you can make an adjustment (such as using more or less fill light) if necessary. You can even use a hand-held light meter to measure the light yourself.

- **Exposure calculation—Con: electronic flash.** Electronic flash illumination doesn't exist until the flash fires, and so it can't be measured by the D5200's exposure sensor when the mirror is flipped up during the exposure. Instead, the light must be measured by metering the intensity of a pre-flash that is triggered an instant before the main flash, as it is reflected back to the camera and through the lens. An alternative is to use a sensor built into an external flash and measure reflected light that has not traveled through the lens. If you have a do-it-yourself bent, there are hand-held flash meters, too, including models that measure both flash and continuous light.

- **Evenness of illumination—Pro/con: continuous lighting.** Of continuous light sources, daylight, in particular, provides illumination that tends to fill an image completely, lighting up the foreground, background, and your subject almost equally. Shadows do come into play, of course, so you might need to use reflectors or fill-in light sources to even out the illumination further, but barring objects that block large sections of your image from daylight, the light is spread fairly evenly. Indoors, however, continuous lighting is commonly less evenly distributed. The average living room, for example, has hot spots and dark corners. But on the plus side, you can *see* this uneven illumination and compensate with additional lamps.

- **Evenness of illumination—Con: electronic flash.** Electronic flash units (like continuous light sources such as lamps that don't have the advantage of being located 93 million miles from the subject) suffer from the effects of their proximity. The *inverse square law*, first applied to both gravity and light by Sir Isaac Newton, dictates that as a light source's distance increases from the subject, the amount of light reaching the subject falls off proportionately to the square of the distance. In plain English, that means that a flash or lamp that's six feet away from a subject provides only one-quarter as much illumination as a source that's 12 feet away (rather than half as much). (See Figure 12.3.) This translates into relatively shallow "depth-of-light."

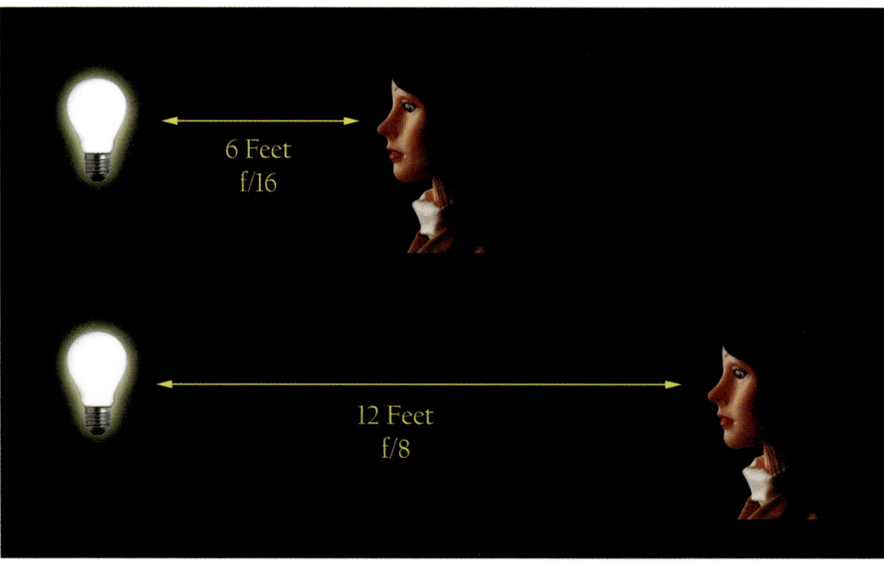


**Figure 12.3**
A light source that is twice as far away provides only one-quarter as much illumination.

- **Action stopping—Con: continuous lighting.** Action stopping with continuous light sources is completely dependent on the shutter speed you've dialed in on the camera. And the speeds available are dependent on the amount of light available and your ISO sensitivity setting. Outdoors in daylight, there will probably be enough sunlight to let you shoot at 1/2,000th second and f/6.3 with a non-grainy sensitivity setting of ISO 400. That's a fairly useful combination of settings if you're not using a super-telephoto with a small maximum aperture. But inside, the reduced illumination quickly has you pushing your D5200 to its limits. For example, if you're shooting indoor sports, there probably won't be enough available light to allow you to use a 1/2,000th second shutter speed (although I routinely shoot indoor basketball with my D5200 at ISO 1600 and 1/500th second at f/4). In many indoor sports situations, you may find yourself limited to 1/500th second or slower.

- **Action stopping—Pro: electronic flash.** When it comes to the ability to freeze moving objects in their tracks, the advantage goes to electronic flash. The brief duration of electronic flash serves as a very high "shutter speed" when the flash is the main or only source of illumination for the photo. Your D5200's shutter speed may be set for 1/200th second during a flash exposure, but if the flash illumination predominates, the *effective* exposure time will be the 1/1,000th to 1/50,000th second or less duration of the flash, as you can see in Figure 12.4, because the flash unit reduces the amount of light released by cutting short the duration of the flash. The only fly in the ointment is that, if the ambient light is strong enough, it may produce a secondary, "ghost" exposure, as I'll explain later in this chapter.

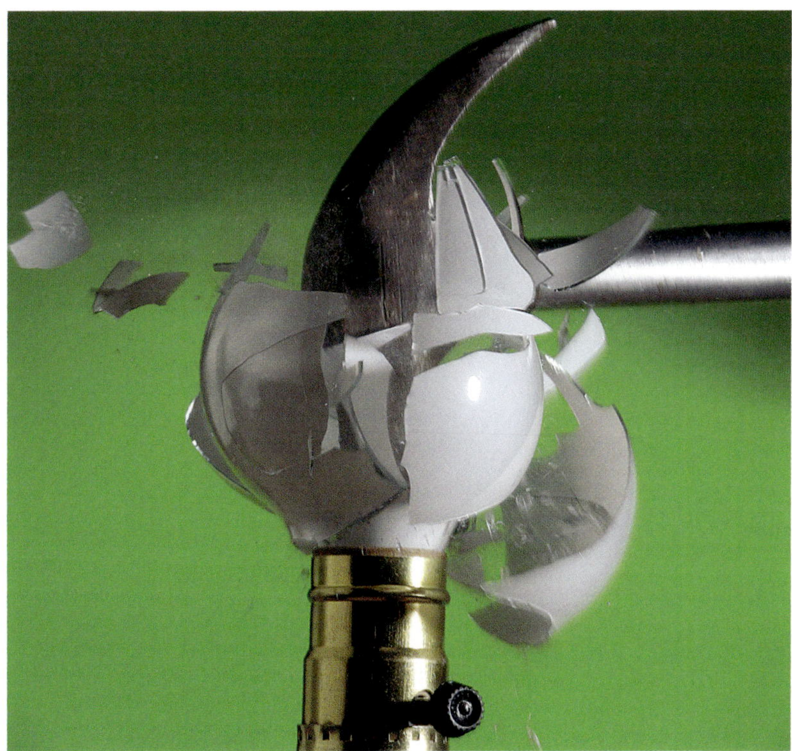

**Figure 12.4**
Electronic flash can freeze almost any action, as this dramatic shot by Cleveland photographer Kris Bosworth proves.

- **Cost—Pro: continuous lighting.** Incandescent or fluorescent lamps are generally much less expensive than electronic flash units, which can easily cost several hundred dollars. I've used everything from desktop high-intensity lamps to reflector flood lights for continuous illumination at very little cost. There are lamps made especially for photographic purposes, too, priced up to $50 or so. Maintenance is economical, too: many incandescent or fluorescents use bulbs that cost only a few dollars.

- **Cost—Con: electronic flash.** Electronic flash units aren't particularly cheap. The lowest-cost dedicated flash designed specifically for Nikon dSLRs is about $120. Such units are limited in features, however, and intended for those with entry-level cameras. Plan on spending some money to get the features that a sophisticated electronic flash offers.

- **Flexibility—Con: continuous lighting.** Because incandescent and fluorescent lamps are not as bright as electronic flash, the slower shutter speeds required (see "Action stopping," above) mean that you may have to use a tripod more often, especially when shooting portraits. The incandescent variety of continuous lighting gets hot, especially in the studio, and the side effects range from discomfort (for your human models) to disintegration (if you happen to be shooting perishable foods like ice cream). The heat also makes it more difficult to add filtration to incandescent sources.

- **Flexibility—Pro: electronic flash.** Electronic flash's action-freezing power allows you to work without a tripod in the studio (and elsewhere), adding flexibility and speed when choosing angles and positions. Flash units can be easily filtered, and, because the filtration is placed over the light source rather than the lens, you don't need to use high-quality filter material. Roscoe or Lee lighting gels, which may be too flimsy to use in front of the lens, can be mounted or taped in front of your flash with ease.

# Continuous Lighting Basics

While continuous lighting and its effects are generally much easier to visualize and use than electronic flash, there are some factors you need to take into account, particularly the color temperature of the light. (Color temperature concerns aren't exclusive to continuous light sources, of course, but the variations tend to be more extreme and less predictable than those of electronic flash, which output relatively consistent daylight-like illumination.)

Color temperature, in practical terms, is how "bluish" or how "reddish" the light appears to be to the digital camera's sensor. Indoor illumination is quite warm, comparatively, and appears reddish to the sensor. Daylight, in contrast, seems much bluer to the sensor. Our eyes (our brains, actually) are quite adaptable to these variations, so white objects don't appear to have an orange tinge when viewed indoors, nor do they seem excessively blue outdoors in full daylight. Yet, these color temperature variations are real and the sensor is not fooled. To capture the most accurate colors, we need to take the color temperature into account in setting the color balance (or *white balance*) of the D5200—either automatically using the camera's smarts or manually using our own knowledge and experience.

When using the Nikon D5200, you don't need to think in terms of actual color temperature (although you can measure existing color temperature using the Preset feature described later), because the camera won't let you set white balance using color temperature values, which are measured in *degrees Kelvin.* But it is useful to know that warmer (more reddish) color temperatures (measured in degrees Kelvin) are the *lower* numbers, while cooler (bluer) color temperatures are *higher* numbers. It might not make sense to say that 3,400K is warmer than 6,000K, but that's the way it is. If it helps, think of a glowing red ember contrasted with a white-hot welder's torch, rather than fire and ice.

You can set white balance by type of illumination, and then fine-tune it in the D5200 using the Shooting menu's White Balance option, as described in Chapter 8. In most cases, however, the Nikon D5200 will do an acceptable job of calculating white balance for you, so Auto can be used as your choice most of the time. Use the preset values or set a custom white balance that matches the current shooting conditions when you need to. The only really problematic light sources are likely to be fluorescents.

Remember that if you shoot RAW, you can specify the white balance of your image when you import it into Photoshop, Photoshop Elements, or another image editor using Nikon Capture NX, Adobe Camera Raw, or your preferred RAW converter. While color-balancing filters that fit on the front of the lens exist, they are primarily useful for film cameras, because film's color balance can't be tweaked as extensively as that of a sensor.

## Daylight

Daylight is produced by the sun, and so is moonlight (which is just reflected sunlight). Daylight is present, of course, even when you can't see the sun. When sunlight is direct, it can be bright and harsh. If daylight is diffused by clouds, softened by bouncing off objects such as walls or your photo reflectors, or filtered by shade, it can be much dimmer and less contrasty.

Daylight's color temperature can vary quite widely. It is highest in temperature (most blue) at noon when the sun is directly overhead, because the light is traveling through a minimum amount of the filtering layer we call the atmosphere. The color temperature at high noon may be 6,000K. At other times of day, the sun is lower in the sky and the particles in the air provide a filtering effect that warms the illumination to about 5,500K for most of the day. Starting an hour before dusk and for an hour after sunrise, the warm appearance of the sunlight is even visible to our eyes when the color temperature may dip to 5,000–4,500K, as shown in Figure 12.5.

## Incandescent/Tungsten Light

The term *incandescent* or *tungsten illumination* is usually applied to the direct descendents of Thomas Edison's original electric lamp. Such lights consist of a glass bulb that contains a vacuum, or is filled with a halogen gas, and contains a tungsten filament that is heated by an electrical current, producing photons and heat. Tungsten-halogen lamps are a variation on the basic light bulb, using a more rugged (and longer-lasting) filament that can be heated to a higher temperature,

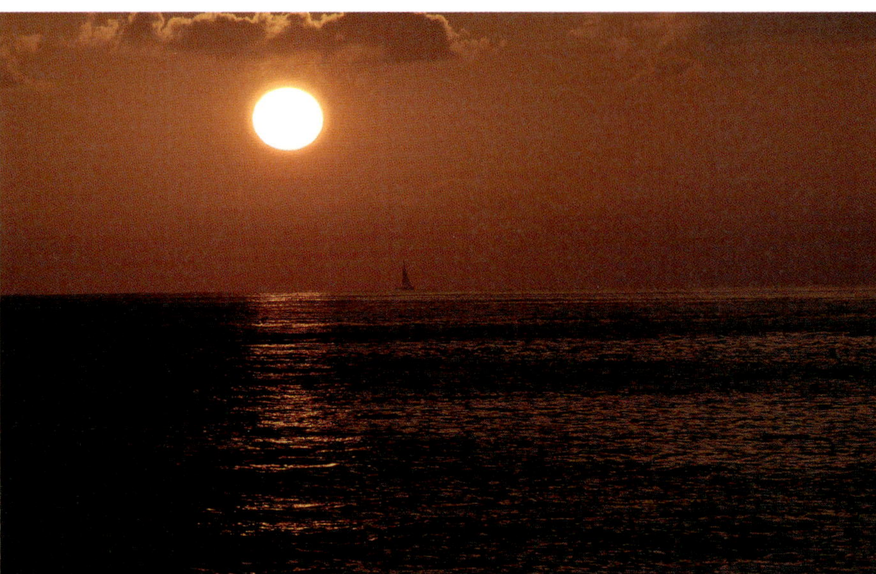

**Figure 12.5**
At dawn and dusk, the color temperature of daylight may dip as low as 4,500K, and at sunset can go even lower.

housed in a thicker glass or quartz envelope, and filled with iodine or bromine ("halogen") gases. The higher temperature allows tungsten-halogen (or quartz-halogen/quartz-iodine, depending on their construction) lamps to burn "hotter" and whiter. Although popular for automobile headlamps today, they've also been used for photographic illumination.

The other qualities of this type of lighting, such as contrast, are dependent on the distance of the lamp from the subject, type of reflectors used, and other factors that I'll explain later in this chapter.

## Fluorescent Light/Other Light Sources

Fluorescent light has some advantages in terms of illumination, but some disadvantages from a photographic standpoint. This type of lamp generates light through an electro-chemical reaction that emits most of its energy as visible light, rather than heat, which is why the bulbs don't get as hot. The type of light produced varies depending on the phosphor coatings and type of gas in the tube. So, the illumination fluorescent bulbs produce can vary widely in its characteristics.

That's not great news for photographers. Different types of lamps have different "color temperatures" that can't be precisely measured in degrees Kelvin, because the light isn't produced by heating. Worse, fluorescent lamps have a discontinuous spectrum of light that can have some colors missing entirely. A particular type of tube can lack certain shades of red or other colors (see Figure 12.6), which is why fluorescent lamps and other alternative technologies such as sodium-vapor illumination can produce ghastly looking human skin tones if the white balance isn't set correctly. Their spectra can lack the reddish tones we associate with healthy skin and emphasize the blues and greens popular in horror movies.

**Figure 12.6**
The uncorrected fluorescent lighting in the gym added a distinct greenish cast to this image when exposed with a daylight white balance setting.

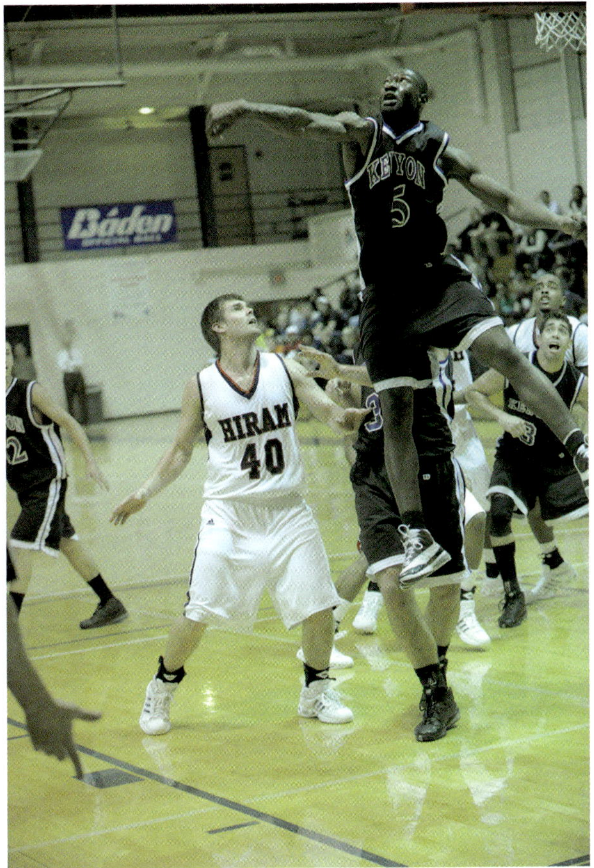


There *is* good news, however. There are special fluorescent and LED lamps compatible with the Spiderlite lighting fixtures sold through dealers affiliated with the F. J. Westcott Company (www.fjwestcott.com), designed especially for photography, with the color balance and other properties required. They can be used for direct light, placed in soft boxes (described later), and used in other ways.

## Adjusting White Balance

I showed you how to adjust white balance in Chapter 4, using the D5200's built-in presets, white balance shift capabilities, and white balance bracketing (there's more on bracketing in Chapter 4, too).

In most cases, however, the D5200 will do a good job of calculating white balance for you, so Auto can be used as your choice most of the time. Use the preset values or set a custom white balance that matches the current shooting conditions when you need to. The only really problematic light sources are likely to be fluorescents. Vendors, such as GE and Sylvania, may actually provide a figure known as the *color rendering index* (or CRI), which is a measure of how accurately a particular light source represents standard colors, using a scale of 0 (some sodium-vapor lamps) to 100 (daylight and most incandescent lamps). Daylight fluorescents and deluxe cool white fluorescents might have a CRI of about 79 to 95, which is perfectly acceptable for most photographic applications. Warm white fluorescents might have a CRI of 55. White deluxe mercury vapor lights are less suitable with a CRI of 45, while low-pressure sodium lamps can vary from CRI 0–18.

Remember that if you shoot RAW, you can specify the white balance of your image when you import it into Photoshop, Photoshop Elements, or another image editor using your preferred RAW converter. While color-balancing filters that fit on the front of the lens exist, they are primarily useful for film cameras, because film's color balance can't be tweaked as extensively as that of a sensor.

# Electronic Flash Basics

Until you delve into the situation deeply enough, it might appear that serious photographers have a love/hate relationship with electronic flash. You'll often hear that flash photography is less natural looking, and that the built-in flash in most cameras should never be used as the primary source of illumination because it provides a harsh, garish look. Indeed, most "pro" cameras like the Nikon D4 don't have a built-in flash at all. Available ("continuous") lighting is praised, and built-in flash photography seems to be roundly denounced.

In truth, however, the bias is against *bad* flash photography. Indeed, flash has become the studio light source of choice for pro photographers, because it's more intense (and its intensity can be varied to order by the photographer), freezes action, frees you from using a tripod (unless you want to use one to lock down a composition), and has a snappy, consistent light quality that matches daylight. (While color balance changes as the flash duration shortens, some Nikon flash units can communicate to the camera the exact white balance provided for that shot.) And even pros will cede that the built-in flash of the Nikon D5200 has some important uses as an adjunct to existing light, particularly to illuminate dark shadows using a technique called *fill flash*.

But electronic flash isn't as inherently easy to use as continuous lighting. As I noted earlier, electronic flash units are more expensive, don't show you exactly what the lighting effect will be (unless you use a second source called a *modeling light* for a preview), and the exposure of electronic flash units is more difficult to calculate accurately.

# How Electronic Flash Works

The bursts of light we call electronic flash are produced by a flash of photons generated by an electrical charge that is accumulated in a component called a *capacitor* and then directed through a glass tube containing xenon gas, which absorbs the energy and emits the brief flash. For the pop-up flash built into the D5200, the full burst of light lasts about 1/1,000th second and provides enough illumination to shoot a subject 10 feet away at f/4 using the ISO 100 setting. In a more typical situation, you'd use ISO 200, f/5.6 to f/8 and photograph something 8 to 10 feet away. As you can see, the built-in flash is somewhat limited in range; you'll see why external flash units are often a good idea later in this chapter.

An electronic flash (whether built in or connected to the D5200 through a cable plugged into a hot shoe adapter) is triggered at the instant of exposure, during a period when the sensor is fully exposed by the shutter. As I mentioned earlier in this book, the D5200 has a vertically traveling shutter that consists of two curtains. The first curtain opens and moves to the opposite side of the frame, at which point the shutter is completely open. The flash can be triggered at this point (so-called *first-curtain sync*), making the flash exposure. Then, after a delay that can vary from 30 seconds to 1/200th second (with the D5200; other cameras may sync at a faster or slower speed), a second curtain begins moving across the sensor plane, covering up the sensor again. If the flash is triggered just before the second curtain starts to close, then *rear-curtain sync* (also called *second-curtain sync*) is used. In both cases, though, a shutter speed of 1/200th second is the maximum that can be used to take a photo.

Figure 12.7 illustrates how this works, with a fanciful illustration of a generic shutter (your D5200's shutter does *not* look like this, and some vertically traveling shutters move bottom to top rather than the top-to-bottom motion shown). Both curtains are tightly closed at upper left. At upper right, the first curtain begins to move downward, starting to expose a narrow slit that reveals the sensor behind the shutter. At lower left, the first curtain moves downward farther until, as you can see at lower right in the figure, the sensor is fully exposed.

When first-curtain sync is used, the flash is triggered at the instant that the sensor is completely exposed. The shutter then remains open for an additional length of time (from 30 seconds to 1/200th second), and the second curtain begins to move downward, covering the sensor once more. When second-curtain sync is activated, the flash is triggered *after* the main exposure is over, just before the second curtain begins to move downward.

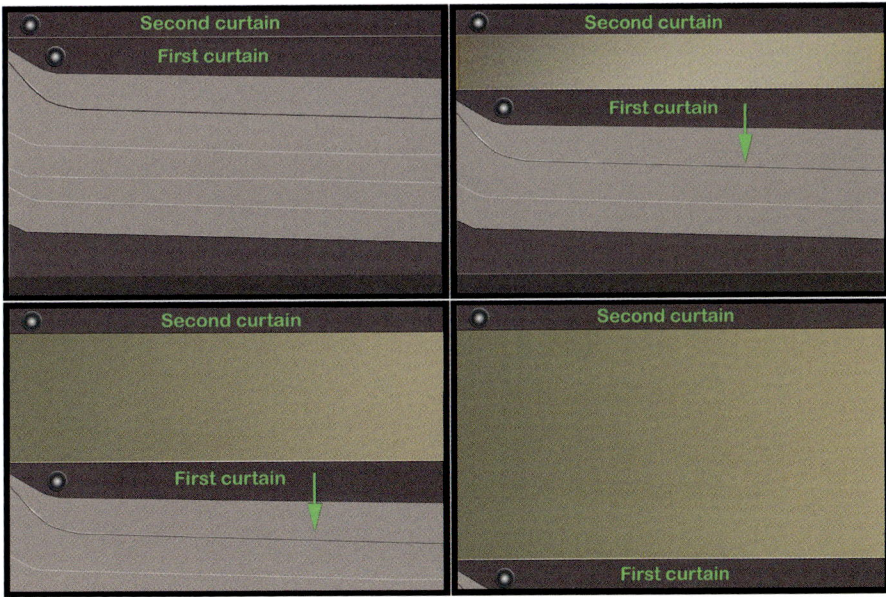


**Figure 12.7**
A focal plane shutter has two curtains, the lower, or front curtain, and an upper, second curtain.

## Ghost Images

The difference between triggering the flash when the shutter just opens, or just when it begins to close might not seem like much. But whether you use first-curtain sync (the default setting) or second-curtain sync (an optional setting) can make a significant difference to your photograph *if the ambient light in your scene also contributes to the image.*

At faster shutter speeds, particularly 1/200th second, there isn't much time for the ambient light to register, unless it is very bright. It's likely that the electronic flash will provide almost all the illumination, so first-curtain sync or second-curtain sync isn't very important. However, at slower shutter speeds, or with very bright ambient light levels, there is a significant difference, particularly if your subject is moving, or the camera isn't steady.

In any of those situations, the ambient light will register as a second image accompanying the flash exposure, and if there is movement (camera or subject), that additional image will not be in the same place as the flash exposure. It will show as a ghost image and, if the movement is significant enough, as a blurred ghost image trailing in front of or behind your subject in the direction of the movement.

As I noted, when you're using first-curtain sync, the flash's main burst goes off the instant the shutter opens fully (a pre-flash used to measure exposure in auto flash modes fires *before* the shutter opens). This produces an image of the subject on the sensor. Then, the shutter remains open for an additional period (30 seconds to 1/200th second, as I said). If your subject is moving, say, toward the right side of the frame, the ghost image produced by the ambient light will produce a blur on the right side of the original subject image, making it look as if your sharp (flash-produced) image is chasing the ghost. For those of us who grew up with lightning-fast superheroes who always left a ghost trail *behind them*, that looks unnatural (see Figure 12.8).

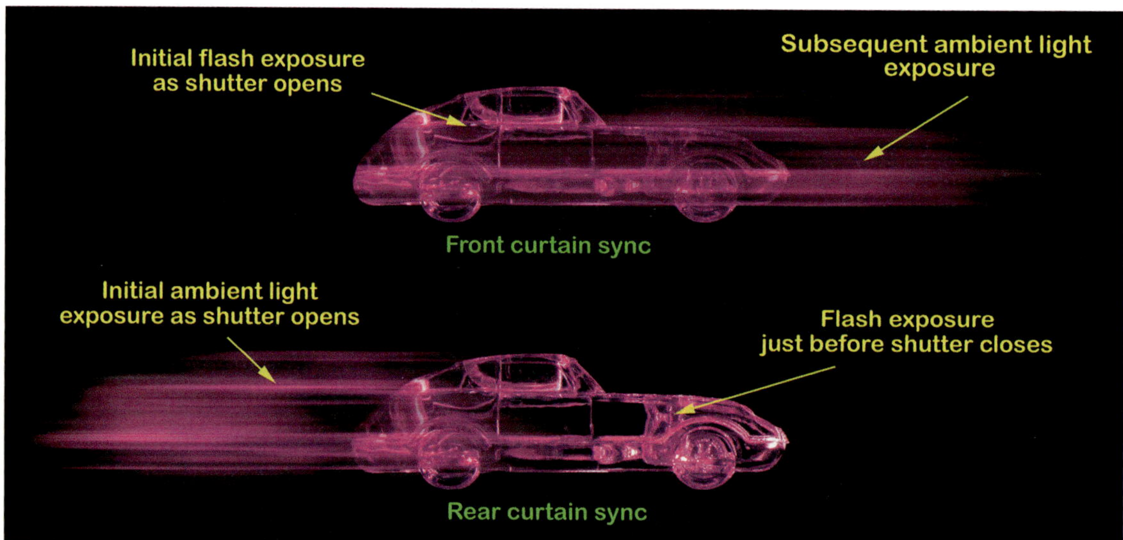


**Figure 12.8** First-curtain sync produces an image that trails in front of the flash exposure (top), while second-curtain sync creates a more "natural looking" trail behind the flash image.

So, Nikon uses second-curtain sync to remedy the situation. In that mode, the shutter opens, as before. The shutter remains open for its designated duration, and the ghost image forms. If your subject moves from the left side of the frame to the right side, the ghost will move from left to right, too. *Then*, about 1.5 milliseconds before the second shutter curtain closes, the flash is triggered, producing a nice, sharp flash image *ahead* of the ghost image. Voilà! We have monsieur *Speed Racer* outdriving his own trailing image.

## Avoiding Sync Speed Problems

Using a shutter speed faster than 1/200th second can cause problems. Triggering the electronic flash only when the shutter is completely open makes a lot of sense if you think about what's going on. To obtain shutter speeds faster than 1/200th second, the D5200 exposes only part of the sensor at one time, by starting the second curtain on its journey before the first curtain has completely opened, as shown in Figure 12.9. That effectively provides a briefer exposure as a slit that's narrower than the full height of the sensor passes over the surface of the sensor. If the flash were to fire during the time when the first and second curtains partially obscured the sensor, only the slit that was actually open would be exposed.

You'd end up with only a narrow band, representing the portion of the sensor that was exposed when the picture is taken. For shutter speeds *faster* than 1/200th second, the second curtain begins moving *before* the first curtain reaches the bottom of the frame. As a result, a moving slit, the distance between the first and second curtains, exposes one portion of the sensor at a time as it moves from the bottom to the top. Figure 12.9 shows three views of our typical (but imaginary) focal plane shutter. At left is pictured the closed shutter; in the middle version you can see the first curtain has moved up about 1/4 of the distance from the top; and in the right-hand version, the second curtain has started to "chase" the first curtain across the frame toward the bottom.

If the flash is triggered while this slit is moving, only the exposed portion of the sensor will receive any illumination. You end up with a photo like the one shown in Figure 12.10. Note that a band across the bottom of the image is black. That's a shadow of the second shutter curtain, which had started to move when the flash was triggered. Sharp-eyed readers will wonder why the black band is at the *bottom* of the frame rather than at the top, where the second curtain begins its journey. The answer is simple: your lens flips the image upside down and forms it on the sensor in a reversed position. You never notice that, because the camera is smart enough to show you the pixels that

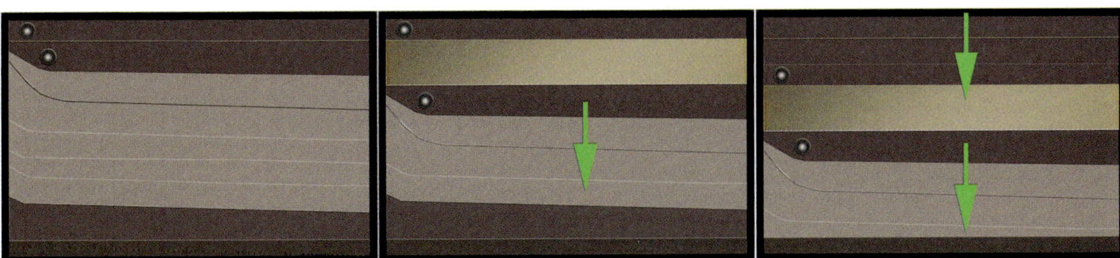

**Figure 12.9** A closed shutter (left); partially open shutter as the first curtain begins to move downward (middle); only part of the sensor is exposed as the slit moves (right).

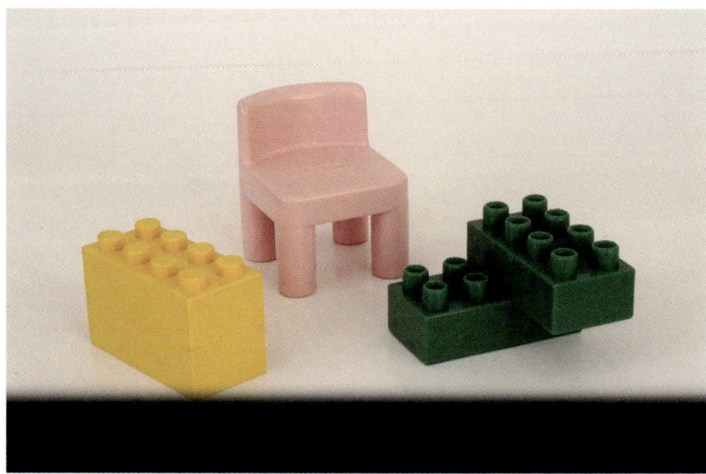

**Figure 12.10**
If a shutter speed faster than 1/200th second is used, you can end up photographing only a portion of the image.

make up your photo in their proper orientation during picture review. But this image flip is why, if your sensor gets dirty and you detect a spot of dust in the upper half of a test photo, if cleaning manually, you need to look for the speck in the *bottom* half of the sensor.

I generally end up with sync speed problems only when shooting in the studio, using studio flash units rather than my D5200's built-in flash or a Nikon dedicated Speedlight. That's because if you're using either type of "smart" flash, the camera knows that a strobe is attached, and remedies any unintentional goof in shutter speed settings. If you happen to set the D5200's shutter to a faster speed in S or M mode, the camera will automatically adjust the shutter speed down to 1/200th second. In A, P, or any of the scene modes, where the D5200 selects the shutter speed, it will never choose a shutter speed higher than 1/200th second when using flash. In P mode, shutter speed is automatically set between 1/60th to 1/200th second when using flash. But when using a non-dedicated flash, such as a studio unit plugged into the D5200's hot shoe connector, the camera has no way of knowing that a flash is connected, so shutter speeds faster than 1/200th second can be set inadvertently.

## Determining Exposure

Calculating the proper exposure for an electronic flash photograph is a bit more complicated than determining the settings for continuous light. The right exposure isn't simply a function of how far away your subject is (which the D5200 can figure out based on the autofocus distance that's locked in just prior to taking the picture). Various objects reflect more or less light at the same distance so, obviously, the camera needs to measure the amount of light reflected back and through the lens. Yet, as the flash itself isn't available for measuring until it's triggered, the D5200 has nothing to measure.

The solution is to fire the flash twice. The initial shot is a *monitor pre-flash* that can be analyzed, then followed virtually instantaneously by a main flash (to the eye the bursts appear to be a single flash) that's given exactly the calculated intensity needed to provide a correct exposure. As a result, the primary flash may be longer in duration for distant objects and shorter in duration for closer subjects, depending on the required intensity for exposure. This through-the-lens evaluative flash exposure system is called i-TTL (intelligent Through-The-Lens), and it operates whenever the pop-up internal flash is used, or you have attached a Nikon dedicated flash unit to the D5200.

## Guide Numbers

Guide numbers, usually abbreviated GN, are a way of specifying the power of an electronic flash in a way that can be used to determine the right f/stop to use at a particular shooting distance and ISO setting. In fact, before automatic flash units became prevalent, the GN was actually used to do just that. A GN is usually given as a pair of numbers for both feet and meters that represent the range at ISO 100. For example, the Nikon D5200's built-in flash has a GN in i-TTL mode of 12/39 (meters/feet) at ISO 100. In Manual mode, the true guide number is a fraction higher: 13/43 meters/feet. To calculate the right exposure at that ISO setting, you'd divide the guide number by the distance to arrive at the appropriate f/stop.

Using the D5200's built-in flash as an example, at ISO 100 with its GN of 43 in Manual mode, if you wanted to shoot a subject at a distance of 10 feet, you'd use f/4.3 (43 divided by 10), or, in practice, f/4.0. At 5 feet, an f/stop of f/8 would be used. Some quick mental calculations with the GN will give you any particular electronic flash's range. You can easily see that the built-in flash would begin to peter out at about 13 feet if you stuck to the lowest ISO of 100, because you'd need an aperture of f/2.8. Of course, in the real world you'd probably bump the sensitivity up to a setting of ISO 800 so you could use a more practical f/8 at 13 feet, and the flash would be effective all the way out to 20 feet or more at wider f/stops.

Today, guide numbers are most useful for comparing the power of various flash units, rather than actually calculating what exposure to use. You don't need to be a math genius to see that an electronic flash with a GN in feet of, say, 111.5 at ISO 100 (like the SB-910) would be *a lot* more powerful than your built-in flash. At ISO 100, you could use f/5.6 to shoot as far as 20 feet.

## Flash Control

The Nikon D5200's built-in flash has two modes, TTL and Manual. It does not have a repeating flash option, nor can it be used to trigger other Nikon flashes in wireless Commander mode, unlike its siblings the Nikon D90 and above. You can choose between TTL and Manual modes using Custom Setting e1, Flash Control for Built-In Flash, as first described in Chapter 9. Other Nikon external flash units, such as the Nikon SB-700 or SB-910, have additional exposure modes, which I'll discuss later in this chapter. Your Flash Control options are as follows:

- **TTL.** When the built-in flash is triggered, the D5200 first fires a pre-flash and measures the light reflected back and through the lens to calculate the proper exposure when the full flash is emitted a fraction of a second later.

- **Manual.** You can set the level of the built-in flash from full power to 1/32 power. A flash icon blinks in the viewfinder and on the shooting information display when you're using Manual mode, and the built-in flash has been flipped up.

# Flash Metering Mode

You don't select the way your flash meters the exposure directly; the two modes, i-TTL Balanced Fill-in Flash and Standard i-TTL Fill-Flash, are determined by the camera metering mode—Matrix, Center-weighted, or Spot—that you select. Indeed, the built-in flash in the Nikon D5200, as well as external flash units attached to the camera, use the same three metering modes that are available for continuous light sources: Matrix, Center-weighted, and Spot. So, you can choose the flash's metering mode based on the same subject factors as those explained in Chapter 4 (for example, use Spot metering to measure exposure from an isolated subject within the frame). Choice of a metering mode determines how the flash reacts to balance the existing light with the light from the electronic unit:

- **i-TTL balanced fill-flash.** This flash mode is used automatically when you choose Matrix or Center-weighted exposure metering. The Nikon D5200 measures the available light and then adjusts the flash output to produce a natural balance between main subject and background. This setting is useful for most photographic situations.
- **Standard i-TTL fill-flash.** This mode is activated when you use Spot metering or choose the standard mode with an external flash unit's controls. The flash output is adjusted only for the main subject of your photograph, and the brightness of the background is not factored in. Use this mode when you want to emphasize the main subject at the expense of proper exposure for the background.

# Choosing a Flash Sync Mode

The Nikon D5200 has five flash sync modes that determine when and how the flash is fired (as I'll explain shortly). They are selected from the information edit screen, or by holding down the Flash button on the front of the camera lens housing while rotating the command dial. In both cases, the mode chosen appears in the information edit screen as the selection is made.

Not all sync modes are available with all exposure modes. Depending on whether you're using scene modes, or Program, Aperture-priority, Shutter-priority, or Manual exposure modes, one or more of the following sync modes may not be available. I'm going to list the sync options available for each exposure mode separately, although that produces a little duplication among the options that are available with several exposure modes. However, this approach should reduce the confusion over which sync method is available with which exposure mode.

In Program and Aperture-priority modes you can select these flash modes:

- **Front-curtain sync/fill flash.** In this mode, represented by a lightning bolt symbol, the flash fires as soon as the front curtain opens completely. The shutter then remains open for the duration of the exposure, until the rear curtain closes. If the subject is moving and ambient light levels are high enough, the movement will cause a secondary "ghost" exposure that appears to be a stream of light advancing ahead of the flash exposure of the same subject. You'll find more on "ghost" exposures next.

- **Rear-curtain sync.** With this setting, the front curtain opens completely and remains open for the duration of the exposure. Then, the flash is fired and the rear curtain closes. If the subject is moving and ambient light levels are high enough, the movement will cause a secondary "ghost" exposure that appears to stream *behind* the flash exposure. In Program and Aperture-priority modes, the D5200 will combine rear-curtain sync with slow shutter speeds (just like slow sync, discussed below) to balance ambient light with flash illumination. (It's best to use a tripod to avoid blur at these slow shutter speeds.)

- **Red-eye reduction.** In this mode, there is a one-second lag after pressing the shutter release before the picture is actually taken, during which the D5200's red-eye reduction lamp lights, causing the subject's pupils to contract (assuming they are looking at the camera), and thus reducing potential red-eye effects. Don't use with moving subjects or when you can't abide the delay.

- **Slow sync.** This setting allows the D5200 in Program and Aperture-priority modes to use shutter speeds as slow as 30 seconds with the flash to help balance a background illuminated with ambient light with your main subject, which will be lit by the electronic flash. You'll want to use a tripod at slower shutter speeds, of course. As shown in Figure 12.11, it's common that the ambient light will be much warmer than the electronic flash's "daylight" balance, so, if you want the two sources to match, you may want to use a warming filter on the flash. That can be done with a gel if you're using an external flash like the SB-900, or by taping an appropriate warm filter over the D5200's built-in flash. (That's not a convenient approach, and many find the warm/cool mismatch not objectionable and don't bother with filtration.)

- **Red-eye reduction with slow sync.** This mode combines slow sync with the D5200's red-eye reduction behavior when using Program or Aperture-priority modes.

**Figure 12.11**
I deliberately used flash and slow sync with a scene otherwise illuminated by tungsten light to create this unconventional mixed-lighting image.

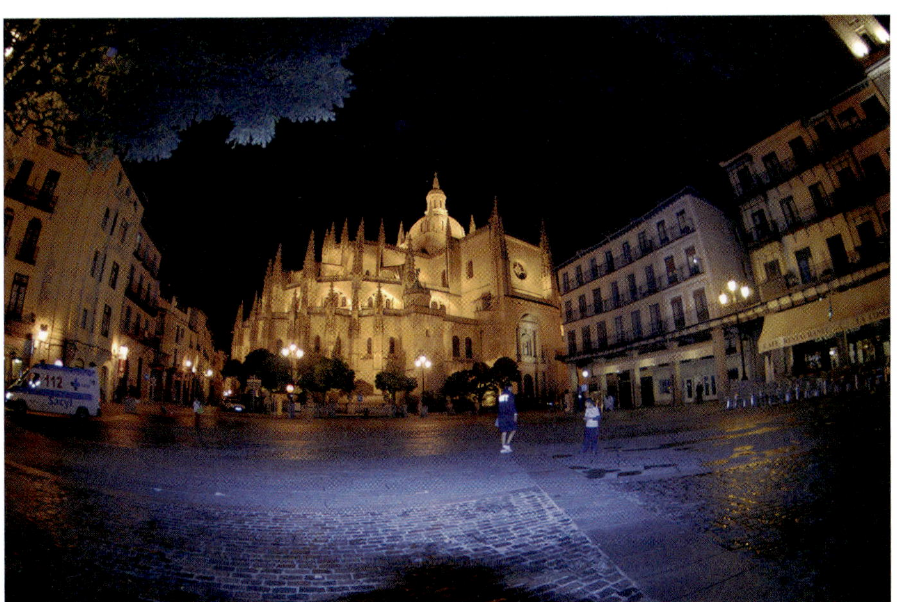

In Shutter-priority and Manual exposure modes, you can select the following three flash synchronization settings:

- **Front-curtain sync/fill flash.** This setting should be your default setting. This mode is also available in Program and Aperture-priority mode, as described above, and, with high ambient light levels, can produce ghost images, discussed below.

- **Red-eye reduction.** This mode, with its one-second lag and red-eye lamp flash, is described above.

- **Rear-curtain sync.** As noted previously, in this sync mode, the front curtain opens completely and remains open for the duration of the exposure. Then, the flash is fired and the rear curtain closes. If the subject is moving and ambient light levels are high enough, the movement will cause that "ghost" exposure that appears to be trailing the flash exposure.

In Auto, Portrait, Child, Close-Up, Party, and Pet Scene modes, the following flash sync options are available:

- **Auto.** This setting is the same as front-curtain sync, but the flash pops up automatically in dim lighting conditions.

- **Red-eye reduction auto.** In this mode, there is a one-second lag after pressing the shutter release before the picture is actually taken, during which the D5200's red-eye reduction lamp lights, causing the subject's pupils to contract (assuming they are looking at the camera), and thus reducing potential red-eye effects. Don't use with moving subjects or when you can't abide the delay.

- **Flash Off.** This is not really a sync setting, although it is available from the same selection screen. It disables the flash for those situations in which you absolutely do not want it to pop up and fire.

In Night Portrait mode, only slow synchronization flash and flash off modes are available:

- **Auto slow sync.** This setting allows the D5200 to select shutter speeds as slow as 30 seconds with the flash to help balance a background illuminated with ambient light with your main subject, which will be lit by the electronic flash. Best for shooting pictures at night when the subjects in the foreground are important, and you want to avoid a pitch-black background. I recommend using a tripod in this mode.

- **Auto red-eye reduction with slow sync.** Another mode that calls for a tripod, this sync setting mode combines slow sync with the D5200's red-eye reduction pre-flash. This is the one to use when your subjects are people who will be facing the camera.

- **Flash off.** Disables the flash in museums, concerts, religious ceremonies, and other situations in which you absolutely do not want it to pop up and fire.

When using the Food scene mode, you can't change sync modes; only Fill Flash mode is available. Other scene and Effects modes not mentioned, such as Silhouette, Miniature Effect, etc., disable the flash, and so have no sync mode options.

# A Typical Electronic Flash Sequence

Here's what happens when you take a photo using electronic flash, either the unit built into the Nikon D5200 or an external flash like the Nikon SB-900:

1. **Sync mode.** Choose the flash sync mode by holding down the Flash button and rotating the command dial to choose the sync mode, as described previously.

2. **Metering method.** Choose the metering method you want, from Matrix, Center-weighted, or Spot metering, using the information edit screen.

3. **Activate flash.** Press the flash pop-up button to flip up the built-in flash, or mount (or connect with a cable) an external flash and turn it on. A ready light appears in the viewfinder or on the back of the flash when the unit is ready to take a picture.

4. **Check exposure.** Select a shutter speed when using Manual, Program, or Shutter-priority modes; select an aperture when using Aperture-priority and Manual exposure modes. The D5200 will set both shutter speed and aperture if you're using a scene mode.

5. **Take photo.** Press the shutter release down all the way.

6. **D5200 receives distance data.** A D- or G-series lens now supplies focus distance to the D5200.

7. **Pre-flash emitted.** The internal flash, if used, or external flash sends out one pre-flash burst used to determine exposure.

8. **Exposure calculated.** The pre-flash bounces back and is measured by the 420-pixel RGB sensor in the viewfinder. It measures brightness and contrast of the image to calculate exposure. If you're using Matrix metering, the D5200 evaluates the scene to determine whether the subject may be backlit (for fill flash), or a subject that requires extra ambient light exposure to balance the scene with the flash exposure, or classifies the scene in some other way. The camera to subject information as well as the degree of sharp focus of the subject matter is used to locate the subject within the frame. If you've selected Spot metering, only standard i-TTL (without balanced fill-flash) is used.

9. **Mirror up.** The mirror flips up. At this point exposure and focus are locked in.

10. **Flash fired.** At the correct triggering moment (depending on whether front or rear sync is used), the camera sends a signal to one or more flashes to start flash discharge. The flash is quenched as soon as the correct exposure has been achieved.

11. **Shutter closes.** The shutter closes and mirror flips down. You're ready to take another picture.

12. **Exposure confirmed.** Ordinarily, the full charge in the flash may not be required. If the flash indicator in the viewfinder blinks for about three seconds after the exposure, that means that the entire flash charge was required, and it *could* mean that the full charge wasn't enough for a proper exposure. Be sure to review your image on the LCD to make sure it's not underexposed, and, if it is, make adjustments (such as increasing the ISO setting of the D5200) to remedy the situation.

# Working with Nikon Flash Units

If you want to work with dedicated Nikon flash units, at this time you have five choices: the D5200's built-in flash, the Nikon SB-900/910, SB-700, SB-400 on-camera flash units, and the SB-R200/R1 wireless remote flash systems. These share certain features, which I'll discuss while pointing out differences among them. Nikon may introduce additional flash units during the life of this book, but the current batch and the Nikon Creative Lighting System ushered in with them were significant steps forward.

## Nikon D5200 Built-in Flash

In automatic mode, the built-in flash has a guide number of 12/39 (meters/feet) at ISO 100, and must be activated by manually flipping it up when not using one of the scene modes that feature automatic pop-up. This flash is powerful enough to provide primary direct flash illumination when required, but can't be angled up for diffuse bounce flash off the ceiling. It's useful for balanced fill flash, but cannot operate in Commander mode, which allows the built-in flash to trigger one or more off-camera flash units. You can use Manual flash mode and the Built-in Flash settings in the Shooting menu to dial down the intensity of the built-in flash to 1/32 power.

Changing settings is easy:

- **Elevate the built-in flash.** Press the Flash button on the front left side of the viewfinder housing to pop up the flash.

- **Choose sync mode.** If you want to change the flash sync mode, after the flash is elevated, hold down the Flash button and rotate the command dial. The sync mode you've selected will appear on the shooting information screen.

- **Apply flash exposure compensation.** If your pictures in a session are consistently overexposed or underexposed, you can dial in flash compensation by holding down the compensation button (just southeast of the shutter release) and the Flash button at the same time, and rotating the main dial. The amount of compensation from +1.0 to −3.0EV is displayed on the shooting information screen.

- **Use the information edit screen.** You can also choose sync mode and flash compensation using the information edit screen. Press the Info button twice, navigate to the function you want to adjust, press OK, and use the up/down buttons to enter the value.

- **Set color temperature.** The D5200's Auto color temperature setting will adjust for the built-in flash nicely. But there might be times when you want to set the color temperature manually. For example, you might be shooting under incandescent illumination and have put an orange gel over your internal or external flash so both light sources match. You'd want to set the color temperature manually to incandescent. Or, you might want to use an oddball setting as a special effect. Use the information edit screen to adjust the color temperature to Flash, Incandescent, or any of the other choices, as described in Chapter 2.

Because the built-in flash draws its power from the D5200's battery, extensive use will reduce the power available to take pictures. For that reason alone, use of an external flash unit can be a good idea when you plan to take a lot of flash pictures.

# Nikon Add-On Flash Units

Nikon offers a broad range of accessory electronic Speedlight flash units that will work with the D5200. You can mount a Speedlight in the flash accessory shoe, or use it off-camera with a dedicated cord like the SC-29 TTL Off-Camera Shoe Cord that plugs into the flash shoe. The other end of the cable is equipped with its own flash shoe where you can plug in your external flash unit. When that cable connects the external flash unit to the camera, full communications between the two is maintained and all the flash features available with on-camera flash continue to function. Here is a quick summary of the available units:

## Nikon SB-400

This entry-level Speedlight (see Figure 12.12) is the smallest and most basic of the series. The SB-400 has a limited, easy-to-use feature set suited for point-and-shoot photography and some slightly more advanced techniques. Do note however that it does not support wireless off-camera flash. The SB-400 has a moderate guide number of 21/69 at ISO 100 when the zooming head (which can be set to match the coverage angle of the lens) is at the 18mm position. It tilts up to 90 degrees, allowing you to bounce the light off of a ceiling, but it cannot be rotated to the side.

## Nikon SB-700

This slightly more expensive unit has a guide number of 28/92 (meters/feet) at ISO 100 when set to the 35mm zoom position. The SB-700 offers many of the features of its big brother, the SB-910, including the zooming flash head, a thermal protection feature that slows recycling when the flash gets hot, and compatibility with filters (included) for fluorescent and incandescent color temperature balancing. Other accessories included with this Speedlight include a stand, a diffuser dome, and a soft case. However, it does not support non-TTL Autoflash or Repeating flash.

You can tilt the flash head up and rotate it to the side for bouncing flash from a ceiling or a side wall, for example. As with the other large Speedlights, the flash head zooms automatically to match the angle of view of the lens at any focal length and is equipped with a powerful focus assist lamp to aid autofocus in dim lighting. It has a Commander mode to allow it to trigger other Nikon flash units wirelessly. Like any flash tube that sits high above the axis of the lens, the SB-700 minimizes the risk of red-eye caused by reflections from the blood vessels in the eye. (See Figure 12.13.)

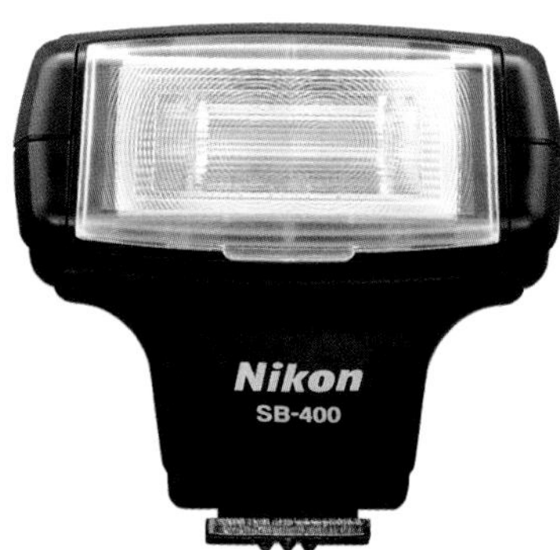

**Figure 12.12** The Nikon SB-400 is an entry-level flash that supports the basic flash features of the camera.

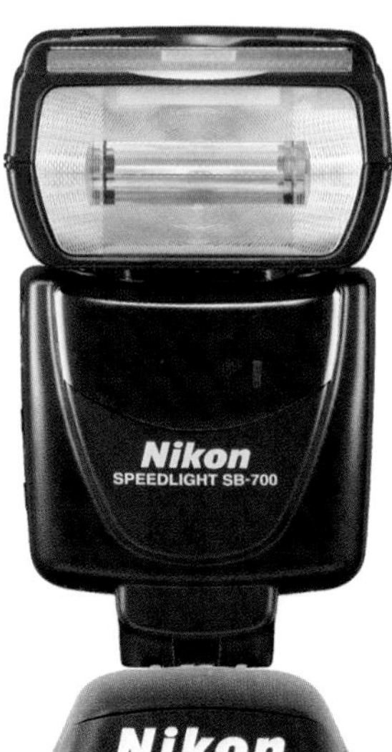

**Figure 12.13** The Nikon SB-700 is an affordable full-featured flash.

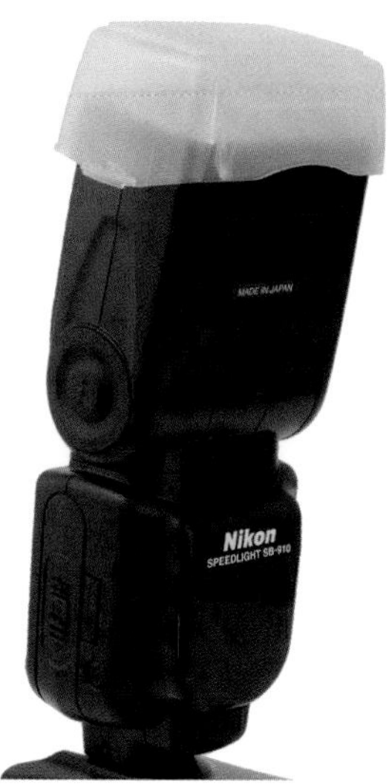

**Figure 12.14** The Nikon SB-910 is currently the flagship of the Nikon electronic flash line up.

# Nikon SB-900/SB-910

The Nikon SB-900 was the flagship of the Speedlight line and may still be available from some retailers, but it has been replaced by the SB-910 (see Figure 12.14). The two models are identical in terms of functionality, providing everything the SB-700 does, and also a few extra features. Those include repeating flash and non-TTL Autoflash; also, a diffuser dome accessory is included in the kit. The difference between the SB-900 and SB-910 is that the latter has thermal protection technology to minimize the risk of overheating when you shoot a lot of flash photos in a series. The guide number is 34/111.5 (meters/feet) at ISO 100 when the zooming flash head is set to the 35mm position.

# Nikon SB-R200

This is a specialized wireless-only flash that's especially useful for close-up photography, and is often purchased in pairs for use with the Nikon R1 and R1C1 Wireless Close-Up Speedlight systems. With a Nikon dSLR camera, you can attach the SB-R200 to the lens, but that's not possible with the D5200. (There's no method for attaching this flash unit to a camera's accessory shoe.) Hold it in one hand or attach it to the optional (inexpensive) Nikon Speedlight Stand AS-20.

Power output is low at 10/33 (meters/feet) at ISO 100 as you might expect for a unit used to photograph subjects that are often inches from the camera. The coverage angle is fixed at 78 degrees horizontal and 60 degrees vertical because the flash head cannot zoom, but the head can be tilted up or tilted downward. When used with the D5200, the SB-R200 supports the high tech i-TTL flash metering and Manual flash mode.

# Flash Techniques

This next section will discuss using specific features of the Nikon D5200's built-in flash, as well as those of the Nikon dedicated external flash units. It's not possible to discuss every feature and setting of the external flash units in this chapter (entire books have been written to do that), so I'll simply provide an overview here.

## Using the Zoom Head

Some external flash zoom heads can adjust themselves automatically to match lens focal lengths in use reported by the D5200 to the flash unit, or you can adjust the zoom head position manually. With flash units prior to the SB-900, automatic zoom adjustment wasted some of your flash's power, because the flash unit assumed that the focal length reported comes from a full-frame camera. Because of the 1.5X crop factor, the flash coverage when the flash is set to a particular focal length was wider than is required by the D5200's cropped image. The SB-900, on the other hand, automatically determines whether your camera is an FX-format, full-frame model, or is a DX "cropped sensor" model like the Nikon D5200, and adjusts coverage angle to suit.

You can manually adjust the zoom position yourself, if you want the flash coverage to correspond to something other than the focal length in use. Just press the Zoom button on the SB-910, and turn the selector dial clockwise to increase the zoom value, or counterclockwise to decrease the zoom value. You can also adjust the zoom position by repeatedly pressing the Zoom button.

## Flash Modes

The TTL automatic flash modes available for the SB-900/910 are as follows:

- **AA.** Auto Aperture flash. The SB-900 uses a built-in light sensor to measure the amount of flash illumination reflected back from the subject, and adjusts the output to produce an appropriate exposure based on the ISO, aperture, focal length, and flash compensation values set on the D5200. This setting on the flash can be used with the D5200 in Program or Aperture-priority modes.

- **A.** Non-TTL auto flash. The SB-900's sensor measures the flash illumination reflected back from the subject, and adjusts the output to provide an appropriate exposure. This setting on the flash can be used when the D5200 is set to Aperture-priority or Manual modes. You can use this setting to manually "bracket" exposures, as adjusting the aperture value of the lens will produce more or less exposure.

- **GN.** Distance priority manual. You enter a distance value, and the SB-900 adjusts light output based on distance, ISO, and aperture to produce the right exposure in either Aperture-priority or Manual exposure modes. Press the Mode button on the flash until the GN indicator appears, then press the SEL button to highlight the distance display, using the plus and minus buttons to enter the distance value you want (from 1 to 65.6 feet, or 0.3 to 20 meters). The SB-800 will indicate a recommended aperture, which you then set on the lens mounted on the D5200.

- **M.** Manual flash. The flash fires at a fixed output level. Press the Mode button until M appears on the SB-900's LCD panel. Press the SEL button and the plus or minus buttons to increase or decrease the output value of the flash. Use the table in the flash manual to determine a suggested aperture setting for a given distance. Then, set that aperture on the D5200 in either Aperture-priority or Manual exposure modes.

- **RPT.** Repeating flash. The flash fires repeatedly to produce a multiple flash strobing effect. To use this mode, set the D5200's exposure mode to Manual. Then set up the number of repeating flashes per frame, frequency, and flash output level on the SB-900/SB-910.

## BURN OUT

When using repeating flash with the SB-900, or *any* large number of consecutive flashes in any mode (more than about 15 shots at full power), allow the flash to cool off (Nikon recommends a 10-minute time out) to avoid overheating the flash. The SB-900 will signal you with a warning chime that rings twice when it's time for a cooling-off period. The flash will actually disable itself, if necessary, to prevent damage. The newer SB-910 has circuitry that allows longer usage cycles.

# Working with Wireless Commander Mode

The D5200's built-in flash cannot be set to Commander mode and used to control other compatible flash units. However, if you mount one of several compatible external dedicated flash units, such as the Nikon SB-700 or SB-910, it can serve as a flash "Commander" to communicate with and trigger other flash units. Nikon offers a unit called the SU-800, which is a commander unit that has no built-in visible flash, and which controls other units using infrared signals.

The SU-800 has several advantages. It's useful for cameras like the D5200, which lacks a Commander mode, and several "pro" cameras, like the D4, D3x, D3, and D2xs, which have no built-in flash to function in Commander mode. The real advantage the SU-800 has is its "reach." Because it uses IR illumination rather than visible light to communicate with remote flashes, the infrared burst can be much stronger, doubling its effective control range to 66 feet.

Once you have set the SB-910 or other flash as the Master/Commander, you can specify a shooting mode, either Manual with a power output setting you determine from 1/1 to 1/128, or for TTL automatic exposure. When using TTL, you can dial in from −1.0 to +3.0 flash exposure compensation for the master flash. You can also specify a channel (1, 2, 3, or 4) that all flashes will use to communicate among themselves. (If other Nikon photographers are present, choosing a different channel prevents your flash from triggering their remotes, and vice versa.)

Each remote flash unit can also be set to one of three groups (A, B, or C), so you can set the exposure compensation and exposure mode of each group separately. For example, one or more flashes in one group can be reduced in output compared to the flashes in the other group, to produce a particular lighting ratio of effect. You'll find instructions for setting exposure mode, channel, and compensation next (for the built-in flash).

# Connecting External Flash

You have three basic choices for linking an external flash unit to your Nikon D5200. They are as follows:

- **Mount on the accessory shoe.** Sliding a compatible flash unit into the Nikon D5200's accessory shoe provides a direct connection. With a Nikon dedicated flash, all functions of the flash are supported.

- **Connect to the accessory shoe with a cable or adapter.** The Nikon SC-28 and SC-29 TTL coiled remote cords have an accessory shoe on one end of a nine-foot cable to accept a flash, and a foot that slides into the camera accessory shoe on the other end, providing a link that is the same as when the flash is mounted directly on the camera. The SC-29 version also includes a focus assist lamp, like that on the camera and SB-900/910. You can also use an adapter in the accessory shoe that accepts a standard flash cable. In all cases, you should make sure that the external flash doesn't use a triggering voltage high enough to "fry" your camera's circuitry. You'll find more information on this, and recommendations for a voltage isolator to prevent problems, later in this chapter.

- **Wireless link.** Certain external Nikon electronic flash can be triggered by another Master flash such as the Nikon SB-700/900/910 in Commander mode or by the SU-800 infrared unit.

# More Advanced Lighting Techniques

As you advance in your Nikon D5200 photography, you'll want to learn more sophisticated lighting techniques, using more than just straight-on flash, or using just a single flash unit. Entire books have been written on lighting techniques (check out *David Busch's Quick Snap Guide to Lighting*). I'm going to provide a quick introduction to some of the techniques you should be considering.

## Diffusing and Softening the Light

Direct light can be harsh and glaring, especially if you're using the flash built in to your camera, or an auxiliary flash mounted in the hot shoe and pointed directly at your subject. The first thing you should do is stop using direct light (unless you're looking for a stark, contrasty appearance as a creative effect). There are a number of simple things you can do with both continuous and flash illumination.

- **Use window light.** Light coming in a window can be soft and flattering, and a good choice for human subjects. Move your subject close enough to the window that its light provides the primary source of illumination. You might want to turn off other lights in the room, particularly to avoid mixing daylight and incandescent light (see Figure 12.15).

- **Use fill light.** Your D5200's built-in flash makes a perfect fill-in light for the shadows, brightening inky depths with a kicker of illumination (see Figure 12.16).

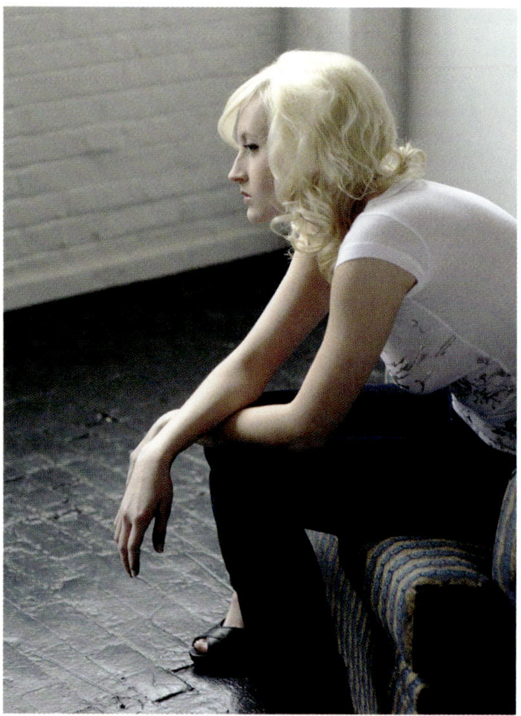

**Figure 12.15** Light from the window located off to the upper left makes the perfect diffuse illumination for informal soft-focus portraits like this one.

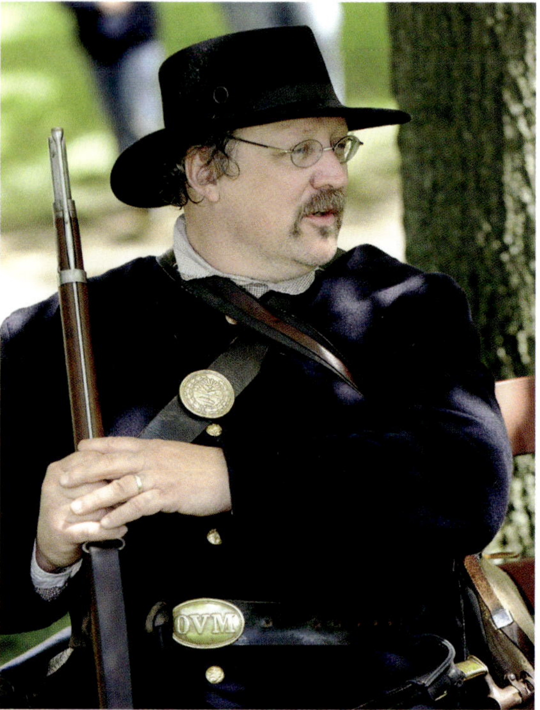

**Figure 12.16** Fill flash illuminated the shadows for this candid portrait.

- **Bounce the light.** External electronic flash units mounted on the D5200 usually have a swivel that allows them to be pointed up at a ceiling for a bounce light effect. You can also bounce the light off a wall. You'll want the ceiling or wall to be white or have a neutral gray color to avoid a color cast.

- **Use reflectors.** Another way to bounce the light is to use reflectors or umbrellas that you can position yourself to provide a greater degree of control over the quantity and direction of the bounced light. Good reflectors can be pieces of foamboard, Mylar, or a reflective disk held in place by a clamp and stand. Although some expensive umbrellas and reflectors are available, spending a lot isn't necessary. A simple piece of white foamboard does the job beautifully. Umbrellas have the advantage of being compact and foldable, while providing a soft, even kind of light. They're relatively cheap, too, with a good 40-inch umbrella available for as little as $20.

- **Use diffusers.** Nikon supplies a Sto-Fen-style diffuser dome with the SB-900/910 and SB-700 flash units. You can purchase a similar diffuser for other flash from Nikon, Sto-Fen, and some other vendors that offer clip-on diffusers. The two examples shown in Figures 12.17 and 12.18 fit over your electronic flash head and provide a soft, flattering light. These add-ons are more portable than umbrellas and other reflectors, yet provide a nice diffuse lighting effect.

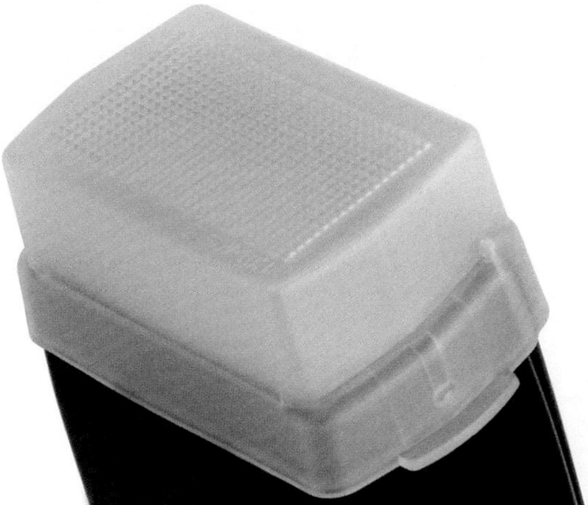

**Figure 12.17** This diffuser dome is provided by Nikon with several of their strobes, and softens the light of an external flash unit.

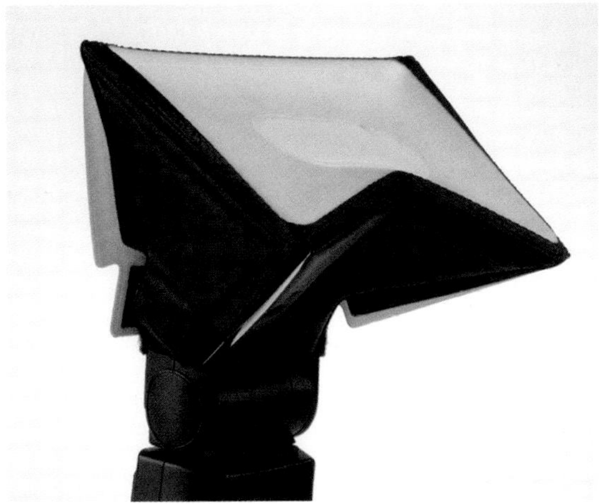

**Figure 12.18** Soft boxes use Velcro strips to attach them to just about any shoe-mount flash unit.

# Using Multiple Light Sources

Once you gain control over the qualities and effects you get with a single light source, you'll want to graduate to using multiple light sources. Using several lights allows you to shape and mold the illumination of your subjects to provide a variety of effects, from backlighting to side lighting to more formal portrait lighting. You can start simply with several incandescent light sources, bounced off umbrellas or reflectors that you construct. Or you can use more flexible multiple electronic flash setups.

Effective lighting is the one element that differentiates great photography from candid or snapshot shooting. Lighting can make a mundane subject look a little more glamorous. It can make subjects appear to be soft when you want a soft look, or bright and sparkly when you want a vivid look, or strong and dramatic if that's what you desire. As you might guess, having control over your lighting means that you probably can't use the lights that are already in the room. You'll need separate, discrete lighting fixtures that can be moved, aimed, brightened, and dimmed on command.

Selecting your lighting gear will depend on the type of photography you do, and the budget you have to support it. It's entirely possible for a beginning D5200 photographer to create a basic, inexpensive lighting system capable of delivering high-quality results for a few hundred dollars, just as you can spend megabucks ($1,000 and up) for a sophisticated lighting system.

## Basic Flash Setups

If you want to use multiple electronic flash units, the Nikon Speedlights described earlier will serve admirably. The higher-end models can be used with Nikon's wireless i-TTL features, which allow you to set up to three separate groups of flash units (several flashes can be included in each group) and trigger them using a master flash and the camera. Just set up one master unit, and arrange the compatible slave units around your subject. You can set the relative power of each unit separately, thereby controlling how much of the scene's illumination comes from the main flash, and how much from the auxiliary flash units, which can be used as fill flash, background lights, or, if you're careful, to illuminate the hair of portrait subjects.

## Studio Flash

If you're serious about using multiple flash units, a studio flash setup might be more practical. The traditional studio flash is a multi-part unit, consisting of a flash head that mounts on your light stand, and is tethered to an AC (or sometimes battery) power supply. A single power supply can feed two or more flash heads at a time, with separate control over the output of each head.

When they are operating off AC power, studio flash don't have to be frugal with the juice, and are often powerful enough to illuminate very large subjects or to supply lots and lots of light to smaller subjects. The output of such units is measured in watt seconds (ws), so you could purchase a 200ws, 400ws, or 800ws unit, and a power pack to match.

Their advantages include greater power output, much faster recycling, built-in modeling lamps, multiple power levels, and ruggedness that can stand up to transport, because many photographers pack up these kits and tote them around as location lighting rigs. Studio lighting kits can range in price from a few hundred dollars for a set of lights, stands, and reflectors, to thousands for a high-end lighting system complete with all the necessary accessories.

A more practical choice these days is *monolights* (see Figure 12.19), which are "all-in-one" studio lights that sell for about $200–$400. They have the flash tube, modeling light, and power supply built into a single unit that can be mounted on a light stand. Monolights are available in AC-only and battery-pack versions, although an external battery eliminates some of the advantages of having a flash with everything in one unit. They are very portable, because all you need is a case for the monolight itself, plus the stands and other accessories you want to carry along. Because these units are so popular with photographers who are not full-time professionals, the lower-cost monolights are often designed more for lighter duty than professional studio flash. That doesn't mean they aren't rugged; you'll just need to handle them with a little more care, and, perhaps, not expect them to be used eight hours a day for weeks on end. In most other respects, however, monolights are the equal of traditional studio flash units in terms of fast recycling, built-in modeling lamps, adjustable power, and so forth.

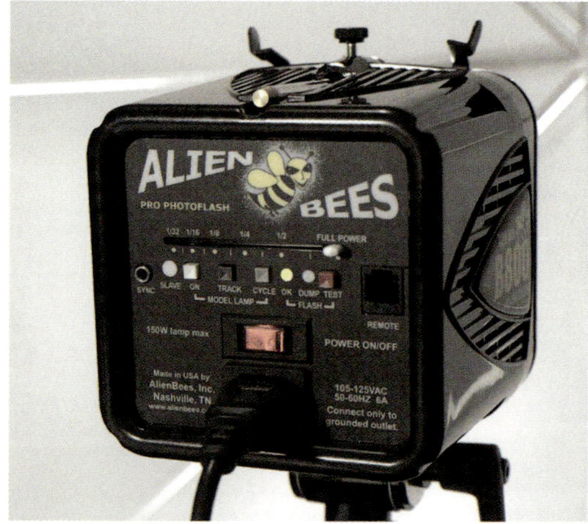


**Figure 12.19** All-in-one "monolights" contain flash, power supply, and a modeling light in one compact package (umbrella not included).

## Connecting Multiple Non-Dedicated Units to Your Nikon D5200

Non-dedicated electronic flash units can't use the automated i-TTL features of your Nikon D5200; you'll need to calculate exposure manually, through test shots evaluated on your camera's LCD, or by using an electronic flash meter. Moreover, you don't have to connect them to the accessory shoe on top of the camera. Instead, you can remove them from the camera and plug in an adaptor like the Nikon AS-15 onto the accessory shoe to provide a PC/X connector for use with an old-style camera sync cord.

You should be aware that older electronic flash units sometimes use a triggering voltage that is too much for your D5200 to handle. You can actually damage the camera's electronics if the voltage is too high. You won't need to worry about this if you purchase brand-new units from Alien Bees, Adorama, or other vendors. But if you must connect an external flash with an unknown triggering voltage, I recommend using a Wein Safe Sync, which isolates the flash's voltage from the camera triggering circuit.

Finally, some flash units have an optical slave trigger built in, or can be fitted with one, so that they fire automatically when another flash, including your camera's built-in unit, fires. Or, you can use radio control devices such as those available from PocketWizard and RadioPopper.

# Other Lighting Accessories

Once you start working with light, you'll find there are plenty of useful accessories that can help you. Here are some of the most popular that you might want to consider.

## Soft Boxes

Soft boxes are large square or rectangular devices that may resemble a square umbrella with a front cover, and produce a similar lighting effect. They can extend from a few feet square to massive boxes that stand five or six feet tall—virtually a wall of light. With a flash unit or two inside a soft box, you have a very large, semi-directional light source that's very diffuse and very flattering for portraiture and other people photography.

Soft boxes are also handy for photographing shiny objects. They not only provide a soft light, but if the box itself happens to reflect in the subject (say you're photographing a chromium toaster), the box will provide an interesting highlight that's indistinct and not distracting.

You can buy soft boxes or make your own. Some lengths of friction-fit plastic pipe and a lot of muslin cut and sewed just so may be all that you need.

## Light Stands

Both electronic flash and incandescent lamps can benefit from light stands. These are lightweight, tripod-like devices (but without a swiveling or tilting head) that can be set on the floor, tabletops, or other elevated surfaces and positioned as needed. Light stands should be strong enough to support an external lighting unit, up to and including a relatively heavy flash with a soft box or umbrella reflectors. You want the supports to be capable of raising the lights high enough to be effective. Look for light stands capable of extending six to seven feet high. The nine-foot units usually have larger, steadier bases, and extend high enough that you can use them as background supports. You'll be using these stands for a lifetime, so invest in good ones.

## Backgrounds

Backgrounds can be backdrops of cloth, sheets of muslin you've painted yourself using a sponge dipped in paint, rolls of seamless paper, or any other suitable surface your mind can dream up. Backgrounds provide a complementary and non-distracting area behind subjects (especially portraits) and can be lit separately to provide contrast and separation that outlines the subject, or which helps set a mood.

I like to use plain-colored backgrounds for portraits, and white seamless backgrounds for product photography. You can usually construct these yourself from cheap materials and tape them up on the wall behind your subject, or mount them on a pole stretched between a pair of light stands.

## Snoots and Barn Doors

These fit over the flash unit and direct the light at your subject. Snoots are excellent for converting a flash unit into a hair light, while barn doors give you enough control over the illumination by opening and closing their flaps that you can use another flash as a background light, with the capability of feathering the light exactly where you want it on the background.

# 13

# Troubleshooting and Prevention

One of the nice things about modern electronic cameras like the Nikon D5200 is that they have fewer mechanical moving parts to fail, so they are less likely to "wear out." No film transport mechanism, no wind lever or motor drive, no complicated mechanical linkages from camera to lens to physically stop down the lens aperture. Instead, tiny, reliable motors are built into each lens (and you lose the use of only that lens should something fail), and one of the few major moving parts in the camera itself is a lightweight mirror (its small size is one of the advantages of the D5200's 1.5X crop factor) that flips up and down with each shot.

Of course, the camera also has a moving shutter that can fail, but the shutter is built rugged enough that you can expect it to last 100,000 shutter cycles or more. Unless you're shooting sports in continuous mode day in and day out, the shutter on your D5200 is likely to last as long as you expect to use the camera.

The only other things on the camera that move are switches, dials, buttons, the flip-up electronic flash, and the door that slides open to allow you to remove and insert the Secure Digital card. Unless you're extraordinarily clumsy or unlucky, or give your built-in flash a good whack while it is in use, there's not a lot that can go wrong mechanically with your Nikon D5200.

On the other hand, one of the chief drawbacks of modern electronic cameras is that they are modern *electronic* cameras. Your D5200 is fully dependent on two different batteries. Without them, the camera can't be used. There are numerous other electrical and electronic connections in the camera (many connected to those mechanical switches and dials), and components like the color LCD that can potentially fail or suffer damage. The camera also relies on its "operating system," or *firmware*, which can be plagued by bugs that cause unexpected behavior. Luckily, electronic components are generally more reliable and trouble-free, especially when compared to their mechanical counterparts from the pre-electronic film camera days. (Film cameras of the last 10 to 20 years have had almost as many electronic features as digital cameras, but, believe it or not, there were whole generations of film cameras that had *no* electronics or batteries.)

Digital cameras have problems unique to their breed, too; the most troublesome being the need to clean the sensor of dust and grime periodically. This chapter will show you how to diagnose problems, fix some common ills, and, importantly, learn how to avoid them in the future.

# Battery Powered

I've grown to live with the need for batteries even though I shot for years using all-mechanical Nikon cameras that had no batteries (or even a built-in light meter!). The need for electrical power is the price we pay for modern conveniences like autofocus, autoexposure, LCD image display, backlit menus, and, of course, digital images.

One of the batteries you rely on is the EN-EL14 battery installed in the grip. It's rechargeable, can last for 500 or more shots, and is user-replaceable if you have a spare. The second power cell in your camera is a so-called *clock battery,* which is also rechargeable, but is tucked away within the innards of the camera and can't be replaced by the user. The clock battery retains the settings of the camera when it's powered down, and, even, when the main battery is removed for charging. If you remove the EN-EL14 for long periods, the clock battery may discharge, but it will be quickly rejuvenated when you replace the main battery. (It's recharged by juice supplied by the EN-EL14.) Although you can't replace this battery yourself, you can expect it to last for the useful life of the camera.

So, your main concern will be to provide a continuous, reliable source of power for your D5200. As I noted in Chapter 1, you should always have a spare battery or two so you won't need to stop shooting when your internal battery dies. I recommend buying Nikon-brand batteries: saving $20 or so for an after-market battery may save you a few dollars, but can cost you much more than that if the battery malfunctions and damages your camera.

## KEEPING TRACK OF YOUR BATTERIES AND MEMORY CARDS

Here's a trick I use to keep track of which batteries are fresh/discharged, and which memory cards are blank/exposed. I cut up some small slips of paper and fold them in half, forming a tiny "booklet." Then I write EXPOSED in red on the "inside" pages of the booklet and UNEXPOSED in green on the outside pages. Folded one way, the slips read EXPOSED; folded the other way, the slips read UNEXPOSED. I slip them inside the plastic battery cover, which you should *always* use when the batteries are not in the camera (to avoid shorting out the contacts), folded so the appropriate "state" of the batteries is visible. The same slips are used in the translucent plastic cases I use for my memory cards. (See Figure 13.1.) For my purposes, EXPOSED means the same as DISCHARGED, and UNEXPOSED is the equivalent of CHARGED. The color coding is an additional clue as to which batteries/memory cards are good to go, or not ready for use.

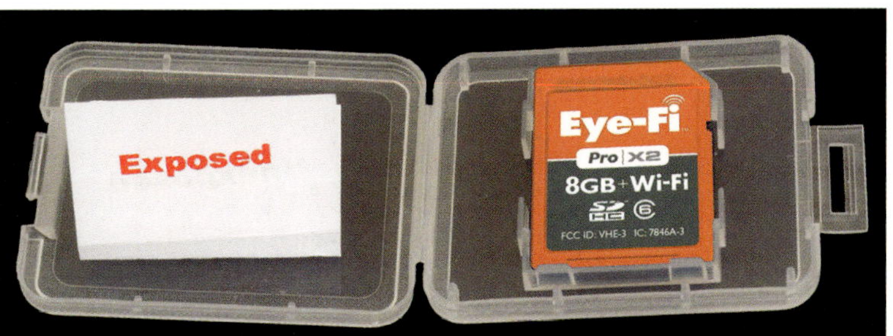


**Figure 13.1**
Mark your batteries—or memory cards—so you'll know which are ready for use.

There are several settings techniques you can use to stretch the longevity of your D5200's battery. To get the most from each charge, consider these steps:

- **Playback menu: Image Review.** Turn off automatic image review after each shot using this menu option. You can still review your images by pressing the Playback button. Or, leave image review on, but set the display for the minimum 4 seconds as described next.

- **Auto off timers.** In CSM c2, set for the minimum, Short, which produces automatic shut-off in 12 seconds for playback and menus, 4 seconds for image review and exposure meters, and three minutes for live view. That three-inch LCD uses a lot of juice, so reducing the amount of time it is active when you don't turn it off manually can boost the effectiveness of your battery.

- **Reduce LCD brightness.** In the Setup menu's LCD Brightness option, select the lowest of the seven brightness settings that work for you under most conditions. If you're willing to shade the LCD with your hand, you can often get away with lower brightness settings outdoors, which will further increase the useful life of your battery.

- **Turn off the shooting information display.** Turn it on or off manually as needed by pressing the Info button on top of the camera (*not* the information edit button next to the viewfinder).

- **Reduce internal flash use.** No flash at all or fill flash use less power than a full blast.

- **Cancel VR.** Turn off vibration reduction if your lens (such as the 18-200mm VR II lens) has that feature and you feel you don't need it.

- **Use a card reader.** When transferring pictures from your D5200 to your computer, use a card reader instead of the USB cable. Linking your camera to your computer and transferring images using the cable takes longer and uses a lot more power.

# Upgrading Your Firmware

The camera relies on its "operating system," or *firmware*, which should be updated in a reasonable fashion as new releases become available. The firmware in your Nikon D5200 handles everything from menu display (including fonts, colors, and the actual entries themselves), what languages are available, and even support for specific devices and features. Upgrading the firmware to a new version makes it possible to add or fine-tune features while fixing some of the bugs that sneak in.

Firmware upgrades are used most frequently to fix bugs in the software, and much less frequently to add or enhance features. As I write this, the D5200 has received no firmware updates. The exact changes made to the firmware are generally spelled out in the firmware release announcement. You can examine the remedies provided and decide if a given firmware patch is important to you. If not, you can usually safely wait a while before going through the bother of upgrading your firmware—at least long enough for the early adopters (such as those who haunt the Digital Photography Review forums at www.dpreview.com) to report whether the bug fixes have introduced new bugs of their own. Each new firmware release incorporates the changes from previous releases, so if you skip a minor upgrade you should have no problems.

### WHEN TO UPGRADE YOUR FIRMWARE

I *always* recommend waiting at least two weeks after a firmware upgrade is announced before changing the software in your camera. This is often in direct contradiction to the online Nikon "gurus" who breathlessly announce each new firmware release on their web pages, usually with links to where you can download the latest software. *Don't do it!* Yet. Nikon has, in the past, introduced firmware upgrades that were buggy and added problems of their own. If you own a camera affected by a new round of firmware upgrades, I urge you to wait and let a few million over-eager fellow users "beta test" this upgrade for you. Within a few weeks, any problems (although I don't expect there will be any) will surface and you'll know whether the update is safe. Your camera is working fine right now, so why take the chance?

## How It Works

If you're computer savvy, you might wonder how your Nikon D5200 is able to overwrite its own operating system—that is, how can the existing firmware be used to load the new version on top of itself? It's a little like lifting yourself by reaching down and pulling up on your bootstraps.

Not ironically, that's almost exactly what happens: At your command (when you start the upgrade process), the D5200 shifts into a special mode in which it is no longer operating from its firmware but, rather, from a small piece of software called a *bootstrap loader*, a separate, protected software program that functions only at startup or when upgrading firmware. The loader's function is to look for firmware to launch or, when directed, to copy new firmware from a memory card to the internal memory space where the old firmware is located. Once the new firmware has replaced the old, you can "reboot" the camera using the new operating system.

## Why Three Firmware Modules?

Your Nikon D5200's firmware is divided into three parts, C (for camera); L (for lens); and S (for strobe/Speedlight). Most early Nikon digital SLRs had the firmware in just two sections, labeled A and B, and some recent cameras had A, B, L, and S. With the D5200, Nikon has combined the A and B modules into one C firmware module.

But, why chop the firmware up in the first place? You might have owned a previous Nikon camera that had an A and B firmware listing, located in the Firmware Version entry in the Setup menu. There's a good reason why the firmware was previously divided in twain. Each of the two modules was "in charge" of particular parts of the camera's operating system. So, when a bug was found, or a new feature added, it was possible, in many cases, to offer only an upgrade for either Firmware A or Firmware B, depending on which module was affected. Although mistakes in upgrading firmware are rare, you cut the opportunities for user errors in half when only one of the modules needs to be replaced. However, Nikon has decided that a single "camera" module is enough and doesn't provide A and B options for the D5200.

So, what are Firmware L and Firmware S, found in some of the most current Nikon models, like the D5200? The L firmware is a database of lens information that helps the camera integrate new lenses with its features, such as barrel and pincushion distortion, while the S firmware provides a similar database for strobes (or Speedlights, take your pick). Nikon regularly updates the C (camera) firmware to correct for mistakes or add features/support for new accessories, and the L and S modules to account for new lens and electronic flash introductions. Note that the S firmware will be shown in the Firmware Version menu *only* if you have an external dedicated flash unit installed and powered up. (See Figure 13.2.)

---

### WARNING

Use a fully charged EN-EL14 charged battery or an AC adapter to ensure that you'll have enough power to operate the camera for the entire upgrade. Moreover, you should not turn off the camera while your old firmware is being overwritten. Don't open the memory card door or do anything else that might disrupt operation of the D5200 while the firmware is being installed.

---

## Getting Ready

Before you get started, I have to emphasize that at the time this book was written, no new firmware release has been made available. So, the procedure I am going to describe is the recommended process used for previous updates to other Nikon cameras. But when it comes time to do an actual firmware upgrade for your D5200, you should double-check the instructions below against the recommended procedure that Nikon implements at that time. It should be very close to the steps I outline, but there may be some small differences.

The first thing to do is determine whether you need the current firmware update. First, confirm the version number of your Nikon D5200's current firmware:

1. Turn on the D5200.

2. Press the MENU button and select Firmware Version from the Setup menu. The camera's firmware version will be displayed. (See Figure 13.2.)

3. Write down the Version number for Parts C, L, and S.

4. Turn off the D5200.

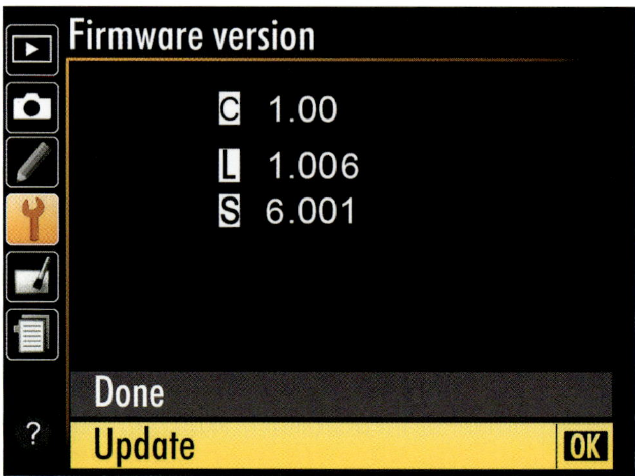



**Figure 13.2**
View your current firmware versions before upgrading.

Next, go to the Nikon support site, locate, and download the firmware update. In the USA, the place to go is http://support.nikontech.com/, which will offer a list of choices, including one that says Current Firmware Downloads available for Nikon Products. Click that link, then click the DSLR link on the page displayed next. Scroll down to the D5200 row in the table, and review the version number for the current update.

If the version is later than the one you noted in your camera, click the firmware link in either the Windows or Macintosh columns (depending on your computer) to download the file. It will have a name like D5200-V101W.exe (Windows) or F-D5200-V101M.dmg (Macintosh). Extract the file to a folder on your computer using the unzipping or unstuffing software of your choice. The actual update files will be named something like:

**D5200_0101.bin**

The final preparation you need to make is to decide whether you'd like to upgrade your firmware using a memory card reader, or by transferring the software to the D5200 using the UC-E4 USB cable. In either case, you'll need to format a memory card in the D5200. Then, perform one of the sets of steps in the sections that follow.

## Updating from a Card Reader

To update from a card reader, use a reader connected to your computer with a USB cable. Then, follow these steps:

1. Insert a formatted memory card into the card reader. If you have been using Nikon Transfer or the "autoplay" features of your operating system to transfer images from your memory card to the computer, the automated transfer dialog box may appear. Close it.

2. The memory card will appear on your Macintosh desktop, or in the Computer/My Computer folders under Windows 8/Windows 7/Windows Vista/Windows XP.

3. Drag one of the firmware files to the memory card. You can install either one first (if two files are provided); or, only the L file if that is the only one included. It doesn't matter. If your particular upgrade consists of only one of the two files, drag that to the memory card. Remember to copy the firmware to the *root* (top) directory of the memory card. The D5200 will be unable to find it if you place it in a folder.

## Updating with a USB Connection

You can also copy the firmware to the D5200's memory card using a USB connection. Just follow these steps:

1. With the camera turned off, insert the formatted memory card. Then, turn the camera back on.

2. Press the MENU button and navigate to the Setup menu.

3. Turn the D5200 off and connect it to your computer using the UC-E4 USB cable.

4. Turn the camera back on. If you have been using Nikon Transfer or the "autoplay" features of your operating system to transfer images from your memory card to the computer, the automated transfer dialog box may appear. Close it.

5. The camera will appear on the Macintosh desktop, or in the Computer/My Computer folders under Windows 8/Windows 7/Windows Vista/Windows XP.

6. Drag one of the firmware files to the memory card. It doesn't matter which you install first. If your particular upgrade consists of only one .bin file, drag that to the memory card. Remember to copy the firmware to the *root* (top) directory of the memory card. The D5200 will be unable to find it if you place it in a folder.

7. Disconnect the camera from the computer.

## Starting the Update

To perform the actual update, follow these steps:

1. With the memory card containing the firmware update software in the camera, turn the camera on.

2. Press the MENU button and select Firmware Version in the Setup menu.

3. Select Update and press the multi selector button to the right.

4. When the Firmware Update screen appears, highlight Yes and press OK to begin the update.

5. The actual process may take a few minutes (from two to five). Be sure not to turn off the camera or perform any other operations while it is underway. (See Figure 13.3.)

6. When the update is completed, the warning message will no longer be displayed on the screen. You can turn off the camera when the message disappears. (See Figure 13.4.)

7. Remove the memory card.

8. Turn the D5200 back on to load the updated firmware.

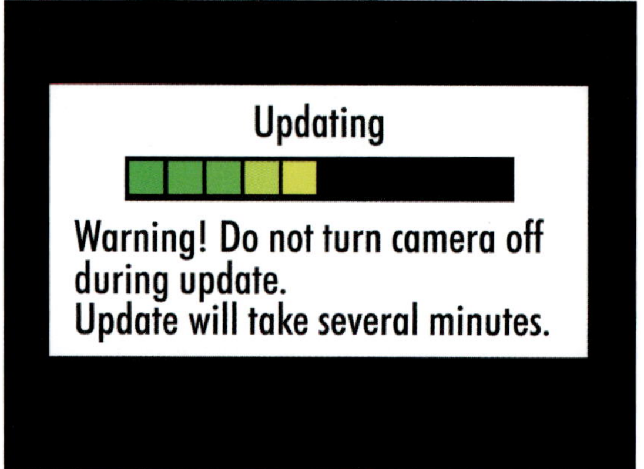


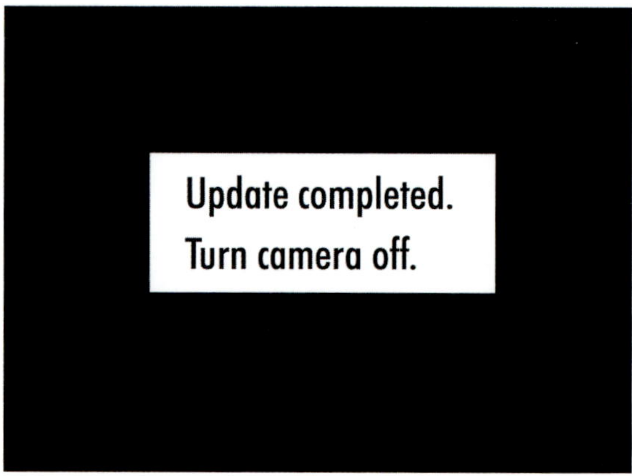


**Figure 13.3** Don't turn the camera off while updating is underway.

**Figure 13.4** Turn the camera off when update is finished.

9. Press the MENU button and select Firmware Version in the Setup menu to view the current firmware number. If it matches the update, you've successfully upgraded that portion of the firmware.

10. Reformat the memory card.

11. If there is a second part to your firmware upgrade, then repeat all the steps for the additional firmware software.

12. Reformat the memory card to return it to a "clean" condition.

# Protecting Your LCD

The massive three-inch color LCD on the back of your Nikon D5200 almost seems like a target for banging, scratching, and other abuse. The LCD itself is quite rugged, and a few errant knocks are unlikely to shatter the protective cover over the LCD, and scratches won't easily mar its tempered glass surface. However, if you want to be on the safe side, there are a number of protective products you can purchase to keep your LCD safe—and, in some cases, make it a little easier to view. Here's a quick overview of your options.

- **Plastic overlays.** The simplest solution (although not always the cheapest) is to apply a plastic overlay sheet or "skin" cut to fit your LCD. These adhere either by static electricity or through a light adhesive coating that's even less clingy than stick-it notes. You can cut down overlays made for PDAs (although these can be pricey at up to $19.95 for a set of several sheets), or purchase overlays sold specifically for digital cameras. Vendors such as Hoodman (www.hoodmanusa.com) offer overlays of this type. These products will do a good job of shielding your D5200's LCD screen from scratches and minor impacts, but will not offer much protection from a good whack.

- **Glass/Acrylic shields.** These scratch-resistant panels, laser cut to fit your camera perfectly, are my choice as the best protection solution, and what I use on my own D5200. At about $12 each, they also happen to be the least expensive option as well. They attach using strips of sticky adhesive that hold the panel flush and tight, but which allow the panel to be pried off and the adhesive removed easily if you want to remove or replace the shield. They don't attenuate your view of the LCD and are non-reflective enough for use under a variety of lighting conditions. I like the glass covers from GGS, available from a variety of sources, and shown in Figure 13.5. Depending on their thickness, these shields may interfere with your ability to reverse the D5200's LCD and store it facing the camera back. However, with transparent protection in place, you might feel less of a need to store the LCD in that position.

- **Flip-up hoods.** These protectors slip on using the flanges around your D5200's eyepiece, and provide a cover that completely shields the LCD, but unfolds to provide a three-sided hood that allows viewing the LCD while minimizing the extraneous light falling on it and reducing contrast. They're sold for about $40 from Hoodman. If you want to completely protect your LCD from hard knocks and need to view the screen outdoors in bright sunlight, there is nothing better. However, I have a couple problems with these devices. First, with the cover closed, you can't peek down after taking a shot to see what your image looks like during picture review. You must open the cap each time you want to look at the LCD. Moreover, with the hood unfolded, it's difficult to look through the viewfinder: Don't count on being able to use the viewfinder *and* the LCD at the same time with one of these hoods in place.

- **Magnifiers.** If you look hard enough, you should be able to find an LCD magnifier that fits over the monitor panel and provides a 2X magnification. These often strap on clumsily, and serve better as a way to get an enlarged view of the LCD than as protection. Hoodman and other suppliers offer these specialized devices.

**Figure 13.5**
A tough glass shield can protect your LCD from scratches.

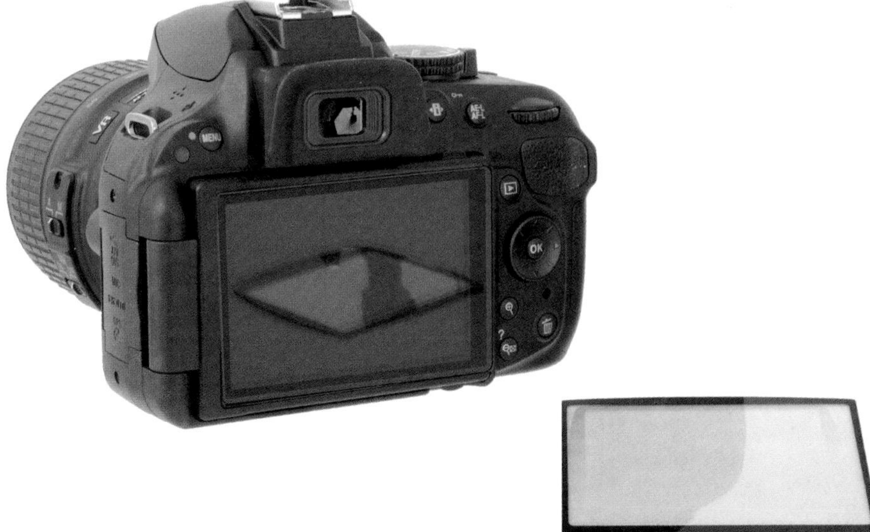

# Troubleshooting Memory Cards

Sometimes good memory cards go bad. Sometimes good photographers can treat their memory cards badly. It's possible that a memory card that works fine in one camera won't be recognized when inserted into another. In the worst case, you can have a card full of important photos and find that the card seems to be corrupted and you can't access any of them. Don't panic! If these scenarios sound horrific to you, there are lots of things you can do to prevent them from happening, and a variety of remedies available if they do occur. You'll want to take some time—before disaster strikes—to consider your options.

## All Your Eggs in One Basket?

The debate about whether it's better to use one large memory card or several smaller ones has been going on since even before there were memory cards. I can remember when computer users wondered whether it was smarter to install a pair of 200MB (not *gigabyte*) hard drives in their computer, or if they should go for one of those new-fangled 500MB models. By the same token, a few years ago the user groups were full of proponents who insisted that you ought to use 128MB memory cards rather than the huge 512MB versions. Today, most of the arguments involve 8GB cards versus 16GB cards, and I expect that as prices for 32GB and 64GB memory cards continue to drop, they'll find their way into the debate as well.

Why all the fuss? Are 16GB memory cards more likely to fail than 8GB cards? Are you risking all your photos if you trust your images to a larger card? Isn't it better to use several smaller cards, so that if one fails you lose only half as many photos? Or, isn't it wiser to put all your photos onto one larger card, because the more cards you use, the better your odds of misplacing or damaging one and losing at least some pictures?

In the end, the "eggs in one basket" argument boils down to statistics, and how you happen to use your D5200. The rationales can go both ways. If you have multiple smaller cards, you do increase your chances of something happening to one of them, so, arguably, you might be boosting the odds of losing some pictures. If all your images are important, the fact that you've lost 100 rather than 200 pictures isn't very comforting.

After all, the myth assumes that a damaged card will always be full before it becomes corrupted. Fortunately, memory cards don't magically wait until they are full before they fail. In a typical shooting session, it doesn't matter whether you've shot 3.5GB worth of pictures on an 8GB card or 3.5GB worth of pictures on a 16GB card. If either card fails, you've lost the same number of images. Your risk increases *only* when you start shooting additional photos on the larger card. In the real world, most of us who use larger memory cards don't fill them up very often. We just like having the extra capacity there when we need it.

The myth also says that by using several smaller cards, you're spreading the risk around so that only some pictures will be lost in case of a failure. What is more important to you, your photographs or the members of your family? When going on vacation, do you insist on splitting your kin up and driving several smaller cars?

If you shoot photojournalist-type pictures, you probably change memory cards when they're less than completely full in order to avoid the need to do so at a crucial moment. (When I shoot sports, my cards rarely reach 80 to 90 percent of capacity before I change them.) Using multiple smaller cards means you have to change them that more often, which can be a real pain when you're taking a lot of photos. In my book, I prefer keeping all my eggs in one basket, and then making very sure that nothing happens to that basket.

## Preventive Measures

Here are some options for preventing loss of valuable images:

- **Interleaving.** One option is to *interleave* your shots. Say you don't shoot weddings, but you do go on vacation from time to time. Take 50 or so pictures on one card, or whatever number of images might fill about 25 percent of its capacity. Then, replace it with a different card and shoot about 25 percent of that card's available space. Repeat these steps with diligence (you'd have to be determined to go through this inconvenience), and, if you use four or more memory cards you'll find your pictures from each location scattered among the different memory cards. If you lose or damage one, you'll still have *some* pictures from all the various stops on your trip on the other cards. That's more work than I like to do (I usually tote around a portable hard disk and copy the files to the drive as I go), but it's an option.

- **Transmit your images.** Another option is to transmit your images, as they are shot, over a network to your laptop, assuming a network and a laptop are available. You can use the Nikon WU-1a Wi-Fi transmitter if you like; Nikon offers a free app for uploading pictures from the D5200 to your iOS or Android phone. A company called Eye-Fi (www.eye.fi) markets a clever Secure Digital card with wireless capabilities built-in. Transcend has recently introduced a similar card, although I have not had a chance to test it. I do have experience with Eye-Fi cards, currently offered in four models, including the basic Eye-Fi Home (about $50), which can be used to transmit your photos from the D5200 to a computer on your home network (or any other network you set up somewhere, say, at a family reunion). Eye-Fi Share and Eye-Fi Share Video (about $60 and $80, respectively), which are basically exactly the same (Share Video is 4GB instead of 2GB in capacity), include software to allow you to upload your images from your camera through your computer network directly to websites such as Flickr, Facebook, Shutterfly, Nikon's own Image Space (which replaced My Picturetown), and digital printing services that include Walmart Digital Photo Center. The most sophisticated option is Eye-Fi Explore and X2 Pro cards, which I use, in sizes up to 8GB, with the ability to add geographic location labels to your photo (so you'll know where you took it), and frees you from your own computer network by allowing uploads from more than 10,000 Wi-Fi hotspots around the USA. Very cool, and the ultimate in picture backup.

- **External backup.** You can purchase external hard disk gadgets called Personal Storage Devices, which can copy files from your memory cards automatically. More expensive models have color LCD screens so you can review your images. I tend to prefer using an ultrabook, like the one shown in Figure 13.6. I can store images on the ultrabook's internal hard disk or SSD (solid state disk), and make an extra backup copy to an external drive as well. Plus, I can access the Internet from Wi-Fi hotspots, all using a very compact device. Lately, I've been backing up many images on my iPad, which has 64GB of storage—enough for short trips.

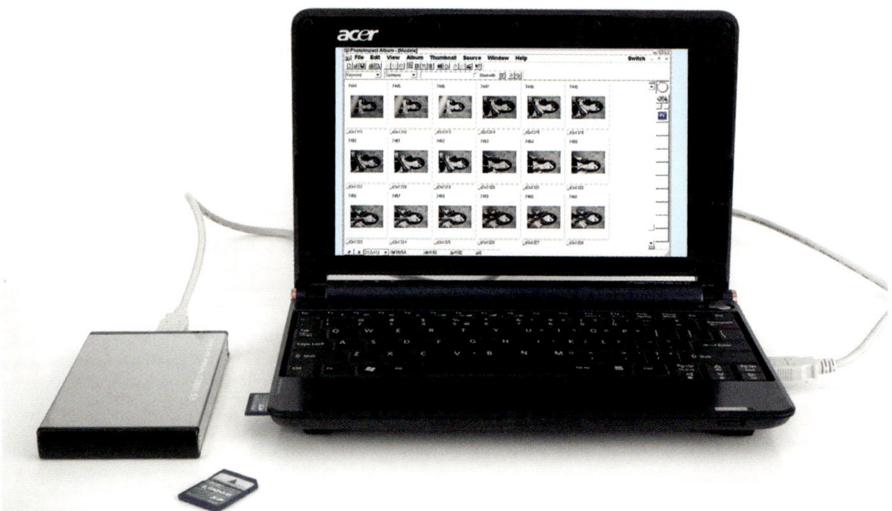

**Figure 13.6**
A small netbook, with or without an external hard drive, is another backup option.

## What Can Go Wrong?

There are lots of things that can go wrong with your memory card, but the ones that aren't caused by human stupidity are statistically very rare. Yes, a memory card's internal bit bin or controller can suddenly fail due to a manufacturing error or some inexplicable event caused by old age. However, if your card works for the first week or two that you own it, it should work forever. There's really not a lot that can wear out.

The typical memory card is rated for a Mean Time Between Failures of 1,000,000 hours of use. That's constant use 24/7 for more than 100 years! According to the manufacturers, they are good for 10,000 insertions in your camera, and should be able to retain their data (and that's without an external power source) for something on the order of 11 years. Of course, with the millions of cards in use, there are bound to be a few lemons here or there.

Given the reliability of solid-state memory compared to magnetic memory, though, it's more likely that your problems will stem from something that you do. Secure Digital and Secure Digital cards are small and easy to misplace if you're not careful. For that reason, it's a good idea to keep them in their original cases or a "card safe" offered by Gepe (www.gepe.com), Pelican (www.pelican.com), and others. Always placing your memory card in a case can provide protection from the second-most common mishap that befalls memory cards: the common household laundry. If you slip a card in a pocket, rather than a case or your camera bag often enough, sooner or later it's going to end up in the washing machine and probably the clothes dryer, too. There are plenty of reports of relieved digital camera owners who've laundered their memory cards and found they still worked fine, but it's not uncommon for such mistreatment to do some damage. Memory cards can also be stomped on, accidentally bent, dropped into the ocean, chewed by pets, and otherwise rendered unusable in myriad ways.

Or, if the card is formatted in your computer with a memory card reader, your D5200 may fail to recognize it. Occasionally, I've found that a memory card used in one camera would fail if used in a different camera (until I reformatted it in Windows, and then again in the camera). Every once in awhile, a card goes completely bad and—seemingly—can't be salvaged.

Another way to lose images is to do commonplace things with your card at an inopportune time. If you remove the card from the D5200 while the camera is writing images to the card, you'll lose any photos in the buffer and may damage the file structure of the card, making it difficult or impossible to retrieve the other pictures you've taken. The same thing can happen if you remove the memory card from your computer's card reader while the computer is writing to the card (say, to erase files you've already moved to your computer). You can avoid this by *not* using your computer to erase files on a memory card but, instead, always reformatting the card in your D5200 before you use it again.

## What Can You Do?

Pay attention: If you're having problems, the *first* thing you should do is *stop* using that memory card. Don't take any more pictures. Don't do anything with the card until you've figured out what's wrong. Your second line of defense (your first line is to be sufficiently careful with your cards that you avoid problems in the first place) is to *do no harm* that hasn't already been done. Read the rest of this section and then, if necessary, decide on a course of action (such as using a data recovery service or software described later) before you risk damaging the data on your card further.

Now that you've calmed down, the first thing to check is whether you've actually inserted a card in the camera. If you've set the camera so that shooting without a card has been turned on, it's entirely possible (although not particularly plausible) that you've been snapping away with no memory card to store the pictures to, which can lead to massive disappointment later on. Of course, the –E- warning appears on the LCD when the camera is powered up, and the Demo message is superimposed on the review image after every shot (assuming you've enabled the D5200 to take photos when a card is not inserted), but maybe you're inattentive, aren't using picture review, or have purchased one of those LCD fold-up hoods mentioned earlier in this chapter. You can avoid all this by setting the Slot Empty Release Lock (CSM f4) feature to Release Locked, and leaving it there.

Things get more exciting when the card itself is put in jeopardy. If you lose a card, there's not a lot you can do other than take a picture of a similar card and print up some Have You Seen This Lost Flash Memory? flyers to post on utility poles all around town.

If all you care about is reusing the card, and have resigned yourself to losing the pictures, try reformatting the card in your camera. You may find that reformatting removes the corrupted data and restores your card to health. Sometimes I've had success reformatting a card in my computer using a memory card reader (this is normally a no-no because your operating system doesn't understand the needs of your D5200), and *then* reformatting again in the camera.

If your memory card is not behaving properly, and you *do* want to recover your images, things get a little more complicated. If your pictures are very valuable, either to you or to others (for example, a wedding), you can always turn to professional data recovery firms. Be prepared to pay hundreds of dollars to get your pictures back, but these pros often do an amazing job. You wouldn't want them working on your memory card on behalf of the police if you'd tried to erase some incriminating pictures. There are many firms of this type, and I've never used them myself, so I can't offer a recommendation. Use a Google search to turn up a ton of them.

A more reasonable approach is to try special data recovery software you can install on your computer and use to attempt to resurrect your "lost" images yourself. They may not actually be gone completely. Perhaps your card's "table of contents" is jumbled, or only a few pictures are damaged in such a way that your camera and computer can't read some or any of the pictures on the card. Some of the available software was written specifically to reconstruct lost pictures, while other utilities are more general-purpose applications that can be used with any media, including floppy disks and hard disk drives. They have names like OnTrack, Photo Rescue 2, Digital Image Recovery, MediaRecover, Image Recall, and the aptly named Recover My Photos. You'll find a comprehensive list and links, as well as some picture-recovery tips at www.ultimateslr.com/memory-card-recovery.php. I like the RescuePro software that SanDisk supplies, especially since it came on a mini-CD that I was totally unable to erase by mistake, rather than on the memory card itself.

## DIMINISHING RETURNS

Usually, once you've recovered any images on a memory card, reformatted it, and returned it to service, it will function reliably for the rest of its useful life. However, if you find a particular card going bad more than once, you'll almost certainly want to stop using it forever. See if you can get it replaced by the manufacturer if you can, but, in the case of Secure Digital card failures, the third time is never the charm.

# Cleaning Your Sensor

Yes, the Nikon D5200 has a two-pronged sensor dust prevention scheme: an innovative air control system that keeps dust away from the sensor in the first place, and a sensor-shaking cleaning mechanism. But no dust-busting technology is 100-percent effective.

Indeed, there's no avoiding dust. No matter how careful you are, some of it is going to settle on your camera and on the mounts of your lenses, eventually making its way inside your camera to settle in the mirror chamber. As you take photos, the mirror flipping up and down causes the dust to become airborne and eventually make its way past the shutter curtain to come to rest on the anti-aliasing filter atop your sensor. There, dust and particles can show up in every single picture you take at a small enough aperture to bring the foreign matter into sharp focus. No matter how careful you are and how cleanly you work, eventually you will get some of this dust on your camera's sensor. Some say that CMOS sensors, like the one found in the Nikon D5200, "attract" less dust than CCD sensors found in cameras from other vendors. But even the cleanest-working photographers using the Nikon D5200 are far from immune.

Fortunately, one of the Nikon D5200's most useful features is the automatic sensor cleaning system that reduces or eliminates the need to clean your camera's sensor manually. The sensor vibrates ultrasonically each time the D5200 is powered either on or off (or both, at your option), shaking loose any dust.

Although the automatic sensor cleaning feature operates when you power the camera up or turn it off (depending on the behavior you specify in the Setup menu), you can activate it manually at any time. Choose Clean Image Sensor from the Setup menu, and select Clean Now. If you'd rather specify when automatic cleaning occurs, choose On (clean at power up), Off (clean when the camera is switched off), On/Off (clean at both power up and power down), or Cleaning Off (no automatic sensor cleaning will take place).

If some dust does collect on your sensor, you can often map it out of your images (making it invisible) using software techniques with the Image Dust Off Ref Photo feature in the Setup menu. Operation of this feature is described in Chapter 10.

Of course, even with the Nikon D5200's automatic sensor cleaning/dust resistance features, you may still be required to manually clean your sensor from time to time. This section explains the phenomenon and provides some tips on minimizing dust and eliminating it when it begins to affect your shots.

## Dust the FAQs, Ma'am

Here are some of the most frequently asked questions about sensor dust issues.

**Q. I see tiny specks in my viewfinder. Do I have dust on my sensor?**

**A.** If you see sharp, well-defined specks, they are clinging to the underside of your focus screen and not on your sensor. They have absolutely no effect on your photographs, and are merely annoying or distracting.

**Q. I can see dust on my mirror. How can I remove it?**

**A.** Like focus-screen dust, any artifacts that have settled on your mirror won't affect your photos. You can often remove dust on the mirror or focus screen with a bulb air blower, which will loosen it and whisk it away. Stubborn dust on the focus screen can sometimes be gently flicked away with a soft brush designed for cleaning lenses. I don't recommend brushing the mirror or touching it in any way. The mirror is a special front-surface-silvered optical device (unlike conventional mirrors, which are silvered on the back side of a piece of glass or plastic) and can be easily scratched. If you can't blow mirror dust off, it's best to just forget about it. You can't see it in the viewfinder, anyway.

**Q. I see a bright spot in the same place in all of my photos. Is that sensor dust?**

**A.** You've probably got either a "hot" pixel or one that is permanently "stuck" due to a defect in the sensor. A hot pixel is one that shows up as a bright spot only during long exposures as the sensor warms. A pixel stuck in the "on" position always appears in the image. Both show up as bright red, green, or blue pixels, usually surrounded by a small cluster of other improperly illuminated pixels, caused by the camera's interpolating the hot or stuck pixel into its surroundings, as shown in Figure 13.7. A stuck pixel can also be permanently dark. Either kind is likely to show up when they contrast with plain, evenly colored areas of your image.

**Figure 13.7** A stuck pixel is surrounded by improperly interpolated pixels created by the D5200's demosaicing algorithm.

Finding one or two hot or stuck pixels in your sensor is unfortunately fairly common. They can be "removed" by telling the D5200 to ignore them through a simple process called *pixel mapping*. If the bad pixels become bothersome, Nikon can remap your sensor's pixels with a quick trip to a service center.

Bad pixels can also show up on your camera's color LCD panel, but, unless they are abundant, the wisest course is to just ignore them.

**Q. I see an irregular out-of-focus blob in the same place in my photos. Is that sensor dust?**

**A.** Yes. Sensor contaminants can take the form of tiny spots, larger blobs, or even curvy lines if they are caused by minuscule fibers that have settled on the sensor. They'll appear out of focus because they aren't actually on the sensor surface but, rather, a fraction of a millimeter above it on the filter that covers the sensor. The smaller the f/stop used, the more in-focus the dust becomes. At large apertures, it may not be visible at all.

**Q. I never see any dust on my sensor. What's all the fuss about?**

**A.** Those who never have dust problems with their Nikon D5200 fall into one of four categories: those for whom the camera's automatic dust removal features are working well; those who seldom change their lenses and have clean working habits that minimize the amount of dust that invades their cameras in the first place; those who simply don't notice the dust (often because they don't shoot many macro photos or other pictures using the small f/stops that makes dust evident in their images); and those who are very, very lucky.

## Identifying and Dealing with Dust

Sensor dust is less of a problem than it might be because it shows up only under certain circumstances. Indeed, you might have dust on your sensor right now and not be aware of it. The dust doesn't actually settle on the sensor itself, but, rather, on a protective filter a very tiny distance above the sensor, subjecting it to the phenomenon of *depth-of-focus*. Depth-of-focus is the distance the focal plane can be moved and still render an object in sharp focus. At f/2.8 to f/5.6 or even smaller, sensor dust, particularly if small, is likely to be outside the range of depth-of-focus and blur into an unnoticeable dot.

However, if you're shooting at f/16 to f/22 or smaller, those dust motes suddenly pop into focus. Forget about trying to spot them by peering directly at your sensor with the shutter open and the lens removed. The period at the end of this sentence, about .33mm in diameter, could block a group of pixels measuring 40 × 40 pixels (160 pixels in all!). Dust spots that are even smaller than that can easily show up in your images if you're shooting large, empty areas that are light colored. Dust motes are most likely to show up in the sky, as in Figure 13.8, or in white backgrounds of your seamless product shots and are less likely to be a problem in images that contain lots of dark areas and detail.

To see if you have dust on your sensor, take a few test shots of a plain, blank surface (such as a piece of paper or a cloudless sky) at small f/stops, such as f/22, and a few wide open. Open Photoshop or another image editor, copy several shots into a single document in separate layers, then flip back and forth between layers to see if any spots you see are present in all layers. You may have to boost contrast and sharpness to make the dust easier to spot.

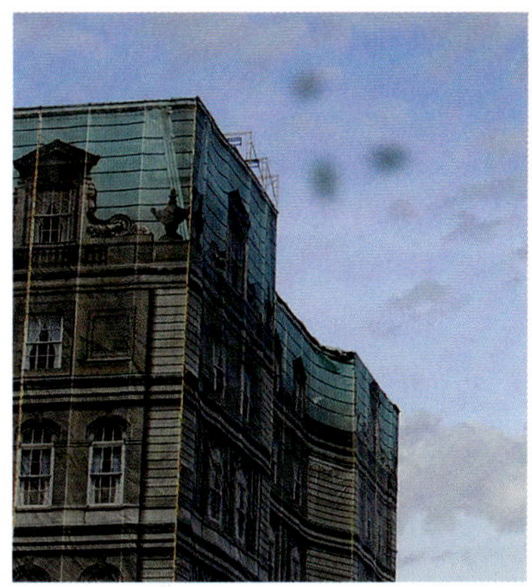

**Figure 13.8**  Only the dust spots in the sky are apparent in this shot.

## Avoiding Dust

Of course, the easiest way to protect your sensor from dust is to prevent it from settling on the sensor in the first place. Here are my stock tips for eliminating the problem before it begins.

- **Clean environment.** Avoid working in dusty areas if you can do so. Hah! Serious photographers will take this one with a grain of salt, because it usually makes sense to go where the pictures are. Only a few of us are so paranoid about sensor dust (considering that it is so easily removed) that we'll avoid moderately grimy locations just to protect something that is, when you get down to it, just a tool. If you find a great picture opportunity at a raging fire, during a sandstorm, or while surrounded by dust clouds, you might hesitate to take the picture, but, with a little caution (don't remove your lens in these situations, and clean the camera afterward!) you can still shoot. However, it still makes sense to store your camera in a clean environment. One placc cameras and lenses pick up a lot of dust is inside a camera bag. Clean your bag from time to time, and you can avoid problems.

- **Clean lenses.** There are a few paranoid types that avoid swapping lenses in order to minimize the chance of dust getting inside their cameras. It makes more sense just to use a blower or brush to dust off the rear lens mount of the replacement lens first, so you won't be introducing dust into your camera simply by attaching a new, dusty lens. Do this before you remove the current lens from your camera, and then avoid stirring up dust before making the exchange.

- **Work fast.** Minimize the time your camera is lens-less and exposed to dust. That means having your replacement lens ready and dusted off, and a place to set down the old lens as soon as it is removed, so you can quickly attach the new lens.

- **Let gravity help you.** Face the camera downward when the lens is detached so any dust in the mirror box will tend to fall away from the sensor. Turn your back to any breezes, indoor forced air vents, fans, or other sources of dust to minimize infiltration.

- **Protect the lens you just removed.** Once you've attached the new lens, quickly put the end cap on the one you just removed to reduce the dust that might fall on it.

- **Clean out the vestibule.** From time to time, remove the lens while in a relatively dust-free environment and use a blower bulb like the one shown in Figure 13.9 (*not* compressed air or a vacuum hose) to clean out the mirror box area. A blower bulb is generally safer than a can of compressed air, or a strong positive/negative airflow, which can tend to drive dust further into nooks and crannies.

- **Be prepared.** If you're embarking on an important shooting session, it's a good idea to clean your sensor *now*, rather than come home with hundreds or thousands of images with dust spots caused by flecks that were sitting on your sensor before you even started.

- **Clone out existing spots in your image editor.** Photoshop and other editors have a clone tool or healing brush you can use to copy pixels from surrounding areas over the dust spot or dead pixel. This process can be tedious, especially if you have lots of dust spots and/or lots of images to be corrected. The advantage is that this sort of manual fix-it probably will do the least damage to the rest of your photo. Only the damaged pixels will be affected.

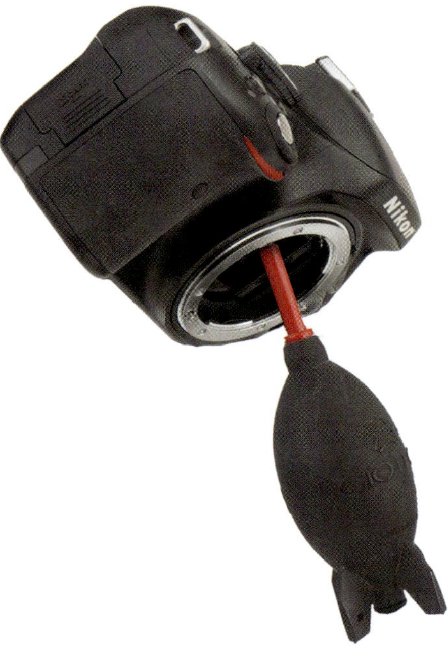

**Figure 13.9** Use a robust air bulb for cleaning your sensor.

- **Use filtration in your image editor.** A semi-smart filter like Photoshop's Dust & Scratches filter can remove dust and other artifacts by selectively blurring areas that the plug-in decides represent dust spots. This method can work well if you have many dust spots, because you won't need to patch them manually. However, any automated method like this has the possibility of blurring areas of your image that you didn't intend to soften.

# Sensor Cleaning

Those new to the concept of sensor dust actually hesitate before deciding to clean their camera themselves. Isn't it a better idea to pack up your D5200 and send it to a Nikon service center so their crack technical staff can do the job for you? Or, at the very least, shouldn't you let the friendly folks at your local camera store do it?

Of course, if you choose to let someone else clean your sensor, they will be using methods that are more or less identical to the techniques you would use yourself. None of these techniques are difficult, and the only difference between their cleaning and your cleaning is that they might have done it dozens or hundreds of times. If you're careful, you can do just as good a job.

Of course vendors like Nikon won't tell you this, but it's not because they don't trust you. It's not that difficult for a real goofball to mess up their camera by hurrying or taking a shortcut. Perhaps the person uses the "Bulb" method of holding the shutter open and a finger slips, allowing the shutter curtain to close on top of a sensor cleaning brush. Or, someone tries to clean the sensor using masking tape, and ends up with goo all over its surface. If Nikon recommended *any* method that's mildly risky, someone would do it wrong, and then the company would face lawsuits from those who'd contend they did it exactly in the way the vendor suggested, so the ruined camera is not their fault.

You can see that vendors like Nikon tend to be conservative in their recommendations, and, in doing so, make it seem as if sensor cleaning is more daunting and dangerous than it really is. Some vendors recommend only dust-off cleaning, through the use of reasonably gentle blasts of air, while condemning more serious scrubbing with swabs and cleaning fluids. However, these cleaning kits for the exact types of cleaning they recommended against are for sale in Japan only, where, apparently, your average photographer is more dexterous than those of us in the rest of the world. These kits are similar to those used by official repair staff to clean your sensor if you decide to send your camera in for a dust-up.

As I noted, sensors can be affected by dust particles that are much smaller than you might be able to spot visually on the surface of your lens. The filters that cover sensors tend to be fairly hard compared to optical glass. Cleaning the 24.6mm × 15.6mm sensor in your Nikon D5200 within the tight confines of the mirror box can call for a steady hand and careful touch. If your sensor's filter becomes scratched through inept cleaning, you can't simply remove it yourself and replace it with a new one.

There are four basic kinds of cleaning processes that can be used to remove dusty and sticky stuff that settles on your dSLR's sensor. All of these must be performed with the shutter locked open. I'll describe these methods and provide instructions for locking the shutter later in this section.

- **Air cleaning.** This process involves squirting blasts of air inside your camera with the shutter locked open. This works well for dust that's not clinging stubbornly to your sensor.
- **Brushing.** A soft, very fine brush is passed across the surface of the sensor's filter, dislodging mildly persistent dust particles and sweeping them off the imager.

- **Liquid cleaning.** A soft swab dipped in a cleaning solution such as ethanol is used to wipe the sensor filter, removing more obstinate particles.

- **Tape cleaning.** There are some who get good results by applying a special form of tape to the surface of their sensor. When the tape is peeled off, all the dust goes with it. Supposedly. I'd be remiss if I didn't point out right now that this form of cleaning is somewhat controversial; the other three methods are much more widely accepted.

## Placing the Mirror/Shutter in the Locked and Fully Upright Position for Landing

Make sure you're using a fully charged battery or an AC adapter. Fortunately, the Nikon D5200 is smart enough that it won't let you try to clean the sensor manually unless the battery has a sufficient charge.

1. Remove the lens from the camera and then turn on the camera.

2. You'll find the Lock Mirror Up for Cleaning menu choice in the Setup menu. Select it.

3. Choose Start. The mirror will flip up and the shutter will open.

4. Use one of the methods described below to remove dust and grime from your sensor. Be careful not to accidentally switch the power off or open the Secure Digital card or battery compartment doors as you work. If that happens, the shutter may be damaged if it closes onto your cleaning tool.

5. When you're finished, turn off the power, replace your lens, and switch your camera back on.

## Air Cleaning

Your first attempts at cleaning your sensor should always involve gentle blasts of air. Many times, you'll be able to dislodge dust spots, which will fall off the sensor and, with luck, out of the mirror box. Attempt one of the other methods only when you've already tried air cleaning and it didn't remove all the dust.

Here are some tips for doing air cleaning:

- **Use a clean, powerful air bulb.** Your best bet is bulb cleaners designed for the job, like the Giottos Rocket. Smaller bulbs, like those air bulbs with a brush attached sometimes sold for lens cleaning or weak nasal aspirators may not provide sufficient air or a strong enough blast to do much good. (See Figure 13.9, earlier.)

- **Hold the camera upside down.** Then look up into the mirror box as you squirt your air blasts, increasing the odds that gravity will help pull the expelled dust downward, away from the sensor. You may have to use some imagination in positioning yourself.

- **Never use air canisters.** The propellant inside these cans can permanently coat your sensor if you tilt the can while spraying. It's not worth taking a chance.

- **Avoid air compressors.** Super-strong blasts of air are likely to force dust under the sensor filter.

## Brush Cleaning

If your dust is a little more stubborn and can't be dislodged by air alone, you may want to try a brush, charged with static electricity, which can pick off dust spots by electrical attraction. One good, but expensive, option is the Arctic Butterfly sold at www.visibledust.com. A motor built into the brush is used to "flutter" the tip for a few seconds prior to cleaning (see Figure 13.10, left), charging the brush's anti-static properties. Then, the motor is turned off (Figure 13.10, right) and the brush tip is passed above the surface of the sensor. (It's not necessary to touch the sensor.) The dust is attracted to the brush and removed by another quick flutter once you've removed the brush from the mirror chamber. A cheaper, inanimate, sensor cleaning brush can be purchased at www.copperhillimages.com. You need a 16mm version. It can be stroked across the short dimension of your D5200's sensor.

Ordinary artist's brushes are much too coarse and stiff and have fibers that are tangled or can come loose and settle on your sensor. A good sensor brush's fibers are resilient and described as "thinner than a human hair." Brush cleaning is done with a dry brush by gently swiping across the surface of the sensor filter with the tip. The dust particles are attracted to the brush particles and cling to them. You should clean the brush with compressed air before and after each use, and store it in an appropriate air-tight container between applications to keep it clean and dust-free. Although these special brushes are expensive, one should last you a long time.

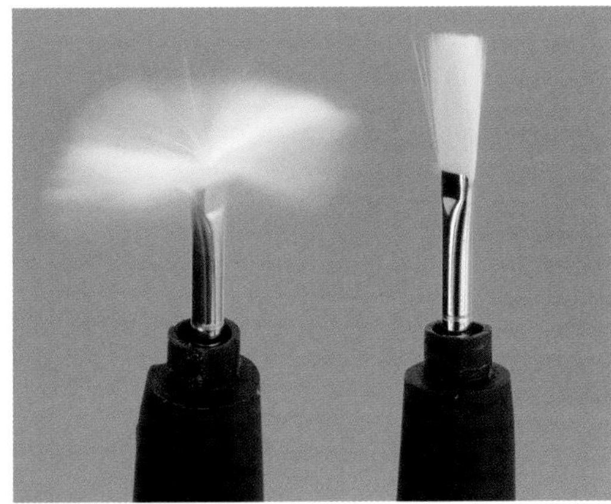

**Figure 13.10** A proper brush like this Arctic Butterfly is required for dusting off your sensor.

## Liquid Cleaning

Unfortunately, you'll often encounter really stubborn dust spots that can't be removed with a blast of air or flick of a brush. These spots may be combined with some grease or a liquid that causes them to stick to the sensor filter's surface. In such cases, liquid cleaning with a swab may be necessary. During my first clumsy attempts to clean my own sensor, I accidentally got my blower bulb tip too close to the sensor, and some sort of deposit from the tip of the bulb ended up on the sensor. I panicked until I discovered that liquid cleaning did a good job of removing whatever it was that took up residence on my sensor.

You want a sturdy swab that won't bend or break so you can apply gentle pressure to the swab as you wipe the sensor surface. Use the swab with methanol (as pure as you can get it, particularly medical grade; other ingredients can leave a residue), or the Eclipse solution also sold by Photographic Solutions. Eclipse is actually quite a bit purer than even medical-grade methanol. A couple drops of solution should be enough, unless you have a spot that's extremely difficult to remove. In that case, you may need to use extra solution on the swab to help "soak" the dirt off.

You can make your own swabs out of pieces of plastic (some use fast-food restaurant knives, with the tip cut at an angle to the proper size) covered with a soft cloth or Pec-Pad, as shown in Figure 13.11. However, if you've got the bucks to spend, you can't go wrong with good-quality commercial sensor cleaning swabs, such as those sold by Photographic Solutions, Inc. (www.photosol.com/swabproduct.htm).

Once you overcome your nervousness at touching your D5200's sensor, the process is easy. You'll wipe continuously with the swab in one direction, then flip it over and wipe in the other direction. You need to completely wipe the entire surface; otherwise, you may end up depositing the dust you collect at the far end of your stroke. Wipe; don't rub.

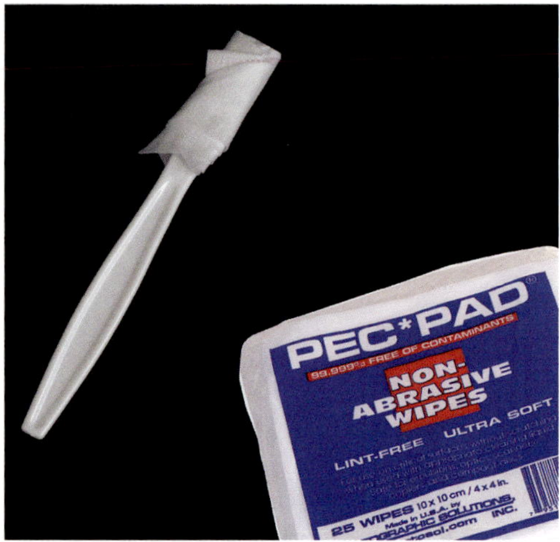

**Figure 13.11** Carefully wrap a Pec-Pad around a plastic knife that you've truncated.

## Tape Cleaning

There are people who absolutely swear by the tape method of sensor cleaning. The concept seems totally wacky, and I have never tried it personally, so I can't say with certainty that it either does or does not work. In the interest of completeness, I'm including it here. I can't give you a positive recommendation, so if you have problems, please don't blame me. The Nikon D5200 is still too new to have generated any reports of users accidentally damaging the anti-dust coating on the sensor filter using this method.

Tape cleaning works by applying a layer of Scotch Brand Magic Tape to the sensor. This is a minimally sticky tape that some of the tape cleaning proponents claim contains no adhesive. I did check this out with 3M, and can say that Magic Tape certainly *does* contain an adhesive. The question is whether the adhesive comes off when you peel back the tape, taking any dust spots on your sensor with it. The folks who love this method claim there is no residue. There have been reports from those who don't like the method that residue is left behind. This is all anecdotal evidence, so you're pretty much on your own in making the decision whether to try out the tape cleaning method.

## Magnifier Assisted Cleaning

Using a magnifier to view your sensor as you clean it is a good idea. I rely on two types. I have four Carson MiniBrite PO-55 5X magnifiers (see Figure 13.12), and keep one in each camera bag. So, no matter where I am shooting, I have one of these $8.95 gadgets with me. You can read more about this great tool at my blog (http://dslrguides.com/blog/carson). When I'm not traveling, I use a SensorKlear loupe. It's a magnifier with a built-in LED illuminator. There's an opening on one side that allows you to insert a SensorKlear cleaning wand, a lens pen-like stylus with a surface treated to capture dust particles. (See Figure 13.13.) Both the SensorKlear loupe and the SensorKlear wand are available from www.lenspen.com.

**Figure 13.12**
The Carson
MiniBrite is a good
value sensor
magnifier.

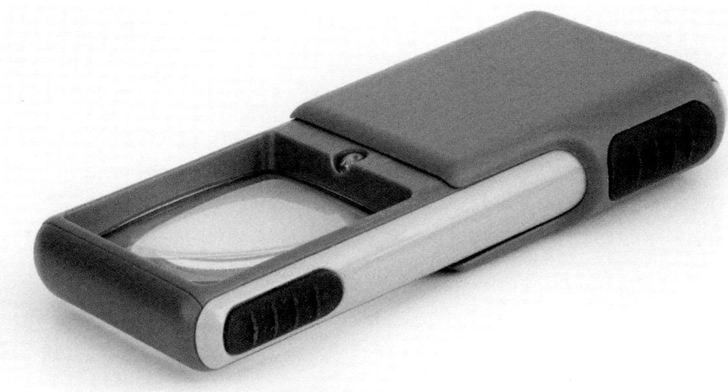

**Figure 13.13**
The SensorKlear
Loupe provides
an illuminated,
magnified view of
your sensor.

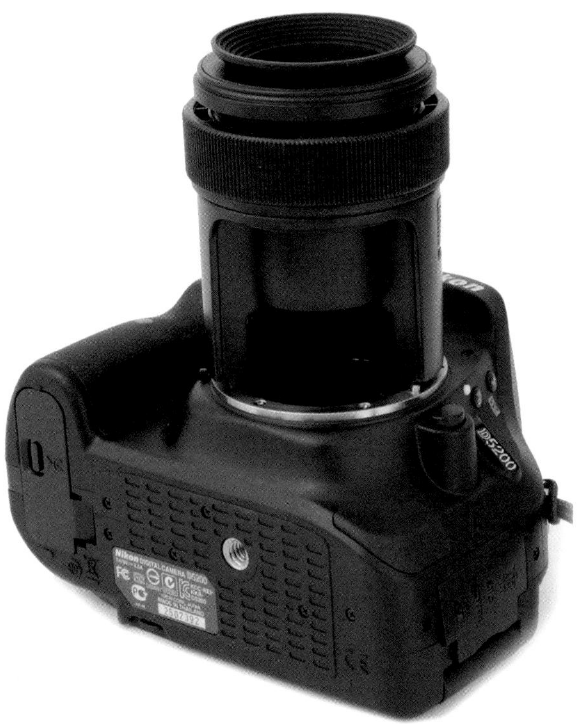

When I'm using the MiniBrite, I locate the dust on the sensor with the magnifier, remembering that the position of the dust will be *reversed* from what I might have seen on an image on the camera's LCD (because the camera lens flips the image when making the exposure). Then, I use the SensorKlear wand or the blower brush to remove the artifact.

The SensorKlear loupe actually allows you to keep your eye on the prize as you do the cleaning. You can peer through the viewer, rotate the opening to the side opposite the position of the dust, then insert the hinged wand to tap the dust while you're watching. This method allows removing a bunch of dust particles quickly, so it's my preferred procedure when I have the loupe with me.

# Glossary

It's always handy to have a single resource where you can look up various terms you'll encounter while working with your digital camera. Here is the latest update of a glossary I've compiled over the years, with some new additions specifically for the Nikon D5200.

**AE-L/AF-L** A button on the D5200 that allows locking exposure and/or focus point prior to taking a photo.

**ambient lighting** Diffuse, non-directional lighting that doesn't appear to come from a specific source but, rather, bounces off walls, ceilings, and other objects in the scene when a picture is taken.

**analog/digital converter** The EXPEED module in the camera that electronically converts the analog information captured by the D5200's sensor into digital bits that can be stored as an image.

**angle of view** The area of a scene that a lens can capture, determined by the focal length of the lens. Lenses with a shorter focal length have a wider angle of view than lenses with a longer focal length.

**anti-alias** A process that smoothes the look of rough edges in images (called *jaggies* or *staircasing*) by adding partially transparent pixels along the boundaries of diagonal lines that are merged into a smoother line by our eyes. *See also* jaggies.

**aperture** The size of the opening in the iris or diaphragm of a lens, relative to the lens's focal length. Also called an *f/stop*. For example, with a lens having a focal length of 100mm, an f/stop with a diameter of 12.5mm would produce an aperture value of f/8.

**Aperture-priority** A camera setting that allows you to specify the lens opening or f/stop that you want to use, with the camera selecting the required shutter speed automatically based on its light-meter reading. *See also* Shutter-priority.

**artifact** A type of noise in an image, or an unintentional image component produced in error by a digital camera during processing, usually caused by the JPEG compression process in digital cameras, or, in some cases, by dust settling on the sensor.

**aspect ratio** The proportions of an image as printed, displayed on a monitor, or captured by a digital camera.

**Autofocus** A camera setting that allows the Nikon D5200 to choose the correct focus distance for you, based on the contrast of an image (the image will be at maximum contrast when in sharp focus). The camera can be set for *Single Servo Autofocus (AF-S),* in which the lens is not focused until the shutter release is partially depressed; *Continuous Servo Autofocus (AF-C),* in which the lens refocuses constantly as you frame and reframe the image; and *Automatic Autofocus (AF-A),* in which the D5200 focuses using AF-S mode, but switches to AF-C mode if the subject starts to move. The D5200 can also be set for *Manual* focus.

**backlighting** A lighting effect produced when the main light source is located behind the subject. Backlighting can be used to create a silhouette effect, or to illuminate translucent objects. *See also* front lighting and side lighting.

**barrel distortion** A lens defect that causes straight lines at the top or side edges of an image to bow outward into a barrel shape. *See also* pincushion distortion.

**blooming** An image distortion caused when a photosite in an image sensor has absorbed all the photons it can handle so that additional photons reaching that pixel overflow to affect surrounding pixels, producing unwanted brightness and overexposure around the edges of objects.

**blur** To soften an image or part of an image by throwing it out of focus, or by allowing it to become soft due to subject or camera motion. Blur can also be applied creatively in an image-editing program.

**bokeh** A term derived from the Japanese word for blur, which describes the aesthetic qualities of the out-of-focus parts of an image. Some lenses produce "good" bokeh and others offer "bad" bokeh. Some lenses produce uniformly illuminated out-of-focus discs. Others produce a disc that has a bright edge and a dark center, producing a "doughnut" effect, which is the worst from a bokeh standpoint. Lenses that generate a bright center that fades to a darker edge are favored, because their bokeh allows the circle of confusion to blend more smoothly with the surroundings. The bokeh characteristics of a lens are most important when you're using selective focus (say, when shooting a portrait) to deemphasize the background, or when shallow depth-of-field is a given because you're working with a macro lens, with a long telephoto, or with a wide-open aperture. *See also* circle of confusion.

**bounce lighting** Light bounced off a reflector, including ceiling and walls, to provide a soft, natural-looking light.

**buffer** The digital camera's internal memory where an image is stored immediately after it is taken until it can be written to the camera's non-volatile (semi-permanent) memory card.

**burst mode** The digital camera's equivalent of the film camera's motor drive, used to take multiple shots within a short period of time, each stored in a memory buffer temporarily before writing them to the media.

**calibration** A process used to correct for the differences in the output of a printer or monitor when compared to the original image. Once you've calibrated your scanner, monitor, and/or your image editor, the images you see on the screen more closely represent what you'll get from your printer, even though calibration is never perfect.

**Camera Raw** A plug-in included with Photoshop and Photoshop Elements that can manipulate the unprocessed images captured by digital cameras, such as the Nikon D5200's NEF files. The latest versions of this module can also work with JPEG and TIFF images.

**camera shake** Movement of the camera, aggravated by slower shutter speeds, which produces a blurred image.

**Center-weighted metering** A light-measuring method that emphasizes the area in the middle of the frame when calculating the correct exposure for an image. *See also* Matrix metering and Spot metering.

**channel** In an electronic flash, a channel is a protocol used to communicate wirelessly between a master flash unit and the remote units slaved to that main flash. The ability to change channels allows several master flash units to operate in the same environment without interfering with each other.

**chromatic aberration** An image defect, often seen as green or purple fringing around the edges of an object, caused by a lens failing to focus all colors of a light source at the same point. *See also* fringing.

**circle of confusion** A term applied to the fuzzy discs produced when a point of light is out of focus. The circle of confusion is not a fixed size. The viewing distance and amount of enlargement of the image determine whether we see a particular spot on the image as a point or as a disc. *See also* bokeh.

**close-up lens** A lens add-on that allows you to take pictures at a distance that is less than the closest-focusing distance of the lens alone.

**color correction** Changing the relative amounts of color in an image to produce a desired effect, typically a more accurate representation of those colors. Color correction can fix faulty color balance in the original image, or compensate for the deficiencies of the inks used to reproduce the image.

**compression** Reducing the size of a file by encoding using fewer bits of information to represent the original. Some compression schemes, such as JPEG, operate by discarding some image information, while others have options that preserve all the detail in the original, discarding only redundant data.

**continuous-servo autofocus** An automatic focusing setting (AF-C) in which the camera constantly refocuses the image as you frame the picture. This setting is often the best choice for moving subjects. *See also* single-servo autofocus.

**contrast** The range between the lightest and darkest tones in an image. A high-contrast image is one in which the shades fall at the extremes of the range between white and black. In a low-contrast image, the tones are closer together.

**Creative Lighting System (CLS)** Nikon's electronic flash system used to coordinate exposure, camera information, and timing between a camera's built-in flash (if present) and external flash units, which can be linked through direct electrical connections or wirelessly. Some external flash units can act as a "master" to command other external units.

**dedicated flash** An electronic flash unit, such as the Nikon SB-400 Speedlight, designed to work with the automatic exposure features of a specific camera.

**depth-of-field** A distance range in a photograph in which all included portions of an image are at least acceptably sharp.

**diaphragm** An adjustable component, similar to the iris in the human eye, which can open and close to provide specific-sized lens openings, or f/stops, and thus control the amount of light reaching the sensor or film.

**diffuse lighting** Soft, low-contrast lighting.

**digital processing chip** A solid-state device found in digital cameras that is in charge of applying the image algorithms to the raw picture data prior to storage on the memory card.

**diopter** A value used to represent the magnification power of a lens, calculated as the reciprocal of a lens's focal length (in meters). Diopters are most often used to represent the optical correction used in a viewfinder to adjust for limitations of the photographer's eyesight, and to describe the magnification of a close-up lens attachment.

**equivalent focal length** A digital camera's focal length translated into the corresponding values for a 35mm film camera. This value can be calculated for lenses used with the Nikon D5200 by multiplying by 1.5.

**exchangeable image file format (Exif)** Developed to standardize the exchange of image data between hardware devices and software. A variation on JPEG, Exif is used by most digital cameras, and includes information such as the date and time a photo was taken, the camera settings, resolution, amount of compression, and other data.

**Exif** *See* exchangeable image file format (Exif).

**exposure** The amount of light allowed to reach the film or sensor, determined by the intensity of the light, the amount admitted by the iris of the lens, the length of time determined by the shutter speed, and the sensitivity of the sensor or film to light.

**exposure compensation** Exposure compensation, which uses exposure value (EV) settings, is a way of adding or decreasing exposure without the need to reference f/stops or shutter speeds. For example, if you tell your camera to add +1EV, it will provide twice as much exposure, by using a larger f/stop, slower shutter speed, or both. The D5200 offers both conventional exposure compensation and flash exposure compensation.

**fill lighting** In photography, lighting used to illuminate shadows. Reflectors or additional incandescent lighting or electronic flash can be used to brighten shadows. One common technique outdoors is to use the camera's flash as a fill in sunlit situations.

**filter** In photography, a device that fits over the lens, changing the light in some way. In image editing, a feature that changes the pixels in an image to produce blurring, sharpening, and other special effects. Photoshop includes several interesting filter effects, including Lens Blur and Photo Filters.

**flash sync** The timing mechanism that ensures that an internal or external electronic flash fires at the correct time during the exposure cycle. A digital SLR's flash sync speed is the highest shutter speed that can be used with flash, ordinarily 1/200th of a second with the Nikon D5200. *See also* front-curtain sync and rear-curtain sync.

**focal length** The distance between the film and the optical center of the lens when the lens is focused on infinity, usually measured in millimeters.

**focal plane** A line, perpendicular to the optical axis, which passes through the focal point forming a plane of sharp focus when the lens is set at infinity. A focal plane indicator is etched into the Nikon D5200 on the top panel.

**focus tracking** The ability of the automatic focus feature of a camera to change focus as the distance between the subject and the camera changes. One type of focus tracking is *predictive,* in which the mechanism anticipates the motion of the object being focused on, and adjusts the focus to suit.

**format** To erase a memory card and prepare it to accept files.

**fringing** A chromatic aberration that produces fringes of color around the edges of subjects, caused by a lens's inability to focus the various wavelengths of light onto the same spot. Purple fringing is especially troublesome with backlit images.

**front-curtain sync (first-curtain sync)** The default kind of electronic flash synchronization technique, originally associated with focal plane shutters, which consists of a traveling set of curtains, including a *front curtain*, which opens to reveal the film or sensor, and a *rear curtain*, which follows at a distance determined by shutter speed to conceal the film or sensor at the conclusion of the exposure. For a flash picture to be taken, the entire sensor must be exposed at one time to the brief flash exposure, so the image is exposed after the front curtain has reached the other side of the focal plane, but before the rear curtain begins to move. Front-curtain sync causes the flash to fire at the beginning of this period when the shutter is completely open, in the instant that the first curtain of the focal plane shutter finishes its movement across the film or sensor plane. With slow shutter speeds, this feature can create a blur effect from the ambient light, showing as patterns that follow a moving subject with the subject shown sharply frozen at the beginning of the blur trail. *See also* rear-curtain sync.

**front lighting** Illumination that comes from the direction of the camera. *See also* backlighting and side lighting.

**f/stop** The relative size of the lens aperture, which helps determine both exposure and depth-of-field. The larger the f/stop number, the smaller the f/stop itself.

**graduated filter** A lens attachment with variable density or color from one edge to another. A graduated neutral-density filter, for example, can be oriented so the neutral-density portion is concentrated at the top of the lens's view with the less dense or clear portion at the bottom, thus reducing the amount of light from a very bright sky while not interfering with the exposure of the landscape in the foreground. Graduated filters can also be split into several color sections to provide a color gradient between portions of the image.

**gray card** A piece of cardboard or other material with a standardized 18-percent reflectance. Gray cards can be used as a reference for determining correct exposure or for setting white balance.

**group** A way of bundling more than one wireless flash unit into a single cluster that all share the same flash output setting, as controlled by the master flash unit.

**high contrast** A wide range of density in a print, negative, or other image.

**highlights** The brightest parts of an image containing detail.

**histogram** A kind of chart showing the relationship of tones in an image using a series of 256 vertical bars, one for each brightness level. A histogram chart, such as the one the Nikon D5200 can display during picture review, typically looks like a curve with one or more slopes and peaks, depending on how many highlight, midtone, and shadow tones are present in the image.

**hot shoe** A mount on top of a camera used to hold an electronic flash, while providing an electrical connection between the flash and the camera. Also called an accessory shoe.

**hyperfocal distance** A point of focus where everything from half that distance to infinity appears to be acceptably sharp. For example, if your lens has a hyperfocal distance of four feet, everything from two feet to infinity would be sharp. The hyperfocal distance varies by the lens and the aperture in use. If you know you'll be making a grab shot without warning, sometimes it is useful to turn off your camera's automatic focus, and set the lens to infinity, or, better yet, the hyperfocal distance. Then, you can snap off a quick picture without having to wait for the lag that occurs with most digital cameras as their autofocus locks in.

**image rotation** A feature that senses whether a picture was taken in horizontal or vertical orientation. That information is embedded in the picture file so that the camera and compatible software applications can automatically display the image in the correct orientation.

**image stabilization** A technology that compensates for camera shake, usually by adjusting the position of the camera sensor or (with the implementation used by Nikon) by re-arranging the position of certain lens elements in response to movements of the camera.

**incident light** Light falling on a surface.

**International Organization for Standardization (ISO)** A governing body that provides standards used to represent film speed, or the equivalent sensitivity of a digital camera's sensor. Digital camera sensitivity is expressed in ISO settings.

**interpolation** A technique digital cameras, scanners, and image editors use to create new pixels required whenever you resize or change the resolution of an image based on the values of surrounding pixels. Devices such as scanners and digital cameras can also use interpolation to create pixels in addition to those actually captured, thereby increasing the apparent resolution or color information in an image.

**ISO** *See* International Organization for Standardization (ISO).

**i-TTL** Nikon's intelligent through-the-lens flash metering system, which uses pre-flashes to calculate exposure and to communicate between flash units, using the camera's 2016-segment RGB sensor viewfinder exposure meter.

**jaggies** Staircasing effect of lines that are not perfectly horizontal or vertical, caused by pixels that are too large to represent the line accurately. *See also* anti-alias.

**JPEG** A file "lossy" format (short for Joint Photographic Experts Group) that supports 24-bit color and reduces file sizes by selectively discarding image data. Digital cameras generally use JPEG compression to pack more images onto memory cards. You can select how much compression is used (and, therefore, how much information is thrown away) by selecting from among the Standard, Fine, Super Fine, or other quality settings offered by your camera. *See also* RAW.

**Kelvin (K)** A unit of measure based on the absolute temperature scale in which absolute zero is zero; it's used to describe the color of continuous-spectrum light sources and applied when setting white balance. For example, daylight has a color temperature of about 5,500K, and a tungsten lamp has a temperature of about 3,400K.

**lag time** The interval between when the shutter is pressed and when the picture is actually taken. During that span, the camera may be automatically focusing and calculating exposure. With digital SLRs like the Nikon D5200, lag time is generally very short; with non-dSLRs, the elapsed time easily can be one second or more under certain conditions.

**latitude** The degree by which exposure can be varied and still produce an acceptable photo.

**lens flare** A feature of conventional photography that is both a bane and a creative outlet. It is an effect produced by the reflection of light internally among elements of an optical lens. Bright light sources within or just outside the field of view cause lens flare. Flare can be reduced by the use of coatings on the lens elements or with the use of lens hoods. Photographers sometimes use the effect as a creative technique, and Photoshop includes a filter that lets you add lens flare at your whim.

**lighting ratio** The proportional relationship between the amount of light falling on the subject from the main light and other lights, expressed in a ratio, such as 3:1.

**lossless compression** An image-compression scheme, such as TIFF, that preserves all image detail. When the image is decompressed, it is identical to the original version.

**lossy compression** An image-compression scheme, such as JPEG, that creates smaller files by discarding image information, which can affect image quality.

**macro lens** A lens that provides continuous focusing from infinity to extreme close-ups, often to a reproduction ratio of 1:2 (half life-size) or 1:1 (life-size).

**Matrix metering** A system of exposure calculation that looks at many different segments of an image to determine the brightest and darkest portions, and base f/stop and shutter speed on settings derived from a database of images. *See also* Center-weighted metering and Spot metering.

**maximum burst** The number of frames that can be exposed at the current settings until the buffer fills.

**midtones** Parts of an image with tones of an intermediate value, usually in the 25 to 75 percent brightness range. Many image-editing features allow you to manipulate midtones independently from the highlights and shadows.

**mirror lock-up** The ability of the D5200 to retract its mirror out of the light path to allow access to the sensor for cleaning.

**neutral color** A color in which red, green, and blue are present in equal amounts, producing a gray.

**neutral-density filter** A gray camera filter reducing the amount of light entering the camera without affecting the colors.

**noise** In an image, pixels with randomly distributed color values. Noise in digital photographs tends to be the product of low-light conditions and long exposures, particularly when you've set your camera to a higher ISO rating than normal.

**noise reduction** A technology used to cut down on the amount of random information in a digital picture, usually caused by long exposures or increased ISO sensitivity ratings.

**normal lens** A lens that makes the image in a photograph appear in a perspective that is like that of the original scene, typically with a field of view of roughly 45 degrees.

**overexposure** A condition in which too much light reaches the film or sensor, producing a dense negative or a very bright/light print, slide, or digital image.

**pincushion distortion** A type of lens distortion in which lines at the top and side edges of an image are bent inward, producing an effect that looks like a pincushion. *See also* barrel distortion.

**Playback menu** The D5200's list of settings and options that deal with reviewing and printing images that you've shot.

**polarizing filter** A filter that forces light, which normally vibrates in all directions, to vibrate only in a single plane, reducing or removing the specular reflections from the surface of objects and darkening blue skies.

**RAW** An image file format, such as the NEF format in the Nikon D5200, which includes all the unprocessed information captured by the camera after conversion to digital form. RAW files are very large compared to JPEG files and must be processed by a special program such as Nikon Capture NX or Adobe's Camera Raw filter after being downloaded from the camera.

**rear-curtain sync (second-curtain sync)** An optional kind of electronic flash synchronization technique, originally associated with focal plane shutters, which consists of a traveling set of curtains, including a *front (first) curtain* (which opens to reveal the film or sensor) and a *rear (second) curtain* (which follows at a distance determined by shutter speed to conceal the film or sensor at the conclusion of the exposure). For a flash picture to be taken, the entire sensor must be exposed at one time to the brief flash exposure, so the image is exposed after the front curtain has reached the other side of the focal plane, but before the rear curtain begins to move. Rear-curtain sync causes the flash to fire at the end of the exposure, an instant before the second or rear curtain of the focal plane shutter begins to move. With slow shutter speeds, this feature can create a blur effect from the ambient light, showing as patterns that follow a moving subject with the subject shown sharply frozen at the end of the blur trail. If you were shooting a photo of The Flash, the superhero would appear sharp, with a ghostly trail behind him. *See also* front-curtain sync (first-curtain sync).

**red-eye** An effect from flash photography that appears to make a person's eyes glow red, or an animal's yellow or green. It's caused by light bouncing from the retina of the eye and is most pronounced in dim illumination (when the irises are wide open) and when the electronic flash is close to the lens and, therefore, prone to reflect directly back. Image editors can fix red-eye through cloning other pixels over the offending red or orange ones.

**RGB color** A color model that represents the three colors—red, green, and blue—used by devices such as scanners or monitors to reproduce color. Photoshop works in RGB mode by default, and even displays CMYK images by converting them to RGB.

**Retouch menu** The D5200's list of special effects and editing changes you can make to images you've already taken. Choices in this menu allow you to trim/crop photos, and add effects such as fisheye looks.

**saturation** The purity of color; the amount by which a pure color is diluted with white or gray.

**selective focus** Choosing a lens opening that produces a shallow depth-of-field. Usually this is used to isolate a subject in portraits, close-ups, and other types of images, by causing most other elements in the scene to be blurred.

**self-timer** A mechanism that delays the opening of the shutter for some seconds after the release has been operated.

**sensitivity** A measure of the degree of response of a film or sensor to light, measured using the ISO setting.

**Setup menu** The D5200's list of settings and options that deal with overall changes to the camera's operation, such as date/time, LCD brightness, sensor cleaning, self-timer delay, and so forth.

**shadow** The darkest part of an image, represented on a digital image by pixels with low numeric values.

**sharpening** Increasing the apparent sharpness of an image by boosting the contrast between adjacent pixels that form an edge.

**Shooting menu** The D5200's list of settings and options that deal with how the camera behaves as you take pictures, such as image size and quality, white balance, autofocus settings, ISO sensitivity, or movie shooting options.

**shutter** In a conventional film camera, the shutter is a mechanism consisting of blades, a curtain, a plate, or some other movable cover that controls the time during which light reaches the film. Digital cameras can use both a mechanical shutter and an electronic shutter for higher effective speeds.

**Shutter-priority** An exposure mode in which you set the shutter speed and the camera determines the appropriate f/stop. *See also* Aperture-priority.

**side lighting** Applying illumination from the left or right sides of the camera. *See also* backlighting and front lighting.

**single-servo autofocus** An automatic focusing setting (AF-S) in which the camera focuses once when the shutter release is pressed down halfway. *See also* continuous-servo autofocus.

**slave unit** An accessory flash unit that supplements the main flash, usually triggered electronically when the slave senses the light output by the main unit, or through radio waves.

**slow sync** An electronic flash synchronizing method that uses a slow shutter speed so that ambient light is recorded by the camera in addition to the electronic flash illumination. This allows the background to receive more exposure for a more realistic effect.

**specular highlight** Bright spots in an image caused by reflection of light sources.

**Spot metering** An exposure system that concentrates on a small area in the image. *See also* Center-weighted metering and Matrix metering

**through-the-lens (TTL)** A system of providing viewing and exposure calculation through the actual lens taking the picture.

**time exposure** A picture taken by leaving the shutter open for a long period, usually more than one second. The camera is generally locked down with a tripod to prevent blur during the long exposure. The D5200 can automatically shoot time exposures up to 30 seconds, as well as much longer exposures with the camera set to Bulb and the shutter opened/closed manually.

**tungsten light** Light from ordinary room lamps and ceiling fixtures, as opposed to fluorescent illumination.

**underexposure** A condition in which too little light reaches the film or sensor, producing a thin negative, a dark slide, a muddy-looking print, or a dark digital image.

**unsharp masking** The process for increasing the contrast between adjacent pixels in an image, increasing sharpness, especially around edges.

**vignetting** Dark corners of an image, often produced by using a lens hood that is too small for the field of view, a lens that does not completely fill the image frame, or generated artificially using image-editing techniques.

**white balance** The adjustment of a digital camera to the color temperature of the light source. Interior illumination is relatively red; outdoor light is relatively blue. Digital cameras like the Nikon D5200 set correct white balance automatically or let you do it through menus. Image editors can often do some color correction of images that were exposed using the wrong white balance setting, especially when working with RAW files that contain the information originally captured by the camera before white balance was applied.

**zoom head** The capability of an electronic flash to change the area of its coverage to more closely match the focal length setting of a prime or zoom lens.

# Index

# E

E-series lenses, 265

Eclipse solution, 335

ED (extra-low dispersion) lenses, 263, 265

Edgerton, Harold, 145

Edison, Thomas, 291–292

editing. *See also* information edit screen; movies

Picture Controls, 193–197

effects modes, 251–252

18-percent gray cards. *See* gray cards

electronic analog exposure display in viewfinder, 65–66

electronic contacts on lens, 63–64

emitted light, 74

equivalent exposures, 74–76

establishing shots in movies, 134–135

EV (exposure compensation). *See also* FEV (flash exposure compensation)

adjusting, 86

with continuous light, 287

with flash, 288

ISO sensitivity adjustments and, 89

in live view, 126

overlaying images and, 243

Overview data screen showing, 58

shooting information display on, 53–54

viewfinder information display showing, 65–66

working with, 101

EV (exposure compensation) button, 60–61

evenness of illumination

with continuous light, 288

with flash, 288

EXPEED chips, 187

exposure. *See also* EV (exposure compensation); FEV (flash exposure compensation); histograms; long exposures; overexposure; short exposures; underexposure

apps for estimating, 166

calculation of, 76–79

correct exposure, example of, 77

equivalent exposures, 74–76

explanation of, 72–76

flash, calculating for, 298–299

Exposure Delay Mode options, Custom Setting menu, 223

exposure modes, 79, 83–87

Overview data screen showing, 58

selecting, 22–26

extension tubes, 279–280

external backup for memory cards, 326

external flash. *See* Speedlights

external microphones. *See* microphones

extra batteries, 5, 8, 12, 316

extra-low dispersion (ED) elements, 263, 265

extreme close-ups in movies, 134–135

Eye-Fi cards, 325

Setup menu options for uploading, 236

working with, 160–161

Eye-Fi Explore, 325

Eye-Fi Home, 325

Eye-Fi Share/Eye-Fi Share Video, 325

eyecup, 7

eyeglasses, diopter correction for, 14–15

eyepiece, 45–46

cap for, 7

magnifying eyepiece, 9

EZ Share cards, 161

# F

# M

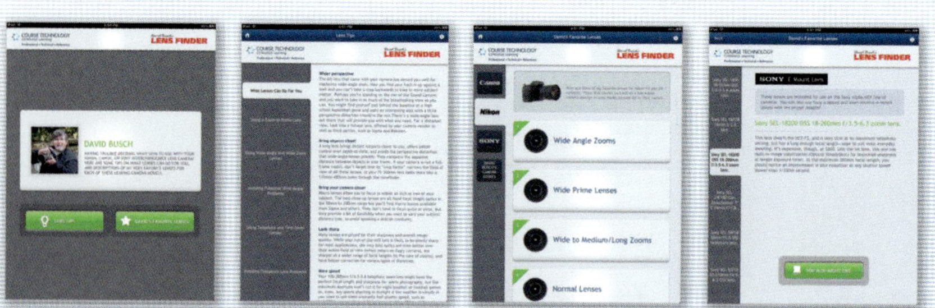

# NEED HELP SELECTING A LENS?
# LET DAVID BUSCH HELP!

The new **FREE** David Busch Lens Finder app for iPhone/iPad is now available for download from the Apple app store. The app will help you learn more about camera lenses and how to select the right ones for various cameras and shooting situations!

Download *David Busch's* Lens Finder now!